Basic Linguistic Theory 3

CW01500092

Basic Linguistic Theory
R. M. W. Dixon

The three volumes of *Basic Linguistic Theory* provide a new and fundamental characterization of the nature of human languages and a comprehensive guide to their description and analysis. The first volume addresses the methodology for recording, analysing, and comparing languages. Volumes 2 and 3 examine and explain every underlying principle of grammatical organization and consider how and why grammars vary.

Volume 1
Methodology

Volume 2
Grammatical Topics

Volume 3
Further Grammatical Topics

"*Basic Linguistic Theory* is destined to be a modern classic."
N.J. Enfield, Max Planck Institute for Psycholinguistics, Nijmegen

"A monumental achievement. Virtually without precedent in the field of linguistics."
Martin Haspelmath, Max Planck Institute for Evolutionary Anthropology, Leipzig

"These books are monumental and destined to become classics, equatable to the two volumes entitled *Language* by Sapir (1921) and Bloomfield (1933), and to Givón's *Syntax*, volumes 1 (1984) and 2 (1990) but in each case surpassing them in scope, detail, rigor, and coherence. Dixon presents a complete, fully articulated, and cohesive explication of grammar, with extensive elaboration on every major grammatical structure found in the world's languages, as well as many minor ones.... This is a masterwork...a lasting reference for grammar writers, typologists, grammatical theorists, and all those fascinated by the complexities of linguistic systems and grammatical analysis."
Carol Genetti, *Language*

"Extremely informative, exceedingly useful, and profoundly inspiring. These are books I can recommend to every graduate student, to every linguistic field worker."
René van den Berg, *Studies in Language*

A complete list of R. M. W. Dixon's books may be found on pp. 546–47

Basic Linguistic Theory

Volume 3 Further Grammatical Topics

R. M. W. DIXON

Cairns Institute
James Cook University

OXFORD
UNIVERSITY PRESS

OXFORD

UNIVERSITY PRESS

Great Clarendon Street, Oxford ox2 6DP

Oxford University Press is a department of the University of Oxford.
It furthers the University's objective of excellence in research, scholarship,
and education by publishing worldwide in

Oxford New York

Auckland Cape Town Dar es Salaam Hong Kong Karachi
Kuala Lumpur Madrid Melbourne Mexico City Nairobi
New Delhi Shanghai Taipei Toronto

With offices in

Argentina Austria Brazil Chile Czech Republic France Greece
Guatemala Hungary Italy Japan Poland Portugal Singapore
South Korea Switzerland Thailand Turkey Ukraine Vietnam

Oxford is a registered trade mark of Oxford University Press
in the UK and in certain other countries

Published in the United States
by Oxford University Press Inc., New York

© R. M. W. Dixon 2012

The moral rights of the author have been asserted
Database right Oxford University Press (maker)

First published 2012

All rights reserved. No part of this publication may be reproduced,
stored in a retrieval system, or transmitted, in any form or by any means,
without the prior permission in writing of Oxford University Press,
or as expressly permitted by law, or under terms agreed with the appropriate
reprographics rights organization. Enquiries concerning reproduction
outside the scope of the above should be sent to the Rights Department,
Oxford University Press, at the address above

You must not circulate this book in any other binding or cover
and you must impose the same condition on any acquirer

British Library Cataloguing in Publication Data
Data available

Library of Congress Cataloging in Publication Data
Data available

Typeset by SPI Publisher Services, Pondicherry, India
Printed in Great Britain
on acid-free paper by
MPG Books Group, Bodmin and King's Lynn

ISBN 978–0–19–957109–3 (Hbk)
          978–0–19–957110–9 (Pbk)

1 3 5 7 9 10 8 6 4 2

Outline contents for whole work

Volume 1 Methodology

Volume 2 Grammatical topics

Volume 3 Further grammatical topics

Contents

List of tables

How to read this book

This book is, of course, designed to be read from first to last page. But other strategies are possible.

Chapter 1 of Volume 1 outlines the approach followed throughout, and should be consulted first. The lengthy Chapter 3 provides an overview of grammatical structures and systems found across the languages of the world. Many of these topics are dealt with in more detail in the chapters of Volumes 2 and 3. Ideally, Chapter 3 should be studied at an early stage, although experienced linguists may choose to skim it.

The remaining chapters of Volume 1, and those of Volumes 2 and 3, could be read in any order. However, recurrent themes are developed across chapters and maximal benefit will be obtained by reading the chapters in the order in which they are presented.

Preface

For more than four decades I have been doing linguistics in the true sense of the word—undertaking immersion fieldwork, writing grammars, compiling lexicons. I've studied, in fair detail, more than two hundred published grammars, and consulted several hundred more. I have worked—by inductive generalization—on a number of topics in typological theory, and have read everything I could lay my hands on that is relevant to this endeavour. However, despite having been learning, learning all along the way, I feel that I know only a fraction of what I would like to know.

This book is a distillation of what I have learned thus far—the most satisfactory and profitable way to work, and what pitfalls to avoid. In short, how best to obtain reliable and satisfactory results which have scientific validity. Volume 1 sets the scene, with chapters on aspects of methodology. Volumes 2 and 3 then deal in fair detail with each of a number of grammatical topics.

The reader will find opinions expressed straightforwardly, without demur. Some of the things that are said may go against certain of the current 'fashions'. I do not expect others to agree with everything I say. But all the points made here have validity, and are worthy of serious consideration.

The languages I know best are those that I have worked on myself and published on—the Australian languages Dyirbal (1971, 1972, 1989), Yidiñ (1977a, 1991b), Warrgamay (1981), and Nyawaygi (1983), plus Boumaa Fijian (1988), Jarawara from Brazil (2004), and English (1991a, 2005a, 2005b). If some point can be illustrated from one of these languages then I do so, rather than using data from another language which I know less well. This applies especially to the general discussions in Volume I. For points which do not occur in these languages, and for further exemplification of points that do, information from many other grammars is used.

Sources are sometimes included in the text and sometimes in notes at the end of a chapter. It has not been thought necessary to always quote sources for well-described languages such as Latin, French, German, Estonian, Turkish, Hebrew, Mandarin Chinese, Quechua, Swahili, Thai, and the like. Specific references are not always given for the languages I have worked on. If, say, an example is taken from Jarawara, the interested reader can easily consult my comprehensive grammar of that language (Dixon 2004) to see how the matter under discussion fits into the overall linguistic system of the language. Sources are provided for information from other languages. A glossary of technical terms is included at the end of each volume.

There is today a fashion in linguistics—and no doubt in other disciplines as well—of what can be called 'quotationitis'. That is, attempting to cite every single thing published on or around a topic, irrespective of its quality or direct relevance. Not unusually, quotations are provided from several sources which are contradictory in assumptions and import, without attention being drawn to this. I have used citations sparingly; these only reflect a small proportion of the grammars and general works which I have studied. The present work is conceived of as being like a well-organized garden; I have tried to avoid it degenerating into an impenetrable jungle.

Volumes 1 and 2 were published together, while Volume 3 followed a couple of years later. Some of the topics discussed briefly in Chapter 3 of Volume 1 are dealt with in more detail here. In just a few instances, further work has led to minor revision of earlier statements.

The Outline Contents in Volumes 1 and 2 anticipated more chapters for Volume 3 than have eventuated. This has been partly to keep the volume to reasonable size and partly because certain topics have been more than adequately dealt with elsewhere:

- Noun categorization devices—see Aikhenvald (2000b) and further references therein.
- Serial verb constructions—see Aikhenvald and Dixon (2006), especially the opening chapter by Aikhenvald (plus the final chapter by Dixon), and further references therein.
- Noun incorporation—see the seminal papers by Mithun (1984, 1986a, b) and further references therein.
- Imperatives—see Aikhenvald (2010) and further references therein.

This book has been envisaged, planned and written in close collaboration with my colleague Alexandra Y. Aikhenvald. We have discussed every topic, often many times. I have benefited from her grammars of Warekena (1998), Tariana (2003), and Manambu (2008a), and from her typological studies (particularly 2000b, 2004, 2010). I am the one who has written the book (and Aikhenvald would not necessarily agree with every single word in it) but the ideas, analyses, and generalizations are in very many instances our joint work.

The Australian Research Council supported a Dixon/Aikhenvald project (1996–8) 'The categories of human languages'. Within this project, articulated grammatical summaries were produced for 66 languages; they have been an invaluable aid to me in writing these volumes. Thanks are due to the scholars who worked on these summaries, particularly Mengistu Amberber, Adam Chapman, Timothy Curnow, Mark Donohue, Geoffrey Haig, Deborah Hill, Suanu Ikoro, Dorothy Jauncey, Knut Olawsky, Masayuki Onishi, Tom Payne,

Regina Pustet, Stuart Robinson, Carl Rubino, Hans-Jürgen Sasse, Mauro Tosco, and Ulrike Zeshan.

Nick Enfield again carefully read almost every chapter and provided the most useful comments, corrections, and suggestions. And I owe a considerable debt to the several score students and colleagues whose grammatical descriptions I have assisted with over the years; having learnt from each of them. Brigitta Flick played an important role in checking the typescript for errors and infelicities.

These volumes have been brought to fruition through the help and encouragement of John Davey, linguistics editor *sans pareil*. Of the several publishers I have worked with over almost five decades, the UK division of Oxford University Press is, in every department, the most efficient and caring. John Davey exudes an enthusiasm which makes one feel valued and wanted, and works in a friendly and unobtrusive way to assist each author in realizing their potential.

And so, I cast my triadic pebble upon the beach.

Abbreviations and conventions, for Volumes 1, 2, and 3

Some abbreviations are used through the book (for example, A, S, and O), others only in chapters where a particular topic is being discussed (for example, RC for relative clause).

There are abbreviations employed in interlinear glossing of examples, such as ERG for ergative and CAUS for causative. However, where an example is short, with plenty of room on the line, a full label ERGATIVE or CAUSATIVE is written out. It would be pedantic (and otiose) to insist on always employing ERG and CAUS when there is no spatial limitation which requires abbreviation. My aim, through the volumes, has been to try to be as reader-friendly as circumstances permit.

-	affix boundary
=	clitic boundary
'	stress (or accent)
1	1st person
2	2nd person
3	3rd person
A	transitive subject
ABS	absolutive
ACC	accusative
AN	animate
APP	applicative
ART	article
ASP	aspect
AUX	auxiliary
CA	common argument (shared by main and relative clauses in a relative clause construction)
CAUS	causative
CC	copula complement
CL, CLASS	classifier

CoCl	complement clause
COM	comitative
COMP	comparative
COMP	complement clause marker
COMPL	completive
CONTIN	continuous
COP	copula
CS	copula subject
CTV	complement-taking verb (Chapter 18)
D	possessed (Chapter 16)
D	specific description in copula construction (§14.4)
DAT	dative
DEC	declarative
DEF	definite
DEM	demonstrative
DEP	dependent
DIFF	different
DIM	diminutive
DIR.EV	direct evidential
DS	different subject
du, DU	dual
E	extension to core
ERG	ergative
exc	exclusive
F	focal clause (§3.11)
FEM, F, f, fem	feminine
FIN	finite
FUT	future
G	general description in copula construction (§14.4)
GEN	genitive
IMM	immediate
IMP	imperative
IMPERV	imperfective

INAN	inanimate
inc	inclusive
INCH	inchoative
INCOMPL	incompletive
INDEF	indefinite
INDIC	indicative
INST	instrumental
INTENT	intentional
INTERROG	interrogative
INTR	intransitive
IP	immediate past
LOC	locative
MASC, M, m, masc	masculine
MC	main clause
Mf	marker attached to focal clause (§3.11)
min	minimal
Ms	marker attached to supporting clause (§3.11)
n	non-eyewitness evidentiality
NEG	negation
NOM	nominative
NOMZR	nominalizer
NON.FIN	non-finite
NP	noun phrase
nsg	non-singular
O	transitive object
ø	zero
OBL	oblique
PART	particle
PERF	perfect
PERFV	perfective
PERI	peripheral function
pl, PL	plural
POS	positive

POSS	possessive, possessor
POSTPOSN	postposition
PRED	predicate, predicate marker
PREP	preposition
PRES	present
PROG	progressive
Q	question
R	possessor (Chapter 16)
R	specific referent in copula construction (§14.4)
RECIP	reciprocal
REDUP	reduplicated
REFL	reflexive
REL	relative clause (marker)
REP	reported
RP	recent past
S	intransitive subject (throughout the work)
S	supporting clause (§3.11)
Sa	'active' S, marked like A
SEQ	sequential
sg, SG	singular
si	standard implicit
SIMULT	simultaneous
So	'stative' S, marked like O
SS	same subject
SUBJ	subject
SUBORD	subordinate
SVC	serial verb construction
TAM	tense, aspect, and modality
TR	transitive
VCC	verbless clause complement
VCS	verbless clause subject
VP	verb phrase

19

Non-spatial setting

19.1 Introduction

Spatial (or locational) specification may be made at many points in a grammar. For example:

(1)   [The man by the gate][looked upwards] [at the bird on the top branch]

The two noun phrases include spatial modifiers *by the gate* and *on the top branch*, while the predicate verb *looked* receives spatial modification by *upwards*. Alternatively, spatial modification may be provided for a complete clause, as in:

(2)   [Mary kissed John] under the mistletoe

It is the complete event 'Mary kissed John' which takes place 'under the mistletoe'.

In English, spatial setting may be made by an adverb (*upwards* in (1), or *outside*, or *there*, and so on) or by an NP introduced by a preposition (*by the gate*, *on the top branch*, *under the mistletoe*, etc.), or by a subordinate clause (for example, *the man standing by the gate*).

There is also the matter of non-spatial setting. A predicate may be specified for whether it refers to something which is realized or unrealized, which happens instantaneously or gradually, which is completed or ongoing, which is habitual or at a specific time, and, if so, what time it is at. These and similar parameters are the topic for this chapter.

Consider the English sentence:

(3)   John was to have given the book to Mary

The predicate of (3) includes the following three bits of information concerning non-spatial setting:

- *be to*, indicating a 'scheduled activity'—this is typically called a 'modality' (§19.4.1);
- *have...-en*, indicating an activity which commenced before the time of speaking—this is often called an 'aspect' (§19.10);

- *was* (rather than *is*), indicating that the activity took place in the past—a tense (§19.3).

The terms 'tense', 'aspect', and 'modality' are used in many different ways (indeed, 'modality' is sometimes confused with 'mood'). These and other parameters of non-spatial setting are often combined with other types of grammatical element in one inflectional system.

Before embarking on an examination of non-spatial settings, it will be useful to summarize a number of distinct types of grammatical markings (leaving aside markers of spatial setting).

I. **Mood,** indicating type of speech act; see (b) in §3.2. In every language, this has three values:

- Imperative, indicating a command (for a comprehensive account see Aikhenvald 2010).
- Interrogative, indicating a question; this is discussed in Chapter 27.
- Declarative (or indicative), indicating a statement.

In a few languages, there is a single morphological system covering all three moods. This is found in Jarawara, where the final slot in predicate structure may include one choice from a system which includes (quoting forms for feminine agreement):

- Imperative suffixes: immediate positive, *-hi*, distant positive *-^{i}jahi*; immediate negative *-rima-na-hi* and distant negative imperative *-ri-ja-hi*.
- Interrogative suffixes: content interrogative *-riha*, general polar interrogative *-ini,* and future polar interrogative *-ibana* (see §27.3).
- Declarative suffix: *-ke*.

However, such a compact morphological system indicating mood is relatively rare. Imperative (and negative imperative) is often shown by affixation, whereas interrogative may be indicated by a clitic (typically, to the first or last word of the sentence), or by constituent order, or just by intonation. Declarative, the default mood, may be left unmarked.

In most instances, the category of mood applies to a complete sentence, which may consist of more than one clause. If there is an embedded clause, then it is the main clause which determines the mood of the sentence; for example, *I$_A$ don't know* [*whether he has come*]$_{CoCl:O}$ is a statement because the main clause *I don't know...*is a statement. If two clauses are linked so as to show a temporal relation, or a relation of consequence, etc., such that one is recognized as Focal clause and the other as Supporting clause (see §3.11), then it is the Focal clause which determines the meaning of the sentence. For example, the sentence *Open the window* [Focal clause] *if you don't* *mind* [Supporting clause]*!* has imperative mood since the Focal clause is a command.

II. Clause linking. Two clauses may be linked together to form one complex sentence. This can involve embedding (relative clause and complement clause) or non-embedded linking indicating a temporal relationship, or one of condition, consequence, contrast, addition, etc. This may be marked on either or both of the clauses involved. The marking may involve a separate grammatical word (such as *after*, *if*, *because*, *although*, or *but* in English), or just apposition, or a verbal suffix. This last can be illustrated from Dyirbal:

(4) ŋajaₛ yanu   ŋabay-gu
     1sg   go:PRESENT   bathe-PURPOSIVE
     I am going (in order) to bathe

The suffix *-gu* on the verb of the second clause indicates purposive clause linking; it corresponds to *(in order) to* in English.

III. Parameters of non-spatial setting. Markers of tense, aspect, modality, etc. can be shown by morphological processes applying to a verb, or just by separate grammatical words.

There has been much discussion in the literature concerning whether markers of non-spatial setting relate just to the predicate, or to the clause as a whole. (Some suggest that tense operates at the level of the predicate and aspect at the level of the clause whereas others say the reverse.) As pointed out in §3.15, there seems little basis for posing this question, on which nothing really hinges. It is most appropriate to consider non-spatial settings to be properties of the predicate *and* of the clause—that is, of *both*, not of one or the other.

Note that whereas a mood specification generally applies to a complete sentence, non-spatial setting—including modality—relates to a clause and to its predicate. A sentence may include several clauses with different choices for non-spatial setting. To give examples from English, main and complement clauses show different tenses in *I think*{PRESENT} [*that John died* {PAST} *last year*], and different modality markers are included in the two clauses of the conditional construction *If John can* {ABILITY/PERMISSION} *go, I will* {PREDICTION} *go too*.

Prime distinctions between mood and modality are that mood has scope over an entire sentence and specifies a type of speech act, whereas modality ('can', 'will', 'must', and so on) relates to a clause and its predicate, and indicates what kind of irrealis specification is appropriate.

It was remarked, at the beginning of §1.9, that there are a myriad contrasts and distinctions applying at the semantic level, to be mapped onto the limited resources of a grammar. As a consequence, one paradigmatic system in the grammar may combine information of several types. One example is where markers of the function of an NP within a clause (nominative, accusative, and other cases) and markers of the function of an NP within an NP (such as genitive) are placed in one paradigm. The great Indian grammarian Pāṇini distinguished between genitive and cases, even though they occur in the same surface structure system for Sanskrit. Other grammarians have considered genitive to be a case—on a par with nominative, accusative, dative, and so on—thus obscuring a basic distinction. (See (f) in §1.10.)

The situation is even more muddied when we turn to markers of types I, II, and III. In a fair number of grammars a system of 'mood' is identified, on morphological grounds, which includes 'true moods' (I) such as declarative and imperative, plus conditional (which is a marker of clause linking, II), plus desire (or optative—expression of a wish, which belongs to non-spatial setting, III), and so on. (See, for example, Mallinson 1986: 284–91 on Rumanian.)

For languages which make a distinction between derivation and inflection—and, as pointed out in §3.13, this is not a distinction which it is useful to invoke for every language—the inflectional system for a verb may combine information of types I, II, and III. This can be illustrated for Dyirbal. A verb root may optionally be followed by one or more of a set of derivational suffixes (antipassive, reflexive, reciprocal, applicative, etc.). And each verb stem *must* make *one choice* from an inflectional system which includes markers of mood, of clause linking, of non-spatial setting, and a couple of suffixes which combine information from two of these parameters. The terms in the inflectional system are shown in Table 19.1, which enlarges on the brief information provided under (d) in §17.3.1.

A cross-linguistic study of non-spatial setting is not an easy task, for a number of reasons. First, opinions differ as to what is and what is not a 'tense', an 'aspect', a 'modality', etc. Our discussion will have to be delimited by specifying exactly what is here considered a type of 'non-spatial setting'. Secondly, a wide range of labels have been employed; for instance, there seems to be no substantive difference between 'durative', 'progressive', and 'continuous'. Thirdly—and most daunting—non-spatial settings are seldom realized through a single compact system at surface level (as 'case' generally is, for instance). We have just shown that one inflectional paradigm may mingle mood, markers of clause linking, and non-spatial setting. The paradigm in Table 19.1, from Dyirbal, is not at all unusual.

This chapter focuses on the parameters of non-spatial setting which we take to apply simultaneously at the level of the predicate and of the clause. Mood, a category of the sentence, is a quite different matter and is only mentioned when it interrelates with non-spatial settings. The same applies to markers of clause linking, such as conditional.

TABLE 19.1. System of inflections on the verb in Dyirbal

I. Mood
  1. Positive imperative, -ø.
  2. Negative imperative, -m (also requires preverbal particle *galga* 'don't').

II. Clause linking
  3. Apprehensive marker -*bila* 'lest'. (For example 'Bury the nuts, rats eat-*bila* them!' for 'Bury the nuts, lest rats eat them!')
  4. Relative clause marker -*ŋu*.

III. Non-spatial setting*
  5. Future tense -*ñ*.
  6. Past tense -*ñu* ∼ -*n*.

Combining II and III
  7. Purposive -*gu* ∼ -*li*. This can occur in a main clause, indicating 'want to do, must do' (a type of non-spatial setting, III), or it can occur as a linker (II) on the second of a sequence of clauses, 'X Y-PURPOSIVE'. This may then indicate either (a) X is done in order that Y can be done or should happen, as in (4), or (b) X is done and Y happens as a natural (and perhaps unintended) consequence, for example 'The woman (who was hiding from the man) burst out laughing and the man found-PURPOSIVE her'.
  8. Suffix -*ŋurra*, in a construction 'X Y-*ŋurra*' indicates both (a) that the A argument of clause X is identical to the S or O argument of clause Y (clause linking, II), and (b) the event described by Y happens immediately after that described by X (a type of relative tense, III).

* Present falls together with future in northern and with past in southern dialects; see §19.3.2.

19.2 Outline of parameters

The ways in which languages code—within their grammars—information on non-spatial setting are manifold. §§19.3–19.13 provide brief discussion of a number of parameters (already listed in §3.15) which recur in many languages:

§19.3 **Tense**—indicating the location in time of an event.

§19.4 **Reality**—distinguishing between irrealis, which roughly covers things which have not (yet) happened, and realis, things which are believed to have happened or to be happening.

§19.5 **Degree of certainty**—likely, unlikely, possible, probable, etc.

§19.6 **Phase of activity**—whether starting, continuing, finishing, etc.

§19.7 **Completion**—whether the event is completed (perfect) or continuing (imperfect).

§19.8 **Boundedness**—whether the activity has a terminal point (telic) or not (atelic).

§19.9 **Temporal extent**—whether the event is more-or-less instantaneous (punctual) or extending over a discernible period of time (durative, progressive, or continuous).

§19.10 **Composition**—whether the event is, in the context of discussion, regarded as having internal temporal constitution (imperfective) or not (perfective).

§19.11 **Degree or frequency**—whether done a bit or a lot, one or many times, etc.

§19.12 **Speed and ease**—whether done quickly or slowly, easily or only with difficulty.

§19.13 **Evidentiality**—the evidence for what is said. This may specify whether the speaker saw it, heard it, assumed it, inferred it, or was told about it, etc.

Individual languages include, within their grammars, a variety of other types of non-spatial setting. For instance, Tarma Quechua (Adelaar 1977: 94–8 and p.c.) has, alongside -*ra*, past tense, suffix -*na*; which indicates 'sudden discovery', as in:

(5) yarga-ra-:ri-na-:
      climbed-PERFECTIVE-PLURAL-SUDDEN.DISCOVERY-1.SUBJECT
         masya:du   karu-ta-m
         very   far-ACCUSATIVE-CERTAIN
      We suddenly realized that we had climbed very far

Before embarking on the survey of parameters we need to consider the status of 'future'. Lyons (1977: 677) suggests that 'futurity is never a purely temporal concept; it necessarily includes an element of prediction or some related modal notion'. Under which of the parameters is future most appropriately placed?

19.2.1 The status of future

One perceives time in terms of a sequence of events. The past can be viewed in either of two ways—retrospectively, looking backwards from this moment; or else moving forwards from some previous event towards the present. These can be exemplified. In the first view, I have just bought a car which I went to see at a house across the river, whose address I obtained by calling the phone number provided in the advert in this morning's paper which I was able to peruse at length since I got up early. In the second view, I got up early which gave me plenty of time to read the paper and I saw an advert for a car. I called the number in the advert which directed me to a house on the other side of the river. I travelled there, inspected the car, and bought it.

Past can be viewed in either of two ways. But—save in exceptional circumstances—future time is perceived only by looking forward from now. That is:

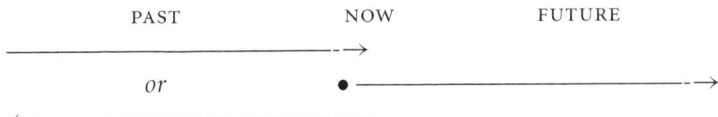

	PAST	NOW	FUTURE

Past events are known (or thought to be known) through observation, inference, assumption, reports, and the like. The future, in contrast, is an interweaving of speculation, prediction, guesses, hopes, possibilities, obligations, and so on.

The question which then arises is: **to which of the parameters of non-spatial setting does future belong?** In terms of the profiles for parameters just presented, there are two alternatives:

I **Future is a tense**, since it does refer to the location in time of an event. For instance, 'John go out hunting tomorrow' states that the event of John going out hunting is located within tomorrow.

II **Future time is shown only by modalities**, within irrealis, since future relates to events which have not yet happened.

Languages divide, fairly neatly, into two groups, depending on which of these alternatives they choose. In a language of type I, there is a grammatical system of tense, one or more of whose terms refer to future time, on a par with terms which refer to past time (and often also present). For instance, the Djabugay language, spoken just to the north of Cairns in North Queensland, Australia, has an inflectional system on verbs which includes suffixes marking past, present, and future tenses. Illustrating for *juŋga-* 'run':

(6) PAST   juŋga-ñ
     PRESENT juŋga-ŋ
     FUTURE   juŋga-na

A language which has a 'future' tense (rather than dealing with future entirely in terms of irrealis modalities) may also have marking for irrealis. A further term in the inflectional system for Djabugay is glossed as 'irrealis', which marks 'an event that could happen or could have happened if not prevented in some way'. For example (Patz 1991: 279):

(7) ŋañji-ñ$_O$ gunday   du:-lbarra,   ŋañji$_s$ juŋga-ñ   jilŋgu
     WE-ACCUSATIVE PERHAPS hit-IRREALIS we   run-PAST DOWN
     (They) would perhaps have hit us, (but) we ran down (the mountain)

In a language of type II, the grammatical system of tense is confined to past and (in many instances) present time. There is no overarching grammatical term referring to 'future'. One has instead to choose the appropriate member from a system of modalities. English is of this type. Past time is shown by past tense inflection on the verb, as in *John went out hunting yesterday*. But if one shifts from 'yesterday' to 'tomorrow' then the speaker of English must choose between stating an obligation (*John should go out hunting tomorrow*), or a necessity (*John must go out hunting tomorrow*), or a prediction (*John will go out hunting tomorrow*), or a conjecture (*John may go out hunting tomorrow*), and so on (there is fuller discussion in §19.4.1).

19.2.2 A note on terminology

There are a number of terms which are used by different writers in such a variety of ways that either one must provide a most careful definition or else decide to avoid possible confusion by declining to employ them. In each case there are clear alternative labels available.

(a) **Subjunctive**. On the basis of morphological realization, four 'moods' are recognized for proto-Indo-European, These are (Lockwood 1969: 108): indicative for 'factual assertion'; imperative for 'giving an order'; subjunctive for 'volition or expectation'; and optative for 'desire or contingency'. The latter two fell together in Latin; Kennedy (1962: 58) states that 'subjunctive mood represents a verbal activity as willed, desired, conditional or prospective'. Palmer (1986: 39) sums this up: 'the subjunctive in Latin is a generalized marker of modality'. So one could just as well employ the label 'modality' (or 'irrealis').

Others provide divergent characterizations. In a survey of Semitic languages, Gray (1934: 86) states that 'subjunctive indicates an act dependent upon the statement of the previous clause, and future to it in terms of time, so that it is used to express purpose, result, etc.'. Kraft and Kirk-Greene (1973: 61) state that, in Hausa, 'subjunctive constructions may usually be literally translated *let one do such-and-such*'. The list could be continued. If a grammar writer is able to do without 'subjunctive', the potentiality of misunderstanding will be avoided.

(b) **Aorist**. Grammars of Ancient Greek recognize an 'aorist aspect' for 'events that have taken place without regard to their extension over time or to the state resulting from them' (Matthews 1997: 20). Describing Takelma, Sapir (1922: 157) states that 'the aorist does duty for the preterite (including the narrative past), the present, and the immediate future'. Other writers accord further senses to this term. In his dictionary of grammatical terms, Trask (1993: 17) summarizes four of these: '1. A verb form marked for past tense but unmarked for aspect. 2. A verb form marked for both past tense and perfective aspect. 3. A verb form marked for perfective aspect. 4. A conventional label used in a highly variable manner among specialists in particular languages to denote some particular verb form or set of verb forms'. For example, Lewis (2000: 116), when discussing Turkish, states that 'the aorist denotes continuing activity'. 'Aorist' is another label which it is easy to avoid, employing instead 'past', 'perfective', and so on. To refrain from employing it does avoid the chance of confusion.

The term 'Aktionsart' is also used in a variety of ways, often overlapping with aspect (for this see §19.10.1). It may refer to lexemes being used in one language to describe some feature of non-spatial setting which is coded grammatically in other languages. Another use is to describe lexical classes of verbs, according to their inherent meaning. Comrie (1976b: 6–7, note 4) explains why he steers clear of using 'Aktionsart', in order to avoid possible confusion; his example is followed in this volume. The label 'preterite' has rather limited currency. Trask (1993: 216) defines it as 'a past-tense form which is unmarked for aspect'. This is another term which I—and many other writers of grammars—are able to do without.

19.3 Tense

All of the parameters for non-spatial setting surveyed in this chapter are expressed in some languages by a grammatical system and in others by lexemes (and in many languages by a combination of these). We are here mainly concerned with grammatical coding.

All languages have some means for indicating the time of an event, with respect to the moment of speaking. It is common for there to be a tense system, with a limited number of choices. However, a fair number of languages do lack a tense system and for time specification have to rely on lexical time words, such as 'earlier', 'later', 'yesterday', and 'tomorrow'. Languages lacking a tense system within their grammar include Mandarin Chinese, Bahasa Indonesian, Tagalog in the Philippines, Akan in Ghana, Lango in Uganda, Tunica in Louisiana, Tzotzil in Mexico, Paumarí in Brazil, Ainu in northern Japan and adjacent regions of Russia, Mundari in India, and Warrgamay in Australia. And, as the grammars of proto-Indo-European and proto-Semitic have been reconstructed, it has been suggested that they did not include a tense system per se (Kuryłowicz 1964; Gray 1934).

Tense may be shown through an obligatory inflectional system applying to the verb or to an auxiliary element which is closely associated with the verb. Or tense may be shown by a system of clitics, or free particles. In Mam (Mayan, Guatemala; England 1983: 161–2, 191–2, 285) tense is shown by sentence-initial particles such as *ma* 'recent past' and *o* 'non-recent past', as in:

(8) o   chin   jaw   tz'aq-a
     NON.RECENT.PAST 1SG.AGENT DIRECTIONAL slip-1sg
     I slipped (a while ago)

Interestingly, if a lexical time adverb—such as *eew* 'yesterday'—occurs sentence-initially, then the appropriate grammatical tense particle is not stated. For example:

(9) eew   chin   jaw   tz'aq-a
     YESTERDAY 1SG.AGENT DIRECTIONAL slip-1sg
     I slipped yesterday

One cannot include *o* and *eew* in the same sentence, only one of them.

As pointed out in §3.7, every language has three varieties of shifters—relating to person, to space, and to time. John may tell Mary *I love you*, where the 1st person pronoun *I* refers to John and 2nd person *you* to Mary. If Mary responds *I love you too*, then the reference of pronouns has been reversed, *I* referring to Mary and *you* to John. The reference of personal pronouns shifts as the identity of the speaker does. Now suppose that John and Mary are looking for a lost object, but in different places. Mary shouts from the bedroom *It's not here!* John responds from the kitchen *No, it's here!* Adverb *here* indicates 'near speaker' and its reference shifts with the identity of the speaker.

Turning now to shifters concerned with time. On a Tuesday, Mary writes in her diary *Yesterday I was a sad spinster, today I am getting married*. The following day, Jane reads this entry and exclaims: *Mary got married yesterday.* Adverb *yesterday* refers to the day before the day of speaking (or writing), this was Monday for Mary's entry but in Jane's report it has shifted to Tuesday. Reference to Mary's wedding uses what can be called the 'particular future' (Dixon 2005a: 212), *am getting married*, on the day it happens but past tense, *got married*, is employed the next day. It will be seen that the category of shifter covers grammatical indicators of tense and also certain temporal adverbs.

It is interesting to enquire whether every language which lacks a tense system does have lexical time shifters. For every instance that has been checked, this is the case. It has always struck me that having items with shifting reference is a highly sophisticated feature of human language. It seems that every human language does have 1st and 2nd person pronouns, at least two demonstrative adverbs ('here' and 'there') and either grammatical or lexical (or both) temporal shifters. No presently-spoken language could be termed 'primitive'; perhaps one criterion for such a designation would be a lack of shifters.

The full tense system is found in a main clause in declarative mood (and positive polarity). This generally extends into interrogative mood but some languages do show special features here. For example, in Kham (Tibeto-Burman, Nepal; Watters 2002: 257–76) -*ke* marks perfect and -*ya* future in a declarative clause:

(10) u-zihm-da   ba-ke   He went home
      3sg-house-ALLATIVE go-PERFECT

(11) u-zihm-da   ba-ya   He might go home
      3sg-house-ALLATIVE go-FUTURE

However, in a content question or in a polar question meanings are switched. Now -*ke* marks future and -*ya* perfect:

(10′) kana   ba-ke   Where will he go?
       WHERE   go-FUTURE

(11′) kana   ba-ya   Where did he go?
       WHERE   go-PERFECT

(Perfect is a parameter within past time, which characterizes an event as non-iterative and complete; it is complementary to imperfect, marked by -*e*/-*ye*. What is here called 'future' is actually a modality indicating potentiality.)

The tense system from declarative mood almost never (perhaps, in fact, never) also applies within imperative mood. There may be a distinction within imperative which relates to time but it is never both functionally and formally congruent with part of the tense system. It was mentioned in §19.1 that Jarawara contrasts 'immediate imperative' and 'distant imperative' (in positive and negative forms). However, the distinction relates to both time and space—'the immediate form gives a command to do something right here and now', whereas 'the distant forms relates to doing something in a different place, or at a different time' (Dixon 2004: 400).

For Takelma (Takelman family, Oregon), Sapir (1922: 157–62) recognizes an inflectional system on the verb covering six 'tense-modes'—aorist, future, potential, inferential, present imperative, and future imperative. 'The present imperative expresses a command which, it is intended, is to pass into more or less immediate fulfilment, as in GO AWAY! while the command expressed by the future imperative is not to be carried out until some stated or implied point of time definitely removed from the present, as in COME TOMORROW!, GIVE HER TO EAT! (when she recovers).' However, there is no similarity of form between inflections for the two imperatives and those for non-imperative, as can be seen from the verb 'run', with 2sg subject, in the six tense modes:

(12) AORIST   yowoʼtʼ   PRESENT IMPERATIVE   yuˋ
      FUTURE   yudaᵋ   FUTURE IMPERATIVE   yuᵋkʼ
      POTENTIAL   yuˋtʼ
      INFERENTIAL   yuˋkǃeīt'

Where tense is (or is part of) an inflectional system on the verb or on a verbal auxiliary, it is likely that the verb of every main clause must be marked for tense or the like. However, not all grammatical systems are obligatorily applied. In Nootka (Wakashan, British Columbia), 'the first sentence of the story locates the time by denoting the tense. After that, tense is not referred to again. The story goes on in a general or present tense, and people know what's what' (Sapir 1994: 109). Fijian is similar to Nootka in this regard. I recorded a number of stories with tense just stated in the first main clause. The story is understood to continue in that tense until the contrary is indicated.

It is interesting to compare (a) tense specification, and (b) statement of subject, between English and Fijian. In English, (a) is obligatory and (b) optional (in the right syntactic circumstance), while the opposite applies in Fijian. A story in English could run as follows: *They went out, shot a deer, brought it home, cooked it, and ate it.* The common subject pronoun, *they*, is stated just once, but each verb must show past tense—*went, shot, brought, cooked,* and *ate.* The same story told in Fijian would be, literally: 'They PAST go out, they shoot a deer, they bring it home, they cook it, they eat it'. Here the subject pronoun 'they' is required in each clause, but it is usual to specify tense just once, at the beginning.

Tense is a grammatical system and time a real-world description. We can now investigate the temporal reference of tense terms.

19.3.1 Temporal realization of tense

Some statements are generic or 'timeless'. If tense marking is optional, then no tense specification need be made, as in Fijian (Dixon 1988: 89):

(13) e   'ata'ata ca'e   [o   Viti]$_S$ [mai.vei Peritania]
      3sgS hot   MORE   ARTICLE Fiji   THAN   Britain
      Fiji is hotter than Britain

This sentence does not include past tense *aa* or future tense *na*, nor any marker of non-spatial setting.

For languages where there is obligatory tense inflection, it is generally the present tense form of the verb which is used for generic statements. In Kannada (Dravidian; Sridhar 1990: 225) non-past is utilized for 'universal time reference' in statements such as 'Eskimos live in igloos' and:

(14) su:rya pu:rvadalli   buTTutta:ne
      sun   east:LOCATIVE rise:NON.PAST:3sg.MASC
      The sun rises in the east

Other languages pursue different strategies. For example Tamil, another Dravidian language, uses the future inflection of a verb in a generic statement such as 'Cows give milk' (Asher 1985: 156).

'Present' is a rather enigmatic tense. Present time is but a moment, yet only an event with duration can properly be described as 'present'. If it were punctual, by the time one could refer to it, the event would be in the past. What is traditionally labelled 'present tense' in English is not generally used for present time reference. If I enquire of John what he is doing, the reply could be *I'm cooking dinner*, employing imperfective *be-... -ing*. He would not say *I cook dinner* (this would be interpreted as a generic statement, implying that John's habitual task in that household is to cook dinner).

In English, one can use the present tense form of the copula *be* to describe a state—*Where is your flashlight?*, and the reply, *It is on a shelf in my hut*. However, other languages operate in a different way. Jarawara deals with future time through an array of modalities and it has three past tenses (immediate, recent, and far past, see §1.7), each bearing an 'eyewitness' or 'non-eyewitness' evidentiality value. There is no present tense, and statements corresponding to (13) and (14) would be tenseless. However, an appropriate reply to 'Where is your flashlight?' would not be tenseless. One day I was visiting a neighbouring Jarawara house and was instructed to say, in reply to this question:

(15) nikiniki   fore-hare-ka
      flashlight(m) lie.on.raised.surface-IMM.PAST-EYEWITNESS(m)-DEC(m)
         [oko jobe   jaa]
         MY   house IN
      The flashlight was seen a short time ago lying on a raised surface in my
         house (that is, I left the flashlight on a shelf in my house)

One must specify the stance of the flashlight, here using verb *fore-* 'lie on a raised surface'. And one should provide full evidence for the statement that the flashlight has been seen in that position a short while in the past, using the immediate past eyewitness suffix *-hare*. (Who knows, during the five minutes since I had left my house someone might have stolen the flashlight, or it might have fallen to the floor.) If we had been talking in my hut, with the flashlight visible on the shelf, then an appropriate response might have been *nikiniki fore-ka ahi*, using verb *fore* 'lie on a raised surface' with no tense/evidentiality suffix (and adding the demonstrative adverb *ahi* 'here and visible').

Even when a tense system includes a 'present' term, there may be alternative ways for referring to present time. In Tamil the response to a command 'Come here' can involve present tense, but an alternative strategy is to express a greater sense of immediacy by using past tense, particularly in combination with a completive marker, meaning 'I'm coming right away' (Asher 1985: 157).

A fairly small number of languages have a three-term tense system {past, present, future}, Lithuanian often being cited as an example. A two-term system {past, non-past} is very common with a {non-future, future} system being encountered less often (some dialects of Dyirbal have the first system and others the second; see (19) in §19.3.2). As mentioned before, future time is often shown just by modalities, discussed in §19.4.1. No language has been reliably reported to have a {present, non-present} system; that is, with one tense covering both past and future time. However, this is attested with lexical time words—see §19.3.4.

A number of languages have several past tenses and a smaller number have several future tenses. Figure 1.1 of §1.7 provides a comparative chart of the five past tenses in the language spoken in the western islands of Torres Strait, the four in Yimas and the three in Jarawara. In each case, temporal realizations are relative—within a particular context, far past refers to events further back than does recent past, but it may be ten years as opposed to two years in one story, and two years as opposed to two months in another.

In some languages, one past tense refers to 'today' and another to 'yesterday'. For instance, Amele (Gum family, Papua New Guinea) includes in its tense system:

- today's past
- yesterday's past
- remote past (before yesterday)
- habitual past—occurred often in past time, such as 'I used to come'

Surely, one might think, 'today's past' and 'yesterday's past' should each refer to a fixed span of time. This is not the case. Roberts (1987: 228–9) remarks on how 'it is interesting to note that the changeover from one past tense to another is not rigid ... Generally, any event that occurred in the hours of darkness the previous night can be referred back to either in the yesterday's past tense or in the today's past tense depending on whether the speaker considers the event relates to other events that occurred on the previous day or to events that occurred on the same day as the utterance ... The same principles apply to the changeover from the remote past tense to the yesterday's past tense.'

Some languages have several future as well as several past tenses. Mithun (1999: 152–3, based on Jacobsen 1964) describes three future and four past tenses in Washo (California/Nevada). The West Torres Strait language has three future tenses (today, including going on now; tomorrow; and beyond tomorrow) alongside five pasts (just completed or going on now; earlier today; last night; yesterday; and before yesterday). Interestingly, languages with multiple tenses have either the same number of specifications in past as in future or more in past, never more in future.

There are a number of special techniques of tense organization. One of the most interesting is a 'cyclic' pattern shown by languages of the Maningrida subgroup in central north Australia. We find two tense suffixes covering four temporal periods. The forms for one conjugation in Burarra (Glasgow 1964; see also Dixon 1977a: 499) are:

(16) REFERRING TO   SUFFIX   LABEL
      now   -nga   contemporary within today
      earlier today   -de   precontemporary within today
      recently before today   -nga   contemporary before today
      long ago   -de   precontemporary before today

The two tense suffixes can be labelled 'contemporary'—for -nga—and 'precontemporary'—for -de. This system applies firstly within today, and secondarily in the past from yesterday on back.

All of the discussion thus far has been of tense which specifies the location in time of an event with respect to the moment of speaking. This is often referred to as 'absolute tense'. There is also 'relative tense' which most often occurs in a subordinate clause and specifies the temporal location of the event described by that subordinate clause with respect to the time established by the main clause. Korean (Sohn 1994: 325–7) has a neat way of dealing with this. A main clause will involve a tense specification. There will be no tense suffix in a subordinate clause if it has the same time reference as the main clause. For example:

(17) emeni-ka   wu-nikka   atul-to   wul-ess-eyo
      mother-NOMINATIVE   cry-BECAUSE   SO-ALSO   cry-PAST-POLITE
      Because the mother cried, (the son) also cried

If the subordinate clause bears a marker of tense, this will be with respect to the time established by the tense marker in the main clause. For example:

(18) Yongho-nun   aph-ass-ta-ko   malhay-ss-ta
      Yongho-TOPIC   sick-PAST-DEC-QUOTATIVE   say-PAST-DEC
      Yongho said that he had been sick

Here, Yongho's having been sick was earlier than his reporting this state, and the report was in the past with respect to the moment of uttering sentence (18).

'Perfect' is often associated with relative tense; see §19.7.

As mentioned in §11.6, in some languages tense suffixes (which are primarily used with verbs) may have their use extended to be occasionally attached to NPs. As an illustration of this, one day some Jarawara came across a clearing in the forest which they were told was the site of an old village, although no trace of the village buildings remained. The storyteller attached the far past non-eyewitness tense suffix (plus reported suffix) to the NP 'their village', giving '(a clearing of) what is reported to be their village in the far past, which cannot now be seen' (Dixon 2004: 308). The tense specification on an NP can be quite different from the tense specification on the predicate of its clause. For a comprehensive account of tense extended to NPs, see Nordlinger and Sadler (2004).

19.3.2 Markedness and neutralization

It is instructive to study the way in which 'tense' was dealt with by the founders of Western scholarship. Aristotle (*De. Int.* 16) stated: 'A *name* is a spoken sound significant by convention, without time, none of whose parts is significant in separation ... A *verb* is what additionally signifies time, no part of it being significant separately, and it is a sign of things said of something else ... 'recovery' is a name, but 'recover' is a verb, because it additionally signifies something's holding *now*. And it is always a sign of what holds, that is, holds of a subject ... 'recovered' and 'will recover' are not verbs but inflexions of verbs. They differ from the verb in that it additionally signifies the present time, they the time outside the present'. Verbs in Greek were bound forms, which had to be cited in *some* inflection; present tense was taken to be the basic form. This applies for ancient grammarians of Greek and Latin and for later grammars of Latin, and of English and other languages, during the Middle Ages and right down to the nineteenth century (Bursill-Hall 1972; Michael 1970).

In §5.7 we described the two varieties of markedness. If a term has zero realization then it is said to be formally unmarked with respect to other terms in its system. Functional markedness is rather different. If each term but one in a system is used in restricted, specifiable circumstances, but the remaining term is used in all other circumstances—and also for citation and perhaps when the system is neutralized—then that term can be said to be functionally unmarked.

Aristotle's focus on present tense was for philosophical, not linguistic, reasons. In some languages we do find one term in the tense system with zero realization. It is sometimes past tense which is formally unmarked; this applies for Ao (Tibeto-Burman, India; Gurubasave Gonda 1975: 49). Alternatively, present tense is formally unmarked; for example, in Upriver Halkomelem (Galloway 1993: 315), 'past tense is marked by {-ł} on a preposed auxiliary verb or syntactically by preposing the subject pronoun affixes...Future tense is marked by verb final {-cε} or syntactically by auxiliary "is going to" ...Present tense is unmarked.' But not only is present tense formally unmarked, it appears also to be the functionally unmarked term in the system for this language. 'Present tense is the catch-all tense, used to indicate present action

(which must be continuing as the speaker speaks—continuative aspect), habitual action (which may be spread over past, present, and future), momentaneous action (which the speaker is about to perform—non-continuative
aspect), and past action (historical present in narratives, legends, etc.)'.

It may be possible to recognize formal but not functional markedness, or
vice versa. And when both kinds of markedness are observed within a tense
system they do not necessarily coincide. It will be useful to repeat the instance
of this for Dyirbal, from §5.7. Illustrating with inflections for the predominantly intransitive conjugation (the Y class), we find the same suffixes across
all dialects but with different meaning distributions. Major tense and mood
choices are (the full paradigm is in Table 19.1):

(19)

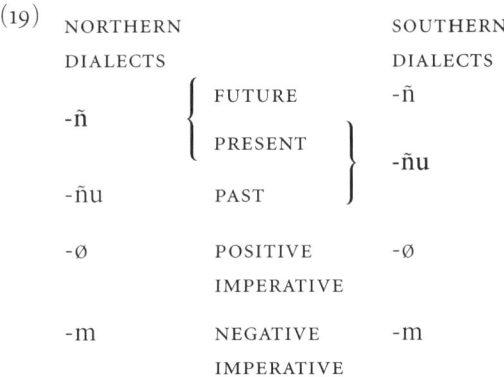

The functionally unmarked term for each set of dialects is in bold type.
This is the suffix which includes present reference—future/present (or non-
past) for northern and past/present (or non-future) for southern dialects. The
functionally unmarked terms are used in citation. A speaker of a northern
dialect will state that the verb for 'come' is *bani-ñ* whereas a southern speaker
will give *bani-ñu*. In each case, the functionally unmarked term is different
from the formally unmarked term, which is positive imperative (with zero
realization). Note that imperative is *never* given as the citation form.

The full roster of tense choices is invariably found in a declarative main clause
with positive polarity. Choice may be more limited in certain contexts, such
as under negation. This can be illustrated for Swahili, whose verb has the
structure:

(20) polarity.prefix-subject.prefix-tense/aspect.prefix-object prefix- ...
     -STEM

The polarity prefix is *hu-* for negative and zero for positive. The major tense-
aspect prefixes are:

(21)		POSITIVE POLARITY	NEGATIVE POLARITY
present		-a-	
progressive		-na-	-si-
past		-li-	
perfect		-me-	-ku-
future		-ta-	-ta-

That is, the contrast between present, progressive, and past is neutralized in negative clauses.

In the Papuan language Nend (Harris 1990: 121–2), the distinction between immediate past and far past is only made in positive, not in negative, clauses. Gondi, a Dravidian language (Subrahmanyam 1968), has a system of verbal inflections that combines mood, reality, modality, tense, and polarity. The terms are:

(22) (a) past realis   (c) future/habitual (e) imperative
     (b) past irrealis   (d) potential
     (f) negative

That is, in a negative clause there can be no specification of mood, reality status, modality, or tense. In other words, the mood/reality/modality/tense distinctions are all neutralized in the negative.

It is not uncommon for some types of subordinate clause to have fewer tense choices available than main clauses. We have already mentioned that a main clause in Jarawara has suffixes which indicate immediate, recent, and far past, combined with eyewitness or non-eyewitness evidentiality. In one variety of dependent clause, this six-term system is neutralized, with the immediate past non-eyewitness suffix used for all past reference. This is exemplified in (Dixon 2004: 469 and see further examples there):

(23) (a) hi-we-himata-mona-ka
         Oc-see-FAR.PAST:NON.EYEWITNESS:M-REPORTED:M-DEC:M
         (she) is said to have seen him

     (b) ka-maki-no-ho
         be.in.motion-FOLLOWING-IMMED.PAST:NON.EYEWITNESS.M-DEP
         as he was following (along the road)

Here (a) is the main clause and (b) a dependent clause, marked as such by final -ho. Although the events reported in both clauses occurred in the far past, the 'neutralized' immediate past non-eyewitness suffix is employed in the dependent clause. (Prefix hi- marks an 'O-construction' where verbal suffixes agree in gender with the O argument, here a man, shown by masculine (M) forms of tense, reported and mood suffixes.)

19.3.3 Space and time

Names for parts of the body play a fundamental role in every language. Very often, their meanings are extended to refer to general spatial notions. In many Oceanic languages, *mata* is 'eye, face' and also 'in front'. (See also the discussion of terms for 'head' in four languages, in §6.5.) Body-part terms may develop into adpositions with spatial meaning, such as *behind* in English (from *hind* 'rear part'). And such adpositions can take on further, non-spatial senses, such as *beside* in English. As discussed in §1.11, alongside spatial use in *Mary is sitting beside the boulder*, this preposition may be used with the meaning 'in addition to', as in *What are you studying beside(s) linguistics?*

Spatial terms—whether related to body-part nouns or independent of them—have a central role. Their meanings may be extended also to refer to time (the reverse, with time words having secondary reference to space, is extremely rare). There was discussion under (a) in §15.2.4 of how demonstratives whose primary meaning is spatial may also have temporal reference.

A number of languages view time in spatial terms. The most common pattern is for past time to be seen as behind and future time as in front of the speaker. In English one may say *That big meeting is now behind us*, with *behind* referring to the past, followed by *However, there are still three minor meetings up ahead*. The future is here seen as 'ahead' and also as 'up'. Many languages are like English in using 'behind' for the past and/or 'ahead' for the future; Haspelmath (1997a: 57) tabulates nineteen, including Latin, Albanian, Tamil, Maori, and Greenlandic.

Time may be viewed not as a flat plain but rather as a slope. It is sloping upwards in some languages (with future higher than present which is higher than past) and downwards in others (here past is higher than present which is higher than future). In Dyirbal time appears to be like a downhill slope: 'earlier on today' is homonymous with 'vertically up' and the expression for 'soon, next week' includes the suffix 'short distance downhill' (Dixon 1972: 115). However, Guugu Yimidhirr, another Australian language, has an idiom in which 'the day before yesterday' is rendered as 'below yesterday', implying an uphill slope (Haviland 1979: 77). And in Motuna, a Papuan language spoken on Bougainville island, local nouns *koto* 'up' and *koho* 'down' are also used for future and past time respectively. For example, 'last year' is literally 'year down' and 'from today onwards' is 'from today up', as in (Onishi 1994: 81):

(24) hoo.hoo irong-ngitee   koto raa'no   toku
     so   today-ABLATIVE up   daytime NOT

    konn-i-mo   tu-heeta-na
    walk.around-2:S-GENERAL.TAM:SAME.SUBJECT be:2:S-FUT-FEM

    So, from today onwards, you will not keep walking around in the
    daytime

19.3.4 Lexical time words

Time words roughly fall into five classes:

  (a) *Duration*. For example, the Australian language Yidiñ has *wudu* 'for a short time', *wayu* 'for a long time', and *muguy* 'all the time, always'.
  (b) *Frequency*. Either general—'usually', 'often', 'occasionally', 'generally', 'habitually', 'indefinitely'—or specific—'monthly', 'annually'.
  (c) *Specific time spans*. These cover units such as 'day', 'month', 'year' and also names for parts of these spans such as 'morning', 'afternoon', 'night-time', 'weekend', 'summer', 'winter', 'wet season'.
  (d) *With respect to expectation*—'already', 'too soon', 'not yet'.
  (e) *Temporal shifters*. These can be located within today—'earlier on today', 'now', 'later on today'—or outside today—'yesterday', 'tomorrow', 'next month', etc.

Languages vary in how they deal with time references. For example, quite different techniques are employed in Dyirbal and Yidiñ, languages which are contiguous but not closely genetically related. For time within today, Dyirbal makes great use of *gala* 'earlier on today' and *gilu* 'later on today'; that is time specification is in relation to *jañja* 'now'. There are lexemes 'dawn' and 'dusk' but nothing like 'morning' or 'afternoon'. (After contact with Europeans, *munin* 'morning' was borrowed from English.) Yidiñ has no words corresponding to Dyirbal's *gala* and *gilu* but instead uses terms relating to where the sun is in the sky, *ŋajagurran* 'morning' and *guygarnguygam* 'afternoon, evening' (Dixon 1977a: 498–9).

Temporal lexemes with shifting reference are particularly interesting. Although there is no tense system with a single 'non-present' term (referring to both past and future), we do find languages—particularly in New Guinea—with one word referring to a certain time in the past and also the corresponding time in the future. Yimas (Lower Sepik family; Foley 1991: 110) provides a canonical instance. It has:

(25) ŋarŋ   'one day removed (yesterday and tomorrow)'
     urakrŋ   'two days removed (day before yesterday and day after tomorrow)'
     tnwantŋ   'three days removed'
     kamprañcŋ   'four days removed'
     manmañcŋ   'five days removed'

The actual time referred to is distinguished by the obligatory tense choice on the verb. Similar systems are found in other Papuan languages, including Alamblak (Bruce 1984: 86) and Kobon (Davies 1981: 140–1, 287).

Another Papuan language, Hua (East-central Highlands family, Haiman 1980: 219), creates a time word referring to the future by adding suffix -'a to one referring to the past. For example:

(26)	ega	'yesterday'	ega-'a	'tomorrow'
	urga	'day before yesterday'	urga-'a	'day after tomorrow'
	kenaga	'long ago'	kenaga-'a	'long time hence'
	fzuga	'earlier'	fzuga-'a	'later'

Other terms taking -'a include 'day after day after tomorrow', 'this morning' and 'last night'.

A further Papuan language, Nend (Harris 1990: 115) has adverbs referring to up to five days distant from today:

(27)	mɨl	one day distant
	ñɨl	two days distant
	ekanj	three days distant
	kambɨl	four days distant
	iki	five days distant

Similarly to Hua, these are used alone for past time reference and have a suffix added, here -ŋam, for future time. It is worth noting that alongside this sophisticated system for referring to number of days distant from the present, the actual set of lexical numbers in Nend reaches only to four, and then only through compounding (Harris 1990: 91):

(28)	'one'	pamoh
	'two'	undamaj
	'three'	undama=pam ('two=one')
	'four'	undamaj=vam ('two=only')

Koasati (Muskogean, Louisiana; Kimball 1991: 408) also relates past and future time lexemes but—unlike Hua and Nend—the basic form is used for future reference with suffix -:kon added to derive the corresponding past term. For example:

(29)	nihtá	'tomorrow'	nihtá-:kon	'yesterday'
	nihtákoła	'day after tomorrow'	nihtákoła-:kon	'day before yesterday'
	hasí mí:ta	'next month'	hasí mí:ta-:kon	'last month'

Suffix -:kon may also be added to names for days of the week; for instance statóklo '(next) Tuesday', statóklo-:kon 'last Tuesday'.

19.4 Realis and irrealis

Some languages mark the 'reality' of an event by means of a grammatical system {realis, irrealis}. These terms are used in the literature in a variety of ways. Their canonical meanings can be characterized as:

- **Realis**—refers to something which has happened or is happening. May be extended to refer something which is certain to happen (for example, 'Tomorrow will be Tuesday').
- **Irrealis**—refers to something which has not (yet) happened. Often also used for something which did not happen in the past, but might have (for example, 'The doctor could have attended to the old man who collapsed right next to him'). Within irrealis, there are generally a number of modality choices, covering necessity, possibility, potential, etc.

Some languages have no tense system, just a realis/irrealis contrast. This applies to the Australian language Wik-Ngathan, where a verb takes one of two inflectional suffixes (Sutton 1978: 294):

(30)   —Realis *-nh* ~ *-ñ* ~ *-n*, for something which has happened, is happening, or will happen.
        —Irrealis *-k*, for something which might happen or is intended to happen (including imperative).

In this language, time and sequence are shown by particles (such as perfective *kan*, past continuous *öyam*) or temporal qualifiers (including *yimaŋk* 'yesterday' and *oñtjan* 'post-wet-season').

Other languages have a realis/irrealis contrast independent of a tense system, but relating to it. In Wardaman (Merlan 1994: 125–36, 175–83), also spoken in Australia, verbs take a three-term system of prefixes, {realis, irrealis, habitual}, and a five-term system of suffixes showing tense, {present, past, future, potential, 'zero'}. These may be combined as follows:

(31) PREFIX+SUFFIX   PREFIX +SUFFIX
      realis   present   irrealis present   = 'ought to'; negative
                                                 imperative
      realis   past   irrealis past   = 'ought to have, would
                                                 have'
      realis   future   irrealis 'zero'   = 'may, might, lest'
      realis   potential   habitual present   = 'always doing'
      realis   'zero'
                  = positive imperative

Tenses show their normal signification if employed with the realis prefix. When this is replaced by irrealis the sense is altered to non-achievement. (Note that irrealis plus present is most commonly used with a negative particle, then meaning 'ought not to, must not'.)

In most languages with a reality system, its semantic scope does not exactly correspond to the canonical characterization provided above. For example, 'potential' is marked as realis in Wardaman whereas in other languages it falls under irrealis.

The ways in which languages vary in their treatment of future time were mentioned in §19.2.1. Where there is a future term in the tense system, it is likely to be included under realis, similar to past and present (as it is in Wardaman). When future time is dealt with only through modalities—which are within irrealis—then realis will be limited to past and present (English is of this type).

Reference to time can be definite or non-definite. What could be more natural than that realis should be used for something which is bound to eventuate in the future, and irrealis for anything which is less certain. Mithun describes a situation of this kind in Central Pomo, where markers of clause linking show a realis/irrealis distinction. Realis forms are used for a certain future happening, as in (Mithun 1999: 180):

(32) šé·   ʔul   ma   ém-aq́=da...
     long already 2.AGENT   old-INCH:PERFECTIVE=DIFF:SIMULT:REALIS
     In the future, when you are older...

For reference to something in the future which is predicted (but which one cannot be absolutely certain will happen), irrealis is appropriate, as in (Mithun 1995: 370):

(33) té:nta=lil   wa-:n-hi...
     town=TO   go-IMPERFECTIVE-SAME:IRREALIS
     I'll go to town...

Some languages keep imperative mood and negative polarity quite separate from realis/irrealis. For instance, in Kiowa the realis/irrealis distinction applies only in declarative—not in imperative—mood and is independent of negation (Watkins 1984: 157–78, Mithun 1999: 173). In other languages a reality contrast may be linked with imperative and/or with negation.

For example, imperatives (both positive and negative) in Wik-Ngathan are marked as irrealis, whereas in Maricopa (Gordon 1986: 19–27) all varieties of imperative take realis. Alongside a simple indicative with realis suffix -*m*, as in (34), we have (35) which adds imperative prefix *k*- and retains the realis suffix:

(34) aham-m 'He hit him'

(35) k-aham-m 'Hit him!'

As mentioned above, choice between realis and irrealis marking may relate to particular kinds of future reference. In similar fashion, the realis/irrealis distinction may relate to different nuances of imperative. For example, in the Yuman language Jamul Tiipay (Miller 2001) casting a command into irrealis makes it softer and more polite, and in the Northeast Caucasian language Tsakhur (Dobrushina 1999) the combination of imperative and irrealis creates a wish or a piece of advice, rather than an order.

There is a different slant in the Tibeto-Burman language rGyalrong (Sun 2007: 809). Here, adding irrealis markers to an imperative indicates that 'the command/request is expected to be realized *during the speaker's absence at a later time*' (italics in original). Compare the plain imperative in (36) with the irrealis variety in (36'):

(36) nə-nɐpriʔ   qʰoʔ   noŋme
      IMPERATIVE-eat.supper SEQUENTIALIZER   only.then
      jɐ-ʃɐ
      IMPERATIVE-go
      Eat supper and then go (I will still be here)!

(36') nə-nɐpriʔ   qʰoʔ   noŋme
      IMPERATIVE-eat.supper SEQUENTIALIZER   only.then
      ɐ-jɐ-tɐ-ʃɐ
      IRREALIS$_1$-IRREALIS$_2$-2-go
      Eat supper and then go (during my absence)!

In some languages, negating a clause does not affect its reality marking. For example, in Wik-Ngathan realis is used for something which has happened, or is happening, or—in the negative—has not happened or is not happening. But in other languages negation ties in with the realis/irrealis system, and a statement that something has not happened or is not happening is naturally coded as irrealis. This applies in Muna (Austronesian, Indonesia; van den Berg 1989: 57).

As mentioned above, in some languages all imperatives are marked as irrealis; in others positive and negative imperatives show different reality marking. In (31) we saw that Wardaman employs the realis prefix (plus 'zero' suffix) for positive imperative but the irrealis prefix (plus present suffix) for negative imperatives. However, in this language negation does not affect the realis/irrealis status of a declarative clause.

Irrealis typically relates to the future, but in many languages it is also used for something which didn't happen (but might have happened) in the past. This can be illustrated from another Australian language, Nyigina:

(37) ŋa-la-MA-na-dyi   miliya marlu
      1SG-IRREALIS-go-PAST-EXPECTATION now   NEGATIVE
      ŋa-la-MA-na
      1SG-IRREALIS-go-PAST
      I was going to go (this morning) but I didn't go

The reference of irrealis does not stop there in Nyigina. Stokes (1982: 281) states that 'some utterances about situations in the past may appear in irrealis mode, presumably to emphasize that the statement does not correspond to present reality.' The following describes certain creatures in the Dreamtime:

(38) wa-la-DI-na-da   idany-barri   magarra
      3-IRREALIS-sit-PAST-HABITUAL long-COMITATIVE tail
      They used to have long tails (but they don't now)

Irrealis may be used for counterfactual statements along the lines of 'If we had known John's phone number, we would have invited him to the party'. The conditional marker 'if' serves as a clause linker; but 'conditional' could—at the same time—be regarded as a kind of modality, on the grounds that it describes something which has not yet happened.

In a language with a reality contrast, there may be non-zero markers (generally, affixes) for both realis and irrealis. But if one term may have zero realization, or a zero allomorph, this is always realis, showing it to be the formally unmarked term in the system; it is often also the functionally unmarked term. Of the languages illustrated above, the prefix system in Wardaman consists of three terms—habitual is basically *ma-*, irrealis is basically *ya-*, and realis is basically zero (there are some irregularities).

In a fair number of languages, realis is unmarked with irrealis being shown not by a single affix but instead by choice from a system of modality markers, which we can now discuss.

19.4.1 Modalities

As mentioned in §1.11—and dealt with in more detail in §18.5.2—we can recognize a number of 'secondary concepts' which are realized in some languages through affixation (or other morphological processes) and in other languages by separate words, called 'secondary verbs'. A secondary verb provides semantic modification for a primary verb, which may be grammatically linked to it within a subordinate clause. For instance, in English one can say *John began to clean the windows*. At the syntactic level, secondary verb *begin* occurs in the main clause and primary verb *clean* in a complement clause which is in O function within the main clause. But semantically, *begin* modifies *clean*. Secondary-A verbs do not add any arguments to those of the primary verb they modify—*John began to clean the windows* has the same two arguments (*John* in A and *the windows* in O function) as does *John cleaned the windows*.

In languages with a rich morphology, non-spatial setting is largely expressed by morphological processes, typically to a verb. But in a language with sparse morphology, such as English, secondary verbs may be used to code modalities within irrealis, and for others of the parameters discussed in §§19.5–19.13. There is always a limited number of modal verbs, so that we can say they constitute a closed grammatical system.

English shows a clear distinction between realis, shown by tense inflection on the verb, and irrealis, shown by a marker for one of a set of nine modalities. The modalities are expressed by two (syntactically different but semantically related) types of words—modals and what we can call semi-modals (both being types of Secondary-A verbs). A modal may only occur as the first of a sequence of verbs within a verb phrase, and may not take tense affixes. In contrast, a semi-modal behaves—syntactically and morphologically—like other verbs. Despite their different grammatical statuses, modals and semi-modals both express modalities, as set out in Table 19.2.

Modals and semi-modals from the same row in Table 19.2 have similar but not absolutely identical meanings. Semi-modals often carry an 'unconditional' sense, while modals may indicate prediction, ability, necessity, etc. subject to certain specifiable circumstances. Compare:

(39)   (a) John will marry his childhood sweetheart (if she'll have him)
       (b) John is going to marry his childhood sweetheart (she has already agreed to this)

TABLE 19.2. Modality expressed by modals and semi-modals in English

MODALITY EXPRESSED (central meaning)	MODAL VERBS	SEMI-MODAL VERBS
A. PREDICTION	will/would shall	be going to
B. OBLIGATION	should ought to	—
C. NECESSITY	must	have to have got to
D. ABILITY	can/could	be able to
E. IMMINENT ACTIVITY	—	be about to
SCHEDULED ACTIVITY	be to	—
ACHIEVEMENT	—	get to
INEVITABILITY	—	be bound to

Modals typically refer to the future. If one wants to talk about the time by which John should get home, this has to be stated in terms of an obligation, a necessity, a prediction, etc:

(40) (a) John should be home by six (dinner is served at that hour and he has an obligation to his partner not to be late for it)
(41) (a) John must be home by six (his boss is coming for dinner and it is absolutely necessary that he be there to greet him)
(42) (a) John will be home by six (based on my knowledge of his regular movements, this is what I predict)

It is possible to use modals with reference to past time. At six o'clock I could say any of:

(40) (b) John should be home by now
(41) (b) John must be home by now
(42) (b) John will be home by now

Much of what has been written on modals and modality is submerged in posh-sounding terminology. Typically, a sentence such as (40a) is said to be 'deontic' (relating to obligation, permission, etc.) while (40b)—and also (41b) and (42b)—are said to be 'epistemic' (relating to probability, possibility, certainty). This is misleading—sentence (40b) relates to obligation in the same way that (40a) does; (40b) simply projects the obligation into the past. It does not simply indicate a possibility/probability; rather it states what the obligation was (and the listener can make up their own mind as to whether the obligation may have been fulfilled). Similarly for necessity in (41b) and prediction in (41c).

Labels such 'deontic', 'epistemic', and the like can create illusory distinctions which may hinder explanation. They are unnecessary and liable to mislead. It is more straightforward to refer directly to modalities, as exemplified in Table 19.2.

Modalities A–E in Table 19.2 each recur in a fair number of languages, and further illustrations will shortly be provided. 'Scheduled activity', 'Achievement', and 'Inevitability' have more limited attestation. There are also 'desire' (or 'optative') and 'intention', which have a rather different status. In English *want*, *wish*, *intend*, and *plan* are classed as Secondary-B verbs since they may add an argument to those of the primary verb for which semantic modification is being provided, as in *I want Mary to go first* and *I intend for John to make the welcoming speech*. Some languages show desire and intention through morphological processes or syntactic particles, and there can then be *no* additional argument. (That is, we must have 'same subject' as in *I want to go first* and *I intend to make the welcoming speech*.) Markers of DESIRE (F) and INTENTION (G) could then be regarded as further types of modalities.

We can now illustrate how some of the modalities are expressed in a number of languages of varying character.

Ika (Chibchan, Colombia; Frank 1990: 59–63) has a suffixal system which includes markers of clause linking (purpose, result), negative imperative (an indicator of mood), and also modality markers:

- B. OBLIGATION   *-ikua*, 'conveys the idea of obligation', as in (43).
- D. ABILITY   *-ikuei*, describing 'what could take place', as in 'You cover over the hole, then you can catch the tiki animal'.
- G. INTENTION   *-iwa*, indicating immediate intention, as in (44).

(43) boko   ás-ik-o?
      where   sit-OBLIGATION-INTERROGATIVE
      Where should I sit?

(44) Pablo   naʔ-nik-ž-eʔ-ri,   iʔba   zor-iwa
      Pablo   come-WHEN-MEDIAL-THEN-TOPIC together go-INTENTION
        ni
      CERTAINTY
      When Pablo comes, we will (immediately) go together

Bini (dialect of Edo, Benue-Congo, Nigeria; Dunn 1968: 216–17, 97–8, 123–5) employs syntactic particles to code modalities, including:

- C. NECESSITY   *ghâ*, for 'action which the speaker feels compelled to do', as in 'I'll have to tell him', 'I'll have to pay that debt'.
- E. IMMINENT ACTIVITY   *khian*, 'about to be done; indicating a resolute commitment to see that the action is done', as in 'We are about to sleep' and (45).
- F. DESIRE   *gha*, indicating 'a desire to perform an action, but with no definite commitment to doing it', as in 'I want to/will follow you'.

(45) ɔ   khian   ti'èbe
      3SG   IMMINENT.ACTIVITY study
      He/she's about to study

Ainu (isolate, Japan; Tamura 2000: 113–19) indicates modality through a series of auxiliary verbs, including

- C. NECESSITY   *easirki*, 'expresses the necessity for an action to occur', as in 'I must write a letter' and 'You must go'.

- E. IMMINENT ACTIVITY *kuni*, as in (46).
- F. DESIRE *rusuy*, 'the desire that an action should occur' as in 'I've always wanted to go and they say we'll finally go tomorrow' and 'Someone probably wants to go home now'.

(46) en-kupa kuni   pekor   ku-yaynu
      1sgO-bite IMMINENT.ACTIVITY AS.THOUGH 1sgA-think
      I feel like (that dog) is about to bite me

Panare (Carib, Venezuela; Payne and Payne 1999: 123–6) has two modality suffixes to the verb:

- D. ABILITY *-poi*, 'indicates that the most agent-like argument has the ability or the potentiality of carrying out the action described by the verb', as in 'You can go', 'I can hear you'.
- F. DESIRE *-jté*, always followed either by *-pe*, indicating immediate (rather than delayed) realization—as in 'I want to bathe you (right now)'—or by negative suffix *-ka*, as in (47).

(47) a-y-ompíku-jté-ka   yu
      2.O-TRANSITIVE-scold-DESIRE-NEGATION 1sg
      I don't want to scold you

The range of meaning of each modality differs between languages; however, a common semantic core can be recognized which does permit cross-linguistic identification. One of the most interesting modalities is that which is here labelled 'ability'. There are two senses to *can* in English: (a) the capacity to do something, as in *John can lift 100 kilos* (he's so strong), and (b) being permitted to do something, as in *Mary can stay out until ten o'clock, no later* (her mother is very strict). Interestingly, corresponding forms in quite a number of other languages have the same two senses; for example *rawa* in Fijian (see Dixon 1988: 282–3).

19.5 Degree of certainty

Two further 'modal verbs' belong in the first column of Table 19.2—*may* and *might*. These are not, strictly speaking, modalities (within irrealis). Rather they describe the chance of some action or state eventuating. Many languages have similar markers, For example, Sapir (1930–1: 169) describes what he calls a 'dubitative' suffix in Southern Paiute (Uto-Aztec), glossed as 'perhaps, it may (might) be that …'.

A rich set of suffixes is described by Boas (1947: 245) for the Wakashan language Kwakiutl under the heading 'degree of certainty':

-ga:nɛm, 'perhaps'   *-lax*, potentiality 'might be'
-ana, 'probably'   *-x:st!ââkᵘ*, 'seemingly, it seems as though ...'
-dzâ, emphatic certainty

For the Salish language Musqueam, Suttles (2004: 373–84) recognizes a set of 'second position predicate particles'. These include *mə* ∼ *me* 'certain', indicating that there is no doubt about a statement, as in (48), and *ćtwaʔ* 'speculative', which indicates that the statement is based on supposition, as in (49).

(48) spéʔeθ mə
      bear   CERTAIN
      It's a bear (certainly, observably)

(49) spéʔeθ ćtwaʔ
      bear   SPECULATIVE
      It might be a bear

Suttles states that the speculative marker *ćtwaʔ* is weaker than the inferential marker *yəxʷ*. He adds a further contrast, with the evidential-type marker *ćə* 'quotative', which indicates that the statement is based on hearsay:

(50) spéʔeθ ćə
      bear   QUOTATIVE
      It is said to be a bear. It is supposed to be a bear.

19.6 Phase of activity

A further parameter of non-spatial setting is to specify whether an activity is beginning, continuing or finishing. A number of languages indicate some of these values. As mentioned in §1.11, Dyirbal has a verbal derivational suffix *-yarray-* meaning 'start to do' or 'do a bit more'. Alamblak (Sepik Hill languages, Papua New Guinea; Bruce 1984: 160–3) has a considerable set of verbal modifiers including 'continuous', 'completive', and 'cessative'. Koasati (Muskogean; Kimball 1991: 90) has a number of forms which function both as lexical verbs and also as auxiliaries, then indicating non-spatial setting. They include *ano:lin* 'finish' (meaning when used as a lexical verb is 'use up, devour') and *á:tan* 'keep on, continue' (lexical meaning 'dwell'). Slave (Athapaskan; Rice 1989: 587–92) includes among its 'aspect prefixes' inceptive *de-*, which 'expresses the start of an action' and terminative/completive *ne-* which 'marks the completion of an activity'.

Carib languages are notable for having verbal affixes which indicate the phase of an activity. For instance, Macushi displays verbal suffixes which

Abbott (1991: 120–1) labels as 'ingressive', meaning 'to begin', and 'terminative', meaning 'to finish', as in

(51) yei   ya'tî-pia'tî-'pî-i-ya
      wood   cut-INGRESSIVE-PAST-3-ERGATIVE
      He began to cut the wood

(52) yei   ya'tî-aretî'k-'pî-i-ya
      wood   cut-TERMINATIVE-PAST-3-ERGATIVE
      He finished cutting the wood

19.7 Completion—perfect and imperfect

The labels 'perfect' and 'imperfect' are used with a wide range of signification. Most typically, 'perfect' is taken to mean 'an action which is completed before the present time', to which is often added 'and which has present relevance'. The complementary label 'imperfect' refers to something which began before the present and is still continuing.

For the Papuan language Kobon, Davies (1981: 168–9) states: 'the perfect forms have both aspectual (present result of past event) and temporal (recent past) semantic values'. He goes on to say: 'the perfect forms are used to express a situation which has held at least once in the period leading up to the present'.

For example, an answer to the question 'Has that old woman borne (PERFECT) any children?' could be:

(53) Yawö, nipe ñi   möhöp rik.dau-ub
      yes   3sg   child two   bear-PERFECT:3sg
      Yes, she has borne two children

In the tradition of Latin and Greek grammar writing, perfect was called a tense—'what, from the point of view of the present moment, has been completed' (Kennedy 1962: 157–8)—alongside pluperfect—'that which, from the point of view of the past, was completed'. Lyons (1977: 704) distinguishes tense and completion, suggesting the following reanalysis for Greek and Latin:

(54) TRADITIONAL 'TENSE' LABELS   LYONS'S RELABELLING

      present   present imperfect
      perfect   present perfect
      imperfect   past imperfect
      pluperfect   past perfect

Jespersen (1924: 269) puts forward a similar opinion. 'The perfect cannot be fitted into the simple series [of tenses], because besides the purely temporal element it contains the element of result. It is a present, but a permansive present: it represents the present state as the outcome of past events, and may therefore be called a retrospective variety of the present. That it is a variety of the present and not of the past is seen by the fact that the adverb *now* can stand with it: *Now I have eaten enough.*'

The term 'perfect' is generally 'used of an action etc. considered as a completed whole' (Matthews 1997: 271). Although English *have -en* has traditionally been labelled 'perfect', this is not an appropriate label. Indeed, in the previous sentence of this paragraph, *has...been labelled* does not imply that this labelling is a thing of the past; it is still very much in use.

Have -en is used of an event or state which commenced previous to the time of speaking. Depending on the verb used and the accompanying adverb (if any) it may or may not be continuing up to—or beyond—the present. Consider:

(55)   John has been in jail for 21 years now

This describes something which commenced in the past and continues up to this moment. But it is not necessarily completed. On hearing (55), one would infer that John is still languishing in his prison cell. Either a different label is needed for *have -en* in English (see the discussion in Dixon 2005a: 211–19) or it should be noted that the conventional meaning of the label is here being extended.

What is of particular interest is the way in which *have -en* interrelates with the tense system in what is called 'back-shifting'. When direct speech is recast as indirect speech, with the framing clause in past tense, then the tense of the quoted clause must be moved back. For example:

(56) (a) 'Mary is ill', John said   (57) (a)   John said that Mary was ill
      (b) 'Mary was ill', John said   (b)
      (c) 'Mary has been ill,' John said   (b) } John said that Mary had been ill
      (d) 'Mary had been ill', John said   (d)

For the (a) sentences, present tense *is* in direct speech, (56), becomes past tense *was* for indirect speech, (57). In (b–d), each of *was*, *has been*, and *had been* becomes *had been* (past plus *have -en*) under back-shifting. In these circumstances, *had -en* does function as a kind of relative tense—'past of past' (one could even say, as 'pluperfect').

The pairs of labels perfect/imperfect and perfective/imperfective (see §19.10) are both well-established, so that it would be incautious to suggest replacing either with something else. But the similarity is unfortunate and most certainly does lead to confusion. Not infrequently, one set of terms is employed, unintentionally, when the other is intended.

19.8 Boundedness—telic and atelic

'Telic' and 'atelic' are often used to describe the inherent meaning of verbs. 'Telic' indicates something with a specific end point, while 'atelic' is used for an activity which does not have any necessary conclusion. *John arrived (in London)* is a telic clause whereas *Mary travelled (all over Europe)* is atelic. Telicity does, of course, depend on what is stated beyond verb and subject—whether there is (and what kind of) object and/or adverbial phrase. For instance *Mary travelled to London* is telic. And while *John wove* is atelic, *John wove a basket* is telic.

There is a considerable literature on the way tenses and other parameters of non-spatial setting have different possibilities (or different kinds of meaning) with verbs which are inherently telic and with those which are atelic. See Holisky (1981) on Georgian and Garey (1957: 105–10) on French.

'Telic' (and sometimes also 'atelic') have also been used as labels for grammatical categories. One of the system of inner suffixes to the verb in Hup (Makú family, Brazil), -*yiʔ*, is labelled 'telic' by Epps (2008: 554–8). Epps explains that this 'relates to a goal which necessarily brings the activity to an end, such as that conveyed by the telic *eat up* (vs. *eat*) in English... Like most Inner Suffixes generally in Hup, the Telic suffix is most frequently followed by the Dynamic [boundary] suffix -*Vy*; the resulting combination (-*yiʔ-iy*) typically indicates a *current state* of having attained the goal relating to the event, by which a participant is now completely affected'. An example is:

(58) húptok   ʔāh gʼɔp-yiʔ-iy
      manioc.beer 1sg   serve-TELIC-DYNAMIC
      I've served all the manioc beer (i.e. it is all gone)

In his survey of the grammars of Semitic languages, Gray (1934: 90–100) examines verb forms commonly called 'perfect' and 'imperfect'. Considering these names inappropriate, he suggests 'telic' and 'atelic', since reference is to an action or state completed or not completed. (However, not all Semiticists would agree with Gray on this matter.)

19.9 Temporal extent—punctual and durative

In his classic text, *Time, tense and the verb*, Bull (1968: 17) divides all events into two categories:

- 'those which are so short that perception cannot be verbalized until after the event is terminated'—punctual
- 'those having sufficient length to permit both perception and verbalization to be simultaneous with some part of them'—durative (or continuous or progressive)

Many languages grammaticalize one or both of these values. For example, Mam (Mayan, Guatemala; England 1983: 16–4) has a 'progressive' verbal prefix *n-*, which 'indicates that the action is in progress', as in:

(59) n-poon   aʔ
      PROGRESSIVE-arrive   water
      The water is arriving

Describing Tunica (isolate, Louisiana), Haas (1941: 39) remarks 'the semelfactive aspect is punctual', illustrating with 'He jumped out' and 'When he had come again'.

Sapir (1930–1: 167) states that in Southern Paiute 'every verb has a durative and a momentaneous form, the former being generally the primary form of the verb, the latter expressed by internal consonant gemination, glottalisation, reduplication, the suffixing of certain elements, or a combination of these'. Compare, for instance, durative *yaɣa'-* 'to cry' and momentaneous (i.e. punctual) *ya-ya'ɣa-* 'to burst into tears'. In Sanuma, from the Yanomami dialect cluster (Brazil and Venezuela; Borgman (1990: 164–79) there is a three-term system of verbal suffixes—durative, punctual (called here 'punctiliar'), and iterative (see §19.11). The durative/punctual contrast is shown in:

(60) a   mi-a-kule
      3sg sleep-DURATIVE-PRESENT
      She is sleeping

(61) a   mi-o-kule
      3sg sleep-PUNCTUAL-PRESENT
      She is asleep (just went to sleep)

19.10 Composition—perfective and imperfective

This parameter relates to the way in which discourse is organized. Each of the terms has significance entirely with respect to the other. A system of composition is pervasive in Slavic languages and also in some others, such as Greek. Wade (1992: 258) states that: 'Most Russian verbs have two aspects, an imperfective and a perfective, formally differentiated in one of the following ways: (i) By prefixation ...; (ii) By internal modification ...; (iii) By derivations from entirely different roots ...; (iv) In a few instances, by stress'.

When perfective aspect is specified, the event is regarded as a whole, without respect for its temporal constituency (even though it may be extended in time). Imperfective focuses on the temporal make-up of the event. The relative meanings of the terms are brought out in the following examples:

(62) Ivan myl   posudu,   (a)
       Ivan wash:IMPERFECTIVE:PAST:MASC:SG dishes:ACC:SG (AND)
          Masha na-pisala   pisjmo
          Masha PREVERB:PERFECTIVE-write:PAST:FEM:SG letter:ACC:SG
       Ivan was washing the dishes and Masha wrote a letter

The activity of Ivan's washing the dishes is marked by imperfective, showing that it is regarded as having temporal composition. In contrast, the event of Masha's writing a letter is marked as perfective showing that its temporal extent is not here under consideration. The sentence thus indicates that Ivan started washing up before Masha wrote the letter and continued after she had finished.

If the letter writing had been protracted and the dish washing shorter, the clauses could, effectively, have been reversed, giving:

(63) Masha pisala   pisjmo,
       Masha write:IMPERFECTIVE:PAST:FEM:SG letter:ACC:SG
          (a)   Ivan   vy-myl
          (AND) Ivan   PREVERB:PERFECTIVE-wash:past:masc:sg
       posudu
       dishes:ACC:SG
       Masha was writing a letter and Ivan washed the dishes

This indicates that Ivan completed washing the dishes (perfective) while Masha was writing a letter (imperfective). (Note that in each of (62) and (63), the two clauses may occur in either order, and the conjunction *a* 'and/but' is optional.)

Like many other grammatical categories, perfective and—even more so—imperfective, have a considerable range of meaning and function which extends well beyond what has been described here.

19.10.1 Aspect

The term 'aspect' has both a narrow and a wider meaning. It is always used of the parameter of composition—perfective and imperfective. Indeed, the label was taken over from a term in grammars of Slavic languages with roughly this general signification. From this focus, 'aspect' has been extended to describe many parameters of non-spatial setting. I have generally avoided using it in this chapter; nevertheless passages quoted above from various grammarians refer to the following 'aspects': punctual, durative, continuative, non-continuative, inceptive, terminative/completed, perfect, and semelfactive. There are similar lists of varieties of aspect in Sapir (1921: 108), Jespersen (1924: 286–9), Nida (1984: 199–200), and Frawley (1992: 294–335), among others.

Aspect is generally contrasted with tense. It is seldom used of modalities or degree of certainty, and never of evidentiality. But its scope often includes the other parameters discussed in this chapter—Phase of activity (§19.6), Completion (§19.7), Boundedness (§19.8), Temporal extent (§19.9), Frequency and degree (§19.11), and Speed and ease (§19.12).

19.11 Frequency and degree

In his fine account of 'aspect', Jespersen (1924: 287) includes: 'the distinction between what takes place only once, and repeated or habitual action or happening'. There can also be specification of the degree of an activity—'a little bit', 'a lot', etc.

Crapo and Aitken (1986: 3–5) list an array of what they call 'modal suffixes' for Bolivian Quechua. These include modalities—Imminent Activity -naya 'be about to, intend to, do as if (start)' and Necessity -na 'must, have to'. Also in the list are:

- -ri 'a little bit, a small amount', as in 'Drink some please' and:

(64)   puñu-ri-ni
       sleep-LITTLE.BIT-PRESENT:1sg.SUBJECT
       I sleep a little bit

- -ykacha 'intermittently, at intervals (frequentative)'. Added to verb root ukya- 'drink' this yields stem ukya-ykacha- 'sip'.

Dyirbal (Dixon 1972: 249) has a verbal derivational suffix -jay- which indicates 'either (a) that an action is repeated (the action often being performed not with respect to some known goal, but blindly, everywhere, in the hope of encountering a goal)', for example 'He called out in all directions (i.e. not knowing if there was anyone there to hear him)'; 'or (b) that an action involves many objects (realizing deep function S or O)'.

As noted in §19.3.1, a statement may be generic or 'timeless'; for instance, *Birds fly and fish swim*. There is also 'habitual' indicating that something happens at regular intervals; this is sometimes restricted to what happened in the past. For Southern Paiute, Sapir (1930–1: 175) explains that what he called the 'usitative' suffix, *-n'ï-ⁿ*, is 'used only before past passive participle'. An example is 'my always saying it'.

For Yuchi (isolate, Oklahoma), Wagner (1934: 355–6) recognizes four 'aspects'. One is essentially spatial, the distributive, as in 'They jumped over here and there'. There is also durative (see §19.9), plus:

- reiterative, shown by reduplication, as in *wɛk'a' yugwa-gwa* 'he was talking now and again'
- habitual, shown by suffix *-nɛ*, as in *honɔndzo'a-nɛ'* 'he used to ask us'

The 'aspect' suffixes given for Kwakiutl by Boas (1947: 241) include:

- *-a*, statement of single act or simple condition, as in 'strike with the fist'
- *=ᵋnakwɛla*, gradual, continued motion, one after another, as in 'to hang one after another'
- *-k'a*, repetitive, as in 'to go again and again'
- *-[x]dala*, to be habitually, as in 'to hurt oneself habitually'
- *-(ɛ)s*, continuously, as in 'to sleep continuously, all the time'

Tariana (Aikhenvald 2003: 366–7) has a set of 'degree markers' including 'a bit', 'really', 'more or less, just about', and 'a lot'.

19.12 Speed and ease

A fair number of languages include in their grammar a morphological process relating to speed. There is suffix *-nbal* ~ *-galiy* 'do it quickly' in Dyirbal (Dixon 1972: 248), suffix *-rpaya* 'rapidly' in Bolivian Quechua (Crapo and Aitken 1986: 3), and suffix *-uri* 'rapid velocity' in Urarina (isolate, Peru: Olawsky 2006: 471–3, 632). The latter is illustrated in:

(65) kwara-uri-a   ku-a
      see-RAPID.VELOCITY-NEUTRAL   go-3sg.A
      She went to see him quickly (e.g. to briefly say goodbye)

The two verbs in (65) make up a serial verb construction. However, the rapid velocity suffix has scope only over 'see'—the seeing was quick, not the going.

Grammatical marking of 'do it slowly' is far less common. Mithun and Ali (1996) list more than twenty 'aspectual categories' for Central Alaskan Yup'ik (Eskimo). Many of them relate to parameters discussed above, including 'customarily', 'always', 'now and then', 'repeatedly', 'keep on, continue', and 'a little at a time'. The list includes *-(g)ar(ar)te-* 'briefly, suddenly', as in 'He left suddenly', and also *-qataar-* 'begin slowly', as in:

(66)   nere-qataar-tu-q   waniwa
       eat-BEGIN.SLOWLY-INTRANSITIVE:INDICATIVE-3sg   now
       He is going to slowly start eating

Another parameter of non-spatial setting relates to manner—the ease with which an action is performed. For Angami (Tibeto-Burman, Nagaland, India), Giridhar (1980: 75–6) identifies what he calls types of mood:

- 'The mood of Ease denotes that the agent considers the action identified by the verb easy to perform'. It is shown by suffix *-sə̄* to the verb.
- 'The Exertive mood denotes that the action identified by the verb is achieved with considerable effort, and hence contrasts with the mood of ease. It is marked by *-liê*.'

From the verb root *dùkrî* 'kill' can be formed:

(67)   dùkŕí-sə̄   'kill with ease (for instance, a domestic animal)'
       dùkŕí-liê   'kill with difficulty (for instance, a tiger)'

The 'ease' suffix is used with transitive verbs, and may indicate that the referent of the O NP is small; for instance *mêlī-sə̄* 'climb a small hill', *pêmhè-sə̄* 'extinguish (a small fire)'.

19.13 Evidentiality

Around one quarter of the world's languages include in their grammar an evidentiality system (discussed in §§1.5–6). For each statement made, there must be obligatory specification of the source of information on which it is based. There may be just a two-term system {eyewitness, non-eyewitness}, as in Jarawara—see (15) in §19.3.1 and (23) in §19.3.2—or else {reported; everything else} as in Estonian.

At the opposite extreme are evidentiality systems with five terms. There is a particular concentration of these in languages spoken in the Vaupes River basin, which spans the Brazil/Colombia border. The system may have originated in Tucanoan languages, and has now diffused into neighbouring languages from the Makú family and into Tariana, from the Arawak family. In Tariana, tense and evidentiality are fused into one set of clitics (Aikhenvald 2003: 289–323, 326–7):

(68)

	REMOTE PAST	RECENT PAST	PRESENT	EVIDENTIALITY (with central meanings)
	=na	=ka	=naka	VISUAL: speaker has seen it, or speaker takes full responsibility for statement
	=mhana	-mahka	=mha	NON-VISUAL: speaker has heard, smelt, tasted, or felt (but not seen) it; for example, a phone ringing
	=sina	=sika	—	INFERRED, GENERIC: not seen, but inferred on the basis of general knowledge
	=nhina	=nihka	—	INFERRED, SPECIFIC: not seen but inferred from specific evidence (for example, the remains of a person are found floating on a lake in which an evil snake is known to live, and the speaker infers that the snake killed the person)
	-pidana	-pidaka	-pida	REPORTED: when someone else informed the speaker of it

It will be seen that the full five-term system only applies for the two past tenses. For present, inferred specifications are not appropriate. And no evidentiality applies for definite future, marked by suffix -*de*, or for less definite future, suffix -*mhade*. Interrogative clauses in past tense employ a three-term system {visual, non-visual, inferred}; for present tense there is no inferred choice in interrogatives, as there is not in declaratives. And there is a special 'reported imperative', marked by -*pida*, meaning 'do what someone else told you to do'.

The wide range of grammatical systems of evidentiality has only been hinted at here. Aikhenvald (2004) provides a detailed and comprehensive survey of types of system, their realizations and meanings, how they intersect with other parts of the grammar, and their origin. The interested reader is directed to her inclusive and incisive account.

19.14 Summary

Every language has some grammatical and lexical means of describing non-spatial setting, although the parameters expressed, and their realization, differ enormously. This chapter deals with relevant grammatical systems, with occasional comments on lexical resources.

Many (but not all) languages include in their grammar a tense system. This may have just two terms—future/non-future or, more commonly, past/non-past. A fairly small number of languages have a three-term system: past, present, and future. There may be several divisions within past tense, and sometimes also several within future. There may be, in a subordinate clause, 'relative tense', indicating time with respect to the time of the main clause.

One important distinction is between 'realis' (things which are believed to have happened or be happening) and 'irrealis' (roughly, things which have not yet happened). Within irrealis there may be a number of modalities, such as prediction, obligation, necessity, and ability. In some languages, reference to future time is through a term in the tense system, in others through a modality.

Other parameters of non-spatial setting include: degree of certainty, phase (starting, continuing, finishing), completion, boundedness, temporal extent, and speaker's view of the composition of an activity. There may also be specification of one or more of degree, frequency, speed, and ease. Evidentiality can also be conveniently included under 'non-spatial setting'.

19.15 What to investigate

It is important to bear in mind that a grammatical system may be realized through affixation or some other morphological process (see §3.13) or through small grammatical words (which may also be distinct phonological words, or may be clitics). For example, there is a four-term system showing non-spatial setting in Mam (England 1983: 161–4). This consists of one prefix—'progressive' *n-* —and three sentence-initial particles—'recent past' *ma*, 'non-recent past' *o* (illustrated at (8) in §19.3), and potential *ok*. Such grammatical words, which make up a closed system, should be distinguished from lexical words (such as 'often' and 'tomorrow').

Where all terms in a system are shown as, say, affixes, they may be realized at different places within a word. We noted in §4.8 that the Australian language Tiwi includes in its grammar a two-term system relating to time of day. However prefix *-atə-* 'happens in the morning' is placed in prefix slot 6, immediately before an object pronominal prefix (in slot 7) whereas *-kə-* 'happens in the evening' comes in slot 11, between the future-imperative suffix (slot 10) and the 'do while walking' suffix (slot 12). Only one of these affixes may occur with a given verb, showing that they make up one grammatical system, albeit with disparate surface realization.

As stated several times before, there is a multiplicity of kinds of information in the world, which has to be mapped onto the limited resources of a grammar.

As a consequence we often find markers of varied sorts combined into one inflectional system; this is illustrated at Table 19.1 in §19.1. Care must be taken to distinguish (a) marking of non-spatial setting, which relates both to a clause and its predicate; (b) marking of mood, relating to a sentence and indicating type of speech act; and (c) marker of type of clause linking.

One must, of course, commence with an examination of surface structure. As the linguist's understanding of the language matures, they will be able to establish the underlying systems and structures, disentangling them from their surface realization.

Of the more than a dozen parameters of non-spatial setting discussed in this chapter, there is none which is found in every language. The fieldworker should not have any presumption that any particular category will be found in the language they are studying, even though it may be present in the neighbours and/or close relatives of the language. (See the discussion of Warrgamay in §4.8.)

The set of recurrent parameters of non-spatial setting is listed in §19.2 and discussed through §§19.3–13. The point to note is that each system—and each term in a system—has an individual character in every language in which it occurs. For example, where there is a category of tense, habitual activity may be shown by the term referring to present time in one language, by the term referring to past time in another, and by neither in a third language. By examination of textual occurrences, and through direct observation within immersion fieldwork, it will be possible to determine the semantic and function scope for each parameter.

A further topic of study is something only alluded to in this chapter, the interrelations between parameters of non-spatial setting. The contrast relating to a certain parameter may only be found in association with some—not all—of the terms of another parameter. For example, the dependency between composition and tense in Russian is described by Comrie (1976b: 71): 'we can say there is a Present tense which is Imperfective, a Past tense with an Imperfective/Perfective opposition, and a Future tense with an Imperfective/Perfective opposition'.

The list given in this chapter of parameters for non-spatial setting, and the descriptions provided for them, are far from exhaustive. Individual languages may show further parameters and/or unusual meanings for some of those listed here.

Sources and notes

There are a number of excellent texts on this topic, of which I have made considerable use. They include Jespersen (1924: 254–89), Bull (1968), Comrie

(1976b), Lyons (1977), Chung and Timberlake (1985), Comrie (1985b), Bhat (1989b), and Elliott (2000). Beyond these, we encounter an array of works which immerse themselves in questionnaires and ersatz terminology.

19.1 Full information on the system of mood suffixes in Jarawara is in Dixon (2004: 233–45).

It has been suggested that, in English, *and*—and perhaps also *but* and *or*—may join clauses with different mood values. However, for many of the proffered examples, *and* is not an intra-clause coordinator but rather an introducer of a separate sentence. For example: *What did you do that for? And don't ever do it again.* Each of the two sentences here has its own mood and its own intonation contour. This is a matter under much debate.

English has one type of complement clause introduced by a *wh*-word, as in *I*$_A$ *don't know* [*whether he has come*]$_{CoCl:O}$. However, this does not mean that the complement clause has interrogative mood.

As one example of the allocation of non-spatial settings to different grammatical levels, Foley and Van Valin (1984) say that aspect applies to the 'nucleus' (i.e. predicate), modality to the 'core' (predicate plus core arguments), and tense to the 'periphery' (whole clause).

Mallinson's (1986: 284–91) discussion of mood in Rumanian is cast in terms of the 'questionnaire' for the series in which his grammar appeared. This questionnaire has a long list of possible moods beginning with—in this order—indicative, conditional, imperative, optional, intentional, debitive ('obligation to do something'), potential (Comrie and Smith 1977: 50–1).

The verbal inflectional paradigm given here is for the Jirrbal dialect of Dyirbal. A fuller account, and information on other dialects, is in Dixon (1972: 246–50).

19.3 It should follow from the discussion in this section that if there is a future tense then this must be a 'shifter', whereas if future time is referred to only through modalities then no shifters are involved. But something which is 'irrealis' (described through a modality) may, as events unfold, become 'realis'. At breakfast one may say *John may/should/must/will come* and then, at noon, *John has come.* We have here something akin to temporal shifting and closely allied to it.

Time specifications are often applied in interesting ways. At a lecture I attended by George van Driem in 2001, he said: *In the first part of the last century (since we are now in the next century)*...The part I have enclosed in parentheses takes as its point of reference the last century (referred to in the main clause), something which in 2001 we had scarcely got used to having moved beyond. And see example (10) in §3.8.

Munro (1987: 127) mentions that in Choctaw (Muskogean) 'there appear to be more tense/aspect distinctions' in polar interrogatives than in the corresponding declaratives. This is highly unusual.

For Kham, Watters (2002) employs labels 'perfective' and 'imperfective'. I have substituted 'perfect' and 'imperfect' which seem more appropriate for the meanings given.

Koasati (Kimball 1991: 266–7) has two 'delayed imperatives'; meaning 'do later' and 'do a lot later'.

19.3.1 For a full account of tense and aspect in English, see Dixon (2005a: 207–29).

Other languages with multiple past tenses include Yagua (Payne and Payne 1990: 364–8), Shipibo-Conibo (Valenzuela 2003: 284–9) and Koasati (Kimball 1991: 161, 207–10).

The 'contemporary/precontemporary' cyclic tense system is found in all four languages of the Maningrida putative subgroup, and appears also to have diffused into contiguous languages of the Yolngu subgroup. See Dixon (2002: 665) and further references there.

19.3.3 It appears that if a tense system includes a term referring just to future time, this is never the formally or functionally unmarked term in the system.

19.4 Elliott (2000) is a most worthwhile discussion of realis and irrealis, with further references to languages showing this grammatical system. She mentions that the distinction has been labelled 'factive/non-factive' or 'actual/potential'. Indeed, labels 'realis' and 'irrealis' have not been employed by some of the sources quoted in this section; nevertheless, it appears that it is a reality system which is being described.

Aikhenvald (2010: §4.2.5) has a fullish discussion of the interrelations between imperatives and realis/irrealis, on which the summary here is based. Chafe (1995) makes the interesting observation that in Caddo content questions are marked as realis but polar questions as irrealis.

19.4.1 There is a useful survey of various scholars' idea about modality in Hladký (1976).

The discussion here of modal and semi-modal verbs in English is closely based on Dixon (2005a: 172–7); more details and exemplification are provided there. Historically, some modals did have present/past tense forms—*will/would, shall/should, can/could* (and *may/might*). However, today each of these forms has its individual meaning. (The original tense distinction is nowadays reflected just in 'back-shifting' in indirect speech—see §19.7.)

Varying techniques which languages employ for same-subject and different-subject 'want' constructions are surveyed in Dixon (2006a: 31–3); and see further references there.

19.7   What were at one time productive past tense forms for a few of the English modals still function as such in back-shifting. Compare the direct speech in *'Mary will go,' said John* with its indirect speech counterpart *John said that Mary would go.*

19.8   Comrie (1976b: 44, note 1) says 'the term "telic" was apparently introduced by Garey (1957)'. In fact, both 'telic' and 'atelic' were used by Gray (1934: 91). And the *OED* cites instances of *telic* from 1846.

19.9   Haas's use of the term 'semelfactive' as an alternative for 'punctual' is unusual. It is generally taken to refer to 'an event which happens just once' (Matthews 1997: 335). In her grammar of Slave, Rice (1989: 798–9) says 'the semelfactive indicates an event isolated from a repetitive process or series of events. It indicates that an action is performed one time and punctually'.

19.10   Sentences (62–3) were provided by Alexandra Aikhenvald.
Note that many otherwise excellent grammars use the terms 'perfective' and 'imperfective' when 'perfect' and 'imperfect' would be appropriate. For instance, Rice (1989: 485) states, for Slave: 'The imperfective mode indicates that the action or state described by the verb is ongoing or about to be done. The perfective mode marks completed actions.' (Grammars of other Athapaskan languages make similar statements.) Schachter and Otanes (1972: 66) recognize a system of three aspects for Tagalog, described as follows: 'The perfective aspect characerizes an event as completed, the imperfective as not completed but begun, and the contemplated as not begun.' And see the note to §19.3 concerning Kham.

19.13   Only a brief summary has been provided here of evidentiality in Tariana. Each term in the system has a much wider range of meanings and functions; a full account is in Aikhenvald (2003: 287–323, 376).

20

Number systems

20.1 Introduction

It is probably the case that every language has some means for showing the number reference of a core (and often also a peripheral) argument of a predicate. This may be coded either through lexical modifiers (number words, etc.)—discussed in §20.9—or through a grammatical system of number, dealt with in the body of this chapter.

Basic linguistic theory focuses on underlying structure. An argument of a predicate can be realized through: (i) an NP, which can have a noun, free pronoun, demonstrative, etc., as head, plus optional modifiers, and/or (ii) a bound pronoun, associated with the predicate.

For a clause in past tense in English, just (i) applies. Orthographic -*s* on the head of an NP indicates plural (referring to two or more), in (2), as opposed to zero marking, which indicates singular, in (1):

(1) [The boy]$_{NP:S}$ [laughed]$_{PREDICATE}$

(2) [The boy-s]$_{NP:S}$ [laughed]$_{PREDICATE}$

In Fijian, there is no grammatical marking of number on a noun (lexical number modifiers are, of course, possible). We have here alternative (ii), where the number of a core argument is shown by choice of the obligatory bound pronoun within the predicate—3rd person singular *e* in (3) and 3rd person plural *era* in (4). (Note that, in this language, 'plural' indicates 'more than a few', within a {singular, dual, paucal, plural} number system—see §20.2.)

(3) [e   aa   dredre]$_{PREDICATE}$ [a   gone]$_{NP:S}$
      3sg PAST laugh   ARTICLE child
      The child laughed

(4) [era aa   dredre]$_{PREDICATE}$ [a   gone]$_{NP:S}$
      3pl   PAST laugh   ARTICLE child
      The children laughed

Swahili utilizes both (i) and (ii), through a set of prefixes which fuse information on number and noun class. Prefix pair *ki-*, singular, and *vi-*, plural, indicate a noun class referring to inanimate things. The appropriate prefix appears on a noun realizing a core argument and also on the verb of the predicate:

(5) [ki-kombe]$_{NP:S}$ [ki-me-vunjika]$_{PREDICATE}$
     INAN:SINGULAR-cup   INAN:SINGULAR.S-PERFECT-be.broken
     A cup is broken

(6) [vi-kombe]$_{NP:S}$ [vi-me-vunjika]$_{PREDICATE}$
     INAN:PLURAL-cup   INAN:PLURAL.S-PERFECT-be.broken
     Cups are broken

In fact, a number/noun-class prefix in Swahili is added not only to the head of an NP (-*kombe* here) but also to words modifying it; see (39) in §20.6.3. Other languages are like English in having number marking just on the head. There are also languages where number marking is on modifiers within an NP, but not on the head. As remarked in §1.10, number is a referential property of an argument—that is, of a complete NP, not just of its head. It is appropriate that in some languages number marking is placed at the end of an NP, on the last word, whatever that should be. These variant possibilities are exemplified in §20.6.

It was emphasized under (c) in §1.10 that, when number or some other category is stated both in an NP and on the predicate—as in (5–6)—it is not useful to enquire whether it is the NP which 'agrees' with the predicate, or vice versa. What we have is an underlying argument specified for number. Within surface structure this may be realized at one or at several places in a clause. There is no reason to attach priority to any one of these. We shall see, in §20.6.4, that there may be further possibilities for specifying the number of a core argument, such as a verbal affix which is not a bound pronoun.

A system of number choices is occasionally found at other places within a language. It was noted in §19.3.4 that Yimas has a set of words which refer to 'X days removed from today' where X ranges over 'one', 'two', 'three', 'four', and 'five'. Combined with past and future tense marking, they indicate 'yesterday' or 'tomorrow', 'the day before yesterday' or 'the day after tomorrow', and so on. Similarly, there may be special terms for 'first-born child', 'second-born child', and so on.

'Number' is sometimes used as a label to refer to frequency or intensity—a type of adverbial modification of a verb, as in 'he did it lots of times'. This kind of specification is excluded from the present discussion.

20.2 Size of systems; absolute and relative reference

Number systems are of varying size and specification of referents.

A. Singular/plural. This is the most common number system, being found in English and other European languages, plus Hausa, Igbo, Swahili, Quechua, Japanese, Tamil, and very many others. The terms are:

- singular   referring to   one
- plural   more than one

B. Singular/dual/plural. The second most common system, found in Egyptian Colloquial Arabic and in many languages of small-scale societies, such as Hua and Alamblak from New Guinea, Ponapean from the Pacific, Dyirbal and Warlpiri from Australia, Yagua from Peru, and Yup'ik Eskimo. The terms here are:

- singular   referring to   one
- dual   two
- plural   more than two

C. Singular/dual/trial/plural. This system is quite uncommon. It is attested in a number of Oceanic languages such as Larike and in a few Australian languages including Wunambal, Ngan'gityemerri, and Marrithiyel (see Laidig and Laidig 1990, Corbett 2000: 21–2, and Dixon 2002: 246). Here we have terms:

- singular   referring to   one
- dual   two
- trial   three
- plural   more than three

Larger systems are extremely rare. The richest number system in pronouns that I have encountered is:

D. Singular/dual/trial/quadruple/quintuple/plural (two varieties) in American Sign Language (Baker-Shenk and Cokley 1996: 205–14, Zeshan 2000: 42–3). This involves:

- singular   referring to   one
- dual   two
- trial   three
- quadruple   four
- quintuple   five
- plural$_1$ more than five, where the referents are conceived of individually
- plural$_2$ more than five, where the referents are conceived of as a group

The difference between plural₁ and plural₂ is said to be similar to that between 'each' and 'all' in English.

It will be seen that 'plural' has a different range of referents in each of A–D 'more than one, two, three, or five respectively'.

The next type of number system involves a quite different type of reference:

E. Singular/dual/paucal/plural.   This is found in a number of languages in the Pacific, New Guinea, and Australia, including Manam (Lichtenberk 1983: 108–10), Paamese (Crowley 1982: 79–81), Longgu (Hill 1992: 91), Fijian (Dixon 1988: 52), Ambrym (Pacon 1971), and Yimas (Foley 1991: 216–25). See also Corbett (2000: 23–6). The terms in the system are:

- singular   referring to   one
- dual   two
- paucal   a relatively smaller number greater than two
- plural   a relatively larger number greater than two

Paucal has sometimes been glossed as 'a few' or 'three to five' and plural as 'many' or 'more than five'. However, in every system of type E which has been systematically examined, we find that paucal and plural have reference *each with respect to the other*. The actual reference of these terms depends on the size of the population under review. If discussing members of a family, paucal may be used to refer to three or four people in contrast to plural for five or six. For a larger population, the reference increases. As mentioned in §15.1.1, there were about sixty adults in my Fijian fieldwork village of Waitabu. A weekly announcement about village work was shouted out from three places within the village, to reach the ears of around one third of the villagers from each point. The village crier said: 'Listen here, you (paucal) people in this part of the village, here are your (plural) tasks of village work'. (Dixon 1988: 52, 351–2). Here paucal referred to about twenty people and plural to sixty, the whole adult population. For Paamese, Crowley (1982: 81) states that paucal most frequently refers to between three and about twelve (depending on the size of the population being discussed), but he had heard it used for all the inhabitants of the island of Paama (about 2,000) then being opposed to plural which referred to the total population of the Republic of Vanuatu (about 100,000). The critical point is that, in this type of system, the references of paucal and plural are relative—paucal refers to a smaller number (more than two) and plural to a larger one.

There are other number systems, some of whose terms have relative reference. For example:

F. Singular/pochal/plural. This is found for the 1st person pronoun in the Muskogean language Choctaw (2nd and 3rd person pronouns make a simpler singular/plural distinction; Nicklas 1972: 29–30, Broadwell 2006: 93–4):

- singular referring to one
- pochal   a relatively smaller number greater than one
- plural   a relatively larger number greater than one

The middle term from this system has been labelled 'dual/paucal'. However, a non-disjunctive label is appropriate and I suggest pochal (based on Italian *pòchi* 'a few'). As with paucal and plural, the reference of pochal and plural are each relative to that of the other.

In systems A–D, each term has absolute reference. In E–F, singular and dual have absolute reference but for the remaining terms reference is relative. That is:

- singular, dual, trial, quadruple, quintuple—always absolute reference
- paucal, pochal—always relative reference

The all-purpose label 'plural' has absolute reference if occurring in a system where all of the other terms have absolute reference (A–D) and relative reference if in a system where one or more of the other terms has relative reference (E–F).

There could be a number system which has more than two terms with relative reference. For instance 'relatively smaller number', 'relatively medium-sized number', and 'relatively larger number'.

Under (d) in §15.1.2, there was discussion of 'minimal/augmented' pronoun systems, where the minimal category covers 1sg, 2sg (3sg if the language has this), and also 'you and me'. Augmented then involves one or more referents in addition to the minimal number. All the terms in attested minimal/augmented systems have absolute reference. There could be terms with relative reference within a system of this type, but none have so far been reported.

20.2.1 Collective, distributive, and associative

We can briefly mention three further quantifier-type categories which may relate to number systems.

(a) **Collective.** This refers to a group or a pile; it is frequently—but by no means exclusively—used on nouns with inanimate reference. Collective may be an alternative to a regular plural or it may be the only type of plural in the language. Describing Tlingit (south-east Alaska), Swanton (1911: 169) writes: 'with animate or inanimate objects, but more often the latter, the sense of

A LOT OF or A HEAP OF is expressed by suffixing *q!* or *q!î*'. For example, *ta* 'stone', *teq!* 'stones lying in a heap'. Swanton goes on to say: 'that this is not a true plural is shown on the one hand by the fact that its employment is not essential, and on the other by the fact that it is occasionally used where no idea of plurality, according to the English understanding of that term, exists. Thus *yuyā'i LAnq!* THE BIG WHALE may be said of a single whale, the suffix indicating that the whale was very large, and that it had many parts to be cut out. Therefore, it may best be called a collective suffix.'

In some languages, a collective suffix is added to an adjective relating to a nation to indicate the inhabitants of that nation;. For example, in Russian one can say (with a slightly derogatory overtone) *nem-čura* ('German-COLLECTIVE') 'the Germans'.

(b) **Distributive**. This refers to things being distributed, either in space or among people (for instance, 'one each'). Investigating the structure of Kwaki-utl (Wakashan family, British Columbia), Boas (1911c: 444) remarked: 'the idea of plurality is not clearly developed. Reduplication of a noun expresses rather the occurrence of an object here and there, or of different kinds of a particular object, than plurality. It is therefore rather a distributive than a true plural.'

Mithun (1999: 88–91) provides examples of a distributive marker being attached to a noun—for example, 'snow here and there'—or to a verb, as in Mohawk (Iroquoian):

(7)   wa'-e-nontar-a-r-<u>onnion</u>'
       FACTUAL-FEMININE.AGENT-soup-EPENTHETIC-put.in-<u>DISTRIBUTIVE</u>
       She kept serving the soup (one ladleful at a time to <u>each</u> diner)

(8)   wa'-k-nata-hr-<u>onnion</u>'
       FACTUAL-1sg.AGENT-visit-ANDATIVE-<u>DISTRIBUTIVE</u>
       I went visiting <u>here and there</u>

(c) **Associative**. An NP whose head is X, if marked for normal plural, refers to 'lots of X'. In contract, if marked for associative plural, the meaning is 'X and associates'. These will make up a compact and coherent group—it may consist of X and their family and/or friends and/or workmates and/or club members, etc. (Associative marking is used predominantly on nouns with human reference.)

Corbett (2000: 102) quotes contrastive sentences in Hungarian (provided by Edith Moravcsik):

(9)   Jànos-ok
       John-PLURAL
       Johns (more than one person called John)

(10)   Jànos-ék
       John-ASSOCIATIVE.PLURAL
       John and associates

In some languages associative plural is an alternative to plain number marking. In others it constitutes a separate parameter. Mithun (1999: 94) shows
how in Central Alaskan Yup'ik (Eskimo), the associative marker -*nku*- may be
followed by dual, as in (11), or by plural, as in (12):

(11)   Cuna-nku-k   ayag-tu-k
       Cuna-ASSOCIATIVE-DUAL   leave-INDICATIVE-3dual
       Cune and his associate (for example, friend) left

(12)   Cuna-nku-t   ayag-tu-t
       Cuna-ASSOCIATIVE-PLURAL leave-INDICATIVE-3plural
       Cune and his associates (friends, family, etc.) left

20.3 Obligatory and optional number systems

In some languages, every NP (or every NP of a certain sort, for example, with
a count noun as head) must have a number specification. In English we have:

(13)   boy-ø   singular, referring to just one boy
       boy-s   plural, referring to more than one boy

There is here a two-term inflectional system of number marking; plural is
shown by orthographic -*s* suffix and singular by the absence of this (or by zero
suffix, ø). If one doesn't know how many boys are involved in some activity,
then it is necessary to employ disjunction and say *boy or boys*.

   Number marking on NPs in Latin is also obligatory and shown through an
inflectional system. Quoting nominative case forms:

(14)   puella   singular, referring to just one girl
       puellae   plural, referring to more than one girl

   In contrast, many languages have optional number marking on NPs. For
example, in Turkish (Lewis 2000: 23):

(15)   kız   neutral, unspecified for number—'one or more girls'
       kız-lar   with plural number suffix—'girls'

The plain noun, *kız*, could refer to any number of girls, as determined by
context. One can optionally added plural suffix -*lar*, to indicate a number
more than one. To unequivocally refer to just one girl, the lexical number word
bir 'one' would be included—*bir kız*.

A similar situation applies for Dyirbal:

(16)   midin   neutral, unspecified for number—'one or more
                        possums'
       midin-jarran   with dual number suffix—'two possums'
       midin-midin   with full reduplication indicating plurality (more
                        than two)—'three or more possums'

Similarly to Turkish, to specify 'one possum' the lexical number word *yuŋgul*
'one' would be added—*yuŋgul midin*.

In Latin, obligatory specification of number is fused with obligatory specification of case in one inflectional system. A sample from the paradigm is:

(17)   SINGULAR   PLURAL
                            'girl'   'more than one girl'
       NOMINATIVE   puella   puellae
       ACCUSATIVE   puellam   puellās
       DATIVE   puellae   puellīs

In Dyirbal, number specification is shown by optional morphological
processes, all derivational in nature. There is an obligatory inflectional system
of cases, and this is added after derivations have applied:

(18)   NEUTRAL   DUAL   PLURAL
                        'possum(s)'   'two possums'   'more than
                                                      two possums'
       ABSOLUTIVE   midin   midin-jarran   midin-midin
       ERGATIVE   midin-du   midin-jarran-du midin-midin-du
       DATIVE   midin-gu   midin-jarran-gu midin-midin-gu

The contrast between obligatory and optional number marking applies
to NPs. It is only very rarely found on pronouns—and then only when
non-singular forms involve a regular morphological process applying to
singulars—or in verbal marking.

20.4 Mixed systems

In §20.2, we surveyed six kinds of number systems (and there are a fair few
more). In each of these, one term was labelled 'plural' but with a different
range of reference—the meaning of 'plural' is with respect to the meanings of
the other terms in that system. Thus, in system A {singular, plural}, plural is
'two or more'; in B {singular, dual, plural}, plural is 'three or more', and so on.
When a language employs just one kind of number system, no problem should

arise. 'Plural' will be used with the appropriate meaning throughout the grammar. However, some languages have a mix of systems, with 'plural' having different signification in each. A problem of terminology will then arise.

Consider the Papuan language Amele, which has system B, {singular, dual, plural}, for personal pronouns but system A, {singular, plural}, for interrogatives 'who' and 'which'. For example (Roberts 1987: 21, 208):

(19)

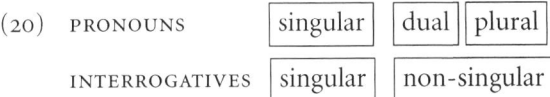

	SINGULAR	DUAL	PLURAL
1 singular	ija	ele	ege
'who'	in	an	

It would be unsatisfactory to employ the label 'plural' both for 1sg form *ege*, here meaning 'three or more' and also for the interrogative form *an*, then meaning 'two or more'. To attach two meanings to the same term at different places in the grammar would be likely to cause confusion, and should be avoided.

The most appropriate course is to employ labels for the larger system, B, and then say that *an* is 'non-singular', a cover term for 'dual-plus-plural':

(20) PRONOUNS   singular dual plural

INTERROGATIVES   singular non-singular

Quite a number of languages include number systems A and B in their grammar, and in each instance the appropriate cover term for 'dual-plus-plural' is 'non-singular'. This point was earlier made in §1.4, there exemplified for Jarawara, which works in terms of a {singular, dual, plural} system for verbal forms relating to number of an S or O argument, and {singular, non-singular} for pronouns.

There can be a more complex mix of systems. Koasati, a Muskogean language, has a singular/plural contrast for pronouns and human nouns. A number of verbs have suppletive stems depending on the number of the S or O argument—some of these have distinct forms for all of singular, dual, and plural, others contrast singular with dual-plural, while a third set recognize singular-dual and plural. For example (Kimball 1991: 323, 417):

(21)

	SINGULAR	DUAL	PLURAL
(a) 'stand', forms for number of S	haccá:lin	hikkí:lin	lokkó:lin
(b) 'put in', forms for number of O	hókfin	állin	
(c) 'die', forms for number of S	íllin		hápkan
1st person free pronoun	anó	isnó	

Once again, we can adopt the labels of the maximal system {singular, dual, plural}, where 'plural' refers to more than two, then using 'non-singular' for 'dual-plus-plural' and 'non-plural' for 'singular-plus-dual'.

(22) (a) 'stand', 'sit', 'dwell'

singular	dual	plural

(b) 'put in', 'hit', 'run', etc.

singular	non-singular

(c) 'die', 'go', 'come', etc.

non-plural	plural

1st person free pronoun

singular	non-singular

There are, however, languages with such a mix of systems that an appropriate set of labels cannot be obtained simply by judicious use of 'non-'. Consider Yimas, another Papuan language (Foley 1991: 111–12):

(23) SYSTEM free and possessive
      E   pronouns;
              exemplified by 1sg
              free forms

SINGULAR	DUAL	PAUCAL	PLURAL
ama	kapa	paŋkt	ipa

      SYSTEM demonstratives,
      B   bound pronouns
              and nouns,
              exemplified by
              'this (near
              speaker)'

SINGULAR	DUAL	PLURAL
pk	plak	piak

'Plural' is here used with two entirely different meanings:

- In system E, it has reference to that of paucal, 'a relatively larger number greater than two'.
- In system B it has absolute reference, 'more than two'.

The third term in System B could be called 'paucal/plural'. But it is surely more felicitous to bring out the fact that Yimas has one number system, B, in which all terms have absolute reference, and another system, E, in which paucal and plural have reference to each other, by employing labels 'absolute plural' and 'relative plural' respectively. That is:

(24)

E free pronouns, etc.

SINGULAR	DUAL	PAUCAL	RELATIVE PLURAL

B demonstratives, etc.

SINGULAR	DUAL	ABSOLUTE PLURAL

Finally, we can examine the number systems in Motuna, a Papuan language spoken on the island of Bougainville (Onishi 1994: 72, 127–33, 315). First of all, free pronouns and bound possessive pronouns make a straightforward singular/non-singular distinction. Illustrating for second person:

(25)

	free form	bound form
2 singular	ro	roko-
2 non-singular	ree	reeko-

Verbs mark number of a core argument through a {singular, dual, paucal, plural} system. We can illustrate with the present tense forms of intransitive verb *paa(h)-* 'cry' where 2nd person subject takes four number values:

(26)

2sg masculine	paakong
2sg feminine	paakana
2 dual	paatikee
2 paucal	paa'kee
2 plural	paa'kong

So far there is no difficulty. We have a maximal four-term system, {singular, dual, paucal, plural}, on verbs, which reduces to {singular, non-singular} for pronouns. Both of these systems are obligatory (as are those just illustrated for Amele, Koasati, and Yimas). However, Motuna also has a number system on nouns and adjectives, and this is of the optional variety. Thus:

(27)

nommai	neutral	one or any number of persons
nommai-karu	dual	two persons
nommai-naa	paucal	a relatively smaller number of persons, greater than two
nommai-ngung	plural	a relatively larger number of persons, greater than two

This is almost identical to the number system on verbs. The difference—and it is a critical one—is that the verbal system is obligatory and includes singular number, whereas the system on nouns is optional, with a neutral term which can have any number reference, depending on context.

Where there is a mixture of number systems, there may be a tendency for the richest set of distinctions to be associated with personal pronouns. But this is far from a rule since many exceptions can be provided; they include Koasati and Motuna.

20.5 Realization

The singular and non-singular forms of pronouns, interrogatives, nouns, and verbs can be formally quite different. This is typically the case with pronouns, as exemplified for Amele in (19), Koasati in (21), and throughout §15.1. When a verb has distinct forms showing number of S and O arguments, these are generally suppletive, as illustrated for Koasati in (21). If a language marks number on just a small set of nouns, some or all of these are likely to have suppletive forms. In Kana (Benue-Congo, Nigeria) just one noun has singular and plural forms and they are suppletive (Ikoro 1996b):

(28) ŋwíí   child
      míɔ́ŋɔ́ children

In Jarawara, just four nouns have non-singular forms. Those for 'spirit', 'man', and 'woman' are based on the singular but the forms for 'child' are rather different (Dixon 2004: 304):

(29) inamatewe child
      matehe   children

   When number is marked on a lexeme—noun, adjective, or verb—any morphological process may be employed (these were listed in §3.13). Affixation is the most common process—as it is for virtually every grammatical category—but others are attested. In English, for example, we find internal change in *man/men, woman/women, mouse/mice, foot/feet, analysis/analyses*, and so on.

   When number marking is obligatory, it may fuse with other obligatory categories, the whole making up one portmanteau inflectional system. This was illustrated for noun class and number on nouns and verbs in Swahili— (5–6) in §20.1—and for case and number on nouns in Latin—(17) in §20.3. We find number fused with both case and gender on adjectives in Latin, while endings on verbs in Latin combine specification of number of subject with person of subject plus tense, mood, and voice.

   Optional number marking is almost always shown by segmentable affixes, which just provide information on number. In some languages, number is shown by clitics which may attach to the periphery of an NP—see §20.6.3.

   As pointed out in §6.4 and §3.13, reduplication may convey many kinds of grammatical information—word-class-changing derivation, tense, possession, syntactic function, and diminutive. But one recurrent use of full or partial reduplication is to mark plural within an optional number system. This was illustrated for Dyirbal in (16) and (18) of §20.3. In Indonesian, the base form of a noun is neutral as to number. Plural may, optionally, be shown by reduplication (Sneddon 1996: 16–17):

(30) rumah   house   rumah-rumah   houses
      perubahan change perubahan-perubahan changes

   The base form of a noun is also neutral as to number in Tamambo (Oceanic Branch of Austronesian, Vanuatu; Jauncey 2011: 113, 134–5). A limited number of nouns have an optional plural form. This is marked by prefix *lo-* for all trees, *na-* for all kin terms, *va-* for 'child' and 'chief', *vai-* for 'male/boy' and 'youth', and *ra-* for 'woman/girl'. Just eight nouns (of diverse meaning) form their plural by partial reduplication; they include:

(31) hinau   some thing   hina-hinau   some things
      tahasi   stone   taha-tahasi   stones
      maranjea   old man   mara-maranjea   old men

Note that in Tamambo reduplication involves just the initial CVCV- of the root, whereas in Indonesian and Dyirbal the whole root is repeated.

Reduplication can often have a distributive (rather than a plain plural) meaning—see Boas's remarks on Kwakiutl, quoted under (b) in §20.2.1. Sapir (1930–1: 274–82) describes the distributive meaning of reduplication with both nouns and verbs in Southern Paiute—from 'father' is formed 'their own fathers', and from 'take hold of' is obtained '(they) each took hold of'.

20.6 Where number is shown

Languages vary as to which constituents bear marking of a grammatical system of number. Returning to the introductory examples from §20.1, Swahili marks number on pronouns, nouns and their modifiers, demonstratives, interrogative words 'which' and 'how many'—but not 'who' and 'what'—and on verbs. In contrast, Fijian shows number just on free pronouns, and on bound pronouns (which occur within the predicate). In English, number is marked only on count nouns, demonstratives (*this/these, that/those*), and the indefinite article (*a* is only used of a singular referent). The present tense form of a verb indicates whether a 3rd person subject is singular or plural—compare *He/she/it fall-s* with *They fall-ø*.

20.6.1 Pronouns

Since this word class was quite extensively discussed in §15.1, here it should suffice to summarize a few major points.

Almost all languages show a number contrast in free pronouns. Under (c) in §15.1.9 we noted that this is lacking from Kiowa, Cayuga, and Acoma Keresan—they have just two free pronouns, for 1st and 2nd person, neutral as to number. But in each instance there is number specification in bound pronouns. These languages are exceptional; in many cases, bound pronouns make fewer distinctions than their free congeners. Also under (c) in §15.1.9, we drew attention to the Australian language Wambaya which has a '1/2/3, sg/du/pl, inc/exc' system for free pronouns and for bound forms in S function, but just two bound pronouns for O function—1st person -*ŋ*- and 2nd person -*ñ*-, neutral as to number.

It is most often the case that a pronoun paradigm cannot be segmented into person and number morphemes. But this is possible in a minority of languages, with plural simply involving the addition of a suffix to the singular form. It was illustrated at (2) in §15.1.1 for Cantonese—where the plural suffix on pronouns, -deih, is not used on nouns, except with yành '(other) person'— and at (18) in §15.1.2 for Lakota—where pronominal plural suffix -pi indicates that a core argument has plural reference.

In some languages where the number system has more than three or more terms, there are two sets of stems, one for singular and the other for non-singular. Specific dual/trial/paucal/plural/etc. forms are then based on the non-singular stems. In the Australian language Ungarinjin, the free pronouns are (Rumsey 1982: 31):

(32)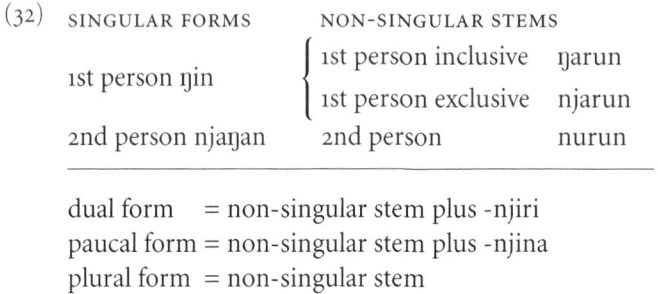

```
       SINGULAR FORMS            NON-SINGULAR STEMS

                              { 1st person inclusive   ŋarun
       1st person ŋin         { 1st person exclusive   njarun
       2nd person njaŋan        2nd person             nurun
```

dual form   = non-singular stem plus -njiri
paucal form = non-singular stem plus -njina
plural form = non-singular stem

Here the non-singular stem is used alone for plural number, with dual and paucal formed from this by the addition of -njiri and -njina respectively. There are a fair number of languages with this profile. (Some others are quoted in Dixon 2002: 247.)

A more unusual paradigm is found in Ponapean (Oceanic subgroup of Austronesian; Rehg 1981: 159) where the subject forms of free pronouns are:

(33)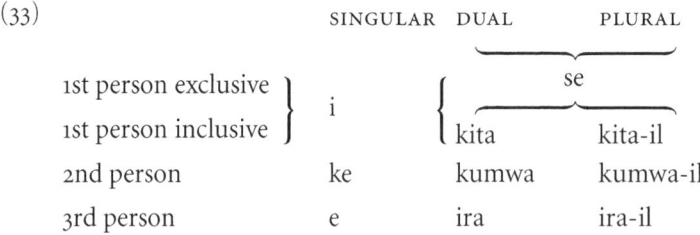

	SINGULAR	DUAL	PLURAL
1st person exclusive }	i	{	se
1st person inclusive }		{ kita	kita-il
2nd person	ke	kumwa	kumwa-il
3rd person	e	ira	ira-il

Here we find that 1st inclusive, 2nd, and 3rd persons use the non-singular stem for dual and add suffix -il for plural forms.

In other languages, all non-singular forms involve an increment to a basic non-singular stem. This can be exemplified from the Papuan language Amele (Roberts 1987: 218) where the distinction between 2nd and 3rd persons is neutralized in dual and plural numbers. The non-singular roots are 1st person *e-* and 2nd/3rd person *a-* to which are suffixed *-le* for dual and *-ge* for plural:

(34)		SINGULAR	DUAL	PLURAL
	1st person	ija	e-le	e-ge
	2nd person	ina	a-le	a-ge
	3rd person	uqa		

Minimal/augmented systems may follow a similar pattern. This is exemplified for the Australian language Mangarayi at (17) in §15.1.2. Here non-minimal stems (1st person *ɲi-*, 2nd *rnu-*, and 1st-plus-2nd *ŋa-*) take suffix *-rr* for unit-augmented and *-rla* for augmented forms.

In some languages, non-singular pronouns may be employed for reference to a single individual—when this individual is to be accorded special respect by virtue of social position or kinship relationship to the speaker. Examples of such usage are provided in §15.1.5; see also Corbett (2000: 220–8).

Cross-linguistically, there is a variety of special uses of non-singular pronouns. Two of these are encountered in Yagua (Peru; Payne and Payne 1990: 377). First, a woman who has had children is referred to by dual (rather than singular) forms of 2nd and 3rd person pronouns. The other special feature is found when there are two plural participants within a stretch of discourse. For ease of identification, one group is referred to by a plural and the other by a singular pronoun. 'In such cases, the more topical or in some sense "salient" group is treated properly in terms of its semantic plurality. The other group is treated as singular. For example, if adults and children are interacting, the adults will be referred to as plural and the children as singular. If humans are interacting with animals, the humans will be plural and the animals singular. If "good guys" are interacting with "bad guys", it is predictably the "good guys" who are treated as plural while the "bad guys" are treated as singular.'

20.6.2 Demonstratives and interrogative words

Some (but far from all) languages mark number on demonstratives and/or on interrogative words. Amharic—with a singular/plural system—does so on both, and the marking has an interesting form (Amberber 1996: 38):

- Plural prefix *inna-* is used on 2nd and 3rd person pronouns, on demonstratives, and on *man* 'who'.
- Plural suffix *-očč* is used on nouns, adjectives, and *min* 'what'.

There are other examples of 'who' being treated like a pronoun and 'what' like a noun, in addition to their overarching membership of the class of interrogative words. See §5.1 and §27.6.4.

In Alamblak, a singular/dual/plural contrast applies in both pronouns and demonstratives. The same number and gender suffixes are used for 3rd person pronouns and for demonstratives (Bruce 1984: 75–81):

(35)		3rd PERSON FREE PRONOUN	BASIC DEMONSTRATIVE
	singular masculine	rë-r	ind-r
	singular feminine	rë-t	ind-t
	dual	rë-f	ind-f
	plural	rë-m	ind-m

A 'proximity marker', -ar- 'near' or -ur- 'far' can optionally be included between demonstrative root and number/gender suffix; for example, ind-ar-f 'this (near) dual'.

Alamblak has interrogative words frëh 'who', fitëh 'which', fiñji 'what (action)' and tamëh 'what (substantive)'. None of these has a dual or plural form. However, there are reduplications with special meanings—fiñji-fiñji is 'how many (with references to substantives rather than to actions)', frëh-frëh is 'who (among many)', fitëh-fitëh is 'which (among many)' and tamëh-tamëhm is 'what (among many)'.

Amele has a quite different marking profile. Demonstratives do not show number (although they may be accompanied by a postposed 3du or 3pl pronoun). A singular/dual/plural system applies to free and bound pronouns, and a singular/non-singular contrast is found in two question words (Roberts 1987: 21):

(36)		SINGULAR	NON-SINGULAR
	'who'	in	an
	'which'	cel	ail

There is no number marking on eeta 'what', nor on nouns or adjectives, providing a further instance of the link between 'who' and pronouns, and between 'what' and nouns.

20.6.3 Noun phrases

Number is a referential property of an argument, which can be fully or partially expressed through an NP. At the level of underlying structure, it is the whole NP which is categorized for number (not its head). Within surface structure, languages adopt many different strategies for the marking of number on an NP. It may be shown at the beginning or end of the NP, or just on the head, or on every word in the NP, or just on modifiers to the head and not on the head itself. We can now briefly illustrate these.

In Tagalog there is an optional plural marker *mga=* which is a proclitic to the first word of an NP (Schachter and Otanes 1972: 111–13). Alamblak has a series of enclitics, attached to the last word of an NP—whatever that may be—which mark person (1st/2nd/3rd), number (singular/dual/plural), and also gender (masculine/feminine) for 3sg. We can illustrate this with the plural clitics in all three persons attached to noun *yima* 'person' (Bruce 1984: 96):

(37) (a) with 3pl enclitic =m   yima-m   'people'
      (b) with 2pl enclitic =kë   yima-kë   'you people'
      (c) with 1pl enclitic =nëm   yima-nëm   'us people'

Tamil has obligatory number marking just on the head of an NP, and then only when it refers to what are called 'rational beings' (humans, gods, and demons). Singular is unmarked, with plural being shown by *-kaḷ*. An interesting point is that case inflections follow the plural suffix. A partial paradigm for *paiyaṉ* 'boy' is (Lehmann 1993: 17–18, 47):

(38)   SINGULAR   PLURAL
      nominative   paiyaṉ   paiyaṅ-kaḷ
      accusative   paiyaṉ-ai   paiyaṅ-kaḷ-ai
      dative   paiyaṉ-ukku   paiyaṅ-kaḷ-ukku

In Swahili the appropriate number/noun-class prefix may go onto every word in an NP. Thus, (6) from §20.1 can be expanded to:

(39) [vi-kombe   vi-dogo   vi-wili]ₙₚ:ₛ
      INAN:PLURAL-cup   INAN:PLURAL-small   INAN:PLURAL-two
          [vi-me-vunjika]ₚᵣₑᵈᵢ𝒸ₐₜₑ
      INAN:PLURALS-PERFECT-be.broken
      The two small cups are broken

Manambu (Ndu family, Papua New Guinea; Aikhenvald 2008a: 130–43, 200–2 and personal communication) makes a singular/dual/plural contrast in pronouns and demonstratives but has no number marking on nouns:

(40) duₛ   yi-na-di
      man/men   go-ACTION.FOCUS-3pl.S
      Men are going

The noun *du* is neutral as to number. If, however, it is modified by a demonstrative—which does mark singular, dual, or plural—this provides a number value for the NP. For example:

(41) [a-di   du]ₛ   yi-na-di
      THAT-PLURAL   man/men   go-ACTION.FOCUS-3pl.S
      Those men are going

Another recurrent phenomenon concerns nouns which only exist in plural form without necessarily having plural meaning. In English they include *heads* and *tails* (on a coin), *brains*, *alms*, and *trousers* (although a wit once remarked that trousers are singular at the top and plural at the bottom). These are known individually as 'plurale tantum', collectively as 'pluralia tantum'. Boas (1911d: 602–3) notes that there are some nouns in Chinook which exist only in plural form, they include 'codfish', 'grasshopper', and 'smoke'. And also some which only have dual form ('dualia tantum'), including 'eel' and 'hawk'.

20.6.4 Verbs

There are a number of ways in which the number of a core argument may be indicated within the predicate, generally by some morphological process applying to the verb. If a language has bound pronouns, these are typically included within the predicate and will show person and number (and often also gender or noun class) or one or more core arguments. This is illustrated in (40–1), from Manambu.

Another technique is for the verb to include an affix which states that one or more of the core arguments has plural reference. For a transitive verb, such marking is three-ways ambiguous, between whether the A argument or the O argument or both are plural. It can be exemplified with plural suffix *-hig* to the verb in Nanti (Campa subgroup of Arawak, Peru; Michael 2008: 260).

(42)   i=kamoso-hig-ak-i=ri
       3masc.S=visit-PLURAL-PERFECT-REALIS=3masc.O
       They visited him OR He visited them OR They visited them

In Musqueam (Salish family; Suttles 2004: 165–6), 'the plural of a transitive form can indicate a plural object as well as a plural subject or event; thus, the plural of $t^\theta íq^w ət$ "hit him with the fist", $t^\theta áləq\acute{q}^w ət$, can mean "one hits several", "several hit one", or "one hits one several times". '

One recurrent and quite fascinating phenomenon is for there to be a small set of verbs which have suppletive form depending on whether a particular core argument has singular or plural reference. The core argument in question is almost always that in O function for a transitive, and that in S function for an intransitive verb.

Gabas (1999: 58) identifies four intransitive verbs in Karo (Tupí family, Brazil) which have suppletive roots relating to whether the S argument has singular or plural reference. For example, the forms for 'cry' are *-wé-* for singular and *-peri-* for plural S, as in:

(43)   ŋa=wé-t   (44)   tap=peri-t
       3sg.femS-cry(sg.S)-INDICATIVE   3pl.S-cry(pl.S)-INDICATIVE
       She cried   They cried

Jarawara has, in my corpus, eleven verbs with suppletive forms depending on the number of the S argument and ten whose suppletive forms depend on the number of the O argument (two of these are ambitransitive). Ten of them (seven intransitive and three transitive) distinguish between singular, dual, and plural reference. They include (see also §1.4):

(45)

	SINGULAR S	DUAL S	PLURAL S
lie on ground	-homa-		
lie on raised surface	-fori-	mata -na-	soo (to-)na(-sa)
lie in water	hofa- ~ -fowa-		

The singular form for 'lie in water' itself has suppletive forms: *hofa-* is used when there is no prefix and *-fowa-* when there is a prefix.

The remaining verbs have two suppletive forms, one for singular and the other for plural S/O. For example:

(46)

	ARGUMENT INVOLVED	SINGULAR	PLURAL
'be big, be much'	S	-nafi(ha)-	-fota-
'take out'	O	-iti-	-jaba-
'pierce'	O	-ita-	saka -na-
'kill'	O	-na(a)boha-	waka -na-

Just like for those verbs which distinguish singular, dual, and plural—exemplified in (45)—'plural' in (46) is 'more than two'. Reference to dual number involves using either the singular or the plural form of the verb, to which is added suffix $-^i kima$ 'two' (Dixon 2004: 543–6).

Number-determined suppletive forms of verbs are found in a wide range of languages—from North America (including the Salish, Uto-Aztecan, Athapaskan, and Muskogean families), the Caucasus, Africa, New Guinea, Australia, and Oceania plus Ainu in Japan and Sumerian in the ancient Middle East. The number of such verbs ranges from one to a couple of dozen.

We find just one transitive verb with suppletive forms in Georgian (Kartvelian; Harris 1981: 125–6)—'throw' is *gadagdeba* with a singular and *gadaqra* with a plural O. The Papuan language Amele (Roberts 1987: 201) has suppletive forms for two verbs—'get, take' is *oc* with a singular and *ced-ec* with a plural O, while 'go' is *nu* for singular and (optionally) *bel-ec* for plural S. Emmi, from north Australia (Ford 1998: 178–9), has a minimal/augmented number system. Two verbs have the number of their O argument shown by a suppletion—'give' is *wut* with minimal and *wurut* with augmented O, while for 'hit' the forms are *gurr* and *parr* respectively. Languages with more than a handful of suppletive verbs of this type generally have some intransitives (according to the number of the S argument) and some transitives (almost always referring to the number of the O argument).

Certain lexemes do recur across lists of number-determined suppletive verbs. Some of the most commonly found are shown, for nine languages, in Table 20.1. For five of the languages there is simply a singular/plural contrast. In Northern Paiute, six verbs (all intransitive) have distinct singular, dual, and plural forms while twelve (seven of which appear to be transitive) just make a singular/non-singular distinction. Verbs in Choctaw follow a similar pattern. The three classes of suppletive verbs in Koasati were shown at (21–2) in §20.4. Set (a) verbs have three forms, singular, dual, and plural, while set (b) contrast singular and non-singular, and set (c) work in terms of non-plural and plural. (The situation in Jarawara was described just above.)

The intransitive verbs which recur with number-determined suppletive forms in many languages include 'sit', 'stand', 'lie', 'enter', 'go', 'be big', and 'die, be dead' (in Table 20.1) and also 'hang', 'arrive', 'run', 'come', 'fall', 'cry', and 'be little'. Besides the two transitive verbs in Table 20.1—'kill' and 'put (put down, put in, etc.)'—other recurring meanings include 'throw', 'give', 'break', 'take', 'bring', and 'carry'. It can be noted—on the basis of the small selection of languages shown in Table 20.1—that the three main posture verbs ('sit', 'stand', and 'lie') tend to be characterized by the richest number system. That is, if some suppletive verbs make a two-term and others a three-term number distinction, posture verbs tend to belong to the latter set.

Meryam Mir (Piper 1989: 81–5, 126–8)—spoken on the eastern islands of Torres Strait, between Australia and New Guinea—shows a fascinating interaction of two techniques for number marking. Verbs with suppletive forms make a distinction between singular-dual and paucal-plural, while bound pronominal prefixes to intransitive atelic verbs have one form covering both singular and plural S and another form for dual and paucal S. This can be illustrated for verb 'be sitting' with 1st/2nd person prefixes. (Note that 1st and 2nd person are distinguished in free pronouns, but fall together for this set of bound pronouns.)

(47)

	SINGULAR	DUAL	PAUCAL	PLURAL
'be sitting' verb root	imi-	imi-	emr-	emr-
1st/2nd person prefix	na-	d-	d-	na-

It can be seen that the combination of this pair of two-term number systems fully specifies the full four-term system, {singular, dual, paucal, plural}.

TABLE 20.1. Some number-determined suppletive verb stems in a sample of nine languages

	NUMBER SYSTEM	NUMBER OF SUPPLETIVE VERBS	'sit'	'stand'	'lie'	'enter'	'go'	'be big'	'die, be dead'	'kill'	'put'
Moses-Columbian (Salish; Kinkade 1977: 148)	sg/pl	22	✓	✓		✓	✓	✓	✓	✓	✓
Northern Paiute (Uto-Aztecan; Thornes 2003: 316)	(a) sg/du/pl (b) sg/nsg	18	a	a	a	b	a		b	b	b
Choctaw (Muskogean; Nicklas 1972: 57–61)	(a) sg/du/pl (b) sg/nsg	15	a	a	a		b	b			a
Koasati (Muskogean; Kimball 1991:322–4)	(a) sg/du/pl (b) sg/nsg (c) npl/pl	15	a	a			c		c		b
Matses (Panoan; Peru; Fleck 2003)	sg/pl	12		✓	✓						✓
Jarawara (Arawá, Brazil; Dixon 2004: 543–6)	(a) sg/du/pl (b) sg/pl	19	a	a	a			b		b	a
Kwaza (isolate, Brazil; Van der Voort 2004: 383–8)	sg/pl	10	✓		✓	✓	✓				
Sumerian (isolate, Mesopotamia; Thomsen 1984: 131–6)	sg/pl	7	✓	✓			✓		✓		
Juǀʼhoan (Khoisan; Botswana and Namibia; Dickens n.d.: 63)	sg/pl	11	✓	✓	✓				✓	✓	✓

20.7 Markedness

In an overwhelming majority of instances, singular is the functionally unmarked term in a number system. If some other grammatical category has different sets of possibilities according to choice from the number system, then the richest set will relate to singular number; see §20.8 and §3.19.

Leaving aside singular, within a {singular, dual, plural} system, dual is often more highly functionally marked than plural. This can be illustrated for the Australian language Yidiñ, which has the following 1st person pronouns:

(48)   1.SINGULAR ŋayu, 1.DUAL ŋali, 1.NON-SINGULAR ŋañji

Pronoun *ŋali* is used for referring to 'two people, one of whom is the speaker'. Interestingly, *ŋali* is not mutually exclusive with 1 non-sg *ŋañji*, which refers to 'two or more people one of whom is the speaker'. What we find is that *ŋañji* is the unmarked non-singular 1st person form whereas *ŋali* is a marked dual form, making a further optional distinction within non-singular (Dixon 1977a: 165–7). In diagrammatic form:

(49)

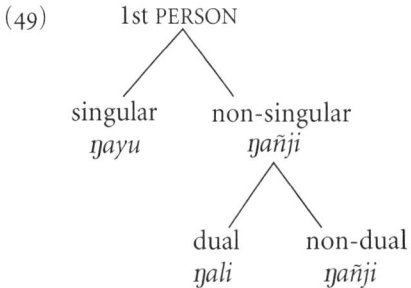

Pronoun *ŋali* is used when it is desired to emphasize two people (rather than three or more). It is often used in a text for first reference to a pair (establishing that there are just two people involved), with *ŋañji* being used for later reference to them. It is thus appropriate to label *ŋañji* as 'non-singular' rather than as 'plural'.

In some languages, gender is marked on singular but not on plural pronouns. If the speaker wishes to refer to a single person without specifying their sex, one option may be to employ the 3pl pronoun. This is done in English, and has been particularly prevalent since the proscription of *he* from being used as general 3sg pronoun (irrespective of the sex of the referent), in addition to its use as 3sg masculine pronoun. Many people prefer to say *When a linguist goes into the field they need two high-quality recorders* in preference to *When a linguist goes into the field he or she* (OR *she or he*) *needs two high-quality recorders*.

Other languages have this as an institutionalized grammatical technique. Alamblak (from the Papuan area) has, for free and bound pronouns, 1/2/3 persons, singular/dual/plural numbers, and masculine/feminine genders just in 3sg. Bruce (1984: 98) comments: 'Given that the gender system is regular and obligatorily a part of an NP in third singular forms, conflicts are bound to arise in situations in which the speaker is either unable or unwilling to indicate the gender of an object. In those circumstances the third-person plural marker is employed as an indefinite gender marker. For example, the plural marker -*m* is used with *yën* "child" in example [(50)] not to indicate plural number, but to avoid specifying the sex of the child':

(50) yën-m   heawrahtm   indom   yamtn
      child-3pl SHE:WILL:bear:THEM another month:IN
      She will bear a child in another month

Although both 3du and 3pl pronouns are unmarked for gender, it is the 3pl form which is used here, showing that plural is functionally unmarked with respect to dual.

If there is a neuter gender within 3sg this is often used as a default form, as in the English sentences *It is raining*, and *I like it that John smokes*. When a complement clause is extraposed to the end of its main clause, pronoun *it* fills the obligatory subject slot before the verb, as in *It$_S$ is well known [that John smokes]*$_{CoCl:S}$. Some languages use a 3pl pronoun as the default form. This is found in Godié (Kru family, Ivory Coast; Marchese 1986: 239), where pronouns distinguish singular and plural number, with noun class marking in 3sg, and human and non-human forms for 3pl. It is the 3pl non-human pronoun, *ι*, which is used as the default form, as in:

(51) ɔ   yì   oo, ɔ̄   wʊ̀   yi   oo nʌ,
      HE came OR   HE:NEGATIVE NEGATIVE come OR NON-FINAL
      àmʉ̆ ʌ̄ nʹɪ   wʊ̀   yì
      ME   I   NEGATIVE:3pl.NON-HUMAN   NEGATIVE know
      Whether he came or not, I don't know it (lit. I don't know them non-human)

Here the 3pl non-human pronoun, *ι*, is used in the second clause to refer back to the whole of the first clause 'whether he came or not'.

If there is formal markedness within a number system, then singular is almost always the unmarked term, with zero realization. This is found on nouns in English (*boy-ø* versus *boy-s*) and on pronouns in Cantonese, illustrated at (2) in §15.1.1. Within non-singular numbers, plural is quite often the unmarked form, with dual/trial/paucal/etc. involving affixes to the plural form; this is illustrated for Ungarinjin at (32) in §20.6.1. However, other scenarios are found, as in the paradigm for Ponapean, at (33), where plural forms involve an increment onto dual.

There are languages—including many from the Cushitic branch of Afroasiatic—where the base form of a noun has collective meaning. Other number specifications require an affix onto the collective form. For example, in Arbore (Zaborski 1986: 105; Hayward 1984: 180) we find:

(52) COLLECTIVE   SINGULAR
     ʔízze   gazelles   ʔízze-t   gazelle
     kónyčo   water-snails   kónyčo-t   water-snail

Zaborski (1986: 3) reports a more complex system in Beja. Again, the plain noun has a collective meaning, with suffixes added for what Zaborski calls 'singulative' (a term here used for morphologically-marked singular) and 'paucal-plural' (the term 'plural' would probably do instead):

(53) COLLECTIVE   tāwig   mosquitos
     'SINGULATIVE'   tāwig-ay a mosquito
     'PAUCAL-PLURAL'   tāwig-ey a few mosquitoes

In a few language there are a number of classes of nouns, each with its own profile for markedness within a {singular, dual, plural} number system. Kiowa provides a seminal instance. There is a suffix -gó which has different number specification according to the class of nouns it is attached to:

(54)

	SINGULAR	DUAL	PLURAL
Class I	∅		-gó
Class II	-gó	∅	
Class III	-gó	∅	-gó

Singular and dual are formally unmarked for Class I, which includes all human nouns and some names for artefacts; plural number is marked by suffix -gó. For class II, which includes plants, plant products, and other inanimates, dual and plural are formally unmarked with -gó indicating singular. The pattern is completed by Class III, where dual is unmarked and -gó is used for singular and plural; just four nouns are reported for this class—'plum, apple', 'orange', 'tomato', and '(head) hair'. (There is also a fourth class which never takes -gó; it includes 'stone', 'meat', 'earring', 'nail' and 'shoe'.)

Used by itself, this pattern of number marking would lead to rampant ambiguity. Watkins (1984: 78–92) explains how it interrelates with a system of intransitive 3rd person prefixes:

(55)   SINGULAR   DUAL   PLURAL
      Class 1   ø   ę̀-   è-
      Class 2   è-   ę̀-   gyà- ~ ø
      Class 3   è-   ę̀-   è-

It will be seen that, by combining the suffix from (54) with the prefixes from (55), there is unambiguous specification for singular, dual, and plural in Classes I and II, although not for Class III. (Class IV does have distinct prefixes for each number.)

20.8 Interrelations with other grammatical categories

There can be interaction between number and other grammatical categories. Information on many of these has been provided in earlier chapters and sections and is recapitulated here.

(a) **Negation.**   As pointed out in §3.19, all specifications of number, and of person, are neutralized in a negative clause for Estonian, Tariana (from the Amazon), and Manambu (from New Guinea).

(b) **Person.**   There are many examples of person distinctions being neutralized in non-singular number(s)—2nd and 3rd person, or 1st and 2nd person, etc. See the paradigm for Chipewyan, in §3.7, and the half-dozen examples given in §15.1.3.

There can also be neutralization in the other direction, where a number contrast is neutralized for a certain person choice. This applies for 2nd person in Standard English; further examples are in §15.1.3.

(c) **Noun class/gender.**   When noun class or gender is marked within a pronoun paradigm, it is rare to find it marked on every single term. Commonly, noun class or gender is found just on 3sg, or just on 2sg, or on both of these, or on all singulars, or on all duals and also 3sg. These and other possibilities are discussed in §15.1.4.

Looking now in the reverse direction, number marking may depend on noun class choice. In Old Church Slavonic, three genders—masculine, feminine, and neuter—were distinguished in the singular, just two in the dual (masculine and neuter having fallen together), while no gender distinctions at all were made in the plural.

In the Australian language Laragia, most nouns bear a noun class suffix (Capell 1984: 62–8):

(56) SINGULAR   PLURAL   Class
      -va   -bira   1a   Humans
            -va   1b   Some animals and birds
            -la   2   Most non-human animates, some
                                    body parts, moon, stone, etc.
            -ma   3   Most plants and their parts, most
                                    body parts, some birds, etc.
            -wa   4   Implements, some body parts,
                                    water, clouds, etc.

Class 1 (marked by suffix -*va*) includes humans and some animals and birds. Plural suffix -*bira* is used only for humans, leading to a division into two subclasses, 1a and 1b. In essence, the suffixes for classes 2, 3, and 4 are not specified for number; that for class 1 is only when its referents are human.

(d) **Human-ness and animateness.** As mentioned earlier, number is almost always marked on pronouns. A number system may apply to all nouns, or to none, or to just some of them. Which type of noun is marked for number, cross-linguistically, can be roughly described in terms of the following hierarchy:

(57) (a) just nouns describing kin relationships
      (b) all nouns with human reference
      (c) all nouns with animate reference; a distinction is often made between higher animates (such as mammals) and lower animates (for example, insects)
      (d) all (count) nouns, whether animate or inanimate

For the Papuan language Kobon 'the only nouns in which number is marked are nouns belonging to the set which describe kin relationships' (Davies 1981: 147). It is more common to find plural marking on all and only those nouns with human reference. This was illustrated for Laragia in (56). And Kimball (1991: 403) reports that: 'A marked nominal plural in Koasati is permitted only for nouns that refer to human beings'.

Languages which restrict plural marking to animate nouns include Jarawara and Southern Paiute. For the latter, Sapir (1930–1: 213–15) mentions that reduplication applies to all nouns, and has a distributive meaning, but that 'properly plural suffixes ... can, for the most part, be appended only to noun stems referring to animate beings (cf. the presence of singular and plural animate forms and the lack of distinctively plural inanimate forms in the third person pronouns).'

In Jarawara (Dixon 2004: 74–5), the number reference of a core argument is shown by a bound pronoun placed at the beginning of the predicate.

3rd person non-singular pronoun *mee* is employed only and obligatorily for animates. A zero in the pronoun slot is used for 3sg animates and for any (singular or plural) number of inanimates. Note that Jarawara cultural beliefs treat as animate the heavenly bodies—'sun/thunder', 'moon', and 'stars'—and also certain afflictions, which are believed to be caused by small animals. For instance, 'rheumatism' is *joki*, an animate noun which only occurs in plural form (marked by *mee*).

The hierarchy set out in (57) is, at best, an indication. As mentioned at the end of §20.5, in the Oceanic language Tamambo plural marking applies just for nouns referring to humans (including kin terms) and for all trees, plus 'stone', 'island', 'piece of coral', and 'thing' (Jauncey 2011: 113, 134–5). The cultural significance of trees is such that they receive number marking, whereas non-human animates do not.

(e) **Other categories.** Many languages have a limited set of case markers in non-singular number(s). For example, nouns in Latin distinguish dative and ablative cases in the singular, but these fall together in the plural. Looking at pronouns, a number of Australian languages have distinct forms for each of S, A, and O functions for 1sg and 2sg (and sometimes also 3sg) but a single form covering S and A for non-singulars; see Dixon (2002: 299–315).

There can also be interaction with parameters of non-spatial setting. For example, number (and person) contrasts are neutralized under negation in analytic past tenses for Estonian.

20.9 Lexical number words and counting

Many languages have an extensive set of number words, with exact reference. As a consequence, anything can be counted, and many kinds of abstract arithmetical operations may be carried out.

There are also a fair number of languages which lack (or recently lacked) such an array of number words. It is often said, of these languages, that 'they can only count "one", "two", "many", or perhaps "one", "two", "three", "many".' This is misconceived. Speakers of such languages did not count. That is, words which are translated as 'one', 'two', and so on, were not used for enumeration.

For the Warlpiri language of Central Australia, Reece (1970: 93) lists four 'numbers' as a subset of the adjective class, glossed as 'one', 'two', 'three or a few' and 'many, a number, a big mob'. In an insightful and incisive account of Warlpiri, Hale (1975: 295–6) suggests that forms which had previously been identified as numbers are better regarded as indefinite determiners, parallel to the system of definite determiners (or demonstratives):

(58)   INDEFINITE DETERMINERS   DEFINITE DETERMINERS
       tjinta 'singular, one'   njampu 'this, singular'
       tjirama 'dual, two'   njampu-tjara 'these, dual'
       wirkardu 'paucal, several'   njampu-patu 'these, paucal'
       panu 'plural, many'   njampu-ra 'these, plural'

(Note that the definite determiners, but not their indefinite counterparts, are morphologically analysable.) This is, essentially, a grammatical number system; note that it is slightly larger than the number system in Warlpiri free and bound pronouns, which is {singular, dual, plural}. Hale emphasizes that neither set of determiners are used for counting in traditional Warlpiri. Before contact with Europeans, the Warlpiri would list items, but they would not count.

Not everything which is a part of the conceptual apparatus of a group of people necessarily finds expression in their language. There is no category of gender in the grammar of Hungarian, but speakers of the language have full cognizance of difference between the sexes. Hale opines that all humans have an innate capacity to count. It is just that in a number of small-scale societies there was no cultural need for things to be counted, and thus no provision in the language for this. 'One might look upon the Warlpiri lack of conventionalized numerals as a gap in the inventory of cultural items—since the principle which underlies counting is present, filling the gap is a rather trivial matter. This view is entirely compatible with the observation that the English counting system is almost instantaneously mastered by Warlpiris who enter into situations where the use of money is important (quite independently of Western-style formal education, incidentally).'

It is believed that humankind developed a sophisticated language system at least 100,000 years ago. Not every portion of the system would have matured at the same rate. Almost certainly, an extensive system of number words, and the notion of counting, came into existence relatively late. For instance, no verb 'count' can be reconstructed for proto-Indo-European or for proto-Austronesian, nor number words beyond 'hundred' ('thousand' has different forms in the various subgroups of each family).

At first, people would just list, rather than count. One would not ask 'How many children do you have?', but rather 'What children do you have?'. Laughren (1981: 29) explains how a Warlpiri would respond to such a question. 'When recounting offspring it is typical to symbolize them in order of birth by marking a straight line in the earth vertical to speaker ... The firstborn is indicated by the line on the leftmost side. So the order is left to right. All lines are of the same length. When all the children are accounted for, a line horizontal to the person marking is made. It is drawn either across the top or the bottom of the strokes, as in:

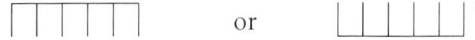

The name of each child would be enunciated, as its line is drawn in the earth. At the pre-counting stage, the language had no number words, and no way of asking 'how many?'.

Other communities would use the fingers, rather than lines drawn in the earth, as symbolic aids to listing. 'What children do you have?' 'John (pointing to one finger), Mary (pointing to the next finger), and Tom (pointing at the third finger in sequence)'. In some communities it is the custom to start with the little finger and move towards the thumb; in others the reverse convention applies (see Seidenberg 1960: 258–69).

The next stage would be to associate a label with each finger, so that the labels might be used for listing, without necessarily pointing to fingers. The labels would now take on an abstract character, and could be called 'numbers'.

Van der Voort (2004: 214) describes a quinary (five-based) set of numbers for Kwaza (Rondonia, Brazil; isolate) 'which suggests a relationship with the fingers of the hand'.

(59) 'one'   tei-   'to be one', 'alone'
      'two'   aky-   'to be two', 'company'
      'three' e'mā   'one more, again', 'without companion'
      'four'   ele'le   'several, many, very, emphatic'
      'five'   bwa-   'to end, to finish'

In many languages, the term for 'five' or for 'ten' refers to 'finish'; that is, all the fingers of one hand, or of both hands, have been used up in the listing.

Another strategy is to work in terms of pairings. In languages of the Makú family, from Amazonia, even numbers between four and ten are described as 'having a brother' (that is, occurring in pairs) and odd numbers are 'one who does not have a brother' (Martins and Martins 1999: 265; Epps 2006). (There is a hint of this in the glosses for 'two' and 'three' in Kwaza.) Such societies have a special type of abstract concept—the opposition between odd and even.

Almost all systems of number words are based on the human body. 'Five' may be, etymologically, 'one hand', with 'ten' being 'two hands', and twenty 'one body' (that is, all fingers and all toes). The most common type of system, right across the world, is decimal, on a base of ten. There are also a fair number of systems on base five, and on base twenty.

Just occasionally, one encounters something different. Evans (2009) describes a six-base system for Nen and other languages from the Morehead-Maro family of New Guinea. In counting, Nen speakers 'first count off the five fingers with a finger of their other hand, and then on the sixth they place their counting finger on the inside of the wrist'. But why take six as the base? For an important cultural reason. The main crop is yams and these are counted in groups of six, each laid out on the ground in star shape, arranged 'so as to radiate from their points, placed together centrally, at sixty degree angles'. So the number of yams which can be conveniently placed together, in symmetrical fashion, with narrow ends together, motives the use of a base of six. Just as in English we have terms for multiples of ten—*hundred* (10^2), *thousand* (10^3), *million* (10^6), and so on—so Nen has terms for multiples of six—*pus* for six, *pria* for 36 (6^2), *taromba* for 216 (6^3), *damno* for 1,296 (6^4), and *wèrèmaka* for 7,776 (6^5).

Some languages in New Guinea are notable for involving further body parts in the operation of counting. For instance, In Kobon (Davies 1981) one starts with the little finger of the left hand, moving along to thumb, then wrist, forearm, inside elbow, biceps, shoulder, collarbone, hole above breastbone, then across to the other side and down, whence the little finger of the right hand is number 23. The process is repeated for higher numbers. Other languages follow a slightly different route, moving up around the head—left ear, left eye, nose, right eye, right ear; see Saxe (1981).

Languages with more conventional bases employ various techniques for specifying numbers. For instance, 'eight' may be, literally, 'four four' and 'nine' may be 'lacking one to reach ten'. Yoruba is particularly adept at this. For instance, '16' is a contraction of 'four short of twenty' and '215' is '20 plus 200 minus 5'. (See Rowlands 1969: 105–12; Ogunbọwale 1970: 75–7, 112–15; Hurford 1975: 211–32.)

A further stage is the development of ordinal numbers. These are almost always derived from their cardinal congeners. And in some languages there may be more derived forms besides. For example, in Tamambo (Oceanic branch of Austronesian, Vanuatu; Jauncey 2011: 158–62), suffix *-na* added to a cardinal yields an ordinal (such as 'fourth'), prefix *vaha-* forms a multiplicative ('four times'), while rightwards reduplication of the last two syllables of the cardinal, plus suffix *-hi*, produce a distributive ('four by four'). These derivational processes are illustrated in (60). They apply throughout this decimal set of number words in Tamambo.

(60) | CARDINAL | ORDINAL | MULTIPLICATIVE | DISTRIBUTIVE |
|---|---|---|---|
| atea 'one' | talom 'first' | vaha-tea 'once' | atea-tea-hi 'one by one' |
| arua 'two' | arua-na 'second' | vaha-arua 'twice' | arua-rua-hi 'two by two' |
| atolu 'three' | atolu-na 'third' | vaha-atolu 'three times' | atolu-tolu-hi 'three by three' |
| avati 'four' | avati-na 'fourth' | vaha-avati 'four times' | avati-vati-hi 'four by four' |

One frequently finds that ordinal versions of the lowest numbers are irregular. In Tamambo this applies just to 'first', which is *talom* (where **atea-na* would be expected). In English we find irregular forms *first* and *second* (rather than **one-th* and **two-th*) and abbreviated forms *third* and *fifth* (rather than **three-th* and **five-th*).

How about a word referring to the lack of anything, like *zero* or *nought* in English? In fact, very many languages with a full set of positive number words lack such a 'nothing' term. See, for instance, Urton (1997: 48–50) on the absence of a name for zero in Quechua. In English, *zero* or *nought* plays little role in conventions of counting. Even when counting down, one is most likely to hear something like '*three, two, one, go*' or '*three, two, one, blast-off*' (rather than '*three, two, one, zero*').

In languages with a set of number words which is all-encompassing, quantities are likely to be specified with exactitude. In societies whose members are not used to employing a full set of number words, quantities may be indicated in approximate fashion. Discussing Matsigenka, an Arawak language of the Peruvian Amazon, Johnson (2003: 153) states that a speaker will specify number accurately up to five, but for larger quantities they will estimate in increments of five or ten by opening their fists and flashing their fingers the right number of times.

As stated at the beginning of this section, many small tribal societies had no social need for counting and lacked a full set of number words—or had no number words at all. We can now examine how such people came to gain number words, within a contact situation.

20.9.1 Developing and borrowing number words

Accounts of small-scale societies—which in pre-contact days had little or no need for counting—typically describe a set of number words, the lowest values of which involve native forms, with higher numbers being borrowings from the contact language. In Jarawara (Dixon 2004: 559–60), all numbers are verbs. There are *-ohari(ha)-* 'be one' and *-fama-* 'be two', involving native roots, with other numbers being loans from Portuguese—*terei -na-* 'be three', *kowato -na-* 'be four', *siko -na-* 'be five', *tee -na-* 'be ten', and so on (from Portuguese *três*, *quatro*, *cinco*, and *dez* respectively).

Is it the case that before contact with Europeans, Jarawara had just two number words, 'one' and 'two'? All the evidence suggests that this was *not* the case. There were two verbs, *-ohari(ha)-* 'be alone, be the only (one/thing)'— as in 'I'm going alone'—and *-fama-* 'be a pair, be a couple with'—as in 'These two man's names are a pair' (that is, 'These two men have the same name'). After contact, an extra sense was added to *-ohari(ha)-* and *-fama-*, their meanings being extended to 'be one' and 'be two', in the same semantic set as *terei -na-* 'be three' and the other borrowed number words.

My contention is that many small societies were like Jarawara in having *no number words at all* before contact with a people who did have a full set of number words. Soon after contact they developed their own number words, some of which were extensions of meaning for native roots. I realize that there is no way of 'proving' this assertion beyond any possibility of doubt. For definitive verification a linguist would have to be the first outsider to get in touch with such a small-scale society and would have to learn the language before they had any further contact with outsiders. This has never happened. In the nature of things, by the time a linguist or anthropologist commences work with a small-scale society, they have had some years of contact with people like miners, traders, missionaries, government officials; and the nature of the contact has been such that a set of number words is in place.

Nevertheless, the evidence supporting the hypothesis is extremely strong. First, there are languages where all numbers, even the smallest, have been borrowed. Vidal (2001: 179) states that Pilagá (Guaykuruan family; Argentina) 'has no native numeral words. The words for "one" are *onole'* (fem.) and *onolek* (masc.), and the word for "two" is *dosolqa*. They come from Spanish *uno* and *dos*, and have been phonologically and morphologically adapted into Pilagá, as the terminations *-le'*, *-lek*, and *-qa*, respectively demonstrate. The rest of the numerals have been borrowed without phonological or morphological nativization.'

And in languages like Jarawara where 'one' and 'two' use native forms, their original meanings are clear. 'One' is typically an extension of '(be) alone'. There is more variation concerning the original meaning of the word extended to cover 'two'. This was 'to face each other' in Wari' (Chapacuran family, Brazil; Everett and Kern 1997: 347–8), and 'be equal, be the same' in Jabutí (Brazil; Pires 1992: 66). Green (1993: 1) reports that in Xerente (Jê family, Brazil) *ponkwane* 'deer track' has been taken over as the number 'two', 'since the cloven deer hoof is made up of two parts that go together'.

Interrogative words relating to quantity provide an interesting topic. Some languages have different forms for 'how many' (referring to countables) and 'how much' (uncountables) but in many languages a single word covers both concepts. This applies to French, Spanish, Russian, German, Basque, Arabic, Japanese, and Igbo among many other languages. See (II) in §27.6.4.

One can imagine a language without lexical number words having a question word 'how much', which could be answered 'a lot' or 'a little'. However, in the majority of cases, languages of small societies extended the meaning of an existing interrogative to also cover 'how many/much' at about the same time that they innovated a set of number words. Jarawara has an interrogative verb *ee (-na-)* with a broad general meaning, 'what about?' It can be used for 'how about?' (as in 'How are you?') and for 'where'. (When bilingual speakers are asked to gloss *ee (-na-)* outside a textual discourse, they always give 'where'.) Its use has now been extended to cover 'How many?' Some of the Jarawara gather rubber latex and sell it to a local trader. In one text someone asks *Kilo ee-ri?* ('Kilo do.what-CONTENT.INTERROG.MOOD'). This is, literally 'What about the kilos (of rubber latex)' but in the context of utterance it means 'How many kilos are there?'. (Also see (91) and (94) in §27.6.4.)

Other languages appear to have initiated a similar extension of meaning in order to develop a way of asking 'how many?'. In Sanuma, a Yanomami dialect, *wi* ('how') *na* ('like') is used for manner ('How was that?', 'What should I do?') and for number. A sentence is ambiguous between 'What kind of machetes does he want?' and 'How many machetes does he want?' (Borgman 1990: 66–9). In Kalam, spoken in New Guinea, *etp* is 'what' and *etp etp* is 'what sort of things', now extended to 'how many' (Pawley 1995: 2).

English is rather unusual is combining an interrogative adverb, *how*, with a quantifier, *many* or *much*, to produce a compound form. *How many apples are there in the basket?* and *How much honey is there in the jar?* are parallel to *How long is it?* and *How clever is she?*, where *how* occurs with a non-number adjective.

While on the topic of borrowing, the idea that names for lower numbers may not be borrowed should be laid to rest. Safford (1909: 48–56) recorded the original set of number words for Chamorro, spoken on Guam. This is a decimal set with regular reflexes of proto-Oceanic forms. It has now been completely replaced by loans from Spanish, so that today no one remembers the original forms. A sample of old and new number words is (Topping 1973: 166–9):

(61)		ORIGINAL CHAMORRO	SPANISH LOANS
	one	hacha	un, unu
	two	hu-gua	dos
	three	tulu, tulo	tres
	four	fatfat	kuatro
	five	lima	sinko
	six	gunum	sais
	seven	fiti	siete
	eight	gualu	ocho
	nine	sigua	nuebe
	ten	manot	dies

20.9.2 Grammatical status of lexical number words

Languages vary as to which word class lexical number words are associated with. They are a subset of nouns in Tamambo, of adjectives in Turkish, and of verbs in Choctaw (Broadwell 2006: 235), and Jarawara. As discussed in §4.4, in Fijian the lower number words—plus 'many', 'few', 'some of', and 'how many/how much'—are best analysed as making up a separate small word class, whose properties are rather similar to those of verbs (alternatively, numbers could be regarded as a divergent subset of verbs). In Finnish, numbers are also placed in a class of their own, together with quantifiers such as 'more', 'several', and 'every' (Sulkala and Karjalainen 1992: 206).

In some languages, lexical number words have mixed word class membership. Jespersen (1937: 119) noted that 'numerals are generally treated as adjectives ... but not infrequently the higher ones or some of them are substantives [that is, nouns]'. Along these lines we can report:

- As mentioned in §8.3, 'in Semitic, the cardinal numbers for "one" and "two" are adjectives; those from "three" to "ten" are abstract nouns' (Gray 1934: 68).
- In Baniwa of Içana (Arawak, Brazil; Alexandra Aikhenvald, personal communication), number words 'one', 'two', and 'three' are adjectives, 'four' is a verb, and 'five' to 'ten' are nouns.
- In Koasati (Muskogean; Kimball 1991: 354), lexical number words 'are verbs, with the exception of the terms *cokpi* "hundred" and *cokpacó:ba* "thousand" which are nouns and require a following verbal numeral' (this can be just 'one').
- In Fijian, number words (and quantifiers) make up a small word class—with grammatical properties similar to those of the verb class—except for *drau* 'hundred' and *udolu* 'thousand' which are nouns. Thus, for 'five hundred' one says, literally 'the hundred(s) are five'. (See Dixon 1988: 141–2.)

It will be seen that, if word class membership is mixed, it is the relatively higher numbers which are nouns.

In many languages, number words have a fixed position within an NP. They precede the head in English, German, Hebrew, and Indonesian, and follow it in Hausa, Swahili, and Burmese, among many other examples.

Yoruba is of particular interest. In this language, modifying nouns precede the head noun and adjectives follow it. Numbers show a split character. Those up to 'nineteen' come after the head, like adjectives, but single-word numbers from 'twenty' up come before, like nouns (Ogunbọwale 1970: 75–7, 112–15). Compare:

(62) (a) iwé kan   one book
      (b) òjìlúgba iwé   240 books

In (62a) *kan* 'one' follows the head noun *iwé* 'book' but in (62b) *òjìlúgba* precedes the head. This is a single word meaning '240', etymologically a combination of 'twelve' and 'twenty' in a number set which is partially twenty-based. To express '241 books', one adds *àti ọkan*, literally 'and one' to *òjìlúgba iwé*, giving:

(62)   (c) òjìlúgba iwé àti ọkan   241 books (literally 240 books and one)

Again, the number below twenty follows the head and the number above twenty precedes it. This provides a further instance of Jespersen's dictum—that often lower numbers are more like adjectives and higher ones like nouns.

In some languages certain adjectives may either precede or follow the head noun in an NP, with a difference of meaning. For example (as mentioned in notes to §12.4), in French *un curieux homme* is 'a curious/strange man' while *un homme curieux* is 'a curious/inquisitive man'. Along similar lines, there are examples of variable positioning for number modifiers. In Russian, for instance, in neutral contexts a number preceding the head indicates an exact quantity and when it follows the meaning is an approximation. Thus, with *korov* 'cows' and *vosem'* 'eight', we get:

(63)   (a) vosem' korov   exactly eight cows
       (b) korov vosem'   about eight cows

In Slave (Athapaskan; Rice 1989: 373–80), a number word follows a head noun which has concrete reference—such as 'egg', 'child'—and precedes one with abstract meaning—such as 'dollar', 'night'. Some words can have two senses, one concrete and one abstract; for instance *sadzée* is 'watch' and 'time'. Which sense is intended in an instance of use can be inferred from the position of a modifying number word such as *tai* 'three', as in:

(64)   (a) sadzée tai   three watches   [number follows, concrete sense]
       (b) tai sadzée   three o'clock   [number precedes, abstract sense]

20.9.3 Verb 'count' and noun 'number'

No verb 'count' can with certainty be reconstructed for proto-Indo-European (or for proto-Austronesian). The etymologies of verbs for counting in individual subgroups and languages are interesting. There is often a link between words for counting and for telling. For example English *recount* (originally *re*-plus *count*) means 'provide a detailed account of something'. The English verb *tell* originally had a second sense 'count' and goes back to proto-Indo-European verb **del-*, one of whose senses was 'cut, split, carve' (Watkins 1985: 11). The verb *tally* 'count, reckon up' goes back to a form meaning 'cutting, rod'. It is quite likely that counting was originally associated with cutting notches on a stick, and words describing such a cutting action have now taken on the meaning 'count'.

In the Pintupi dialect of the Western Desert language from Australia (Hansen and Hansen 1974: 289, 1992: 193), the present-day word for counting is *yiltjirripungu*, a verb whose original meaning was 'mark the ground with one finger' as when making parallel marks in connection with the kind of listing described above for the neighbour language Warlpiri. It appears that, at the evolution of the use of numbers, varied societies employed different aids for listing—touching fingers, making marks on the ground, cutting notches on a stick. A fair number of modern words for counting have developed from verbs describing such practices.

Many languages with a full set of lexical number words (enabling one to count any quantity) lack an abstract noun 'number'. Indeed, the first recorded occurrence of *number* in English is about 1300 CE, as a loan from Old French *nombre*, itself a descendent of Latin *numerus* 'number, portion, part' (this may go back to proto-Indo-European **nem-* 'assign, allot, take'; Watkins 1985: 44). No noun 'number' can be reconstructed for proto-Indo-European.

On the other side of the world, Fijian has a comprehensive decimal array of numbers, and a verb *wili-* 'count, read'. But there was no word 'number'. Fiji has recently taken in loans—*naba* (pronounced [namba]) in some dialects and *fika* in others—from English *number* and *figure* respectively.

In summary, lexical number words appear to have developed before a general verb 'count'. And an abstract noun 'number' was probably an even later introduction.

20.10 Historical development

Grammatical number systems and lexical number words are quite different entities. But they can interrelate in diachronic development. Proto-Austronesian simply had a singular/plural contrast in pronouns. Its descendent proto-Eastern-Oceanic developed a four-term system, adding dual and trial forms. Thus (Pawley 1972: 37):

(65)   Proto-Eastern Oceanic pronouns (focal forms)

	SINGULAR		DUAL	TRIAL	PLURAL
1st person	*i-nau	inclusive	*ki(n)ta-dua	*ki(n)ta-tolu	*ki(n)ta
		exclusive	*kami-dua	*kami-tolu	*kami
2nd person	*i-koe		*kamu-dua	*kamu-tolu	*kam(i)u
3rd person	*inia, ia		*(k)ida-dua	*(k)ida-tolu	*(k)ida

What has happened here is that lexical numbers **dua* 'two' and **tolu* 'three' have become suffixed to plural forms, creating new dual and trial pronouns.

There have been further developments in individual languages—both shortening of forms and shifting of meanings. For example, in Fijian, pronouns
ending in -*dou* (a reflex of *tolu* 'three') now have a paucal meaning, 'a relatively
smaller number greater than two'—within a system of type E from §20.2,
{singular, dual, paucal, plural}—although lexical number *tolu* retains its exact
reference 'three'. And in Polynesian languages the original plural pronouns
have been lost, with forms based on -*tolu* taking over the plural meaning
within a {singular, dual, plural} system.

The Eastern Oceanic example shows lexical number words being used to
augment a grammatical number system. One also encounters developments
in the opposite direction. In Australia, the three languages from the North
Kimberley region—Worora, Ungarinjin, and Wunambal—employ a number
system from the grammar to generate lexical number words.

We can illustrate with Worora. This language has suffixes:

(66)   -warndu   'two'   dual
       -oorri   'three or a few'   paucal

The number system is optional (see §20.3)—the base form of a noun is neutral; that is, unspecified for number. Pronouns and nouns have special non-
singular forms. A non-singular form used alone has plural meaning; dual and
paucal are shown by the addition of a suffix from (66) to the non-singular
form. The dual and paucal suffixes may also be added to verbs, indicating the
number of a core argument (or arguments). All this is intriguing. The point
of particular interest for our present discussion is the way in which lexical
number words are created. One takes the 'quantifier root' -*yarrungu*, adds the
appropriate noun class prefix and number suffix from (66), or plural -*ya*. For
example, masculine forms are:

(67)   i-yarrungu   one
       i-yarrungu-warndu   two
       i-yarrungu-oorri   three or a few
       a-jarrungu-ya   many

The first three numbers commence with masculine prefix *i*-; the alternatives
are *njin*- for feminine, *ma*- for one neuter class, and *ø*- for the other neuter
class. For 'many', prefix *a*- is used across all noun classes. (This discussion
of Worora is based on Love 2000: 20, 24; Clendon 2000: 183–4, 259–89; and
Capell and Coate 1984: 153–5.)

As would be expected, some lexical numbers are based on body-part terms.
Diakonoff (1988: 67) mentions that the Common Cushitic and Common
Omotic number **lam'*- 'two' comes from 'index finger'. This suggests that
listing or early counting was accompanied by first touching the thumb ('one')

and then the adjacent index finger ('two'). In many Austronesian languages, *lima* is both 'five' and 'hand' (the same synonymy is found in languages from the Semitic subgroup of Afroasiatic, from the Arawak family of South America, and from the Ndu family of New Guinea, among many others).

Emphatic plural marker -*nawi* in Warekena (Arawak; Brazil; Aikhenvald 1998: 301) is probably cognate with noun *nawiki* 'people' in the close genetic relatives Baniwa and Tariana. Heine and Kuteva (2002: 230–1, 67, 36) gives further examples of a plural marker coming from noun 'people', and also from 'children', and from 'all'.

20.11 Summary

All languages have, within their grammar, one or more number systems. These vary in size, in whether their terms have absolute or relative reference, and in whether the system is obligatory or optional. Some languages include more than one number system in the grammar, and care must then be taken in choice of terminology (for example, 'plural' should not be used for 'more than two' in one section of the grammar, and for 'more than three' in another). There are special plural-type specifications in some languages—collective, distributive, and associative.

Number may be shown by affixation or any other morphological process (and its realization may then be fused with one or more other grammatical categories) or through clitics. Number marking is always found on pronouns, and sometimes also on demonstratives and interrogative words. Most—but not all—languages have number marking on an NP. This may be realized on the head, or on every word, or just at the beginning or end of the NP. Verbs may mark the number reference of their arguments in a variety of ways—through bound pronouns which are attached to them, through special number-marking affixes, and through having suppletive root forms, the use of which is determined by the number reference of the S or O argument.

Singular is almost always the functionally (and sometimes also the formally) unmarked term in a number system. In a three-term system, dual is often—although not always—more marked than plural. But when, say, a 3sg pronoun must carry information concerning gender, 3pl may be employed as the default form. There are some languages in which a non-singular number is the unmarked term in specified circumstances. Other grammatical categories may have their range of contrasts reduced in non-singular numbers. And a number system may itself have reduced contrasts in a negative clause, or in the context of a certain person or noun class choice, etc.

Evidence was presented that many small tribal societies had no need of counting (they would just list) or of lexical number words. Hale suggests that what had been called lexical numbers in Warlpiri are more appropriately analysed as a grammatical system of indefinite determiners. On contact with larger-scale societies—having an extensive set of lexical numbers, and counting practices—the need for counting does arise and a set of number words quickly evolves. Some native forms may have their meanings extended to cover the lower numbers (for example, 'alone' becoming 'one' and 'face each other' becoming 'two') with names for higher numbers being simply borrowed. A general interrogative word may extend its meaning to include 'how many/how much'.

Counting is typically associated with parts of the body, leading to the most common bases for lexical number sets being ten (fingers on both hands), or five (fingers on one hand), or twenty (all fingers and all toes). Different bases are attested, but are relatively rare.

Lexical number words are most typically a subset of adjectives, but in some languages they relate to nouns, or to verbs, or make up a word class of their own. There are languages whose number words relate to several major word classes; there is then a clear tendency for larger numbers to be nouns. A verb 'count' appears to have been a late development. An abstract noun 'number' is rather rare across the languages of the world, being found only in some 'counting' societies.

An interesting observation can be made. There is a tendency for languages with complex number systems within their grammar to have few or no number words in their lexicon. Is this a valid correlation? Well, in a sense it is, but the connection is of a social, rather than of a linguistic, nature. (That is, it is unlikely to be the case that the human mind can only handle so much 'number information', so that if there is extensive number specification in the grammar there is little capacity for number words in the lexicon, and vice versa.)

Right across the world, the most intricate grammars are found in small-scale tribal societies. These often include number systems with three, four, or five terms. Value is placed on having pronouns which specify whether a person is coming alone, or with one companion, or with more than one. Such small societies are typically hunters and gatherers or slash-and-burn agriculturalists. They have no trade (only exchange), no exact measuring, no money or taxes, no armies or unions, no need to talk of how many hours or days or months have elapsed, no need to identify dwellings in a village by assigning street name and house number. That is, they have no need of counting, or of more than a few numbers. Languages spoken by millions of people do tend to have relatively simple grammars, typically with just a two-term number system. These societies are organized around counting, and numbers—what is the price of bread, how many cans of fish will we need to buy to last us the six weeks we will be away camping, how many people must be present to maintain a quorum at the meeting? There are social reasons why large-scale societies require numbers and counting, where small-scale ones have no such need. This is quite different from the inductive observation—not yet fully explained—that smaller societies tend to have more complex grammars which are likely to include larger number systems. (And see §28.2.)

20.12 What to investigate

One should carefully examine where number systems appear in the grammar—on free and bound pronouns, on demonstratives, on interrogatives/indefinites, in an NP, and/or in a verb. There may be one system throughout the grammar or there could be several systems, each in a different portion. In such an eventuality, care must be taken to choose appropriate labels so as to ensure overall consistency.

The reference of each term in a number system must be ascertained. Some terms may have absolute reference (for instance, 'trial' always refers to three participants) and others relative reference ('paucal' indicates a smallish number greater than two, relative to 'plural' which relates to a biggish number greater than two). This can seldom be achieved just by elicitation; it requires detailed observation of language use. For example, I was once told by an intelligent speaker that what is actually a paucal pronoun refers just to three participants, whereas on one occasion I heard it used for a group of four or five (contrasting with 'plural', referring to eight or ten) and on another occasion for a gathering of several score people (again contrasting with plural, which here referred to several hundred).

A number system applying to nouns may be optional, and is likely to be shown by segmentable affixes or by clitics. The bare stem of a noun will then be neutral with respect to number—as in Turkish, where *kız* is 'any number of girls (can be one or more than one)'. When number specification is obligatory, it is generally shown by an inflectional system, which may combine specification of number with other grammatical information (for instance, person, case, tense, aspect, voice).

There may be dependencies between a number system and other grammatical categories, such that the range of choices available in one system depends on what term is chosen in the other. This generally interrelates with the functional markedness within each system. Within a number system, 'singular' is generally the functionally unmarked term, but other possibilities do occur.

If there is a large set of lexical number words, they should be thoroughly investigated and the manner of their organization worked out. What is basically a decimal system may include some portions which have a different base. For instance, French uses *vingt* 'twenty' sparingly as a subsidiary base, expressing 'eighty' as *quatre-vingts* 'four twenties'. And English has special terms *dozen* for 'twelve' and *gross* for 'twelve twelves'.

Any language which a field linguist is likely to encounter will have some lexical number words. But, in the case of small-scale societies, these may be a recent development, motivated by contact with the language of an invading group. Lower numbers may be expressed by native forms, which in many cases originally had a non-numerical meaning.

Lexical number words may belong to any of the major word classes, or be spread across several. This must be fully investigated. There will be some way of asking 'how many/how much' but this may be through a more general interrogative word; its word class membership should be ascertained. (And see §27.6.4.)

Sources and notes

There is much useful information on this topic in Corbett (2000). However, a fair amount of the material quoted is just from 'personal communication' and so cannot be followed up in a full grammar of the language in question. The East Cushitic language Bayso is referred to on no less than twenty pages. However, we read that 'Hayward's account is invaluable, but he had limited time to work on the language in the field, and there are tantalising questions left open' (Corbett 2000: 127; see also Corbett and Hayward 1987: 3). One wonders whether so much should be made of data over which a considerable question mark must hover, when there are so many full and reliable grammars available.

An excellent source on number systems in languages from North America is Mithun (1999: 79–92).

20.1   In English one could say that 'singular' refers to one while 'plural' refers to 'other than one' (as in *No dogs are allowed here*).

Fijian has no number marking on nouns; there are just seven adjectives which indicate non-singular reference by reduplicating their first syllables; for example, *levu* 'big', *le-levu* 'lots of big (things)'. See Dixon (1988: 231–2).

20.2   I have not tried here to list every possible type of number system. Corbett (2000: 26–30) reports a {singular, dual, trial, quadral, plural} system for a few languages, including the Oceanic language Sursurunga (based on Hutchisson 1986). However, this 'quadral' (or quadruple) term is not a full member of the number system. It can be used with certain kin terms (such as 'we four (exclusive) who are in an uncle-nephew/niece relationship'; note that plural cannot be used with kin terms, so that there is here no contrast between quadral and plural. The only other use of a quadral pronoun is in hortatory discourse, and here it may refer just to four people or to more than four (then intruding into the zone of reference usually reserved for plural). Corbett later suggests that the system in Sursurunga could be restated as paucal, greater paucal and plural; that is, including three terms with relative reference.

Boas (1911b: 38) mentions that, in the native languages of North America, dual number is common and 'it happens also that a trialis and paucalis— expressions for *three* and *a few*—are distinguished'. Later writers shortened these terms to *trial* and *paucal*. The newly-coined term *pochal* has the same etymological origin as *paucal*; it is entirely appropriate that this should be so.

Nicklas, in his grammar of Choctaw (1972: 29–30), sensibly allows 'plural' to have only one meaning, 'more than one', using 'multiple' for 'a relatively large number greater than one'. He sets out the number systems for 1st and 2nd person pronouns:

1st person	SINGULAR ano	PAUCAL pishno	MULTIPLE hapishno
2nd person	SINGULAR chishno	PLURAL hachishno	

Nicklas contrasts the two 1st person non-singular forms as follows: '*pishno* means "we few" or "the few of us", while *hapishno* means "we many" or "the many of us". It is this contrast which suggests the names "paucal" and "multiple".' We also find *pishno* used for 'some of us here' and *hapishno* for 'all of us here'.

Hale (1997b: 72–6) considers three-term number systems, {singular, dual, plural} in Hopi, Navajo, Tanoan languages, and Warlpiri. He concludes that there is—in each language—justification for analysing these in terms of binary features '±singular' and '±plural', with dual being '–singular, –plural'. For example, in Hopi pronominal subjects operate on a singular/non-singular basis while perfect endings on the verb show a non-plural/plural contrast.

20.2.1   There is further discussion and exemplification of collectives, distributives, and associatives in Mithun (1999: 88–94) and Corbett (2000: 101–20). Moravcsik (2003) has an incisive discussion of associatives, featuring a hierarchy describing their preferences of usage.

20.3   Corbett (2000: 9–19, and see references therein) refers to what I here call 'neutral' forms as 'general number', mentioning that 'transnumeral' is an alternative label.

20.5   We sometimes find 'double marking', where a regular and productive number-marking process applies to a form which involves irregular (and archaic) number marking. The plural form of *kind* 'child' in Dutch was *kinder* but today the regular plural suffix *-en* is added to this, giving *kinderen* (Corbett 2000: 154). Some dialects of English add regular plural suffix *-s* to irregular plural forms *men*, *women*, and *children*, giving *mens*, *womens*, and *childrens*. Anderson (1993) is a survey of types of 'double-marking' for number and for other grammatical categories.

20.6.3   In Swahili, number-plus-noun-class prefixes occur on adjectives of native origin, but not on those borrowed from Arabic (Dixon 1982: 37).

Aikhenvald (2003: 170–1) has an account of pluralia tantum nouns in the Arawak language Tariana, and Haspelmath (1993: 81–2) discusses this phenomenon in the North-east Caucasian language Lezgian.

20.6.4   As pointed out in Appendix to Chapter 13, the association between S and O arguments for number-determined suppletive verbs should not be taken as a type of 'ergativity'. (See also Aikhenvald and Dixon 2011b.)

Durie (1986) is a classic study on number-determined suppletive verb roots. Veselinova (2003, 2005) also deals with this topic; however, care should be taken to check back to primary sources for information from her publications.

20.7   The description which Jespersen (1924: 205) provides of the use of dual in Greenlandic Eskimo is very similar to that in Yidiñ.

Mithun (1999: 81–2) describes number marking in Jemez (also from the Kiowa-Tanoan family), which is similar to that in Kiowa (her account is based on Sprott 1992).

20.8   Smith-Stark (1974) is an important early study of how and why number marking occurs. He suggests the following hierarchy: speaker, addressee, kin, human, animate (to which there are a fair few exceptions).

Number marking on kin terms is quite complex in Kobon: 'The suffix *-l* together with the postposed numeral *möhau* "two" indicates that two persons who share the kin relationship specified by the noun are involved. The suffix *-l* and postposed noun *bɨ* "man" or the morphologically related suffix *-lipi- ~ lip- ~ -lap* indicates that three or more persons related as specified are involved' (Davies 1981: 147).

20.9   The term *numeral* is generally used for a written symbol used to express a number. However, linguists have come to use *numeral* in a different sense, to refer to any lexical number word; this does help to avoid confusion with a grammatical system of number. For instance, one variety of classifiers is always called numeral classifiers (never number classifiers). I have here preferred to employ the label 'lexical number word'.

There are useful surveys of the range of bases used in sets of number words in Comrie (2005), and Heine (1997: 18–34). See also Hymes (1955) on Athapaskan languages, and Mazaudon (2009) on Tibeto-Burman languages. Greenberg (1978) provides references to early studies on the nature and development of 'numeral systems'.

With respect to (60), Jauncey (2011: 161) states that cardinal and ordinal numbers function as nouns, but *talom* 'first' is an exception, functioning as an adverb.

20.9.1   In Swahili, 'one' to 'five' and 'eight' are native Bantu forms, and take noun class prefixes, while other numbers are loans from Arabic and do not accept prefixes.

20.9.2   Corbett (1978) suggests two 'universals'. The first is that 'the syntactic behaviour of simple cardinal numbers will always fall between those of adjectives and nouns'. This is disconfirmed by the several examples, quoted in this section, of cardinal number words belonging to the verb class. His second generalization is similar to that of Jespersen (although Corbett does not mention Jespersen): 'if the simple cardinal numbers of a given language vary in their syntactic behaviour, the numerals showing nounier behaviour will denote higher numerals than those with less nouny behaviour.' He then provides a detailed and insightful discussion of how this applies to lexical number words in Russia, plus useful information on other languages. See also Hurford (1987: 187–238).

20.9.3   I am most grateful to George Cardona, Hans Henrich Hock, Jay Jasanoff, Craig Melchert, and Vyacheslav V. Ivanov for providing information on verb 'count' and noun 'number' in Indo-European languages. And to Robert Blust for information on Austronesian.

21

Negation

21.1 Introduction

Negation is an intrinsic notion in the world, and in language. It is not something which can be defined or even explained (in the way that 'demonstrative' and 'relative clause construction' can be). There are scarcely any absolutes in the world; most things we want to talk about have a relative meaning. These can be described (in slightly different ways) by lexical opposites—for example, *tall* versus *short*—or through a grammatical operator of negation—*tall* versus *not tall*.

One does encounter, in the literature, peculiar statements about negation. For example 'a proposition must be existing in the mind of the speaker in some way or the other before he can express a corresponding negative proposition' (Bhat 2000a: 147). But if I say *Napoleon was not tall*, surely the proposition *Napoleon was tall* is not existing in my mind. If it is, then presumably when I say *Abraham Lincoln was tall*, the proposition *Abraham Lincoln was not tall* is also existing in my mind.

In another source one comes across: 'semantically speaking, attributive negation indicates conflicting views on a given thing. On a pragmatic level, there is a debate between the speaker and his co-speaker on the degree of validity of the statement...' (Mettouchi 2005: 266). But if I say *Napoleon was not tall* does this indicate that there must be a conflicting view? Or that there is some inherent debate between me and a co-speaker on the matter?

Leaving aside such unproductive fantasy, we can note that a sentence with negative marking does not necessarily carry negative meaning. Suppose that Mary, John and I are planning a visit to a fun fair, and Mary mentions that she often enjoys consulting the fortune teller. John responds with (negative elements are underlined throughout the chapter):

(1) I wouldn't ever go to a fortune teller

Later, at the fun fair, Mary and I notice John emerging from the fortune teller's tent. Mary says:

(2) Hmm! John wouldn't ever go to a fortune teller!

Mary's declaiming (2)—as an echo of John's earlier statement (1)—uttered with a derisory intonation tune, carries the meaning 'John *does* go to a fortune teller', showing his earlier assertion, (1), to be unfounded.

Sometimes the linguistic conventions of a particular society include using a sentence which is grammatically negative as a positive suggestion. For instance: *Wouldn't it be nice if we went to visit Mother on Sunday?* Or a negative introducer may serve to soften some unpleasantness, as in *I don't know how to say this but the firm no longer requires your services*. In neither instance would the corresponding positive sentence be at all felicitous.

Negation is a term in a two-member polarity system {positive, negative}. 'Positive' is always the formally unmarked term, with zero realization. When another grammatical system is dependent on polarity, there is almost always a fuller set of contrasts available in positive than in negative clauses.

However, polarity is not really a clear-cut yes-or-no matter. Negation can be hedged—*maybe not* or *probably not* or *I don't really agree* and so on. In British Sign Language, clausal negation is shown by a combination of head shaking and facial expression. 'There are different degrees of general negation facial expression. At its mildest level, negation...facial expression can be signed by having the lips pushed out a little bit and the eyes slightly narrowed. At a very extreme level, the eyes can be almost closed, the nose very wrinkled and the mouth very turned down or the lip very curled' (Sutton-Spence and Woll 1999: 73).

Other languages have alternative markers of negation with varying pragmatic implications. The Papuan language Namia has verb prefix *ao-* as neutral negator, and also verb prefix *awara-* 'not, contrary to expectations' (Feldspausch and Feldspausch 1992: 70–1). In Indo-Pakistani Sign Language there are two clausal negators—one neutral and one contrastive, as in 'Villages are good, (in contrast) cities are not' (Zeshan 2004a: 34).

English has other means of negation as an alternative to the standard *not*. The phrase *like hell* was originally an emphatic adverb, as in *They paddled like hell to get home before dark* (meaning that they paddled very strongly). *Like hell* has now evolved into a sentence-initial emphatic negator, as in:

(3) (a) Will you go to the party?
     (b) <u>Like hell</u> I'll go (meaning: I most definitely won't go)

Negation may be shown at several places in a sentence. It is important to distinguish between (a) multiple markers of a single negation (sometimes called 'negative concord'); and (b) several distinct negations, each with its own scope.

(a) **Multiple marking.**   In Spanish, for instance, the basic clausal negator *no* 'not' is placed before the verb (and its pronominal proclitics, if there are any). Other negative elements include *nadie* 'no one', *nada* 'nothing', *nunca* 'never' and *ninguno*(masc)/*ninguna*(fem) 'no, none, nobody'. If one of these precedes the verb, *no* will not be included:

(4) (a) <u>Nadie</u> vino   No one came

However, *nadie* (or any other negative word) can follow the verb, and in that circumstance *no* must also be included before the verb:

(4) (b) <u>No</u> vino <u>nadie</u>   No one came

Note that (4a) and (4b) are simply stylistic variants, and have essentially the same meaning. A further characteristic of Spanish is that if one word in a clause is negated, all following words must be in negative form (if they have one). For example (Butt and Benjamin 2004: 344):

(5) <u>Nunca</u> hay <u>nada</u>   nuevo en <u>ningum</u> parte
     NEVER IS   NOTHING new   IN NO   part
     There's never anything new anywhere

   Old English had multiple marking of a single negation. This continued into Middle English and is retained in many so-called 'non-standard' varieties of the modern language. For example (Anderwald 2002: 109):

(6) <u>Nobody</u> do<u>n't</u> bother with them, do they?

(b) **Double negation.**   There can be several negators within a sentence; for instance, one in the main clause and one in a complement clause. If someone said that they suspected John had failed to attend an important meeting which you had been at, and asked about it, you might reply:

(7) (a) I did<u>n't</u> notice that John was <u>not</u> at the meeting

This has a quite different meaning from:

(7) (b) I noticed that John was at the meeting.

On hearing (7a), one might infer that the speaker was too preoccupied with other matters to pay attention to who was at the meeting and thus didn't know whether John was present or absent. (See also (43a–b) in §18.3.)
   Multiple marking of negation is discussed in §21.2.5 and double negation in §21.5.

The interrelations of negation with mood are interesting. In some languages the same negator element is used in a negative imperative as in a negative declarative. However, many languages negate an imperative in a different manner from a declarative—see §21.2.7.

In the great majority of cases, there is no difference between the way declaratives and interrogatives are negated. But a few exceptions do exist. For example, Karo (Tupí family, Brazil; Gabas 1999: 184–94) has the following negators:

- In a declarative clause, *iʔke* which comes after the verb phrase, as in (8). (This also serves to negate a clausal constituent, which is placed in focus position at the beginning of the clause and followed by *iʔke*.)
- In an imperative or a content question, *yahmãm* which follows the verb, as in (9) and (10).
- In a polar interrogative, negation is marked by particle *taykit*, which occurs at the beginning of the clause, as in (11).

(8) ar   o=top-t   i̱ʔke
     3sg:A 1sg:o=see-INDICATIVE NEGATIVE
     He/it did not see me

(9) e=wé-t   yahmãm
     2sg:S=cry-INDICATIVE   NEGATIVE
     Don't cry!

(10) kõm at   o=top-t   yahmãm
      HOW 3sg:A 1sg:O=see-INDICATIVE   NEGATIVE
      How (come) he did not see me?

(11) taykit   iʔ=wirup$_O$ top-a
      NEGATIVE   1pl.inc=food   see-GERUND
      Aren't/weren't (you) watching our food?

Where negation is shown by a verbal affix, this sometimes belongs to the same inflectional system as positive imperative and as tense/aspect/modality markers—see Table 19.1 in §19.1. Mỹky (isolate, Brazil, Monserrat 2000) is unusual in having an optional system of verbal suffixes which includes three evidentiality markers and the clausal negator:

(12) *-ə́ra, -rə́ra*—negator
      -maka—reported evidential ('someone said this'), typically used in
         myths and traditional stories
      -aka—inferred evidential ('it appears that')
      -hé (with allomorph *-étiro*)—speculative evidential ('it is likely that')

That is, one can specify that a statement is negative. Or, if it is positive, one may specify what type of evidence it is based on. (Alternatively, this slot in verb structure may be left blank. But note that visual/non-visual evidentiality is obligatory shown through the form of subject pronominal suffixes. See Monserrat and Dixon 2003.)

There are a number of different types of negators; some languages display a wide range, while others restrict themselves to a single variety. The majority of languages have an independent polarity item 'no', which can function as the complete answer to a question. However, a fair number of languages lack this. One is instead required to use a complete clause—the negative reply to 'Will you go?' can only be 'I will not go'; see §21.8. In many—but not all—languages a constituent within a clause may be negated; literally 'it wasn't the cow that John shot (it was the horse)'; see §21.3.2. In most languages every variety of subordinate clauses may be negated, quite independently of whether the main clause to which they are attached is positive or negative; an exception to this is discussed in § 21.3.1.

The only universal negator is that which pertains to a main clause. It always applies to every variety of main clause—of all transitivity profiles, plus copula clauses and/or verbless clauses (although these may have special properties, discussed in §21.2.6).

§21.2 deals with negators applying to a main clause and their realizations. In §21.3 we examine negators with different scopes—over a sentence, over a subordinate clause, over a clausal constituent, or within an NP. §21.4 looks at other kinds of negative words, including such items as English *neither*, *never*, *no one*, *nobody*, *nothing*, and *nowhere*. We also consider lexemes with an inherently negative meaning—such as *forbid* and *forget* in English—and derivational processes which yield negative lexemes (along the lines of *un-* and *dis-* in English). Later sections discuss double negation (§21.5), tags (§21.6), and dependencies between the polarity system and other grammatical systems (§21.7).

Recent work had provided a number of tests for whether a sentence in English should be considered negative—addition of a positive tag, or an addition commencing with *and neither*, or one commencing with *not even* (Klima 1964; Payne 1985; Pullum and Huddleston 2002: 786–7). For example:

(13)   (a) John won't go, will he?
         (b) John won't go, and <u>neither</u> will Mary
         (c) John won't go, <u>not even</u> when his mother pleads with him to

The tests are not watertight. For instance, it is scarcely felicitous to append a *not even* element to *He wasn't rumoured to have resigned*, or *Alcoholism doesn't result from bad living conditions. Seldom* is regarded as a negative word on the basis of the tag test—*John seldom arrives on time, does he?* However an *and neither* addition is at best marginally acceptable—**John seldom arrives on time and neither does Mary*. Tests for negation must be established on an individual basis for each language; they seldom provide cut-and-dried results.

An idiom is an idiosyncratic expression which in some ways functions as a lexical item in its own right. Some idioms do include a negator, but the corresponding positive expression is not used. For example (placing the idiom in bold type): *He pushed and pushed but the door wouldn't budge* and *He did not lift a hand to help*. Idioms including negation lie outside our scope here.

The historical origin of markers of negation is also outside the scope of this chapter. They may develop out of negatively-orientated lexemes such as 'lack', 'leave', 'fail', or 'cease, stop', or from a negative existential. To mention just one development in the opposite direction, in some Tibeto-Burman languages clausal negator prefix *ma-* has developed a second function as marker of a polar question (see, for example Watters 2002: 96 on Kham).

21.2 Negation of main clause

It is not profitable to say that a negative clause is 'derived' from the corresponding positive. They exist side-by-side, albeit that there will always be some explicit marker of negative, but not of positive, polarity. Often, a negative main clause has the same structure as the corresponding positive clause with the addition of a negative particle or morphological process. In a number of languages a special negative construction type is employed, with an auxiliary verb. Or the negator may be a main verb, taking a complement clause. These various mechanisms are considered in §§21.2.1–4. We then discuss multiple marking of a single negation, negation of copula and verbless clauses, negative imperatives, and grammatical features of negative clauses.

An interrogative construction may, in some languages, differ from the corresponding declarative just through word order (plus, of course, distinctive questioning intonation)—for example, the statement *She will come* and the question *Will she come?* in English. There are no reports of negation being marked solely by word order, although sometimes a main clause negator may require a special ordering of words (see Payne 1985: 229).

It is not unheard of for the same form to be used both as marker of negation and of a polar question. Cole (1982: 15, 83) reports that, in Imbabura Quechua, non-imperative main clauses are negated by particle *mana* and suffix *-chu* (it appears that the scope of the negation comprises those elements between *mana* and *-chu*):

(14) [ñuka wawki]$_A$ <u>mana</u>   [jatun wasi-ta]$_O$ chari-n-<u>chu</u>
      MY   brother   NEGATOR big   house-ACC have-3:A-NEGATOR
      My brother does not have a big house

Mana is also 'used to express "no", while *-chu* is otherwise used to form polar questions... If *mana* is omitted a polar question results' (using the appropriate question intonation):

(15) [kan-paj   wawki]$_A$ [jatun wasi-ta]$_O$ chari-n-chu
      YOU-POSS brother   big   house-ACC have-3:A-POLAR.QUESTION
      Does your brother have a big house?

Negative questions may involve *-chu* directly attached to *na*, a shorter form of *mana*, as in:

(16) <u>na</u>-chu   Juzi-ka   Agato-pi kawsa-n?
      NEGATOR-POLAR.QUESTION José-TOPIC Agato-IN   live-3:S
      Doesn't José live in Agato? (Isn't it true that José lives in Agato?)

The expectation of a negative reply requires placing *nachu* at the end of a negative clause which is marked by *mana* and *-chu*:

(17) Juzi <u>mana</u>   Agato-pi-<u>chu</u>   kawsa-n <u>na</u>-chu
      José NEGATOR Agato-IN-NEGATOR live-3:S   NEG-POLAR.Q
      José doesn't live in Agato, does he? (Isn't it true that José doesn't
        live in Agato?)

21.2.1 Shown by syntactic particles

Many languages have, for main clause negation, an independent grammatical word (commonly called a 'particle'), similar to Spanish *no* which was illustrated above. Cross-linguistically, there is a strong tendency for negative particles to occur early in the clause. They may be clause-initial, as in Yagua (Payne and Payne 1990: 317). Or they may occur anywhere before the verb. In Ainu, negators *somo* 'not' and *iteke* 'don't' (in negative imperatives) must precede the verb. Within this constraint there appears to be a degree of freedom as to their positioning. Tamura (2000: 28) notes that the following two sentences have identical meaning:

(18) (a) ku=yapo$_A$ <u>somo</u>   cep$_O$ koyki
           1sg.NOMINATIVE=elder.brother NEGATOR fish   catch
           My elder brother did not catch fish

      (b) ku=yapo cep <u>somo</u> koyki

In Dyirbal, words can occur in almost any order in a clause (and also in a sentence). The only real restriction is that—as pointed out in §2.4—eight particles must precede the verb; they include *gulu* 'not', and *galga*, *ŋarru* (dialect variants) 'don't' (Dixon 1972: 121, 291).

There are in fact a number of exceptions to the early-in-the-clause preference for main clause negators. For instance, in Kisi (Southern Atlantic group, Guinea, Liberia, and Sierra Leone; Childs 1995: 125), the negative particle *lé* (when the preceding word ends in a vowel) ~ *té* (after a word ending in a consonant) occurs at the end of a clause:

(19) kèítláŋ á   nèì   yòndòó là   nǐŋ   táú   lé
      pass   TO   road forest   IT   good very NEGATOR
      It is not very easy to pass by [using] the forest path

In Mupun (Chadic branch of Afroasiatic, Nigeria) main clause negation is shown by particle *kas*, which is always sentence-final and obligatory, plus particle *ba* which is clause-initial and optional. 'In a simple or matrix sentence the initial *ba* may be omitted without any change of meaning' (Frajzyngier 1993: 353). For example:

(20) (ba)   kə   n-se   [lua   nyer]ₒ kas
      (NEGATOR) PERFECTIVE 1sg:A-eat   meat bird   NEGATOR
      I did not eat the bird meat

We saw in (14) and (17) that Imbabura Quechua marks main clause negation by a combination of particle *mana* and suffix *-chu*.

It was mentioned in §1.11 and §3.19 that Amele (Gum family, Papuan region) distinguishes two future and three (non-habitual) past tenses in positive clauses, but neutralizes these to a single past and a single future form under negation. Amele uses a combination of negative particle *qee*, which can occur anywhere before the verb, and special negative forms of the verb. We find (Roberts 1987: 110–11, 223–32):

- (absolute) future
- relative future ('about to happen')
  both are negated by *qee* plus negative future form of the verb, which involves infixing *-u-* into the positive absolute future form. Compare:
  —1pl subject positive absolute future of 'come'   ho-q-an
  —1pl subject negative future of 'come'   hoq-a-u̱-n
- today's past
- yesterday's past
- remote past
  all three are negated by *qee* plus negative past form of the verb, which involves infixing *-l(o)-* into the positive remote past form. Compare:

—1pl subject positive remote past of 'come'   ho-m
—1pl subject negative past of 'come'   ho-<u>lo</u>-m
- habitual past
- present
   each is negated just with *qee*, there being no change to the verb form in a negative clause.

21.2.2 Shown by morphological processes

As with other grammatical categories, the most common morphological process to mark main clause negation is affixation, predominantly by a prefix or a suffix. However, other processes are attested. For example, we find infixation and reduplication in Tabasaran (North-east Caucasian family; Khanmagomedov 1967: 556, 2001: 393). The main clause negator is *dar*. This is simply suffixed to a verb form which includes a pronominal subject (with slight adjustment to the verb form), as in (21a). In other circumstances, *dar* occurs as a prefix, as in (21b), or (in shortened form) as an infix, as in (21c). For three-syllable verbs with preverbs, negative forms are created by reduplicating the second syllable, as in (21d).

(21) (a) ɣafnu 'he came'   ɣafun-<u>dar</u>   'he didn't come'
      (b) anub 'to do'   <u>dar</u>-anub   'not to do'
      (c) ursub 'to jump in(side)'   u-<u>dr</u>-sub   'not to jump in(side)'
      (d) ilipub 'to throw over'   i-<u>li</u>-lipub   'not to throw over'

(In (21c) we have -*dr*- infixed into *ursub*, with *udrrsub* becoming *udrsub*. The -*r*- could be analysed as part of the verb or of the negator. The negative form in (21d) could be analysed as *i-<u>li</u>-lipub* or as *ili-<u>li</u>-pub*.)

In many languages, especially from Africa, negation is shown by segmental elements with associated tone changes. There are also examples of it being shown entirely by tone shift. For example, in Kana (Benue-Congo family, Nigeria; Ikoro 1996a: 173, 337–49), perfective verb forms use negative particle *síì* (best glossed as 'not yet') as enclitic to the first constituent in the clause. But the negation of imperfective verb forms is shown by just by tone. Compare:

(22) (a) m̀-wēè   lū
           1sg:S-PAST   come
           I came

      (b) m̀m̄   wèè   lū
           1sg:S:NEGATIVE   PAST:NEGATIVE   come
           I did not come

There are two tonal changes here. The positive sentence (22a), uses the short form of the 1sg pronoun with low tone (shown as m̀). In contrast, the negative sentence (22b) uses the long form of this pronoun with raised mid tones (shown as m̂m̄). And the past tense marker has canonical form wēè, with mid-low tones, in (22a); in the negative sentence (22b) the tones shift to low-low, wèè.

Negation may be shown by a prefix or suffix attached to the verb. In some languages a negator is placed within a series of verbal affixes. For example, in (23) from Turkish, negative suffix -ma- follows causative suffix -t- and is itself followed by perfective-dı and 1st person plural subject bound pronoun -k (Göksel and Kerslake 2005: 146).

(23) Ev-i_O   çoltandır   boya-t-<u>ma</u>-dı-k
      house-ACC   for.a.long.time   paint-CAUS-NEG-PERFECTIVE-1pl:A
      We haven't *had* the house painted for a long time

In Mỹky, the negative/evidential system—shown in (12) above—belongs in the fourth of eleven suffix slots (Monserrat and Dixon 2003).

A negative affix is, in many languages, on the edge of a verb. That is, it may be last suffix, as in Iraqw (Cushitic, Tanzania: Mous 1993: 168), or the first prefix, as in Swahili (Vitale 1981: 14–17). A more complex situation is found in Yimas (Lower Sepik family, Papuan area). The negator ta- is first prefix to a verb. This is added directly to an intransitive verb (retaining the S pronominal prefix, which now follows ta-). But with a transitive verb, adding negator ta- engenders rearrangement of pronominal-type affixes. Basically, a prefix referring to the O argument is replaced by a corresponding suffix. Compare:

(24) (a) takiŋkat_O   ya-kay-wampak-ɲan
          rock:PLURAL   plO-1plA-throw-NEAR.PAST
          We threw the rocks yesterday

      (b) takiŋkat_O   <u>ta</u>-kay-wampak-ɲa-ra
          rock:PLURAL   NEGATOR-1plA-throw-NEAR.PAST-plO
          We didn't throw the rocks yesterday

(This is only a part of the story. See the full account in Foley 1991: 251–63.)

Main clause negation may be shown by a circumfix to the verb (combination of prefix and suffix). In Cairene Egyptian Colloquial Arabic (Gary and Gamal-Eldin 1982: 38–40) circumfix ma-...-ʃ is used with perfect, imperfect, and also imperative forms of the verb. For example:

(25) <u>ma</u>-gaa-<u>ʃ</u>   imbaarih
      NEGATOR-come:perfect:3sg.masculine:S-NEGATOR   yesterday
      He didn't come yesterday

There may be a number of negative affixes, depending on the choice made for some other grammatical category. For instance, Aguaruna (Jivaroan family, Peru; Overall 2007: 324–6, 357–9, 481–2) has three negative suffixes:

- *-tsu,* used in present and future tenses, as in (26)
- *-tʃa,* used with other tenses, as in (27)
- *-(a)i,* used in apprehensive and negative imperative constructions.

(26) wi-ka   buuta-<u>tsu</u>-ha-i
      1sg-FOCUS cry:IMPERFECTIVE-NEGATOR-1sgS-DECLARATIVE
      I am not crying

(27) daka-sa-<u>tʃa</u>-tata-ha-i
      wait-ATTENUATIVE-NEGATOR-FUTURE-1sgS-DECLARATIVE
      I will not wait

Note that the negator follows a tense-aspect suffix and is itself followed by pronominal subject marker and mood suffixes.

Like other grammatical systems, indicators of polarity may be fused with some other category. In Koasati (Muskogean, Louisiana; Kimball 1991: 56–110), verbs have different paradigms for person and number of subject in positive and in negative clauses. A sample of forms for conjugation 1A is:

(28) | SUBJECT | AFFIRMATIVE | NEGATIVE |
      |---|---|---|
      | 1sg | ROOT-l(i) | ak-ROOT-ǫ |
      | 2sg | is-ROOT | cik-ROOT-ǫ |
      | 3 | ROOT | ik-ROOT-ǫ |

Illustrating for verb *ha:l(o)-* 'hear':

(29) | I hear | há:lo-l | I don't hear | ak-há:l-ǫ |
      |---|---|---|---|
      | You (sg) hear | is-há:l | You (sg) don't hear | cik-há:l-ǫ |
      | He/she/they hear | há:l | He/she/they don't hear | ik-há:l-ǫ |

21.2.3 Requiring an auxiliary verb

In English, the positioning of the main clause negator *not* is as follows:

- After the first word of the auxiliary if there is one, whether or not there is a copula, as in *He will <u>not</u> have gone* and *She will <u>not</u> be angry.*
- If the corresponding positive clause has no auxiliary and the verb is the copula *be,* after the copula, as in *John was<u>n't</u> tall.*
- If there is no auxiliary and the verb is not a copula, then a dummy element *do* (a surrogate auxiliary) must be included, and *not* follows this. Corresponding to *She laughed* we get *She did <u>not</u> laugh.*

As in positive clauses, tense is shown on the first verb within the verb phrase, be it auxiliary or lexical verb. *Not* is frequently reduced to be a clitic, written *-n't*, which attaches to the preceding auxiliary (sometimes with phonological reduction of the combination), as in *He won't have gone* and *She didn't laugh*.

In questions, the first word of the auxiliary is fronted before the subject, and again *do* is added if there is no existing auxiliary: *Will he have gone?* and *Did she laugh?* Interestingly, the process of reduction to a clitic appears to precede that of fronting. That is, a negative clitic is fronted with the auxiliary to which it is attached, as in *Won't he have gone?* and *Didn't she laugh?* In contrast, the particle *not* may not move—one must say *Will he not have gone?* and *Did she not laugh?*, rather than **Will not he have gone?* and **Did not she laugh?*

In Evenki (Tungusic, Siberia; Nedjalkov 1994, 1997: 96–101) the main clause negator is an auxiliary verb *e-*, to which tense and bound pronominal suffixes are transferred from the lexical verb (this is now in participle form). Compare:

(30) nuŋan$_A$ min-du   purta-va$_O$ bū-che-n
      HE   1sg-DATIVE knife-ACC   give-PAST-3sgA
      He gave me the knife

(31) nuŋan$_A$ min-du   purta-va$_O$ e-che-n   bū-re
      HE   1sg-DATIVE knife-ACC   NEG-PAST-3sgA give-PART
      He did not give me the knife

Many languages from the Uralic family follow a similar plan, with subtle individual variations; Payne (1985: 214–21) provides a well-illustrated and insightful discussion.

A different strategy is found in Apalai (Carib, Brazil; Koehn and Koehn 1986: 64–7). In this language, bound pronominal prefix and tense suffix are transferred from lexical verb to verb 'be'. The lexical verb now bears negator suffix *-pyra*, plus a pronominal prefix relating to the O argument (this was not included in the corresponding positive). Thus:

(32) isapokara$_O$ ene-no
      jakuruaru.lizard 1.A:see-IMMEDIATE.PAST
      I saw a jakuruaru lizard

(33) isapokara$_O$ on-ene-pyra   a-ken
      jakuruaru.lizard 3.O-see-NEGATOR   1.A-be:IMMEDIATE.PAST
      I didn't see a jakuruaru lizard

Sentence (33) could be analysed as involving 'be' as an auxiliary, or else (as Koehn and Koehn suggest) as being a copula clause, with *on-ene-pyra* being a nominalized verb functioning as copula complement. It would then be, literally, 'I am not-seeing-jakuruaru-lizard'.

21.2.4 *Negator as a main verb*

There are a number of languages in which the canonical negator is an intransitive main verb. The main clause of the corresponding affirmative sentence is coded as a complement clause in S function to the negator verb. Thus, 'John will not come' is rendered by, literally, '[That John will come]$_{CoCl:S}$ is not the case'.

This construction type is an areal feature of languages in the north-west USA and south-west Canada, from the Chimakuan, Salish, and Wakashan families. It was illustrated at (60) in §18.5.2 for the Wakashan language Makah. Andrade (1933: 268–9) describes it for the Quileute, a Chimakuan language (see §3.12), and Kuipers (1974: 81) for the Salish language Shuswap, among several other sources.

An example from another Salish language, Lillooet, is:

(34) x̣ʷʔaz   [kʷ=š=ʔacʼx̣-ən-cí-haš]$_{CoCl:S}$
      NEGATOR   COMPLEMENTIZER=NOM=see-TRANSITIVE-2sgO-3A
      He didn't see you (lit. His seeing you was not the case)

The prefix $k^w(u)$- functions as a complementizer with a complement clause, as in (34) and (35), and as a determiner in an NP, as in (36).

Davis (2005) provides persuasive argumentation in support of this analysis. Evidence in favour of $x^w\hspace{-1pt}?az$ functioning as predicate is (i) that it 'participates freely in derivational processes characteristic of other intransitive verbs, including inchoative formation . . . and suffixation of regular causative and directive transitivizers'; and (ii) that it 'can be modified by sentence-level auxiliaries . . . just like any other main predicate, while it cannot be an auxiliary itself.' Davis also points out that $k^w(u)$ plus 'nominalization is the standard means of clausal subordination in Lillooet', as illustrated in (van Eijk 1997: 233; Davis 2005: 18):

(35) qaʼním-ɬkan   [kʷ=š=núkʼʷ-an-axʷ
      hear-1sgA   COMPLEMENTIZER=NOM=help-TRANSITIVE-2sgA
        ni=n-šqácəzʔ=a$_O$]$_{CoCl:O}$
      DETERMINER=1sgPOSS-father=EXISTENTIAL
      I heard that you helped my father

The negator $x^w\hspace{-1pt}?az$ may also take a plain NP as S argument:

(36) x̣ʷʔaz   kʷu=šx̣ʷəlálp$_{NP:S}$
      NEGATOR   DETERMINER-ghost
      There are no ghosts

The negative verb *sega* 'it is not the case' in Fijian behaves in an almost identical manner, taking either a complement clause or an NP as its S argument; see Dixon (1988: 281). A similar pattern is found in languages of the related Polynesian subgroup, as exemplified and discussed by Payne (1985: 208–12).

21.2.5 Multiple marking of a negation

As explained in §21.1, there is an important distinction between having two separate negations within a sentence and there being multiple realizations of a single underlying negation. Consider:

(37)   You couldn't not realize that he was lying

The -*n't* negates the whole sentence while the following *not* simply negates the predicate—see §21.3.2. We have here two distinct negators which provide an overall positive sense 'You could (= had to) realize that he was lying'.

This contrasts with a sentence such as (6), *Nobody don't bother with them, do they?*, and:

(38)   The dog did not never eat

In these sentences there is a single negation, realized twice. The overall meaning is negative (as opposed to the overall meaning of (37), which is positive). The fact that (6) is negative can be seen from the inclusion of a positive tag.

Some writers treat sentences like (6) and (38) as if they involved two separate negators. For instance, in a textbook of otherwise high standard, Frawley (1992: 391) states 'The dog did not never eat (= the dog ate)'.

The point at issue is that sentences such as (6) and (38) occur in many varieties of 'non-standard English' but not in the standard variety. Speakers of the standard variety would not use such constructions. The grammar of their dialect does not allow for multiple realizations of a single negation and when they observe such a sentence they treat it as a double negation ('two negatives make a positive', as in (37)). People who do use sentences such as (6) and (38) speak a dialect with a slightly different grammar, which does allow for multiple marking. One must be aware that a dialect other than one's own may work in terms of different grammatical principles. As Pullum and Huddleston (2002: 847) so nicely put it: 'Someone who thinks that the song title *I can't get no satisfaction* means "It is impossible for me to lack satisfaction" does not know English.'

There is an historical explanation for the proscription on multiple realization of a negation in present-day standard English. Old English did in fact have multiple marking and so did Middle English, as do many other languages across the world. It was mentioned in §21.1 that, in Spanish, if a negative word follows the verb, then *no* 'not' must also be included before the verb, as illustrated in (4b).

It appears that the habit of multiple marking began to wane from the beginning of the Modern English period, and accelerated during the sixteenth century. Nevalainen (1996: 273) counted the proportion of multiple markings in comparable sets of written texts over two thirty-year periods. The figures were 40 per cent for 1520–50 and just 12 per cent for 1590–1620. It seems that teachers of grammar had been inveighing against multiple marking, with considerable success. In stanza LXIII of Sir Philip Sydney's long poem 'Astrophel and Stella' (composed about 1580) we read:

(39)   But grammers force with sweet successe confirme:
        For grammer says, (Oh this, deare *Stella*, say,)
        For grammer sayes, (to grammer who sayes nay?)
        That in one speech two negatiues affirme!

If two negatives must (in all circumstances) mean a positive, then if you mean the whole to be negative only one negative marker should be used.

There are a few instances of multiple marking in Shakespeare; see Singh (1973). But the habit was soon lost—and strongly criticized—with regard to the 'standard dialect'. Its presence in other varieties is in many cases an historical continuation (in just a few dialects it may be an innovation).

The placement of negative markers is of interest. In her survey of multiple marking ('negative concord') in non-standard British English, Anderwald (2002: 106–9) found that, in about 97 per cent of instances, one of the negators is *not* or *-n't* or *never* in the canonical position (for English) of following the first word of the auxiliary. This undoubtedly relates to the universal tendency to place a main clause negator before the verb (often, immediately before it), which in turn may be linked to the association between focus and negation.

The development of multiple negation in French is well-known. Originally there was just *ne* 'not' before the verb. For verbs of motion the noun *pas* 'step' could be added after the verb—*Il ne va (pas)*, 'He doesn't go (a step)'. In time, *pas* lost its lexical meaning and simply became a second negator, used with every kind of verb: *Il ne sait pas* 'He doesn't know'. There has been phonetic reduction of the *ne* and this element is often omitted altogether in colloquial speech, yielding *Il sait pas*, where *pas* carries the whole burden of negation. There is a further development, in a number of French-based creoles: the sole negator element *pa* (from *pas*) has moved into the cross-linguistically favourite position, before the verb. Bernini and Ramat (1996: 35) provide examples from Seychelles Creole, Guyana Creole, and the following from Mauritius Creole:

(40) [me mõte]ₛ   pa   pe   travaj
      MY watch   NEGATOR   PROGRESSIVE   work
      My watch doesn't work

There is thus a cycle of change. First of all, just negator X. Then second negator Y is called in. The original element X is reduced and eventually lost, leaving Y as sole negator. The first person to draw attention to such a cycle appears to have been Jespersen (1917/1962: 4). Such a cycle of change has been noted for a number of other languages, including Arabic and Berber (see Lucas 2007 and further references therein).

    If a language has a choice available, then multiple marking of negation is likely to carry greater negative force than single marking. In Tariana (Arawak family, Brazil; Aikhenvald 2003: 421–4), main clause negation is generally achieved through circumfix *ma-. . . -kade* on the verb. Negative proclitic *ne =* (also used in 'neither . . . nor' constructions) may be added before negative prefix *ma-* to make the negation stronger; for example 'She was not at all satisfied'.

    In Dhimal (Tibeto-Burman, Nepal; King 2009: 109–10) plain negation involves prefix *ma-* to the verb:

(41) ka   te   ma-han-aŋ-ka
      1sg TOPIC NEGATOR-go-FUTURE-1sgS
      As for me, I won't go

A further negative prefix *mha-* can be added before *ma-* for absolutely categorical denial:

(42) mha-ma-hiŋ-khe
      ABSOLUTE.NEGATOR-PLAIN.NEGATOR-listen-IMPERFECTIVE
      [He] is not listening at all

    Main clause negation in Brazilian Portuguese may involve just *não* before the verb, or there may also be a second occurrence of *não* at the end of the clause. The two alternatives carry a pragmatic difference in terms of 'expectation'. Schwenter (2005: 1443) discusses variant responses to the statement 'João has stopped smoking':

(43) (a) Ele não   deixou   de   fumar   (*não),
          HE   NOT   leave:3sg.PAST FROM   to.smoke   (not)

          ele nunca fumou
          HE   NEVER smoke:3sg.PAST
      He hasn't stopped smoking, he never smoked

(b) Ele <u>não</u> deixou de fumar (<u>não</u>),   eleainda fuma

                                    STILL smoke-3sg.PRESENT

He hasn't stopped smoking, he still smokes

In (43b), the optional inclusion of a second *não* indicates that there is an expectation that he has stopped smoking. In contrast, for (43a) there is no expectation that he has stopped smoking since he never smoked in the first place. For the 'no expectation' reading, it is not permissible to include a second *não*, at the end of the clause.

Sign languages typically show multiple realization of negation; the combination of head shaking and facial expression in British Sign Language was mentioned in §21.1. Zeshan (2004a, 2006b) distinguishes between sign languages that require a manual sign for negation—which may be augmented by non-manual means—and those which may show negation entirely non-manually (although, generally, a manual sign can also be employed).

Some spoken languages also have more than two realizations of a single negation. For example, Lewo (Oceanic branch of Austronesian, Vanuatu; Early (1994) has: (i) particle *ve* (irrealis) or *pe* (realis) before the item being negated; (ii) particle *re*, immediately after the item being negated; and (iii) clause-final particle *poli*. Only *re* is obligatory, *ve/pe* and *poli* being omissible under specified circumstances. Triple realization is also reported for Sentani (Papuan region; Hartzler 1994). And familiar languages can have three or more realizations of a single negation. There are three in the Spanish sentence at (5) in §21.1.

Discussing the Ozark dialect—spoken in a mountainous region of central USA—Randolph (1927: 8) comments as follows. 'The double negative, as in *I never done nothin'*, is the rule rather than the exception. Often the word *nohow* is added for greater emphasis, and we have a triple negative. Even the quadruple form—*I ain't never done nothin' nohow*—is not at all uncommon. Occasionally, one hears the quintuple—*I ain't never done no dirt of no kind to nobody*.'

21.2.6 Negation in copula and verbless clauses

As pointed out in §14.5.1, in most languages copula clauses (and verbless clauses) are negated in the same way as transitives and intransitives. However, a number of languages employ a different technique. For example, in Alamblak (Sepik Hill family, Papua New Guinea; Bruce 1984: 191–4), non-copula clauses are negated by particle *fiñji* 'not' (in non-future tenses), or *afë* 'not' (in future irrealis), or *tafitë* 'not yet'. However, copula clauses are negated by particle *nhai*, which also functions as an independent polarity form 'no' (see §21.8). Thus:

(44)   yima-r_{CS}   nhai   bro-e-r
      person-3.MASCULINE   NEGATION   big(CC)-COPULA-3.MASCULINE
      The man is not big

Some languages have a special negative form of the copula. This is found in
Koromfe and Awa Pit, mentioned in §14.5.1. In Dagbani (Gur family, Ghana;
Olawsky 1999: 17, 49–50), there are three verbs which have special negative
form:

(45)   POSITIVE FORM   NEGATIVE FORM
    'be' (copula)   nye-   pa-
    'be in a place, exist'   be- ⎫
    'have'   mali- ⎬   ka-

It is interesting to note that *be-*, the copula used when the CC (copula complement) is a locational phrase or when there is no CC at all, has the same
negative form as the non-copula verb *mali-* 'have'.

In Hungarian (Groot 1994) copulas also divide into two types in terms of
the relations they represent (see Chapter 14):

   (i) showing identity or attribution, where the CC is an NP, a noun, or an
       adjective;
  (ii) showing location or existence, where the CC is a locational phrase, or
       there is no CC at all.

In a copula construction of type (i), the copula verb may be omitted when
the clause is in present tense and declarative mood, and the CS (copula subject) is 3rd person; the copula verb must be included in other circumstances.
This variety of copula construction is negated in the same way as a verbal
clause—negator *nem* 'not' is placed immediately before the copula verb if this
is stated, as in (46), and before the CC if there is no copula verb, as in (47).

(46) (a) Mari_{CS} okos_{CC} volt
         Mary   clever   COPULA:PAST:3sgCS
         Mary was clever

    (b) Mari_{CS} nem   volt   okos_{CC}
         Mary   NEGATOR   COPULA:PAST:3sgCS   clever
         Mary was not clever

(47) (a) Mari_{CS} okos_{CC}
         Mary   clever
         Mary is clever

    (b) Mari_{CS} nem   okos_{CC}
         Mary   NEGATOR   clever
         Mary is not clever

Note that the copula verb and the CC argument occur in different orders in the positive and negative sentences (46a/b).

Copula constructions of type (ii) behave in a quite different manner. They do not include the regular negative particle *nem*, but instead employ a special negative form of the copula. Compare:

(48) (a) Fák$_{CS}$ vannak   [a   ház   mögött]$_{CC}$
          trees   COPULA:PRES:3pl   THE   house   BEHIND
          There are trees behind the house

      (b) Fák$_{CS}$ nincs-enek   [a   ház   mögött]$_{CC}$
          trees   NEGATIVE.COPULA-PRES:3pl   THE   house   BEHIND
          There are no trees behind the house

As exemplified in §14.5.1, in some languages negative copula constructions make fewer grammatical distinctions than their positive counterparts, and in other languages more distinctions.

21.2.7 Negative imperatives

Every language has a grammatical construction used for telling someone what to do—a (positive) imperative—and also some means for telling what not to do—a negative imperative, or prohibitive.

In many instances, a negative imperative relates to a positive imperative in the same way that a negative declarative relates to a positive declarative. The use of tone to mark a negative declarative in Kana was illustrated at (22) in §21.2.2. A negative imperative is also shown by floating raised-mid tone. However, unlike in the declarative 'where it is attached to pronominal subject clitics, here it is attached to the progressive marker, $\bar{a}\,\bar{a}$' (Ikoro 1996a: 349).

Where negation in a declarative main clause is shown by a particle or affix, the same device may be employed in a negative imperative. This applies for *no* 'not, don't' in Spanish, and for *not* ~ *n't* in English (where it must be added to *do*). It also holds for circumfix *ma-*...*-ʃ(i)* in Egyptian Colloquial Arabic. Compare (25) in §21.2.2 with (Gary and Gamal-Eldin 1982: 38–40):

(49)   ma-truħ-ʃi   ʔinnaharda!
       NEGATOR-go:2sg.masculine:S-NEGATOR   today
       Don't you go today!

In some languages, a marker of prohibition has its own special form but goes into the same slot as a marker of plain negation. This was described in §21.2.2 for Aguaruna where there are three negative suffixes to a verb: *-tsu*, with present and future tenses, *-tʃa*, with other tenses, and *-(a)i*, used in apprehensive and negative imperative constructions. In Hungarian, a negative declarative takes *nem* 'not' before the verb and a negative imperative has *ne* 'don't' in the same position. In Ainu, negation of a declarative main clause involves placing *somo* 'not' somewhere before the verb, as illustrated in (18), while a negative imperative is formed by putting *iteki* 'don't' before the verb (Tamura 2000: 28).

The array of negative techniques in Amele was set out at the end of §21.2.1. Negative imperative involves particle *cain* 'don't' followed by the verb in negative future form, for example (Roberts 1987: 41):

(50) <u>cain</u>   nu-ag-a<u>u</u>n!

     PROHIBITION   go-2sgS-NEGATIVE.FUTURE

     Don't go!

If a declarative negator is a main verb, then a prohibitive negator is likely to be a different main verb. This can be illustrated for Boumaa Fijian:

(51) (a) POS. DECLARATIVE   au   la'o

                    1sgS go

                    I go

     (b) NEG. DECLARATIVE   e   <u>sega</u>   [ni-u   la'o]_S

                    3sgS   NEGATOR   THAT-1sgS go

                    I don't go (lit. It is not the case that I go)

     (c) POS. IMPERATIVE   m-o   la'o!

                    SHOULD-2sgS go

                    You (sg) go!

     (d) NEG. IMPERATIVE   <u>'ua</u>   [ni   m-o   la'o]_S!

                    NEGATOR   THAT SHOULD-2sgS go

                    Don't you (sg) go! (Lit. It is not the case that you should go)

Both *sega* in (51b) and *'ua* in (51d) are verbs which here take a complement clause as S argument. In each sentence the S pronoun within the complement clause can be raised into the subject pronominal slot before the main verb—*au sega ni la'o* and *mo 'ua ni la'o*—with no change in meaning. Verb *waa'ua* is an alternative to *'ua* and appears to have slightly stronger negative force.

A negative imperative may use the same marker(s) as a negative declarative (or a part of them) plus something additional. In Imbabura Quechua, negation of a declarative main clause involves particle *mana* and suffix *-chu*. as illustrated in (14) and (17). A negative imperative requires the same suffix *-chu* and also preverbal particle *ama*, as in (Cole 1982: 84):

(52) <u>ama</u>   shamu-y-<u>chu</u>!

     NEGATOR   come-2sg.IMPERATIVE-NEGATOR

     Don't come!

As shown in (19), negation of a declarative main clause in Kisi is marked by clause-final particle *lé* ~ *té*. This same particle is used in a negative imperative, plus a high-low tone pattern on the verb (Childs 1995: 228).

The negation of a declarative clause in Dyirbal requires particle *gulu* somewhere before the verb. For a negative imperative we must have particle *galga* before the verb, plus a special negative imperative inflection, -*m*, on the verb (see Table 19.1 in 19.1). Compare:

(53) (a) POS. DEC. ŋaja$_A$ waguli$_O$ guñja-n
                      1sg   blood   drink-PAST
                      I drank the blood

       (b) NEG. DEC. ŋaja$_A$ waguli$_O$ <u>gulu</u>   guñja-n
                      1sg   blood   <u>NEGATOR</u>   drink-PAST
                      I didn't drink the blood

       (c) POS. IMP. (ŋinda$_A$) waguli$_O$ guñja-ø!
                      2sg   blood   drink-POS.IMP
                      (You) drink the blood!

       (d) NEG. IMP. (ŋinda$_A$) waguli$_O$ <u>galga</u>   guñja-<u>m</u>
                      2sg   blood   <u>NEGATOR</u>   drink-NEG.IMP
                      (You) don't drink the blood!

There are languages where negative imperative is constructed in a quite different way from negative declarative. In §21.2.2, we saw that in Koasati verbs have distinct paradigms for person and number of subject in positive and in negative declarative clauses. However, negative imperative simply involves suffix -*V́n* (in the twelfth of fifteen suffix slots to the verb); this is used with the positive set of person/number subject markers. Thus (Kimball 1991: 266):

(54) ís-híska-V́n
      2sg.POSITIVE-drink-NEGATIVE.IMPERATIVE
      Do not drink it!

If a language has a contrast between several varieties of positive imperative, then in many cases the contrast does not carry over into negative imperative. There are a number of instances of immediate and delayed positive imperatives (for instance, 'Eat now!' and 'Eat later!'). In most, but not all, cases there is a single negative imperative. (See Aikhenvald 2010: §5.2.2 for discussion and exemplification.) One language where a contrast of this type spans both polarity values is Jarawara—the 'immediate' imperative gives a command to do something right here and now, while the 'distant' imperative relates to doing something in a different place or at a distant time (Dixon 2004: 396–402, 611). An example of a distant negative imperative comes from an instruction an old man gives to some people to whom he has entrusted his newly-made canoe:

(55) kanawaa$_O$ tee   ita-rija-hi!
      canoe(fem)   2nsgA   pierce-DISTANT.NEGATIVE-IMPERATIVE:fem
      Don't you-all make a hole in (my) canoe (at some later time and/or in
         some different place)!

As described in §1.5. Tucano has a five-term evidentiality system in declarative clauses. Like in a number of other languages, only the reported evidentiality marker carries over into imperatives, and it does occur in both the positive and negative varieties. Examples of positive and negative reported imperatives—directed at a 3rd person addressee—are (Aikhenvald 2010: §5.2.2):

(56) (a) dãâ$_A$ basâ-ato
           3pl   dance-REPORTED.IMPERATIVE
           May they dance! (on someone else's order)

      (b) dãâ$_A$ basâ-tikâ'-ato
           3pl   dance-NEGATIVE-REPORTED.IMPERATIVE
           May they not dance! (on someone else's order)

Quite often, a negative imperative may show fewer distinctions for a particular category than its positive counterpart. For example, positive imperatives in Manambu may relate to all three persons and to three numbers, but negative imperative forms exist only for 2nd person. However, this language does have three negative imperative suffixes which differ in their illocutionary force (as compared with a single positive form), for example (Aikhenvald 2010: §5.2.2; see also 2008a: 317–24):

(57) (a) wukə-tukwa!
           listen-GENERAL.PROHIBITION
           Don't listen! (a neutral prohibition)

      (b) wukə-way!
           listen-STRONG.PROHIBITION
           Don't listen under any circumstances! (a strong prohibition)

      (c) wukə-wayik!
           listen-EXTRA.STRONG.PROHIBITION
           Don't listen no matter what (or else)! (a very strong and
              threatening prohibition)

In Zhuang (Tai-Kadai family, China; Luo 2008: 339) there is one positive but several negative imperatives, with different shades of meaning including 'don't do ... yet (but do it later)'.

Sometimes a negative imperative is more felicitous with certain types of verbs than with others, simply because of their meaning and pragmatic effect. In English, one is likely often to hear *Don't be angry!*, but very special circumstances would be required for it to be appropriate to tell someone *Be angry!* There are also preferences in the opposite direction. Situations in which it might be appropriate to tell someone *Listen carefully!* are much more frequent than those giving rise to *Don't listen carefully!* In Tariana, no stative verb may form a positive imperative; however there are negative imperatives for verbs of quality, such as 'be bad' and 'be cold' (although not for verbs referring to physical and mental states, such as 'be unwilling' and 'be lazy').

21.2.8 Grammatical features

Negative clauses may have special syntactic properties. For example, it was mentioned in §13.6 that in Estonian an O NP relating to a completely involved object is marked by genitive case in a positive and by partitive in a negative clause. Compare (Erelt 2007: 111):

(58) (a) Ma$_A$ ehita-si-n   paadi$_O$
           1sg:NOMINATIVE   build-PAST-1sg   boat:SG:GENITIVE
           I built a boat

      (b) Ma$_A$ ei   ehita-<u>nud</u>   paati$_O$
           1sg:NOMINATIVE   NEG   build-PAST:NEG   boat:SG:PARTITIVE
           I did not build a boat

Copula subjects in Finnish and Russian are marked like S in a positive clause but—as mentioned in §14.3—for certain copula relations, CS is in partitive case in Finnish and in genitive in Russian.

A negative clause may exhibit different functional properties as compared with the corresponding positive. To give just one example, compare:

(59)   It took a long time

(60)   (a) It did<u>n't</u> take a long time
       (b) It did<u>n't</u> take long

The negative statement, (60), can include either the NP *a long time* or the adverbial-type element *long*. Only the former is possible for the positive statement; one cannot say *It took long*.

In some languages a marker of negation falls in the same inflectional system as modalities and so cannot co-occur with such specifications—see the discussion of Ika in §19.4.1. In other languages there is dependency between choices in realis/irrealis and in polarity systems. For example, in Muna (Austronesian; van den Berg 1989: 207) 'when a verbal clause referring to the past or present is negated, the word *miina* is put before the verb' and 'the verb form changes from realis to irrealis'. The Australian language Maung requires that positive declarative clauses should take a realis suffix and negative clauses an irrealis one. Compare (Capell and Hinch 1970: 67, charts XIV, XV):

(61) (a) ŋi-udba-n
          1sgA:3sgO-put-PAST:REALIS
          I put it

      (b) marig   ŋi-udba-nji
          NEGATOR   1sgA:3sgO-put-PAST:IRREALIS
          I did not put it

Interestingly, reality values are reversed for imperatives—positive imperative occurs with irrealis and negative imperative with realis suffixes in Maung. The wide cross-linguistic variation in reality/polarity interrelations can be seen by comparing Maung with Wardaman, another Australian language. As shown at (31) in §19.4, in Wardaman negative imperative takes an irrealis and positive imperative a realis verbal prefix.

21.3 Scope

Generally, in a coordinated sentence each clause will be negated on an individual basis; this is illustrated for Japanese by Hinds (1986: 105). However, in non-coordinate clause linking, negation can extend over both Focal clause and Supporting clause (see §3.11), as in (62a), or just over Focal clause, as in (62b):

(62) (a) You must<u>n't</u> go to the synagogue because you're a Jew (, you should only go because you believe)
      (b) You must<u>n't</u> go to the synagogue, because you're a Christian

In (62a) the negator *-n't* has scope over the whole biclausal construction *You must go to the synagogue because you're a Jew*, but in (62b) the scope of the negator is only the Focal clause, *You must go to the synagogue*. The contrast is shown in writing by inclusion of a comma after *synagogue* just in (62b), and in speaking by intonation. (A similar pair of examples is given at (1–2) in §3.12.)

A serial verb construction involves two (or more) verbs functioning together like a single predicate and being conceived of as describing a single action (see §3.4 and §18.6.1). In most instances a serial verb construction may only be negated as a whole; this is exemplified for Tariana in Aikhenvald (2003: 40–408) and for Mupun in Frajzyngier (1993: 231–2). Newār (Tibeto-Burman, Nepal; Hale and Shrestha 2006: 185) may be an exception in that verbs in what is reported to be a serial verb construction may be negated separately. Example (63a) shows a plain serial verb construction; the first component is negated in (63b) and the second one in (63c).

(63) (a) ji_S wən-e   phu
         I   go-INFINITIVE   able:IMPERFECT.DISJUNCT
         I am able to go / it is possible that I will go

      (b) ji_S wən-e   mə-phu
         I   go-INFINITIVE   NEGATOR-able:IMPERFECT.DISJUNCT
         I am not able to go

      (c) ji_S mə-wən-e   phu
         I   NEGATOR-go-INFINITIVE   able:IMPERFECT.DISJUNCT
         It is possible that I may not go

We can now briefly examine the possibilities for negating subordinate clauses, and then NPs and other constituents of a main clause.

21.3.1 Negating a subordinate clause

It is almost always the case that all types of subordinate clause may be negated—sometimes in the same way as a main clause, sometimes in a different way. In English we find *not*~ *-n't* used in every kind of clause. For example, it negates the main clause in (64a) and the complement clause in (64b):

(64) (a) Mary_A did<u>n</u>'t know [that John_{CS} was dead]_{CoCl:O}
      (b) Mary_A knew [that John_{CS} was<u>n</u>'t dead]_{CoCl:O}

Jarawara is a rare exception. This language shows a wide variety of types of subordinate clause and all may be negated (like a main clause, by verbal suffix -*ra*) except for complement clauses. As mentioned in §18.3, Jarawara has a considerable number of 'miscellaneous suffixes' to the verb, which fall into six 'echelons'. The verb in a complement clause may only include suffixes from the first four echelons ('coming', 'in the morning', 'still', 'do without stopping', etc.) The negator -*ra* falls into the sixth echelon and so may *not* be included in a complement clause. One can straightforwardly translate (64a) into Jarawara but not (64b); here a circuitous paraphrase would be required.

In Amharic, negation of a main clause is expressed with verbal prefix *a(l)-* and suffix -*mm*. In a subordinate clause, only the prefix is used. (Amberber 1996: 50; note that *ind-* 'that' marks a complement clause.)

(65) (a) MAIN CLAUSE   al-səbbərə-mm he did not break
     (b) COMPLEMENT CLAUSE ind-al-səbbərə   that he did not break

As shown in §21.2.1, Mupun shows negation by obligatory sentence-final particle *kas* and optional clause-initial particle *ba*, illustrated in (20). In a complex sentence (Frajzyngier 1993: 354), *ba* precedes the clause to be negated. This is the main clause in (66a) and the complement clause in (66b):

(66) (a) ba   mo$_A$ sat [nə   mo$_S$ cin   ji
         NEG 3pl   say THAT 3pl   do.again come
         ḍin-mopun]$_{CoCl:O}$ kas
         PREP-Mupun   NEG
         They$_1$ did not say that they$_2$ came again to Mupun area

     (b) mo$_A$ sat [nə   ba   mo$_S$ cin   ji
         3pl   say THAT NEG 3pl   do.again come
         ḍin-mopun]$_{CoCl:O}$ kas
         PREP-Mupun   NEG
         They$_1$ said that they$_2$ did not come again to Mupun area

Languages which negate subordinate clauses differently from main clauses were mentioned under (e) in §17.3.2 and under (e) in §18.3. For example, in Mojave a main clause is generally negated with suffix *-mot-* but suffix *-m-* is used with dependent clauses and also in the negation of NPs (Munro 1976: 65, 213–17).

Somali (Saeed 1993: 234, 248) also exhibits different mechanisms. All types of clause use a preverbal negator particle and also a special negative form of the verb. The particle is *má* in a main clause, as in (67a), and *aan* in a subordinate clause, as in (67b). Each of these particles may fuse with a following pronominal. A further use of *aan* is in a main clause where one constituent is focussed, this being fronted and followed by focus marker *baa-* (which may fuse with *aan*), as in (67c).

(67) (a) máan   keenin
         NEGATOR:1sg bring:NEGATIVE
         I did not bring [it]

     (b) hílibka   [áanad   cúni   karín]$_{RC}$
         meat:ARTICLE NEGATOR:2sg eat:INFINITIVE can:NEGATIVE
         The meat that you cannot eat

     (c) Cáli báan   tegín
         Ali FOCUS:NEGATOR go:NEGATIVE
         It wasn't Ali that went

With certain choices of verb, negation of a main clause and of a complement clause carry quite different meanings and need to be carefully distinguished. This applies to (62a/b). But with other verbs the two negations are less strongly distinguished and there can be a tendency to 'raise' negator from subordinate to main clause. Consider the English example (Jespersen 1940: 444):

(68)   (a)   I$_A$think [that John$_S$ didn't come]$_{CoCl:O}$

In keeping with the universal tendency to place a negator before the verb of the main clause, speakers often say, instead of (68a):

(68)   (b)   I$_A$ don't think [that John$_S$ came]$_{CoCl:O}$

The literal meaning of (68b) is 'I don't have any idea as to whether John came or not'. People would seldom need to express such a thought. It is undoubtedly because of this that (68b) may be used in the meaning of (68a), to cast doubt on whether John came.

21.3.2 Negating a clausal constituent

Most—but perhaps not all—languages have some mechanism for negating a constituent within a clause. In Awtuw (Ram family, Papua New Guinea; Feldman 1986: 145–7), plain main clause negation requires *ka-* ∼ *kæ-* in the first prefix slot to the verb:

(69)   Awtiy-re$_O$ wan$_A$ ka-d-uwpo-ka
       Awtiy-OBJECT   1sg   NEGATOR-FACTIVE-see-PERFECT
       I haven't seen Awtiy

A quite different strategy is used to negate a constituent within a clause. Particle *yene* is placed before the constituent, which may be a verb or an NP, as in:

(70)   wan$_A$ [yene   Yawmən-re]$_O$ du-puy-e,
       1sg   NEGATOR   Yawmen-OBJECT   FACTIVE-hit-PAST

       wan$_A$ Naytow-re$_O$ du-puy-e
       1sg   Naytow-OBJECT   FACTIVE-hit-PAST
       I didn't hit Yawmen (lit. It wasn't Yawmen I hit), I hit Naytow

A fair number of languages use the same particle to negate a main clause and to negate one of its constituents; see the discussion of Karo in §21.1. In Hungarian, a clause is negated by placing *nem* before its verb. For negation of a constituent, this must be moved to a position before the verb and preceded by *nem* (Groot 1994: 150):

(71)   [Nem   Ildikó-val]   találkoz-t-am
       NEGATOR   Ildikó-COMITATIVE   meet-PAST-1sg
       It was not Ildikó whom I met

As described in §21.2, in Quechua a non-imperative main clause is negated by placing particle *mana* before the verb and suffixing -*chu* to the verb, illustrated for Imbabura Quechua in (14). Weber (1989: 336, 410) describes two techniques of negating a constituent in Huallaga Quechua. One is to have *mana* before the verb and affix -*chu* to the constituent in question:

(72) mana   rura-ra-n Hwan-paq-<u>chu</u>
      NEGATOR do-PAST-3 John-PURPOSE-NEGATOR

      rura-ra-n Pablo-paq-mi
      do-PAST-3 Paul-PURPOSE-DIRECT.INFORMATION

      He didn't do it for John (lit. It was not John he did it for), he did it for
      Paul

A more common method is to negate the main clause in the usual way, and highlight the constituent in question by attaching topic marker -*qa*. Describing the burial of a child (in contrast to that of an adult):

(73) mana   hatipan-<u>chu</u>   yana-ta-qa
      NEGATOR they.put.on.him-NEGATOR black-OBJECT-TOPIC

      paykuna kabritillu-ta
      THEY   linen-OBJECT

      They don't dress him in black, they [dress him] in linen

It is often the case that, as in (73), in order to negate a clausal constituent it must be topicalized. This can be illustrated from Colloquial Welsh (Jones and Thomas 1977: 324–5). Compare main clause negation in (74a) with negation of the O NP in (74b):

(74) (a) 'doedd   John <u>ddim</u>   yn   golchi'r   car
           NEGATOR:was:3sg John NEGATOR PROG wash-THE car
           John wasn't washing the car

      (b) [<u>dim</u>   y   car] oedd   John yn   ei   olchi
           NEGATOR THE car   was:3sg John PROG ITS wash
           It wasn't the car that John was washing

A particular point of interest about English is that *not* has the following two functions:

   (a) to negate a complete clause, then following the first word of the auxiliary, as in (75a)
   (b) to negate just a verb, then immediately preceding the verb, as in (75b).

(75) (a) Mary could <u>not</u> (OR couldn<u>'t</u>) have climbed the mountain (she is incapable of doing so, being bound to a wheelchair)
      (b) Mary could have <u>not</u> climbed the mountain (she should have just refused to go, instead of going and grumbling about it afterwards)

Another 'minimal pair'—of clause negation in (76a) and verb negation in (76b)—is:

(76) (a) We do<u>n't</u> have to put the alarm on (we can choose whether to do so or not)
      (b) We have to <u>not</u> put the alarm on (we have been instructed not to do so)

An alternative to (76b), with the same meaning, is *We have <u>not</u> to put the alarm on*.

When used as clause negator *not* can reduce to *-n't*, attached to the preceding auxiliary. *Not* as verb negator may never reduce to *-n't*.

The two functions of *not* can occur together in one clause. For example (Francis 1982: 216):

(77) I knew logically that I could<u>n't</u> have <u>not</u> done what I did.

Another example relates to it being doubtful whether an invited visitor was actually going to arrive. One academic remarked: *If JN does<u>n't</u> come, we can spend the money put aside for her on EB*. His colleague responded:

(78) But JN has<u>n't</u> <u>not</u> come yet

English lacks any technique of formal marking for negating an NP constituent, instead using prosodic means. Consider:

(79) (a) The old lady did<u>n't</u> feed the cat in the kitchen yesterday

If one wanted to negate the subject NP, *the old lady*, this should be stressed (indicated by bold type):

(79) (b) **The old lady** did<u>n't</u> feed the cat in the kitchen yesterday (the old man did)

Similarly if one wanted to negate *the cat* (she had instead fed the dog) or *in the kitchen* (it had taken place on the verandah) or *yesterday* (it had been the day before yesterday)—that constituent should be accorded special stress.

An alternative, as in many other languages, is to topicalize the constituent:

(79) (c) It was<u>n't</u> the old lady who fed the cat yesterday (it was the old man)

21.3.3 Negation within an NP

In English, determiners such as *all* and *some* can directly modify a noun and then have a general sense, as in [*All men*] *are mortal* and [*Some animals*] *hibernate in winter*. Or they may be followed by *of the X* and then relate to a specific population X—[*All (of) the men in this platoon*] *are tall* and [*Some of the animals in the zoo*] *are kept in separate cages*. In similar fashion, *no* may directly modify a noun and then has a general meaning:

(80)   [No man]$_A$ may bear [a child]$_O$

Or we may have *none of the X* (a reduction from *no one of the X*) relating to a specified population, *X*:

(81)   [None of the men in our street]$_A$ has [a job]$_O$

There is another use of *no* as modifier which appears to be limited to an NP in copula complement (CC) function. We can first examine a copula clause with regular main clause negation. As noted in §21.2.3, the *not* ~ *-n't* particle is attached to the copula verb:

(82)   John$_{CS}$ isn't [a linguist]$_{CC}$ (he's an historian)

This is quite different from (83), where *no* is modifier within the NP in CC function:

(83)   John$_{CS}$ is [no linguist]$_{CC}$

This implies that, although John may be employed by the linguistics department, in fact he has little competence in the discipline.

   Only some languages—predominantly a number spoken in Europe—have a technique for negating within an NP, each in its own particular manner.

21.4 Negative words

Never is an alternative to *not* as negator of both main and subordinate clauses in English. It comes from *ne* 'not' in Old and Middle English plus *ever*. Unlike *not*, *never* does not require a preceding auxiliary—compare *He never tells lies* with *He does not ever tell lies*. *Never* may not negate a verb but it may negate a clause in concert with *not* negating the verb, as in:

(84)   I have never not paid my credit card on time

Some other languages, predominantly in Europe, have a simple or complex negator 'never'; each has its special functional characteristics.

   The English word *neither* (which is underlyingly *not either*) has a variety of grammatical roles. First, it can negate an NP argument. Consider a situation where there is an armchair and a folding chair. Someone says:

(85)   You may sit in either of the chairs

The constituent *either of the chairs* may be negated, and *either* then becomes *neither*:

(86)   (a) You may sit in neither of the chairs

As mentioned before—and illustrated for a subordinate clause in (68) of §21.3.1—there is a tendency to raise a negator, which is not in the favoured position of following the first word of the auxiliary in the main clause, into that position. This may apply for the *not* of *neither* in (86a), giving

(86) (b) You may <u>not</u> sit in either of the chairs

This is an instruction not to sit in the armchair and not to sit in the folding chair. But suppose that the requirement was that you cannot choose where to sit but must sit in one particular chair, say the armchair. Main clause negation of (85) will express this:

(87) You may <u>not</u> sit in either of the chairs

We thus have *You may <u>not</u> sit in either of the chairs* being ambiguous between a negated NP (with raising of *not*), in (86b), and a negated main clause, in (87). In speech, the difference would be likely to be shown by contrastive stress.

Turning now to clausal connective function, *either* may be used—with a meaning like 'also'—at the end of a clause, as in:

(88) (a) Mary shoul<u>dn't</u> have gone and John shoul<u>dn't</u> (have (gone)) either

Either can be fused with the *not*, yielding *neither*, which comes clause-initially and requires the first word of the auxiliary to jump to the left over the subject:

(88) (b) Mary shoul<u>dn't</u> have gone and <u>n</u>either should John (have (gone))

Nor is linked with *neither* as the negated forms of *either... or*. For instance, in (86a), *neither of the chairs* could be replaced by *neither the armchair nor the folding chair*. It may also be used in clause linking—another way of saying (88b) is *Mary shoul<u>dn't</u> have gone and <u>n</u>or should John (have (gone))* (However, there is no *not... or* sentence corresponding to (88a).)

Some languages have complex negators, of varying types. Those for English include *not only*, *not just*, and *not even*. Although these commence with *not*, they do not require a preceding auxiliary. For example *John <u>not only</u> climbed the Matterhorn, he also climbed Everest*. And, like *neither* and *never*, they may occur clause-initially, again requiring the first word of the auxiliary to move before the subject (if there is no auxiliary, then *do* is supplied)—*<u>Not only</u> did John climb the Matterhorn...*

21.4.1 Negative indefinites

English has a fine array of indefinite words, with a negative member corresponding to each row (and see §27.6.1):

(89) someone   anyone   no one
      somebody   anybody   nobody
      something anything   nothing
      somewhere anywhere   nowhere

Main clause negator *not* may move from its preferred position, after the first auxiliary word, to fuse with *anyone* or *anybody* or *anything* in O function. One can say either of the following, with no significant difference in meaning:

(90) (a) They did<u>n't</u> see anybody
      (b) They saw <u>n</u>obody

However, when such an indefinite form is in subject function, it must fuse with *not*. One has to say:

(91) <u>N</u>obody saw them

rather than **Anybody did<u>n't</u> see them*, although this is the underlying structure of (91). (One can say *Somebody did<u>n't</u> see them* but this has a quite different meaning with *somebody* referring to a specified but indefinite individual.)

   The reason for this restriction may be that if negator *not* and an indefinite *any-* form co-occur, then the negator must come first. This applies for *-n't...anybody* in (90a) and for the fused form *nobody* in (90b) and (91). The requirement is contravened in **Anybody did<u>n't</u> see them*, and this may be why such a sentence is unacceptable.

   In Chapter 7 of Lewis Carroll's *Through the Looking Glass*, Alice has a memorable conversation with the White King:

(92) 'I see <u>n</u>obody on the road,' said Alice.
      'I only wish *I* had such eyes,' the King replied in a fretful tone. 'To be able to see <u>N</u>obody! And at that distance too! Why, it's as much as *I* can do to see real people, by this light!'

The King was responding to the surface structure, assuming the *nobody* was the object of *see*. In fact the underlying structure is *I did<u>n't</u> see anybody*.

   A little later, the King's messenger appears and is asked who he passed on the road:

(93) '<u>N</u>obody,' said the messenger.
      'Quite right,' said the King, 'this young lady saw him too. So of course <u>N</u>obody walks slower than you.'
      'I do my best', the Messenger said and in a sullen tone. 'I'm sure <u>n</u>obody walks much faster than me.'
      'He ca<u>n't</u> do that,' said the King, 'or else he'd have been here first.'

The meaning of _Nobody walks slower than you_ is 'There isn't anybody who walks slower than you.' As mentioned just above, one cannot say *_Anybody doesn't walk slower than you_; the _not_ must fuse with _anybody_, giving _nobody_.

Passive constructions show very clearly the functional limitations of _any_ forms. We can go back to (90). Only the (b) alternative has a corresponding passive:

(94)   Nobody was seen (by them)

One cannot have a passive of (90a), *_Anybody wasn't seen (by them)_, simply because _anybody_, in this meaning, may not occur in surface subject slot.

Just as _not...anybody_ can be replaced by _nobody_, so _not . . . any_ may be replaced by _no_. A prohibition may be phrased in either of two ways:

(95)   (a) Don't light any fires!
       (b) Light no fires!

These two sentences have the same basic meaning, but (95b)—being shorter (and not requiring auxiliary _do_)—has greater pragmatic vigour.

A well-known characteristic of indefinite forms in English is that _some_ in a post-verbal constituent is replaced by _any_ under clausal negation (and also in a question). Compare:

(96)   (a) Mary put some money in some bank somewhere in some Scandi-
            navian country
       (b) Mary didn't put any money in any bank anywhere in any Scandina-
            vian country

Much has been written about the ramifications of the 'some-any' rule. See, among many others, Klima (1964), Lakoff (1969), Bolinger (1977: 21–36), and Hirtle (1988). One important point is that the rule applies only to one of several senses of _some_, and relates only to one of the several senses of _any_ (see Dixon 2005a: 438–40).

Negative indefinite words are fairly rare across the world's languages. Most often, the clausal negator 'not' is used with a generic noun such as 'person' or 'thing'. Or else with a specific indefinite form such as 'someone' or 'something'. This can be exemplified from Huallaga Quechua (Weber 1989: 346):

(97)   [aqcha suwa]$_A$ mana   ima-ta-pis$_O$ malubra-n-chu
        hair   thief   NEG   WHAT-ACC-INDEFINITE   damage-3-NEG
       The hair thief (an insect with very long legs, which gets tangled in
          them) doesn't damage anything (i.e. damages nothing)

A similar scheme is used in Basque (Saltarelli 1988: 92–3).

In Lezgian (North-east Caucasian; Haspelmath 1993: 197–8), there is a special set of negative indefinites, which are derived from specific indefinites 'by means of a phrase-final suffix -*ni* ("also, even").' For example:

(98)   SPECIFIC INDEFINITES   NEGATIVE INDEFINITES
        sa kas   someone, a certain person   sa kas-ni   nobody
        sa zat' something, a certain thing sa-zat'-ni nothing
        sana   somewhere   sana-ni   nowhere
        sadra   once   sadra-ni   never

Component elements of these forms include *sa* 'one', *kas* 'person', *zat'* 'thing', and -*na* 'place'. They always require clausal negator -*č*. For example:

(99)   k'wal-e   sa kas-ni   awa- č
        house-INESSIVE   NOBODY   be-NEGATOR
        There is nobody at home

In Dyirbal, the only way of saying 'nobody' is to add the regular nominal suffix -*ŋaŋgay* 'without' to *waña* 'who, someone', giving *waña-ŋaŋgay* which is literally 'without anyone'. In one story, people bewail the fact that an American agricultural company is bulldozing traditional sites. One speaker says:

(100)   bala   waña-ŋaŋgay   mija
        THERE-ABSOLUTIVE-NEUTER   SOMEONE-WITHOUT   place/camp

        bala$_O$ bilmba-n
        THERE-ABSOLUTIVE-NEUTER   push.down-PRESENT

This was translated by the speaker as 'There was no one to own the camp and so it was pushed down'. Literally 'the place/camp there (was) without anyone (and) it was pushed down'.

21.4.2 Inherently negative lexemes

Some lexemes are inherently negative so that a clause including them has the properties of a negative clause. This can apply to verbs (including modals), adjectives, and adverbs.

Inherently negative verbs fall into two sets, according as to whether the implicit negation relates to complement clause or to main clause. We can illustrate from English.

I. One set of verbs carries implicit negation of a complement clause. They include:

(101)   doubt [that . . .]   =   think [that not]
        forbid [to/from . . .] =   order [not to . . .]
        deny [that . . .]   =   state/say [that not . . .]
        dissuade [from . . .]   =   persuade [not to . . .]

For example:

(102)   (a) I$_A$ think [that he$_A$ ate something$_O$]$_{CoCl:O}$
       (b) I$_A$ think [that he$_A$ did<u>n't</u> eat anything$_O$]$_{CoCl:O}$
       (c) I$_A$ <u>doubt</u> [that he$_A$ ate anything$_O$]$_{CoCl:O}$

The complement clause O NP is *something* for main verb *think* in (102a), *anything* for *think* plus *not* in the complement clause in (102b), and also *anything* for main verb *doubt* in (102c). This confirms that *doubt* has a similar meaning to *think* taking a negated complement clause.

   II. A second set of verbs carries implicit negation of the main clause. These include:

(103)   forget = not remember
       fail   = not succeed
       reject = not accept

For example:

(104)   (a) I$_A$ remembered [that I$_A$'d written something$_O$]$_{CoCl:O}$
       (b) I$_A$ didn't remember [that I$_A$'d written anything$_O$]$_{CoCl:O}$
       (c) I$_A$ <u>forgot</u> [that I$_A$'d written anything$_O$]$_{CoCl:O}$

In these sentences, *something* is used after *remember* and *anything* after both *not remember* and *forget*, showing the similarity between the latter two.

   Quite a few languages have a small set of inherently negative verbs—never more than a dozen and sometimes just one or two. A survey of sixteen such languages shows the most common meaning to be 'know' (in seven languages), followed by 'want' (in six) and 'can, be able to' (in four).

   Ainu has a negative copula and also four negative verbs (Bugaeva 2004: 83–4):

(105)   (a) e-askay   'be able to do something, be good at something'
            e-aykap   'be unable to do something, be bad at something'
       (b) amkir   'remember/know'
            eramiskari   'not remember/know'
       (c) eramuan   'understand/know'
            erampewtek   'not understand/know'
       (d) kor   'have (something/someone)'
            sak   'not have (something/someone)'

The positive member of each of the pairs in (105) cannot be negated. Instead, one must use the corresponding negative verb. A similar situation applies with respect to the half-dozen or so inherently negative verbs in Anywa (Nilotic, Sudan and Ethiopia; Reh 1996: 204–5).

Tamambo (Austronesian, Vanuatu; Jauncey 2011: 271) adopts a different profile for its single negative lexeme, the modifying verb *wati* 'unable'. This 'can only be used in conjunction with the pre-head negative marker *te*', as in:

(106)   ku-<u>te</u>   sile   <u>wati</u>-a   telei-ho
        1sgA-NEGATOR give   unable-3sgO   TO-2sgO
        I am unable to give it to you

In English there are some adjectives with an inherently negative meaning. For example, *reluctant* is similar to *not eager* in using an *any-* form:

(107)   (a) He was eager to do something about it
        (b) He wasn'<u>t</u> eager to do anything about it
        (c) He was <u>reluctant</u> to do anything about it

On the *some/any* test, *difficult* can be shown to have a similar meaning to *not easy*. Compare *It was easy to find something relevant* with *It was difficult/<u>not easy to find anything relevant</u>*.

Grammars of English typically describe a small set of negative adverbs. These include *hardly*—said by Jespersen (1917/1962: 38) to mean 'almost not'— *barely*, and *scarcely*. Compare the positive sentence in (108a), plain negative in (108b), and the sentence with *scarcely* in (108c):

(108)   (a) He'd said something, had<u>n't</u> he?
        (b) He had<u>n't</u> said anything, had he?
        (c) He'd <u>scarcely</u> said anything, had he?

In (108c), *scarcely* satisfies two criteria for being considered a negative word— the use of *anything*, and the positive tag.

At the end of §21.1, it was mentioned that time adverb *seldom* has some negative characteristics (as also does *rarely*). We also pointed out there that none of the tests for negation is really watertight. There are—in English, and doubtless in many other languages—degrees of 'inherent negativity'. This would be a fertile field for detailed study.

21.4.3 Deriving negative lexemes

Some languages have a large number of derivational processes for creating negative lexemes, others only a few, and a further set none at all. Lexical means may be used in one language for what is achieved morphologically in another. For example, in Jarawara *Etina maki* is 'Etina's husband' and *Etina maki botee* is 'Edina's ex-husband'. In these circumstances, adjective *botee* 'old' carries the meaning 'former'.

Among the ways of deriving negative lexemes in Japanese are the following prefixes (of Sino-Japanese origin):

(109)   *mu-* 'without, lacking', as in *mu-kee* 'formlessness'
      hu- 'un-, non-', as in *hu-wa* 'unfriendliness'
      hi- 'un-, non-' (with negative connotations), as in *hi-ree* 'lack of
        courtesy'
      han- 'anti', as in *han-taisee* 'anti-establishment'

English has a considerable array of prefixes for deriving negative lexemes. Some of the more important are summarized in Table 21.1.

These have varied properties:

- Those in rows 4 and 11 are of Greek origin; 1, 7, and most instances of 8 are Germanic; while the remainder come from Latin or French.
- All the prefixes may be used with nouns, 1–7 and 11–13 with adjectives, 6–8 and 12–13 with verbs, and 1–2 with derived adverbs.
- Prefixes 5–7 may change word class membership while the remainder preserve this.
- Those in rows 1, 3, and 7 are highly productive; 5, 8, 10, 11, and 12 are fairly productive and 4 and 9 are productive in medical/scientific work.

As can be seen in Table 21.1, the range of negative prefixes in English covers a number of subtypes of negation. Just a few adjectives from the HUMAN PROPENSITY subtype (§12.4) have a negative form—through prefix *un-*(1)— which is similar to inherently negative lexemes in terms of the *some-any* test (but not necessarily in terms of other tests). They include *uncertain* and *unsure*, as in:

(110)   (a) John was sure that someone would come
      (b) John was<u>n't</u> sure whether anyone would come
      (c) John was <u>un</u>sure whether anyone would come

A negative derivation may not have the same import as the clausal negator 'not'. If it is not the case that someone is happy than it must be the case that they are not happy. But they may not necessarily be unhappy. This can be illustrated in:

(111)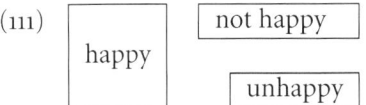

Happy and *unhappy* relate to opposite ends of a parameter of 'happiness'. The scope of *not happy* is complementary to that of *happy*. But one can say:

(112)   John is<u>n't</u> happy and he is<u>n't</u> unhappy either

This relates to the blank space between *happy* and *unhappy* in the bottom row of (111).

TABLE 21.1. Summary of negative prefixes in English

	FORM	MEANING	EXAMPLES
1	un-(1)	lacking a (valued) quality	un-clean
2	in/-im-/il-/ir-		in-capable
3	non-	not a member of a specified class	non-fiction
4	a(n)-	not relating to a parameter	a-political
5	de-	a. get off a vehicle	de-plane
		b. deprive of	de-frost
6	dis-	a. deprive of	dis-mast
		b. lacking a (valued) quality	dis-loyal
		c. not	dis-approve
		d. reverse state or process	dis-arm
7	un-(2)	a. deprive of	un-frock
		b. reverse process or state,	un-dress
8	mis-	do wrongly, improperly	mis-govern
9	mal-	defective, inadequate	mal-nutrition
10	ex-	former	ex-husband
11	anti-	a. reverse of	anti-climax
		b. opposed to	anti-abortion
12	counter-	do/be the opposite	counter-attack
13	contra-	opposed to	contra-distinction

21.5 Double negation

As has already been stated, there are three ways in which a clause may include more than one mark of negation.

First, there can be independent negation of a main clause and of a subordinate clause—as in *We$_S$ weren't surprised* [*that John$_S$ didn't show up*]$_{CoCl}$—or of a main clause and an NP constituent—as in [*John's non-arrival*]$_A$ *didn't surprise us*$_O$. In Cantonese (Matthews and Yip 1994: 259–60), including two types of negation in a single sentence is used 'typically to make a point in an indirect or subtle way' where 'the two negatives make a (qualified) positive statement':

(113)   Ngoh mhaih   mséung   heui
        I   NOT:be NOT:want go
        It's not that I don't want to go

Discussion of negation of both a clause and a clausal constituent is in §21.3.2.

Secondly, as shown in §21.2.5, there may be multiple realization of a single negation, as in *John didn't eat nothing, did he?*, where the inclusion of a positive tag, *did he?*, indicates that *John didn't eat nothing* has an overall negative meaning.

Then there are true double negatives—a clause where the inclusion of two negators gives an overall positive meaning. In Newār (Hale and Shrestha 2006: 185–6) 'double negatives function as strong assertives':

(114)   ji mə-wɔ̄:-se
        I   NEGATOR-go:IMPERFECT.DISJUNCT-ASSOCIATED.ACTION/STATE

        cwən-e   ma-phu
        stay-INFINITIVE   NEGATOR-able-IMPERFECT.DISJUNCT

        I am unable to remain without going = It is absolutely essential that
           I go

In Tuyuca (Tucanoan, Colombia; Barnes 1994: 340), a double negative may yield 'a semantically strong positive statement':

(115)   nĩyéru   kĩo-rí-hã   tii-rí-a
        money   have-NEGATOR-EMPHATIC do-NEGATOR-EVIDENTIAL
        I certainly do have money

Other languages in which a double negative shows a positive meaning include Korean (Sohn 1994: 135, 1999: 393–4), Awtuw (Feldman 1986: 147), Sanuma (Yanomami, Brazil/Venezuela; Borgman 1990: 88), and Canela-Krahô (Jê family, Brazil; Popjes and Popjes 1986: 160).

21.6 Tags

As mentioned at the end of §21.1, the 'tag test' is quite useful as an indicator of negation in English. A positive statement takes a negative tag and a negative statement requires a positive tag. See (108c) in §21.4.2, where the positive tag, *had he?*, in *He'd scarcely said anything, had he?* confirms the negative character of *scarcely* (this being confirmed by the occurrence of *anything* here, rather than *something*). A tag involves a pronoun referring to the subject of the main clause and the first word of the auxiliary (or *do*, if there is no auxiliary), to which -*n't* may be attached:

(116)   (a) John resigned, did<u>n't</u> he?
         (b) John did<u>n't</u> resign, did he?

The positive/negative tag association applies only in neutral circumstances, when there was no particular presupposition. Suppose that I consider John's resigning to be the least likely of events. Then someone tells me: *John resigned.* In this situation, I would add a positive tag to a positive statement as an indication of surprise:

(116)   (c) John resigned, did he?

It can be seen that the tag test must be applied with caution. (There are excellent discussions in Quirk et al. 1985: 810–16, and Huddleston 2002: 891–5.)

   Amharic appears to have tags very much like the English system (Amberber 1996). A number of languages do have a negative tag after a positive statement, but a positive tag after a negative statement is rather rare.

   Other languages have tags of a different hue. In Oromo (Cushitic branch of Afroasiatic, Ethiopia and Kenya; Owens 1985: 205), the negative equative form *miti* functions as a tag and is attached to the end of the verb in both positive and negative clauses. 'In general, a positive verb assumes a "yes" answer and a negative one a "no".' For example:

(117)   inníi   hin-d'úfúu-miti
         HE   NEGATOR-come-NEGATIVE.EQUATIVE
         He's not coming, is he (lit. isn't he)?—expecting 'no'

(118)   foddá   bantíi-miti
         window   open-NEGATIVE.EQUATIVE
         She will open the window, won't she?—expecting 'yes'

A similar technique is found in Tamil (Asher 1985: 5), and in Ika (Frank 1990: 89–90).

21.7 Dependencies with other grammatical systems

Polarity is the most fundamental of grammatical systems. Many other systems may depend on it, in various ways, but it is exceptional for polarity to depend on anything else.

One frequently finds that there are fewer tense/aspect choices in a negative than in a positive clause. It was shown in §21.2.1 that in Amele there are three past tenses and two futures within positive polarity, but just one of each in a negative clause. There is illustration in §19.3.2 of the possibilities for tense/aspect marking being reduced in negative polarity for Swahili, Nend and Gondi. In Turkana (Nilotic, Kenya; Dimmendaal 1983: 441–4) a positive clause in declarative mood has five tense/aspect choices available, but a negative one only has four.

In §3.19, 'Dependencies between grammatical systems', examples are given of choice in a variety of systems depending on polarity—tense, aspect, evidentiality, person, noun class, number, and case. One often finds a number distinction neutralized under negation. For example, the intransitive verb 'exist' in Ainu has distinct forms for singular and plural subject in a positive clause but a single form in a negative one (Refsing 1986:152):

(119)   'exist'   POSITIVE NEGATIVE

    SINGULAR SUBJECT   an ⎫

                                   ⎬ isam

    PLURAL SUBJECT   oka ⎭

A rare instance of there being more choices in negative than in positive polarity was shown in §14.5.1. Mangghuer has separate forms for Identity and Attribution relations in negative copula constructions, but a single form in positive clauses.

21.8 Independent polarity forms, 'no' and 'yes'

Most—but not quite all—languages have independent polarity forms 'no' and 'yes' which can provide a one-word response to a polar question. We will here mostly be concerned with 'no'.

Where main clause is negated with a particle, 'not', the same form may be used for 'no'. This applies for *no* in Spanish, for *somo* in Ainu (the 'not' function is illustrated is (18)), for *ez* in Basque (Saltarelli 1988: 92, 26) and for *không* in Vietnamese (Thompson 1965: 211, 309), among many other languages.

There are languages where the word for 'no' involves just a part of the main clause negator, or just one of the possibilities for clausal negation. As shown in (14), Quechua negates a main clause through particle *mana* and verbal suffix *-chu*; just *mana* is used for 'no'. At the end of §21.2.1, the complex principles for negating a main clause in Amele were described—particle *qee* plus a special negative form of the verb; just *qee* is used for 'no'. In §21.2.6, the various negative particles in Alamblak were listed: *fiñji*, *afe*, and *tafitë* in non-copula clauses and *nhai* in copula clauses. It is *nhai* which functions as independent polarity form 'no'.

Or 'no' may have a quite different form from the particle(s) used for main-clause negation. We saw at (20) in §21.2.1 that Mupun uses particles *ba* and *kas* in a main clause; 'no' is *hayi*. Indonesian has *tidak* 'not' and *bukan* 'no'.

Languages in which main clause negation involves a morphological process necessarily employ a distinct form for 'no'. The circumfix *ma-...-ʃ* 'not' in Egyptian Colloquial Arabic was illustrated at (25) in §21.2.2; 'no' is *laʔ*. Main clause negation in Koasati is rendered by a special paradigm for person and number of subject, illustrated at (28–9) in §21.2.2. As shown at (54) in §21.2.7, negative imperative is marked by verbal suffix *-V́n*. 'No' is different again, being *ínkọ*.

A number of languages—scattered across the globe—lack an independent polarity form 'no'. What one has to do is respond with a full clause, marked for negation. For example, the only negator in Jarawara is verbal suffix *-ra*. One day while in the field I asked whether the village chief Okomobi had returned from a trip, and was answered with:

(120) Okomobiṣ ka-ma-ka-<u>ra</u>
       Okomobi   move-RETURN-DEC:MASCULINE-NEGATOR:MASCULINE
       No (lit. Okomobi has not returned)

Jarawara lacks any word 'no'. In Dumi (Tibeto-Burman, Nepal; van Driem 1993: 149, 324), there is a form *moːnə* 'no' but it must be accompanied by a negative clause (the negative clause is obligatory, *moːnə* being the optional element). A typical conversational exchange went:

(121) (a) gu   ya   a-sir-i̧?
            clothes TOO   MARKED.SCENARIO-wash-3sgO:PRETERITE
            Did you wash the clothes too?

       (b) gu   <u>mə</u>-sir-i̧-<u>nə</u>
            clothes NEGATOR:PRETERITE-wash-3sgO:PRETERITE-NEGATOR
            No (lit. I didn't wash the clothes)

Other languages lacking 'no'—and having to use a negated full clause for the negative answer to a question—include Balinese (Clynes 1992), Awa Pit (Barbacoan family, Ecuador/Colombia; Curnow 1997: 314), and Tuyuca (Barnes 1994: 339). Some languages—including Jarawara—have neither 'no' nor 'yes'; a full clause must be used for both a negative and a positive reply to a question. Tuyuca differs in that it lacks 'no' but does have a one-word positive response item *ɨhɨ* 'uh-huh/yes'.

In languages with several kinds of negator, the same or similar forms may recur. This is illustrated in Table 21.2 for six North Queensland languages/dialects, set out in roughly north to south order. We should note

TABLE 21.2. Negative forms in some North Queensland languages

	A nominal suffix 'without'	B independent polarity item 'no'	C clausal negator 'not'	D negative imperative 'don't'
Guugu Yimidirr	-mul	gaari	gaari	gaari
Kuku-Yalanji	-gari	gari	gari	gari
Yidiñ	-gimbal	ŋuju	ŋuju	giyi
Dyirbal, Mamu dialect	-ŋaŋgay	yimba	gulu	ŋarru*
Warrgamay, inland dialect	-biray	maya	ŋaa	ŋarru*
Warrgamay, Biyay dialect	-biyay	biyay	ŋaa	ŋarru*

*In Dyirbal and Warrgamay, negative imperative is shown by a combination of particle 'don't' and negative imperative inflection on the verb. See (53) in §21.2.7, and notes to that section.

that many Australian languages have nominal derivational suffixes 'with' and 'without'; for example in Dyirbal we get *yara yugu-bila* 'man with a stick' and *yara yugu-ŋaŋgay* 'man without a stick'. Table 21.2 gives forms for (A) privative suffix 'without', (B) one-word negative response 'no', (C) main and subordinate clause negator particle 'not', and (D) negative imperative particle 'don't'.

It will be seen—from the boxes in Table 21.2—that the forms for these four types of negator fall together in various ways: B–D coincide in Guugu Yimidirr, all of A–D are identical in Kuku-Yalanji, B–C fall together in Yidiñ, and A–B do so in the Biyay dialect of Warrgamay. Only in (all dialects of) Dyirbal and in the inland dialect of Warrgamay are there four distinct negator forms.

There is a further interesting parameter of variation concerning the use of 'no' and 'yes' (for languages which have these items). This relates to the technique for responding to a negative question. In English one says:

(122)   (a) QUESTION Are<u>n't</u> you going?   ANSWERS (b) <u>No</u> (, I'm <u>not</u> going)
                                                        (c) Yes (, I'm going)

In (122b) the answer can be just 'no', repeating the negator from the question, to agree with the negative expectation of the question. Here 'no' states that the speaker is not going.

Japanese adopts an opposite strategy, as seen in:

(123)   QUESTION

    (a) Anata   wa   iku-mase-<u>n</u>   ka?
        YOU:POLITE TOPIC go-FORMAL-NEG QUESTION
        Aren't you going?

    ANSWERS

    (b) hei (, iki-mase-<u>n</u>)
        yes   go-FORMAL-NEGATOR
        Yes (, I'm not going)

    (c) <u>iya</u> (, iki-masu)
        no   go-FORMAL
        No (, I'm going)

In (123b) answer 'yes' indicates agreement with the negation of the question and in (123c) 'no' indicates disagreement with it. Here 'no' states that the speaker is going.

This difference can make for frustrating communication difficulties between a speaker of English and a speaker of a language with the Japanese-style convention who learns to speak English. In fact, a great majority of languages behave like Japanese. The minority to use an English-type answering technique include Romanian, Tamil, and Dhaasanac (Cushitic branch of Afroasiatic, Ethiopia, and Kenya; Tosco 1999a: 89–90). Egyptian Colloquial Arabic appears to be basically on an English-type system; see Gary and Gamal-Eldin (1982: 5).

21.9 Summary

Every language has a technique for negating main clauses. For some this is all there is. Such a language has no single word 'no' as response to a question; one has to employ a full sentence, suitably negated. And in such a language the only means of negating a clausal constituent may be by topicalizing it (through stress or fronting or a segmental topic marker) within a regular negative clause.

The same method of negation almost always applies to interrogative as to declarative clauses. In many cases it also applies to imperatives, with the normal negator added to a positive imperative. But, in a significant number of languages, negative imperatives are on a quite different basis. In most—but not quite all—languages, all types of subordinate clause may be negated, either in the same way as a main clause, or in a slightly or radically different way. There is sometimes special means for negating copula and/or verbless clauses.

There are many alternative ways of marking negation—by a particle (almost always placed before the main verb), by a prefix or suffix or infix or circumfix to the verb, by reduplication, or by change of tone (there may also be shift in constituent order). In some languages a special auxiliary verb is required to handle negation, and in a few languages negation is achieved through a main verb 'it is not the case' with the sentiment to be negated functioning as a complement clause in S function ('[That I am hungry]$_S$ is not the case' to render 'I am not hungry').

Many languages have special negative words. These include negative versions of indefinites ('nobody' and 'nothing') and also lexemes with an inherent negative meaning (such as *forbid* and *reject* in English). There may be morphological processes for deriving negative words (as by prefixes such as *un-* and *non-* in English).

A negative construction may have special grammatical properties in terms of case marking, or specification of non-spatial setting. Quite often, one or more grammatical categories may have more limited paradigmatic possibilities in a negative than in a positive clause; this can apply to (at least) tense, aspect, evidentiality, number, person, noun class, and case.

There are a number of explanations for there being more than one marker of negation in a sentence. There may be independent negation of main clause and of either a subordinate clause or a constituent NP. There may be multiple realization of a single underlying negation. Or there may be two negators within a main clause which combine to produce an emphatic affirmative effect.

21.10 What to investigate

Overt markers of negation are generally easy to detect. For each marker, its form and placement, and its scope, should be investigated.

- For a negative particle one needs to check whether it applies to main clause, subordinate clauses (and what types), clausal constituents, or internally within an NP.
- If negation be shown by a morphological process (including affixation), what types of word does it apply to and what is its syntagmatic scope?
- If there is a special negative construction—involving an auxiliary or a negative main verb—this should be carefully described.

Any negative construction may have special grammatical properties, in terms of surface structure, marking of arguments, tense-aspect choices, etc.; all need to be examined. This applies in particular to negative imperatives, and negative copula and verbless clauses. The fieldworker needs to systematically investigate the co-occurrence with negation of all manner of other grammatical categories, to see whether their possibilities are restricted.

A negation construction may have—on a language-particular basis—certain criterial properties. For instance, a positive tag and *any* in place of *some* for English. These can be of assistance for recognizing lexemes which do not have an overtly negative form but can be classed as inherently negative in meaning. Other items may be negative by their form (for instance, *nobody* in English) and also show criterial grammatical properties.

To fully study the range of types and uses of negation, a fieldworker requires a goodly corpus of text material and also information from participant observation. For example, in Jarawara, more than half the examples I gathered of polar questions involve the negative suffix—people tend to ask 'Isn't it a plane?' rather than 'Is it a plane? (Dixon 2004: 411). This kind of information would be unlikely to show up through elicitation.

One underlying instance of negation may be realized by more than one particle, or by particle and affix, or in a variety of other ways. It can be a difficult (but fascinating) task to separate out (a) multiple marking of a single negation, (b) several negations in a sentence, each with its own scope, and (c) two negators with the same scope which effectively cancel each other out, creating a positive outcome.

Sources and notes

21.1   The pre-eminent source is Jespersen (1917/1962); Jespersen (1940: 426–66) is 'to a great extent an extract' of the English parts of the earlier work. Jespersen covers considerably more topics than are dealt with in this chapter, some of them in great detail; his work well repays detailed study.

Payne (1985) is an invaluable survey. Pullum and Huddleston (2002) provide a thorough and insightful account of negation in English. Kahrel and van den Berg (1994) is an excellent compendium of studies of negation in sixteen individual languages. Dahl (1979) essentially surveys the surface placement of negators in approximately 240 languages. Miestamo (2005) looks just at the negation of main clauses, distinguishing between cases where a negator is simply added to a positive clause and those where there is a fundamental structural difference. Bernini and Ramat (1996) survey negation in the languages of Europe, employing a questionnaire of thirty-eight items. There are many further studies of negation; 3,147 of these are listed in Seifert and Weite (1987), cross-indexed by languages.

A fair proportion of the literature on linguistic negation deals in terms of 'truth value', a notion taken over from logic; for example, Horn (1989). Language is—in the present book—viewed as social behaviour, fluid and permeable, for which 'truth' is a matter of attitude and judgment. One hears *There may be an element of truth in it*, or *That's essentially true as far as it goes, but looking at it from another angle* . . . The notions of 'truth' and 'truth value' need not feature prominently in a discussion of negation.

Durie (1985:269) states: 'it is common in Acehnese to use a negative exclamatory sentence to imply a positive meaning'. For example, 'not really stupid=you very' meaning 'You are really stupid'.

An interrogative sentence, with positive polarity, can be used to convey a negative meaning. For example, *How do you expect me to be able to lend you ten thousand dollars?*, with the meaning 'I cannot lend you ten thousand dollars.'

There is in the literature one report of a language in which negative is said to be unmarked and positive marked. Discussing Karitiana (Tupí family, Brazil), Landin (1984: 237) gives the sentences

(a)	Y	ta-oty-j	ỹn	(b) Y	oty	ỹn
	I	AFFIRMATIVE-bathe-TENSE	I	I	bathe	I
	I will bathe			I will not bathe		

Landin states that a positive statement includes affirmative marker *ta-* plus a tense suffix, while the corresponding negative statement lacks both of these.

Perusal of two other sources on Karitiana sheds doubt on Landin's claim that negative is unmarked. Storto (1999: 164) states that what she calls 'declarative clauses' are always prefixed by *ta(ka)-/na(ka)-*, and explains that 'non-declarative clauses include exclamatives, negatives, imperatives, interrogatives, quotes and direct speech'. Everett (2006: 285, 328–9) points out that prefix *ta(ka)-* or *na(ka)-* occurs 'in many, though certainly not all, declarative clauses'. He also describes the clausal negator as a verbal suffix with allomorph *-i* after a consonant, and zero allomorph 'in the case of some vowel-final verbs', such as Landin's *oty-* in (a–b), written as *oti-* by Everett.

21.2   §27.2 includes discussion of questions in Imbabura Quechua.

A fair number of languages have several negating devices whose use is conditional by a variety of grammatical factors. Examples include Bafut (Bantu, Cameroon; Chumbow and Tamanji (1994), Igbo (Benue-Congo, Nigeria; Emenanjọ (1978: 172–96) and Tamil (Dravidian; Asher 1985: 76–9; Lehmann 1993: 228–31).

21.2.3   There is a historical reason for the *do*-requirement on the negator. In Middle English, *not* would generally follow a non-copula verb, as in *I say not*. The Elizabethans used *do* a good deal, for all sorts of purposes, and the negator naturally followed it, as in *I did not say*. Gradually, *do* became restricted to marking emphasis (*I did say that*) and to use in polar questions (*Did he say that?*). It was also retained in sentential negation with a non-copula verb when there was no auxiliary (see Jespersen 1917/1962: 9–10).

21.2.5   It has been suggested that 'prescriptive norms' against the use of multiple negation in Modern English 'began to be enforced in the eighteenth century', on the basis of published treatises from that time (see, for example, Nevalainen 1996: 263). It is in fact likely that the prescriptive norms were enforced by oral instruction a couple of centuries earlier—see the quotation from Philip Sydney's poem.

21.2.7   There is a full and illuminating account of negative imperatives in Aikhenvald (2010; Chapter 5) on which some of the discussion in this section is based.

   For further details on negation in Boumaa Fijian see Dixon (1988: 279–82).

   There is cross-dialectal difference in the form of markers used for negative imperative in Dyirbal. First, we can note that the particle 'not' used in negative declaratives is *gulu* in all dialects, and the positive imperative verbal inflection is always zero (ø). Preverbal particle 'don't' and negative imperative inflection are:

DIALECT	'DON'T'	NEGATIVE IMPERATIVE INFLECTION
Girramay	ŋarru	-mu ∼ -lmu
Jirrbal	galga	-m
Mamu	ŋarru	-m

It is likely that the particle 'don't' was originally *ŋarru* with this being replaced just in the Jirrbal dialect by *galga* (which is probably a development from transitive verb *galga-l* 'leave'—see Dixon 1972: 111–12). It is also likely that the negative imperative verbal inflection was *-mu* ∼ *-lmu*, as in modern-day Girramay, with this reducing to *-m* in other dialects.

21.2.8   Miestamo (2005: 96–109) includes a number of examples illustrating the link between reality and polarity.

   It is interesting that, as far as I am aware, no language has different techniques for negating intransitive and transitive clauses.

21.3   The construction from Newār, illustrated in (63a–c), might not be recognized as a true serial verb construction by some linguists, since the first verb bears an infinitive suffix.

Ameka (2006: 138–9) describes a serial clause construction in Ewe (Kwa family, Ghana) in which negation markers are placed before and after the sequence of serial verbs but the scope of the negation is ambiguous, relating just to the first verb, or just to the second, or to the combination of two verbs.

21.3.2   There is further discussion and exemplification of negation in English in Dixon (2005a: 432–45).

21.4.1   There is, of course, a fourth column to the paradigm in (89): *everyone, everybody, everything, everywhere*. These do not relate to negation in the way that *any-* and *some-* forms do.

21.4.2   It is possible to say *I doubt that he ate something* but this would refer to a specific unidentified thing (see §27.6.1) and has a quite different meaning from *I think that he didn't eat anything* and *I doubt that he ate anything* in (102b/c). A similar comment applies with respect to (104), (107), and (110).

The sixteen languages surveyed for inherently negative verbs are Ainu, Anywa, Basque, British Sign Language, Diegueño, Evenki, Kurdish, Lewo, Longgo, Mam, Marathi, Sm'algyax, Swahili, Tagalog, Tamambo, Tukang Besi.

21.8   Bariai (Austronesian; Papua New Guinea; Gallagher and Baehr 2005: 133–9) is particularly interesting in that particle *mao* is used as clausal negator 'not', as independent polarity form 'no', and as marker of disjunction 'or'.

21.9   Negation can also be indicated (especially in answer to a question) by an interjection, or a gesture such as a head shake (see §27.8).

22

Reflexive and reciprocal constructions

22.1 Introduction

Reflexive and reciprocal constructions share the property of referring to activities where the participants are not all distinct from one another. This can be roughly illustrated from English.

The transitive verb *paint* requires two arguments, in A and O function. These are generally distinct, as in $John_A$ *painted* $Bill_O$. But the A and O arguments may have the same reference—as in the underlying $John_A$ *painted* $John_O$—and then a reflexive construction is used, with the reflexive pronoun *himself* in O slot, giving $John_A$ *painted* $himself_O$. The fully-specified NP—here John—will be referred to as the **controller** (an alternative label is 'antecedent').

We can have two clauses with the same verb as head of each predicate; there will be four arguments in all and these will generally be distinct, as in $John_A$ *painted* $Bill_O$ and Tom_A *painted* $Harry_O$. But if the A argument of each verb has the same reference as the O arguments of the other—as in the underlying $John_A$ *painted* $Bill_O$ and $Bill_A$ *painted* $John_O$—then we must use a reciprocal construction, $[John \; and \; Bill]_A$ *painted* $[each \; other]_O$. Here the two participants are conjoined, *John and Bill*, as the A argument, with the O slot being filled by reciprocal pronoun *each other*. (The underlying semantics of reciprocal constructions is in fact more complex than this when more than two participants are involved; see §22.2.2.) The fully specified NP will again be called the controller (or antecedent). In a reciprocal construction the controller must have plural reference (it can be a noun with non-plural form but plural meaning, such as *people* in English).

All languages have some way of indicating reflexive and reciprocal relations, generally by special construction types. They may employ different construction types, or identical ones. We begin by providing illustrations of languages which use the same grammatical techniques and the same forms for both reflexive and reciprocal.

One of the two major mechanisms is to employ special reflexive and recip-rocal pronouns in the O slot (or, sometimes, in another non-subject slot). This was just illustrated for English, where reflexive and reciprocal pronouns have different form. There are languages in which they have the same form. For instance, in West Greenlandic (Eskimo; Fortescue 1984: 155–67, 283–9), the reflexive/reciprocal pronoun has form *immi-* if the controller is singular and *immiC-* if it is plural. (The *C* 'indicates an indeterminate non-uvular consonant that undergoes assimilation'.) These take case inflections in the normal way. For example (throughout this chapter, reflexive and reciprocal markers in example sentences are underlined):

(1) immi-nut   tuqup-puq
     REFLEXIVE/RECIPROCAL:SG-ALLATIVE kill-3sgS:INDICATIVE
     He killed himself

In (1) the reflexive/reciprocal marker functions as a full NP. Alternatively, it can function (here in reduced form *-mi-*) as reflexive possessor within an NP, as in:

(2) savim-mi-nik   kapi-yaa
     knife-REFL/RECIP:SG-INSTRUMENTAL   stab-3sgA:3sgO:INDICATIVE
     He stabbed it with his own knife

Example (2) is, literally, 'He stabbed it with self's knife'. English is unlike West Greenlandic in that a reflexive pronoun cannot function as possessor; instead, one must employ *own* (see §22.4.5).

In (1) and (2) the controller is singular with only a reflexive interpretation being possible. If the controller is plural, then a reciprocal sense is most likely, as in:

(3) immin-nut   tuqup-put
     REFLEXIVE/RECIPROCAL:PL-ALLATIVE kill-3plS:INDICATIVE
     They killed each other

However, a sentence such as (3) is essentially ambiguous between a reciprocal and a plural reflexive meaning: 'Each of them killed themself (i.e. committed suicide)'. A clearly reciprocal sense can be brought out by inserting iterative suffix *-rar-* 'repetition of an action':

(4) immin-nut   tuqu-rar-put
     REFL/RECIP:PL-ALLATIVE   kill-ITERATIVE-3plS:INDICATIVE
     They killed each other

Note that in West Greenlandic the reflexive/reciprocal pronoun does not vary for the person of the controller, as the reflexive pronoun does in English (*myself, yourself, herself,* and so on). The same reflexive/reciprocal pronoun is used in (1), with 3sg controller, and in (5), where the controller is 1sg:

(5) <u>immi</u>-nut   uqarviga-anga
     REFL/RECIP:SG-ALLATIVE   speak.to-1sgS:INDICATIVE
     I spoke to myself

Reflexive and reciprocal constructions in West Greenlandic are discussed further in §22.4.1.

The other major mechanism is for a morphological process to be applied to a transitive verb, deriving an intransitive stem which takes as S argument the underlying A = O (for a reflexive) or the conjunction of participants (for a reciprocal).

In the Australian language Guugu Yimidhirr (Haviland 1979: 119–26, 60–1), transitive verb *gunda-* 'hit' takes NPs in A and O function, as in:

(6) bama-al$_A$ nganhi$_O$ gunda-y
     person-ERGATIVE   1sg:ACCUSATIVE   hit-PAST
     A person hit me

Derivational suffix -*Vdhi* (where V lengthens the preceding vowel), when added to a transitive verb, creates an intransitive form which takes a single core argument in S function. In (7) the S argument is singular and the sentence has a reflexive meaning; in (8) it is plural, producing a reciprocal sense.

(7) ngayu(ugu)$_S$ gunda-<u>adhi</u>
     1sg:NOMINATIVE   hit-REFLEXIVE/RECIPROCAL:PAST
     I hit myself

(8) bula(agu)$_S$ gunda-<u>adhi</u>
     3du:NOMINATIVE   hit-REFLEXIVE/RECIPROCAL:PAST
     The two of them hit each other

As in West Greenlandic, there is an alternative plural reflexive reading for (8) 'Each of the two of them hit themself'. (Both reflexive and reciprocal clauses may optionally add post-inflectional suffix -*Vgu* after the S argument; this has emphatic effect, and strengthens the reflexive or reciprocal reading.)

There are a number of grammatical profiles languages employ for the expression of reflexive and reciprocal situations. The main ones can be outlined.

A Pronouns for both reflexive and reciprocal within a transitive clause.

Ai. Same form for reflexive and reciprocal pronouns. This is illustrated by free reflexive/reciprocal pronoun *immi(C)-* in West Greenlandic, by free pronoun *ti* in Iraqw (Cushitic branch of Afroasiatic, Tanzania; Mous 1993: 139), and by bound pronominal suffix (to the verb) *-rninyi-* in Nyangumarta (Australian area; Sharp 2004: 252–3)

Aii. Different forms for reflexive and reciprocal pronouns. One illustration is provided by English. In Oromo (Cushitic, Ethiopia and Kenya; Owens 1985: 187–92) the reflexive and reciprocal free pronouns have invariant forms *if(i)* and *wali* respectively. Koasati (Muskogean; Kimball 1991: 127–9) uses bound pronouns, placed in prefix slot 4 (that used for O and So functions); the forms are *ili-* for reflexive and *-itti-* for reciprocal.

B Verbal derivation for both reflexive and reciprocal, creating an intransitive clause.

Bi. Same form for reflexive and reciprocal derivations. This is illustrated by verbal suffix *-Vdhi* in Guugu Yimidhirr, by verbal prefix *mat-* in Maricopa (Yuman, Arizona; Gordon 1986: 65–7)—see §22.4.3 below—and by verbal suffix *-na-* in Warekena (Arawak, Brazil; Aikhenvald 1998: 371–4; 2007).

Bii. Different forms for reflexive and reciprocal derivations. Ainu (isolate, Japan; Tamura 2000: 204) employs verbal prefixes *yay-* and *u-* to derive intransitive reflexive and reciprocal verbal stems respectively, while Huallaga Quechua (Weber 1989: 167) has reflexive suffix *-kU* and reciprocal suffix *-nakU*.

C Different constructions types for reflexive and reciprocal.

Ci. Pronominal construction for reflexive, verbal derivation for reciprocal. There are a fair number of languages with this profile. Kugu Nganhcara (Northern Paman, Australia; Smith and Johnson 2000: 397–9, 411–12) has a full set of reflexive free pronouns, reflecting person and number of the controller. It employs a morphological process for deriving reciprocal verb stems, substituting *o* for the stem thematic vowel (with assimilation to an *a* in the preceding syllable); for example *peka-* 'throw (missile) at', reciprocal *peko-* 'throw at each other', *patha-* 'bite', reciprocal *potho-* 'bite each other'. A further example is provided by Swahili, discussed just below.

Note that there are, to the best of my knowledge, no languages which reverse these construction types, with reciprocal pronoun(s) and an intransitivizing derivation for reflexive.

Intransitivizing derivations and reflexive/reciprocal pronouns are the major construction types, but there are a fair number of other possibilities, each found in just a few languages; these are described in §22.6.

Many grammars are not as neat and tidy as is implied by the examples given thus far. There is often a combination of several techniques for reflexive and/or for reciprocal. To mention one instance, in Kugu Nganhcara (Smith and

Johnson 2000: 398, 426–7) a reciprocal construction can optionally include—
in addition to the derived reciprocal verb form—a reflexive pronoun as part
of the S NP:

(9) [pula   pama kuce pulan<u>mala</u>-la]_S   yen<u>to</u>
     3du:NOM   man   two   3duREFL-3du:NOM   spear:RECIP
     Those two men speared each other

If a language has bound pronouns—which are generally attached to the verb—
there may be a reflexive and/or reciprocal bound pronoun going into the O
slot. It is important to distinguish the following, which may appear similar on
the surface but are in fact phenomena of quite different natures:

(A) Reflexive or reciprocal bound pronouns, filling an established bound
     pronoun slot within a transitive verb which maintains its transitivity.
(B) Morphological processes applying to a transitive verb, deriving an
     intransitive stem which bears reflexive and/or reciprocal meaning.
     (It often has other meanings as well; see §22.5.1.)

Swahili is of particular interest (see, among other sources, Vitale 1981:
136–52; Ashton 1947: 43, 240–3). For reflexive it has (A) a bound pronoun in
O slot, and for reciprocal it has (B) an intransitivizing derivation. We can first
compare the plain transitive clause in (10) with the corresponding reflexive
in (11).

(10) Ahmed_A a-na-m-penda   Halima_O
      Ahmed   3sgA-PRESENT-3sgO-love   Halima
      Ahmed loves Halima (lit: Ahmed he-her-loves Halima)

(11) Ahmed a-na-<u>ji</u>-penda
      Ahmed 3sgA-PRESENT-REFLEXIVE-love
      Ahmed loves himself (lit: Ahmed he-self-loves)

In both sentences, the 3sg subject bound pronoun, *a-* 'he/she', fills the first
slot in the verb. The third slot, following present tense prefix *-na-*, bears 3sg O
bound pronoun *-m-* 'him/her' in (10) and the reflexive bound pronoun *-ji-* in
(11). Note that the reflexive bound pronoun has invariant form; it is *-ji-* for all
persons and numbers of the controller. Reflexive in Swahili is further discussed
in §22.4.1.

There are also 'emphatic reflexive' free pronouns (agreeing with the number
and noun class of the controller) which may follow the verb in (11), in the
position corresponding to Halima in (10). That is, (11) could be extended to
Ahmed anajipenda mwenyewe 'Ahmed loves *himself*'.

For reciprocal there is verbal suffix -*na* which derives an intransitive stem taking just one argument, shown by the subject bound pronoun in the first prefix slot:

(12) [Juma   na   Halima]$_S$ wa-na-penda-<u>na</u>
      Juma   AND   Halima   3plS-PRESENT-love-RECIPROCAL
      Juma and Halima love each other

We have said several times in previous chapters that the great majority of grammatical forms have a range of meanings and functions. This applies to intransitivizing reflexive/reciprocal processes and also to free reflexive/reciprocal pronouns (but much less to bound pronouns). For example, verbal suffix -*Vdhi* in Guugu Yimidhirr covers reflexive, reciprocal, and also a kind of passive. In Warekena, suffix -*na*- is used for reflexive, reciprocal, and also an agentless passive. In her fine grammar of Swahili, Ashton (1947: 240–3) prefers the term 'associative' rather than 'reciprocal' since 'in addition to reciprocity, -*na* expresses other aspects of association such as concerted action, interaction and interdependence (and in some cases dissociation)'.

The reflexive pronouns in English have a further function, emphasizing the identity of the referent of an argument, as in *John himself solved the problem* or—with extraposition of *himself* to the end of the clause, creating a slightly different nuance of meaning—*John solved the problem himself*; that is, no one helped him with it. This is further discussed in §22.4.5. Similar meanings apply for reflexive pronouns in Cairene Egyptian Colloquial Arabic (Gary and Gamal-Eldin 1982: 44, 82) and Indonesian (Sneddon 1996: 152, 205–6). In Maricopa, reflexive/reciprocal form *mat*- also has a non-reflexive meaning in sentences like 'Jeni made it all by herself' (Gordon 1986: 66).

In some languages a grammatical form whose central employment is to mark reflexive and/or reciprocal may have further functions. We also encounter the reverse situation, where reflexive or reciprocal is a subsidiary function of some grammatical form which has wider significance. This can be illustrated from Boumaa Fijian (Dixon 1988: 177–9).

Most verbs in Fijian may be used in both intransitive and transitive clauses, with S corresponding either to A or to O. When used transitively the verb bears a suffix, and this suffix is omitted when it is used intransitively. Verb '*oti(va)* 'cut'—of type S = O—is illustrated in an intransitive clause in (13) and in a transitive one in (14).

(13) e   sa   'oti [a   ulu-i   Elia]$_S$
      3sgS ASPECT cut   ARTICLE head-PERTENSIVE   Elia
      Elia's hair is being cut

(14) au   sa   'oti-va   [a   ulu-i   Elia]$_O$
     1sgA ASPECT cut-TRANS:3sgO   ART   head-PERTENSIVE Elia
     I am cutting Elia's hair

A verb may take derivational prefix *vei-* which derives an intransitive stem with a 'collective' meaning. The verb refers to a two-participant activity. The collection of core participants (agent plus patient) are coded as the S argument. Thus:

(15) erau   sa   vei-'oti   [o   Sepo vata.'ei Elia]$_S$
     3duS ASPECT   COLLECTIVE-cut   ART Sepo WITH   Elia
     Sepo and Elia are involved in an activity of (hair-)cutting

One cannot tell, just from (15), who is cutting whose hair. But everyone in the village of Waitabu—where the sentence was recorded—knows that Sepo often cuts people's hair, including that of his son Elia. Such sociocultural knowledge enables villagers to deduce who is doing what to who.

As a particular subtype of *vei-* sentences, one can add the passive form, *-vi*, of transitive suffix *-va*, to *vei-'oti* and the meaning is then reciprocal:

(16) erau sa <u>vei-</u>'oti-<u>vi</u> [a Sepo vata 'ei Elia]$_S$
     Sepo and Elia are cutting each other's hair

Sentence (16) states that Sepo cuts Elia's hair and also Elia cuts Sepo's hair. (These two activities could take place in either order). It can be seen that in Fijian reciprocal is a particular subtype of *vei-*construction. (*Vei-* has a wide range of uses, being also added to nouns, time words, and kin terms; see §22.2.2, and Dixon 1988: 175–81.)

There are some languages which lack any kind of reflexive construction. How can they indicate that someone is doing something to themself? Simply by using plain pronouns. This can be exemplified from the Australian language Gumbaynggirr (Smythe 1948/9: 74; Eades 1979: 312–13):

(17) ŋa:ja gi:li   ŋa:ña bu:m-gu   dulúlbi-wu
     1sgA today   1sgO hit-PURPOSIVE gun-INSTRUMENT
     I'm going to shoot me today (lit. hit me with a gun)

When A and O are both 3rd person, the sentence is ambiguous between a reflexive and a non-reflexive meaning:

(18) gula:-du$_A$ bu:rwa-ŋ   gula:-na$_O$ magay-u
     3sg-ERGATIVE   paint-PAST 3sg-ABSOLUTIVE   red.ochre-INST
     EITHER: He painted him (himself) with red ochre
     OR: He painted him (someone else) with red ochre

A reflexive reading can be secured by adding reflexive marker -*w* to the 3rd person O pronoun, giving *gula:du bu:rwa-ŋ gula:na-w̱ magayu* 'He painted himself with red ochre'.

A number of familiar languages employ plain pronouns for 1st and 2nd person reflexives, using a special reflexive pronoun only for 3rd person; they include French, Spanish, and Portuguese (see §22.4.3).

Some languages without specific reflexive pronouns require a body part or some other inalienably possessed noun to be included as part of the O argument. Whereas in English one may say *I cut myself* or *I am looking at myself in the mirror*, a speaker of Jarawara has to say what exactly is being cut or seen; for example 'I cut my hand', 'I saw my face in the mirror'. And corresponding to *I am smelling myself* in English, in Jarawara one has to say 'I am sniffing my own smell' (Dixon 2004: 328–9).

The next section discusses the ranges of meaning associated with reflexive and with reciprocal constructions. The following one puts forward some preliminary generalizations comparing the two construction types. There is then, in §§22.4–5, more detailed discussion of the two major techniques for coding reflexive and reciprocal relationships—by pronouns and by verbal derivation. §22.6 deals with a number of other techniques and §22.7 surveys the combination of techniques found in individual languages. Some languages exhibit a number of inherently reflexive and/or inherently reciprocal verbs (such as *wash* and *meet* in English), discussed in §22.8. In §22.9 we look at the origins of reflexive and reciprocal markers, and their relationships with space and time. As with other chapters, there is then a summary section and advice on 'what to investigate'.

22.2 Meanings

A reflexive or reciprocal construction is only available for a certain verb if its two relevant arguments may have the same kind of referent. If, for a given verb, the A argument must be animate and the O argument can only be non-animate, then it is implausible that the verb should appear in a reflexive or reciprocal frame. Looking at English, this applies to transitive verbs such as *breathe, nibble, affirm,* and *make up* (in both of the senses *make up a story* and *make up a bed for the visitor*), among many others. For *swallow*, both A and O can be animate but the referent of A must be substantially larger than that of O. We do read, in legend, *The whale swallowed Jonah*; however, it is implausible to have **The whale swallowed itself* or **The whale and Jonah swallowed each other*.

22.2.1 The semantics of reflexives

A reflexive situation occurs when two arguments of a verb have identical reference. The canonical construction involves a transitive verb, with A and O arguments coreferential. However, there is a diverse selection of transitive verbs which would not—in normal circumstances—feature in a reflexive construction (but are perfectly acceptable in a reciprocal construction). They include (in English) *hunt, overpower, approach, marry, threaten, annoy,* and *tease*. (Note that there is no absolute prohibition against a reflexive construction including such a verb. With ingenuity, suitable contexts might well be devised, but this would be an unusual occurrence.)

The most frequent controller of a reflexive construction is human, or else animate, seldom inanimate. Some languages have a constraint concerning the identity of the controller. In Finnish, for example, it *must* be animate (Sulkala and Karjalainen 1992: 135). Kuno (1973: 290) observes that in English the controller can be inanimate, as in *History repeats itself* and *The newspaper unfolded itself in the wind*, but in Japanese it 'must be something that is animate and has will power'.

In Ainu, the regular reflexive prefix on verbs, *yay-*, 'usually expresses an intentional action made on oneself'. A reflexive-type action which is 'without intention' is likely to involve a different verbal prefix, *si-* (Tamura 2000: 204). In the Australian language Walmatjari (Hudson 1978: 66), a reflexive construction 'carries the meaning that the action was intentional'. Thus:

(19) lan-i   ma-rna-nyanu   jina$_O$ ngaju-ngu$_A$
      pierce-PAST AUXILIARY-1sgA-REFL/RECIP foot   1sg-ERGATIVE
      I poked my foot (intentionally)

In contrast, if the action was unintentional a plain transitive construction is used, with no reflexive marking:

(20) jina$_O$ pa-ø-ja   lan-i   mana-ngu$_A$
      foot   AUXILIARY-3sgA-1sgO pierce-PAST stick-ERGATIVE
      A stick poked my foot (i.e. I poked my foot accidentally on a stick)

Note that in Walmatjari bound pronouns are attached to an auxiliary root. These examples feature the declarative auxiliary, which has form *ma-* when the next consonant is a nasal and *pa-* elsewhere. In (20), bound pronouns mark A and O arguments. In the reflexive construction (19), reflexive/reciprocal suffix *-nyanu* could be said to be used in place of an O bound pronoun.

A number of Salish languages have distinct derivational suffixes to the verb depending on whether a reflexive action involves full control or limited control. In Halkolemem the forms are -θət and -namət respectively (Gerdts 2000; also see Suttles 2004: 243–6; Watanabe 2003: 262–8). Thus:

(21) q̓ay-θət   'kill self'
      q̓ay-námət 'kill self accidentally'

Generally, the two arguments in a reflexive relationship have identical reference. Just a few languages show a variation on this pattern, where the referents may be overlapping. For instance, Newman (2000: 524) provides a number of examples from Hausa, including:

(22) à   yâu   dau,   nā   bā   wà <u>kânmù</u> kunyà
      AT today MOREOVER 1sg:COMPLETIVE give to   1pl:REFL   shame
      Today I embarrassed ourselves

Here the reflexive pronouns *kânmù* 'ourselves' includes within its reference the controller pronoun, in subject function, *nā* 'I'. Note that the translation is scarcely felicitous in English; one would have to say something like *I embarrassed us*.

22.2.2 The semantics of reciprocals

The meaning of reflexive construction is easy to characterize—someone directs an activity or feeling towards themself. A two-participant reciprocal is also straightforward: X acts in a certain way towards Y and Y acts in the same way towards X. If one hears *John and Bill painted <u>each other</u>* then it can be inferred that *John painted Bill* and *Bill painted John*.

But what if a reciprocal construction features more than two participants, as in *John, Bill, and Harry painted <u>each other</u>*, or:

(23) The boys in the class painted <u>each other</u>

Sentence (23) could be used if the speaker did not know the exact size of the class. But suppose that there are thirty boys. (23) does not necessarily imply that each of the thirty boys painted every one of the others (that there were $30 \times 29 = 870$ individual acts of painting). What (23) does imply is that some of the boys were painters and some were paintees, with there being an element of overlap between the two groups.

I suggest that the underlying semantic basis for a reciprocal construction which is expressed schematically as:

(24) [the set of B]$_A$ did action P to [each other]$_O$

is as follows:

(25)   —a subset of set B were referents of the A argument for action P
        —another subset of set B were referents of the O argument for action P
        —there is some overlap between these two subsets

This implies that if the boys in the class were divided into 15 pairs, with one member of each pair painting the other—but with no boy being both painter and paintee—then (23) should not be an appropriate description of the activity. (However, the semantic scope for both reciprocal and reflexive constructions may be extended in particular pragmatic circumstances so that it is not impossible that the interpretation just rejected *could* be encountered.)

A putative counter-example to the characterization just suggested is:

(26)   All the guests at the party were married to <u>each other</u>

That is, the guests comprised a number of married couples. But this sense of *marry* is a symmetric verb—if *John is married to Mary* then it follows that *Mary is married to John*. Each of the guests is referent for both of the arguments in 'X is married to Y'. Thus, (26) does not constitute a counter-example.

The relation between the members of the set of participants in a reciprocal relationship may vary. Suppose that three poles are erected in a garden, each at the vertex of an equilateral triangle whose sides are ten metres. Each of the poles is ten metres from the other two. This can be described by:

(27)   The poles are ten metres from <u>each other</u>

Now suppose a different scenario. The poles are placed in a line, the second ten metres from the first, and the third ten metres from the second. Note that the third is now twenty metres from the first. This arrangement can also be described by (27).

That is, a sentence like (27) is ambiguous between a 'full reciprocal' and a 'linear' interpretation. The appropriate interpretation for a reciprocal construction is in many instances obvious from the meaning of the verb. In *The plates are piled on top of each other* or *These Russian dolls fit inside one another* it is plain that linear situations are being described. (Interestingly, I know of no language which has distinct ways of marking the two kinds of reciprocal relationship.)

I have heard *Those crocodiles are lying over each other* used to describe one crocodile lying over another (it is scarcely possible to also have the other lying over the one). And *John and Mary followed each other through forest and glen* when, in fact, Mary was in front and John behind the whole way. Such sentences in English extend the meaning of reciprocal markers to non-reciprocal situations, simply indicating a close and cohesive relationship between the participants. Similar extensions of meaning occur in other languages. (This can relate to the fact that in many languages a reciprocal marker also has a 'sociative' or 'together' sense; see §22.4.5 and §22.5.1.)

Verbs occurring in a reciprocal construction are of various kinds. Some have symmetric arguments and a reciprocal clause including them describes a single unit of activity. *Mary and Jane met each other outside the town hall* can be rephrased as *Mary met Jane outside the town hall* or *Jane met Mary outside the town hall*. Similarly, one could say *China and Japan are fighting each other* or *China is fighting Japan* or *Japan is fighting China* (the difference is purely pragmatic, relating to which participant is being focussed on).

With some verbs there must be several units of activity. If *John and Bill are punching each other* then the punches may be delivered simultaneously or sequentially. That is, they may be each punching the other at the same time, or else in sequence—John delivers a punch to Bill, then Bill delivers one to John and so on, in turn.

The sentence *John and Mary are kissing* has two interpretations. There may be one unit of activity, a romantic mouth-on-mouth kiss. Or it can be an instance of social kissing, John kissing Mary's cheek and then she in turn kissing his cheek.

In English—as in many, but not all, other languages—some verbs referring to symmetric activities typically omit the *each other* (or *one another*); we can refer to them as 'inherently reciprocal' verbs; see §22.8. This applies to *Mary and Jane met (each other) outside the town hall*, to *China and Japan are fighting (each other)*, and to the romantic mouth-on-mouth sense (but not the sequential mouth-on-cheek sense) of *John and Mary kissed (each other)*.

John and Mary love each other implies that John loves Mary and Mary loves John simultaneously. (If Mary loved John one year but the feeling was not reciprocated, and John loved Mary the following year but the feeling was not reciprocated, then it would not be appropriate to say *John and Mary love(d) each other*.) The verb *love* does not require symmetric arguments. It may be for this reason that when it does, as in *John and Mary love each other*, the *each other* may not be omitted.

As mentioned above, if John is married to Mary than it must also be the case that Mary is married to John. The arguments are symmetric and so *to each other* may be omitted from *John and Mary are married (to each other)*. But we can also say *John is married* (not specifying who to) and *Mary is married* (not specifying who to). These can be conjoined, *John is married and Mary is married* reducing to *John and Mary are married*. It can be seen that the sentence:

(28)   John and Mary are married

is ambiguous between a symmetric reciprocal sense implying that they are married to each other and a conjoined sense, when each is married to someone else. (Jokes are often fashioned upon this ambiguity.)

Some reciprocal constructions necessarily refer to a series of activities. If one hears *John and Bill are throwing a ball to each other*—when only one ball is involved—then John must throw it to Bill, Bill throw it back to John, and so on. If, on the other hand, one hears *John and Bill are throwing balls to each other*, the actions could be sequential or simultaneous—John throws one ball to Bill at the same time as Bill throws another ball to John.

For many reciprocal constructions, either a simultaneous or a sequential interpretation is possible. This applies—in English—for many verbs, including *scrape, grab, console, entertain*, and *question*. If it is considered necessary to specify, then a suitable adverb may be used. For instance *ataatsikkut* 'at the same time' or *tulliriillutik* 'one after the other' in West Greenlandic (Fortescue 2007: 829), and similarly in other languages.

'In German there are two main and regular means of expressing reciprocity.' First, the reflexive/reciprocal pronoun *sich*. And secondly, the reciprocal pronoun *einander* which is (a) used instead of *sich* in the high (written) style, and (b) combines with most prepositions—for example *gegen-* 'against' plus *einander* gives *gegeneinander* 'against each other'. Wiemer and Nedjalkov (2007: 507) show that with verb *küß-* 'kiss', *sich* indicates simultaneous activity while *einander* is most likely to be used in the case of serial activity. Thus:

(29) [Hans und Maria]$_A$ küßten sich$_O$
      Hans AND Maria   kissed   REFLEXIVE/RECIPROCAL
      Hans and Maria kissed (simultaneously)

(30) [Hans und Maria]$_A$ küßten einander$_O$
      Hans AND Maria   kissed   RECIPROCAL
      Hans and Maria kissed (most likely, one after the other)

However, Wiemer and Nedjalkov state that the distinction does not hold for verbs of similar meaning, such as 'shake hands', 'embrace', and 'toast'.

A reciprocal construction can involve an intransitive verb, as in *The contestants ran towards one another* and *The cousins grumbled at each other*. Certain types of adjectives (see §12.4) may also feature. We have already illustrated with *be married to (each other)*. A number of HUMAN PROPENSITY adjectives take a prepositional argument and can be used reciprocally, including *be angry with each other* and *be jealous of each other*. Also some in the SIMILARITY type, such as *be independent of each other*, *be similar to each other*, and *be different from each other* (*similar* and *different* are further examples of 'inherent recip-rocals', where the *each other/one another* can be omitted).

As pointed out in §1.8 and §8.3.1, kinship terms necessarily refer to two people—'X is Y's father'. In some languages, a number of kin terms are verbs, 'be a father to'. And it is surely appropriate that in a few of the many languages in which kinship terms are nouns, some or all of them may take the same affix that marks a verb as reciprocal. We have mentioned prefix *u-* in Ainu, which is added to a verb and derives a reciprocal form. This is also used, not only with symmetric kin terms such as 'brother', but with other symmetric nouns such as 'friend' and 'stranger'. Thus (Alpatov, Bugaeva, and Nedjalkov 2007: 1812):

(31) irwak 'brother'   u-irwak 'both brothers'
       tokoy 'friend'   u-tokoy 'friends'
       anun 'stranger'   u-anun 'mutual strangers'

As described in §22.1, prefix *vei-* in Fijian, when added to a verb, conveys a 'collective' meaning, which includes reciprocal. It may also be added to an inalienably possessed kin term, together with suffix *-ni* (which appears to have no other function in the grammar) producing a noun that describes a collection of people in that kin relation. For example (Dixon 1988: 170–1):

(32) wati-   'spouse'
       vei-wati-ni   'married couple'

(33) tama-   'father'
       vei-tama-ni   'man and one (real or classificatory) child' or 'man and
                      several children' or 'child and several fathers (father's
                      brothers are treated as classificatory fathers)' or 'a
                      group of children and a group of men who is each in
                      a "father" relationship to every one of the children'

22.3 Preliminary generalizations

Before wading into the details of grammatical techniques for expressing reflex-ive and reciprocal constructions—plus particulars of coreferentiality con-straints, and the like—it will be useful to present a number of preliminary generalizations.

We can note that transitive subject (A), intransitive subject (S), and copula subject (CS) generally behave in the same way with respect to reflexives and reciprocals. The distinction between A, S, and CS—so critical in other parts of the grammar—has less import here, so that we can conveniently refer just to 'subject'.

The generalizations given here are not 'absolute laws' (this is not the kind of thing one encounters in the study of a social phenomenon such as language) but rather strong tendencies. Exceptions can no doubt be found for them (some are mentioned below) but these are few and far between.

GENERALIZATION A. If, of the two arguments involved in a reflexive or reciprocal relation, one is in subject function, then that argument will be the controller.

This applies to all kinds of subject, however they are shown. Attention was drawn, in §13.6, to non-canonical marking. The canonical marking of transitive subject is by nominative case in a nominative-accusative system and by ergative in an absolutive-ergative system. But, in particular circumstances, subject may be marked in some other way—by genitive, or by dative, or by locative. Such non-canonically marked subjects behave in exactly the same way as their canonically marked confrères with respect to reflexives and reciprocals. (Indeed, this is often given as one reason for considering them to be bona fide subjects; see §13.6 and references mentioned there. But it is not the sole reason, so that the argumentation is not circular.)

A canonical reflexive construction in Russian, with nominative controller and accusative reflexive pronoun, is:

(34) Ja$_A$ sebja$_O$ nenavizhu
      1sg:NOM   REFL:ACCUSATIVE hate:1sgA:PRESENT:IMPERFECTIVE
      I hate myself

Dative subject is used with a limited set of verbs referring to emotional and physical states. Just like nominative subject, the dative subject is always controller of a reflexive construction, as in:

(35) Mne$_A$ sebja$_O$ zhalko
      1sg:DATIVE REFL:ACCUSATIVE pity:SG:NEUTER
      I pity myself

In some languages, the arguments involved in a reflexive or reciprocal relation need not include that in subject function. This can be illustrated for English:

(36) [The chairperson]$_A$ introduced [John and Mary]$_O$ [to each other]

Here, the argument in O function is the controller, with reciprocal pronoun placed in 'indirect object' slot. (See Haspelmath 2007 for discussion of general principles for choosing the controller.)

Generalization A only applies to full arguments, not to a reflexive or reciprocal marker which is possessor within an argument. In such a circumstance, an O—or even a peripheral—argument may be controller and a possessor within a subject NP may be the reflexive or reciprocal cataphor or anaphor. For example, in English one can say (at a pinch):

(37) [Her <u>own</u> son]$_A$ hit Mary$_O$

In English the reflexive form in possessive function, *own*, is different from those functioning as a full argument, the *-self* forms (see §22.4.5). However, in the Papuan language Kobon (Davies 1981: 84–7) the same reflexive marker, *ke*, is used. Sentence (37) would be translated as:

(38) [ñi   nipe <u>ke</u>]$_A$ Nabaub$_O$ pak-öp
       boy   3sg   REFLEXIVE Nabaub   hit-3sgA:PERFECT
       Her own son hit Nabaub

The remaining generalizations compare reflexive and reciprocal constructions. B, C, D, E, and G describe how, in a number of ways, reflexive is the more basic, while F and H show how certain wider possibilities are associated with reciprocal.

GENERALIZATION B. This applies when reflexive and reciprocal employ the same technique—either both using pronouns, or both verbal derivations. If one type of marking is related to the other, then in the majority of cases it is the reflexive marking which is the simplest, with reciprocal being based on it.
  We can first illustrate with intransitivizing verbal derivations:

- In Apalai (Carib, Brazil; Koehn and Koehn 1986: 43–7), reflexive requires verbal prefix *os-* ~ *ot-* ~ *at-* ~ *e-*. For reciprocal, the same prefix is used plus reduplication of the first syllable of the stem (which indicates repeated action).
- In Amharic, reflexive is shown by verbal prefix *ta-*. For reciprocal, the same prefix is again used, plus verbal reduplication; see §22.5.1 for details.
- As mentioned in §22.1, Huallaga Quechua has reflexive suffix *-kU* and reciprocal *-nakU* (where *U* becomes *a* when certain suffixes follow in the word and is *u* otherwise—Weber 1989: 462–4).
- In Uradhi (Northern Paman genetic group, Australia; Crowley 1983: 364–6) reflexive is marked by verbal suffix *-:ni* while reciprocal is *-:niβa* (in three conjugations) and *-yβa* (in the fourth conjugation).

The following examples involve reflexive and reciprocal pronouns:

- In Akan (Kwa family, Ghana; Christaller 1875: 41) the reflexive pronoun involves *-hó* suffixed to the appropriate free pronoun, as in (39). This whole form is reduplicated for the reciprocal pronoun, as in (40).

(39) ɔ-do   ne-<u>ho</u>ₒ
      3sgA-love   3sg-REFLEXIVE
      He loves himself OR She loves herself

(40) wɔ-do   won-<u>ho</u>-won-<u>ho</u>
      3plA-love   3pl-REFLEXIVE-3pl-REFLEXIVE
      They love each other

- Korafe (Binandere family, Papua New Guinea; Farr 1991) has invariant *tofu* as reflexive free pronoun and the reduplicated form *tofu-tofu* as reciprocal free pronoun.
- A transitive verb in Tonkawa (isolate, Texas; Hoijer 1933: 67–77) carries a bound pronominal prefix for O and a bound pronominal suffix for A. In a reflexive construction, invariant prefix *he-* goes into the O slot. Reciprocal again requires prefix *he-*, and also suffix *-yew* ∼ *-yo·* to the verb.

Fox (Algonquian, Dahlstrom n.d.: 210–13) presents an exception to Generalization B. There is a reflexive intransitivizing suffix *-(e)tiso-* which appears to involve an increment on the reciprocal intransitivizing suffix *-(e)ti*.

GENERALIZATION C. As mentioned in §22.1, the pronoun technique may be used for reflexive and the intransitivizing technique for reciprocals (I know of no language where the reverse applies). Instances of this—besides Kugu Nganhcara and Swahili (discussed in §22.1)—include Indonesian (Sneddon 1996: 105–6, 152) and Ponapean (Oceanic subgroup of Austronesian; Rehg 1981: 208–9, 300).

GENERALIZATION D. When the pronoun technique is employed, a reflexive or reciprocal pronoun may be 'invariant'—having the same form for all person choices of the controller—or 'informative'—copying information about the person and number of the controller. Invariant pronouns sometimes mark plural (as illustrated for West Greenlandic in §22.1) but most often do not.

The generalization is as follows. Reflexive and reciprocal pronouns may both be invariant (as are free pronouns in Oromo and bound ones in Koasati) or both informative (as in Colloquial Welsh). But if only one is informative, then this is reflexive. That is, there are languages with informative reflexive pronouns and an invariant reciprocal pronoun (not the reverse). Languages of this type include English, Basque (Saltarelli 1988: 104–18), and Dagbani (Gur family, Ghana; Olawsky 1999: 24–5).

GENERALIZATION E. In each language employing the pronoun technique, there are a number of possible combinations of syntactic function for controller and reflexive/reciprocal anaphor or cataphor. The generalization is that the number of possibilities available for reflexive may be about the same as the number for reciprocal but it is often larger.

In the *Questionnaire* for their *Lingua* (later Croom Helm, later still Routledge) *Descriptive Series*, Comrie and Smith (1977: 21–4) list 212 possible combinations, for both reflexive and reciprocal. A number of the thirty-six grammars published in this series consider each of these possibilities, stating whether it is found in their language of description.

In Cairene Egyptian Colloquial Arabic, for example, Gary and Gamal-Eldin (1982: 43–6) illustrate ten possibilities for a reflexive construction but only seven for a reciprocal. In each instance, the controller must be subject, and the anaphor may be chosen from: direct object, indirect object, copula complement, peripheral NP, or a modifier within one of these constituents. Other languages showing more possibilities for reflexive than for reciprocal include Rumanian (Mallinson 1986: 151–65) and Basque (Saltarelli 1988: 104–28).

Finnish appears to be an exception, with Sulkala and Karjalainen (1992: 132–65) listing more possibilities for reciprocals than for reflexives.

GENERALIZATION F. In virtually every language, the number of verbs which may plausibly feature in a reciprocal construction is greater than the number which may occur in a reflexive construction.

At the beginning of §22.2.1, a number of English verbs were mentioned which may be used in a reciprocal construction but scarcely (save within some unusual and extravagant scenario) within a reflexive. Many more can be added to this list: for example, *capture, believe, encourage, greet, insult, offend, assist, disturb*, and *envy*. In contrast, there are very few verbs which are plausible in a reflexive but not in a reciprocal construction. (Apart from verbs which may function transitively—in an idiomatic kind of way—only with a reflexive pronoun in O slot, such as *pride oneself on being honest*, and *cry oneself to sleep*.)

GENERALIZATION G. It is perhaps surprising, in view of Generalization F, that—in languages with bone fide construction types for both reflexive and reciprocal—reflexive constructions appear generally to be much more frequent in texts than reciprocal ones.

This is a definite impression, which I have gained from perusing information on these construction types in several score languages. Two sets of specific figures can be offered. In the Lancaster-Oslo-Bergen corpus of English, there are seven or eight times as many reflexive uses of *-self* forms as there are of the reciprocal markers, *each other* and *one another*. Dyirbal employs a different technique with intransitivizing suffixes for both construction types. On a textual count, there are five times as many reflexive as there are reciprocal constructions. Investigation of relative frequencies across a fair number of other languages would be needed to confirm (or deny) this tentative generalization.

GENERALIZATION H. It is rare to find a marker of a reflexive or reciprocal construction which has *just* this function. A reflexive pronoun often also has an emphatic/intensifying sense (as do -*self* forms in English), and a reciprocal pronoun may also indicate 'together'. Reflexive and reciprocal verbal affixes typically fulfil a general intransitivizing function, often also covering passive and/or antipassive. A reciprocal derivation may also have a 'collective', or a 'competitive' sense. And so on. (These issues are discussed in §22.4.4 and §22.5.1.)

The generalization is that, cross-linguistically, a reciprocal marker tends to have a wider range of further functions and meanings than does a reflexive marker.

22.4 The pronoun technique

It is convenient to use the label 'reflexive pronoun' or 'reciprocal pronoun' for anything which can fill an argument slot in clause structure and create a reflexive or reciprocal meaning.

'Pronoun' was characterized, in §15.1, as 'a small closed class of grammatical words which vary for person'. Some reflexive and reciprocal pronouns (what we have called the 'informative' variety) copy person and number from the controller. Some just mark person, some just number, and some a restricted set of person/number specifications. Others mark neither—the 'invariant' variety. It is convenient to have the same label covering all of these and we will refer to them all as reflexive or reciprocal pronouns, even though a number do not strictly satisfy the criterion for 'pronoun'.

Reflexive and reciprocal pronouns generally function as anaphor for the controller. Just occasionally they may be cataphor for a controller which follows. Most instances of this are when the reflexive or reciprocal pronoun is possessor within an NP, as in (37) and (38).

22.4.1 Transitivity

In most instances, a reflexive or reciprocal pronoun is used within a transitive clause. It fills the O argument slot and the clause remains transitive. This is what we get in English. It can be further illustrated from Dagbani (Gur family, Ghana; Olawsky 1999: 24–5). Basic constituent order is AVO, as in:

(41) o_A bɔri namba$_O$
     3sg want sandals
     He/she wants sandals

The reflexive pronoun is of the informative variety, involving suffix -*maŋa* added to the appropriate plain pronoun:

(42) o$_A$ ŋmaagi o-maŋa$_O$
      3sg cut   3sg-REFLEXIVE
      He cut himself OR She cut herself

The reciprocal pronoun is invariant *taba*:

(43) bɛ$_A$ ku   taba$_O$
      3pl   kill RECIPROCAL
      They killed each other

Note that both *o-maŋa* in (42) and *taba* in (43) go into the regular slot for an O NP, immediately after the verb.

   Just occasionally, we encounter an unusual constituent order. Transitive clauses in Vietnamese are generally AVO. In accord with this, the invariant reciprocal pronoun *nhau* follows the verb Thompson (1965: 271, 357):

(44) [hai đứa   con]$_A$ đánh nhau$_O$
      two CLASSIFIER child   hit   RECIPROCAL
      The two children are hitting each other

However, the invariant reflexive pronoun *tự* is unusual in that it precedes the verb:

(45) nó$_A$ tự$_O$ nói
      3sg REFLEXIVE talk.to
      He is talking to himself OR She is talking to herself

Mandarin Chinese behaves in a similar manner.

   All languages have free pronouns which can make up an NP, outside the predicate. For those that also have bound pronouns, and use the pronoun technique for reflexive and/or reciprocal constructions, there are two possibilities. Reflexive/reciprocal may be shown by a free pronoun, or by a bound pronoun. We investigate these alternatives in turn.

   Hua has bound pronouns but shows reflexive by a free pronoun, as in (Haiman 1980: 225):

(46) dgai-'di   d-go-e
      1sg-1sgPOSSESSOR 1sgO-see:1:A-INDICATIVE
      I saw myself (lit. Myself, me-saw-I)

Reflexive pronouns in Hua are created by taking a free pronoun (here *dgai* 'I') and suffixing the appropriate possessive pronoun (here -'di 'my'); hence *dgai-'di* 'myself'. The verb in (46) commences with bound pronoun in O function, *d-* 'me'. The verb stem, *-go-* fuses together lexeme 'see' and information that the subject argument is 1st person (of any number).

For Hua the verb in (46) remains in transitive form—including an O bound pronoun. West Greenlandic also has bound pronouns and also shows reflexive (and reciprocal) by a free pronoun. But here the verb assumes intransitive form. Compare (Fortescue 2007: 815):

(47)   nukappiaqqa-t$_A$ niviarsiaqqa-t$_O$
       boy-ERGATIVE:PL   girl-ABSOLUTIVE:PL
         saap-pai
         turn.to.face-3plA:3plO:INDICATIVE
       The boys turned to face the girls

(48)   nukappiaqqa-t$_S$ immun-nut
       boy-ABSOLUTIVE:PL   REFLEXIVE/RECIPROCAL:PL:ALLATIVE
         saap-put
         turn.to.face-3plS:INDICATIVE
       The boys turned to face each other

In the transitive clause, (47), the verb bears a fused suffix *-pai*, showing 3pl A and 3pl O (in indicative mood). The verb in the reflexive construction, (48), shows suffix *-put* for 3pl S (in indicative), indicating that this clause is intransitive. Transitive construction (47) has an A NP, marked by ergative case suffix, and an O NP (absolutive case is used for O, and also for S function in an intransitive clause). Note that ergative and absolutive are distinct in singular number, but fall together as *-(i)t* in the plural (there are other criteria for distinguishing A and O NPs). The intransitive reflexive, (48), has the controller NP in S function (absolutive case) with the reflexive pronoun marked by allative. Examples (1) and (3–5), in §22.1, show a similar profile.

In the Australian language Wambaya (Nordlinger 1998: 139–42, 193; Evans, Gaby, and Nordlinger 2007: 564–7), reflexive/reciprocal is shown by *-ngg-* in the bound pronoun slot. Compare:

(49)   ngajbi   gini-ng-a
       see   3sg.mascA-1.O-PAST
       He saw me

(50)   ngajbi   gini-ngg-a
       see   3sg.mascA-REFLEXIVE/RECIPROCAL-PAST
       He saw himself

In this language, bound pronouns are shown through an auxiliary constituent which follows the verb. It commences with a bound subject (A or S) pronoun, then (if transitive) a bound pronoun indicating the person of the O argument, followed by a TAM element. The auxiliary in (50) includes the A form, *gini-*, of the 3sg masculine bound pronoun (rather than the S form, *gi-*), suggesting that (50) is a transitive clause. However, a measure of indeterminacy enters when we consider the forms of NPs. Compare:

(51) daguma   irr-ø-a   janji-ø$_O$ alangmiminji-ni$_A$
      hit   3plA-3.O-PAST   dog-ABSOLUTIVE   children-ERGATIVE
      The children hit the dog

(52) daguma   irri-ngg-a   alangmiminji-ø
      hit   3plA-REFL/RECIP-PAST   children-ABSOLUTIVE
      The children hit themselves/each other

The NP 'children' in (52) is in absolutive form, which indicates O or S function. We could say that (52)—and also, presumably, (50)—are basically intransitive clauses, with an S NP, in absolutive case, but with a transitive set of bound pronouns. The alternative is to regard (52) as fully transitive, but—since A and O are coreferential—just the O NP is stated, in absolutive case. (See Evans, Gaby, and Nordlinger 2007: 564–7, 583 for further discussion.)

The Wambaya data exemplifies difficulties involved when reflexive and/or reciprocal is shown by a bound pronoun in O slot. What sort of NPs would we get, outside the predicate, and how to analyse them? Another example of this was given for Swahili at (10–11) in §22.1.

(10) Ahmed$_A$ a-na-m-penda   Halima$_O$
      Ahmed   3sgA-PRESENT-3sgO-love   Halima
      Ahmed loves Halima (lit: Ahmed he-her-loves Halima)

(11) Ahmed   a-na-ji-penda
      Ahmed   3sgA-PRESENT-REFL-love
      Ahmed loves himself (lit: Ahmed he-self-loves)

Swahili does not employ case marking on NPs. It does generally place an NP in A or S function before the verb and one in O function after it. How then should we analyse NP *Ahmed* in (11)? Is it an A NP within a transitive clause—having a transitive verb—with the O NP not stated (as it doesn't need to be, since it has the same reference as the A NP)? Or is it an intransitive clause with an NP in S function, but the verb having the reflexive affix -*ji* in the slot generally filled by an O bound pronoun, indicating a transitive verb form? It may be that a thorough examination of all aspects of the grammar would help decide between these two alternatives.

As shown in (19) from §22.2.1, Walmatjari also employs a reflexive marker in place of an O bound pronoun:

(19) lan-i   ma-rna-<u>nyanu</u>   jina_O ngaju-ngu_A
      pierce-PAST AUXILIARY-1sgA-REFL/RECIP foot 1sg-ERGATIVE
      I poked my foot (intentionally)

Here the controller is the A argument, shown jointly by free pronoun *ngaju*
'I', making up an NP in A function (marked by ergative case) and by bound
pronoun *-rna* 'I'. And there is an O NP, *jina* 'foot' indicating the body part
being affected. Reflexive/reciprocal marker *-nyanu* within the auxiliary shows
that it is *my* foot which is being pierced by me. It seems clear that (19), which
involves a bound pronoun fulfilling O function, remains transitive.

22.4.2 *Coreference possibilities*

For a reflexive or reciprocal construction, there must be two underlying arguments. Under the pronoun technique, there will be a controller (fully specified) and a reflexive or reciprocal anaphor (which may not be fully specified).
For the great majority of languages the two arguments should be within the
same clause. Exceptions to this are discussed at the end of the section.

In very many languages the controller must be in subject function. The
possible functions for the reflexive/reciprocal anaphor vary.

- *The anaphor must be in O function.* I know of no language which is so limited in its pronoun technique. Perhaps the nearest is Tamil which prefers
  the reflexive pronoun—this is only used for a 3rd person controller—to
  be in O function; 'as indirect object its use is unlikely but grammatical'
  (Asher 1985: 86). However, many languages employing the intransitivizing technique are limited to A–O; see §22.5.1.
- *The anaphor can be in O function or an argument marked by an adposition.*
  This applies in Punjabi (Bhatia 1993: 131–4) where a reflexive or reciprocal
  pronoun in 'indirect object' function takes 'dative' postposition *nüü*,
  as in:

(53) [ó   ne]_A   [apNe nüü]   voT_O
      3sg:REMOTE ERGATIVE   REFL POSTPOSN vote
      dittaa
      give:PAST:MASC:SG
      He cast a vote for himself OR She cast a vote for herself

Supyire (Gur family, Mali; Carlson 1994: 157–8, 416–17) provides further neat
examples of this type.

As noted in §13.5.3, in English the O argument for *give* can be either Gift
or Recipient. For a reflexive construction where Donor (always in A function)
is coreferential with Gift, the preferred construction is that with Gift as O.

One would tend to favour *Mary*~A~ *gave herself*~O~ [*the prize*] over *Mary*~A~ *gave* [*the prize*]~O~ [*to herself*]. That is, there appears to be a liking for the reflexive anaphor to be in O function, rather than in some other function.

- *The anaphor may be in almost any non-subject function—O, CC, peripheral argument, or a possessive modifier within any of these.* This applies to many languages, including West Greenlandic, Rumanian, Basque, Finnish, and the Papuan language Amele (Roberts 1987: 122–34).

In a rather limited set of languages, the controller may be something other than the subject. It is the O argument, *John and Mary*, in (36) from §22.3, [*The chairperson*]~A~ *introduced* [*John and Mary*]~O~ [*to each other*]. In (54) the controller is the E argument, *Mary*, of an extended transitive construction, with the reflexive anaphor being a later NP marked by a preposition. (E is 'extension to core'—see §3.2 and §13.1—otherwise 'indirect object'.)

(54)   I~A~ gave [the cake]~O~ [to Mary]~E~ [for herself]

What is extremely rare is to have an O argument as controller and a full A argument as reflexive or reciprocal anaphor. This is reported for Basque (Saltarelli 1988: 113) and Finnish (Sulkala and Karjalainen 1992: 138) but the parsings offered there are not uncontroversial.

When we extend coverage to possessors within core (or peripheral) arguments, the coreference possibilities are wider. The O argument can be controller over a possessor within the A NP, as illustrated in (37) from English and (38) from Kobon, in §22.3. Another example from Kobon, (55), has the controller as possessor within the O NP and the reflexive anaphor as possessor within the A NP (Davies 1981: 87).

(55)   [Kulua kain]~O~ [ñi   nipe ke]~A~   al-öp
        Kulua dog   boy   3sg   REFLEXIVE   shoot-3sgA:PERFECT
        Kulua's son shot his (Kulua's) dog (lit. Himself's son shot Kulua's
           dog)

All of the examples of coreference so far in this section have involved free pronouns. Bound pronouns tend to have more restricted possibilities, often just A (controller) – O (reflexive/reciprocal anaphor). Some languages do show wider possibilities, through employing a number of bound reflexive/reciprocal forms. The Australian language Nyangumarta (Sharp 2004: 252–6) has the same forms for reflexive and reciprocal, filling the O bound pronoun slot in verb structure. There are two suffixes:

-rninyi, for coreference of A and O, as in (56)
-rningu, for coreference of A and an argument other than O, as in (57)

(56)   <u>wirla</u>-rna-rna-rninyi
       shoot-NON.FUTURE-1sgA-REFLEXIVE/RECIPROCAL:O
       I shot myself

(57)   <u>wirla</u>-rna-rna-rningu-a
       shoot-NON.FUTURE-1sgA-REFLEXIVE/RECIPROCAL:NON.O-PURPOSIVE
       I shot it for myself OR I shot my own

'Secondary concepts' were mentioned in §18.5.2—meanings such as 'can', 'begin', 'try', and 'want'. These are expressed through verbal suffixes or clausal particles in some languages, but by lexical verbs taking complement clauses in others, such as English. Secondary-A verbs do not add any argument to those of the verb in the complement clause. The whole complex appears to function as a single unit for reflexive/reciprocal purposes. That is, the subject of the secondary verb may be controller over the O NP (or some other NP) in the complement clause. For example: *John tried to paint <u>himself</u>*, *People began punching <u>each other</u>*. (One could suggest that the underlying structures are *John$_A$ tried [John$_A$ paint John$_O$]$_O$* and *People$_A$ began [people$_A$ punch [people]$_O$]$_O$*, with coreference applying just to the underlying A–O couplet within the complement clause.)

At the end of §18.3 we drew attention to complement clause constructions in English such as:

(58)   John reminded Tom [that Bill should paint Fred]

(59)   John$_{CONTROLLER}$ reminded <u>himself</u>$_{ANAPHOR}$ [that Bill should paint Fred]

(60)   John reminded Tom [that Bill$_{CONTROLLER}$ should paint <u>himself</u>$_{ANAPHOR}$]

The controller and the reflexive anaphor must be in the same clause—both in the main clause, as in (59), or both in the complement clause, as in (60). English does not allow the controller to be in the main clause with the anaphor in the complement clause. That is, one cannot say, where the *himself* relates back to *John*:

(61)   *John$_{CONTROLLER}$ reminded Tom [that Bill should paint <u>himself</u>$_{ANAPHOR}$]

A limited number of languages do permit reflexive/reciprocal coreference between a main clause and a complement clause. That is, they allow a construction like (61). But it may be ambiguous between the *himself* referring back to the subject of the main clause (here *John*), or to the object of the main clause (*Tom*), or to the subject of the complement clause (*Bill*), as controller.

This can be exemplified from Korean (Sohn 1994: 152–3):

(62) Yongho-nun   Minca-eykey [Ilmin-i   caki   cip-ulo
      Yongho-TOPIC   Minca-TO   Ilmin-NOM   REFLEXIVE   house-TO
      ka-ss-ta]-ko   malhay-ss-tn
      go-PAST-DECLARATIVE]-QUOTATION   say-PAST-DECLARATIVE
      Yongho told Minca that Ilmin went to self's house

Here *caki* 'self' could refer to the house belonging to Yongho, or to Minca, or to Ilmin.

Similar possibilities are found in Japanese (Kuno 1973: 291–6) and in Copala Trique (Hollenbach 1984: 278–9). See also Givón (1990: 641–4; 2001: 112–16).

To the best of my knowledge, the only instances of reflexive/reciprocal coreference between clauses are within complement clause constructions.

22.4.3 Forms

What we are calling 'informative' reflexive and reciprocal pronouns typically convey the same information as plain pronouns—person and number, some-times also gender or noun class. In Dagbani—illustrated by (42) in §22.4.1—reflexive pronouns involve suffix -*maŋa* added to non-emphatic preverbal pronouns: *m-maŋa* 'myself', *o-maŋa* 'himself/herself', and so on (Olawsky 1999: 24). In Hua—illustrated by (46) in §22.4.1—reflexive pronouns involve pos-sessive pronominal prefixes added to plain pronoun forms: *dgai-'di* 'myself', *kgai-'Ka* 'yourself', *rgai-'ri* 'ourselves', and so on (Haiman 1980: 225).

However, informative reflexive/reciprocal pronouns may provide either more information than is given by plain pronouns, or else less. English falls into the former set. To illustrate this, the English pronoun paradigm is set out in Table 22.1.

It will be seen that reflexive pronouns *himself*, *themself*, and *themselves* are based on the 'other functions' column while the remainder are based on the possessive (although *herself* and *itself* could be taken as related to either). The important point about Table 22.1 is that all ten rows are distinguished for reflexives while there are only seven distinctions in the other columns. *You* has both singular and plural reference; when one hears *You go and wash!* it is unclear how many people are being addressed. But adding a reflexive pronoun creates a contrast between singular *You go and wash yourself!* and plural *You go and wash yourselves!* *We* is sometimes used with singular reference, referring either to the speaker—as when Queen Victoria is reputed to have said *We are not amused*—or to the addressee—as when a doctor asks a patient *How are we today?* It then has reflexive form *ourself.* An example of the addressee sense comes from J. M. Coetzee's prize-winning novel *Disgrace* (2000: 48), when a lawyer advises his client

TABLE 22.1. Pronouns in English

	SUBJECT FUNCTION	OTHER FUNCTIONS	POSSESSIVE	REFLEXIVE
SINGULAR REFERENCE	I	me	my	my-self
	we	us	our	our-self
	you	you	your	your-self
	he	him	his	him-self
	she	her	her	her-self
	it	it	its	it-self
	they	them	their	them-self
PLURAL REFERENCE	we	us	our	our-selves
	you	you	your	your-selves
	they	them	their	them-selves

(63)   I think we had better restrict <u>ourself</u> to the legal sense

They has long been used, in a limited way with non-plural reference, as in *If anyone calls, tell them I'm busy and, if they persist, tell them they'll just have to sit themself down and wait.* In recent years, *they* has replaced generic *he* for non-gender-specified 3rd person singular (as an alternative to the ugly *he/she* or *she/he*). It naturally takes on reflexive form *themself*, as in *When a student begins to study linguistics, the first question they ask themself is* ... The functions of *-self* forms in English are discussed in §22.4.5.

A further row can be added to Table 22.1, involving the indefinite form *one*. This behaves like a pronoun in forming a reflexive, *oneself*. For example, *One should apply oneself and get on with it, instead of grumbling.* The Chadic language Hausa has a pronoun system with 1/2/3, sg/pl, plus m/f just in 2sg and 3sg. There is also 'impersonal' *à* (the shortest form of any pronoun), similar in meaning to English *one*. Reflexive pronouns in Hausa are based on the noun *kâi* 'head', adding masculine possessive linker *-n* and then a possessive pronoun suffix; for example *kâ-n-mù* 'ourselves', as in (22) of §22.2.1. The reflexive of *à* 'one' is simply *kâi*, as in (Jagger 2001: 218):

(64)   gārā   à_A   dógarà   gà   <u>kâi_O</u>
       better ONE   rely   ON REFLEXIVE
       One should rely on oneself

At the end of §22.1, attention was drawn to languages lacking a reflexive or reciprocal construction per se for 1st and 2nd persons, just employing plain pronouns. That is, saying 'I cut me' for 'I cut myself'. Such languages often—although not always—do have a reflexive/reciprocal pronoun for 3rd person, and this typically has a wide range of use. For instance, in Portuguese *se* is employed for 3rd person (singular and plural) reflexive and reciprocal, and is also—among other functions—impersonal 'one', as in *Em Lisboa vive-se muito bem* 'One lives rather well in Lisbon' (Azevedo 2005: 123). To translate a 'one ... oneself' reflexive, a single instance of *se* is included, as in *Precisa se organizar* 'One needs to organize oneself'.

Sochiapan Chinantec (Otomanguean, Mexico; Foris 2000: 171) is an example of the opposite sort to English. There is a pronoun system with 1/2/3, sg/pl, but reflexive pronouns do not reflect all these distinctions, having but three forms (raised letters indicate tones):

(65) ʔuẽ[M]   1sg, 2sg
      ʔŋá[M]   3sg
      ʔmóu[LM]   1pl, 2pl, 3pl

Reflexive pronouns in English are based on *self*, which also has limited function as a noun (for example, *You're starting to look like your old self*). It also occurs as the first element in very many compounds, including *self-esteem*, *self-confident*, *self-styled*, *self-sufficient*, and *self-catering*.

In many languages, a reflexive/reciprocal pronoun is based on a common noun. Hdi (Chadic subgroup of Afroasiatic, Cameroon; Frajzyngier 2002: 195–8) uses *vghá* 'body' in the O slot to indicate reflexive and reciprocal meaning. For example:

(66) dzàˈá   gùy-éy-mú
      FUTURE   meet-POTENTIAL.OBJECT.EXTENSION-1plA

      [tá   vghá]$_O$ màxtsím
      OBJECT MARKER   REFLEXIVE/RECIPROCAL   tomorrow

      We will meet one another tomorrow

In Dime (Omotic subgroup of Afroasiatic, Ethiopia; Seyoum 2008: 70–1), reflexive pronouns involve the object or genitive pronoun prefixed to *mát*, which is plainly related to *máte* 'head'. For example:

(67) ʔatí$_A$ ʔa-mát$_O$ tičinɗ-i-t
      1sg   1sg.OBJECT-REFLEXIVE   cut-PERFECTIVE-1
      I cut myself

An intransitive verb in Maricopa (Yuman, Arizona; Gordon 1986: 65–6) bears a pronominal prefix coding the S argument and a transitive verb bears a prefix which fuses information on A and O arguments. Reflexives and reciprocals are expressed with prefix *mat-* before a verb which bears an S prefix. Thus:

(68) mat-ˈ-aqar-m
      REFLEXIVE/RECIPROCAL- 1sgS-cut-REALIS
      I cut myself

Interestingly, Gordon states that reflexive/reciprocal *mat-* is historically derived from the noun *iimaat* 'body'.

Heine (2000: 9) surveys reflexive/reciprocal markers in sixty-two African languages and finds that thirty-seven of them have a nominal source. This is 'body' in twenty languages, 'head' in seven, 'owner' in three, 'comrade' and 'life' each in two, and 'relative', 'soul' and 'person' each in one. (In Colloquial Welsh, the reciprocal pronoun is based on noun 'fellow'—see (121) in §22.9.)

There was discussion, in §15.1.5, of languages which show 'social niceties' of respect and authority within their pronoun systems. In some, this extends into reflexives. For example, Sohn (1994: 148–9) describes how 'Korean has several 3rd person reflexive forms with the animate meaning "(one)self", which are sensitive to social stratification: (a) the neutral *caki* (*ca* "self", *ki* "animate body"), which is used for persons in all ages, (b) the deferential *tangsin* (*tang* "proper", *sin* "human body") which is used only for adult social superiors, and (c) the plain *ce*, which is used only for social inferiors, children, or animals. There is yet another neutral reflexive form *casin* (*ca* "self", *sin* "human body") "one's own self", which is used for all persons, either by standing alone, or as part of a compound.'

22.4.4 Extended meanings of reflexive and reciprocal pronouns

In very many languages, a reflexive pronoun may also function as an emphatic or intensifying item. Compare reflexive use of *myself* in I_A *will wash myself*$_O$ with intensifying use in [*I myself*]$_A$ *will wash* [*the dog*]$_O$. Languages discussed thus far in this chapter whose reflexive pronoun also has an emphatic use include Cairene Egyptian Colloquial Arabic and Indonesian (mentioned in §22.1), plus Hausa, Kobon, Korafe, Dagbani, Amele, Copala Trique, and Dime.

In Chaozhou (Sinitic; Xu 2007: 82–4) *ka³³ki¹¹* functions as an invariant reflexive pronoun, as in (69), as an emphatic modifier, as in (70), and in an adverbial-type function 'by -self' or 'alone', as in (71).

(69) i³³   [kai⁵⁵⁻¹¹   (i³³)   ka̱³³ki¹¹]ₑ   poi⁵³⁻³⁵   liau⁵³⁻³⁵   lʼa³³
      3sg   FOR   3sg   REFL   buy   PERF   CL
          kai²¹³⁻⁵³tsi⁵³
          ring
      She bought a ring for herself

(70) i³³   ka³³ki¹¹   aĩ²¹³⁻⁵³   kʼɯ²¹³   kai⁵⁵⁻¹¹
      3sg   REFL   want   go   PARTICLE
      He himself volunteered to go (no one asked him to go, you know)

(71) (luɯ⁵³) kim³³zek⁵ ka³³ki¹¹ k'uɯ²¹³⁻⁵³ hak⁵⁻²hau³⁵
    2sg   today   REFL   go   school
    Today (you) go to school by yourself (because I am busy)

However, not all reflexive pronouns also have an emphatic sense—reflexive and emphatic forms are quite distinct in Rumanian and Supyire, for instance.

    Reciprocal pronouns can have further meanings; a common one is 'together'. In Lao, *kan³* may indicate a simultaneous or sequential reciprocal construction, as in 'They butt each other with their heads'. Or it can have the sense 'together', as in 'They celebrated together'. Or it may be used for a situation where two people participate in an event in different but complementary ways; if one person gives another a watch one can say, literally 'Take watch give *kan³*' (Enfield 2007a: 317–29).

22.4.5 *Reflexives* -self *and* own *in English*

A form *X-self* in English marks a contrast 'X rather than someone/something else'. It has two functions:

(a) As the full filler of an argument slot other than subject. It is then a 'reflexive pronoun' with anaphoric reference to the subject, as in *Mary*$_A$ *burnt herself*$_O$ (she didn't burn anyone else).

(b) In apposition to the head (noun or pronoun) of an NP in any core or peripheral function. For example [*John himself*]$_A$ *burnt* [*the cakes*]$_O$ (no one else burnt them) and *Mary*$_A$ *believes* [*that no one has such a good fashion sense as* [*Mary herself/she herself*]]$_O$.

    Subject is the only function which is not available for a reflexive pronoun, (a), and it is the most frequent slot in which to find an appositional *-self* form, (b). An appositional *-self* item which is underlyingly in subject slot may, alternatively, occur at one of a number of other positions in the clause. This can be illustrated by (where *himself* may appear at any one—but only one—of the positions indicated):

(72) [John (himself-1)]$_A$ had (himself-2) solved [the puzzle]$_O$ (himself-3) in the physics class (himself-4)

The canonical position for *himself* is in apposition to John within the subject NP, *himself*-1. Or it could be placed after the first word of the auxiliary, *himself*-2, or after the verb (plus O NP if there is one), *himself*-3, or after a peripheral constituent, *himself*-4. The four alternatives have essentially the same meaning but differ in pragmatic orientation. Note that a *-self* form which is in apposition within an NP that is in a function other than subject does not have any alternative placement. One can say *John showed the baby crocodile itself to Mary*, but not **John showed the baby crocodile to Mary itself.*

Placement of (b), *X-self*, which relates to the subject of the clause is limited by coreferential constraints. As an alternative to *John himself painted Mary* one may say *John painted Mary himself*. The masculine form *himself* could only relate to *John* not to *Mary*. But in *John painted Bill himself*, the *himself* is likely to be understood as relating to the nearest masculine noun, which is here *Bill*; that is *John*$_A$ *painted* [*Bill himself*]$_O$.

There is an interesting property of appositional *-self* forms in English. If such a form occurs in an NP which is in a function other than subject or object, and if the NP has anaphoric reference back to an earlier NP in the clause, then the head noun or pronoun to which it is in apposition may be omitted, leaving the *-self* form as making up the full NP. For example:

(73)   Mary believes that no one has such good fashion sense as
$$\begin{Bmatrix} \text{her} \\ \text{Mary herself} \\ \text{she herself} \\ \text{herself} \end{Bmatrix}$$

Note that if a plain pronoun is used here it must be *her*, but if a *-self* form is added we get *she herself* (never *her herself). The final NP can omit the head element, *she* or *Mary*, and becomes just *herself*. Other examples are *Mary considers that Jane is more beautiful than her/she herself/Mary herself/herself* and *John suggests that the payment should be made jointly to him and Mary/he himself and Mary/John himself and Mary/himself and Mary*. Note that all instances of *-self* forms in these examples are taken to be the appositional, rather than the reflexive, sense (an analysis which might be considered controversial).

There are further uses of *-self* forms. Whereas in Chaozhou, reflexive pronoun *ka³³ki¹¹* may also function as an adverbial-type form 'alone'—illustrated in (71)—in English one must add *by* or *all by*. *All by himself* or *by himself* could be used in place of *himself* in any of the four slots indicated in (72). And *all by himself* or *by himself* may also be placed clause-initially, a position generally not possible for plain *himself*.

English has a number of combinations where nothing else could be substituted for a *-self* form. These include (among very many others): *She cried herself to sleep*, *He drank himself to death/into a stupor*, *She prided herself on her honesty*, *They made themselves at home*, and *He pulled himself together*.

In a fair number of languages, a reflexive or reciprocal pronoun may function as a full NP or as possessor within an NP. In Kobon (Kalam family, Papua New Guinea), reflexive marker *ke* is used with the appropriate pronoun as a full NP, or as possessor within an NP. Two examples were given above, both with

the reflexive functioning as possessor within an NP in A function—in (38) of
§22.3 the controller is the full O NP, and in (55) of §22.4.2 it is the possessor
within the O NP.

We find a similar situation in Amele (Gum family, Papua New Guinea;
Roberts 1987: 122–31). Invariant reflexive marker *dodoc* follows a plain pronoun
as a reflexive anaphor in O function in:

(74) uga$_A$ [uga <u>dodoc</u>]$_O$ qo-i-a
      3sg   3sg   REFLEXIVE hit-3sgA-TODAY.PAST
      He hit himself

The same reflexive pronoun may also be modifier within an NP. In (75) it is
possessor within the NP in E function, with the O NP being the controller:

(75) ija$_A$ [uga <u>dodoc</u>   meme-g]$_E$ Dege$_O$
      1sg   3sg   REFLEXIVE father-3sg Dege
         ihac-du-g-a
         show-3sgO-1sgA-TODAY.PAST
      I showed Dege to his own father

There are similar examples from Kammu at (34) in §24.3.2, and from Piapoco
at (88–9) in §24.6.1

Some languages employ a special reflexive marker for use in possessive
function. For example, Tamil has reflexive pronoun *taan-* 'self', used as a full
NP, and also possessive reflexive form *conta* 'one's own', employed as modifier
within an NP (Asher 1985: 83–5).

In English, a *-self* form may not function as possessor; for this function we
have *own*. For example:

(76) John$_A$ ignored [his (<u>own</u>) sister]$_O$

(77) [His (<u>own</u>) sister]$_A$ ignored John$_O$

The *own* may be omitted from (76–7). Indeed, it is only likely to be included
in a situation of contrast, for example: *Bill's sister paid a lot of attention to John*
but his <u>own</u> sister ignored him (here *his own* must be *John's*).

Now consider:

(78) [John's brother]$_A$ gave [a book]$_O$ [to his (<u>own</u>) wife]$_E$

If *own* is omitted from (78) the anaphoric reference of *his* is ambiguous—it
could be John or the brother. But if *own* is included in (78) then the sentence
becomes unambiguous—the book is given to the brother's wife. Including
reflexive marker *own* indicates that the controller of the possessive anaphor
his must be the head of the subject NP (*brother*) not the modifier within the
subject (*John*).

Own occurs in a variety of other expressions, each with a reflexive slant. For example, *They have ideas of their own, He's living on his own, She has a house of her own,* and *from our own correspondent.* And there is the verb *own*, from which the reflexive marker evolved in distant times.

22.4.6 *Reciprocal pronouns* each other *and* one another *in English*

A reciprocal construction in English is shown by the inclusion of either *each other* or *one another*; these two forms are virtually always substitutable for each other/one another. Although they are invariant (not showing person and number of the controller) it is convenient to refer to *each other* and *one another* as 'reciprocal pronouns'.

If the controller is in subject function, a reciprocal pronoun may be in O function, as in (79), or within a prepositional NP, as in (80) and (81).

(79)   [John and Mary]$_A$ painted [each other/one another]$_O$

(80)   [The cousins]$_A$ gave presents$_O$ [to each other/one another]

(81)   [The combatants]$_S$ ran [towards each other/one another]

The controller can be in O function and the reciprocal pronoun then in a peripheral role, as in:

(82)   John$_A$ introduced [Mary and Fred]$_O$ [to each other/one another]

Unlike *-self* reflexive pronouns, the reciprocal pronouns can function as possessor, marked by *'s* (but scarcely by *of*) as in:

(83)   [The delegates]$_S$ flirted [with each other's wives]

Reciprocal pronouns are like *-self* reflexive pronouns in that they may not appear as passive subject. Alongside (79) we cannot have *Each other/ one another were painted by John and Mary.*

As with *-self* forms, reciprocal pronouns *one another* and *each other* can be extended from their canonical templates. I recently heard someone say to two people:

(84)   Do you$_A$ know [who$_{CC}$ [each other]$_{CS}$ is]$_{CoCl:O}$?

The reciprocal pronoun, *each other*, is here in CS function and the controller, *who*, is in CC function. But *each other* follows *who* (which has been fronted within its clause) and it is this which makes the sentence acceptable.

It is interesting to investigate the properties of the constituent words of the two reciprocal pronouns. First, *each* may occur as a modifier within an NP (*each word*, or *each of the words*) or as an adverb, then being placed either after the first word of the auxiliary, as in (85), or after the verb (plus object NP, if there is one), as in (86).

Suppose a linguist decides that two words are synonymous, having the same meaning and function. He might say either of

(85)   These two words can each be substituted for the other

(86)   These two words can be substituted each for the other

The reciprocal construction, in (87), is similar to (86), having *each* moved next to *other* and *the* omitted.

(87)   These two words can be substituted for each other

An alternative statement of (85–6) is:

(88)   These two words can be substituted one for the other

If there are three words regarded as synonymous, then instead of (88) one should say:

(89)   These three words can be substituted one for another

The reciprocal construction in (90) is similar to (89), simply having *one* moved next to *another*:

(90)   These three words can be substituted for one another

This kind of similarity may have given rise to the belief that *each other* is generally used for a reciprocal circumstance involving two participants and *one another* when there are more than two. In fact, there is at most a slight preference for such an association, with a large number of counter-examples. A few other tendencies have been mooted. First, that *each other* (which is the more common) is most favoured in non-formal discourse and writing, with there being a discernable preference for *one another* in more formal use of language. Another idea is that *each other* often has a positive, more cohesive, sense—one may hear *John and Mary love each other* but *Tom and Jane hate one another*, and also *These two cars are similar to each other* but *those two cars are different from one another*.

However, exceptions to such tendencies abound. It seems that choice between *each other* and *one another* is basically a matter of speaker's whim. An accomplished writer prefers not to use the same form twice in one sentence— *each other* and *one another* may be alternated for stylistic felicity. Jespersen (1914: 202–3) provides half-a-dozen examples, including the following from *Ann Veronica* by H. G. Wells (1909: 334):

(91)   They were enormously pleased with one another; they found each
       other beyond measure better than they had expected

22.5 The verbal derivation technique

When reflexive or reciprocal is shown by a derivational process applying to a verb, this is generally realized by prefix or suffix. Kugu Nganhcara is rather unusual; as described in §22.1, it substitutes *o* for the stem thematic vowel to create a reciprocal stem, thus *waa-* 'scold', *woo-* 'argue' (lit. scold each other).

In a fair number of languages, a derivational affix must be accompanied by some kind of reduplication of the verb in the case of reciprocal (never for reflexive). For example:

- In Motuna (Buin family, Papua New Guinea; Onishi 1994: 432–4) the first two moras of the verb stem are reduplicated before it, and suffix *-tuh* added, to form a reciprocal. For example, *rorongee* 'talk about (someone)', *roro-rorongee-tuh-* 'talk about one another'.
- As mentioned under Generalization B in §22.3, Apalai uses prefix *os-* ~ *ot-* ~ *at-* ~ *e-* for both reflexive and reciprocal. Just reciprocal also involves reduplication of the first syllable of the verb root.
- In Madurese (Austronesian; Indonesia; Davies 2000) reciprocal involves the last syllable of the verbal stem being repeated before it, plus suffix *-an*. Thus: *tambuk* 'throw stones at', *buk-tambuk-an* 'throw stones at each other'.

Reduplication by itself may indicate an iterative or repeated action, thus making it appropriate for use within a reciprocal construction (which often refers to a sequence of actions). This is so in Madurese. A derived reciprocal, such as *buk-tambuk-an-* is intransitive, taking just one core argument, in S function. If this same kind of reduplication is applied to a transitive verb without suffix *-an*, it indicates 'do several times'; for example *mokol-* 'hit', and *kol-mokol-* 'hit several times' (still transitive, taking A and O arguments). There are, however, exceptions. In Dyirbal, reciprocal involves reduplication of the first two syllables of the verb plus suffix *-barri-*, for example *ñunjal-ñunjal-barri-* 'kiss each other' whereas plain reduplication of a verb has the rather special meaning 'do more than is appropriate' (Dixon 1972: 92–3, 252–1).

A reciprocal construction must always have a subject with non-singular reference. Most languages do not indicate whether such a subject refers to two people or more than two. However, this is achieved in the Austronesian language Muna by means of reduplication (van den Berg 1989: 206):

- Subject with dual reference—simply use reciprocal prefix *po-*, as in (92).
- Subject referring to more than two—reciprocal prefix *po-* plus reduplication of first two syllables of the root, as in (93).

(92) do-po-semba
3pl-RECIPROCAL-kick
They (two) kick each other

(93) do-po-feta-fetapa
3pl-RECIPROCAL-REDUPLICATION-ask
They (more than two) ask each other

Note that these two sentences have the same 3pl subject prefix *do-*, referring to 'two or more'. Only the lack or presence of reduplication distinguishes 'two' from 'more than two'.

There was discussion in §22.4.3 of how the forms of some reflexive/reciprocal pronouns relate to common nouns. Little of this nature is found for verbal derivational affixes. However, §22.9 mentions some similarities of form with nominal affixes.

22.5.1 Range of functions and meanings

A transitive clause has two core arguments, in A and O functions. A morphological process may apply to a transitive verb, creating an intransitive stem which takes a single core argument, in S function. Table 22.2 summarizes the possibilities for what happens to the erstwhile A and O arguments.

For languages which employ the verbal derivation technique, an intransitivizing suffix which marks (e) reflexive and/or (f) reciprocal typically also shows some of the other functions from Table 22.2.

TABLE 22.2. What may happen to transitive arguments under an intransitivizing derivation

(a)	PASSIVE	O → S, original A becomes a peripheral argument, which may be omitted
(b)	AGENTLESS PASSIVE	O → S, original A not stated
(c)	ANTIPASSIVE	A → S, original O becomes a peripheral argument, which may be omitted
(d)	PATIENTLESS ANTIPASSIVE	A → S, original O not stated
(e)	REFLEXIVE	(A = O) → S
(f)	RECIPROCAL	S refers to a set, one subset of which is in A function and one subset in O function for tokens of a certain activity, with some overlap between the subsets (see (24–5) in §22.2.2)

- In Amharic (Amberber 1996), verbal prefix *t(ə)-* marks both (e) reflexive and (a) passive. Thus a derived verb *tə-səkk'ələ* is ambiguous between a reflexive interpretation 'he hanged himself' and a passive reading 'he was hanged (by someone)'. For (f), reciprocal, the same prefix is used together with a special variety of reduplication (repeating the middle consonant of a triradical root: $C_1C_2C_3 \rightarrow C_1C_2C_2C_3$).
- Warekena, uses verbal suffix *-na-* for (e) reflexive, (f) reciprocal, and also (b) agentless passive.
- Derivational suffix *-(yi)rriy-* ~ *-marriy-* in Dyirbal marks (e) reflexive and also (c) antipassive. There is a slight but significant semantic difference between the antipassive use of *-(yi)rriy-* ~ *-marri-* and the dedicated antipassive suffix *-ŋay-* ~ *-nay-*; this is discussed in §23.2.5.
- In Latvian and Lithuanian, intransitivizing suffix *-s(i)* is used for (e) reflexive, (f) reciprocal, (b) agentless passive, and (d) patientless antipassive (Geniušienė 1987: 65–178).

In the Australian language Kuku Yalanji, verbal suffix *-ji-* marks (e) reflexive, (a) passive, and (c) antipassive, each of which is semantically conditioned. Patz (2002: 144–54, 52, 106) explains that four basic conditions must be met for a transitive clause:

(i) A NP and O NP must not be coreferential.
(ii) The described action must be intentional.
(iii) The agent must be stated and should be the most prominent clause constituent.
(iv) The described action must be discrete and performed on a specific object.

A transitive clause has its A NP marked by ergative case and its O by absolutive (with zero realization). For example:

(94) ŋamu-ŋgu$_A$ kuyu$_O$ mani-ñ
      mother-ERGATIVE fish   get-PAST
      Mother caught a fish

If any of conditions (i–iv) is not satisfied then the verb is marked by suffix *-ji-* which intransitivizes it. There is then just one core argument, in S function which is shown by absolutive case (with zero realization).

Firstly, if A and O are coreferential, then condition (i) is not satisfied and *-ji-* marks a reflexive:

(95) kaarkay$_S$ julurri-ji-y
      child   wash-INTRANSITIVIZER-NONPAST
      The child is washing itself

If something happens accidentally, contravening condition (ii), then a transitive construction is not available. One has to use a passive clause, marked by -*ji*-, in which underlying O becomes S. Underlying A may be included, marked by locative case, or may be omitted. For example, if a man deliberately stepped on my foot, then I would use a transitive construction 'man-ERGATIVE$_A$ [my foot]$_O$ stepped on'. But if he stepped on it accidentally, then a -*ji*-passive is required:

(96) diŋkar-anda   [ŋayu jina]$_S$ narri-ji-ñ
      man-LOCATIVE   1sg   foot   step.on-INTRANSITIVIZER-PAST
      The man happened to stand on my foot (lit. My foot was stood on by
          the man)

If the underlying A is unknown or irrelevant, or lower than O on the nominal hierarchy (see §3.9 and §13.5.4), then condition (iii) is not satisfied and a passive intransitive construction marked by -*ji*- is required. Since 'crocodile' is lower on the hierarchy than 'I', one must use—rather than the transitive construction 'A crocodile frightened me'—a passive construction. Again, the underlying A argument takes locative marking (or may be omitted):

(97) ŋayu$_S$ yinilkaŋa-ji-ñ   biliŋkama-ndu
      1sg   frighten-INTRANSITIVIZER-PAST crocodile-LOCATIVE
      I was frightened by a crocodile

Finally, if condition (iv) is not satisfied, with the action or patient being 'generalized', then an anti-passive construction is employed, again marked by -*ji*-. Underlying A is now in S function and underlying O may be included, marked by locative. For example:

(98) jalbu$_S$ [bayan-ba   yindu-yinduy-mbu]
      woman   house-LOCATIVE   REDUPLICATED-other-LOCATIVE
          nuri-nuri-ji-y
      REDUPLICATED-peep-INTRANSITIVIZER-NONPAST
      The woman keeps on peeping into all the other houses

Verbal reduplication in Kuku-Yalanji indicates 'an ongoing, repeated or habitual action and/or a certain intensity in action'. Nominal reduplication appears to be used for plurality.

   We can now look in a different direction, towards the semantics of reciprocals. The subject of a reciprocal construction refers to the collection of participants involved in A and O functions. It was shown in §22.1 that in Fijian 'reciprocal' is one sense of verbal prefix *vei*-, which has a general meaning 'collective'. In some languages a certain verbal affix functions as reciprocal with a transitive verb (then deriving an intransitive stem) and signifies 'together' when used with an intransitive verb (not then affecting transitivity).

For example, in Yakut (Turkic, Siberia; Nedjalkov and Nedjalkov 2007a: 1111, 1132–5), verbal suffix -(s)əs- has reciprocal meaning with transitive verb baləj- 'slander' in baləj-səs- 'slander each other' and a simple collective sense with intransitive taxs- 'go out' in taxs-əs- 'go out together'. Interestingly, the 'together' sense may in this language also be used with a transitive verb, leading to ambiguity. Thus ann'-əs- can mean either 'push each other' or 'push somebody/something together'.

A rather unusual secondary sense of a reciprocal verbal affix is to indicate 'competitive'. In Japanese, for example, suffix -at- can be ambiguous between a reciprocal meaning and 'in competition', as in (Alpatov and Nedjalkov 2007: 1046):

(99) [kankookyaku wa]$_A$ [miyage   o]$_O$ kai-<u>at</u>-ta
       sightseer   TOPIC   souvenir ACCUSATIVE buy-RECIP-PAST
       EITHER   The sightseers bought souvenirs for each other
           OR   The sightseers bought souvenirs as if in competition

Another example of reciprocal being extended to competitive meaning is provided by Nedjalkov and Nedjalkov (2007b: 1006) for the Turkic language Karachay-Balkar.

There are a number of other secondary meanings reported for reciprocal verbal affixes. One of the fullest is that given by Moyse-Faurie (2007) for the Polynesian language East Futunan. Prefix fe- (cognate with vei- in Fijian) plus transitive suffix -(C)aki is used for reciprocal. It is also associated with (this list is not exhaustive):

- 'together' ('sociative'), as in 'Children are running together after the ball'
- 'with difficulty', as in 'Samino carries his bag in his hand with difficulty'
- 'in turn', as in 'Children put on my loin-cloth in turn'
- iterative, as in 'Lightning flashes again and again in the sky'
- dispersive, as in 'The wall of the house is full of holes'

Note that at least some of the non-reciprocal senses may accept plural or singular subject.

Finally, we can draw attention to lexical roots with what we can call 'in-built' reflexives or reciprocals. That is, the root includes a reflexive or reciprocal affix, and the form without this affix does not exist. These are particularly prevalent in the Australian language, Guugu Yimidhirr. As illustrated in (7–8) of §22.1, verbal suffix -Vdhi- marks both reflexive and reciprocal. Haviland (1979: 98) notes that about thirty intransitive roots have an in-built -*Vdhi*-. They include *madha-adhi*- 'climb', *buurngga-adhi*- 'enter', and *dumba-adhi*- 'be frightened'. (One imagines that the plain forms *madha*-, *buurngga*-, and *dumba*- were probably there in an earlier stage of the language, and have since dropped out of use.)

Used productively, a reflexive or reciprocal verbal affix may engender a specialized meaning with certain roots. For example, in Dyirbal *ŋamba*- is 'hear, listen to' and its derived reflexive *ŋamba-yirri*- is 'think' (literally, 'listen to oneself'). Another example is *miju*- 'take no notice of' with reflexive *miju-yirri*- 'wait' (literally, 'take no notice of oneself').

22.5.2 Coreference possibilities and transitivity

In a language employing the verbal derivation technique, underlying A and O arguments (which are coreferential) are mapped onto S argument of the derived intransitive verb. In §13.2 we described how a number of languages have two ways of marking S. In a 'split-S' language, some verbs have their S argument marked like A; this is called Sa (or 'active'), while others have S marked like O—So (or 'stative'). A few languages are 'fluid-S' where a single intransitive verb may take either Sa or So marking, with a difference in meaning. We now need to enquire: if a split-S or fluid-S language forms reflexives and/or reciprocals by the verbal derivation technique, whereby (A = O) → S, will this S be Sa or So? The answer is (in all the languages I have been able to examine) that it is Sa.

The split-S systems of Mali (Baining family; Papua New Guinea; Stebbins forthcoming) was illustrated by examples (5–7) in §13.2. In a transitive clause, the A argument precedes the verb and the O argument follows it. For an Sa intransitive verb (such as 'lie down') the subject has the same form as A and precedes the verb, whereas for an So verb (such as 'be sad'), it follows the verb and has the same form as O. A typical reflexive construction is:

(100)   asik   ngi$_{Sa}$ tluvēt-<u>nas</u>   mamēr
           IRREALIS 2sg   look.after-REFLEXIVE properly
           You must look after yourself properly!

Note that the 2sg S pronoun comes before the verb (like an A argument) and has form *ngi*, like A. An O/So NP would follow the verb and have form *nge*.

Other split-S languages which have (A = O) → Sa for a derived reflexive/reciprocal include Warekena, from the Arawak family Aikhenvald (1998: 371–4) and Kamaiurá, from the Tupí-Guaraní branch of the Tupí family (Seki 2000: 279–85), both spoken in Brazil. And also the Argentinean language Mocovi, as illustrated in (123–4) of §22.9.

In §22.4.2 we surveyed the often considerable coreference possibilities for languages which employ the pronoun technique for reflexive/reciprocal constructions. When the verbal derivation technique is utilized, coreference possibilities are considerably slimmer.

Some languages restrict coreference possibilities to A = O. Fox is of this type but it has available ways of circumventing the constraint (Dahlstrom n.d.: 210–16). If coreference is desired between A and an argument whose underlying function is something other than O, then this argument may be brought into surface O function through applying an applicative derivation (see Chapter 25). We can say that the applicative derivation 'feeds' the coreference constraint on reflexive/reciprocal constructions; see §23.2.4. Amongst other languages restricted to A = O coreference are many from Australia, including Mangarayi (Merlan 1982: 105, 135–6) and Dyirbal.

The controller of a reflexive or reciprocal construction, using the verbal derivation technique, must be A. But in some languages, coreference possibilities can extend beyond A = O, to A = E (E is 'extension to core'—see §3.2 and §13.1—otherwise 'indirect object'). This was exemplified for Japanese by (99) in §22.5.1, 'The sightseers bought presents for each other'. In this sentence reciprocal suffix -at- on the verb indicates the coreference of Buyer (A) and Recipient (E). The Gift, 'souvenirs', in O function, is left untouched; as a consequence, (99) is still transitive, with subject and object NPs. But when -at- marks A = O coreference, there is just one NP (in subject function) and the construction then appears to be intransitive.

In Lithuanian (Geniušienė 1987: 126), reflexive and reciprocal are marked by verbal derivational prefix -si. This is used for A = O and also A = E coreference. The latter can be seen by comparing the plain three-argument clause in (101) with the reflexive in (102), where the NP in E function has gone, prefix -si indicating that it is coreferential with A.

(101)   On-a$_A$ pa-siuvo   dukr-ai$_E$ suknel-ę$_O$
        Ann-NOM   PERFECT-sew   daughter-DATIVE   dress-ACCUSATIVE
        Ann (has) made a dress for her daughter

(102)   On-a$_A$ pa-<u>si</u>-siuvo   suknel-ę$_O$
        Ann-NOM   PERFECT-REFLEXIVE-sew   dress-ACCUSATIVE
        Ann (has) made a dress for herself

In §22.4.2 we showed how, within the pronoun technique, coreference can involve a possessor within an NP (as in 'John's daughter hates his new wife'). Could such coreference be possible under the verb derivation technique? The answer is: only if some special ploy is used. In Guaymi (Chibchan family, Panama and Costa Rica; Payne 1982) reflexive/reciprocal prefix ha-, added to a verb, derives an intransitive stem. And *ha-* may also be added to a noun, then indicating that the possessor of the noun is coreferential with the subject of the clause. For example:

(103) Davi(-gwe)   ha-hu-e-te   hadïg-aba
       David(-NOM) REFLEXIVE-house-PERTENSIVE-LOCATIVE   sleep-PAST
       David slept in his own house

22.6 Other techniques

There are a number of other grammatical techniques for creating reflexive and reciprocal constructions, each of which is found in a small number of languages. Just a sample is illustrated here.

   (a) *Using a transitive verb in an intransitive syntactic frame.*

In the Australian language Warrgamay (Dixon 1981: 64), verbs divide into transitive and intransitive sets. Five of the seven verbal inflections have different allomorphs in transitive and intransitive clauses. For example:

(104)   TRANSITIVE   INTRANSITIVE
                        ALLOMORPH   ALLOMORPH
       irrealis   -lma   -ma
       perfect   -ñu   -gi

   A reflexive construction has no special reflexive pronoun, nor any verbal derivational affix. What happens—in all dialects—is simply that a transitive verb is placed within an intransitive clause. Compare verb *ganda-* 'burn' used in a canonical transitive clause in (105) and in an intransitive clause—conveying reflexive meaning—in (106):

(105) ŋadja waguno ganda-ñu
       1sgA   wood   burn-PERFECT:TRANSITIVE
       I've burnt the wood

(106) [ŋayba mala]s ganda-gi
       1sgS   hand   burn-PERFECT:INTRANSITIVE
       I've burnt myself on the hand

   In the Biyay dialect of Warrgamay, reciprocal is shown by verbal derivational suffix *-ba-* (Dixon 1981: 74–5). However, in the Warrgamay proper dialect, technique (a)—using a transitive verb in an intransitive construction—covers both reflexive and reciprocal.

   Unlike Warrgamay, Mawng (Dineen 1992)—another Australian language— has bound pronouns, and these have different forms for each of S, A, and O.

A transitive verb normally takes A and O pronominal prefixes. If, instead, it is supplied with an S prefix, then the clause is interpreted as reflexive (like Warrgamay, there is no separate reflexive marker). Compare verb *-wuña-* ~ *-puña* 'cook, burn' used in a canonical transitive construction in (107) and in an intransitive construction, with reflexive meaning, in (108).

(107) ki-i-ŋa-wuña [ja karnjawarra]$_O$
PRESENT-3mascO-3femA-cook/burn MASC crab(generic)
She's cooking crabs

(108) iñ-puña-n
3femS-cook/burn-PAST
She burnt herself'

(b) *Leaving blank the O slot.*

This can be illustrated from a further Australian language, Malak-Malak (Green 1991). Each lexical verb is followed by an obligatory auxiliary which takes a pronominal prefix for A or S and a suffix for O. We can illustrate a canonical construction with transitive verb *yir* 'scratch' plus auxiliary *-ni-* 'sit':

(109) yir-ma e-ni-nginj-nœnœ
scratch-DURATIVE 1sgA-sit-IMPERFECTIVE-2sgO
I was scratching you (sg)

To create a reflexive construction, one simply leaves the O bound pronoun slot blank, as in:

(110) yir-ma e-ni-nginj
scratch-DURATIVE 1sgA-sit-IMPERFECTIVE
I was scratching myself

Note that it is not admissible to add 1sg O bound pronoun, *-arriny*, to (110). (This would be, literally 'I-scratch-me'.)

(c) *A sequence of verbs.*

A sequential reciprocal, with dual subject, involves two actions. In the Papuan language Amele one has to describe two actions. For example (Roberts 1987: 132):

(111) ale qo-co-b qo-co-b esi-a
3du hit-DS-3sg hit-DS-3sg 3du-TODAY.PAST
They (two) hit each other (lit. They two, one hit, another hit)

This consists of two medial clauses, each with suffix *-co-* which indicates 'different subject (DS) from that of following predicate'. Interestingly, if one were describing a group of more than two people hitting one another, the only adjustments to (111) would be 3pl free pronoun *age* in place of 3du *ale* at the beginning, and 3pl bound pronoun *eig-* in place of 3du *esi-* at the end. Similar two-verb constructions are used in a number of other Papuan languages, including Hua (Haiman 1980: 431–9).

When I was doing fieldwork on Yidiñ, an Australian language, the texts gathered included many instances of reflexives but no reciprocals at all. It seems that just one verb forms a reciprocal by reduplication, *bunja-bunja-* 'hit each other' (with other verbs, reduplication has a different meaning). For other verbs one simply has to use two clauses, linked by particle 'in turn'. Thus, to say 'We told each other stories', this has to be spelled out in full: 'I told him a story and he, in turn, told me a story' (Dixon 1977a: 345, 380–1).

(d) *Using a reciprocal adverb.*

Many languages have one or more adverbs with reciprocal meaning. In most, a reciprocal adverb can occur with a reciprocal pronoun but cannot replace it. In English, for instance, one can say *John and Mary hate* <u>*each other*</u> *mutually*, but not **John and Mary hate mutually*. In other languages, an adverb of this type can be the sole marker of a reciprocal construction. Compare the plain transitive clause in Mandarin Chinese, in (112), with the reciprocal construction in (113). (From (Nedjalkov, and Geniušienė 2007: 387; see also Hoa, Nedjalkov, and Nikitina 2007:2001–12.)

(112) wǒ [xiàng tā] dào.qiàn-le
       1sg   TO   3sg apologize-PERFECT
       I apologized to him/her

(113) tāmen <u>hùxiāng</u>   dào.qiàn-le
       3pl   MUTUALLY   apologize-PERFECT
       They apologized to each other

The Papuan language Kobon combines strategies (c) and (d). A reciprocal construction requires two clauses with a reciprocal adverb in each. For example (Davies 1981: 90):

(114) ne_A <u>pen(pen)</u>   ip   ñi-mön
       2sg   RECIPROCALLY   1sgO   give-PRESCRIPTIVE.MOOD:2sgA

       yada_A <u>pen(pen)</u>   nöp   ñi-nam
       1sg   RECIPROCALLY   2sgO   give-PRESCRIPTIVE.MOOD:1sgA

       Let us exchange! (lit. Let you reciprocally give to me and let me reciprocally give to you!)

The word *pen* as a nominal means 'reciprocation', 'debt', or 'compensation'. It also functions as an adverbial, as in (114), and is then often reduplicated.

22.7 Combining techniques

The main techniques for expressing a reflexive or reciprocal relation are reflexive and/or reciprocal pronouns—which can be free or bound, invariant or informative—and verbal derivations. We mentioned under Generalization C in §22.3 that the pronoun technique may be used for reflexive and verbal derivation for reciprocal, but the reverse is not attested. And, under Generalization D, that the reflexive pronoun may be informative and the reciprocal one invariant, but the reverse of this is not attested. Taking these into account, rows A–R of Table 22.3 list all possible combinations of varieties of the two main techniques, with illustrative languages from among those discussed thus far in this chapter. (Where a box extends over both reflexive and reciprocal columns, this means that a single form combines these two functions.) It can be seen that no language is quoted for rows H, J, and R; however, it

TABLE 22.3. Types of combination of techniques

	REFLEXIVE	RECIPROCAL	EXAMPLE LANGUAGES
A	invariant free pronoun		Hdi, Iraqw, West Greenlandic
B	invariant free pronoun	invariant free pronoun	Kashmiri, Korafe, Korean, Lao, Oromo, Vietnamese
C	informative free pronoun		Supyire
D	informative free pronoun	informative free pronoun	Akan, Copala Trique, Hausa, Colloquial Welsh
E	informative free pronoun	invariant free pronoun	Basque, Dagbani, English
F	invariant bound pronoun		Nyangumarta, Walmatjari, Wambaya
G	invariant bound pronoun	invariant bound pronoun	Koasati
H	informative bound pronoun		\<none attested thus far\>
J	informative bound pronoun	informative bound pronoun	\<none attested thus far\>

TABLE 22.3. Continued

	REFLEXIVE	RECIPROCAL	EXAMPLE LANGUAGES
K	informative bound pronoun	invariant bound pronoun	Abkhaz
L	verbal derivation		Guaymi, Guugu Yimidhirr, Mangarayi, Maricopa, Warekena
M	verbal derivation	verbal derivation	Ainu, Amharic, Apalai, Dyirbal, Halkomelem Salish, Kamaiurá, Kuku Yalanji, Mali, Motuna, Huallaga Quechua, Uradhi
N	invariant free pronoun	verbal derivation	Indonesian, Ponapean
P	informative free pronoun	verbal derivation	Dime, Kugu Nganhcara, Muna
Q	invariant bound pronoun	verbal derivation	Swahili
R	informative bound pronoun	verbal derivation	<none attested thus far>
S	transitive verb in intransitive frame		Warrgamay (main dialect)
T	transitive verb in intransitive frame	verbal derivation	Mawng, Warrgamay (Biyay dialect)
U	informative free pronoun	sequence of verbs	Amele, Hua, Kobon
V	verbal derivation	sequence of verbs	Yidiñ
W	invariant free pronoun	reciprocal adverb	Mandarin Chinese

is likely that a wider search would throw up examples of these. Rows S–W provide ad hoc exemplification of languages which include some of the minor techniques described in the last section. (As mentioned at the end of §22.1, some languages lack any sort of reflexive and/or reciprocal construction and just use plain pronouns, saying something like 'I cut me'. These are not covered by Table 22.3.)

It might be inferred from the discussion thus far that there is just one technique available in a given language for reflexive and one for reciprocal. This is the case in many languages, but there are some which have alternative techniques available. As described in §22.1, Kugu Nganhcara has an informative free pronoun for reflexive, and a verbal derivation for reciprocal. But, as illustrated in (9), it is permissible (but not obligatory) to also include the reflexive pronoun in a reciprocal construction.

The Algonquian language Fox has both verbal derivation and pronoun techniques available for reflexive (reciprocal employs just verbal derivation). These are illustrated in:

(115)   wa·pa-tiso-wa
        look.at-REFLEXIVE-3.INDEPENDENT.INDICATIVE
        He looked at himself

(116)   wa·patammwa   ow-i·yawio
        look.at:3:INAN.PROXIMATE:INDEPENDENT.INDICATIVE   3sg-REFL
        He looked at himself

Sentence (115) is intransitive while (116) remains transitive. Dahlstrom (n.d.: 215–16) states that her consultant reported the two sentences to 'mean the same' and adds 'it is not clear what conditions the choice between them'. However, the pronoun technique has wider functional possibilities than verbal derivation:

- Whereas for verbal derivation coreference can only be A = O, a reflexive pronoun can handle A = O, A = E, and also O = E, as in 'They told me about myself'.
- Only reflexive pronouns may be used for overlapping reference, of the type illustrated for Hausa in (22) of §22.2.1. For example, 'You(pl) destroyed us(inclusive)-REFLEXIVE'.
- 'If the reflexive object is contrastively focused', it must be expressed by a reflexive free pronoun.

For Fox, only one technique can be employed, not both at once. In contrast, either the verbal derivation technique, or the pronoun technique, or both of them at the same time, are reported to be possible for reciprocals in the Tungusic language Udehe (Nikolaeva 2007). The Turkic language Yakut (Nedjalkov and Nedjalkov 2007a) has both techniques available for reflexive and also for reciprocal, and again they can be combined. The forms employed in Yakut are of interest:

REFLEXIVE
    verbal derivation suffix -*n*
    reflexive pronoun *beje*-PLUS-POSSESSIVE-PRONOUN:CASE
RECIPROCAL
    verbal derivation suffix -*s*
    reciprocal pronoun *beje-beje*-PLUS-POSSESSIVE-PRONOUN:CASE

The pronouns are based on *beje* 'self' (an ancient borrowing from Mongolian *bie* 'body, person') with this being reduplicated for the reciprocal.

22.8 Inherently reciprocal and inherently reflexive verbs

There may be a number of basically two-argument verbs which can be used in a reciprocal construction and may then omit the reciprocal pronoun, still retaining a reciprocal meaning. For instance, in English:

(117)   Bill and Tom fought (<u>each other</u>)

(118)   John and Mary hugged (<u>each other</u>)

(119)   The bus and the car collided (with <u>each other</u>)

Some of these verbs may only occur with a single argument when they have a reciprocal meaning; they include *hug, adjoin, match, collide (with), differ (from)*. The list can be extended to adjectives with a copula complement, including (*be*) *similar (to)*, and (*be*) *equal (to)*. There are also ambitransitive verbs which may occur with either one or two arguments; for some of these, if they have just a subject and this has plural reference, then reciprocal is the default reading. They include *fight, play, agree*. (See Dixon 2005a: 65–6 for a fuller account of inherently reciprocal verbs in English.)

Many languages do have a smallish set of inherently reciprocal verbs, but others lack these. In Lao (Enfield 2007a: 315), for instance, a reciprocal pronoun must always be included, even for verbs such as 'kiss' and 'meet'. If the reciprocal pronoun were omitted, the clause would be 'interpreted as having an ellipsed, definite object argument whose referent is not included in the plural subject', e.g. 'They kissed/met (him/her/them)'.

Inherently reciprocal verbs are such by virtue of the meanings. It is thus not surprising that the same meanings recur across languages. For example, the set in the Uto-Aztecan language Ute includes 'meet (with)', 'quarrel (with)', 'fight (with)', 'kiss', and 'mate' (Givón 1980: 158), and those in the Oceanic language

Tamambo include 'quarrel', 'chat', 'share out', and 'play chasings' (Jauncey 1997: 60, 2011: 274).

Alongside the inherently reciprocal verbs, we also get a smallish number of inherently reflexive verbs, for which a reflexive pronoun can be omitted and the reflexive meaning retained, as in *John hid (himself)*. When *hide* and *dress* are used with no object, the only interpretation is reflexive. However, when *wash* and *shave* are used with just a subject stated, there is ambiguity. *Mary is washing* could mean either that she is washing herself or that she is doing the weekly clothes wash. Other languages have different ways of dealing with verbs which typically relate to a reflexive activity. For instance, the Oceanic language Longgu has two distinct verb roots, transitive *po-a* 'hide (something)' and intransitive *obwa* 'hide oneself' (Hill 1997: 78).

In contrast to English and other languages, where a reflexive pronoun may be omitted after certain verbs, the Chadic language Mupun (Frajzyngier 1993: 189–90) *requires* a reflexive pronoun to be always stated with *mūn* 'forget about something' and *nók* 'ignore something'.

22.9 Origins, space and time

The origin of reflexive and reciprocal markers is an interesting topic. As shown in §22.4.3, many reflexive and some reciprocal markers are based on common nouns such as 'body' and 'head'.

The origin of the reciprocal pronouns in English—*each other* and *one another*—is plainly evident, as discussed in §22.4.6. 'One' is a recurrent etymon. In Tamil 'the most usual way of expressing reciprocality involves the use of nominal forms based on the number adjective *oru* "one"' (Asher 1985: 87). French has a 'compound reciprocal pronoun *l'un à l'autre* "each other" (marked for gender and number)'. This is, literally 'the one to the other'. An example is (Guentchéva and Rivière 2007: 564):

(120) [Pierre et   Marie]$_A$ pensent [l'un.à.l'autre]$_O$
       Pierre AND Marie   think   RECIPROCAL
       Pierre and Marie think of each other

In a number of languages, reciprocal pronouns are based on a common noun 'friend' or 'comrade' (see the examples quoted in Heine and Kuteva 2002: 92–3). Colloquial Welsh bases its reciprocal pronouns on the noun *gilydd* 'fellow' preceded by the appropriate possessive pronoun, thus 'our/your/their fellow'. For example (King 2008: 104):

(121) siaradwch   â'ch.gilydd   am ^{n}ddeng munud
       talk:IMPERATIVE:PL TO:YOUR:PL.FELLOW FOR ten   minute
       Talk to each other [amongst yourselves] for ten minutes!

Less information is available concerning the origin of verbal derivations which mark reflexive and reciprocal constructions. Sometimes there is similarity between the reflexive/reciprocal affix to a verb and the comitative affix ('having') to a noun. For Djapu from north Australia, the reflexive/reciprocal verbal suffix is -*mi*- (taking unmarked/potential inflection -*rr*) while the 'having' suffix is -*mirr*. Morphy (1983: 17–21) suggests that the verbal suffix is 'almost certainly derived historically' from the nominal one.

As languages evolve, forms which had concrete reference—say, to place or space—take on a grammatical role. For example, one kind of reciprocal construction in Mandarin Chinese involves linking two occurrences of the appropriate verbal root with verbs 'come' and 'go', 'V-come-V-go', as in (Liu 2000: 124):

(122)   tamen   da-<u>lai</u>-da-qu
        3pl   hit-COME-hit-GO
        They hit each other

Manambu (Ndu family, Papua New Guinea; Aikhenvald 2008a: 418–19, 2008b: 158), has a reciprocal/associative marker *awar-wa* 'each other, all together' which comes from comitative case-form of the inherently locational noun *awar* 'side, sideways direction'. In Mocovi (Waikurúan, Argentina; Grondona 1998: 116–25), verbal prefix *n*- marks a reflexive derivation with a transitive verb (creating an intransitive stem), as in (123), and has the meaning 'hither' with an intransitive, illustrated by (124).

(123)   i-<u>n</u>-oʔwet   (124)   i-n-owir
        1sgSa-REFLEXIVE-dress   1sgSa-HITHER-arrive
        I dress myself   I arrive here

Some reflexive/reciprocal markers have a secondary sense, relating to time. In The Yuman language Hualapai (Sohn 1995), verbal suffix -*v*, added to a transitive verb, marks reflexive (with a singular subject) or reciprocal (the most normal interpretation when the subject is plural). This suffix -*v* may also be added to a certain set of intransitive verbs, then adding a temporal nuance 'just now', as in 'The toy just broke'.

22.10 Summary

Every language must have some means for marking such things as negation, questions, and commands. But there is really little need for a special reflexive construction. At least as far as 1st and 2nd persons are concerned, what is wrong with saying just 'Don't cut you with that axe!' and 'I saw me in the mirror'? And if a reciprocal involves just two participants and sequential activities, it should be perfectly adequate to say 'John hit me and then I hit John'. (Indeed, this states the order of events, which a reciprocal construction such as *John and I hit each other* fails to do.)

Yet most languages do have special marking for showing that someone is acting on themselves. Since, in a canonical reflexive, A and O arguments have the same reference, the A argument (the controller) may be left as is with a reflexive pronoun being placed in the (free or bound) pronoun O slot. The reflexive pronoun may be 'informative', including as much information about person, number, and gender as the controller—or sometimes even more, as it does in English (see §22.4.3)—or less information (often, none at all; it is then called 'invariant').

Since A and O have the same reference, there is no need to state this twice. The alternative to the reflexive pronoun technique is to apply a morphological process to the verb, deriving an intransitive stem with reflexive meaning, which takes a single core argument in S function. It codes underlying A = O. There can be variants on this technique—for example, using a transitive verb in an intransitive clause without any special marking, or maintaining a transitive construction but just stating the A argument, with the O slot left blank.

Under the reflexive pronoun technique, coreference possibilities may extend beyond A = O, into A = E and even O = E. In addition, a possessor within an NP may enter into reflexive coreference. In some languages the controller of a reflexive can only be animate, in others only human. In some, the controller must be acting intentionally; and there are languages with different marking for intentional and accidental control. Under the verbal derivation technique, coreference is often restricted to A = O, sometimes extended to A = E.

Basically the same possibilities apply for reciprocal as for reflexive constructions. But the number of participants may be more than two—may be any large, perhaps unspecified, number. The actions described may be sequential ('John and Mary told each other jokes'), or simultaneous ('John and Mary kissed each other on the lips'), or linear ('The children formed a circle and held one another's hands'). The marker of a clausal reciprocal may be extended to nouns which indicate a reciprocal relationship, such a 'friend' or a kinship term like 'sister'.

In some languages reflexive and reciprocal markings coincide—a singular subject implies reflexive, while with a non-singular subject reciprocal is the most likely interpretation (the alternative is a plural reflexive, such as 'The boys each looked at himself in his own mirror'). When the markings are different, reciprocal is often built upon reflexive (quite often, by reduplication), seldom the reverse. A form used to indicate reflexive or reciprocal typically has further functions. A reflexive pronoun may have an emphatic sense. Reciprocal pronouns and reciprocal verbal derivations can also indicate 'together' or 'in competition'. Within some grammars, reflexive or reciprocal is most appropriately regarded as one sense of a broader grammatical category; for instance, a general intransitivizing process.

Reflexives and reciprocals contrast in interesting ways. The set of verbs which may plausibly be used in a reciprocal construction is generally larger than the set which may be used in a reflexive construction. There are typically more 'inherently reciprocal' verbs (such as 'meet') than 'inherently reflexive' ones (such as 'hide'). But preliminary results suggest that, on a text count, reflexives tend to be far more frequent than reciprocals.

22.11 What to investigate

Information on reflexive and reciprocal constructions can be gathered from analysis of recorded texts, or from observations of how the language is used in everyday conversation, within an 'immersion' fieldwork technique. It is not advisable to try to gather data by asking for translation of reflexive or reciprocal constructions from a lingua franca, or by showing videos clips of activities in some alien culture.

Not all languages have special construction types for both reflexive and reciprocal situations. Someone acting on themself may be shown just by plain pronouns—'He hit him' or 'He cut his hand'. (There may be some other grammatical clue—or some pragmatic hint—as to whether or not 'he' is coreferential with 'him/his' in such a clause.) And reciprocal activities may only be describable though a sequence of clauses: 'Mary gave a present to Jane and then Jane gave one to Mary'.

However, most languages do have both reflexive and reciprocal constructions. These may be marked in the same way—a singular subject then indicates reflexive and a non-singular subject is likely to indicate reciprocal. Or they may be marked in different ways. Quite often, a reciprocal marker involves an addition to the corresponding reflexive marker (this addition may be reduplication).

The following points should be investigated.

A. Are these constructions marked by special (free) reflexive/reciprocal pronouns, or by some affix (or other morphological process) applied to the verb?

B. If the latter, care must be taken to distinguish between a reflexive or reciprocal bound pronominal form, which replaces an O bound pronoun in its slot, and a derivational process which generally changes the transitivity of the verb, typically deriving an intransitive reflexive/reciprocal stem from an underlying transitive root. (Distinguishing these two possibilities is sometimes a straightforward matter, other times a little tricky.)

C. When the pronoun technique applies, if the reflexive or reciprocal relationship involves the A argument, then this will be 'controller' (otherwise called 'antecedent') and is stated in full. The other argument in the relationship will be shown by a reflexive or reciprocal free or bound pronoun, which has anaphoric reference back to the controller. The transitivity of the clause is, as a rule, not affected.

Questions to address include:

- Are there any semantic limitations on the controller? For example, must it be animate, or can it only be human? Or does the activity have to be intentional, rather than accidental?
- What coreference relationships are permitted? Some languages allow only A = O; others also permit A = E ('indirect object'), A = peripheral argument and even O = E, or O = peripheral argument (O will then be controller). Or a possessor within (any kind of) an NP may be involved, and there may then be a measure of choice as to what is controller and what is reflexive/reciprocal element. In some languages there is a special reflexive form for possessor (for example, *own* in English).
- How much information about person, number, gender, inclusive/ exclusive nature of the controller is included in the reflexive or reciprocal pronoun? This pronoun may be 'informative', repeating all or most information, or 'invariant' simply showing that this *is* a reflexive or reciprocal construction, nothing more.

D. When the verbal derivation technique applies, two underlying arguments are coded as S of the derived intransitive. (The notion of 'controller' is then scarcely relevant.)

- Once again, are there any semantic restrictions on this A = O element— animate/human, or must be acting intentionally?
- What coreference pairs occur? There is always A = O and sometimes also A = E. If both are allowed, how are these distinguished? (It may be by different derivational affixes on the verb.)
- What is the transitivity of a derived reflexive/reciprocal construction? When (A = O) → S, then the clause is invariably intransitive. When A = E, then O may remain and the clause stays transitive (that is, we get (A = E) → A). Further factors may intrude and tests for transitivity in the language should be most carefully applied.

E. Do reflexive/reciprocal markers also have other roles in the grammar? For instance:

- A reflexive pronoun may also function as an emphatic modifier, or as an adverb, indicating 'all by oneself'.
- A reflexive (and sometimes also a reciprocal) verbal derivation may have general intransitivizing function, also covering full or agentless passive, full or patientless antipassive, and perhaps more besides.
- Reciprocal markers—whether pronouns or derivational processes— may have one or more further meanings such as 'together' (what Nedjalkov 2007 calls 'sociative'), comitative ('with'), and 'in competition'.
- There are languages in which reciprocal markers may also be used with nouns, typically kin terms and items like 'neighbour' and 'friend' which refer to a symmetrical two-participant relationship.

(A reciprocal construction requires a plural subject. But when a reciprocal marker is used with an extended meaning—such as 'together'—it may be able to occur with a singular subject. This is something which should be carefully investigated.)

In some languages, reflexive or reciprocal is best regarded as a secondary sense of some more general category, such as 'collective' or general intransitivizer.

F. One should ascertain which types of verbs may occur in reflexive and in reciprocal constructions. It may be that reciprocals are restricted to verbs which refer to actions performed sequentially (such as 'hit', 'dress', 'tell'). They may not be applicable with verbs referring to feelings, such as 'love' and 'hate'. A sentence like 'John and Mary love each other' necessarily implies that 'John loves Mary' and 'Mary loves John' apply simultaneously (rather than sequentially).

G. The productivity of a verbal derivation technique should be investigated. It may pertain to all verbs which have an appropriate meaning, or just to a restricted set (which may or may not show semantic homogeneity).

H. There may be further ways of marking a reflexive or reciprocal relationship, beyond the standard pronoun and verbal derivation techniques. Some were illustrated in §22.6, but there could be further possibilities. If something of this nature turns up, it should be studied from every angle, in great detail.

J. A given language may have more than one technique available for showing reflexive and/or reciprocal. There could be a verbal derivation which has restricted productivity, the pronoun technique being used beyond its boundary. Or two techniques may both be productive. The fieldworker should then endeavour to examine which is used when, and for what.

K. Some—but not all—languages have a limited set of inherently reflexive verbs and a somewhat larger set of inherently reciprocal verbs. These are verbs which basically have two arguments and, if used with just a subject, then take on a reflexive or reciprocal meaning.

L. Finally, it is of course interesting to investigate what the etymology might be for each reflexive and reciprocal marker.

M. If time allows, check on the textual frequency of (different kinds of) reflexive and reciprocal markers

Sources and notes

Reflexive and reciprocal constructions are only of middling importance within any grammar. But there is considerable variation in the means which different languages employ to express reflexive and reciprocal relationships. Despite its length, this chapter has only been able to deal with some of the major issues.

There have been a large number of publications on reflexive or reciprocal constructions (but rather few, surprisingly, on both together) both in general terms and with respect to individual languages. On reflexives, Geniušienė (1987) is particularly recommended. Although referred to a good deal, Faltz (1985) is now somewhat dated. Nedjalkov's (2007) five-volume compendium on reciprocals is a monumental work of lasting value; some authors also provide information concerning reflexives, which enhances the interest of their contributions. Other useful discussions of reciprocals include Evans (2008), Evans, Gaby, and Nordlinger (2007), Frajzyngier and Curl (2000), and Lichtenberk (1985).

A comment is in order on the term 'middle'. This was first used for Classical Greek where a system of three voices was recognized—active, passive, and middle (so-called since it was considered intermediate between active and passive). Passive and middle forms were distinguished only in aorist and future (falling together in present and imperfect). The scope of 'middle' in Greek includes: reflexive, reciprocal, a number of O → S intransitivizations, and 'doing it for oneself'; middle verbs are generally intransitive, sometimes transitive. The term 'middle' is best reserved for this enigmatic language-specific category in Greek. Recent attempts to apply the term to other languages (including English) have led to a degree of confusion (see Dixon and Aikhenvald 2000b: 11–12). This has been compounded by Kemmer's (1993) monograph *The middle voice*, which defines neither 'voice' nor 'middle', and identifies instances of 'middle' on semantic grounds, rather than on internal grammatical criteria for each language. Some of her citations are misleading and a number of interpretations open to question. Unless defined very clearly within the grammar of a particular language, the term 'middle' is best avoided (for languages other than Greek).

22.1   The short mentions of reflexive and reciprocal constructions in this section are not absolutely complete; references should be made to the primary sources for full details.

Vitale (1981: 145) points out an alternative form of the reciprocal construction in Swahili. For 'Juma and Halima love each other' one could say, instead of (12) [*Juma na Halima*]$_S$ *wa-na-penda-na*:

(12′)   Juma$_S$ a-na-penda-na   [na   Halima]
        Juma   3sgS-PRESENT-love-RECIPROCAL   AND   Halima
        Juma and Halima love each other

That is, the second part of the A NP, *na Halima*, is extraposed to the end of the clause and the verb retains reciprocal suffix -*na* but now takes 3sg rather than 3pl S pronominal prefix.

22.2.1   Fox (Dahlstrom n.d: 216) also allows controller and reflexive anaphor to have overlapping reference, the second including the first, as in 'I have the say over ourselves (inclusive)'. See also §22.7.

22.3   Another clear example of dative subject functioning as reflexive controller is Kashmiri (Wali and Koul 1997: 126).

Abkhaz (North-west Caucasian; Hewitt 1979: 77–90) provides a superficial counter-example to Generalization A. As shown by example (28) in §17.2.3, a transitive verb bears a bound pronoun for O function followed by one for A function. In a reflexive construction, a reflexive pronoun (marking person and number) fills the first prefix slot, for O, and a plain pronoun is in the second slot, for A. However, the situation is different for reciprocals. Here the first (O) slot bears a normal pronoun with an invariant reciprocal pronoun being placed in the second prefix slot, for A function. Such an 'exception' to Generalization A is perhaps only likely to be encountered with bound pronouns. Since both bound pronoun slots must be filled, it scarcely matters which takes the reciprocal pronoun. Abkhaz opts to have the fully specified pronoun stated first, followed by the invariant reciprocal form. (It appears that Kabardian, a close genetic relative of Abkhaz, behaves in a similar way; see Kazenin 2007.)

22.4   Some writers describe invariant reflexive and reciprocal pronouns— which do not show person or number of the controller—as a type of noun. Cross-linguistically, it is most convenient to use the same label (reflex- ive/reciprocal pronoun) for all forms that can fill an argument slot in clause structure and convey a reflexive or reciprocal meaning.

22.4.2   Alongside a THAT complement clause construction such as *John reminded Tom that Bill should paint Fred*, the verb *remind* may enter into a (FOR) TO complement construction. If main clause object and complement clause subject coincide, this may be stated just once, as in John *reminded Tom to paint Fred*. The underlying structure for this is *John reminded Tom (for) Tom to paint Fred*. This analysis is supported by the acceptability of both *John reminded himself to paint Fred* (an A–O couplet in the main clause) and *John reminded Tom to paint himself* (an A–O couplet within the TO complement clause).

22.4.3   Some grammars of Hausa (see Newman 2000: 486; Jagger 2001) refer to *à* 'one' as 'fourth person'. This is an addition to the confusing list of uses for the term 'fourth person' given in §15.1.6.
    An example of a language which has no reflexive construction and uses plain pronouns for *all* persons is Tamambo (Oceanic subgroup of Austrone- sian, Vanuatu; Jauncey 2011: 272). Sentences such as 'He cut him' and 'They cut them' are ambiguous between 'he'/'him' and 'they'/'them' being coreferential or having separate reference. A distinction can only be made from context or through additional information being supplied.

22.4.5   Although *himself* could not be placed at the beginning of a construc- tion such as (72), there are sentences such as *Myself, I never vote* (an alternative to *Me, I never vote*). This is parallel to *John, he never votes* and *Hamlet, Bill has never read it*, where an argument is placed in focus, stated first and then referred to within the clause by the appropriate pronoun. It is interesting that either *myself* or *me* may be used as the 1sg focus form. Such a construction is also possible with *ourselves* (but scarcely with *yourself* or any of the other *-self* forms).
    Baker (1995) and Stirling and Huddleston (2002) were of particular use in connection with this section; they can be consulted for further discussion of *-self* forms.

22.4.6   Erades (1950) has useful discussion concerning the difference in meaning and use between *each other* and *one another*.

22.5.1   A few grammars use the label 'anticausative' for one variety of O → S derivation with the A argument from the corresponding transitive not stated. One infers that an agentless antipassive implies an underlying agent (even though this cannot be stated in the construction), something like 'The branch was broken'. In contrast an 'anti-causative' describes something that happened all by itself, such as 'The branch broke'. This is, there is an implicit causer for an impersonal passive but not for an 'anti-causative', something which makes the latter label wholly inscrutable.

Derivational suffix *-Vji-* in Yidiñ has a similar range of functions to *-ji-* (with which it is cognate) in Kuku-Yalanji, with the addition that it may also be used with an intransitive verb, then having the meaning 'continuous action, extending into the past and future' (Dixon 1977a: 273–93).

Other instances of a reciprocal verbal affix also having the sense 'together' include Swahili (Givón 1990: 635; 2001: 109) and Austronesian languages such as Nêlêmwa (New Caledonia; Bril 2007) and Tongan (Churchward 1953: 255–8). See also Lichtenberk (2000). In the Australian language Martuthunira (Dench 1995: 152–5), the reciprocal suffix can be used for plain 'collective' and also to 'emphasize the existence of a particular kin relationship between the participants of the clause'.

The five volumes of Nedjalkov (2007) provide a rich and detailed study of the multiple meanings of reciprocal markers in a variety of languages, with special attention to 'sociative' ('together').

Some other examples of 'in-built' reciprocals are 'believe', 'be pretty, be good', 'be very much, be best', 'curse', 'be stuck up', 'fast, have one's first menstrual period', and 'be angry' in Mojave (Yuman, California; Munro 1976: 46–7).

Nyangumarta (Australian; Sharp 2004: 255) has a bound pronominal which covers reflexive and reciprocal. The following verbs require this: 'join together for mourning' (reciprocal sense) and 'lay oneself open to payback', 'transform oneself into something', and 'rotate (of a wheel etc.)', the last three having a reflexive sense.

22.6   There are further examples of reciprocal adverbs in Evans (2008: 76- 8).

22.7   Other languages with alternative techniques available for reflexive include Kannada (Dravidian; South India; Sridhar 1990: 118–24). Those with alternative techniques for reciprocal include Madurese (Austronesian; Davies 2000), Lithuanian (Geniušienė 2007), and Nivkh (isolate; Otaina and Nedjalkov 2007). The Turkic language Karachay-Balkar also has both techniques available for reciprocals, but Nedjalkov and Nedjalkov (2007b: 971–2) report that the verbal derivation is 'in the process of losing its productivity as a reciprocal marker and being ousted by the pronoun'.

22.9 Further examples of cognation between reflexive/reciprocal affixes to verbs and comitative affixes to nouns in Australian languages are in Dixon (1980: 433–40). Maslova (2000) compares reciprocal and comitative across a range of languages.

23

Pivots, passives
and antipassives

23.1 Topic and pivot

Much linguistic work focuses on 'sentence' as a prime unit. But linguistics purports to examine how people use language, and no one speaks in a sequence of
self-contained sentences. Typically, a discourse can be divided into a number
of segments, whose (full or partial) clauses are linked together through a
shared topic.

In the great majority of instances, the topic is a predicate argument, which
recurs in each clause from that discourse segment. Just occasionally, the topic
may be a repeated predicate, such as *likes* in *John likes Mary and Mary likes
Tom and Tom likes Jane and Jane likes Fred, and Fred likes Susan, but Susan
can't stand Tom.*

There may be overlap between two topics which are arguments. For
example, there may be twenty or so clauses with 'the giant' as topic and then a
dozen with 'the dwarf' as topic, linked by:

(1)   (a) ... The giant destroyed the castle on the hill
      (b) Then he came down into the valley
      (c) There he met a dwarf doing good works
      (d) The dwarf turned the giant to stone
      (e) Then the dwarf climbed the mountain
      (f) He gave succour to the people from the castle...

'The giant'—shown by a single underline—was topic for a long sequence of
clauses finishing with (1a-d); it is indicated just by anaphoric *he* in (1b–c).
Then 'the dwarf'—marked with a double underline—takes over as topic for a
lengthy sequence of clauses commencing with (1c–f), and it is indicated just
by anaphoric pronoun *he* in (1f). Clauses (1c–d) provide an overlap between
the two topics.

Sometimes a text has two topics which 'leapfrog' over each other, such as
'the youth' and 'the maiden' in:

(2) (a) The youth ran down the street
     (b) The maiden took off in pursuit
     (c) He turned into a small alley
     (d) She ran past the alley entrance, then looked back and espied it
     (e) He opened a door, went in, and turned the key
     (f) She noticed an open window and vaulted through it

The identity of the topic in a sentence may sometimes be evident only when the sentence is considered within the context of the discourse in which is appears. Consider the following discourse segment in English:

(3) (a) Mary$_S$ came out of the back door
     (b) Mary$_A$ saw John$_O$ lurking at the bottom of the garden
     (c) And she$_S$ was scared by his actions
     (d) And so she$_S$ went back into the house
     (e) and ø$_S$ locked the door

'Mary' is the topic argument (underlined) which recurs in each clause of (3a–e), and is in S or A subject function in each. It is realized by proper name *Mary* in (3a–b), by pronoun *she* in (3c–d), and by an empty S slot—shown as ø—in (3e).

Now consider a description of the same scenario from a different angle:

(4) (a) John$_A$ was surveying [the house]$_O$ with a view to breaking in
     (b) Mary$_A$ saw John$_O$ lurking at the bottom of the garden
     (c) He$_S$ was intimidated by the look she gave him
     (d) And so he$_S$ jumped over the back fence
     (e) and ø$_S$ ran away

'John' is topic argument (underlined) for the segment of discourse (4a–e). It is realized by proper name *John* in (4a–b), by pronoun *he* in (4c–d) and by an empty S slot in (4e). We can see that 'John' is in (A or S) subject for four of the clauses. In (4b) the focus is on 'Mary' which is in A slot, with the discourse topic, 'John', being here placed in O function.

Comparing the two segments of discourse, we can note that (3b) and (4b) are identical: *Mary$_A$ saw John$_O$ lurking at the bottom of the garden*. In (3b) *Mary* is the topic argument and in (4b) *John* is. That is, in English we may only be able to perceive what the topic is for a particular clause by examining it within the discourse segment in which it occurs.

Not every language is organized in the same way. Jarawara differs from English in that topic marking is grammaticalized. That is, for every clause a listener can tell what the topic is, even when the clause is quoted outside of its discourse context. It is useful to employ the term 'pivot' for such a fully grammaticalized topic.

In every clause, the final element of the predicate agrees in gender with the pivot argument. For a copula construction, it is always the copula subject (CS) which is pivot, and for an intransitive one it is always the intransitive subject (S), as in:

(5) Haimoto_S   kija   ne-mari
     Haimoto(m) be.feverish AUX-FAR.PAST.EYEWITNESS:m
     Haimoto was visibly feverish

(6) Jane_S   kija   na-maro
     Jane(f) be.feverish AUX-FAR.PAST.EYEWITNESS:f
     Jane was visibly feverish

Intransitive verb *kija* 'be feverish' requires a following auxiliary, *-na-*, to which affixes are attached. As mentioned in §1.7—see Figure 1.1—Jarawara has three past tenses ('immediate past', 'recent past', and 'far past') each of which is fused with a value from the evidentiality system 'eyewitness'/'non-eyewitness'. (5–6) describe something that happened more than two years in the past, which the narrator witnessed, and so employs far past eyewitness. This has masculine (m) form *-himari*, used in (5) since the pivot argument is a man's name, and feminine (f) form *-hamoro*, used in (6) since the pivot is here a woman's name. The combinations of auxiliary plus tense/evidentiality reduce in this environment, by regular phonological rules: *-na-himari* to *ne-mari* and *na-hamaro* to *na-maro*.

There are two transitive construction types:

- an A-construction (Ac), in which the A argument is pivot, and the final element of the predicate agrees with the A
- an O-construction (Oc), in which the O argument is pivot and the final element of the predicate agrees with the O

As mentioned in §5.7, feminine is the unmarked value of the Jarawara gender system. As one instance of this, all pronouns—whatever the sex of the person(s) they are referring to—take feminine agreement. Compare:

(7) (a: Ac) Haimoto_O   o-josiha
              Haimoto(m)   1sgA-order:f
              I ordered Haimoto (where 'I' is pivot)

     (b: Oc) Haimoto_O   o-josihi
              Haimoto(m)   1sgA-order:m
              I ordered Haimoto (where 'Haimoto' is pivot)

Transitive verb 'order' is here predicate-final. It is in feminine form, *-josiha*, in
(7a), agreeing in gender with the pronoun in A function, and in masculine
form, *-josihi*, in (7b), agreeing in gender with the masculine noun in O
function.

We can now examine the following segment of discourse from a narrative
which village chief Okomobi recorded concerning a trip with his brother
Haimoto up the Ituxi river (a tributary of the Purús, itself a major tributary of
the Amazon):

(8) (a) $\underline{\text{Haimoto}}_S$ kija   ne-mari
          Haimoto(m) be.feverish AUX-FAR.PAST.EYEWITNESS:m
          Haimoto was visibly feverish

    (b) $\underline{\text{Haimoto}}_A$ [jama   kome]$_O$ awe
          Haimoto(m)   thing(f) fever:f   feel:m
          Haimoto felt the fever (in fact, he had a bout of malaria)

    (c) $\underline{\emptyset}_O$ o-josihi
          [Haimoto(m)]   1sgA-order:m
          I ordered him (to go back down the river to get medical attention)

    (d) $\underline{\emptyset}_S$ to-kisa-me-himari
          [Haimoto(m)]   AWAY-go.downstream-BACK-FAR.PAST.EYEWITNESS:m
          He was seen going back downstream

'Haimoto' is the pivot argument for all four clauses—it is in S function for
the intransitive clause (8a), in A function for the transitive A-construction
(8b)—as shown by masculine agreement on the verb—in O-function for the
transitive O-construction (8c)—again shown by masculine agreement—and
in S function again for the final intransitive clause (8d).

The important point here is that, in Jarawara, the pivot can be recognized
for each clause even when it is quoted outside a discourse context. (8b) is
marked as an A-construction by masculine gender agreement and there is
no question that the A argument ('Haimoto') is pivot. Similarly, masculine
gender agreement at the end of the predicate marks (8c) as an O-construction,
and the pivot is the O argument (which is again 'Haimoto') rather than the A
argument (1sg pronoun, shown by prefix *o-* to the verb, which would engender
feminine agreement).

This is in marked contrast with English. The sentence *Mary$_A$ saw John$_O$
lurking at the bottom of the garden* occurs as (3b) in discourse sequence (3) and
as (4b) in discourse segment (4). One cannot tell which of 'Mary' and 'John'
is topic without referring to the stretch of discourse in which the sentence
appears.

One of the main functions, for the grammar of any language, is to integrate together successive clauses of a discourse. A topic need only be stated, by a full NP, for the first clause in which it features. It may thereafter be shown just by a pronoun, as *she* is used for 'Mary' in (3c–d) and *he* for 'John' in (4c–d).

Most economical of all, a speaker may omit any statement of a topic from any clause, after the first, within its topic chain. For this to lead to efficient communication, a listener must be able to infer what is the topic and what its function is, for each clause. There must be some grammatical convention within the language to facilitate this.

In Jarawara, each clause is **pivot-specified**. That is, the identity and function of the pivot is inferable from the grammatical structure of the clause. In (8c), verbal prefix *o-* indicates 1sg A, which (like all pronouns) takes feminine agreement. But the end of the predicate shows masculine gender, indicating that this must be an O-construction—that the O argument is masculine and is the pivot. This must be the man's name *Haimoto*, stated as pivot in the previous two clauses but ellipsed from (8c). The argument in pivot function (an A NP in an A-construction and an O NP in an O-construction) is typically omitted, unless the clause is initial in a pivot chain.

Omission is optional. *Haimoto* could have been omitted from (8b)—since it is stated in (8a)—but is included there. From their knowledge of the world and of the structure of their language, the Jarawara know that *jama kome* 'fever', which is feminine, can only be in O function for verb *-awa-* 'feel, see'. Since the predicate shows masculine gender, this must be an A-construction with the pivot being *Haimoto*, in A function.

(Note that in Jarawara the 3sg pronoun has zero realization, there being nothing like *he* and *she* in English. Note also that if A and O arguments have the same gender, there can be a measure of indeterminacy in parsing, with pragmatic clues being resorted to. Discourse segment (8) was chosen for exemplification partly in view of its gender contrast.)

Rather than a strong pivot specification for each clause, as in Jarawara, other languages employ a **pivot condition** which will motivate and control clause combination and omission of a repeated topic argument.

English works in terms of an **S/A pivot condition**. What this means is that, if an S or A slot is left blank in any clause, then the omitted argument is understood to be identical with the S or A argument of the previous clause. This is 'Mary' for (3e)—it was Mary who locked the door—and 'John' for (4e)—it was John who ran away. But consider what the interpretation would be if (4c–d) were omitted so that (4e) followed directly after (4b), giving *Mary$_A$ saw John$_O$ lurking at the bottom of the garden and ø$_S$ ran away*. In this instance, the omitted S argument of *and ø$_S$ ran away* would be inferred to be identical with the A argument of the previous clause, *Mary$_A$ saw John$_O$ lurking at the bottom of the garden*. That is, it would then be understood that it was Mary who ran away.

For a discourse segment where 'John' is pivot, one can say:

(9)   (a)   John$_S$ went into the forest
      (b)   and ø$_A$ shot [a jaguar]$_O$

Since 'John' is in pivot function for each clause (S in the first, A in the second), statement of it can be omitted from (9b).

If a topic is in O function in one clause of a topic sequence then it may be shown just by a pronoun (there are few syntactic conditions on the use of pronouns in English) but may not be omitted, since it is not in one of the allowed pivot functions, A or S. Suppose that following after (9a) we have [*and a jaguar*]$_A$ *ate John$_O$*. 'John' is here in a non-pivot function, O, for the second clause and cannot be omitted. That is, one cannot say **John$_S$ went into the forest and [a jaguar]$_A$ate ø$_O$*.

English has a grammatical device for dealing with such a situation. The passive derivation applies, putting the underlying O argument into derived S function, and placing the erstwhile A argument into peripheral function (from which it can be omitted). Thus, *John$_S$ was eaten (by a jaguar)*. We can link this to (9a) and omit *John* from the second clause since the S/A pivot condition is now met:

(10)   (a)   John$_S$ went into the forest
      (b)   and ø$_S$ was eaten (by a jaguar)

One function of the passive derivation in English is to 'feed' its S/A syntactic pivot.

A number of languages—especially some with an ergative profile (see §3.9)—work in terms of an **S/O pivot condition**. This means that if an S or O slot is left blank in any clause, then the omitted argument is understood to be identical with the S or O argument of the previous clause. Consider the following clause sequence in Dyirbal:

(11)   (a)   yara-ø$_O$ yibi-ŋgu$_A$ bura-n
            man-ABSOLUTIVE   woman-ERGATIVE   see-PAST
            The woman saw the man

      (b)   ø$_S$ juda-ñu
            [man]   run.away-PAST
            (and) the man ran away

There is a further example of an S/O pivot chain in Dyirbal at (40–2) in §25.6.

In English, if one hears *The woman saw the man and ø ran away*, it is understood—in terms of English's S/A pivot—to be the woman who ran away. But the equivalent pair of sentences in Dyirbal, (11a/b), is understood to mean that the man ran away. The zero (ø) S element in (11b) is taken to be identical to the O argument in (11a).

Just as a language with an S/A pivot may employ a passive derivation to put an underlying O argument into derived S function, thereby 'feeding' the pivot, so may a language with an S/O pivot include an antipassive derivation, with similar 'feeding' function. Antipassive puts an underlying A argument into derived S function, and makes the original O into a peripheral constituent (which may be omitted). The antipassive in Dyirbal, and its role in creating a pivot chain, were exemplified in §§3.20–21.

Yidiñ, which is Dyirbal's northern neighbour (but not a close genetic relative), has an S/O pivot constraint on the formation of subordinate clauses. The argument common to main clause and relative clause—see Chapter 17—must be in S or O function in each of the clauses.

Suppose that we wanted to create a construction in which the main clause is (12) and the relative clause is based on (13):

(12) ŋayu$_A$ [yiŋu   bama-ø]$_O$ banji-ili-ñu
      1sg   THIS:ABSOLUTIVE person-ABSOLUTIVE   find-GOING-PAST
      I went and found these people

(13) [yiñju-uŋ   bama-al]$_A$ mayi-ø$_O$ jula-al
      THIS-ERGATIVE   person-ERGATIVE   vegetable-ABSOLUTIVE   dig-PAST
      These people dug up vegetables (i.e. potatoes)

The common argument is 'these people', which is in a correct pivot function, O, in (12) but in A, a non-pivot function, in (13). What we must do is derive the antipassive version of (13). This involves putting the underlying A (which was in ergative case) into S function (shown by absolutive case, with ø realization), marking the underlying O with—in this instance—locative case, and adding the antipassive derivational suffix -*Vji*- to the verb, between root and tense inflection:

(13ap) [yiŋu   bama-ø]$_S$ mayi-i
        THIS:ABSOLUTIVE person-ABSOLUTIVE   vegetable-LOCATIVE
        jula-aji-ñu
        dig-ANTIPASSIVE-PAST

(12) can then be combined with (13ap) in one complex sentence, replacing the past tense inflection, -*ñu*, on (13ap) with relative clause inflection, -*ñuun* (Dixon 1977a: 278–9):

(14) ŋayu$_A$ [yiŋu   bama-ø]$_O$ banji-ili-ñu
      1sg   THIS:ABSOLUTIVE person-ABSOLUTIVE find-GOING-PAST
      [mayi-i   jula-aji-ñuun]$_{RELATIVE.CLAUSE}$
      vegetable-LOCATIVE   dig-ANTIPASSIVE-RELATIVE.CLAUSE
      I went and found these people who were digging up vegetables

Pivot constraints have a different profile for every language in which they occur. In Yidiñ, the common argument linking relative and main clause must be in S or O surface function in each clause. But for coordination of clauses this language employs a mixed strategy. It works in terms of an S/O pivot if the topic argument is a noun and an S/A pivot if it is a pronoun. This mirrors the fact that nouns inflect on an ergative pattern and pronouns on an accusative one.

In Dyirbal, a relative clause construction requires that the common argument be in S or O surface function within the relative clause, but it can be in almost any function within the main clauses (S, A, O, dative, instrumental, or locative). However, in Dyirbal all coordination of clauses to make one sentence utilizes an S/O pivot—the repeated argument must be in S or O function in each clause, whether it is a noun or a pronoun. (This applies even though, like Yidiñ, nouns show an ergative and pronouns an accusative morphology. The reason for this difference is suggested in §28.2.5.)

In comparison, the S/A pivot in English has a relatively weak nature. It does not restrict coordination of clauses (since pronouns can occur in any function), only the omission of a repeated argument.

Some languages lack any pivot specification in their grammar. If an argument is left unstated, its identity has to be inferred from common sense or pragmatic knowledge. If, in such a language, one heard [*The lion*]$_A$ *bit* [*the zebra*]$_O$ *and then ø$_S$ slept peacefully*, one would suppose that it was the lion who slept peacefully. And if one heard [*The lion*]$_A$ *bit* [*the zebra*]$_O$ *and then ø$_S$ died*, it would be fair conjecture that it must be the zebra who died. However, in English the S/A pivot requires one to understand that it was the lion who slept peacefully, in the first sentence, and who died, in the second (however counterintuitive this might be). And for a language with Dyirbal with an S/O pivot for coordination, it would have to be the zebra who slept peacefully (albeit that this is rather surprising) and who died.

There are other grammatical devices for integrating clauses together within a discourse, many of them language-particular. One recurrent method is 'switch-reference marking', indicating whether a certain clause has the same or different subject (A or S) as the following one. A straightforward example can be quoted from Manambu (Ndu family; Papua New Guinea; Aikhenvald, personal communication, and see 2008a: 452–6):

(15)   (a) a-di   jǝb   kur-ku
           THAT-PL   design   make-COMPLETIVE:SAME.SUBJECT
           ata   ya:d
           THEN   go:3sg.m
           After he had made these designs, he [*same* he] went off

       (b) a-di   jǝb   kur-de-k
           THAT-PL   design   make-3sg.m-COMPLETIVE:DIFFERENT.SUBJECT
           ata   ya:d
           THEN   go:3sg.m
           After he had made these designs, he [*different* he] went off

Preceding the completive different subject suffix, in (15b) there is specification of what the subject of this clause actually is, 3sg masculine. No such element is required in (15a) since the subject is stated to be the same as that of the following clause, shown on the verb 'go'.

Interestingly, 'switch' systems along these lines—of which there are many variants, occurring predominantly in New Guinea, Australia, and the Americas—always operate on an S/A basis. No language has yet been encountered with 'switch-S/O' marking. Such a system may well be discovered, as more languages are described in detail.

We have outlined the 'pivot-feeding' functions of passive and antipassive. The remainder of the chapter looks at these syntactic derivations in fair detail, examining their forms, functions, and meanings.

23.2 Passives and antipassives

In Classical Greek, the grammatical category {active, middle, passive} was referred to as *diathesis* 'state, disposition, function'. The modern label 'voice' for an {active, passive} system comes from a shift in meaning of one sense of *vox* 'voice' in Latin 'the "form" of a word (that is, what it "sounded" like) as opposed to its "meaning"' (Lyons 1968: 371–2). Since active and passive were in Latin shown by inflectional forms of the verb, voice was taken to be a category of the verb. Nowadays, it is generally regarded as relating to the clause.

Passive and active can be considered as independent clause types. Or, as here, passive may be looked upon as a syntactic derivation from active, which is the basic, unmarked construction type. Every—or almost every—verb may occur in an active clause, whereas there are limitations on the verbs that may enter into a passive construction.

An active/passive distinction is typically found in languages of nominative/accusative mien. But there are also languages whose grammar is organized on an absolutive/ergative principle. In 1969, William H. Jacobsen, Jr. gave a conference presentation: 'The analog of the passive-transformation in ergative-type languages' (published in 1985). A name for this 'analog' soon came into general use—'antipassive'.

I take 'voice' as covering active, passive, and antipassive (and also 'middle', in Classical Greek and a few more languages; see Sources and Notes to Chapter 22). A voice contrast may be {active/passive} or {active/antipassive} or {active/passive/antipassive} or {active/middle/passive}. We must also note that many languages have no system of voice at all.

Diverse linguists extend the term 'voice' in various (and different) ways. It may be employed for valency-increasing derivations such as applicative and causative, for impersonal constructions (for example, *One would sympathize with him* in English), for argument-focusing constructions in Philippines languages and for inverse systems in Athapaskan, Algonquian, and other languages, for ambitransitive verbs, and even for 'promotion to subject' constructions such as *These umbrellas are selling fast* in English (see Dixon 1991a: 322–35; 2005a: 446–8).

We can repeat, from §3.20, the four basic characteristics of a canonical passive derivation:

Canonical passive derivation (applying to a transitive clause)

(a) Applies to an underlying transitive clause and forms a derived intransitive.
(b) The underlying O becomes S of the passive.
(c) The underlying A goes into a peripheral function, being marked by a non-core case, adposition, etc.; this argument can be omitted, although there is always the option of including it.
(d) There is some explicit (that is, non-zero) formal marking of a passive construction; this can be a morphological process applying to the verb, or a periphrastic verbal construction (as in English, where it involves auxiliary verb *be*, plus suffix *-en* or *-ed* on the verb).

There is a variant on the canonical passive in which the underlying A is obligatorily omitted, Such 'agentless passives' are discussed in §23.2.6.

In English (and in some other languages), it is important to distinguish between a passive construction, as in (16a) and a copula construction where the copula complement is a derived adjective (with the same form as a passive participle), as in (16b).

(16)   (a) [The box]$_S$ was broken (by the gardener)
         (b) [The box]$_{CS}$ is [broken]$_{CC}$

The fact that *broken* is an adjective in (16b) can be shown as follows:

   (i)   It can be modified by *very*, *quite*, or *rather*, as in *The box is rather broken.*
   (ii) It can be coordinated with another adjective, as in *The box is dirty and broken.*
   (iii) It can be negated with prefix *un-* (or *dis-*, etc.); for example, *The box is unbroken.*

None of these properties applies to *broken* in the passive construction (16a).
   Consider a similar pair of sentences:

(17)   (a) John$_S$ was interested (by the news that his ex-wife had remarried)
         (b) John$_{CS}$ is [interested in gardening]$_{CC}$

Properties (i–iii) again apply for *interested* as an adjective in (17b) but not as a passive participle in (17a). Note also that the passive construction may include a *by*-phrase (corresponding to the subject NP of the active, [*The news that his ex-wife had remarried*]$_A$ *interested John*$_O$.) *Interested (in)* is one of a group of adjectives which may be followed by a prepositional phrase; they include *terrified (of)*, *pleased (with* or *about)*, *surprised (at)*. The point to note is that the passive construction, (17a), employs *by* while in the copula construction, (17b), a different preposition is used, *in*. (There are in fact a couple of adjectives which take *by*, including *impressed (by)*; but then criteria (i–iii) serve to distinguish passive participle and adjective.)

   A passive construction, such as (16a) or (17a), is most likely to describe some particular activity or state of mind. In contrast, copula constructions, such as (16b) and (17b), more often describe a general state. We do of course encounter short sentences—such as *The box was broken* or *John was interested*—which are ambiguous between passive and copula analyses when quoted out of context. But within their context of utterance—and every sentence should be so considered—ambiguity is likely to disappear.

   Some linguists have described constructions like (16b) and (17b) as 'stative passives'. This obscures the fundamental difference between such copula-plus-derived-adjective clauses and true passives. And it draws attention to an important precept in grammatical analysis—the need to clearly distinguish between morphological derivations such as nominalizations, and forms involved in syntactic derivations such as passives.

   It may be surprising to people mainly familiar with the languages of Europe to learn that a canonical passive derivation is relatively rare in other areas. It appears to occur in little more than a quarter of languages worldwide.

We can now repeat, again from §3.20, the four basic characteristics of a canonical antipassive derivation:

Canonical antipassive derivation (applying to a transitive clause)

  (a) Applies to an underlying transitive clause and forms a derived intransitive.
  (b) The underlying A becomes S of the antipassive.
  (c) The underlying O goes into a peripheral function, being marked by a non-core case, adposition, etc.; this argument can be omitted, although there is always the option of including it.
  (d) There is some explicit formal marking of an antipassive construction (similar possibilities as for passive).

There is a variant on the canonical antipassive in which the underlying O is obligatorily omitted, Such 'patientless antipassives' are discussed in §23.2.6.

Canonical antipassives have thus far been reported for just a few dozen languages. A number of them—Eskimo, and some from the Mayan family—include in their grammars both passive and antipassive derivations. Many languages have neither.

The label 'antipassive' is in some ways misleading, but it is now so well established that an attempt to replace it would be counter-productive. The 'anti' implies that antipassive is the opposite of passive. Indeed, looking just at their syntactic statements, the two derivations appear to be parallel, save that A and O are interchanged. However, we shall see below that there are significant differences in function and meaning.

Table 22.2 in §22.5.1 summarizes 'what happens to transitive arguments' in passive, agentless passive, antipassive, patientless antipassive, reflexive, and reciprocal derivations. Although each of these has a basic intransitivizing effect, their grammatical and semantic roles are quite diverse. Reflexive indicates coreference of arguments within a single clause, and reciprocal has similar function with respect to a number of underlying clauses, coded into one surface structure. Passive may indicate the result of some action, and/or it may highlight the underlying O and/or background the underlying A. Antipassive focuses on the action itself, and the agent who is controlling it. In many languages, antipassive and passive carry aspectual nuances, of contrasting kinds. Both passive and antipassive may play a role in the integration of discourse, by feeding a pivot constraint (but note that not all passives and antipassives include feeding among their roster of functions).

Passive and antipassive can have a disambiguating function. In Quiché (Mayan, Guatemala; Mondloch 1978), a clause may be ambiguous if both

A and O are third person and of the same number, in terms of cross-referencing on the verb. This is exemplified in (18) and (19).

(18) š-ø-u:-kuna-x   [ri: ačih] [ri: išoq]
      COMPLETIVE-3sgO-3sgA-cure-ACTIVE   THE man   THE woman
      Either The woman cured the man *or* The man cured the woman

(19) xačin š-ø-u:-kuna-x   [ri: ačih]?
      WHO   COMPLETIVE-3sgO-3sgA-cure-ACTIVE   THE man
      Either Who cured the man? *or* Who did the man cure?

Sentence (18) is, literally 'he/she cured him/her the-man the-woman' and (19) is 'he/she cured him/her who the-man'. Constituent order is fairly fluid and cannot be relied upon for disambiguation. What a speaker of Quiché may do is employ antipassive or passive voice; each of these ensures that underlying A and O are treated in distinct ways. Only one argument will be cross-referenced on the verb—underlying O for passive and underlying A for antipassive—with the other being accorded an oblique marking—the demoted A in a passive by prepositional *-umal* 'by', and the demoted O in an antipassive by *če:* 'for'. The passive version of (18) is (20) and the antipassive version of (19) is (21). Both are unambiguous.

(20) š-ø-kuna-š   [ri: ačih]ₛ
      COMPLETIVE-3sgS-cure-PASSIVE   THE man
          [r-umal ri: išoq]
          3sg-BY   THE woman
      The man was cured by the woman

(21) xačinₛ š-ø-kuna-n   [če: ri: ačih]
      WHO   COMPLETIVE-3sgS-cure-ANTIPASSIVE   FOR:HIM THE man
      Who cured (for) the man?

Justification must of course be provided for each analytic decision, such as that passive and antipassive derive intransitive stems. There may be various kinds of criteria. Looking again at the Quiché examples, a transitive verb must include two bound pronominal prefixes, for O and A arguments, as in (18) and (19). In contrast, a (simple or derived) intransitive verb bears a single pronominal prefix, for the S argument, as in (20) and (21).

Similar argumentation applies for another Mayan language, Tzotzil (Robinson 1999; Haviland 1981). A further criterion for Tzotzil is that an intransitive verb is obligatorily marked by suffix *-uk* when used with an auxiliary, as in (22), whereas *-uk* is not included with a transitive verb, as in (23). The auxiliary here is *-tal* 'coming'.

(22) ch-tal   k'opoj-uk-ø
      INCOMPLETE-coming   speak-INTRANSITIVE-3.S
      He's coming to talk

(23) ch-tal   x-mil-ø
      INCOMPLETE-coming   3.A-kill-3.O
      He's coming to kill him

Passive requires -uk when used with an auxiliary, confirming its intransitive status:

(24) ch-tal   mil-e-uk-ø
      INCOMPLETE-coming   kill-PASSIVE-INTRANSITIVE-3.S
      He's coming to be killed

The underlying A argument could be included in (24)—as in any passive—marked by relational noun -u'un 'for, by virtue of' to show that it is now in peripheral function.

   Another criterion is transitivity agreement. Dyirbal has a type of asymmetrical serial verb construction, where one of a small class of verbs with adverbial-type meaning is combined with some other verb (Dixon 2006a, b). The two verbs must take the same inflection and also share the same transitivity value. Suppose one wanted to combine adverbial-type verb *gurrma-y* 'take a long time doing something', which is intransitive, and *nudi-l* 'cut', which is transitive. A derivation has to be applied to one of the verbs, so that it takes on the same transitivity value as the other. Either the intransitive verb can be made transitive (by an applicative-type derivation) or the transitive verb, *nudi-l*, can be intransitivized through the antipassive derivation, which inserts suffix -*ŋa*- between root and inflection, as in:

(25) ŋaja$_S$ [gurrma-ñu   nudil-ŋa-ñu]$_{SERIAL\ VERB}$
      1sg   take.a.long.time-PAST cut-ANTIPASSIVE-PAST
      I was cutting for a long time

The occurrence of antipassive form *nudil-ŋa-ñu* in a serial verb construction with intransitive *gurrma-ñu* shows that the antipassive is a derived intransitive.

23.2.1 Types of marking

Active is always the unmarked member of a voice system. There is seldom any special marking for active, but there always is for other voice possibilities. Passive and antipassive can be shown by a morphological process applying to the verb—typically affixation. Passive may also be shown by an auxiliary construction, or by a serial verb construction (these mechanisms have not yet been reported for a canonical antipassive).

Verbal affixation is the most common method for marking a clause as passive. The majority of examples involve a derivational suffix which comes after the root and is followed by an appropriate inflection. Examples of this presented so far are:

- antipassive *-Vji-* in Yidiñ, in (13ap), followed by past tense inflection
- passive *-e-* in Tzotzil, in (24), followed by intransitive suffix *-ul* and a bound pronoun indicating the S argument (in (24) this has zero realization for 3sg but with other person/number combinations it would have non-zero form)
- antipassive *-ŋa-* in Dyirbal, in (25), also followed by past tense inflection

In (20) and (21), from Quiché, we find passive *-š* and antipassive *-n* as the only suffixes on the verb. However, generally in Mayan languages voice suffixes may be followed by a 'mood or mode' marker (see, for example, Dayley 1981; England 1983: 172–4).

Passive in Korean (Sohn 1994: 300–9, 359) is shown by a verbal suffix which can be followed by a variety of other suffixes. Compare the active sentence in (26a) with the passive in (26b):

(26) (a) kay-ka$_A$ apeci-lul$_O$ mwul-ess-ta
          dog-NOMINATIVE father-ACCUSATIVE bite-PAST-DECLARATIVE
          A dog bit my father

      (b) apeci-ka$_S$ kay-hanthey mwul-li-si-ess-ta
          father-NOMINATIVE dog-BY   bite-PASSIVE-SH-PAST-DEC
          My father was bitten by a dog

'SH' is the 'subject honorific', *-(u)si-*, which is used when the referent of the subject is 'one or more adults who deserve the speaker's deference, such as a social or familiar superior'. It is used in (26b) by virtue of the subject being 'father' but is not required in (26a) where the subject is 'dog'.

Amharic (Amberber 2002: 9) is one of a relatively small number of languages which marks a passive with a verbal prefix, here *t(ə)-*. Compare active in (27a) with passive in (27b):

(27) (a) Aster$_A$ dinggay-u-n$_O$ wərəwwər-əčč
          Aster   stone-DEFINITE-ACCUSATIVE throw:PERFECT-3:f
          Aster threw the stone

(b) dinggay-u$_S$ (bə-Aster) tə-wərəwwər-ə
     stone-DEFINITE   BY-Aster   PASSIVE-throw:PERFECT-3:m
     The stone was thrown (by Aster)

The final suffix on the verb indicates the gender of the (A or S) subject—feminine -əčč for Aster in (27a) and masculine -ə for 'stone' as subject in (27b).

Many grammatical elements have several functions. §22.5.1 mentioned that verbal prefix $t(ə)$- in Amharic marks both passive and reflexive, and that derivational suffix -(yi)rriy- ~ -marriy- in Dyirbal is used for reflexive and also a second type of antipassive (see (42c) in §23.2.5). Suffix -Vji- in Yidiñ covers reflexive and antipassive while—as exemplified in §22.5.1—the scope of -ji- in Kuku-Yalanji includes reflexive, passive, and antipassive.

Somewhat surprisingly, in a number of languages the verbal marking for passive is homonymous with that for causative. For example, in Sonrai (or Songhai; Shopen and Konaré 1970: 238) verbal suffix -ndi can mark either causative or agentless passive on the same verb, and a verb can take two tokens of -ndi, one causative and one agentless passive, so that ŋa-ndi-ndi is literally '[the rice] was made to be eaten [by someone: causee] [by someone: causer]'. Further examples are discussed in §24.6.2.

Another way of marking a passive is through an auxiliary construction, such as be- ...-en in English. In every instance, the form used as a passive auxiliary has some other function in the language. It is often a copula 'be' or 'become' or a verb such as 'get' or 'receive'. Punjabi uses 'go' (Bhatia 1993: 234–6).

Auxiliary marking for passive is common in modern Indo-European languages (though not in the classical tongues) and rather rare elsewhere. An interesting instance comes from the Dravidian language Tamil (Lehmann 1993: 218–19; Asher 1985: 151–2), where the verb paṭu 'experience, suffer, undergo' functions as passive auxiliary. Compare the active sentence in (28a) with passive in (28b):

(28) (a) appaa$_A$ Kumaar-ai$_O$ aṭi-tt-aan̲
           father:NOMINATIVE   Kumar-ACCUSATIVE beat-PAST-3sgm
           Father beat Kumar

      (b) Kumaar$_S$ apaa·v-aal   aṭi·kk-a·p
           Kumar:NOMINATIVE   father-INSTRUMENTAL beat-INFINITIVE
               paṭ-ṭ-aan̲
               AUXILIARY('experience')-PAST-3sgm
           Kumar was beaten by father

Such a passive construction appears in the oldest written records for Tamil (from more than two thousand years ago) and is maintained in the literary language but is scarcely encountered in colloquial Tamil today.

Just a few languages create a passive through a serial verb construction. This involves two (or more) verbs, each of which could occur on its own. When combined, the verbs make up a single predicate, which describes a single action (see (b) in §3.4, and §18.6.1). In Kristang (a Portuguese-based creole spoken in Malacca, Malaysia) verb *toka* means 'touch' when used alone, but signals passive when employed as first element in an asymmetrical serial verb construction (Baxter 1988: 211; Aikhenvald 2006: 26):

(29) [aké   pesi]$_S$ ja   [toka   kumi]$_{SERIAL.VERB}$
      THAT fish   PERFECT   touch eat
      [di   gatu]
      SOURCE   cat
      The fish got eaten by the cat

23.2.2 Which arguments may become S

Passive and antipassive place an argument in S function. What are the possible arguments which this can apply to? For antipassive it is always underlying A which goes into surface S. For passive, most languages only permit underlying O to be placed in surface S function. This applies to, among many others, Rumanian, Marathi, Turkish, Tamil, Kannada, Swahili, Korean, and Evenki.

But some languages do allow wider possibilities. Consider the following active sentence in New Zealand Maori (Bauer 1993: 402–3):

(30) i   paatai [te   kaiako]$_A$ [i   te   paatai]$_O$
      PAST ask   THE   teacher   OBJECT THE question
      [ki   te   tamaiti]
      TO   THE child
      The teacher asked a question of (lit. to) the child

A regular passive marks the verb with suffix -*tia*, places the original O NP into S function, and moves the erstwhile A NP into peripheral function, marked by preposition *e*:

(31) i   paatai-tia   [e   te   kaiako] [he paatai]$_S$
      PAST ask-PASSIVE BY   THE teacher   A   question
      [ki   te   tamaiti]
      TO   THE child
      A question was asked by the teacher of (lit. to) the child

The indirect object 'the child' was marked by preposition *ki* 'to' in (30) and retained in the same form in (31). However, a further possibility is to place the indirect object into S function:

(32) i   paatai-tia   [te   tamaiti]ₛ [ki te   paatai]
      PAST ask-PASSIVE   THE child   TO THE question
      [e   te   kaiako]
      BY THE teacher
      The child was asked (to) a question by the teacher

Interestingly, (32) appears to be—like (31)—an intransitive clause. The under-lying A argument, 'the teacher' is again marked by preposition *e* 'by' and the original O, 'the question', which appeared with O-function marker *i* in the active sentence (30), is now marked by preposition *ki* 'to'.

(Note that since the syntactic function of each phrase in Maori is indicated by an initial marker—or the lack of one—the order of phrases is not fixed. The alternation between *te* 'the' and *he* 'a' with noun *paatai* 'question' is as given by Bauer's consultants.)

In some languages there can be two NPs which each have the surface characteristics of 'object'. A general criterion for an NP being in O function is that it can become passive subject. In Tariana (Arawak, Brazil) a clause may include two NPs which can each 'take the topical non-subject marker *-nuku* and, if expressed with a personal pronoun, the non-subject case *-na*'. But only one may be the 'target' of a passive and it is this which is thus shown to be the true O argument (Aikhenvald 2003: 511).

But what might happen if an indirect object could be placed in subject func-tion within a passive construction, the A moved into a peripheral function, but the original O argument left as is? Would not the passive then be transitive, since it has subject and object? To investigate this question we need look no further than English.

There are two constructions available in English for 'extended transitive' (or 'ditransitive') verbs such as *give*, *show*, and *tell*, illustrated by:

(33)   Fredₐ showed [the million dollar picture]ₒ [to Tom]

(34)   Fredₐ showed Tomₒ [the million dollar picture]

In (33), *the million dollar picture* is O argument and can be placed in S function in a passive:

(33p) [The million dollar picture]ₛ was shown [to Tom] ([by Fred])

The prepositional NP *to Tom* is unaffected by the passive derivation. Note that *Tom* from (33) cannot be passivized. That is, one cannot say **Tom was shown the million dollar picture to by Fred.*

Grammarians of English have been much exercised concerning analysis of a sentence such as (34). Plainly, *Tom* has moved into position immediately after the verb and is now the O argument. *The million dollar picture* follows Tom. Is it a second object (and if so what would this mean)? Or is it a peripheral NP which just does not have any prepositional marking? Note that *Tom* from (34) can become S in a passive:

(34p)   Tom$_S$was shown [the million dollar picture] ([by Fred])

If *the million dollar picture* is some kind of object in (34) then it would also be one in (34p). This would mean that (34p) has subject and object arguments and is, presumably, transitive.

Now if *the million dollar picture* in (34) were a type of object then this should passivize from (34), giving:

(34pp)   ?[The million dollar picture] was shown Tom by Fred

Native speakers of English disagree concerning the acceptability of a sentence such as (34pp); some accept and others reject it. (Note that (34pp) differs from (33p) simply by the omission of *to* from before *Tom*.)

There are the following alternative analyses:

- In (34) *the million dollar picture* is a peripheral argument. It follows that (34p) is intransitive and (34pp) should be unacceptable.
- Sentence (34) has two O arguments, *Tom* and *the million dollar picture*, each of which can be passivized. We would then infer that (34pp) should be an acceptable sentence and that both it and (34p) retain one object and must thus be considered transitive. (They would be exceptions to the general statement that a passive construction should be intransitive.)

This provides an example of an analytical problem for which two solutions are possible. Which should be preferred may hinge on the acceptability of (34pp). Those native speakers of English who consider this sentence acceptable and those who reject it might, as a consequence, opt for different analyses. (Or there may be further factors which could be brought into play.)

A number of S = A ambitransitive verbs in English may occur with a peripheral argument. For example:

(35)   (a) [The dirty Martians]$_S$ have eaten [off this plate]
       (b) [The dirty Martians]$_A$ have eaten gruel$_O$ [off this plate]

If someone were to be offered such a plate, and was horrified by it, they might express indignation by placing *this plate* from (35a) into passive subject function:

(35) (a-p)   [This plate] has been eaten off ([by the dirty Martians])

However, it is not possible to passivize *this plate* from (35b). That is, one cannot say **This plate had been eaten gruel off (by the dirty Martians)*. The principle appears to be: an NP marked by a preposition can become passive S only if there is no O NP in the sentence. This does, of course, ensure that all of this class of passives are intransitive. (See also (46–7) in §23.2.6.)

23.2.3 Argument moved out of the core

The underlying A argument from a passive and the underlying O from an antipassive are placed in peripheral function, marked with a suitable case or adposition (and may be omitted). The way in which they are marked shows considerable variation.

Underlying A for a passive is marked by instrumental case in Tamil and in Sinhala—illustrated in (28b) and (37b). Other possibilities include locative and genitive; see Keenan (1985: 262) and Keenan and Dryer (2007: 343–5). When the erstwhile A argument is included in a passive construction in Evenki (Tungusic, Russia; Nedjalkov 1997: 219) it is generally marked with dative case but nowadays occasionally with instrumental, under the influence of Russian. Fleisch (2005) provides a survey of 'agent phrases in Bantu languages'. He shows that, although Bantu languages exhibit considerable homogeneity in the way passive is marked on the verb, they vary a great deal in the treatment of underlying A; it may be marked as comitative, locative, instrumental, or by means of a copula (literally 'the snake is being seen, it is the woman' for 'the snake is being seen by the woman').

Similar peripheral cases are used to mark the underlying O in an antipassive. Yidiñ (Dixon 1977a: 110–11) may always use dative, but the lower the referent of the NP is on the animacy scale, the more likely it is to instead employ locative, as it does for 'vegetable' in (13ap). Other Australian languages employ instrumental, dative, purposive, locative, perlative (Dixon 2002: 539). West Greenlandic (Eskimo; Fortescue 1984: 212, 265) uses ablative.

Many languages employ adpositions. Marker *e* 'by' in Maori—illustrated in (31–2)—appears to be used only for passive agent. But in most languages such a marker has a wide range of other functions. Prepositional element *bə-* in Amharic not only marks passive agent—as in (27b)—but is also used for instrument/means ('by a knife'), location of an event ('at the market'), time ('at two o'clock') and with malefactive sense ('(they judged) against him'). In Kristang, illustrated in (29), passive agent is shown by the 'source' preposition. Rumanian uses preposition *de* 'by, from, of' or *de către*, which is literally 'by towards' (Mallinson 1986: 211–12), while Modern Greek utilizes preposition *apó* 'from, by', which requires the following noun to be in genitive case (Joseph and Philippaki-Warburton 1987: 128).

For the passive in Korean there are three ways of marking the underlying A argument. Particle *ey* is used if it is inanimate (for example, 'blown by the wind'), *eykey* or *hanthey*—as in (26b)—if animate, and *kkey* for honorific effect (for example, when referring to grandfather). 'Notice that the agentive particles are the same as dative, static locative and goal particles' (Sohn 1994: 242–3).

There are fewer examples of antipassives. In Päri (Western Nilotic, Sudan; Andersen 1988: 303) we find that the erstwhile O argument is marked by preposition *ki* which is also used for instrument, accompaniment ('(cook) the meat with oil'), space ('(far) from here'), time ('at night'), and fear ('(afraid) of the leopard').

23.2.4 Rationale

In many—but not all—instances, a main function of a passive derivation is to place the underlying O argument into derived S function, to assist the formation of a topic sequence (sometimes, an S/A grammatical pivot condition). Writing of English, Jespersen (1924: 168) explained: 'the passive turn may facilitate the connexion of one sentence with another: *He rose to speak and was listened to with enthusiasm by the great crowd present*.' This is further illustrated in (3c), (4c), and (10b) of §23.1. For Swahili, 'the passive is frequently a useful device to maintain continuity of grammatical subject both within and across sentence boundaries' (Whitely 1970: 403; see also Loogman 1965: 406–7).

In similar fashion, a major function of antipassive is to place the underlying A argument into derived S function in order to satisfy some S/O condition within the grammar. England (1988: 532) reports, for the Mayan language Mam, that 'the most purely syntactic' of the functions of antipassive is to put underlying A argument into surface S function 'which is used obligatorily for interrogation, negation, or focus of an A, for answering a question about an A, and to express certain temporal sequences in relative clauses formed on an A'. This is similar to the 'S/O pivot feeding' described for Yidiñ in (12–14) of §23.1 and for Dyirbal in (7–11) of §3.21.

Most typically, passive is found in languages with an accusative and antipassive in those with an ergative profile. But there are exceptions. And we noted in §23.1 that a number of languages from the Mayan and Eskimo genetic groups include both canonical passives and canonical antipassives. In Kuku-Yalanji, as illustrated in §22.5.1, verbal suffix *-ji* is used for both passive and antipassive (plus reflexive, etc.).

In a number of languages, passive and antipassive appear not to have a strong topic-feeding role. And even in those where they do, these syntactic derivations have several further functions. A pithy summary of the reason for 'passivizing a transitive verb' in Turkish is provided by Göksel and Kerslake (2005: 149): 'for purposes of topicalizing the direct object and suppressing the agent or perpetrator of the action denoted by the verb'.

If the O argument of a transitive clause is lower than the A argument on the nominal hierarchy (see §3.9, §13.5.4) then it is likely to be passivized and placed in focus function. One is more likely to hear *I was really annoyed by some dog's barking* than *Some dog's barking really annoyed me*. Passive may also be preferred if the referent of the O argument is someone or something better known than the referent of the A argument; for example *John Lennon was murdered by Mark David Chapman* (just about everyone knows John Lennon but scarcely anyone is familiar with the name of the person who murdered him).

There are other means for highlighting the reference of the O argument. Some grammars include an 'inverse system' where core arguments are cross-referenced on the verb in different fashion depending on whether the referent of the A argument is higher than that of the O on the nominal hierarchy (direct marking) or lower (inverse marking). Sochiapan Chinantec (Chinantec family, Mexico; Foris 2000: 270–82) has a system of inverse cross-referencing. As a consequence, the passive derivation is unusual in that it does not have— as a primary function—focussing on underlying O and placing it in derived S function. Instead 'the main function of Chinantec passives appears to be to background the subject [underlying A argument] because it is unimportant or unknown; sometimes it is used to purposely avoid specifying an agent. The passive is also the most productive strategy for encoding inanimate agents'.

Similar comments on 'backgrounding' the underlying A argument apply for passives in virtually all languages in which they occur. In fact, this is a major reason for employing a passive construction. And it explains why, although the canonical passive *can* include the original A (in peripheral function), more often than not it omits it. For Evenki, we read 'the agent in passive constructions is seldom expressed' (Nedjalkov 1997: 152), and for Modern Greek 'agent nominals corresponding to the active version may be expressed, though truncated passives without overt expression of the agent are preferred and are more frequent' (Joseph and Philippaki-Warburton 1987: 168). In English, agent phrases are included in less then 20 per cent of passive clauses overall, and in far less than that for colloquial speech.

Some of the reasons for employing a passive construction, and often also omitting statement of the 'agent phrase' (the original A argument), include the following.

(a) **When the identity of the agent is not known.**   If one hears *John was attacked last night*, the fact that an agent is not specified implies that the speaker does not know who did it. A policeman preparing a report on the incident might employ a more pedantic style and write *John Smith was attacked by person or persons unknown*, the last phrase making explicit what would normally be inferred from non-inclusion of an agent phrase.

(b) **When the identity of the agent is obvious.**   For example, *Mary was breastfed until she was six months old*; since no agent is specified we assume that it was Mary's mother. Another example is *The soldiers were confined to barracks for the remainder of the week*; the agent must be the only person able to issue such an order, their commanding officer.

In scientific publications use of the passive is de rigueur—to background the agent and give an appearance of total objectivity. One must say *An experiment was devised to test* ... rather than *We devised an experiment to test* ... In fact, this is simply a matter of style; it is clear who the agent is.

(c) **To conceal the identity of the agent.**   When the CEO of an advertising agency calls the staff together and says *I have been told that one of you has been selling some of our ideas to a competitor*, the CEO is taking care not to reveal the identify of the informer (see also §3.20).

Since the 'agent phrase' of a passive clause is an optional component, it may be omitted on purely grammatical grounds. These may be anaphoric, as in *John crept up on Mary with a loaded pistol. Next thing she was lying on the floor in a pool of blood, shot in the head* (sc. by John). Or they may be cataphoric, as in *After all the biscuits had been eaten* (sc. by Little Tommy), *Little Tommy crept back to bed*.

When they are included, agent phrases carry an important semantic load. Looking back at the discourse segments in §23.1, the agent phrase *by his actions* in (3c), *And she was scared by his actions*, is a necessary link in motivating the sequence of events.

In many languages, a passive construction is used to focus on the result of some activity (and its effect on the patient), paying little attention to who the agent may have been; for example *Mary has been shot*. In contrast, an antipassive focuses on the activity itself and the agent (referent of A argument) who is controlling it. There must be some patient (O argument) but their identity may be either obvious or unimportant. In Nez Perce (Sahaptian, Idaho; Rude 1982) an antipassive is typically used when the underlying O is 'indefinite, non-referential or plural'.

A Dyirbal myth tells how two brothers chop a rotten log (starting at opposite ends) to see if it contains any edible grubs. The narrator uses transitive verb *bañi-* 'chop' in an antipassive construction in which the underlying O argument is not included:

(36) (a) balagarra$_S$ bañil-ŋa-ñu
            3dual   chop-ANTIPASSIVE-PAST
            The two of them were chopping

The fact that an underlying O argument is not stated would lead a listener to infer that it is the default O for 'chop', i.e. *yugu* 'wood, timber, log'. Dative NP *yugu-gu* could have been included in (36a) but is not necessary.

Then the brothers do come across some grubs in the rotten log, and chop them out. Now a 'patient phrase' is included:

(36) (b) ø$_S$ bañil-ŋa-ñu   jambun-gu
            [3dual]   chop-ANTIPASSIVE-PAST   grub-DATIVE
            They were chopping out grubs

It is necessary to here specify what is being chopped out, but an antipassive construction is maintained—no S argument is stated for (36b) since it is understood to be the same as the preceding clause in discourse, (36a)—since the emphasis of the story is still on the brothers chopping. (Very soon, as they reach each other in the middle of the log, the elder brother chops the younger one, killing him.)

Antipassive may be used to satisfy some syntactic constraint (pivot feeding), or to focus on what the A argument is doing, or to avoid stating the O argument. An examination of 200 antipassive clauses in Dyirbal texts shows that about 65 per cent of them include a patient phrase, in dative case. (Compare this with canonical passives where—in virtually every language in which they occur—agent phrases are rather seldom included.) It would be interesting to obtain figures for canonical antipassives in other languages.

One factor determining whether a particular NP can become passive subject relates to its nature and reference. In the last chapter it was noted that neither a reflexive nor a reciprocal pronoun may become S in a passive construction. In order to be passivized, an argument must have independent reference and be affected by the activity. Bolinger (1977: 10) describes this most succinctly: 'We can say *George turned the pages* or *The pages were turned by George*; something happens to the pages in the process. But when we say *George turned the corner* we cannot say **The corner was turned by George*—the corner is not affected, it is only where George was at the time. On the other hand, if one were speaking of some kind of marathon or race or game in which a particular corner is thought of as an objective to be taken, then one might say *That corner hasn't been turned yet*. I can say *The stranger approached me* or *I was approached by the stranger* because I am thinking of how his approach may affect me— perhaps he is a panhandler. But if a train approaches me I do not say **I was approached by the train*, because all I am talking about is the geometry of two positions.'

In similar vein an O NP from an idiom is unlikely to be passivizable. One may say *John met his fate in the examination room* but not **His fate was met by John* ... or **John's fate was met by him* ...

For Evenki (Nedjalkov 1997: 218)—as for many other languages—the verbs 'most commonly passivized' describe an activity which affects the patient, such as 'kill', 'make/build', 'cut off', 'tie', 'put/lay down', 'finish', 'find', and 'see' (if someone wishes to remain unobserved, then for them to 'be seen' is a significant happening).

In every language there are a number of verbs which do not allow a passive, or have one in very limited circumstances. For English these include (there is a fuller account in Dixon 1991a: 305–13, 2005a: 360–7):

- Symmetric verbs, referring to a state or activity that relates equally to two entities. Thus, if it is the case that *Mary resembles John* it must also be the case that *John resembles Mary*. (Alternatively, we can use a reciprocal construction *John and Mary resemble each other* or *Mary and John resemble each other*.) Either of the roles may be placed in subject slot, and so there is no possible need for a passive construction.
- Verbs such as *contain, cost, weigh* which refer to a static relationship as in *The bottle contains beer, These strawberries cost ten euros a kilo,* and *I weigh seventy kilos*. Nothing 'happens' and so a passive construction, which normally describes the result of an activity, could not be used. (Note also that in a passive construction the *by* phrase is always omissible, and for these verbs both poles of the relationship must be stated.)

Other languages show similar restrictions. In some, no verb with a 'stative' meaning may passivize. For languages with a verb 'have', it is often—although not always—the case that it cannot be passivized. (Very little work has been done on verbs that may not antipassivize, in languages which include an antipassive derivation. This is a worthwhile topic for future work.)

Some languages have a fair number of verbs which only occur in passive form. There are perhaps only two such in English—*rumour* and *repute*. One can say *He is reputed to earn a million dollars a year* but scarcely **They repute him to earn a million dollars a year*. (Note also that a *by*-phrase is not permitted with such 'inherent passive' verbs.)

23.2.5 Meanings

An active construction is always functionally unmarked, and is used in neutral circumstances. Passive or antipassive will only be employed to meet some specific syntactic, semantic, or pragmatic purpose. We have already looked at pivot constraints, at highlighting O or A, and at backgrounding A or O. There may be other, semantic, reasons for employing a non-active construction. For example, in the North-east Caucasian language Bezhta the antipassive carries a potential meaning—'Brother boils the water' would be expressed by a regular transitive, with 'brother' in ergative and 'water' in absolutive case, but 'Brother can boil the water' requires an antipassive, with 'brother' in absolutive and 'water' in an oblique case, instrumental (Kibrik 1990: 27).

A passive or antipassive construction may have concomitant semantic properties. In Swahili, 'a passive verb may be used when the action suffered is viewed as proceeding from an intelligent, free and responsible agent' (Loogman 1965: 406). In Marathi a passive construction 'always expresses a volitional act' and also 'the capability of the agent to perform/not perform the action expressed by the verb' (Pandharipande 1997: 395).

In Colloquial Sinhala (Wijayawardhana, Wickramasinghe, and Byron 1995: 113), for a verb such as 'break' the passive construction is used if the result was achieved accidentally. Compare active clause in (37a) with passive in (37b):

(37)   (a) laməya$_A$ kooppe$_O$ binda
           child   cup   break:PAST:ACTIVE
           The child (deliberately) broke the cup (e.g. in a fit of anger)

       (b) laməya-atin   kooppe$_S$ biñduna
           child-INSTRUMENTAL   cup   break:PAST:PASSIVE
           The child (accidentally) broke the cup (e.g. when trying to wash it)

If the agent phase were omitted from (37b), giving just *kooppe biñduna*, this could describe the cup breaking without any direct agent being involved (for example, on having hot water poured into it).

In some languages there is a passive which indicates that the underlying O (passive S) is adversely affected by the activity. Alongside the normal passive, marked by a verbal suffix—which has neutral connotations—Fijian also has an 'adversely affected patient' passive, shown by verbal prefix *lau-*. My Fijian mentor, Josefa Cookanacagi, explained the difference through the following 'minimal pair':

(38)   (a) sa   sivi-ti   [a   matakau   yai]$_S$
           ASPECT   carve-PASSIVE   ARTICLE   statue   THIS
           This statue has been (properly) carved

(b) sa   lau-sivi
    ASPECT   ADVERSATIVE.PASSIVE-carve
    [a   matakau yai]$_S$
      ARTICLE statue   THIS
    This statue has been badly carved (as if someone tried to spoil it)

In (38a/b) the two passives involve the same underlying O. For other verbs different types of NPs trigger contrastive passives. For instance with *rabe* 'kick', passive *rabe-ti* would be used for 'the ball was kicked' but passive *lau-rabe* for 'the door was kicked in'. (All of these sentences can include an agent phrase, marked by preposition *mai* 'from', although this may be a calque from English; see Dixon 1988: 222–5). A number of East Asian languages have what is called an 'adversative passive'. However, this involves valency increase, not decrease; see (g) in §23.2.7.

Antipassive in Päri was mentioned at the end of §23.2.3. The 'patient phrase' is marked by preposition *ki* which is also used for instrument, accompaniment, space, time, and fear. Verbs have a fusional structure. Antipassive is always combined with one value from a three-term system 'go and do', 'come and do', and 'do many times' (this can also be used with active transitive and with intransitive verbs). 'Go and do' is the functionally unmarked term, to be used for a single action where no going or coming is involved. A sample paradigm is (Andersen 1988: 300–1 and personal communication):

(39)   verb root 'steal'   kwal
       antipassive plus 'go and do'   kwʌt
       antipassive plus 'come and do'   kwʌnn
       antipassive plus 'do many times' kwʌd

Compare the active in (40a) with the three antipassives in (40b–d):

(40) (a) dhòk$_O$ á-kwàl   ùbúrr-i$_A$
        COWS   COMPLETIVE-steal Ubur-ERGATIVE
        Ubur stole the cows (and took them away)

    (b) ùbúr$_S$ á-kwʌt-ò
        Ubur   COMPLETIVE-steal:GO:ANTIPASSIVE-SUFFIX
        Ubur went to steal *or* Ubur stole

    (c) ùbúr$_S$ á-kwʌnn-ò
        Ubur   COMPLETIVE-steal:COME:ANTIPASSIVE-SUFFIX
        Ubur came to steal

    (d) ùbúr$_S$ á-kwʌd-ò
        Ubur   COMPLETIVE-steal:MULTIPLICATIVE:ANTIPASSIVE-SUFFIX
        Ubur used to steal

To each of (40a–d) could be added *ki dhok* (with cows), the erstwhile O NP now being placed in peripheral function. (Verbal ending *-ò* appears to be a default suffix used on derived intransitive verbs.)

If a language has two (or more) passive or antipassive constructions, then there will be some meaning difference between them. Besides the main passive construction in English, shown by *be-. . . -en*, there is a second one, marked by *got-. . . -en*. Compare:

(41)   (a) John was accepted by the medical board for pilot training
       (b) John got accepted by the medical board for pilot training

Sentence (41a) simply states a fact. In contrast, (41b) implies that John did something special to make sure he was selected (maybe he was a family friend of the chairperson of the medical board, and personal pressure was applied through this channel).

Some European (and other) languages have two copula verbs—roughly 'be' and 'become'—each of which may function as passive auxiliary, more or less carrying over their contrastive copula meanings. (See Siewierska 1984: 129–39 and the primary sources referred to there.) Several Mayan languages include several canonical passives. For example, Tzutujil has both a 'completive passive', which 'emphasizes the result of the activity on the patient as well as the termination of the activity' and a 'simple passive' which simply 'defines and describes the activity' (Dayley 1985: 342; see also Dayley 1978).

Other languages have several canonical antipassives. Bittner (1987) maintains that the various antipassive suffixes in Eskimo are not suppletive variants (as had previously been thought) but carry semantic information, indicating 'imperfective', 'inceptive', and so on.

In Dyirbal there is a dedicated antipassive, marked by derivational suffix *-ŋa-y* ∼ *-na-y* on the verb. Compare active clause (42a) with antipassive (42b):

(42)   (a) jaban$_O$ [ba-ŋgu-l   yara-ŋgu]$_A$
           eel   THERE-ERGATIVE-MASC   man-ERGATIVE
           waga-ñu
           spear-PRESENT
           The man is spearing eels

       (b) [bayi   yara]$_S$ waga-na-ñu   (jaban-gu)
           THERE:MASC   man   spear-ANTIPASSIVE-PRES   eel-DATIVE
           Man is spearing (eels)

As mentioned in §22.5.1, there is a further derivational suffix *-(yi)rri-y* ~ *-marri-y* which marks reflexive and also functions as a second antipassive. For example:

(42) (c) [bayi   yara]$_S$ wagay-marri-ñu   (jaban-gu)
          THERE:MASC man   spear-ANTIPASSIVE-PRES eel-DATIVE
          Man is spearing (eels)

Both (42b) and (42c) focus on the agent and what he is doing. The difference is that the *-ŋa-y* ~ *-na-y* antipassive refers to an *actual* action, whereas *-(yi)rri-y* ~ *-marri-y* refers to the *potentiality* of some action taking place. That is, (42c) could describe a man who has gone out on an eel-spearing expedition, but is not actually spearing any at the moment, whereas (42b) would be appropriately used if he has just found some eels and is presently spearing them. (See Dixon 1972: 91–2 for further exemplification.)

On listening to Dyirbal conversation, one set of verbs appear to 'prefer' one variety of antipassive and a second set the other variety. In fact, this relates to whether the verb refers to something which is actually done here and now (cutting a tree or chopping a log—as in (25) and (36) above—or telling a story, or looking at something) or some activity which has the potential to produce results (for example, hunting for an animal, or searching for something lost).

23.2.6 Non-canonical passive and antipassives

Many languages have what appears to be a type of passive where the agent (underlying A) may *not* be included, although there is an implication that some agent was involved. There is also a type of antipassive where statement of the patient is excluded, although it is understood that there was a patient. Care must be taken to distinguish such 'agentless passives' and 'patientless antipassives' from copula-type constructions involving nominalizations, as illustrated above by (16a/b) and (17a/b) in English.

Such non-canonical constructions have properties similar to those of the canonical varieties. They may be marked by a verbal affix (which often has further functions in the grammar) or by an auxiliary (which is virtually always homonymous with a copula or some lexical verb). The rationale for their use is also similar. For example, an agentless passive will focus on the underlying O argument (now passive S), and background the erstwhile A argument to the extent that it may not be mentioned (although it is understood that there *was* an agent).

There may also be a semantic or pragmatic reason for using one of the non-canonical constructions. For example, Spanish (Hidalgo 1994: 170–3) has a canonical passive marked by auxiliary *ser* (identical to one of the copulas 'be'), with the agent optionally included and introduced by preposition *por* 'by, for, through, in'. It 'tends to be used more often with highly topical ("pragmatically promoted") patients: definite, anaphor, human', as in:

(43) [El   museo]ₛ fue   inaugurado
      THE museum be:PAST:3sg open:PARTICIPLE:MASC:SINGULAR
      ([por el   ministro español])
        BY   THE minister Spanish
      The museum was opened (by the Spanish Minister)

In contrast, the agentless passive involves auxiliary *estar* (homonymous with a further copula 'be') and is likely to be used when the original patient is 'indefinite, non-anaphoric, non-human'. It is understood that there was an agent, but this is not considered important enough to state. For example:

(44) [La   puerta]ₛ está   quebrado
      THE door   be:PRESENT:3sg break-PARTICIPLE:FEM:SINGULAR
      The door is broken

There is discussion of the different meanings and uses of *ser* and *estar* as copulas in §14.4.1; see also, for example, Butt and Benjamin (2004: 418–27).

A non-canonical construction may be restricted in terms of the possible reference of one of its arguments. Matses (Panoan, Peru) has a patientless antipassive marked by suffix *-an* on the verb. There are a number of syntactic tests to show that this derives an intransitive verb. The underlying A argument is placed in S function, and the original O argument (now not stated), may be either (a) plural or singular 1st person, or (b) indefinite. Compare the active clause in (45a) with the corresponding patientless antipassive in (45b):

(45) (a) [aid   opa-n]ₐ   matses-ø₀   pe-e-k
           THAT dog-ERGATIVE people-ABSOLUTIVE bite-NONPAST-DEC
           That dog bites people
      (b) [aid   opa-ø]ₛ   pe-an-e-k
           THAT dog-ABSOLUTIVE bite-ANTIPASSIVE-NONPAST-DEC
           (a) That dog always bites/is biting (me/us)
           (b) That dog bites

'The first person patient reading is readily used in any tense-aspect' whereas the indefinite patient reading 'occurs mostly in generic statements' such as 'scorpions sting'. Fleck (2006) distinguishes three sets of verbs:

- Set 1 verbs may not be antipassivized; they include: 'drink', 'eat', 'steal', 'pick (fruit)', 'sharpen'.

- Set 2 verbs can be antipassivized only with a 1st person reading; they include 'see', 'visit', 'find', 'follow', 'give to', 'tell', 'wait for'.
- Set 3 verbs can be antipassivized with either 1st person or indefinite reading; these include 'kill', 'bite', 'grab, capture, take', 'curse to die', 'hug'.

Another non-canonical construction type is when a passive is formed from an intransitive verb (no instances have yet been reported of this happening with antipassive). In a few languages, the marking on the transitive verb in a canonical antipassive may also be added to an intransitive verb. There are, basically, two ways in which this may happen.

In English, an NP marked by a preposition in an intransitive clause can become passive S, with the original S now marked with *by*. The meaning of the construction is quite different, depending on whether the *by*-phrase is included or omitted. If I am shown an hotel room with a dirty, unmade bed, I could use the active intransitive clause *Someone has slept in this bed*, or the passive version:

(46)   This bed has been slept in

Such an agentless passive of an intransitive clause is most likely to be used when the passive S (here, *the bed*) has been adversely affected by the activity. (Note that an adverse meaning is not always implied. Suppose that Little Timmy does not appear at breakfast and cannot be found anywhere. His room is checked, and mother tells father: *Well, his bed has been slept in*.)

Now suppose you are shown a beautifully made-up bed in a quite different type of hotel and told that some well-known person slept there in the past. The bellboy could use an active intransitive clause such as *Winston Churchill slept in this bed*, but is perhaps more likely to employ a passive construction with the agent specified:

(47)   This bed was slept in by Winston Churchill

A similar example was given at (35a–p) in §23.2.2, involving the passive of an ambitransitive verb used in an intransitive clause (with no O NP stated).

In other languages, an intransitive verb may be passivized with nothing going into the S slot (and no indication of an underlying S). For instance, in German the passive auxiliary construction may be used with intransitive verb 'dance' as in (Keenan 1985: 274; Keenan and Dryer 2007: 346):

(48)   Gestern   wurde   getanzt
        yesterday become:PAST:3sg   dance:PARTICIPLE
        Yesterday there was dancing

An engaging example in Turkish of intransitive verbs 'laugh' and 'die' being used in intransitive form comes from a novel (Haig 1999: 88–9):

(49) [Böyle bir nokta-da]   ya   gül-ün-ür
      such a   point-LOCATIVE EITHER laugh-PASSIVE-AORIST
      ya öl-ün-ür
      OR die-PASSIVE AORIST
      In a situation like this, one either (has to) laugh or (to) die (literally, either laughing or dying)

Constructions such as (48) and (49) are sometimes called 'impersonal passives' (and this term is used for more besides; see Keenan 1985: 272–7; Keenan and Dryer 2007: 345–8; Siewierska 1984: 98–112).

23.2.7 What is not a passive or antipassive

Labels 'passive' and 'antipassive' have been applied—by a minority of scholars—to construction types which do not correspond to the 'canonical' or 'non-canonical' chacterizations set out in this chapter. Some of them can be briefly noted.

(a) **Ambitransitive as antipassive (or passive).**   As stated in §13.3, many languages have a set of verbs which can occur in either transitive or intransitive clauses. Such ambitransitive (a.k.a. labile) verbs may be of type S = A—for example $John_A$ has eaten $lunch_O$ and $John_S$ has eaten—or of type S = O—as in $John_A$ raced $[the\ horse]_O$ and $[The\ horse]_S$ raced. It has been suggested that the intransitive form of an S = A ambitransitive is an 'antipassive'. The transitive A argument does become S, but there is no special marking, and the original O cannot be included in the intransitive. (See Heath 1976 for this unfortunate idea and Hewitt 1982 for a rebuttal, relating to North Caucasian languages.) On the same principle, one would have to—equally erroneously—label the intransitive form of an S = O ambitransitive as 'passive'.

(b) **Object incorporation as antipassive.**   Object incorporation takes various forms. In some languages it involves incorporating an object noun within a transitive verb, creating an intransitive stem. Roughly I_A cut $firewood_O$ becomes I_S firewood-cut. (See Mithun 1984.) In Mayan linguistics the tradition has arisen (perhaps emanating from Dayley 1981) of classing object incorporation as a kind of antipassive. However, this is a morphological, not a syntactic, derivation.

(c) **Ergative as passive.**   When Western scholars first became acquainted with ergative systems, they experienced some difficulty in dealing with them. One solution (which continues to recur, even today) is to say that an ergative construction is a kind of obligatory passive. But in languages in which it occurs, ergative-case marking is the unmarked profile for an active clause (not some sort of secondary derivation). See the discussion in Dixon (1994: 189) and further references therein.

(d) **Inverse system as passive.**   These were briefly mentioned, for Sochiapan Chinantec, in §23.2.4, and are quite different from active/passive contrasts. Whistler (1985) shows that what had been called 'passives' for Nootka are in fact parts of an inverse case-marking system.

(e) **Focus system in Philippines languages as passive.**   There was brief mention in §11.5 of focus systems in Philippines languages. In each clause, one argument must be put in 'focus', this being shown by an appropriate focus marking on the verb. In one of his early publications, on Tagalog, Bloomfield (1917: 154) described the focus system as 'active', 'direct passive', 'instrumental passive', and 'local passive'. Modern writers appear to be unanimous that the term 'passive' is not suitable here—see, among others, Shibatani (1988b) and De Wolf (1988) (but note that both of these authors do consider the focus system to be a type of 'voice').

(f) **Complement clause construction as passive.**   Thai and Lao are very similar—either dialects of one language, or else two closely related languages. Iwasaki and Ingkaphirom (2005), among others, recognize a passive construction in Thai, marked by one of a number of auxiliary verbs, notably *thùuk* which also has a lexical use 'touch, come into contact with, strike'. However, Enfield (2007a: 438–41)—dealing with corresponding sentences in Lao—provides persuasive arguments that these are better analysed as complement clause constructions: '*thùùk5* takes a verb phrase or sentence complement, where the subject of *thùùk5* is coreferential with the object of the lower complement'. One says, literally 'He strike [fish eat him]' for 'He got eaten by fish'.

(g) **'Adversative passive'.**   In Japanese, for example, there is a syntactic derivation generally called 'adversative passive'. This involves the addition of a new argument (in subject function within the derived clause) to either an intransitive or transitive clause. Compare the plain intransitive in (50a) with its 'adversative passive' in (50b) and the plain transitive in (51a) with its 'adversative passive' in (51b) (Shibatani 1990: 317–19).

(50) (a) [Kodomo ga]ₛ   nak-u
           child   NOMINATIVE   cry-PRESENT
           The child cries

      (b) [Taroo wa]ₛ   [kodomo ni] nake-re-ta
           Taro   TOPIC child   BY   cry-'ADVERSATIVE.PASSIVE'-PAST
           Taroo was adversely affected by the child's crying

(51) (a) [Ziroo ga]ₐ   [doramu o]ₒ   rensyuusu-ru
           Jiro   NOMINATIVE   drum   ACCUSATIVE practise-PRESENT
           Jiro practises the drums

      (b) [Taroo wa]ₐ [Ziroo ni] [doramu o]ₒ
           Taro   TOPIC   Jiro   BY   drum   ACCUSATIVE
           rensyuusu-re-ta
           practise-'ADVERSATIVE.PASSIVE'-PAST
           Taro was adversely affected by Jiro's practising the drums

Note that the 'adversely affected' argument—in S function in (50b) and in
A function in (51b)—receives topic marker *wa* rather than nominative *ga*.

Sentences (50b) and (51b) each add an argument and are plainly not 'passives' as the term is used in the chapter (or in most literature on the topic).
The interesting point is that the verbal suffix used to mark them, *-(ra)re*, is also
used to mark a canonical passive. And the suffix is polysemous, also indicating
spontaneity, politeness, and potentiality.

A number of other languages in East and South-east Asia (including Chinese and Vietnamese) are reported to have a canonical passive which indicates
adversative effect on the derived S and/or a valency-increasing adversative
construction similar to those just illustrated for Japanese.

23.3 Summary

This chapter is mainly about discourse and how passive and antipassive derivations facilitate its smooth organization. The labels 'passive' and 'antipassive'
have been used in a variety of (not always consistent) ways, so that we needed
to characterize canonical passive and antipassive derivations. Each operates
on an underlying transitive structure, and places one of the core transitive
arguments (O for passive, A for antipassive) into surface S function. The
other transitive argument becomes a peripheral element (marked by a case
inflection or an adposition); it is often omitted but there is always the possibility of including it. Both types of derivation involve some explicit formal marking—either a derivational affix to the verb or (these two are so
far attested only for passive) an auxiliary verb construction or a serial verb
construction.

There can be additions to, and variations on, the canonical schemes. Just
a few languages also permit an indirect object (argument in E function)—or
a locative or some other peripheral argument—to become passive S. Sometimes passive marking may also be used with a number of intransitive verbs;

either an original peripheral argument becomes passive S or else the passive construction includes no S at all (or just a dummy one). Quite a number of languages have only agentless passive and/or patientless antipassive.

Antipassive is the 'opposite' of passive in a limited syntactic sense, with A being exchanged for O within their profiles. However, they differ markedly in semantic and pragmatic effect. Passive typically focuses on the result of some activity, and the effect this has on the patient, whereas antipassive emphasizes the fact that an activity is taking place, controlled by a particular agent.

There can be further semantic connotations in individual languages. Antipassive sometimes carries a potential meaning (the referent of the underlying A *can* do this) or completive or perfective/imperfective. The English *get*-passive is used when the underlying O was in some way responsible for their being affected by the activity. In contrast, passive in Swahili requires that the action emanates from 'an intelligent, free, and responsible agent'. In some languages passive is used for a result obtained accidentally, in others only when the agent acts volitionally. A recurring theme is for one type of passive to indicate an 'adversely affected patient'.

In all languages in which they occur, passive and antipassive serve to highlight one argument—that which is placed in S function. It is likely to be the topic argument for the clause, within a segment of discourse characterized by having this recurrent topic. Some languages work in terms of a grammaticalized topic or 'pivot'. English utilizes an S/A pivot: if an argument is repeated in two successive clauses, it may be omitted from the second only if it is in surface S or A function in each clause. The S/O pivot in Dyirbal is stronger in that it governs not only argument omission but also clause coordination. That is, two clauses can only be joined into one sentence (a single intonation group) if they share an argument which is in S or O function in each clause. Some languages lack grammatical constraints of this type; potentially, any argument may be left unstated, so that its identity can only be inferred from context of use (or just from common sense).

The chapter began with a brief account of Jarawara which has full specification of pivot. That is, for each clause (considered on its own, outside discourse context) the identity of the pivot argument is stated. To say 'John came in and John saw Mary', the second clause must be expressed as an 'A-construction', for which the A argument ('John') is pivot. And to say 'John came in and Mary saw John', the second clause must be coded as an 'O-construction', where the O ('John') argument is identified as pivot. The grammar of this language can only be understood if each clause is considered within the context of the discourse in which it occurred.

The same principle should be followed in the analysis of every language. A linguist must work in terms of spontaneous discourse, rather than just eliciting (ugh!) sentences through a lingua franca.

23.4 What to investigate

In order to ascertain whether there are pivot conditions within the grammar of a language under investigation, it is useful to investigate (preferably through examination of texts) biclausal sentences where the two clauses share a core argument. We can use subscript $_1$ for occurrence of an argument in the first and $_2$ for occurrence in the second clause. There are the following possibilities:

> *Possible functions of a common NP in two syntactically linked clauses:*
>   both clauses intransitive
> (a) $S_1 = S_2$
>
>   first clause intransitive, second transitive
> (b) $S_1 = O_2$
> (c) $S_1 = A_2$
>
>   first clause transitive, second intransitive
> (d) $O_1 = S_2$
> (e) $A_1 = S_2$
>
>   both clauses transitive, one common NP
> (f) $O_1 = O_2$
> (g) $A_1 = A_2$
> (h) $O_1 = A_2$
> (i) $A_1 = O_2$
>
>   both clauses transitive, two common NPs
> (j) $O_1 = O_2$ and $A_1 = A_2$
> (k) $O_1 = A_2$ and $A_1 = O_2$

There is no pivot constraint on actual clause linking in English. In the case of coordination we can say (i) *John returned and saw Mary* (where $S_1 = A_2$) or (ii) *John returned and Mary saw him* (where $S_1 = O_2$). But there is a constraint on the omission of the second occurrence of a common NP—it must be in S or A function in each clause. Thus (i) satisfies this pivot condition and the occurrence of *John* from the second clause has been omitted; but (ii) does not satisfy it and here we had to retain the pronoun *him* in O slot. If we wished to fully omit mention of John from the second clause in (ii) then this must be passivized, putting underlying O into derived S function, so that the pivot condition is now met, i.e. *John returned and was seen by Mary*. English thus has a weak S/A pivot.

The operation of the pivot condition on NP omission in English can be illustrated by constructing examples for each of (a)–(k):

Illustration of S/A pivot in English

(a) $S_1 = S_2$ Bill entered and sat down
(b) $S_1 = O_2$ Bill entered and was seen by Fred
(c) $S_1 = A_2$ Bill entered and saw Fred
(d) $O_1 = S_2$ Bill was seen by Fred and laughed
(e) $A_1 = S_2$ Fred saw Bill and laughed
(f) $O_1 = O_2$ Bill was kicked by Tom and punched by Bob
                            (*or* Tom kicked and Bob punched Bill)
(g) $A_1 = A_2$ Bob kicked Jim and punched Bill
(h) $O_1 = A_2$ Bob was kicked by Tom and punched Bill
(i) $A_1 = O_2$ Bob punched Bill and was kicked by Tom
(j) $O_1 = O_2, A_1 = A_2$ Fred punched and kicked Bill
(k) $O_1 = A_2, A_1 = O_2$ Fred punched Bill and was kicked by him
                            (*or* Fred punched and was kicked by Bill)

Omission is straightforward—with no syntactic derivations required—when the common NP is in S or A function in each clause, in (a), (c), (e), (g), and (j). But when the common NP is in O function in one clause then that clause must be passivized for NP omission to be allowed; this applies to (b), (d), (f), (h), (i), and (k). In (f) it was necessary to passivize both clauses. Note that English has a further clause-linking strategy—if two clauses differ only in their verbs, the verbs can simply be coordinated. Thus, from *Fred punched Bill* and *Fred kicked Bill* we can get *Fred punched and kicked Bill* in (j), in which both *Fred* and *Bill* are stated only once (*Fred punched Bill and kicked him* is a possible alternative). In (k), as an alternative to *Fred punched Bill and was kicked by him*, some (but not all) native speakers are happy with *Fred punched and was kicked by Bill*. There is also the possibility of combining A-NP-plus-verb from two clauses which have the same O NP so that, as an alternative to *Bill was kicked by Tom and punched by Bob* in (f), it is also possible to say *Tom kicked and Bob punched Bill* (although, again, not all native speakers are happy with this).

It must be stressed that this scheme only provides a basic framework for the investigation of whether a language has a pivot and, if so, what it is. The framework will need to be refined according to the grammatical organization of each specific language. For example, the syntactic condition on functions allowed to a common NP may vary according to the semantic/syntactic nature of the head of the NP: whether it is a pronoun or a noun, or whether, if a noun, it has human reference, and so on. Different pivots may apply (or a given pivot may apply in varying ways) for different kinds of clause combining—coordination, relativization, complementation, or other varieties of subordination. There may also be pivot conditions on the formation of negative or interrogative constructions.

As an alternative to pivot constraints, some languages operate in terms of a switch-reference system—(a), (c), (e), (g), and (j) would receive the marking for 'same S/A' while (b), (d), (f), (h), (i), and (k) would be marked for 'different S/A' (this marking generally goes onto the verb of the second clause). The second occurrence of the common NP could then be omitted, and would be retrievable by hearers.

To check whether a particular construction type is a passive or an antipassive derivation, the following points must be checked.

(i) There should be some explicit formal marking for passive/antipassive. This may involve a morphological process (typically, affixation) applying to the verb from an underlying transitive active clause, or an auxiliary or serial verb construction. Check whether this marking has any other function (it is often also used for reflexive and/or reciprocal). Examine whether the marking may also apply to intransitive verbs—in what circumstances and with what syntactic and semantic effect.

(ii) There must be criteria for establishing that a putative passive or antipassive construction is intransitive, with just one core argument that is in S function. These criteria may include: case or adpositional marking, forms of free and/or bound pronouns, linking with underived intransitive verbs, different allomorphs of some morphemes for intransitive and transitive clauses.

(iii) One needs to ascertain which arguments from a corresponding transitive active construction may become S in a passive or antipassive. For a passive, for instance, all languages allow active O to become passive S, and some have wider possibilities ('indirect object' in E function, locative, etc.).

(iv) The fieldworker should investigate what happens to the other argument from the transitive active clause—A for passive and O for antipassive. In a canonical passive/antipassive this argument is often omitted but *may* be retained, marked by some peripheral case or adposition (investigate the full range of functions for this). If the 'other argument' *must* be omitted, we have an agentless passive or patientless antipassive.

(v) It is most important to analyse the functions and conditions of use of each passive and antipassive derivation. They are likely to include:

- Highlighting one argument—generally topicalizing it, often to feed some pivot constraint.

- Backgrounding another argument, sometimes avoiding having to specify it. This may be because its identity is not known, or is obvious, or the speaker wishes not to reveal what it is.

(vi) If there is more than one passive/antipassive derivation in a language, these will differ in meaning and in pragmatic effect—for example, actual versus potential activity, ongoing versus completed. Single derivations have their own semantic overtones, which differ from language to language—the agent acting purposely or accidentally, having the potential to act, and so on. There may be restrictions on the reference of NPs within a passive/antipassive construction (in terms of human, inanimate, etc.). Such semantic factors must be carefully investigated.

(vii) Depending in large part on its functions and meanings, an antipassive or passive derivation may only apply to—or is most likely to apply to—a limited selection of verbs. It may be that a few verbs *must* occur in passive or antipassive form. Such restrictions should be looked into, and semantic motivations investigated.

(viii) Finally, care must be taken to distinguish true passive and antipassive constructions from such things as plain nominalizations (as in English *She was very worried*), ambitransitives, object incorporation, inverse systems, focus systems, so-called 'adversative passives' (which actually increase valency), and so on.

Sources and notes

A great deal has been published on passives, only a small portion of it being referred to here. Keenan (1985) includes much good discussion and data, although he takes the canonical passive construction to be agentless. Keenan and Dryer (2007) constitutes a minor revision of this, with some omissions and the addition of a section on 'constructions that resemble passives'. There have been a number of anthologies relating to voice which include some useful material but are overall—as is often the nature of such volumes—of uneven quality. They include Nichols and Woodbury (1985), Shibatani (1988a), Fox and Hopper (1994), and Givón (1994). Particularly worthwhile studies relating to specific language families include Dayley (1981) on Mayan and Fleisch (2005) on Bantu.

Siewierska (1984), the revision of an MA thesis, is confused about what is a passive construction and generally lacks insight. Siewierska (2005), on 'passive constructions', and Polinsky (2005b), on antipassive constructions—two contributions to *The World Atlas of Language Structures*—are unreliable as to criteria and attestation. Cooreman (1994) purports to be a typology of antipassives but much of the data she considers would not be accepted as antipassives by most other linguists, nor do her analyses stand scrutiny. A great deal has been published by Tasaku Tsunoda on antipassives in the Australian language Warungu. However, the only consultant Tsunoda used (who I also worked with) was more proficient in Dyirbal than in Warungu and much of the material Tasaku recorded appears to involve calques from Dyirbal. (There were at that time other speakers of Warungu, but Tsunoda did not work with them.)

Parts of this chapter are based on material in chapter 6 of Dixon (1994) and chapter 11 of Dixon (2005a).

23.1   There are several other criterial features which distinguish A-constructions and O-constructions in Jarawara. For example, when both A and O arguments are 3rd person, then the verb or auxiliary takes prefix *hi-* just for an O-construction; this is illustrated by (43-ap) in §25.6. A full account is in Dixon (2004: 417–45, 2000b).

There is fuller cross-linguistic discussion and exemplification of pivots in Dixon (1994: 152–81). Under (b) of §15.2.3 it was noted that Dyirbal nominal demonstratives may only be used in S and O functions; a demonstrative in underlying A function must be put into surface S function through an antipassive derivation. Refer back to §3.21 for a survey of the different means which languages employ for marking an argument as topic.

There is no standard reference on switch-reference marking. The introduction and most of the papers in Haiman and Munro (1983) are useful. Roberts (1997) is an excellent survey of switch-references in the languages of Papua New Guinea. For switch-reference in Australian languages, see Austin (1981b), Dixon (1980: 465–6; 2002: 527–9), and further references therein. The term 'switch-reference' was introduced in an influential paper by Jacobsen (1967). Note that switch-reference marking is an excellent test for subject identification.

23.2   The label 'antipassive' was coined in late 1968 by Michael Silverstein to describe the *-ŋa-y* derivation in Dyirbal, while he was taking part in a course I conducted at Harvard University on 'The native languages of Australia'. It gradually gained wide acceptance. I did not employ it in my 1972 grammar of Dyirbal (sticking with '-ŋa-y construction') but five years later 'antipassive' was sufficiently well-established that it seemed appropriate to use it in the grammar of Yidiñ (Dixon 1977a).

Here are a few examples of what various linguists have grouped under 'voice' (in addition to passive, antipassive, and sometimes also 'middle'). Palmer (1984) includes causative and applicative; Dayley (1981) has instrumental applicative; Trask (1993: 9, 299) has reflexive, causative, and adjutative ('someone helping someone to do something'); Klaiman (1991) has argument focusing in Philippines languages and inverse systems; Shibatani (1988b) also includes argument focussing.

A quarter-century ago, Marantz (1984) was under the impression that passive only occurred in a syntactically accusative and antipassive only in a syntactically ergative language. He suggested that in a syntactically ergative language, S and O functions should be recognized as subject and A function as object. Ergo, passive and antipassive coincide. At about the same time, there was much discussion of passive and antipassive within the framework of 'relational grammar'. There is brief consideration of all this in Dixon (1994: 232–6).

23.2.1   A number of other types of verbs have taken on the additional role of becoming an auxiliary in a passive construction. For example, Heine and Kuteva (2002) list 'eat', 'fall', and 'see' (it would be necessary, for each of these, to check back in primary sources that it does occur in a bona fide canonical passive construction).

23.2.2   Other languages with a passive, for which arguments other than O may become derived S, include Egyptian Colloquial Arabic (Gary and Gamal-Eldin 1982: 89–90) and Gamo (Omotic, Ethiopia; Éva 1990: 394).

A lot of attention has been focussed on Bantu languages in which two noun phrases, without any case or adpositional marking, may follow the verb (see §13.5.3). Either of them can be in O function, but only one NP will be O in a particular clause, in which circumstance this NP will immediately follow the verb and is then passivizable (and cliticizable). See Hyman and Duranti (1982); Gary and Keenan (1977).

23.2.4   For a succinct overview of inverse systems, see Dixon and Aikhenvald (1997: 98–100).

Figures on the percentages of passives in English for which no agent is given are quoted in Svartvik (1966), Givón (1979), and Thompson (1987).

23.2.5   For further discussion of the *get* passive in English see Chappell (1980), Ward, Birner, and Huddleston (2002: 1440–3), and Dixon (1991a: 302–4, 2005a: 358–9). Givón and Yang (1994) offer an instructive account of its historical origin.

23.2.6   Other languages which apply passive marking to an intransitive verb include Punjabi (Bhatia 1993: 234–6, 177–8) and Evenki (Nedjalkov 1997: 222–5). The label 'impersonal passive' should be used with care. For example, it is not appropriate to apply it to a transitive clause with a generic A argument, such as *One shouldn't eat raw meat* (cf. some of the examples in Siewierska 1984).

23.2.7   In some languages (including Indonesian) there is a passive-like construction in which underlying A *must* be included (that is, it cannot be omitted); this does not qualify as a canonical passive.

Since Dayley (1981), Mayanists have recognized what they call an 'absolutive antipassive' and also a 'focus antipassive'. The former is a canonical antipassive in some languages and a patientless antipassive in others. However, Hale and Storto (1997) have shown that the so-called 'focus antipassive' is still transitive and thus scarcely an antipassive.

23.4   The section on pivots here is repeated, in condensed form, from Dixon (1994: 157–9); see that account for fuller information.

24

Causatives

24.1 Introduction

There are two main ways of changing the valency of a verb. The previous two chapters discussed derivations which reduce valency—reflexive and reciprocal (when marked by the verbal derivation technique), passive, agentless passive, antipassive, and patientless antipassive. Their canonical effects are summarized in Table 22.2 of §22.5.1. All of these processes basically apply to a transitive verb and derive an intransitive stem. In a number of languages, passive can—as a rather minor function—also be used with some intransitive verbs.

It is now time to consider derivations which increase valency—causatives, in the present chapter, and applicatives, in the next. Each of these may act on an intransitive verb, adding a core argument. An intransitive clause has one core argument, in S function, and a transitive verb has two, in A and O functions. There are thus two basic possibilities:

- S becomes O—causative, new argument in A function
- S becomes A—applicative, new argument in O function

In the last chapter it was pointed out that—despite the (rather inopportune) similarity of name, there are significant syntactic, semantic, and pragmatic differences between passive and antipassive. As will become apparent over this chapter and the next, the differences between causative and applicative are considerably greater than those between passive and antipassive.

One important point is that applicative—like passive and antipassive—may 'feed' a pivot constraint, through making something which was a peripheral argument within the original intransitive construction, into a core argument (in O function) within the derived applicative construction.

A causative derivation takes an S argument (which is a pivot function for both syntactically accusative and syntactically ergative languages) and places it in derived O function. This suggests that a causative would be unlikely to be used to feed a pivot or for similar discourse effect, and will normally be employed just for semantic reasons or for pragmatic effect. Study of grammars bears out this idea, that a causative construction will seldom be used to satisfy the demands of discourse organization.

Causatives may have a syntactic function in fostering transitivity agreement. For example, in Tariana a causative construction can be used to satisfy the 'same subject and same object constraint' on serial verb constructions (Aikhenvald 2003: 435–7). Oswalt (1977), O'Connor (1992), and Nichols (1985) describe a similar function in some Pomo languages and in Chechen-Ingush.

The characterization of a canonical causative derivation may be repeated here from §3.20:

Canonical causative derivation (applying to an intransitive clause)

(a) Applies to an underlying intransitive clause and forms a derived transitive.
(b) The argument in underlying S function goes into O function in the causative.
(c) A new argument (the causer) is introduced in A function.
(d) There is some explicit formal marking of the causative construction.

We find a variety of semantic nuances associated with each causative derivation in every language in which they occur (§28.2.4 discusses languages which lack a grammatical causative). Parameters of variation include the following. Whether or not the causee has control over the activity they are being 'made' to do, whether or not they perform it willingly, whether the causee is completely or only partially affected. Whether the causer acts directly or indirectly, whether they achieve the result accidentally or on purpose. Whether the caused event happens fairly naturally or is only achieved with effort. And whether or not the causer is also involved in the activity. The semantics of causation is discussed in §24.4.

There are a number of alternative ways of providing formal marking for a causative construction. Most typically, a morphological process applies to the verb which is predicate head. Or the language may combine two verbs in one predicate, either as a serial verb construction or in some other manner. Some languages employ periphrastic means (for example, the *make* construction in English, as in *She made him run*). A rarer technique is to exchange the auxiliary which must accompany a verb. There are also lexical causatives, either where one verb root may be used as intransitive and as its own causative (an example from English is *hurt*, as in *My leg hurts* and *John hurt my leg*), or where there are distinct lexemes with one being causative of the other (English *kill* meaning *make die*). §24.2 provides a survey of these formal mechanisms. Later in the chapter, §24.5 explores correlations between the 'degree of compactness' of formal mechanisms and values of semantic parameters.

A causative derivation always applies to intransitive verbs. In some languages this is its limit. In others it may also—like applicative—apply to some transitive (and perhaps even extended transitive) verbs. Most often, causative adds an argument to a transitive, as it does to an intransitive. The new causer argument is always in A function. What then happens to the original A and O arguments? Five different possibilities are described in §24.3.2, within the general discussion (in §24.3) of the syntax of causatives. Multiple applications of a causative process are mentioned in §24.3.4.

In a not insignificant number of languages, a process which has valency-increasing causative effect with an intransitive verb (together with specific semantic overtones) also applies to transitive verbs—sometimes also to intransitives—but without engendering any increase in valency. It simply has semantic effect, in terms of some of the semantic parameters which are associated with the causative of an intransitive. For example, an action being performed forcefully or over a long period, and/or completely affecting the patient. These are discussed in §24.6.1. There is then, in §24.6.2, brief mention of formal markings which have double function as both causative and passive. (The same marking used for both causative and applicative is dealt with in §25.8.)

A causative construction is sometimes described as involving 'two events'. Frawley (1992: 159) talks of 'a precipitating event' and 'a result', and Shibatani (1976b: 1) of 'a causing event' and 'a caused event'. A quite different characterization is preferred here. In §1.11, §3.10, and §18.5.2, we explained the notion of 'secondary concept', which adds some semantic modification to a lexical verb. A secondary concept may be realized by an affix or some other morphological process or (typically, in a language with meagre morphology) by a separate word. Some secondary concepts—such as 'begin' and 'try'— do not add any argument to those of the verb they modify. Secondary-C concepts, such as 'make' and 'help', do add an argument, the 'causer/helper', which is in A syntactic function. That is, a causative construction involves the specification of an additional argument, a causer, onto a basic clause. A causer refers to someone or something (which can be an event or state) that initiates or controls the activity. This is the defining property of the syntactic-semantic function A (transitive subject).

In this chapter, a narrow interpretation of prototypical 'causative construction' is adopted—it must involve a morphological process, or a verb which only has an abstract, causative meaning (or a lexical pair whose members are in causative relation). In English, *make* only has causative meaning while *order* also refers to an act of speaking. In view of this, *Mary made John go* is treated as a causative construction, but *Mary ordered John to go* is not. Other investigators permit a wider scope for the label 'causative'. For instance,

Song (1996: 36) accepts as a causative construction a sentence which is literally translated as 'I speak and child eats'. The difficulty then is in knowing where to draw the line.

'Causative' has been in use as a grammatical label since about 1600. From it has arisen the misconception that *cause* is the prototypical causative verb in English. It is not; *make* is. *Cause* is a causative verb but it has a more specialized meaning than *make* and is much less common. Many grammatical terms in English end in *-(at)ive* and as a productive suffix this is almost exclusively used with verbs of Romance origin, such as *cause*. A straightforward Germanic verb such as *make* would not sound right with *-(at)ive* (giving **make-ative*).

Following on from the illicit inference that *cause* is the main causing verb in English, it has been suggested that *kill* is equivalent to *cause to die*. Fodor (1970) presented a number of arguments against this analysis; for example, one can say *John caused Bill to die on Sunday by stabbing him on Saturday* but not **John killed Bill on Sunday by stabbing him on Saturday*. This is because *cause* has a rather special meaning, referring to indirect causation which can involve a time lapse. In fact, the meaning of *kill* is the same as that of the unmarked causative verb *make* plus *be dead*. All of the difficulties experienced with *cause to die* are eliminated if *make (be) dead* is used instead.

24.2 Formal mechanisms

We begin (in §24.2.1) by describing causatives marked by a morphological process applied to the verb of the underlying clause, then go on (in §24.2.2) to discuss causatives that involve two verbs making up a single predicate and (in §24.2.3) biclausal (or periphrastic) causative constructions. §24.2.4 looks at lexical pairs that are in causative relation, and at ambitransitive verbs of type S = O, which can be regarded as causatives. In §24.2.5 we mention languages that achieve a causative effect by exchanging the auxiliaries which accompany a lexical verb.

24.2.1 Morphological processes

A causative construction may be marked by a morphological process applied to the verb of the clause. Such a process can consist of (a) internal change, for example in vowel quality or consonant mutation; (b) repeating a consonant; (c) lengthening a vowel; (d) tone change; (e) reduplication; or various processes of affixation, with (f) a prefix, (g) a suffix, (h) a circumfix (combination of prefix and suffix), or (j) an infix. Each of these processes is illustrated, for one sample language, in Table 24.1.

In some languages, an affix with the same form as the causative derivation used on a verb may also be added to an adjective or noun, creating a transitive

TABLE 24.1. Morphological processes for marking causatives

	Process	Basic verb	Causative form	Language (source)
(a)	internal change	*tikti* 'be suitable'	*táiktyi* 'make suitable'	Lithuanian (Senn 1966: 283)
(b)	consonant repetition	*xarab* 'go bad'	*xarrab* 'make go bad, ruin'	Gulf Arabic (Holes 1990: 185)
(c)	vowel lengthening	*mar* 'die'	*ma:r* 'kill'	Kashmiri (Wali and Koul 1997: 211)
(d)	tone change	*nɔ̂* (high falling) 'be awake'	*nɔ̄* (low level) 'awaken, rouse'	Lahu (Matisoff 1973: 33)
(e)	reduplication	*bengok* 'shout'	*be-bengok* 'make shout'	Javanese (Suhandano 1994: 64–5)
(f)	prefix	*gəbba* 'enter'	*a-gəbba* 'insert'	Amharic (Amberber 2000: 318)
(g)	suffix	*xachíi* 'be moving'	*xachíi-a* 'move, set in motion'	Crow (Graczyk 2007: 141)
(h)	circumfix	*-č'am-* 'eat'	*-a-č'am-ev-* 'feed (make eat)'	Georgian (Aronson 1991: 260)
(j)	infix	*buebae* 'lose way'	*bue-da-bae* 'make lose way, mislead'	Rabha (Joseph 2005: 83)

verb with causative-type meaning. For instance, varieties of Quechua employ *-či* both with verbs—illustrated in (55–6)—and with adjectives and nouns. From *ali* 'good' we get *ali-či* 'make good', and from *pampa* 'flat place' is derived *pampa-či* 'make be a flat place, bury' (Cole 1982: 180).

24.2.2 Two verbs in one predicate

A serial verb construction (SVC) involves two or more verbs, each of which could make up a full predicate on its own. Within an SVC, the verbs function together as one predicate and are conceived of as describing a single action. Criteria for an SVC are that there must be no mark of linkage or subordination within it, and there will be at least one argument shared by the constituent verbs. Any grammatical category which in this language has the predicate as its scope is likely to have the whole SVC as its scope (these may include tense, aspect, evidentiality, modality, and—as discussed in §21.3—generally also negation).

There are two broad divisions of SVCs. In the symmetrical variety each verb comes from an unrestricted class and has equal status; no verb can be regarded as 'head' of the SVC. The combination of verbs may convey a 'cause-effect' meaning, as in the following from the Central Khoisan language Khwe (which has seventy phonemes, including thirty-five clicks; Kilian-Hatz 2006: 113).

(1) tí_A ǁˈámá ǀxˈǚá-té   [córò-hὲ   ὲ]_O
     1sg beat   kill-PRESENT   rock.monitor-3sg.f OBJECT
     I beat the rock monitor to death (lit. I beat-kill rock monitor)

Such 'cause-effect' combinations do not involve a strictly causative verb, and so fall outside the characterization of 'causative construction' followed in this chapter.

In the asymmetrical variety of SVC, the 'major member' (which is head of the SVC) comes from an unrestricted class, while the 'minor member' is chosen from a small closed class of verbs. The minor member may indicate position or direction (for example, 'run' plus 'go out' yields 'run out'), or some kind of non-spatial setting ('write' plus 'stay' is 'be writing for a continuous period'). Some languages have a kind of asymmetrical SVC where the minor member is a verb of causation. For example, in Tetun Dili (Austronesian; East Timor; Hajek 2006: 242) we find:

(2) labele   [fó   sai]_SVC [lia   neˈe]!
     NEGATIVE:CAN give exist   voice THIS
     You can't reveal this matter!

In Tetun Dili, *fó* 'give' functions as a causative verb within an SVC, so that (2) can be regarded as a type of causative construction. In most SVCs the constituent verbs share the same subject, but there are exceptions, called 'switch function'. (2) is of this type—the underlying O argument for 'give' is the same as the underlying S for 'exist'.

Tariana has causative clauses of the asymmetrical SVC variety. But Tariana requires that every verb in an SVC bears the same pronominal prefix. The way in which the language deals with this is illustrated in (Aikhenvald 2000a: 160):

(3) nu-inipe-nuku   kwaka-mhade [nu-a   nu-hña]_SVC
     1sg-children-TOPIC.NON.A/S how-FUTURE   1sg-make   1sg-eat
     How will I get my children to eat?

It is the children (not the speaker) who do the eating, and the sentence is understood in this way. But, since a surface structure constraint in Tariana requires that each verb in an SVC show the same subject pronoun, 1sg prefix *nu-* is on 'make' and is also attached to 'eat'. (Examples (67–8), from Yimas, in §24.4 below, illustrate a type of serial verb construction in which there is a single set of pronominal prefixes for the two verbs, which are effectively compounded together.)

There is another type of analytic causative which, in a quite different manner from SVCs, involves a predicate that includes two verbs. For instance, French has a causative verb *faire*, which appears to make up a single predicate with a following verb. The second verb is in a subordinate form, infinitive, showing that this is not an SVC.

As Comrie (1976a: 262–3) points out, the causee NP cannot come between *faire* and the following verb (which must be in infinitive form) but must be placed in oblique function (marked by preposition *à*) as normally happens with morphologically marked causatives. For instance:

(4) je   ferai   manger   [les   gâteaux] [à   Jean]
     1sg   make:FUT:1sg   eat:INFINITIVE   THE   cakes   PREP   name
     I shall make Jean eat the cakes

Italian, Spanish, and Catalan have constructions of similar type.

24.2.3 Periphrastic causatives

The third type of causative construction involves two verbs in separate clauses. Generally, the causative verb is in the main clause while the lexical verb is in a complement clause—see the discussion in §18.5.2—or some other kind of subordinate clause. In Macushi (Carib family, Brazil) the causee maintains its original function in the subordinate clause. Thus, in (5) 'Satan' is marked by ergative case since it is in A function in the main clause (with causative verb *emapu'tî*), and 'Jesus' is also marked by ergative since it is in A function in the subordinate clause (Abbott 1991: 40):

(5) [imakui'pî kupî   Jesus-ya$_A$]
      bad   do   Jesus-ERGATIVE
      emapu'tî   yonpa-'pî makui-ya$_A$ teuren
      CAUSATIVE TRY-PAST   Satan-ERGATIVE   FRUSTRATIVE
     Satan unsuccessfully tried to make Jesus do bad

Persian also has a periphrastic causative in which the causee retains its function in the 'that' subordinate clause (Mahootian 1997: 225).

Canela-Kraho (Jê family, Brazil) employs a subordinate construction for causatives, but with a difference. The causee maintains its normal function in the subordinate clause and is also marked as the O argument of the causative verb, the causer being the A argument. This language has a pronominal prefix to the verb which marks the O argument in a transitive clause and the S argument in an intransitive (an ergative strategy). Thus in (6) the causee ('me') is marked as O for the causative verb -to and as S for the lexical verb -jot 'sleep' (Popjes and Popjes 1986: 143).

(6) Capi_A te   [i-jōt   na]   i-to
     Capi   PAST:A   1sgS-sleep SUBORDINATOR   1sgO-CAUSATIVE
     Capi made me sleep

English differs from Macushi, Persian, and Canela-Kraho in that a causative verb is followed by a *to*-type complement clause, e.g. *I forced him to go, I made him go*. The causee is original subject of the subordinate clause (with verb *go*) but is coded with non-subject case, as the object of the causative verb.

We thus have three different ways of marking the causee within a periphrastic causative construction. In Macushi it is marked for its function in the subordinate clause, as in (5); in English it is marked for its function in the main clause (the clause with the causative verb); and in Canela-Kraho, shown in (6), it is marked for both of these.

It is interesting to compare Portuguese with the other Western Romance languages. Portuguese is like English in that the causee can come between the causative verb *fazer* and the lexical verb in infinitive form. Thus (cf. Aissen 1974: 354):

(7) Eu fiz   José comer   [os   bolos]
     1sg make:PAST:1sg José eat:INFINITIVE   THE cakes
     I made José eat the cakes

Compare with (4) in French, which has moved towards a more synthetic structure in which nothing can now intervene between the causative verb *faire* and the following infinitive *manger*. But note that French maintains a structure like (7) for other causative-type verbs such as *laisser* 'let, allow'.

Hale (1997a) discusses periphrastic causative constructions in languages of the Misumalpan family (Nicaragua and Honduras). These are unusual in that it is the causative verb which is in the subordinate clause, as in:

(8) yang baka kau   ât-ing   wauhdi-da
     1sg   child ACCUSATIVE CAUS-DIFF.SUBJ:1sg fall-PAST:3sg
     I made the child fall

Hale notes that causative constructions have different grammatical properties from other kinds of clause sequences with switch-reference marking. For instance, if the verb 'fall' in (8) is negated, this has scope over the whole sentence (that is, we get 'I did not make the child fall' rather than 'I made the child not fall'). If the verb in the subordinate clause were non-causative, a negator applied to the main verb would have scope only over that clause. This suggests that in a Misumalpan causative construction the two clauses are more tightly integrated than in a normal switch-reference construction. It could be the first stage in a process of grammaticalization, which might lead to a 'two verbs in one predicate' construction, and perhaps from that to the development of causative as a verbal affix.

Just as a morphological process of causation may also apply to an adjective or noun (§24.2.1), so may a periphrastic mechanism. In English, the complement clause to a verb of causation can be a copula construction, whose copula complement argument is an adjective or an NP. The copula verb *be* may optionally be omitted with an adjective as CC—for example, *I tried to make him (be) confident*—and is even more likely to be omitted with an NP as CC—thus, *The teacher is going to make me (be) the best dancer in the class.*

24.2.4 Lexical causatives

We can now consider a kind of causative that involves neither a morphological process nor separate causative verbs—lexical causatives. These are of two kinds: (a) when a single lexeme can be used in either a causative or a non-causative function; and (b) when there are two unrelated forms, that appear to be in causative relation.

(a) ONE LEXEME

As discussed in §13.3, in some languages every verb is either strictly transitive (appearing only in transitive clauses) or strictly intransitive (appearing only in intransitive clauses). Other languages have a number of ambitransitive (or 'labile') verbs that can occur in either clause type. There are two varieties of ambitransitives:

(i) S = A, for example *paint* in English, as in *Mary* (S)*is painting*, and *Mary* (A) *is painting the kitchen*(O).

(ii)' S = O, for example *walk* and *spill* in English, as in *The horse* (S) *walked around the paddock* and *John* (A) *walked the horse* (O) *around the paddock*; and in *John* (A) *spilled the milk* (O) and *The milk* (S) *spilled*.

Now for some S = O verbs native speakers' intuitions are that the lexeme is primarily transitive and only secondarily intransitive; this applies to *spill, smash,* and *extend*, among other verbs. For other S = O verbs the intransitive sense is considered to be primary; these include *trip, explode, melt, dissolve, walk,* and *march* (see Dixon 1991a: 291–3; 2005a: 309–11). For some of those in the latter set it is plausible to suggest that we have a causative relationship.

That is, verbs like *trip, dissolve,* and *walk* are basically intransitive but can be used in a transitive clause and then take on a causative meaning, similar to that marked by a morphological process or by a periphrastic verb in other languages.

Examples similar to those just given for English are provided for Greek by Joseph and Philippaki-Warburton (1987: 170). For the North American language Tunica, Haas (1941: 46) states that any non-causative intransitive stem may become causative through being inflected like a transitive verb. For instance 'we find that *ha'pa* has the function of an intransitive stem meaning "to stop, cease" when it undergoes non-causative inflection but assumes the function of a transitive stem meaning "to cause ... to stop, cease" when it undergoes causative inflection.' Li and Thompson (1976: 478) list a number of verbs of this type in Classical Chinese.

(b) TWO LEXEMES

In quite a number of languages one can assemble pairs of lexemes (with quite different forms), one intransitive and the other appearing to be a causative correspondent of it.

Thus, for Yimas (Lower Sepik family, Papua New Guinea), Foley (1991: 289) provides a number of lexical pairs, including the following:

(9) intransitive   transitive
       mal-   'die'   tu-   'kill'
       awa-   'burn'   ampu-   'burn'
       aypu-   'lie down'   ti-   'lay down'

In the Australian language Dyirbal, lexical pairs of this type include:

(10) intransitive   transitive
       mayi-   'come out'   bundi-   'take out'
       gaynyja-   'break'   bana-   'break'
       jana-   'stand'   jarra-   'put standing'

And in English we get:

(11) intransitive/copula-plus-adjective   transitive
       be dead   kill
       go in   put in
       lie   lay

It is relevant to enquire what the criteria are for linking distinct lexemes in this way. A major one is semantic, as can be seen by translation between languages. In English we have a single lexeme *burn*, with intransitive and causative senses, for example *The grass burned* and *I burned the grass*. Yimas would use *awa-* in translation of the first sentence and *ampu-* in translation of the second.

In Dyirbal there is a further criterion. The verbs given in (10) are from the everyday speech style, called Guwal. There is also a 'mother-in-law' speech style, Jalnguy, used in the presence of taboo relatives. As described in §5.1 and §8.1, Jalnguy has fewer lexemes than Guwal. In the case of two Guwal verbs which have the same meaning but just differ in transitivity, Jalnguy simply has a transitive verb, which corresponds to the transitive member of the Guwal pair. Derivational suffix *-(yi)rri-* ~*-marri-* marks reflexive and antipassive constructions (see §22.5.1 and §23.2.5) and can also have a general intransitivizing function. In these Jalnguy pairs, it is used for the correspondent of the intransitive member. Thus, the verbs in (10) have Jalnguy correspondents as follows (Dixon 1972: 297, 1982: 83):

			everyday style (Guwal)	mother-in-law style (Jalnguy)	
(12)	(a)	transitive	bundi-	yilwu-	'take out'
		intransitive	mayi-	yilwu-rri-	'come out'
	(b)	transitive	bana-	yuwa-	'break'
		intransitive	gaynyja-	yuwa-rri-	'break'
	(c)	transitive	jarra-	dinda-	'put standing'
		intransitive	jana-	dinda-rri-	'stand'

The fact that Jalnguy uses a single verbal form for each pair of verbs in Guwal indicates that they do have the same meaning, and differ just in transitivity.

24.2.5 Exchanging auxiliaries

In the Australian language Ngan'gityemerri (Reid 2000) a predicate generally includes a lexical verb and one of a closed set of thirty-one auxiliaries. Pronominal prefixes for S and A arguments, and suffixes for O argument, are added to the auxiliary, with the lexical verb appended to this auxiliary complex. Each lexical verb and each auxiliary has its own transitivity value. An intransitive verb will prototypically be used with an intransitive auxiliary. However, it can be used with a transitive auxiliary, which then has causative effect.

Thus the verb 'slip' plus the intransitive GO auxiliary is used to describe a simple act of slipping, as in (13). When 'slip' is used with the transitive auxiliary MOVE, the predicate has the meaning 'make slip', as in (14).

(13) ye-nim-purity
      3sgS-GO-slip
      He slipped

(14) ngu-di-nyi-purity-pe
      1sgA-MOVE-2sgO-slip-FUTURE
      I'll make you slip

This is not a prototypical causative since there is no derivation involved. Rather, Ngan'gityemerri employs a causative strategy, which is functionally and semantically equivalent to causative derivations in other languages.

24.3 Syntax

The various varieties of causatives, according to the way in which they are marked, have different syntactic possibilities.

The reported examples of forming causatives by exchanging auxiliaries apply just to intransitive verbs. For lexical causatives involving two forms (such as *be dead/kill* in English or *mal-/tu-* in Yimas) the non-causative member is always intransitive; it appears that this mechanism is also limited to providing causatives of intransitives.

A similar restriction is likely to apply for lexical causatives involving a single form which can be used in two syntactic frames, such as English *trip*, whose basic function is in an intransitive clause, for example *John* (S) *tripped*, but may also be used—with causative function—in a transitive clause, for example *Mary* (causer: A) *tripped John*(O).

The applicability of this kind of causative construction—in a language like English, where syntactic function is shown by place in constituent order—is limited by the surface structure possibilities available. Alongside the intransitive *John tripped* and its causative counterpart *Mary tripped John*, it is not possible to construct a causative counterpart for a transitive clause, for example *John ate the apple*. We cannot say **Mary John ate the apple* or **Mary ate John the apple* (with the meaning 'Mary made John eat the apple'), simply because no verb in English can be preceded by two independent NPs, and *eat* cannot be followed by two NPs.

There is, however, one circumstance where English does allow a causative of a transitive simply by change in constituent order. Secondary-A verbs were discussed in §18.5.2. These simply provide semantic modification but add no semantic role to the clause to which they are attached, for example, the Secondary-A verb *start*, as in *The maid started cleaning the bathroom at ten o'clock*. Here we can form a causative, with the causer (the new A) coming before *start* and the causee (the original A) coming between *start* and the following verb, for example *Mother started the maid cleaning the bathroom at ten o'clock*. (There is fuller discussion in Dixon 1991a: 172–9, 296–7; 2005a: 177–83, 314–15.)

Periphrastic causatives generally apply to any intransitive or transitive (including extended transitive) verb. In §24.2.3 we mentioned that in some languages the causee is the surface O of the transitive verb, while in others it still maintains its original function with respect to the lexical verb, and in some it may be marked for both functions. The other arguments of the lexical verb are retained, for example, in English *He gave the bone to the dog in the garden after lunch*, and *Mary made him give the bone to the dog in the garden after lunch*.

Periphrastic causatives may sometimes also apply to copula clauses. As mentioned at the end of §24.2.3, they do in English, but here the copula verb *be* can be omitted, for example *John was jealous* and the causative *Mary made John (be) jealous*. There is only a little information on languages that have serial causative constructions, with two verbs in one predicate. In Tariana this causative mechanism can apply to verbs of any transitivity (but not to a copula); see Aikhenvald (2003).

Morphological causatives are syntactically varied. In some languages they apply only to intransitives, in others only to intransitives and simple transitives (but not extended transitives), and in others to all verbs. (Examples are given in §24.4, §24.3.3, and §24.3.2 below.)

Hetzron (1976: 383) notes that, in Hungarian, impersonal verbs (of zero valency) such as *fagy* '[it] freezes' and *esik* '[it] rains' 'cannot be causativized for the simple reason that they have no subject that could become a causee'. However, causatives of impersonal verbs are possible in Nivkh (or Gilyak, isolate, north-east Russia; Nedjalkov, Otaina, and Xolodovič 1995: 77–8).

It is not usual for a morphological causative to apply to a copula verb, but this does sometimes happen. Example (15) gives a plain copula clause in Petats (Austronesian, Papua New Guinea) and (16) the causative version (information from Evelyn Gitey, via Alexandra Aikhenvald).

(15) [u   taul] e   ka-nou
      ARTICLE towel ASPECT COPULA-3sg:PRESENT
      [taru   lekleki-ta-guan]
      on:ARTICLE shoulder-POSS-1sg
      There is a towel on my shoulder (lit. A towel is on my shoulder)

(16) eyaw$_A$ e   ha-ka-nou
      3sg   ASPECT CAUSATIVE-COPULA-3sg:PRESENT
      [u   taul]$_O$ [taru   lekleki-ta-guan]
      ARTICLE towel   on:ARTICLE shoulder-POSS-1sg
      He put a towel on my shoulder (lit. He made a towel be on my shoulder)

Other languages in which a morphological causative can apply to a copula include Hebrew (Alcalay 1974: 519), and Turkana (Nilo-Saharan; Gerrit Dimmendaal, personal communication).

Many languages do not allow a transitive verb to be directly causativized. One strategy is to first detransitivize the verb, and then apply the causative derivation. Examples (17–20) are from Paumarí (Arawá family, Brazil; Chapman and Derbyshire 1991: 185–6).

(17) bi-noki-hi   [ida   gora]$_O$
      3sgA-see-THEME   ARTICLE(f) house(f)
      He saw the house

(18) noki-a-hi   [ida   gora]$_S$
      see-DETRANSITIVIZER-THEME   ARTICLE(f) house(f)
      The house is visible

(19) bi-na-noki-a-hi
      3sgA-CAUSATIVE-see-DETRANSITIVIZER-THEME
        [ida   gora]$_O$
        ARTICLE(f) house(f)
      He made the house become visible

(20) ho-ra$_O$ na-noki-a-hi-vini
      1sg-ACC   CAUSATIVE-see-DETRANSITIVIZER-APPLICATIVE-DEP
        hi-hi   [ida   gora]$_{2nd.O}$
        AUXILIARY-THEME   ARTICLE(f) house(f)
      He showed me the house (lit. He made the house become visible to me)

Sentence (17) is a straightforward transitive with root *noki-* 'see'. In (18) the detransitivizing suffix *-a* has been added, giving *noki-a-* with the O argument of (17) becoming S of (18) and the original A dropping out. In (19) causative prefix *na-* is added, giving *na-noki-a-* with the S of (18) becoming O of (19) and a causer brought in as A. In (20) a further derivational suffix is added, the applicative *-hi-* (a different suffix from *-hi* 'theme'), producing verb stem *na-noki-a-hi-*. This brings a beneficiary (here 'me') into O function with the original O NP from (19), 'house', becoming second object. In summary:

		she	house	he	me
(17)	transitive	A	O		
(18)	add detransitivizer, becomes intransitive		S		
(19)	add causative, becomes transitive		O	A	
(20)	add benefactive, becomes extended transitive		2nd O	A	O

Other languages in which a transitive verb must be made intransitive before a causative suffix can be added include Bandjalang (Australian;

Crowley 1978: 87–8) where an antipassive derivation must first apply, and Southern Tiwa (Kiowa-Tanoan family; Allen, Gardiner, and Frantz, 1984) where a noun in O function must be incorporated into the transitive verb, producing an intransitive stem, which then accepts the causative suffix. Further examples are mentioned in Baker (1988: 193–8) and Song (1996: 179–81).

The discussion that follows, in §§24.3.1–3, relates to intransitive, transitive, and extended transitive clauses whose arguments receive what is the canonical case marking for that language. It was mentioned in §13.6 that in some languages there is a small class of verbs (typically, verbs of ATTENTION and LIKING, plus those describing physical and mental states) which take non-canonical marking; the subject may receive dative or genitive inflection (instead of the canonical nominative or ergative). In Kannada (Dravidian) a dative-marked subject retains its marking when the clause is made transitive, for example 'I-DATIVE$_S$ got.a.headache', and 'you-NOMINATIVE$_A$ (causer) I-DATIVE$_O$ got.a.headache:CAUSATIVE' ('you made me get a headache') (Sridhar 1979: 111, 1990: 219). Note that in this language there is difficulty in deciding on the transitivity status of both non-causative and causative clauses with a dative subject.

24.3.1 Of intransitives

Virtually every causative mechanism applies to intransitive verbs (quite a few apply only to intransitives). In every language we get the original S becoming O of the causative construction:

(21)   CAUSATIVE OF INTRANSITIVE

underlying clause (intransitive)   S
                                                          |
causative construction (transitive)   causer: A   O

This is exemplified in (18–19).

While every language has the schema shown in (21), a number also have an alternative marking for the original S, which carries a semantic difference.

(a) Japanese allows the original S to be either in O function, marked by accusative postposition *o*, or to be marked by dative postposition *ni*. The dative alternative indicates that the causee (the original S) does it willingly, 'let do', while the accusative alternative indicates that the causee's intentions were ignored by the causer, 'make do'. See (52–4) in §24.4 below.

(b) In Hungarian the original S can be marked as O, by accusative case, indicating that the causer acts directly, for example 'The nurse (causer: A) walked him (original S: accusative) for an hour every day', where the nurse accompanied him on the walk. Or, for some verbs, it can be marked by instrumental case, implying that the causer acted indirectly, for example 'The doctor (causer: A) had him (original S: instrumental) walk for an hour each day', where the doctor just told him to do so. (Hetzron 1976: 394, and see the discussion of parameter 6, Directness, in §24.4 below.) Sumbatova (1993: 259–60) describes a similar alternation in Svan (Kartvelian).

Nivkh constitutes a partial exception to schema (21). In this language a causee (whether originally S or A) is marked by a special 'causee case suffix', -ax, if it is animate; if inanimate it receives zero marking (like an O argument). See (a) under (i) in §24.3.2.

There can be another sort of variation on the prototypical schema for causatives of intransitives, shown in (21). As described in §3.9 and §13.2, a number of languages have a split-S system, where some intransitive verbs have their S argument marked like the A of a transitive (Sa) and other intransitive verbs have S marked like O (So). For two languages from the Carib family in Brazil, Ikpeng (Pacheco 1997) and Wayana (Tavares 1995), in the causative of an So-type intransitive, the original So goes into O function. In the causative of a transitive, the original O stays as is and the original A (the causee) is marked by dative suffix. In the causative of an Sa-type intransitive, the causer is A and the original Sa is now marked by dative, just like the original A in the causative of a transitive.

For the great majority of languages each causative construction is syntactically similar to an existing non-causative clause type. Only very occasionally does a causative form a new construction type, not found elsewhere in the grammar. This does occur in Tariana, a split-S language. Transitive and Sa-type intransitive verbs take a pronominal prefix marking the A or Sa argument while So-type intransitives have no prefix.

Causatives of Sa-type intransitives are normal transitive clauses with a prefix marking A (the causer). Just So-type intransitives in Tariana have two alternative causative constructions: either (a) with a prefix (for the causer, in A function), indicating that the causer achieved the result intentionally (for example 'He frightened them, on purpose'); or (b) with no prefix (the causer being shown just by an NP), indicating that the result was obtained unintentionally (for example 'The dog's barking made me frightened' when the dog didn't mean to frighten me). (See examples (22–7) in Aikhenvald 2000a.) Thus, in Tariana a transitive clause with no pronominal prefix is a special construction type, found only with an 'unintentional' causative of an So-type intransitive.

24.3.2 Of transitives

This section provides a general discussion of the syntax of morphological causatives of transitive verbs (including extended transitives as a subclass). §24.3.3 then looks in more detail at extended transitives.

It is almost always the case that a causative adds an argument; that is, it increases the valency of the verb by one. Mishmi (Bodic branch of Tibeto-Burman; north-east India) is noteworthy in that the causative of a transitive appears to have at most two arguments. There are in fact two causative suffixes: with *-bo*, just the causee (not the causer) is stated, and with *-syig*, just the causer (not the causee) is stated. Thus (Sastry 1984: 155–6):

(22) hã   tapẽ thá-de-bo
      1sg:NOMINATIVE rice   eat-TENSE-CAUSATIVE$_1$
      I (causee) was made to eat rice (by someone—unstated but
         implied causer)

(23) hã   tapẽ thá-syig-a
      1sg:NOMINATIVE rice   eat-CAUSATIVE$_2$-AFFIX
      I (causer) made (someone—unstated but implied causee) eat rice

If one wishes to specify both causer and causee, then the verb must be stated twice, once with each of the causative suffixes:

(24) hã   thá-syig-a,
      1sg:NOMINATIVE eat-CAUSATIVE$_2$-AFFIX
       nyú   thá-de-bo
       2sg:NOMINATIVE eat-TENSE-CAUSATIVE$_1$
      I made you eat

(The source grammar does not say how the original O argument, 'rice', would be specified in (24).)

Mishmi is highly unusual. In virtually every other language all the original arguments may be stated, together with the new argument, the causer. As already described, the causative of an intransitive is a straightforward matter, with the causer coming in as A and—in almost every instance—the original S becoming O. The causative of a transitive is often less straightforward, and shows more variation.

A transitive clause already has two core arguments, in A and O functions. The causer is always placed in A function (I know of no putative causative that could be an exception to this). Now in a periphrastic causative construction, where there are two clauses involved, there is no difficulty in making provision for all the arguments. As shown in §24.2.3, the causee can be marked as O of the causative verb or still as A of the lexical verb, or both at once; the other arguments of the lexical verb remain unchanged.

A morphological causative of a transitive verb is itself a transitive clause. The question now is: what happens to the A and O arguments of the original clause. There are five main possibilities, shown in (25).

(25)   CAUSATIVE OF TRANSITIVE

type	causer	original A (causee)	original O
(i)	A	special marking	O
(ii)	A	retains A-marking	O
(iii)	A	has O-marking	has O-marking
(iv)	A	O	non-core
(v)	A	non-core	O

In type (i) there is a special marking, used just for the causee in a causative construction. In (ii) both causer and original A receive A-marking. In (iii) the original A and the original O both receive O-marking. In (iv) the original A becomes O, and the original O now takes non-core marking. And in (v) the original O remains as is, while the original A takes peripheral marking. Types (i) and (ii) are relatively rare, with type (iii) being rather well attested, while types (iv) and (v) occur with medium frequency.

The five possibilities will now be discussed in turn.

TYPE (i)—SPECIAL MARKING FOR CAUSEE

(a) Nivkh has no case marking for S, A, O or indirect object. However, there is a special case suffix -*ax*, which is used just to mark an animate causee (whether original A or S) in a causative construction. (An inanimate causee takes no marking.) The suffix -*ax* is generally optional but it is obligatory when there are already three unmarked NPs as in (27), the causative counterpart of the extended transitive clause in (26) (Nedjalkov, Otaina, and Xolodovič, 1995: 78, and Comrie 1976a: 267, 274).

(26)   ōla   lep   pʰnanak   xim-dʹ
        child   bread   his.older.sister   give-FINITE
        The child gave the bread to his older sister

(27)   ətək   ōla-ax   lep   pʰnanak   xim-gu-dʹ
        father   child-CAUSEE   bread   his.older.sister   give-CAUS-FINITE
        The father made/let the child give the bread to his older sister

(b) The causative of a transitive verb in Telugu (Dravidian) has the original O remaining as is with the original A (the causee) being followed by a special marker, *ceeta*. This is in fact the instrumental case form of the noun *ceeyi* 'hand' (lit. 'with the hand') but here functions as a postposition marking the causee argument in the causative of a transitive. Note that for the causative of an intransitive the original S can either be placed in accusative case or can be marked by *ceeta*; there is a semantic difference, the first alternative indicating direct and the second indicating indirect causative—see parameter 6, Directness, in §24.4 below (Krishnamurti and Gwynn 1985: 202, and Bh. Krishnamurti, personal communication).

TYPE (ii)—CAUSEE RETAINS A-MARKING

(a) In Kabardian (North-west Caucasian), a language with an ergative case system, the causee retains its case marking. Thus the S of an intransitive clause (marked by absolutive case) becomes O in the corresponding causative (still marked by absolutive). In the causative of a transitive the causer takes ergative inflection and the causee (original A) retains its ergative inflection (Abitov et al. 1957: 126).

(b) In another ergative language, Trumai (isolate, Upper Xingu region, Brazil) we encounter a similar situation (Guirardello 1999a, 1999b: 301–4):

(28) Alaweru-k   hai-ts   axos   disi ka
      Alaweru-ERGATIVE 1sg-ERGATIVE   child:ABSOLUTIVE   beat CAUS
      Alaweru made me beat the child

Note that the causer and the causee (original A) are both marked by an ergative enclitic (this has the form *-ts* after the 1sg pronoun and *-(e/a)k* elsewhere); they are distinguished by their order in the clause, causer before causee. Guirardello states that speakers tend to omit one of the ergative-marked NPs if, say, the information can be inferred from context, or it does not matter who the causee is. If this is not the case, then both ergative NPs will be included.

Kabardian and Trumai each have two NPs in ergative case, in the causative of a transitive. Abitov et al. (1957: 126) state that in Kabardian the ergative-marked causer is in A function while the ergative-marked causee is now an 'oblique agent' (although the term is not further explained). Further investigation is required to tell whether this also applies for Trumai.

TYPE (iii)—ORIGINAL A TAKES ON O-MARKING, ORIGINAL O RETAINS O-MARKING

There are a fair number of languages in which the original A (the causee) takes on the marking of an O in a causative construction, while the original O appears to retain its marking. That is, it seems on the surface that we have two Os.

Further investigation shows that, for most of these languages, only one of the arguments has the full properties of an O—for example, it can be passivized—(this could be called the 'full O') while the other NP that is marked like an O lacks these properties (it could be called a 'second object'). It is generally the original A which is the full O while the original O has become the second object (making these ostensibly type (iii) languages perhaps a special case of type (iv), where A becomes O and the original O moves out of the core).

In Hebrew there are three syntactic possibilities for the causative of a transitive: type (iv), original A becomes O and original O is marked by locative; type (v) original O stays as is and original A is marked by dative; and type (iii), both original A and original O are marked by the accusative preposition *et*. An example of the third alternative is (Cole 1976: 99):

(29)   hirkadə-ti   [et   ha-talmid-im]
       dance:CAUS:PAST-1sgA   ACCUSATIVE   ARTICLE-student-PLURAL
       [et   ha-rikud   ha-xadaš]
       ACCUSATIVE   ARTICLE-dance   ARTICLE-new
       I made the students dance the new dance

Here the causee NP, 'the students', can passivize and is thus identified as the full O while 'the new dance' cannot passivize and is identified as second object. Similar conclusions apply for morphological causatives in Tariana (Aikhenvald 2000a, 2003) and in Imbabura Quechua (Cole 1982: 136–7).

Having two NPs marked in the same way, as object, may lead to ambiguity. For Ute, Givón (1980: 164–5) states that although the case-marking of both objects is identical, their relative order tells them apart, with the causee preceding the underlying object. Thus:

(30)   [mamá-ci̱   'u]   [ta'wá-ci   'uwáy] ['áapa-ci   'uwáy]
       woman-SUBJECT   SHE   man-OBJECT   HIM   boy-OBJECT   HIM
       maĝá-ti-pu̱gá
       feed-CAUSATIVE-REMOTE
       The woman made the man feed the boy

If the order of the two object NPs, *ta'wá-ci 'uwáy* and *'áapa-ci 'uwáy* were reversed, the sentence would mean 'The woman made the boy feed the man'.

Amharic (Semitic, Ethiopia) has an interesting set of possibilities. In this language an NP in O function can take accusative marking only if it is definite. As Amberber (2000) shows, there are two basic possibilities for the causative of a transitive clause:

   (i) Original A becomes O; it must be definite, and takes accusative marking. The original O can be omitted but it may be retained and is then generally indefinite (it cannot take accusative marking). The original A is plainly a full O, with the original O becoming second object. Thus we can have, in a simple transitive clause, either 'He cut the meat (definite, accusative)' or 'He cut some meat (indefinite, no marking)'. Only the second of these (that in which the O is indefinite) is likely to be causativized.

(ii) If the original O is inherently definite (for example, a proper noun) it stays as is, in which case the original A (the causee) is generally omitted (but its identity may be inferable from the context).

There are a number of languages where original A takes on O-marking and original O retains O-marking and it is, on the information available, impossible to distinguish between the two objects. In Oromo (Cushitic branch of Afroasiatic family, Ethiopia; Owens 1985: 172–81) passive can apply to the O NP in a plain transitive or in the causative of an intransitive but to neither of the O-marked NPs in the causative of a transitive. In Yagua (Peru; Payne and Payne 1990: 284–7), either or both of the O-marked arguments can be specific and referred to by a clitic; there seems to be no criterial way of deciding between them. In Gamo (Omotic, Ethiopia; Éva 1990: 395) the two O-marked NPs can occur in either order and no criteria are given for distinguishing between them. Misantla Totonac (Totonacan, Mexico) also has two objects in the causative of a transitive clause, and MacKay (1999: 303) explicitly states that 'multiple object marking may result in ambiguity'.

The causative of a transitive is a kind of extended transitive clause. In many languages it has essentially the same syntax as a non-causative extended transitive (involving a verb like 'give' or 'show' or 'tell'). It is relevant to enquire whether languages with 'two objects' in the causative of a transitive also have 'two objects' in a regular extended transitive, that is, with both 'gift' and 'recipient' marked as object for a verb of giving, etc. It appears that this does apply in the case of Tariana, Yagua, and Misantla Totonac, but not for the other languages surveyed here. There is different marking for object and indirect object of an underived extended transitive verb in Hebrew, Imbabura Quechua, Ute, Amharic, Oromo and Gamo. It appears that in these languages 'double object' is a characteristic just of the causative-of-a-transitive construction.

TYPE (iv)—ORIGINAL A BECOMES NEW O, ORIGINAL O MOVES OUT OF THE CORE

In this variety of morphological causative of a transitive verb each of the arguments shifts its function, the original A (the causee) taking on O function within the causative construction and the original O moving out of the core into a peripheral function.

In Javanese, core syntactic relations are shown by the constituent order AVO, SV (very like English). In a extended transitive clause the indirect object (for example, the recipient in an activity of giving) is marked by the dative preposition *marang*. Example (31) shows a simple transitive clause and (32) its causative counterpart, which has the structure of a normal extended transitive, with original A becoming O (shown by its positioning immediately after the verb) and original O now taking dative preposition *marang* (Suhandano 1994: 67).

(31) asu-ne$_A$ nguyak Bambang$_O$
      dog-DEFINITE chase   Bambang
      The dog chased Bambang

(32) Sri$_A$ nguyak-ake   asu-ne$_O$ [marang Bambang]
      Sri   chase-CAUSATIVE dog-DEFINITE   DATIVE   Bambang
      Sri got the dog to chase Bambang

There is a similar causative mechanism, also involving constituent order, in Tolai, another Austronesian language (Papua New Guinea; Mosel 1984: 154–5).

Swahili (Bantu, East Africa) has similar syntax. Here the fact that the original A takes on O function in the causative construction is shown by its being cross-referenced by O pronominals in the verb, while the original O loses its cross-referencing (Vitale 1981: 155–6). Jarawara (Arawá family, Brazil) is like Swahili in having A and O arguments expressed by bound pronominals within the predicate. It has a general postposition *jaa* which marks any non-core argument. In the causative of a transitive the original A is now cross-referenced as O while the original O loses its cross-referencing and is marked by *jaa* (see Dixon and Aikhenvald 1997: 83, and Dixon 2004: 251–2).

Within a causative construction in Bora (Bora-Witotoan family, Peru and Colombia; Thiesen and Weber 2000: 234–5), the causee goes into O function and the underlying O is now marked by suffix -*βu̇*. The causative of a transitive now has similar marking on NPs as a plain extended transitive but with one important difference from the languages just mentioned. With a ditransitive verb such as give, the 'recipient' is in O function, with 'gift' marked by -*βu̇* (rather than 'gift' being in O function).

Kammu (Austroasiatic, Laos; Svantesson 1983: 103–5) is another language with this kind of causative construction. Here the original O is often omitted but can be included for some verbs, marked by the instrumental preposition. Compare the plain transitive in (33) with its causative counterpart in (34).

(33) [kɔ́ɔn Tɛ́ɛk]$_A$ màh któŋ$_O$
      child Tɛ́ɛk   eat   egg
      Tɛ́ɛk's children eat eggs

(34) Tɛ́ɛk pń-màh   [kɔ́ɔn tèe]   [yʌ̀ʌ   któŋ]
      Tɛ́ɛk CAUS-eat child REFLEXIVE INSTRUMENTAL egg
      Tɛ́ɛk gave his children eggs to eat (lit: Tɛ́ɛk made his children eat eggs)

Interestingly, 'give' is expressed in Kammu as the causative of 'have', with
the recipient being in O function and the gift marked by the instrumental
preposition. Compare (33–4) with:

(35) nàa$_A$ ʔàh   tráak$_O$
      she   have buffalo
      She has a buffalo

(36) kə̀ə$_A$ pń-ʔàh   nàa$_O$ [yʌ̀ʌ   tráak]
      he   CAUSATIVE-have she   INSTRUMENTAL buffalo
      He gave her a buffalo

Babungo (Grassfields Bantu, Cameroon; Schaub 1985: 211) is like Kammu
in that the original O is generally omitted but can be included as an optional
adverbial, marked by preposition *nə̀* 'with'. And, as mentioned under type
(iii), those languages in which original A becomes full O and the original O
(which still retains object-marking) is syntactically a 'second object' are also
essentially of this type.

TYPE (V)—ORIGINAL O STAYS AS O, ORIGINAL A MOVES OUT OF THE CORE

There are two subtypes here: (a) where the original A goes into the first empty
slot on a hierarchy of clausal functions; (b) where the original A goes into a
fixed function. The first has been made much of in the literature but is in fact
rather rare.

(a) Marking of original A is motivated by a hierarchy. In an important and
pioneering paper, Comrie (1975) brought into play a hierarchy that had already
been suggested to explain the syntax of relative clauses (in work published as
Keenan and Comrie 1977):

(37) COMRIE'S HIERARCHY
      subject—direct object—indirect object—oblique—genitive—object of
      comparison

He suggested that in one group of languages the causee goes into the first available slot in the hierarchy. For example, in French we get causatives of intransitive, transitive, and extended transitive clauses as (repeating (4) as (39)):

(38) je_A ferai   courir   Jean_O
     1sg MAKE:FUTURE:1sg run:INFINITIVE Jean
     I shall make Jean run

(39) je_A ferai   manger   [les gâteaux]_O [à   Jean]
     1sg MAKE:FUT:1sg eat:INFINITIVE THE cakes   PREP Jean
     I shall make Jean eat the cakes

(40) je_A ferai   écrire   [une lettre]_O
     1sg MAKE:FUTURE:1sg write:INFINITIVE A   letter
          [au   directeur] [par   Jean]
          PREPOSITION:THE headmaster PREPOSITION Jean
     I shall make Jean write a letter to the headmaster

The causee, 'Jean', fills the O slot in (38). In (39) the O slot is already filled and it goes into the indirect object slot, marked by preposition *à* 'to'. In (40) both O and indirect object slots are filled so the causee goes into an oblique slot, marked by preposition *par* 'by'.

Comrie refers to this as the 'paradigm case' (1975: 8, 1976a: 263–4) or 'the norm' (1989: 174–83) or 'a general tendency' (1985a: 342). These labels have been repeated by other writers; for example, Palmer (1994: 218) uses 'paradigm case'. In fact this pattern is far from common. It is found in Western Romance languages such as French and Italian. Comrie quotes Turkish as a further example, but the literature on this language gives mixed information. For instance, Kornfilt (1997: 331–2) states that the causee goes into dative case in the causative of both simple transitive and extended transitive clauses (the causative of a extended transitive then having two dative NPs). There may be a few other languages of type (v-a) but they are greatly outnumbered by those of type (v-b). When we also take into account types (i–iv), it will be seen that there is no justification for attaching special importance to the pattern illustrated for French in (38–40).

(b) Original A is assigned a fixed non-core function (irrespective of whether the underlying clause is simple transitive or extended transitive). The possibilities here include:

(i) Dative. This is the mechanism in Sanuma (Yanomami family, Brazil/ Venezuela; Borgman 1990: 47–51), Apalai (Carib family, Brazil, Koehn and Koehn 1986: 49–51)—plus two other Carib languages, Ikpeng and Wayana, mentioned in §24.3.1—Kamaiurá (Tupí-Guaraní branch of Tupí family, Brazil; Seki 2000: 291), Turkish (Kornfilt 1997: 331–2), and Japanese. One of the causative strategies in Hebrew involves original A being marked by dative preposition.

Comrie (1976a: 272) mentions this as an alternative strategy in French. That is, most native speakers can say *Je ferai écrire à Jean une lettre au directeur* as an alternative to (40), although he states that the preferred construction type, acceptable to all speakers, is that shown in (40).

We find a variant of this pattern in Sinhalese (Indo-European) where the original A of a simple transitive or extended transitive verb goes into dative case, but this must be followed by the postposition *kiəla* (Gair 1970: 68–70). (We could regard this as a language of type (i), with dative-plus-*kiəla* constituting 'special marking' of original A.)

All of these languages allow a clause to include two dative NPs—the original dative of the extended transitive verb, plus the original O.

(ii) Instrumental. Examples here include Hungarian (Kenesei, Vago, and Fenyvesi 1998: 186–8), Kannada (Sridhar 1990: 217–9), Punjabi (Bhatia 1993: 238–40) and Marathi (Pandharipande 1997: 401–3).

(iii) Locative. For example, in Daghestanian languages (Hewitt 1983).

(iv) Allative. For example, in West Greenlandic Eskimo (Fortescue 1984: 268–9).

(v) Adessive. For example, the morphological causative in Finnish. Interestingly, the original A of the periphrastic causative in Finnish takes the genitive suffix (Sulkala and Karjalainen 1992: 294–6).

(vi) Possessive. Comrie (2000) states that in Tsez (North-east Caucasian) the original A is marked with the possessive case suffix, and this applies whether A was originally marked by lative case (with verbs like 'see' and 'find') or by ergative case (with other verbs).

24.3.3 Of extended transitives

The surface syntactic constraints of a language may limit the syntactic— and also semantic—possibilities for causative constructions. We mentioned in §24.3.1 that, in the causative of an intransitive, Japanese allows the original S to be marked by either dative or accusative postposition, indicating that the causee performed the action willingly (dative) or that the causer ignored the causee's intentions (accusative). However, Japanese does not allow two accusative-marked arguments in a clause. Thus, in the causative of a transitive (including extended transitive), since there is already an O NP, the original A (the causee) must take dative marking. The syntactic alternation for intransitives is not available for transitives, and with it is lost the possibility of a semantic alternation.

Syntactic constraints are especially evident when we look in detail at causatives of extended transitive clauses, which in underlying form have A, O, and indirect object (generally marked by dative case or adposition). As noted under (v-b) in §24.3.2, there are some languages which allow two dative NPs (rather more, in fact, than allow two accusative NPs); for example, Japanese, Turkish, Kamaiurá. But other languages do not permit two dative NPs in a single clause. There are a number of different ways of dealing with this situation.

In Evenki (Tungusic, north Russia; Nedjalkov 1997: 231–2), the original A in the causative of a simple transitive has two possible markings: definite accusative or dative (the difference in meaning is not given in the source grammar). In the causative of an extended transitive the original A can only be definite accusative, not dative. (Interestingly, this language allows two accusative NPs in a clause, but not two dative NPs.)

Causatives of transitives in Svan (Kartvelian, Georgia) are basically of type (v-b) from §24.3.2, where the original O stays as is, and the original A goes into dative case. But Svan does not allow two dative NPs in a clause and in the causative of an extended transitive, which already has a dative NP, what we get is the original A becoming the new dative and the old dative moving down to become an oblique constituent, marked by genitive plus postposition -t' 'for'. Example (41) shows a simple extended transitive clause and (42) its causative correspondent (Sumbatova 1993: 257):

(41) dena-d$_A$ kalaxwem   mare-s   diar$_O$
      girl-ERGATIVE   give:AORIST   man-DATIVE   bread:NOMINATIVE
      The girl gave bread to the man

(42) eže-m$_A$ kalaxawodnune   dena-s
      he-ERGATIVE   give:CAUSATIVE:AORIST   girl-DATIVE
         diar$_O$ mare-š-t'
      bread:NOMINATIVE   man-GENITIVE-FOR
      He made the girl give bread to the man

Other languages have varying ways of responding to the prohibition on two dative NPs in a clause, when attempting to create the causative of an extended transitive. In Hixkaryana (Carib family, Brazil) both causee (original A) and original indirect object should take dative postposition *wya*; but only one *wya* phrase can occur in a clause so that (43a) is ambiguous. In order to disambiguate it one could add a second clause with the same verb 'give', but not in causative form, as in (43b).

(43) (a) kuraha yïmpoye   Waraka   rowya
         bow   3sgA:CAUSATIVE:give:3gO   Waraka   1sg:DATIVE
         either (i)   Waraka made me give a bow (to someone)
            or (ii)   Waraka made (someone) give a bow to me

(b) wimye   [Kaywerye wya]
    1sgA:give:3sgO   Kaywerye DATIVE
    I gave [the bow] to Kaywerye

Taken together, the two clauses of (43) have an unambiguous meaning 'Waraka made me give the bow to Kaywerye' (Derbyshire 1985: 89, cf. 1979: 135). Sonrai behaves in a similar way (Shopen and Konaré 1970). In Basque the prohibition on a clause including two dative NPs means that one simply cannot form a morphological causative of an extended transitive. In this language the morphological causative applies only to intransitive and to many simple transitive clauses (those with an inanimate O). But there is also a periphrastic causative which applies to all types of clauses, including extended transitives (Saltarelli 1988: 220–1).

In Abaza (North-west Caucasian) a predicate can cross-reference up to four arguments. In the morphological causative of an extended transitive such as 'he couldn't make him give it back to her', all of causer (A, 'he'), causee (original A, 'him'), original O ('it'), and original indirect object ('her') can be shown by pronominal prefixes to the verb. This was illustrated by (43) in §15.1.9. However, Abkhaz (another dialect of the same language) avoids four-argument verbs and as a result causatives of extended transitives can only be achieved by using a periphrastic construction (Hewitt 1979: 171).

There is one syntactic possibility which might be expected but has not yet been encountered. Note that we have an extended transitive version of type (iv) from §24.3.2, with:

(44)   underlying clause   A   O   dative
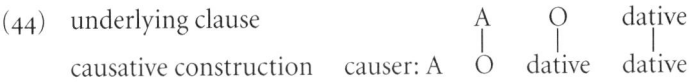
      causative construction   causer: A   O   dative   dative

And we have a variety of type (v) found in Svan (see (41–2)):

(45)   underlying clause   A   O   dative

      causative construction   causer: A   dative   O   oblique marking

The one possibility which is not currently attested is a combination of these, an extension of type (iv) whereby in a causative construction each argument shifts one place down on a hierarchy:

(46)   underlying clause   A   O   dative
                                               | | |
      causative construction   causer: A   O   dative   oblique marking

Note that the data on causatives of extended transitives has many gaps; a high proportion of grammars simply do not mention this topic. When more documentation becomes available, I would predict that a language showing schema (46) will be found.

24.3.4 Double causatives

Some of the varieties of causative mechanisms carry the possibility of being applied twice (although double application may occur only rather occasionally in the daily use of language). This possibility is plainly not available for lexical causatives (§24.2.4) or for the mechanism which involves exchanging auxiliaries (§24.2.5) and it is not reported for the 'two verbs in one predicate' construction (§24.2.2).

One would expect periphrastic causatives to always carry the possibility of being applied iteratively; for example, in English *The king made the general make the captain make the soldiers clean out his goldfish bowl*. We know of no counter-examples to this (although this is not to imply that a detailed search might not uncover some). In fact, whether or not it can be iterated may be one criterion for deciding whether a causative verb enters into a simple predicate or a dual predicate construction type. In Lahu (Tibeto-Burman), for instance, a causative verb such as *ci* 'make' appears to make up a single predicate with the lexical verb (like *faire* in French; see §24.2.2). This is confirmed by the fact that a double causative (for example 'God made the devil spirit make the boy kick the dog') cannot be achieved by using *ci* twice within the same surface clause. 'Rather, one must embed the *ci* clause within a higher causative-purpose clause' (Matisoff 1973: 436).

Turning now to morphological causatives (§24.2.1), we find that some languages (including Jarawara) only allow the causative process to apply once per verb, whereas others may have it apply twice. Double application sometimes indicates a single causative with a special meaning; for example, 'force to do' in Swahili, illustrated in (59) below, and intensive meaning in Oromo (Dubinsky, Lloret, and Newman 1988).

In some languages two morphological causative mechanisms, that have rather different form, can be applied to a single verb. In Nivkh some verbs are causativized by replacing their initial stop or affricate by a corresponding fricative and/or liquid. For example:

(47) t'o-   'bend' (intransitive)   zo-   'bend' (transitive)
      pəkz- 'get lost' (intransitive) vəkz- 'lose' (transitive)
      tʰa-   'fry' (intransitive)   rša-   'fry' (transitive)

The second mechanism involves a suffix *-(g)u-* being added to the verb; for example *nok-* 'be narrow', *nok-u-* 'make narrow'. There is also a class of verbs that combines the two changes to form a single causative: they include *t'oz-* 'go out (e.g. fire)', *zoz-u-* 'put (e.g. fire) out'.

Some verbs in Nivkh can form a causative in either of two ways; we then find that initial consonant mutation (with or without an accompanying suffix) indicates direct causation, as in *pol-* 'fall', *vol-u-* 'make fall (e.g. knock down)';

and the use of a suffix (with no mutation) indicates indirect causation, as in *pol-gu* 'make fall (for example, by not supporting)'. Both causatives may apply to a single root. Nedjalkov, Otaina, and Xolodovič (1995: 67) present this as a symmetrical array:

(48)

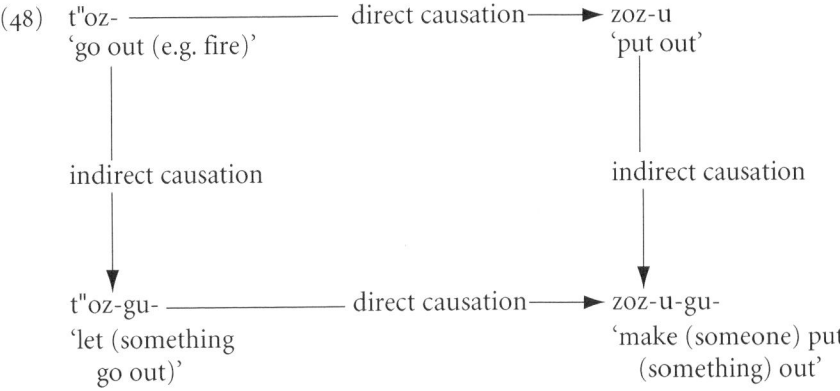

    t"oz- ————————— direct causation———→ zoz-u
    'go out (e.g. fire)'   'put out'

    indirect causation   indirect causation

    t"oz-gu- ——————— direct causation———→ zoz-u-gu-
    'let (something   'make (someone) put
       go out)'   (something) out'

In many languages the same causative process can be applied twice, yielding a causative of a causative. Thus, in Capanawa (Pano family, Peru; Payne 1990: 229) we can get:

(49)   underlying root (intransitive)   -mapet- 'ascend'
       causative (transitive)   -mapet-ma- 'bring [it]up (i.e.
                                                 make ascend)'
       double causative (extended transitive) -mapet-ma-ma- 'make/allow
                                                 [someone] to bring [it] up'

Similar sequences of two causative affixes added to an intransitive verb are reported for a number of languages. These include two tokens of the same causative suffix in Crow (Graczyk 2007: 323), Hungarian, and Turkish—see §10.4—and two tokens of the same prefix in Kabardian (Abitov et al. 1957: 127) and in Karbi (Tibeto-Burman, Assam; Jeyapaul 1987: 111).

In Apalai, different suffixes are used for the causative of an intransitive and of a transitive verb. Some intransitive verbs take *-ma-* (as *nyh-ma-* 'make sleep') while others take *-nohpo-* (as *kuma-nohpo-* 'make rise'). A transitive verb is causativized by adding *-po* (for example, *aro-po-* 'make [someone] take [something]'). An intransitive and a transitive causativizer can be applied in sequence. For example (Koehn and Koehn 1986: 51):

(50)   otuh-   'eat' (intransitive)
       otuh-ma-   'feed [someone], i.e. make [someone] eat' (transitive)
       otuh-ma-po- 'get [someone] to feed [someone]' (extended transitive)

It is also possible to apply the two intransitive causative suffixes in sequence. This produces a single causative but with an indirect meaning:

(51)   otuh-ma-nohpo-   'oversee [someone] eating' (transitive)

24.4 Semantics

Quite a few languages have two or more causative constructions, involving either different formal mechanisms or different marking of the causee (original S or A). There is always a semantic difference and it may involve one or more of nine semantic parameters, set out below.

If a language has just one causative mechanism, then this generally has a wide semantic range, covering all values of most of the parameters. But it is unlikely to cover *all* values of *all* parameters. Many linguists, when writing the grammar of a language, simply state 'there is a causative construction', describing the formal marking and something of the syntax. This is not enough—the meaning must be discussed as well. This is done for Motuna by Onishi (2000) when he specifies 'the Causer acting directly and achieving the result intentionally', and 'the Causee is not in control of the state or activity, and is affected by the result of the whole event'. See also Rice's (2000) comparison of the meanings of morphological causatives across various Athapaskan languages.

There can be further semantic specifications that are not known to enter into any of the contrasts between alternative mechanisms—discussed below—but may need to be stated in the semantic characterization of the single causative in some languages. For instance, in Nivkh a causer must be animate. One cannot, as a rule, say something like 'The mist made us stay in the village', using a causative construction. This has to be expressed in another way; for example, 'We stayed in the village because of the mist' (Nedjalkov, Otaina, and Xolodovič 1995: 76).

The nine semantic parameters are:

(a) RELATING TO THE VERB
    1. *State/action*. Does a causative mechanism apply only to a verb describing a **state**, or also to a verb describing an **action**?
    2. *Transitivity*. Does it apply only to **intransitive** verbs, or to both intransitive and (some or all) simple **transitive** verbs, or to all types of verbs—intransitive, simple transitive, and also **extended transitive**? Note that there are no causatives that apply only to transitives and not to intransitives. However, the form of a causative mechanism may vary depending on whether it applies to an intransitive or to a transitive verb, as in Carib languages such as Apalai—illustrated in (50) just above—and Hixkaryana (Derbyshire 1979: 134–5).

(b) RELATING TO THE CAUSEE (original S or A)

    3. *Control.* Is the causee **lacking control** of the activity (for example, if inanimate, or a young child) or normally **having control**?

    4. *Volition.* Does the causee do it **willingly** ('let') or **unwillingly** ('make')?

    5. *Affectedness.* Is the causee **only partially affected** by the activity, or **completely affected**?

(c) RELATING TO CAUSER (in A function in the causative construction)

    6. *Directness.* Does the causer act **directly** or **indirectly**?

    7. *Intention.* Does the causer achieve the result **intentionally** or **accidentally**?

    8. *Naturalness.* Does it happen **fairly naturally** (the causer just initiating a natural process) or is the result achieved only **with effort** (perhaps, with violence)?

    9. *Involvement.* Is the causer **not also involved** in the activity (in addition to the causee) or are they **also involved**?

For most of the parameters there are many examples available of languages with two causative mechanisms that are distinguished by the parameter; only a selection are given here. Just for 5, Affectedness, is there so far a single instance attested.

The parameters are not fully independent. If **state** is chosen under 1 then parameter 2 is likely to be **intransitive**. Parameter 4, Volition, can only be applied if **control** is chosen under 3. Parameter 8, Naturalness, is only likely to apply if **directly** is chosen under 6. It can sometimes be difficult to distinguish between 3, Control and 4, Volition on the part of the causee, and parameter 8, relating to whether the causer had to act **with effort** or achieved the result **naturally**. In some languages a causative contrast may relate primarily to Control, in another language to Naturalness, but in a third language it may effectively combine these two parameters.

We now discuss and exemplify the nine parameters, in turn.

1. *State/Action.* Whether a causative mechanism applies only to **state** verbs or also to **action** verbs.

In Bahasa Indonesian and Malay (Tampubolon 1983: 45) the causative suffix *-kan* applies only to state and process verbs, e.g. we can get *meleban-kan* 'make wide' and *menggembira-kan* 'make pleased'. For action verbs the only kind of causative is periphrastic, involving a verb like *suruh* 'order', *buat* or *bikin* 'make'.

In Amharic (Amberber 2002: 32–52; Hudson 1997: 476–7) the shorter causative prefix, *a-*, attaches to intransitive verbs of state and change of state, for example 'stand', 'melt' (but not 'dance' or 'laugh'). It is also used with a few transitive verbs 'whose meanings involve benefit to the self', such as 'eat' and 'dress'. However, the longer causative prefix, as-, occurs with all kinds of verbs.

2. *Transitivity*. Whether a causative mechanism applies only to **intransitive** verbs, or to both intransitive and simple **transitive** verbs, or to all types of verbs—intransitive, simple transitive, and also **extended transitive**.

In many languages a causative mechanism applies only to **intransitive** verbs. This is so for Australian languages such as Kayardild (Evans 1995: 279–80), Uradhi (Crowley 1983: 376) and Yidiñ (Dixon 1977a: 311–19), and also for Urubu-Kaapor (Tupí-Guaraní branch of Tupí family, Brazil; Kakumasu 1986: 341). In these languages there is no way of forming an abstract causative of a transitive verb (for example, 'I made John cook the dinner'). One simply has to specify what was done to make the causee act (as in 'I told John to cook the dinner').

In other languages the morphological causative applies only to intransitives but there is also a periphrastic causative which may be used with all verbs; it is the only mechanism available for transitives. Languages of this kind include a number from the Austronesian family, including Maori (New Zealand; Bauer 1993: 409–12), North-east Ambae (Vanuatu; Hyslop 2001: 332–6) and Balinese (Wayan Pastika, personal communication), and a number from the Mayan family such as K'iche' (Campbell 2000). Other languages are mentioned by Nedyalkov and Silnitsky (1973: 7).

Onishi (2000) states that in Motuna a morphological causative can be formed on any plain intransitive (whether of type Sa or type So) and on an extended intransitive (or 'middle'; that is an intransitive with an obligatory peripheral argument) and on just a couple of transitive verbs. There are a number of ambitransitive verbs in Motuna, and a causative is always based on the intransitive sense.

There are a number of languages where a morphological causative applies freely to all intransitive verbs but only rather rarely to transitives and then to just a few verbs. A similar set of verbs is involved, in different languages. For Yimas, Foley (1991: 292) quotes 'weave' and 'eat'. For Tariana, Aikhenvald (2000a, 2003: 270–1) quotes a number of verbs to do with ritual activity, plus 'drink' and 'smoke'. Onishi (2000) mentions two transitive verbs that form a morphological causative in Motuna, 'eat (munchable food)' and 'eat (soft food)/drink'. In Jarawara (Dixon 2004: 251–2), 'eat' and 'drink' are the transitive verbs which occur most often with the causative prefix na-. Nedyalkov and Silnitsky (1973: 16) conclude from their typological survey that if only a few transitive verbs form morphological causatives these are likely to include 'verbs denoting abstract action', such as 'see/show', 'remember/remind' and 'understand/explain', plus 'drink' and 'eat' (their example languages include Chukchee, Arabic, Bats, Hausa, Armenian, and Kurdish).

Rice (2000) surveys the applicability of the causative affix across languages of the Athapaskan family. In all languages it can be used on an intransitive verb with a 'patientive subject'. In some languages it can be used with all intransitives. Only in Koyukon can it be freely used with transitives. For other languages, just a few transitive verbs take the morphological causative; the examples which Rice quotes for Ahtna, Carrier, and Navajo are 'eat' and 'drink'.

There is here a clear generalization—if a morphological causative is used with only a few transitive verbs, these are likely to include 'drink' and 'eat'. It seems that drinking and eating are the transitive activities which people are most likely to make other people do, on every continent.

As mentioned in §24.3.3, we find languages where a morphological causative can apply to intransitive and simple **transitive** verbs, but not to extended transitives. Sonrai, Basque, and Abkhaz are of this type.

3. *Control*. Whether the causee **lacks control** or **has control** of the activity.

Creek (Martin 1991, 2000) has two morphological mechanisms. Roughly: (i) suffix -*ic* is used if the causee **lacks control** or is unwilling (for example, 'feed the baby'); (ii) suffix -*ipa* followed by -*ic* is used if the causee **has control** (e.g. 'make the baby eat'), or if the causee is athematic (as in 'make it rain'). (Martin suggests that this difference between causatives basically relates to the separability of events.)

This parameter underlies the meaning of the morphological causative in a number of languages. For examples, in Marathi (Pandharipande 1997: 406) and in Japanese and Korean (Shibatani 1976b: 33) the causee must have control; as a result, inanimate causees are not permitted.

4. *Volition*. Whether the causee does it **willingly** ('let') or **unwillingly** ('make').

Japanese has intransitive/transitive verb pairs as lexical causatives (these include 'be damaged'/'damage' 'be sold'/'sell', 'become fat'/'fatten'—see Shibatani 1990: 236). These imply that the causee **lacks control**; indeed, with most lexical causatives the causee is inanimate. It also has a morphological causative with suffix -*(s)ase*; this implies that the causee **has control**. With intransitives there are two syntactic possibilities, indicating a difference in the causee's volition. If the original S takes accusative postposition *o* in the causative construction it implies that the intentions of the causee are ignored by the causer, as in (53) below; if the original S takes dative postposition *ni* this implies that the causee is **willing**, as in (54). (See Shibatani 1990: 309 and Tonoike 1978; Tsujimura 1996: 247–9.)

(52) [Taroo ga]$_S$ [konsaato e]   it-ta
      Taroo NOMINATIVE   concert   TO go-PAST
      Taroo went to a concert

(53) [Ryooshin ga]$_A$ [Taroo o]$_O$ [konsaato e]
      parents   NOMINATIVE Taroo ACCUSATIVE   concert   TO
      ik-ase-ta
      go-CAUSATIVE-PAST
      [His] parents made Taroo go to a concert

(54) [Ryooshin ga]$_A$ [Taroo ni]$_O$ [konsaato e]
      parents   NOMINATIVE Taroo DATIVE   concert   TO
      ik-ase-ta
      go-CAUSATIVE-PAST
      [His] parents let Taroo go to a concert

We mentioned in §24.3.2 that Japanese may not have two accusative-marked
NPs in a clause; as a result, in the causative of a transitive the original A can
only have dative marking (since there is already an accusative NP). Thus, the
volitional contrast is only available for the causative of an intransitive.

Bolivian Quechua (Cole 1983: 118) shows a similar contrast, but this time
only with transitive verbs. Here the morphological causative is marked by
verbal suffix -*či*. In the causative of an intransitive the original S must become
O, marked by the accusative postposition -*ta*. However, in the causative
of a transitive the original A can be marked with accusative, showing that
the causee is **unwilling**, as in (55), or with instrumental, -*wan*, showing that the
causee is **willing**, as in (56).

(55) nuqa Fan-ta   rumi-ta   apa-či-ni
      1sgA   Juan-ACCUSATIVE rock-ACCUSATIVE carry-CAUS-1sgA
      I made Juan carry the rock

(56) nuqa Fan-wan   rumi-ta   apa-či-ni
      1sgA   Juan-INSTRUMENTAL rock-ACCUSATIVE carry-CAUS-1sgA
      I had Juan carry the rock (where Juan submits voluntarily to the
         causer's wishes)

In Swahili (Vitale 1981: 156–7) there is a causative suffix, -*isha*/-*esha*, to the
verb; and also a periphrastic apparatus for causation. Where these contrast, the
suffix indicates that the causee acts **willingly** and the periphrastic construction
indicates that the causee acts **unwillingly** (is forced to do it). Thus:

(57) mwalimu hu-wa-som-esha   wanafunzi kurani
      teacher   HABITUAL-3pl-study-CAUSATIVE students   Koran
      The teacher teaches the students the Koran (they want to study it)

(58)   mwalimu   hu-wa-lazimisha   wanafunzi
       teacher   HABITUAL-3pl-FORCE   students
         wa-som-e   kurani
         3pl-study-SUBJUNCTIVE   Koran
       The teacher forces the students to study the Koran (they do not want
       to study it)

Interestingly, an alternative to the periphrastic construction is doubling the
causative suffix on the verb. Sentence (59) has the same meaning as (58):

(59)   mwalimu   hu-wa-som-es(h)-esha   wanafunzi kurani
                 HABITUAL-3pl-study-CAUS-CAUS

In Wappo (Yukian, California; Thompson, Park, and Li, 2006: 123–35), the
suffixal causative contrasts with the periphrastic variety in that the former
indicates 'let do' and the latter 'make do'.

The pragmatic import of 'causation' in a language relates to the societal
profile of its speech community. Writing about Semelai (Aslian branch of Austroasiatic, Malaysia), Kruspe (2004a: 124), emphasizes that 'the degree or force
of causation must be understood against a society where personal autonomy
is paramount at all levels of personal interaction. At most, causation merely
represents the assistance in, or the facilitation of, an event, where the causee
is an animate being, based on the causee's willingness to participate.' (See also
§28.2.4.)

   5. *Affectedness.* Whether the causee is **only partially affected** or is **completely affected** by the activity.

   Tariana has two morphological causatives, suffixes -*i* and -*ita*. They contrast
in a number of ways (Aikhenvald 2000a: 155–66. 2003: 268–70). The longer
causative, -*ita*, is used when the causee is definite and topical, or if the action
is intensive. And the suffixes contrast in terms of affectedness, with shorter
form -*i* used when the causee is only **partially affected**, and longer form -*ita*
when it is **completely affected**. Intransitive verb -*ruku*- 'fall, go down' is used
with short causative -*i* in (60), indicating that only some of the woodchips
were made to fall, and with the long causative -*ita* in (61), where the entire
house was made to fall down:

(60)   na-ruku-i-pidana   naha
       3pl-fall-CAUSATIVE$_1$-REMOTE.PAST.REPORTED   3pl
         itʃida-pe-ne
         turtle-PLURAL-INSTRUMENTAL
       They (the devils) made some (woodchips) fall down, with the help of
         turtles (used as axes)

(61) phia nuha panisi-nuku   pi-ña-bala
      2sg   1sg   house-TOPICAL.NON.A/S 2sg-hit-EVERYWHERE
      pi-ruku-ita-ka
      2sg-fall-CAUSATIVE$_2$-RECENT.PAST.VISUAL
      You destroyed my house completely (lit. hit-everywhere make-all-
      fall) (said the evil spirit to a man in his dream)

6. *Directness*. Whether the causer acts **directly** or **indirectly**.

Hindi (Kachru 1976; Saksena 1982) has two causative suffixes. Both can be
used with all kinds of verbs, implying a causee **having control** and the causer
acting **intentionally**. They differ in terms of directness—suffix -*a* indicates
that the causer acts **directly** and -*va* that they act **indirectly**. The intransitive
clause in (62) is the basis for the **direct** causative in (63), where the labourers
did the job themselves, and for the **indirect** causative in (64), where the
contractor achieved the task indirectly (through 'the labourers', who can be
included in the clause, marked by instrumental case).

(62) Məkan$_S$ bəna
      house   was.made
      The house got built

(63) [Məzduuro ne]$_A$ məkan$_O$ bənaya
      labourers ERGATIVE house   was.made:CAUSATIVE$_1$
      The labourers built the house

(64) [Thekedar ne]$_A$ (məzduuro se)   məkan$_O$
      contractor ERGATIVE labourers INSTRUMENTAL house
      bənvaya
      was.made:CAUSATIVE$_2$
      The contractor got the house built (by the labourers)

A similar distinction between **direct** and **indirect** causatives is found in
many other languages of the region, for example Gojri (Indo-European;
Sharma 1982: 153–4). Masica (1976) surveys **direct** and **indirect** causatives in
the South Asian linguistic area.

Jinghpaw (Tibeto-Burman, Burma; Maran and Clifton 1976) has a causative
prefix, *sha-*, and a causative suffix, *-shangun*. They are often interchangeable,
but contrast with some verbs. If a causative action is **accidental** only the suffix
can be used. If it is **intentional** then the prefix will be preferred if the causer
acts **directly** while the suffix is preferred if they act **indirectly**. For an event
'X killed Y' imagine the following three scenarios:

(a) X decapitated Y (**direct**)—prefix preferred.
(b) X saw Y unconscious in water and didn't rescue them (**indirect**)—suffix
    preferred.
(c) X ordered someone to decapitate Y (**indirect**)—suffix preferred.

In §24.3.4 we mentioned Nivkh, where consonantal mutation (sometimes also accompanied by a suffix) can mark **direct** causation, and a verbal affix (with no mutation) may be used for **indirect** causation. Schema (48) illustrates how these can be combined. Apalai was illustrated in (50–1); here a single causative suffix to an intransitive verb indicates **direct** causation, while a sequence of two suffixes is used for **indirect** causation. In Yanesha' (or Amuesha, Arawak, Peru; Duff-Tripp 1997: 100–1), the causative suffix -*at* when applied once indicates **direct** causation and when repeated it signifies **indirect** causation, for example *muets-at-at-an* 'get (someone else) to kill (someone)'.

There are two derivational suffixes in Crow: -*ee* ~ -*aa* 'direct causative' and -*hche* 'indirect causative'. Graczyk (2007: 322–6) states that 'the distribution of the causatives corresponds fairly closely to the active and stative verb classes in Crow: direct causatives most often combine with stative verbs, indirect causatives with active verbs. Since active verbs have an agentive subject, their causativization is more likely to involve less direct or mediated causation. Nevertheless, it is possible to elicit minimal pairs where both the causative [suffixes] occur with the same stem, with a clear difference in meaning':

(65) bas-lilaalee$_O$ xachi-w-aa-k
      1.POSSESSOR-car   move-1.A-CAUSATIVE$_1$-DECLARATIVE
      I moved my car (e.g. by pushing it, **direct** causative)

(66) bas-lilaalee$_O$ xachi-wa-hche-k
      1.POSSESSOR-car   move-1.A-CAUSATIVE$_2$-DECLARATIVE
      I moved my car (e.g. by turning the ignition key and starting the
           engine, **indirect** causative)

In Telugu (Dravidian) there are two varieties of causative for an intransitive verb: (i) the original S argument is placed in accusative case; or (ii) it is marked by the postposition *ceeta*, which is used to mark the original A in the causative of a transitive, described under type (i) in §24.3.2. Alternative (i) is used to describe **direct** causation such as 'the nurse walked the child (for example, by holding its hands)' while (ii) is used for **indirect** causation, such as 'the nurse got the child to walk (say, by telling it to do so)'. Interestingly, verbs like 'cry' and 'laugh' only accept alternative (i) (Bh. Krishnamurti, personal communication).

Foley (1991: 291) describes causative serial verb constructions in Yimas. There are two verbs which may take on a causative meaning when used in such a construction, *tar-* ~ *tal-* 'hold' and *tmi-* 'say'. The alternative '*tar-* ~ *tal-* marks a **direct** causative, the causing of an event by physically manipulating an object, while *tmi-* is used for an **indirect** causative in which the event is brought about through speech, by verbal commands or requests.' Thus:

(67)   na-ŋa-tar-kwalca-t
       3sgA-1sgO-CAUSATIVE₁-rise-PERFECTIVE
       She woke me up (**directly**, e.g. by shaking me)

(68)   na-ŋa-tmi-kwalca-t
       3sgA-1sgO-CAUSATIVE₂-rise-PERFECTIVE
       She woke me up (**indirectly**, e.g. by calling me)

The Directness parameter may also be shown by alternation of case mark-ing. In the causative of an intransitive, Hungarian normally puts the original S into accusative case, but some verbs allow either accusative or instrumental. The accusative alternative marks **direct** causation, where the causer person-ally directs the activity, while instrumental indicates **indirect** causation (Het-zron 1976: 394). Under (b) in §24.3.1 we contrasted the direct causative 'The nurse walked him (accusative) for an hour each day' with the indirect causative 'The doctor had him (instrumental) walk for an hour each day (by telling him to do so)'.

In Buru (Austronesian, Indonesia; Grimes 1991: 211) a prefix *pe-* is used to indicate **direct** causation, and a periphrastic verb, *puna*, for **indirect** causation, where the causer 'brought about a situation that caused the resulting action or state'. Compare:

(69)   da_A   pe-gosa   ringe_O
       3sg   CAUSATIVE₁-be.good   3sg
       He healed her (**directly**, with spiritual power)

(70)   da_A   puna   ringe_O   gosa
       3sg   CAUSATIVE₂   3sg   be.good
       He [did something which, **indirectly**] made her well

A similar mechanism/meaning correlation is found in another Austrone-sian language, Chrau (Vietnam; Dorothy M. Thomas 1969 and David D. Thomas 1971) where causative prefix *ta-* indicates **direct** action, by physical manipulation (e.g. 'I made the child stand up (by holding him)' while the periphrastic causative verb *ôp* indicates **indirect** causation, e.g. by issuing a command.

From the examples given it will be seen that **indirect** causation can have varying significance. In Telugu, Yimas, Hungarian, and Chrau it appears to involve the causer telling the causee to do something, while in Hindi, Jinghpaw and Crow it can involve acting through a (human or inanimate) intermediary. There is need for a full study of the semantics of indirect causation, taking a much larger sample of languages than those mentioned here, and looking in detail at the meanings and conditions for use of the indirect causative in each language.

7. *Intention*. Whether the causer achieves the result **intentionally** or accidentally.

Kammu (Svantesson 1983: 103–11) has two causative mechanisms, a prefix $p(n)$- and a preverbal particle, *tòk*. If the causer achieves the result **intentionally** the prefix is used, and if they achieve the result **accidentally** the particle is used. Compare:

(71) kə̀ə$_A$ p-háan   tráak$_O$
      3sg:M   CAUSATIVE$_1$-die buffalo
      He slaughtered the buffalo

(72) kə̀ə$_A$ tòk   háan   múuc$_O$
      3sg:M   CAUSATIVE$_2$ die   ant
      He happened to kill an ant (e.g. by accidentally treading on it)

We mentioned above that in Chrau a causative prefix is used for direct and a periphrastic verb for indirect causation. These mechanisms can also be used to mark intention—the causative verb alone for something achieved **intentionally**, with the prefix and verb used together to indicate something that was brought about **accidentally**. For example (Thomas 1969: 100):

(73) ănh$_A$ ôp   dăq$_O$ khlâyh
      1sg   CAUSATIVE$_2$ trap   escape
      I made the trap spring (**on purpose**)

(74) ănh$_A$ ôp   dăq$_O$ ta-khlâyh
      1sg   CAUSATIVE$_2$ trap   CAUSATIVE$_1$-escape
      I made the trap spring (**accidentally**)

As described in §24.3.1, there are two syntactic frames available for the causative of an So intransitive verb in Tariana (Aikhenvald 2000a: 155–7). If the causative verb lacks a pronominal prefix this indicates **lack of intention** on the part of the causer, e.g. 'the dog's barking made me frightened' (the dog didn't bark with the intention of scaring me). If it bears a prefix, then this indicates **intentionality**, e.g. 'he frightened them' (he meant to achieve this end).

In other languages one type of causative construction will mark **intentional** causation while another type is neutral as to whether the activity was made to happen intentionally or accidentally. (Note that the reverse situation—where just accidental is marked—is not attested.) In Spanish the verb *hacer* 'make' can be followed either by a 'that' clause, with the verb in subjunctive form, or by a verb in infinitive form. The subjunctive can be used only when the causer acted intentionally, whereas with an infinitive either an intentional or an accidental reading is possible (Curnow 1993). In Javanese there are three morphological mechanisms for marking a causative—suffix *-ake*, suffix *-i*, and initial reduplication. Most verbs take only one of these. There are, however, some verbs which can take either *-ake* or *-i* and there is then a difference of both intentionality and number. Suffix *-i* indicates **intentional** activity and plural causee, while *-ake* is neutral with respect to both intentionality and number. Thus *pecah-i* is 'intentionally break many (things)' whereas *pecah-ake* is 'intentionally or accidentally break one or many (things)' (Suhandano 1994: 66).

8. *Naturalness.* Whether the activity happens **fairly naturally** (the causer just initiating a natural process) or is achieved only **with effort** (perhaps, with violence).

Russian uses a morphological causative describing something that happens **naturally** and a periphrastic causative where **violence or force** (which can include moral force) is employed. Thus (examples from Alexandra Aikhenvald):

(75) on$_A$ na-poi-l   menja$_O$
      3sg:M   PREVERB$_1$-drink:CAUSATIVE$_1$-sg:M:PAST   1sg:ACCUSATIVE
      vinom
      wine:INSTRUMENTAL:sg
      He got me to drink wine (and I didn't resist)

(76) on$_A$ za-stavi-l   menja$_O$
      3sg:M   PREVERB$_2$-CAUSATIVE$_2$-sg:M:PAST   1sg:ACCUSATIVE
      pitj   vino
      drink   wine:ACCUSATIVE:sg
      He forced me to drink wine (for example, by threats or blows)

Among the causative suffixes which Mithun (2000: 100) lists for Yup'ik is *-cir* which 'indicates causation without direct effort, by waiting and allowing something to happen'.

In English there is a lexical causative (using what is basically an intransitive verb in a transitive construction) and also a periphrastic mechanism with verbs such as *make*. Where these contrast the lexical causative describes something achieved by the causer **naturally** (with the causee being willing, if it is animate) while the *make* construction implies **definite effort** (and an **unwilling** causee). Compare the (a) and (b) alternatives in (77) and (78).

(77) (a)   He walked the dog in the park (it wanted to walk)
      (b)   He made the dog walk in the park (although it didn't want to)

(78) (a)   He opened the door/melted the ice (without difficulty)
      (b)   He made the door open/ice melt (with difficulty)

Aikhenvald (2000a: 162–5, 2003: 276–9) describes how in Tariana the use of a periphrastic causative implies a **special effort** on the part of the causer and/or **unwillingness** of the causee, whereas a morphological causative will be preferred when **no special effort** is needed. (As mentioned above, in some languages alternative causative constructions may link the ideas of control and volition, on the part of the causee, and that of naturalness from the point of view of the causer.)

9. *Involvement.* Whether the causer is **not also involved** in the activity (in addition to the causee) or is **also involved**.

In Nomatsiguenga (Arawak family, Peru; Wise 1986: 593) there is a causative prefix *ogi-* and a causative suffix *-hag*. The prefix is used when the causer was **not involved** in the activity, and the suffix when they were **involved**. Compare:

(79) y-ogi-monti-ë-ri   i-tomi$_O$
3sg:M-CAUSATIVE$_1$-cross.river-NON.FUTURE-3sg:M   3sg:M-son
He made his son cross the river (he told him to)

(80) y-monti-a-hag-ë-ri
3sg:M-cross.river-EPENTHETIC-CAUSATIVE$_2$-NON.FUTURE-3sg:M
i-tomi$_O$
3sg:M-son
He made his son cross the river (he helped him across)

A similar distinction is made in Kamaiurá. Here we find two causative prefixes to the verb: *mo-* indicating that the causee is **not involved** in the activity (e.g. 'he stopped the canoe, when he was outside it'), and *(e)ro-*indicating that the causer was **involved** (e.g. 'he stopped the canoe, when he was inside it'). These examples are given in full in Dixon and Aikhenvald (1997: 84). And Mekens—like Kamaiurá from the Tupí family—also has two causative prefixes: *mo-* ~ *mõ-* does not indicate that the causer is involved in the activity, whereas *ese-* is used when the causer also performs the action 'at the same time as the causee' (Galucio 2001: 96–9).

The Involvement parameter is found in a fair number of South American languages. For instance, Cavineña (Tucanoan, Bolivia; Guillaume 2008: 287–306, Guillaume and Rose 2010: 388–9) has three causative suffixes, which differ in terms of two parameters—2, Transitivity and 9, Involvement:

(81)   causer not involved   causer involved
    onto intransitive verb   -she
                                                               -kere
    onto transitive verb   -mere

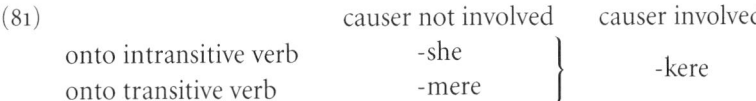

Compare the plain transitive in (82) with the not-involved causative in (83) and the causer-involved causative in (84).

(82) ebakwa=ra=tu   ara-wa   misi
      child=ERGATIVE=3sg   eat-PERFECT   tamale
      The child ate tamale

(83) epuna=ra=tu   ara-mere-wa   misi
      woman=ERGATIVE=3sg   eat-CAUSATIVE$_2$-PERFECT   tamale
          tu-ja   ebakwa
          3sg-GEN   child
      The woman fed the child with tamale

(84) e=ra=tu   era-kere-chine   torta
      1sg=ERGATIVE=3sg   eat-CAUSATIVE$_3$-RECENT.PAST   cake
          [Don   Francisco]
          Mr   Francisco
      I had/invited Mr Francisco (to) eat a cake with me

Examples (83–4) effectively include two objects, the causee (original A) and
the original O. Guillaume (2008: 292–3) states that this shows 'direct causation'. The alternative is for the causee to become an optional general locative
oblique, then indicating 'indirect causation'.

Alamblak has a number of causative prefixes. One of them is *ha-*, used when
the causer is also **involved** in (joins in) the activity which they make the causer
undertake, for example 'He made them enter (something) by entering with
them' (Bruce 1984: 155). Further examples of this parameter (sometimes called
'sociative causative') are discussed in Guillaume and Rose (2010) and Shibatani
and Pardeshi (2002).

The list presented here—of nine semantic parameters that characterize
causative constructions—is a tentative one. Further work may suggest that
it should be reorganized, or that further parameters need to be added. For
instance, Golovko (1993: 386) describes how Aleut has a distributive causative
suffix *-dgu*, indicating that a set of causees is involved (the O NP must take
plural marking), distributed in space; for example, 'the woman is making the
hides dry'. Saksena (1982: 827–8) suggests that in Hindi different case markings
on the causee in a causative construction can indicate whether the aim is to
get the activity done (by anyone), or to get it done specifically by the stated
causee. For the causative of an intransitive in Korean, the original S can take
accusative marking (indicating 'do fully') or dative ('do to some extent'). Thus
'mother (A) child (DATIVE) eat-CAUSATIVE' signifies that the mother fed the
child once, whereas 'mother (A) child (ACCUSATIVE) eat-CAUSATIVE' would
describe her feeding the child for its whole life. Interestingly, 'die' can only
take the accusative alternative, presumably because killing is, by its nature,
something that is done fully (Yunseok Lee, personal communication).

24.5 Meaning-mechanism correlations

We are now in a position to examine the correlation between values of the semantic parameters and types of causative mechanism, for languages that have more than one causative. There is some mention of this in the literature. Comrie (1981: 164–7, 1989: 171–4) recognizes a continuum of causative mechanisms:

(85)   analytic [i.e. periphrastic]—morphological—lexical

He suggests that this correlates with the continuum from less direct to more direct causation, and with that from high control to low control on the part of the causee. Haiman (1983: 783–8, 1985: 108–11) puts forward a 'principle' that if a language has two causatives then 'the conceptual distance between cause and result will correspond to the formal distance between cause and result'. And Givón (1990: 556) makes the following prediction: 'if a language has both a periphrastic—syntactic complementation—causative and a morphological causative, the former is more likely to code causation with a *human-agentive manipulee*, while the latter is more likely to code causation with an *inanimate manipulee*' (his italics).

The present study reveals a correlation between the nine semantic parameters and the degree of 'compactness' of a causative mechanism. We can recognize a scale of compactness, set out in Table 24.2. (Note that the mechanism of exchanging auxiliaries, discussed in §24.2.5, does not contrast with any other mechanism, and is not included in Table 24.2.)

We can, in addition, recognize degrees of compactness within M, morphological causatives. Firstly, a shorter affix is more compact than a longer one. Secondly, a causative mechanism which does not lengthen the word—for example, mutation of an initial consonant in Nivkh, illustrated in (47)—is

TABLE 24.2. Scale of compactness for causatives

		TYPE OF MECHANISM
more compact ↑	L	Lexical (for example, *walk*, *melt* in English).
	M	Morphological—internal or tone change, lengthening, reduplication, affixation, etc.
	CP	Complex Predicate—including serial verbs, *faire* in French, in (4) and (38–40), and the pre-verbal particle construction in Kammu, in (72).
less compact ↓	P	Periphrastic constructions with two verbs (a causative verb and a lexical verb) in separate clauses.

more compact than affixation. When there are two morphological mechanisms that differ in compactness, we use M_1 for the more compact and M_2 for the less compact alternative.

There is a further possibility. One type of causative may be marked by a single mechanism and another by a combination of two mechanisms. Thus in Chrau the intentional causative involves just P (the causative verb *ôp*) whereas something achieved accidentally involves a combination of P plus M (causative prefix *ta-*); see (73–4).The causative involving a single mechanism is plainly more compact than that involving two mechanisms.

We are now in a position to look back over the nine semantic parameters, discussed in §24.4, and examine how each correlates with the scale of compactness. Note that in some instances the two mechanisms marking different values of a semantic parameter do not differ in compactness; for example, Yimas has a single-word serial verb construction for both direct and indirect causation, illustrated in (67–8).

However, for most of the examples of the two causatives with a semantic distinction, given in §24.4, the mechanisms involved do vary in compactness. We find a significant correlation between the values of each parameter and the compactness scale. This is set out in Table 24.3.

The more compact (M_1) and less compact (M_2) morphological mechanisms given in Table 24.3 are set out in Table 24.4.

It will be seen that there is a clear correlation between compactness, as measured by the scale set out in Table 24.2, and each of the semantic parameters. For eight of them we have several examples, and these agree. In Parameter 6, for instance, the direct value of the parameter is always marked by the more compact mechanism, and the indirect value by the less compact one. The actual mechanisms are: short affix versus longer affix in Hindi, Jinghpaw, and Crow, initial mutation versus suffix in Nivkh, one suffix versus two suffixes in Apalai and Yanesha', and morphological versus periphrastic mechanism in Buru and Chrau. Only for parameter 5 is there a single example; in Tariana the suffix *-i* marks causee partially affected while double suffix *-ita* (which could be analysed as causative suffix *-i* plus further causative suffix *-ta*) is used when the causee is completely affected by the activity.

These results agree with Comrie's observations regarding the Directness and Control parameters, mentioned at the beginning of this section. Haiman's principle concerning 'formal distance' and 'conceptual distance' is rather vague, but could be interpreted as applying to the correlations established here. Givón's prediction could be taken to relate to parameter 3, Control—the causee can only be in control if human/animate and this does correlate with a less compact mechanism.

What is particularly interesting is the correlation between 'more compact' and the parameter values in the Type 1 column of Table 24.3—causer not

TABLE 24.3. Correlations of causative meanings with causative mechanisms

PARAMETER	MEANING		MECHANISM		LANGUAGE(S)
	TYPE 1	TYPE 2	TYPE 1	TYPE 2	
1	state	action	M_1	M_2	Amharic
			M	P	Bahasa Indonesian and Malay
2	intransitive	all transitive	M	P	Austronesian, Mayan, etc.
	intransitive and simple transitive	extended transitive	M	P	Basque, Abkhaz
3	causee lacks control	causee has control	L	M	Japanese
			M_1	M_2	Creek
4	causee willing	causee unwilling	M_1	M_2	Swahili
			M	P	Swahili, Wappo
5	causee partially affected	causee fully affected	M_1	M_2	Tariana
6	direct	indirect	M_1	M_2	Hindi, Jinghpaw, Nivkh, Apalai, Yanesha', Crow
			M	P	Buru, Chrau
7	intentional	accidental	M	CP	Kammu
			P	M plus P	Chrau
8	naturally	with effort	L	P	English
			M	P	Russian, Tariana
9	causer not involved	causer involved	M_1	M_2	Mekens, Cavineña

also involved, naturally rather than with effort, intentionally rather than accidentally, directly rather than indirectly; causee only partially affected, willing, lacking control; and applying only to some verbs (at the intransitive and/or state ends of the Parameters 1 and 2). This is surely a ripe field for investigation of cognitive mechanisms.

Finally, it must be noted that this is a tentative and preliminary study of the marking, syntax, and semantics of causative constructions, and of meaning-mechanism correlations. A number of parameters of variation and meaning-mechanism correlations have been suggested, but need to be exhaustively tested against a much wider sample of the world's languages. A few exceptions will of course turn up, but this is always the case. Linguistic theory deals with

TABLE 24.4. More compact (M_1) and less compact (M_2) morphological mechanisms

PARAMETER	LANGUAGE	M_1	M_2
1. State/Action	Amharic	prefix *a-*	longer prefix *as-*
3. Control	Creek	suffix *-ic*	double suffix *-ipa-ic*
4. Volition	Swahili	one suffix *-esha*	repeated suffix *-esh-esha*
5. Affectedness	Tariana	suffix *-i*	longer suffix *-ita*
6. Directness	Hindi	suffix *-a*	longer suffix *-va*
	Jinghpaw	short prefix *sha-*	long suffix *-shangun*
	Nivkh	initial mutation	suffix *-(g)u*
	Apalai	one suffix *-ma*	two suffixes *-ma-nohpo*
	Yanesha'	one suffix *-at*	repeated suffix *-at-at*
	Crow	suffix *-ee* ~ *-aa*	longer suffix *-hche*
9. Involvement	Mekens	prefix *mo-* ~ *mõ-*	longer prefix *ese-*
	Cavineña (on intransitives)	suffix *-she*	longer suffix *-kere*

tendencies—sometimes just significant, sometimes overwhelming—not with absolute rules.

24.6 Other meanings, other functions

Many things in a grammar are not cut and dried. The morphological marking of a causative construction may have a wider range of meaning, briefly discussed in §24.6.1. And a form used to mark causative can have further syntactic function in the language, as exemplified in §24.6.2.

24.6.1 Causatives which don't cause

We have already noted that in some languages causative marking may only apply to intransitive verbs. In others it is used with intransitives and also with (few or many) transitives. There is a further possibility—an affix or other morphological process which increases valency and has causative meaning when applied to an intransitive, and can also be used with a transitive verb but then takes on a quite different character, not altering the valency or indicating causation but instead just adding a semantic feature.

For example, in Piapoco (Arawak, Colombia; Klumpp (1990: 88–90), verbal derivational suffix *-(i)da* may be added to an intransitive verb and then derives a transitive stem with causative meaning, as in:

(86)　i-chàca-ca-wa
　　　3sg-extinguish-POSITIVE-INTRANSITIVIZER
　　　It went out (a fire dies)

(87)   i-chàca-(í)da-ca   lámpara$_O$
       3sg-extinguish-CAUSATIVE-POSITIVE   lamp
       He extinguished the lamp

Suffix -(i)da may also be used with a transitive verb and then does not add
an argument nor have causative effect. Instead, it indicates that the action
was done intensively, and that the patient is fully affected (see Parameter 5
in §24.4). Compare that plain transitive clause in (88) with (89) where -(i)da
is added:

(88)   nu-épùa-ca   nu-ìri-wa$_O$ táiyápi   bàwina
       1sgA-wrap-POSITIVE   1sg-son-REFLEXIVE   at:night   early
       I wrapped my son (in a blanket) early last night

(89)   nu-épùa-(í)da-ca   nu-ìri-wa$_O$
       1sgA-wrap-INTENSIVELY-POSITIVE   1sg-son-REFLEXIVE
         ca-salíni-íri   i-ícha
         ATTRIBUTIVE-CHILL-MASCULINE   3SG-AWAY.FROM
       I (regularly) bundled up my son against the cold

A speaker of Piapoco explained that (88) could be used when 'the boy was
simply covered up with a blanket, probably just one time and on one particular
night', whereas (89) describes 'a regular practice of heavily bundling up the
child against habitual cold', as when staying in the high-altitude capital Bogota.
   In the Australian language Margany (Breen 1981: 319–20), suffix -ma- may
be added to an intransitive verb, producing a transitive stem with causative
meaning. For example, gala- 'be frightened', gala-ma- 'make frightened'. When
-ma- is added to a transitive verb the effect is entirely semantic, indicating
plurality of the O argument. Thus, idha- 'put down' and idha-ma- 'put down
many things'.
   There are a variety of meanings which an affix marking causative with an
intransitive verb may have when added to a transitive. These include: the
referent of the A argument applying special effort or acting intentionally
(see Parameters 8 and 7 in §24.4), or the action done for a long time or
intensively—as in Piapoco—or many times, or involving a large O or a plural
O—as in Margany. There is detailed discussion and exemplification of these
meanings in Aikhenvald (2011), and see further references therein.
   A big question remains. Should we say that there is just one derivational suffix -(i)da in Piapoco, with double function, or instead recognize two distinct
suffixes, which happen to be homonymous; similarly for -ma- in Margany?
This is a matter to be decided separately for each language, based on internal
grammatical considerations.

There are languages in which a certain affix may have either causative or simply semantic effect with an intransitive verb. For example, Nedyalkov and Silnitsky (1973: 17–20) describe how in Zulu *enza-* 'work' can take derivational suffix *-isa*. When this is used with an O argument, it shows that the clause is transitive and thus causative, meaning 'force (someone) to work'. If there is no O argument then the clause is intransitive and *-isa* has an intensive or iterative sense, *enza-isa* then carrying the meaning 'work energetically'.

Choctaw (Muskogean; Mississippi and Oklahoma) has a productive morphological causative suffix *-chi* which 'can be added to nearly every verb in the language' and increases the valency of the verb by one argument. However, there is a second sense to *-chi*, when there is 'neither increase in valency nor a change in grammatical relations'; instead, *-chi* indicates 'either a more completely affected patient or a greater effort on the part of the agent'. For example, 'twist it hard/with difficulty/to break it off', as opposed to just 'twist it', and 'force the shoes into the box', as against 'put the shoes into the box'.

Broadwell (2006: 128–34) argues that 'it is unsatisfying to claim that there are two homophonous morphemes *-chi$_1$* "causative" and *-chi$_2$* "affected" ', preferring to recognize a single suffix with two effects. Choctaw verbs divide into two sets. For one set, *-chi* may only mark causation; they include 'be happy', 'sing', 'take', and 'hit'. For verbs of the second set, *-chi* may have either effect; these include 'be overgrown', 'twist', 'pull', 'whip, spank', and 'boil', as illustrated in:

(90)   akākoshi' hobi-chi-tok
      egg   boil-CAUSATIVE/AFFECTED-PAST
      either: She made someone boil an egg (causative)
      or: She boiled an egg until it was cooked (affected)

24.6.2 Multi-functional forms

This group of chapters (22–25) deals with derivations which change valency. In §22.5.1 and §23.2.1 we saw that one morphological process may mark two (or three or four) of the valency-reducing operations—passive (canonical or agentless), antipassive (canonical or patientless), reflexive, and reciprocal. In similar fashion, a single morphological process may have both causative and applicative effects, the two valency-increasing derivations. This is discussed in §25.8.

What is perhaps a little surprising is that a few languages include an affix which doubles for valency decreasing and valency increasing; most examples involve passive and causative. However, when one thinks about it, this should be quite manageable. If a given transitive verb, plus affix X, is used in an extended transitive clause, then X must here have causative function, adding an argument. If the verb plus affix X is used in an intransitive clause, then here X must have passive function, reducing the number of core arguments from two to one.

In Korean, for example, the suffix *-(h)ita* has causative effect with one set of verbs and passive with another set. The sets do overlap—thus *pota* 'see' has derived form *po-ita*, which can have a passive interpretation 'be seen' or a causative one 'show' (i.e. 'make see'), and *cap-hita* can be 'be held' or 'make hold' (Sohn 1994: 314, and see Kwak 1994). Presumably, the senses are disambiguated by the syntax of the clause in which they occur, and by discourse context.

There is an interesting twist in Ayulta Mixe (Mixe-Zoque family, Mexico; Romero-Méndez (2008: 482–94). This language has two causative prefixes: *-tuk-* is used on transitive (including extended transitive) and *-ak-* on intransitive verbs. Prefix *-ak-* can also be used with transitive verbs and then forms an agentless passive. Thus, *-ak-* always changes valency—added to a verb with valency one, it increases it to two, and added to a verb with valency two it reduces it to one. Also see the example from Sonrai (or Songhai) mentioned in §23.2.1.

Kulikov (2001: 894) suggests that a causative with 'let' meaning (causee willing) could develop into a passive, the permissive 'I let someone grab my hand' shifting to 'I was grabbed by the hand'. Keenan (1985: 262) discusses how passive may have developed from causative in Korean. When a single affixal form has two meanings these may well have developed one from the other. But it must always be borne in mind that there is an alternative possible scenario— that causative and passive developed from quite different earlier forms and through phonological change have just happened to coincide in their modern forms.

24.7 Summary

'Causative' is a variety of secondary concept, which provides modification to a lexical verb and adds an argument that goes into A function, with agent effect (this is the 'causer'). The secondary concept 'causation' may be realized by an affix or other morphological process—in a language with ample morphology—or by a separate word, a 'secondary verb'. The causative verb— which is semantic modifier to the lexical verb—may be the syntactic main verb, one of whose arguments is a complement clause featuring the lexical verb. An example from English is *Jock*$_A$ *made* [*his son eat the porridge*]$_{CoCl:O}$, a sentence which describes the activity of the son eating, with the secondary feature that Jock makes the son eat. Other techniques for the realization of causative include serial verb constructions, further instances of two verbs in one predicate, and—in a number of northern Australian languages—the lexical verb switching its auxiliary.

A grammatical concept of causation is found in most languages, but not quite in all of them—see the discussion in §28.2.4. Irrespective of whether or not there is morphological or syntactic marking of causation, there may be lexical couplets, one member of which is the causative correspondent of the other. For instance, *go in/put in, remain/leave*, and *eat/feed* in English.

A causative construction may be limited to intransitive verbs, or also to transitives but not extended transitives, or may apply to verbs of every transitivity value. The syntactic effect is straightforward with intransitives— underlying S becomes O and the causer is A. Things become more complicated for the causative of a transitive verb, which already had A and O arguments. The causer is always A of a causative construction. The original A (the 'causee') may receive a special marking, or retain its A marking, or be placed in periph- eral function, or become the new O. If the last circumstance, the original O may either retain its marking (now being 'second object') or be shunted out onto the periphery.

There are languages in which causative marking may be applied twice, either two different processes or one process repeated. This may indicate the causative of a causative (as in *Mother made Jock make his son eat the porridge*) or, alternatively, some special semantic nuance such as intensive action, or indirect action on the part of the causer.

A considerable number of languages have more than one causative mech- anism, and there is always a semantic contrast. This may involve any (or a combination) of: (a) nature of the verb, such as whether it can only refer to a state, or must have a certain transitivity; (b) whether the causee is able to exercise control, performs the action willingly, or is partially or fully affected; (c) whether the causer acts directly or indirectly, achieves the result intention- ally or accidentally, has to exert force, or is also involved in the caused event. If there is a single causative mechanism in a language, its semantic profile should be ascertained, in terms of these parameters.

A scale of morphological compactness can be recognized as follows: lexical pairs → shorter morphological process → longer process → two verbs in one predicate → periphrastic means (two verbs in different predicates). Table 24.3 demonstrates a solid correlation between degree of compactness and values of the nine semantic parameters.

As reiterated before, each grammatical element typically has a range of functions and meanings. There are languages in which a given morphological mechanism may mark both causative and passive, or causative and applicative, in each case with different sets of verbs (which may overlap). And a causative affix may also have a non-causative meaning, indicating large size or plural number of the O argument, an action performed over a long time, or the causer acting forcefully or intentionally.

24.8 What to investigate

It is not sufficient, when writing the grammar of a language, just to say that it has a causative construction. All causative constructions have in common the addition of an A argument (the causer) to an underlying clause and this provides the basic semantic/syntactic criterion for recognizing a causative construction in a given language. But languages differ a great deal in the formal marking and syntax of their causatives, and in the specific meanings attached to them.

The following details should be pursued:

(a) The grammatical mechanism which is used to mark a causative construction may have alternate forms, perhaps conditioned phonologically, or else relating to the transitivity of verbs to which they apply. As discussed in §24.2, causative mechanisms include morphological processes, multi-verb predicates, and periphrastic constructions (typically, the causative verb in the main clause, taking a complement clause whose predicate head is the lexical verb being causativized).

There may also be pairs of lexical verbs which appear to be in causative relation (like *go* and *send* in English) although in all such instances language-internal criteria should be sought (rather than just relying on intuitional judgement).

(b) The syntax of each causative mechanism is to be carefully considered. What are the transitivity values of the verbs to which it applies? A new argument is always added, the causer (in A function). What happens to the original arguments of the underlying verb (especially if it is transitive or extended intransitive)? Attested possibilities are presented in §24.3.

(c) There may be several causative constructions, and they will always differ in terms of one or more of the semantic parameters discussed in §24.4—State/action, Transitivity, Control, Volition, Affectedness, Directness, Intention, Naturalness, and Involvement. If there is a single causative mechanism, its meaning must be tested. Single mechanisms do typically have a wide semantic range, but they are unlikely to cover all values of each parameter. For example, a causative may only apply to an animate (or just a human) causee, but may only be used when the causee is willing and the causer acts directly. And so on.

(d) Check, for each grammatical marking of causation—a valency-increasing process—whether it has further functions. It may also mark the other valency-increasing process, applicative, and/or passive, a valency-reducing process. Or, in certain circumstances, it may have no valency-changing effect at all, but just add some semantic element, such as an action intensively performed.

If a certain grammatical form has more than one function, it is often hard to decide whether to analyse it as one item with multiple functions, or as several homonymous items. Often, it does not really matter which path is followed, so long as there is consistency. (There may be more important points to worry about in the grammar than such an issue.) In some cases, a form with disparate meanings or functions may have developed out of an earlier form with narrower scope. In other cases, items which are homonymous today may have developed from quite different forms at an earlier stage of the language.

It should always be borne in mind that the most appropriate synchronic analysis is not necessarily congruent with the diachronic scenario. For example, what were distinct prefixes *ka-* and *kha-* at one stage of a language may (as aspiration is lost) fall together as *ka-*, with the original semantic functions becoming so intertwined that in synchronic analysis it is appropriate to recognize a single prefix *ka-* (rather than two homophonous forms).

Sources and notes

This chapter is a revision and updating of Dixon (2000a). The structural generalizations and semantic parameters have in some instances been finetuned but none have been radically altered. Some examples and discussion from the 2000 chapter are not included here. There was nothing wrong with them; they just had to be omitted to make way for new material, while ensuring that the chapter did not become overlong.

There is a considerable literature on causatives. Nedyalkov and Silnitsky (1973) and Comrie (1975, 1976a, 1985a) made most important contributions. A number of worthwhile case studies are in the individual chapters of Dixon and Aikhenvald (2000a). There are excellent insights in some of the chapters of the following edited volumes: Shibatani (1976a), Comrie and Polinsky (1993) and Shibatani (2002). Caution should be exercised with respect to Song (1996, 2005a, 2005b).

24.1   A main reason why some linguists have put forward the misguided idea that a causative construction involves 'two events' is undoubtedly the fact that English and other familiar languages use a bi-clausal causative construction.

Make is the main verb of causation in English, the others being *force, cause,* one sense of *drive*, and causative senses of *get* and *have*. See Dixon (1991a: 193–8, 2005a: 196–201).

Talk-ative is a rare exception to the rule that suffix *-(at)ive* is confined to Romance verbs. Marchand (1969: 317) mentions that *talkative* 'is difficult to account for. It is probably originally a facetious word, perhaps mock-Latin of the well-known macaronic kind'.

24.2.2   Aikhenvald (2006) provides an inclusive account of serial verb constructions and a full set of references to earlier studies. See also the individual case studies in Aikhenvald and Dixon (2006).

24.2.3   *Make* differs from most other causative verbs, and from most other verbs in English that take *to* complement clauses, in that it omits the *to* in active clauses, although *to* must be included in the passive. (Compare *The nurse made me swallow it* with *I was made to swallow it (by the nurse)*. For fuller discussion see Dixon (1991a: 192–8, 247–8; 2005a: 196–202, 268–9.) This could be the preliminary stage to a diachronic shift which sees *make* become a 'same predicate' causative verb, like *faire* in French.

24.2.5   Other Australian languages with complex predicates—from the same geographical area as Ngan'gityemerri—show a similar mechanism for forming causatives; for instance, Mangarayi (Merlan 1982: 132–4). As a later stage of development, in a further group of Australian languages what was a causative auxiliary has become a causative derivational suffix (Dixon 2002: 676–7).

24.3   In §14.5, Urarina was mentioned as one example of a language in which the causative process may not apply to a copula verb.

24.3.2   Relating to Type (iii), Comrie (1975: 14–17) and Kozinsky and Polinsky (1993: 181) provide further information on languages that have 'two objects' in the causative of a transitive clause.

   The only report we have of the original O staying as full O and the original A taking on O marking but being a second object is Kozinsky and Polinsky's (1993) account of the *bi*-verbal causative in Dutch, which they consider to constitute a single predicate.

   Baker (1988: 164–6, quoting Gibson 1980 and Trithart 1977) mentions Chamorro (Austronesian) and some dialects of Chichewa (Bantu) as also being of type (iv).

24.3.4   Maxmudova (1999) exemplifies multiple application of a periphrastic causative construction in the North-east Caucasian language Rutul. It appears that lexical verb 'give' also functions as causative marker. The translation of 'I made Annie make the girl make her sister throw bread to the dog' is glossed as 'I-ERGATIVE Annie-ADESSIVE girl-ADESSIVE sister-ADESSIVE dog-DATIVE bread:ABSOLUTIVE throw-INFINITIVE give-INFINITIVE give-INFINITIVE give-PAST'.

Further examples of double causatives are quoted in Kulikov (1993: 128–30, 1999).

I have not been able to find a reliable textual (as opposed to elicited) example of a causative affix being added twice to a transitive verb. This relates partly to the fact that many languages restrict morphological causative processes to intransitive verbs, and quite a few of the remainder allow these processes to apply only sparingly to transitive verbs. Note that in Hungarian it may be theoretically possible to apply the causative suffix twice to a transitive verb but the result is judged infelicitous by native speakers; they prefer to use a morphological causative plus a periphrastic causative (Edith Moravcsik, personal communication).

24.4   A number of recent grammars each presents a clear and explicit summary of the meanings of causatives in terms of the nine semantic parameters discussed here (which are the same as those in Dixon 2000a). For example, Urarina (Olawsky 2006: 609–21) and Cavineña (Guillaume 2008: 285–301), both from South America, and Manambu (Aikhenvald 2008a: 407–16) from Papua New Guinea.

Tangkhul Naga (Tibeto-Burman, India, Arokianathan 1987: 65–6) proves a further instance of Parameter 5, Volition.

There are many further examples of parameter 6, Directness. In Alamblak (Papuan region; Bruce 1984: 153–9) there are a number of causative prefixes, including *ka-* 'make do by **direct** physical action' while a causative serial verb construction involving the verb *hay* (whose meaning when used alone is 'give') is employed for **indirect** causation, where the causer and causee need not even be at the same place when the event takes place (rather like the verb *cause* in English). See also Hinton (1982) on Mixtec (Mixtecan), Austin (1981a: 159–60) on Diyari (Australian), Haiman (1983: 786) on Korean, and Payne (2002) on Asheninka (Arawak, Peru).

Kulikov (1993: 134–5) mentions further examples of parameter 7, Intention.

24.5   Shibatani and Pardeshi (2002: 109–11) provide a critical commentary on my discussion of meaning-mechanism correlations.

24.6.1   For Choctaw, Broadwell (2006: 132–3) provides a most helpful list of twenty-five 'type B' verbs for which *-chi* can only have causative meaning, and thirty 'type A', verbs for which it can indicate either causative or 'affect'. (Unfortunately, the transitivity of each verb is not stated.) He then suggests that 'in general, verbs whose meaning includes a component of causation and which are bounded in their temporal semantics will fall into type A'. He does say 'in general'. It is hard to reconcile, for example, why 'whip, spank' and 'pull' should be in type A, but not 'hit' and 'take'.

24.6.2   A number of other languages are reported to have identical (or homonymous) marking for causative and passive, but in most instances scant detail is provided. Thomas (1971: 152) mentions that the 'direct action' prefix *ta-* in Chrau—illustrated in (74)—has passive meaning with one set of verbs. See also Nedyalkov and Silnitsky (1973: 20–1). Kulikov (2001: 894) mentions Manchu and also refers to other languages with this homonymy.

25

Applicatives

Whereas almost every language has one or more varieties of causative, a far smaller number have an applicative construction—probably no more than about a quarter of the world's languages. Many languages have just one type of causative and only a few have more than two mechanisms. In contrast, more than half of the languages with an applicative construction show multiple varieties. There may be two, three, four, or as many as eight or more types of applicative marking, each with its own range of meaning. Other languages have a single morphological derivation for applicative, but that exhibits a wide array of meanings.

As mentioned in the last chapter, virtually every causative mechanism applies to intransitive verbs. In quite a few languages, causative is restricted to intransitives. In others it may also apply to just a few transitives, and in a further set to many transitive verbs. This is in marked contrast to applicatives. Out of a sample of eighty-two languages with either canonical applicative or quasi-applicative (see §25.2), we find that in fifty-four languages (66 per cent), both intransitive and transitive verbs may enter into applicative derivations. For seventeen (21 per cent), applicative is restricted to intransitives, and for eleven (13 per cent) it applies just to transitives.

There has been no inclusive typological framework for the study of applicatives, and the basic information needed for a full account of this grammatical category—as set out below in §25.11, 'What to investigate'—has been supplied for only some of the languages for which applicatives have been reported. As a consequence, the present study is more of a pioneering endeavour than other chapters in this work.

In the canonical applicative derivation, a peripheral argument (what we can called the 'applicative argument') in an underlying intransitive or transitive clause becomes the O argument (referred to as 'AP-O') in the corresponding applicative construction. This is described and exemplified in §25.1. The following section deals with what I call 'quasi-applicatives', where the applicative argument may *only* be expressed as AP-O and there is no underlying non-applicative construction in which the applicative argument has a peripheral role. §25.3 surveys the considerable range of meanings spanned by applicatives, §25.4 provides a sample of languages with multiple applicatives, §25.5 examines the range of argument markings (and the possibility of two different applicative processes applying to the same verb), and §25.6 examines syntactic and pragmatic functions of applicatives.

Applicatives are typically marked by a morphological process applying to a verb. In §25.7 we take a brief look at other possible realizations—serial verb constructions, exchanging auxiliaries, and lexical pairs which have an applicative-type flavour. In some languages, a derivational process may mark causative with one set of verbs and applicative with another set, or else may have applicative meaning in some instances and a purely semantic effect in others; this is surveyed in §25.8. A wide range of labels has been used for what are here called applicatives; discussion of terminology is deferred until §25.9. There is then the usual summary, in §25.10, and specification of what to investigate, in §25.11.

25.1 Canonical applicative derivations

There are distinct specifications for the canonical applicative according to the transitivity of the clause it applies to.

Canonical applicative derivation with an intransitive clause.

(a) Applies to an underlying intransitive clause and forms a derived transitive.
(b) The argument in underlying S function goes into A function in the applicative.
(c) An argument which was in peripheral function in the underlying intransitive (the 'applicative argument') is taken into the core, in O function (called the 'AP-O').
(d) The applicative construction receives some explicit marking. This is predominantly by a morphological process of affixation applying to the verb.

Our first illustration is a Locative applicative from Misantla Totonac (Totonacan family, Mexico; MacKay 1999: 283). Throughout this chapter, the applicative argument is underlined in examples.

(1)   Juan$_S$ ta-wila-la   (laka-<u>tantsi</u>)
        Juan   INCHOATIVE-sit-PERFECTIVE PREPOSITION-bench
        Juan sat (on the bench)

(1-ap) Juan$_A$ puu-ta-wila-la   hun-<u>tantsi</u>$_O$
        Juan   LOC.APP-INCHOATIVE-sit-PERFECTIVE DETERMINER-bench
        Juan sat-on the bench

We begin with an intransitive clause, (1). This has one core argument, *Juan*, in S function and an optional peripheral construction in which *tantsi* 'bench' bears the all-purpose prepositional prefix *laka-*; this is used for location (as here), instrument, comitative, etc. From (1) is derived the transitive applicative clause (1-ap), marked by the Locative applicative prefix *puu-* to the verb. The original S argument, *Juan*, becomes A within the applicative construction and the 'applicative argument', *tantsi* 'bench', is promoted from being a peripheral argument to now being in core function, O. As befits an O argument in Misantla Totonac, *tantsi* now takes determiner prefix *hun-* 'the, that'.

Note that Misantla Totonac has four distinct applicative derivations, the Locative applicative, illustrated here, is marked by derivational prefix *puu-*, Instrumental applicative employs prefix *lii-* (as in 'He peeled the apple with a knife'), Goal applicative has suffix *-ni* (for example, 'She brought your shirts for you'), and Comitative applicative combines prefix *laa-* and suffix *-na* ('We talked with them'). Each may be used with both intransitive and transitive verbs. (There is further discussion in §25.4.)

We can now examine the canonical applicative of a transitive verb.

Canonical applicative derivation with a transitive clause.

(a) Applies to an underlying transitive clause—with A and O core arguments—and the derived applicative remains transitive (in some languages, it may be considered to become extended transitive).

(b) The argument in underlying A function stays as is in the applicative.

(c) An argument which was in peripheral function in the underlying transitive (the 'applicative argument') is taken into the core, in O function (called the 'AP-O'), replacing the original O argument.

(d) There are a variety of possibilities for what happens to the O argument of the original non-applicative clause. In Ainu, the original O is simply omitted. Most often, it is moved out of the core and now marked—by an appropriate adposition or case—as a peripheral argument. In some languages, the original O seems to remain as is, so that there appear on the surface to be two objects, the AP-O and the original O. Generally, grammatical tests show that AP-O is the true argument in O function within the applicative construction, with the original O having a more minor role (as 'second object'). In just a few languages, object properties are shared between AP-O and the original O.

(e) The applicative construction receives some explicit marking. This is predominantly by a morphological process of affixation applying to the verb.

This may be illustrated with an Instrumental applicative from Indonesian (Sneddon 1996: 78):

(2)   Dia$_A$ memukul anjing$_O$ ([dengam tongkat])
        3sg   hit   dog   WITH   stick
        He/she hit the dog (with a stick)

(2-ap) Dia$_A$ memukul-kan   tongkat$_O$ [pada anjing]
        3sg   hit-INSTRUMENTAL.APPLICATIVE stick   AT   dog
        He/she used a stick to hit the dog with (lit. He/she hit-with a stick at
              the dog)

The applicative construction, (2-ap), is marked by Instrumental applicative
suffix -*kan* to the verb. The 3sg A argument remains the same. Erstwhile
peripheral NP *dengam tongkat* sheds its preposition *dengam* 'with' and *tongkat*
'stick' moves into O argument slot in the applicative construction. The original O argument, *anjing* 'dog', becomes a peripheral NP, taking preposition
pada 'at'.

   Applicative suffix -*kan* in Indonesian is used only with transitive verbs and
has a fair range of meanings, also including Goal (for example, 'He fetched
a glass of water for the guest'). There is one other applicative derivation in
Indonesian, shown by suffix -*i* and used with both transitive and intransitive
verbs. It promotes into AP-O slot an argument which was in a locational
function; for example, 'swarm over X', 'fall on X'.

   Misantla Totonac has four applicative affixes and Indonesian has two. Each
has its own range of meaning, relating to the original peripheral function of
the applicative argument. Some languages have a single morphological process
marking applicative but it has wide semantic scope, covering meanings associated with several applicative derivations in languages which do have several.

   In Dyirbal, derivational suffix -*m(b)a*- marks Instrumental (for example,
'hit him with a stick'), and Locative, as in:

(3)   baŋgul$_A$ gaban$_O$ gunda-n   jawun-da
        HE:ERG   grub:ABS put.in-PAST dilly.bag-LOCATIVE
        He put the grubs into the dilly-bag

(3-ap) baŋgul$_A$ jawun$_O$ gundal-ma-n   gaban-gu
        HE:ERG   dilly.bag:ABS put.in-APP-PAST grub-DATIVE
        He put the grubs into the dilly-bag (lit. He put-in grubs to the dilly-
              bag')

The applicative argument, *jawun* 'dilly-bag', is marked by locative case in the
plain transitive clause, (3), and is placed in O function (shown by absolutive
case, with zero realization) in the applicative construction, (3-ap). The original
O argument, *gaban* 'grub(s)' now becomes a peripheral NP, in dative case. The
A argument, *baŋgul* 'he' (in ergative case) remains as is.

Instrumental and Locative senses of applicative -*m*(*b*)*a*- in Dyirbal may be used with both intransitive and transitive verbs. There is a third meaning, Comitative, which is in my corpus attested only with intransitives. For instance:

(4)   bayi$_S$ ŋurba-ñu   barrmba-ba$_S$
        HE:ABSOLUTIVE   return-PAST   quartz-WITH
        He returned with the quartz

(4-ap)   baŋgul$_A$ barrmba$_O$ ŋurbay-ma-n
         HE:ERGATIVE   quartz:ABSOLUTIVE   return-APPLICATIVE-PAST
         He returned-with the quartz

The applicative argument is here *barrmba* 'quartz'. It is marked by suffix -*ba* ∼ -*bila* 'with' in the original intransitive clause, (4), and then goes into O function in the derived applicative (4-ap). Note 'he' is in absolutive case, indicating an S argument, in (4) but in ergative case, showing that it is now in A function, in the transitive clause (4-ap). (The syntactic status of *barrmba-ba* in (4) is discussed in §25.5.1.)

§25.6 discusses the circumstances in which a speaker might employ an applicative construction. Two of the main ones are simply to highlight the applicative argument, or to place it in such a function that it is available for various processes of coordination and subordination (concerning which there are syntactic constraints in the language under study). As described in §23.1, Dyirbal has a pervasive S/O pivot. In fact (4-ap) is the final clause of a multiclause pivot chain (the whole making up one sentence): 'He saw the piece of quartz (O function) glittering, picked it (O) up, to bash it (O) against a rock, so that it (S) split into two pieces, and he returned-with them (O)'. We find that *barrmba* (variously indicating 'piece of quartz' and 'split pieces of quartz') is in S or O pivot function in each of these clauses. The applicative derivation is needed in the final clause to maintain 'quartz' in a pivot function (here, O). (The complete pivot chain is given as sentence 52 in Dixon 1972: 377.)

There are four basic types of meaning associated with applicative derivations (each bearing a number of subdivisions). We have illustrated Locative in (1) and (3), Instrumental in (2), and Comitative in (4). There is also Goal, where the action described by the applicative clause may be for the benefit of the applicative argument (for example, 'Mother knitted a scarf for John') or to else its detriment ('Tom stole the scarf from John'). §25.3 provides a detailed examination of these types of meaning. Before moving on to that, we need to look at what can be called 'quasi-applicatives'.

25.2 Quasi-applicatives

A quasi-applicative differs from a canonical applicative only in that there is no underlying construction for which the applicative argument appears in peripheral function. This can be illustrated from Creek (Muskogean; Martin 2000: 389–93, 2011: 183–96, and personal communication). First consider an intransitive clause:

(5)   cá:ni-t$_S$ opóna:y-ís
        John-NOMINATIVE   talk-INDICATIVE
        John is talking

The preferred way of specifying who Bill is talking to or for is not by adding a peripheral argument to (5), but instead forming a Goal applicative through derivational prefix *im-* to the verb:

(5-ap)   cá:ni-t$_A$ inhíssi-n$_O$ im-ópona:y-ís
         John-NOMINATIVE   friend-OBLIQUE   GOAL.APP-talk-INDICATIVE
         John is talking to/for his friend

Creek has two case-like suffixes: *-t* ('nominative') may mark an S or A argument, while *-n* ('oblique') is used on an NP in O function—as in (5-ap)—or in any peripheral function. We can now provide the quasi-applicative specification:

Quasi-applicative derivation with an intransitive clause.

(a), (b), and (d) as for canonical applicative with an intransitive clause
(c) A new argument (the 'applicative argument'), which did not appear in the underlying intransitive, is taken into the core, in O function (called the 'AP-O').

A quasi-applicative based on a transitive verb can also be illustrated from Creek. We begin with a transitive clause:

(6)   cá:ni-t$_A$ istaha:koci-n$_O$ ha:y-ís
        John-NOMINATIVE   doll-OBLIQUE   make-INDICATIVE
        John is making a doll

For specification of who John is making the doll for, one would not add a dative-type NP to (6), but instead append derivational prefix *in-* to the verb. This allows the applicative argument to be included in O function:

(6-ap)   cá:ni-t$_A$ cími-n$_O$ istaha:koci-n   in-ha:y-ís
         John-NOM   Jim-OBL   doll-OBL   GOAL.APP-make-INDIC
         John is making a doll for Jim

Note that oblique case suffix -*n* is used on both the new O argument (the AP-O), 'Jim', and also on the original O, *istah:koci* 'doll', which has moved into peripheral function. We can now characterize the quasi-applicative based on a transitive clause:

Quasi-applicative derivation with a transitive clause.

(a), (b), (d), and (e) as for canonical applicative with a transitive clause
(c) A new argument (the 'applicative argument'), which did not appear in the original transitive, is taken into the core, in O function (called the 'AP-O'), replacing the original O argument.

Interestingly, the Goal applicative prefix in Creek also marks person and number of the applicative argument. It is *im-* ~ *in-* for 3sg, as in (5-ap) and (6-ap), *am-* ~ *an-* for 1sg, *cim-* ~ *cin-* for 2sg and *pom-* ~ *pon-* for 1pl. Thus, for example, *pom-ópona:y-is* is 'He/she is talking to/for us'. Creek also has an Instrumental applicative, marked by invariable prefix *is-* to the verb.

As already mentioned, many grammars do not provide complete information concerning applicatives. The fullest accounts quote a non-applicative clause in which the applicative argument is in peripheral function and a corresponding applicative construction for which it is in O function (the AP-O), similar to (1–4) above. Some descriptions state that this is what is found but fall short of providing specific examples.

   And then there are grammars which specify that an applicative argument may *only* be in AP-O function. No choice is possible, as there is between (1) and (1-ap), (2) and (2-ap), and so on. These are clear quasi-applicatives. Another way of putting it is that the applicative derivation is obligatory.

   Unfortunately, there are a fair number of partial accounts of applicatives which do not come down on either side. That is, they neither indicate that a non-applicative clause with the applicative argument in peripheral function is possible, nor that it is not allowed. Such scenarios have been classed, by default, as quasi-applicatives. However, it is possible that fuller descriptions would indicate that some of them are of the canonical variety.

We have stated that any kind of applicative is generally marked by a morpho-logical process applying to the verb. (Other kinds of realization are discussed in §25.7.) In almost every instance this involves either a prefix or a suffix. (An applicative suffix is sometimes fused with the verb root, as in (7-ap), (10-ap), and (25-ap).) About three-quarters of the languages I have studied just use suffixes with most of the remainder having just prefixes. There are a handful of languages for which some applicative varieties are shown by suffixes and others by prefixes. As already mentioned, Misantla Totonac employs prefix *puu-* for Locative, prefix *lii-* for Instrumental, and suffix *-ni* for Goal applicative. This language also has a Comitative applicative which is unusual in being marked by a circumfix; that is, a combination of prefix *laa-* and suffix *-na*.

I know of no applicative derivation marked by any of the other kinds of morphological process listed in §3.13—reduplication, shift of stress, change of tone, internal change, or subtraction. It is entirely possible that such processes may be found, as more languages are accorded comprehensive description.

Applicative derivations show varying degrees of productivity; some may apply to many verbs, others to a limited set. The breadth of use of a particular applicative process is determined, in large part, by the meaning associated with it. The next section surveys parameters of meaning.

25.3 Meanings

The meaning of a canonical applicative construction relates to the role the applicative argument has when occurring in peripheral function in the original non-applicative construction. Thus, (3-ap) is a Locative applicative since the applicative argument, *jawun* 'dilly-bag' (which is AP-O in the applicative clause) is marked by locative case in the non-applicative clause, (3). The meaning assigned to a quasi-applicative construction is more a matter of interpretation.

It seems that, cross-linguistically, any type of peripheral argument has the potential to be an applicative argument, and become AP-O in an applicative construction. Each individual language makes use of only a portion of the full set of possibilities. It is useful to recognize four broad categories of applicative meanings—Goal, Instrumental, Comitative, and Locative, each with a number of subtypes. They will be discussed in turn.

Quite a number of studies of applicatives—in individual languages and in general—refer to a 'benefactive' meaning, sometimes also to 'malefactive'. It is true that the action referred to in an applicative construction may be for the benefit of, or to the detriment of, the referent of the applicative argument. But this is always a secondary feature of meaning (usually for some subtypes of Goal).

25.3.1 Goal

The applicative argument may refer to the 'goal' of the activity or state described by the verb of the applicative construction. We can recognize four subdivisions, each with its own abbreviatory code.

(1) *Additional argument*, **G-addition**.

There is here a self-contained clause which may stand alone. A peripheral argument can be added—as a sort of optional extra—specifying a goal. And then an applicative derivation may be applied, putting the applicative argument into AP-O function.

Consider Chi-mwi:ni, a Bantu language closely related to Swahili (Kisseberth and Abasheikh 1977: 194):

(7)   A:sha$_A$ an<u>d</u>ishi<u>l</u>e: xa<u>t</u>i$_O$ ([ka <u>Nu:ru</u>])
        Asha   wrote   letter   TO   Nuru
        Asha wrote a letter (to Nuru)

The point to note is that *A:sha an<u>d</u>ishi<u>l</u>e: xa<u>t</u>i* 'Asha wrote a letter' is a self-contained transitive sentence. The peripheral NP *ka Nu:ru* may optionally be added, indicating who the letter was addressed to. This can then be the basis for an applicative construction, marked by the applicative suffix which has basic form *-il-* and is here fused with the verb root:

(7-ap) A:sha$_A$ mw-an<u>d</u>ikILile   <u>Nu:ru</u>$_O$ xa<u>t</u>i
        Asha   3sgo-wrote:APPLICATIVE Nuru   letter
        Asha wrote Nuru a letter

The applicative argument, *Nu:ru*, is moved into AP-O slot in (7-ap). It shows the properties of an O—occurring immediately after the verb, being cross-referenced on the verb (since it has human reference) by prefix *mw-*, and so on. Sentence (7-ap) could well have beneficial implications for Nuru (say, if it was telling Nuru some good news) or it could have detrimental effect (if the message conveyed were unwelcome). However, this would be a secondary feature to the basic Goal meaning.

Like other Bantu languages, Chi-mwi:ni has a single applicative marker which covers a fair range of meanings within the Goal, Instrumental, and Locative types. Jarawara, from southern Amazonia, also has a single applicative marker, verbal prefix *ka-*, encompassing various subtypes of Goal, Instrumental, and Comitative meaning.

In one Jarawara story, Okomobi tells of how he visited a group of unacculturated Indians, the Sorowahá. The first morning, the Sorowahá get up earlier than Okomobi and his companions (Dixon 2004: 255):

(8)   ([<u>otaa</u>   nijaa])   mee$_S$ bosa
        1pl.exclusive PERIPHERAL 3pl   get.up.early
        na-maki-hete-ke
        AUXILIARY-FOLLOWING-RPn:f-DECLARATIVE:f
        Then they got up early (on us)

Mee bosa na-maki-hete-ke, 'Then they got up early', is a self-contained intransitive sentence. The peripheral NP *otaa nijaa* 'on us' is added, as an optional extra. Note that *(ni)jaa* is an all-purpose preposition in Jarawara, corresponding to English 'at', 'in', 'on', 'into', 'to', 'from', 'with' (and more).

In the next sentence of the text, Okomobi rephrases this as an applicative construction:

(8-ap) ota-ra$_O$ mee$_A$ bosa
      1pl.exclusive-ACCUSATIVE   3pl   get.up.early
        ka-na-hani
        APPLICATIVE-AUXILIARY-IPn:f
      They got-up-early-on us.

The applicative argument, 1st plural exclusive pronoun *otaa*, which was in peripheral function in (8), is marked by accusative case suffix *-ra* and is O argument in (8-ap). (The tense suffixes are recent past, RP, in (8) and immediate past, IP, in (8-ap) in each instance showing non-eyewitness evidentiality (n)—since the narrator did not actually see the Suruwahá people getting up—and feminine gender—since all subject pronouns ((including 3rd plural *mee*)) are cross-referenced by the unmarked gender specification, feminine.)

Okomobi appeared to be mildly unhappy about the Sorowahá getting up before him so that (8-ap) could be called a 'malefactive'. But this would be a secondary nuance to its basic meaning as a Goal applicative.

The quasi-applicative (5-ap), 'Bill is talking to <u>his friend</u>', in Creek is also an instance of G-addition meaning. Other examples from the literature include (where in each case X is the applicative argument): 'bake a cake for X', 'cut the cake for X', 'untie the knot for X', 'open the box for X', 'leave it for X', 'choose a tie for X', 'work for X', and 'make a doll for X', as in (6-ap). For each of these, X might be expected to derive benefit. We also have 'steal the money from X' which is surely to X's detriment; similarly in the case of 'yell at X', 'bark at X'. In the Australian language Ngandi (Heath 1978: 81), intransitive verb *warnʔdhu-* 'look around' may take applicative prefix *bak-*, the AP-O then being that which is looked around for. This does not bear any obvious overtones of benefit or detriment for the referent of the applicative argument.

(2) *Recipient*, **G-recipient**.

Some languages are like English in allowing either Gift or Recipient to be in O slot for a verb such as 'give' (or 'send', 'lend', 'sell', and the like). For example, *Father*$_A$ *gave* [*a necklace*]$_O$ *to mother*, and *Father*$_A$*gave mother*$_O$ [*a necklace*]. In contrast, a considerable number of languages are restricted to having the Gift as O argument. In such cases, there may be a type of Goal applicative which puts Recipient into O function.

Consider the plain transitive clause with 'give' in Toba (Guaycuruan, Argentina; Censabella 2010: 190):

(9)   [so   jaGajkjolek]$_A$ j-an   [so   l-apoʔ]$_O$
        THAT   old.man   3.A-give THAT   3sg.POSS-poncho
        That old man gives the poncho

The use of verb 'give' implies that there should be a recipient. But for this to be stated, an applicative construction is required, marked by suffix -*i* on the verb:

(9-ap) [so   jaGajkjolek]$_A$ j-añ-i   [so   l-qaja]$_O$
        THAT   old.man   3.A-give-APP   THAT   3sg.POSS-brother

        [so   l-apoʔ]
        THAT   3sg.POSS-poncho
        That old man gives his brother the poncho

The source account does not state that the recipient argument could be added to the plain transitive, (9), as a peripheral argument. This must thus be provisionally classified as a quasi-applicative.

   An action of giving (or sending, lending, etc.) may be for the benefit of the recipient (for example 'He gave her a strawberry') or to their detriment ('He gave her syphilis'). As with G-addition, this is at most a secondary feature of a G-recipient applicative.

   In some languages, it is the Recipient which is O argument for 'give'. This applies in West Greenlandic (Eskimo; Fortescue 1984: 88–9). The Gift can be included as a peripheral NP in instrumental case:

(10)   Niisi$_O$ aningaasa-nik   tuni-vaa
        Niisi   money-INSTRUMENTAL:PLURAL   give-3sgA:3sgO:INDIC
        He gave Niisi money (lit. He gave Niisi with money)

The Gift is placed in O function in a further type of Goal applicative construction, with Recipient now being marked by allative case. Applicative suffix -*ut(i)* is fused with verb root *tuni* 'give' to give *tunniut(i)* (which becomes *tunniup* through assimilation):

(10-ap) aningaasa-t$_O$ Niisi-mut   tunniup-pai
        money-PLURAL   Niisi-ALLATIVE   give:APP-3sgA:3plO:INDIC
        He gave-money to Niisi

   (3) *Stimulus for a stative verb*, **G-stimulus**.

In English, the stative verb *worry* can be used alone (*Mother is always worrying*) or with a prepositional phrase introduced by *about*, referring to what motivates the worry, what we can call the 'stimulus' for the worrying (*Mother is always worrying about Michael*). There are relatively few stative verbs of this type in English; instead we find many HUMAN PROPENSITY adjectives, which can be used either alone or with a prepositional phrase stating the stimulus; for example *happy (about X)*, *ashamed (of X)*, *homesick (for X)*.

Other languages express such concepts through stative verbs. Used in intransitive clauses, these can take an optional peripheral argument showing the stimulus. This may become AP-O in a transitive applicative construction. In Motuna (Buin family, Papua New Guinea; Onishi 2000: 132) stative verb *iirong-* 'get angry' may be used in an intransitive clause (this is spoken by a woman):

(11)   nii$_{Sa}$ [ong-jo   pehkoto] iirong-ohna-na
         1sg   THIS:MASC-PURPOSIVE boy   get.angry-1.Sa:PRES.PROG-F
         I am angry for the sake of this boy

In (11), the applicative argument, *pehkoto* 'boy', is in peripheral function shown by purposive suffix *-jo* on the first word of its NP. In the corresponding applicative—the transitive clause (11-ap), marked by suffix *-ee-* on the verb—*pehkoto* is in AP-O function:

(11-ap) nii$_A$ [ong   pehkoto]$_O$ iirong-ee-uhna-na
         1sg   THIS:MASC boy   get.angry-APP-3.O:1.A:PRES.PROG-F
         I am angry-with this boy

Many languages have stative verbs such as 'be annoyed (with X)', 'be frightened (of X)', 'be embarrassed (about X)', 'be homesick (for X)', and 'be fed up (with X)'. Each may be used in an intransitive clause, with the stimulus X optionally stated through a peripheral argument, or else with G-stimulus applicative marking, so that the applicative argument, X, goes into AP-O function. Interestingly, G-stimulus applicatives predominantly indicate a negative stimulus (that is, one is more likely to encounter a G-stimulus applicative with 'be ashamed (of X)' than with 'be proud (of X)').

(4) *Stimulus for a corporeal verb*, **G-corporeal**.

Almost every language describes the corporeal activities of laughing and crying (that is, sobbing or weeping) through an intransitive verb. This may be used alone, or with a peripheral argument stating what is being laughed at or cried over. For example, in Amharic (Amberber 2000: 323):

(12)   atsemari-wa$_S$ bə-lïj-u   sak'ə-čč
         teacher-DEF:F   AT-boy-DEF   laugh:PERF-3.S.F
         The teacher laughed at the boy

The stimulus argument, *lij* 'boy', is marked by prepositional-type prefix *bə-* 'at' in (12). Applicative suffix *-ibb-* derives a transitive clause for which *lij* is in AP-O function:

(12-ap) atsemari-wa_A lij-u-n_O   sak'ə-čč-ibb-ət
         teacher-DEF:F boy-DEF-ACC laugh:PERF-3.A.F-APP-3.O.M
         The teacher laughed-at the boy

The Central Australian language Mparntwe Arrernte (Wilkins 1989: 258) has a valency-increasing suffix *-(lh)ile* which generally has causative effect. However, this suffix shows applicative meaning just with *therre* 'laugh' and *artne-* 'cry'. That is, *therre-lhile* means 'laugh at someone' or 'laugh someone down' (and not 'make someone laugh'). Ngiyambaa, another Australian language (Donaldson 1980: 163), has a dedicated applicative suffix *-ba-* which, in the corpus available, is used with just two verbs, intransitive *ginda-* 'laugh (at)' and *yuŋa-* 'cry (at)'. (See also §25.8.)

25.3.2 Instrumental

The applicative argument may refer to some actual or notional instrument. We can recognize five subdivisions.

(1) *Implement*, I-implement

The applicative argument is a weapon, tool or implement which physically affects the referent of the original object. It is illustrated by (2) from Indonesian, 'hit with a stick' and the following from K'iche' (Mayan, Guatemala; Campbell 2000: 278) which has the same translation but treats the original O in a different way in the applicative construction, (13-ap).

(13)   š-at-in-č'ay   [či   če:ʔ]
         ASPECT-2sgO-1sgA-hit WITH   stick
         I hit you with a stick

(13-ap) če:ʔ_O š-ø-in-č'aya-be'-x   a:w-e:h
         stick ASPECT-3sgO-1sgA-hit-APP-TR   2sg.POSS-GENITIVE
         I used a stick to hit you (lit. I hit-with stick your)

Other instances of I-implement include 'cut it with <u>an axe</u>', 'beat him with a <u>whip</u>', 'slap with <u>the hands</u>' and result statements such as 'kill them with <u>a gun</u>', 'break it using <u>stones</u>'.

(2) *Surface effect*, I-surface.

The effect of the instrument only affects the surface of the referent of the original O, not its material nature. An example based on a transitive clause in Dyirbal is:

(14)   ŋaja_A gayu_O   jurra-n   warrgay-ju
        1sg   bark.bag:ABS wipe-PAST grass.rag-INSTRUMENTAL
        I wiped the bark bag with a grass rag

(14-ap) ŋaja_A warrgay_O   jurral-ma-n   gayu-gu
         1sg   grass.rag:ABS wipe-APP-PAST bark.bag-DATIVE
         I used a grass rag to wipe the bark bag (lit. I wipe-with a grass rag to
             the bark bag)

Other examples of the I-surface meaning include: 'sweep with a <u>broom</u>',
'sprinkle with <u>water</u>', 'touch with the <u>foot</u>'.

   (3) *Something which assists*, **I-assist**.

The applicative argument refers to something which assists the activity
described by the verb. For example, in Olutec (Mixe-Zoque family, Mexico;
Zavala 2000: 741), the intransitive verb *-pet-* 'ascend' may take Instrumental
applicative prefix *toj-* which enables 'new rope', something which assists the
speaker in their ascent, to be placed in AP-O function.

(15-ap) je?   tan=toj-pet-pe   [namʔal tüpxi]_O
         THAT 1sgA=INST.APP-ascend-INCOMPL.TR new   rope
         I used the new rope to ascend (lit. I ascended-with the new rope)

Other instances of G-assist applicative constructions from Olutec include:
'remove grease with <u>a little stick</u>' and 'pull the plant with <u>your hands</u>'. In
other languages we find: 'fish with <u>net</u>', 'catch animal with <u>noose</u>', 'cook it
with <u>pan/spoon</u>', 'make it with <u>a mould</u>', 'see with <u>binoculars</u>', 'walk with
<u>a walking stick</u>', 'travel by <u>car/canoe</u>', 'drink milk with <u>a glass</u>', 'eat with
<u>the hands</u>'.

   (4) *Materials used*, **I-material**.

The materials used in some activity may be coded as applicative argument. For
example, 'cover him with <u>a shawl</u>', 'thatch the hut with <u>straw</u>', 'wrap meat with
<u>leaves</u>', 'build the wall with <u>bricks</u>', 'make a damper with <u>flour and water</u>'.
   Dyirbal has transitive verb *jaŋga-* 'eat'. There is also the intransitive verb
mañja- '(eat to) satisfy hunger'. 'What is eaten' can be included, marked by
instrumental case:

(16)   bayi_S   mañja-ñu   (wuju-ŋgu)
        HE:ABSOLUTIVE satisfy.hunger-PAST vegetables-INST
        He satisfied his hunger (with vegetable food)

Applicative suffix *-ma-*, when added to the verb, creates a transitive construction in which the applicative argument, *wuju* 'vegetable food', is now the AP-O:

(16-ap) baŋgul$_A$ wuju$_O$ mañjay-ma-n
         HE-ERGATIVE vegetables:ABSOLUTIVE satsify.hunger-APP-PAST
         He satisfied-hunger-with vegetable food

Eating verbs in Dyirbal are further discussed in §25.7.

   (5) *Reason or cause*, I-**reason**.

The applicative argument may specify the reason, cause, or motive for the
activity or state described by the verb. This meaning is included here, under
Instrumental, since it is frequently covered by the same applicative process
as subtypes (1–4) just listed. It can be regarded as a figurative variety of
instrumental.
   The I-reason applicative can be illustrated from Chichewa (Bantu branch
of Benue-Congo, Malawi; Mchombo 2004: 88):

(17-ap) ndí-ma-dy-élá   njala$_O$ maûngu
         1sgA-HABITUAL-eat-APPLICATIVE hunger pumpkin
         I eat pumpkin because of hunger

The applicative argument, *njala* 'hunger' becomes AP-O, showing regular
object properties, while the original O, *maûngu* 'pumpkin', follows the O
argument and now has a more peripheral role.
   Other examples of I-reason include: 'cook pumpkins because of hunger',
'die of hunger', 'die from a fall', 'hit him because of a woman', 'can't see because
of tears in the eyes'. For Lakota, Boas and Deloria (1941: 42) mention 'know by
means of', 'be made tired on account of', 'be fat on account of', and 'be angry
on account of'.

25.3.3 Comitative

The referent of the subject argument, which is generally human, is accompanied by some person or thing, specified by the peripheral argument.
   The intransitive verb *wina* 'live' in Jarawara can optionally be accompanied
by an NP marked by the wide-ranging preposition *nijaa* (also used in (8)):

(18)   okobi$_S$ wine   ([otaa   nijaa])
         1sgPOSSESSIVE:father(m) live:m   1pl.exc PERIPHERAL
         My father lived (with us)

Applicative prefix *ka-* derives a transitive verb for which the applicative argument, *otaa* 'we (plural, exclusive)', is in AP-O function (Dixon 2004: 255–6):

(18-ap) okobi$_A$ ota-ra$_O$ ka-wine,
    1sgPOSSESSIVE:father(m)   1pl.exc-ACCUSATIVE   APP-live:m
      otaa$_S$ fota-ra   otaa
      1pl.exc   be.big(plural S)-NEGf   1pl.exc:DEPENDENT.MARKER
      My father lived-with us, when we were small (lit. us being not big)

The applicative construction was used in this textual instance to place the applicative argument in a core function (here O) so that it could be modified by the dependent clause *otaa fota-ra otaa* 'us being not big' (the final *otaa* marks that this is a dependent clause).

An example of Comitative applicative with a verb of motion comes from Yimas (Lower Sepik family, Papuan area; Foley 1991: 303):

(19) [ipa kantk] pu-mampi-wa-k
     1pl   WITH   3plS-AGAIN-go-IRREALIS
     Again they went with us

(19-ap) pu-kra-mampi-taŋ-wa-k
     3plA-1plO-AGAIN-COMITATIVE.APPLICATIVE-go-IRREALIS
     Again they went-with us

The applicative argument, 1pl 'us', is marked by postposition *kantk* 'with' as a peripheral argument of the intransitive clause (19). In the transitive applicative construction, (19-ap), it is in AP-O function, marked by 1pl O bound pronoun *-kra-*.

A Comitative applicative construction can refer to a major participant accompanied by a minor one (for example, 'Mother walked to the river with the baby') or to a number of people joining together in an activity, as in 'John played with his cousins'. Other examples in the literature include 'dance with', 'work with', and 'talk with'.

The applicative argument need not be human. In (4-ap), from Dyirbal, we had 'He returned-with the quartz'. Other examples are 'He stood with a fish (in his hand)', 'He came with some tobacco', and 'I sat with the moon (i.e. I sat in the moonlight)'.

Another possibility is for both subject and applicative arguments to have non-human animate reference, as in Longgu (Austronesian, Solomon Islands; Hill 1992: 59):

(20-ap) mwaa-i$_A$ e   ango-ta'ini-ka   [gale   ngala-gi]$_O$
     snake-SINGULAR   3sgA   crawl-APP-3plO   baby   3sg-PLURAL
     The snake is crawling with its babies (on its back)

Or both arguments can be inanimate, as in Yidiñ (Australian region; Dixon 1977a: 297, 304). We can repeat (5–6) from §3.20:

(21)   marun$_S$ gada-ŋ   bana-mujay$_S$
        cloud:ABSOLUTIVE   come-PRESENT   water-WITH
        A cloud is coming full of rain (lit. cloud water-with is coming)

(21-ap) maru:n-du$_A$ bana$_O$ gada-ŋa-l
         cloud-ERGATIVE   water:ABSOLUTIVE   come-APP-PRESENT
         A cloud full of rain is coming (lit. cloud is coming-with water)

The syntactic status of *bana-mujay* in (21) is discussed in §25.5.1.

25.3.4 Locative

Many types of verbs may be accompanied by an optional peripheral argument providing some kind of locational information—'at', 'on', 'in', 'into', 'to',
'towards', 'from', 'along', and so on. There is often the potential for such a
specification to be treated as an applicative argument, which can be put into
AP-O function through a Locative applicative derivation. This was illustrated
with (1-ap) from Totonac 'Juan sat-on the bench'. A similar example comes
from Tamambo (Austronesian, Vanuatu; Jauncey 2011: 130):

(22)   mo   lua   [ana   tavalu-i   sala]
        3sgS vomit   PREPOSITION   side-LINKER   path
        He vomited on the side of the path (he was there when he vomited)

(22-ap) mo   lua-si   [na   tavalu-i   sala]$_O$
         3sgA vomit-APPLICATIVE   ARTICLE   side-LINKER   path
         He vomited-on the side of the path (his vomit was on the side of the
            path)

The NP *tavalu-i sala*, 'side of the path', is marked by preposition *ana* 'to, from,
at, on' in the intransitive sentence (22), and goes into AP-O function in the
transitive applicative construction (22-ap). Similar examples include 'arrive at
the camp', 'sleep on the ground', 'run from the river'.
   Whereas in English one would say 'The child caught measles', a different
turn of phrase is employed in Nadëb (Makú family, Brazil; Weir 1986: 301):

(23)   salãap$_S$ a-dúng   [kalapéé hã]
        measles   FORMATIVE-fall   child   DATIVE
        Measles fell on the child (i.e. the child caught measles)

(23-ap) kalapéé$_O$ salãap$_A$ ha-dúng
         child   measles   APPLICATIVE-fall
         Measles fell-on the child (i.e. the child caught measles)

The applicative argument, *kalapéé* 'child', is in peripheral function—marked
by 'dative' postposition *hã*—in the intransitive clause, (23) and then becomes

AP-O in (23-ap). Applicative prefix *ha-* has developed from dative postposition *hā*. (This is a common type of development in Amazonian languages.) Note that the most usual constituent order in Nadëb is 'S – predicate', and 'O – A – predicate'.

As is discussed in §25.6, the choice between non-applicative and applicative constructions is likely to depend in part on the nature of the arguments involved. Romero-Méndez (2008: 519–20) provides examples involving the verb *-tëk-* 'enter' in Ayutla Mixe. A plain intransitive construction is employed in (24), with what the ball enters into, *pejk-kemy* 'corral', being marked as a peripheral argument by suffixes *-ojt-* 'inside' and *-py* 'locative'. When the arguments are 'he' and 'car', the applicative construction, (24-ap), is preferred.

(24)   [tuʼuk pelota]$_S$ y-tëk   pejk-kemy-ojt-py
         one   ball   3.S-enter   round-fence-INSIDE-LOCATIVE
         A ball entered the corral

(24-ap) tëë   t-ta-tëk   carro$_O$
         BEFORE.NOW   3.A:3:O-APPLICATIVE-ENTER   car
         He entered (i.e. got into) the car

Locative applicative derivations may also apply to transitive verbs. This was illustrated for Dyirbal in (3-ap), 'He put the grubs into the dilly-bag'. Other instances include 'skin the animal on the ground' and 'push the boy towards the girl'.

There are many other varieties of locative expression which may be used as applicative arguments. For example, 'hit it against a rock', 'walk between two villages', 'swarm over a log'. A rather unusual one is 'in the presence of'. This is reported for one African and several South American languages. In Kisi (Atlantic family; Guinea, Liberia, and Sierra Leone; Childs 1995: 178–83), the applicative suffix *-(l)ul-* (which may fuse with the verb root) marks various types of Goal and also 'in the presence of'. For example:

(25-ap) ò$_A$ yààmál   yá$_O$ [á   yìááŋ]
         she   yawn:APPLICATIVE   me   WITH hunger
         She yawned with hunger in front of me

Nomatsiguenga (Campa branch of Arawak, Peru: Payne 1997: 188; Wise 2002: 336) has eight suffixes showing different types of what appear to be quasi-applicatives. One is *-(i)mo* 'in the presence of', as in 'I gave Richard the headscarf in Irene's presence'. Nanti, a related Campa language (Michael 2008: 285–6), has a cognate applicative suffix *-imo* with similar meaning; for example 'Birari felled (it) in your presence' and 'She arrived in my presence (that is, she arrived where I was)'.

It is relevant to enquire what kinds of verb are likely to co-occur with each subtype of applicative. In some instances, this is straightforward, relating to the meaning of the applicative. For example, I-implement is likely to apply to verbs from the AFFECT semantic type, such as 'hit' and 'cut', I-surface with verbs such as 'wash' and 'wipe', G-recipient with 'give' and its hyponyms, and G-stimulus with stative verbs. I-reason is particularly common with 'die' and 'be tired' but it can be used with any verb describing a state or action for which a reason may be given. Comitative is found with 'go', 'sit', 'live', 'talk', 'walk', and 'dance', and Locative with 'enter', and 'sit', but—essentially—these two applicative types are at risk to be used with almost any verb. And so, pre-eminently, is G-addition. In addition, specific cultural factors may condition the use of a particular applicative.

And how does transitivity relate to applicative meanings? As mentioned before, the great majority of applicative derivations may occur with both intransitive and transitive verbs. However, it is useful to survey those which show a transitivity restriction. We find that, of those instances where only one transitivity value is allowed, transitive is most common for G-addition and, to an even greater extent, for I-implement. And that intransitive is the most common value for Locative, Comitative, I-reason, G-stimulus, and G-corporeal.

25.4 Applicative arrays

We can now examine a number of languages each of which has an array of applicative derivations, indicating the semantic scope of each. (It should be noted that many grammars provide only scanty information on applicatives, with just one or two examples. The languages surveyed below have been chosen since a fair amount of detail is provided; nevertheless, each of these applicative derivations may well have wider scope than indicated here.)

I. Olutec (Mixe-Zoque family, Mexico; Zavala 2000: 656–887)

(a) suffix -ja:y?. Covers types of Goal:
  • G-addition: 'take tortillas to <u>him</u>', 'prepare food for <u>his friend</u>', 'buy meat for <u>him</u>', 'wash clothes for <u>me</u>', 'sing a song to <u>you</u>'. Also 'steal money from <u>me</u>', which is plainly an instance of G-ad͞dition ('me' is an affected additional participant) rather than Locative (where 'me' would be an indication of place).
  • G-recipient: 'sell food to <u>me</u>'.
(b) prefix kuj-. Also relates to G-addition: 'his wife died on <u>him</u>', 'the string of his guitar broke on <u>him</u>', 'the parrot escaped from <u>me</u>'. This may refer to an action which has detrimental effect on the referent of the applicative argument, as in the examples just given, or else a beneficial

effect, as in 'may his money grow on <u>him</u>'. Similarly with (a) suffix *-ja:y?*—this presumably has a beneficial effect with 'wash clothes for' and 'prepare food for' but a detrimental effect with 'steal money from'.

Applicative suffix *-ja:y?* and prefix *kuj-* have similar meanings. One difference is that *-ja:y?* is a canonical applicative, used just when the applicative argument is pragmatically prominent, whereas Zavala (2000: 727) states that, for the sentences he has gathered using *kuj-*, a non-applicative alternative (with the applicative argument in peripheral function) is not acceptable. There is plainly a difference of semantic association between applicative argument and predicate for the two derivations.

(c) prefix *toj-*. Covers types of Instrumental:
  • I-implement: 'stab with <u>knife</u>', 'hit with <u>umbrella</u>', 'dig ground with <u>hoe</u>'.
  • I-surface: 'wash with <u>soap</u>', 'cover with <u>shawl</u>'.
  • I-assist: 'ascend with <u>new rope</u>' as in (15-ap), 'pull with <u>the hands</u>', 'go using <u>the other road</u>'.
(d) prefix *mü:-*. Covers Comitative: 'go with (=take) <u>grilled chicken</u>', 'come with (=bring) <u>corn</u>', 'sit with <u>the woman</u>', 'run with <u>son</u> in arms', 'work with <u>him</u>', 'talk with <u>each other</u>', 'eat gristle with <u>the dog</u>'.
(e) prefix *toko-*. Covers:
  • I-reason: 'give him medicine because (he has) <u>a big belly</u>', Often used with 'why'—'Why (= because of <u>what</u>) aren't you sleeping/eating?'.
  • G-corporeal: 'crying for <u>wife</u>'.

Olutec is unusual in linking 'cry for' with I-reason; in most languages this is linked with other Goal subtypes. It goes to show that, although the categorization of meanings in §25.3 is presented as the most appropriate semantic model for applicative derivations across the eighty or so languages I have examined, there are a (smallish) number of cross-links, such as this.

It is instructive to compare the array of applicatives in Olutec with those in another language from the Mixean branch of the Mixe-Zoque family.

II. Ayutla Mixe (Mixean, Mexico; Romero-Méndez 2008: 397–401, 507–29)

(a) prefix *më-*. Covers Goal-addition: 'work for <u>the boss</u>', 'talk to <u>the woman</u>', 'sow beans for <u>Carlos</u>'.
(b) prefix *ku(j)-*. Only two examples are given in the grammar:
  • G-corporeal: 'cried for <u>his grandma</u>'.
  and a special sense of G-addition: 'his parents died on <u>him</u> (so that he became an orphan)'.

(c) prefix *ta-*. Covers subtypes of Instrumental and also Locative:
- I-implement: 'cut the piece of wood with the machete'.
- I-assist: 'sew the shirt with the needle', 'go by donkey'.
- I-material: 'play with mud'.
- Locative, 'enter into the car' as in (24-ap), 'go to school', 'go through the house'.

We can now consider applicatives in a language which is also spoken in Meso-America but belongs to a quite different genetic group.

III. Misantla Totonac (Totonacan family; Mexico; MacKay 1999: 260–9, 273–302)

(a) suffix -*ni*. Covers subtypes of Goal:
- G-addition: 'throw a stone at the dog', 'cut the dog's hair for me', 'yell at me', 'run from Pedro', 'steal the watch from me', 'stand in place of X' (the last three plainly involve an additional affected argument, rather than just locational specification).
- G-recipient: 'sell it to me', 'send a letter to you'.
- G-stimulus: 'afraid of me'.
(b) prefix *lii-*. Covers subtypes of Instrumental:
- I-implement: 'cut X with a knife', 'kill the dog with a rifle'.
- I-assist: 'see you with my spectacles', 'lie on the bed', 'bring it by mule'.
- I-material: 'make tortillas with X', 'cure using X', 'feed child with bread'.
- I-reason: 'tired because of the work', 'what did your uncle die of?'.
(c) circumfix *laa-* . . . -*na*. This is used for Comitative: 'he comes with me', 'they work with me'.
(d) prefix *puu-*. Locative meaning: 'sat on the bench' as in (1), 'sleep on the bus', 'dance in the main square', 'wash the plate in the kitchen'.

Note that all four applicative derivations for Misantla Totonac, all five for Olutec, and two of those for Ayutla Mixe may be used with both intransitive and transitive verbs. The third in Ayutla Mixe, (b) prefix *kuj-*, is only exemplified with two verbs, both intransitive ('cry' and 'die').

Other languages show different distributions of meanings over their applicative derivations. There are two applicative processes in Indonesian (Sneddon 1996: 69, 78–88). Suffix -*kan* (apprently restricted to use with transitive verbs) covers Instrumental, as in (2-ap), 'hit the dog with a stick' and also G-addition, as in 'fetch a glass of water for the guest'. Suffix -*i* is (besides other functions) a Locative applicative; for instance, 'fall on X'; it is used with verbs of either transitivity value.

In Nadëb (Weir 1986), a number of prepositions may be attached to the verb. Five of these are incorporated into the verb word and function as applicative prefixes; they appear to be used only with intransitive verbs. One has Instrumental meaning, while the other four cover subtypes of Locative: very roughly, 'on top of', 'inside', 'in', and 'on', the last exemplified in (23-ap).

Languages with what appear to be quasi-applicatives may have an array of these. For example:

IV. Creek (Muskogean; Martin 2000: 389–93, 2011: 183–96) has two prefixes, both are attested with intransitive and with transitive verbs.

(a) prefix *im-* ~ *in-* for 3sg (there are other forms for other values of the applicative argument; see §25.2). This relates to Goal:
   • G-addition, exemplified by (5-ap), 'talk to/for <u>his friend</u>', (6-ap) 'make a doll for <u>Jim</u>', and 'move out of the way of <u>X</u>'.
   • Goal-recipient: 'send X to <u>Y</u>'.
(b) prefix *(i)s-* (the form is invariable) covers diverse subtypes:
   • I-assist: 'eat with a <u>spoon</u>', 'write a letter with <u>a pen</u>'.
   • I-material: 'pay someone with <u>money</u>'.
   • I-reason: 'die from <u>thirst</u>'.
   • G-stimulus: 'be angry/happy about <u>something</u>', 'be envious of <u>something</u>'.

It appears that I-reason and G-stimulus are linked in Creek. They are dealt with differently in other languages, such as Misantla Totonac.

   • Comitative: 'go with (= take) <u>me</u>'.

A nifty example of this applicative sense is shown in (Martin 2011: 194):

(26)   siskitá-n$_O$ î:s-ey-s
         cup-OBLIQUE   hold-1sgA-INDICATIVE
         I'm holding a cup (one that's empty)

(26-ap) siskitá-n   (i)s-î:s-ey-s
         cup-OBLIQUE   INSTRUMENTAL.APP-hold-1sgA-INDICATIVE
         I'm holding a cup (one that contains something)

The applicative prefix *(i)s-* indicates 'hold-with'. The applicative argument is omitted from (26-ap). However, it can be included, as AP-O:

(26-ap') <u>ássi</u>-n$_O$ (i)s- î:s-ey-s
         tea-OBLIQUE   INSTRUMENTAL.APP-hold-1sgA-INDICATIVE
         I'm holding tea (in a container) (lit. I'm holding-with tea in something)

We can recall, from §25.2, that there is an 'oblique' (or 'non-subject') suffix -*n* in Creek. This is used on an NP in O function and also on one in peripheral function. It marks 'cup' as O in the non-applicative clause (26), and 'tea' as AP-O in (26-ap'). Within the applicative, the original O argument 'cup' moves into peripheral function, also marked by -*n*, as in (26-ap). One could presumably include both the AP-O and the original O, as happens in (6-ap).

A comparative construction in Creek is marked by the two applicative prefixes used together; see §25.8.

As with canonical applicatives, we find a number of different distributions of meanings in languages with quasi-applicatives. Toba (Guaykuruan family; Argentina; Vidal 2001: 316–29) has four applicative suffixes. One covers G-addition, G-corporeal, and also Locative; a second deals with G-recipient (extended also to include 'tell/explain the problem to the woman'); a third covers I-implement, I-surface, and I-assist, while the fourth is Comitative. (The second and third are exemplified with transitive verbs, the fourth with intransitives, and the first with both; but more data is needed.)

Many languages have a single applicative derivation, but it may have as wide a semantic range as a whole array of applicative affixes, in languages such as those just described. For example:

  V. Chichewa (Bantu branch of Benue-Congo, Malawi; Mchombo 2004: 78–89; Baker 1988: 229–60)
    (a) suffix -*il* ∼ -*el* occurs with both intransitive and transitive verbs and covers at least the following meanings (there may well be more besides):
      • G-addition: 'cook pumpkins for the lion', 'write a letter to my brother', 'steal the bicycle from the lion'.
      • G-recipient: 'send a calabash of beer to the chief'.
      • I-implement: 'cut the rope with a knife'.
      • I-assist: 'cook pumpkins with (using) a spoon', 'walk with a stick'.
      • I reason: 'eat pumpkin because of hunger' in (17-ap).
      • Locative: 'cook pumpkins on the anthill'.

  VI. Yidiñ (Australian region; Dixon 1977a: 302–11, 431–6, 1991b, and field materials)
    (a) suffix -*ŋa* can have a causative reading (see §25.8) and also the following applicative senses:
      • G-addition: 'sneaking up on my wife'.
      • G-stimulus: 'frightened of the man'.
      • G-corporeal: 'laughing at me', 'crying for her husband'.
      • I-implement: 'hit the wallaby with a stick', 'shoot us with bullets'.
      • I-surface: 'clean the camp with a broom'.
      • I-material: 'make the camp with bladey grass'.

- I-assist: 'catch animals with a <u>trap</u>', 'propel the raft with
  the paddle', 'he will swive (copulate with) the woman with
  <u>his erect penis</u>', 'sleep with <u>a blanket</u>'.
- Comitative: 'sit with <u>his wife</u>', 'stand with a stick in <u>his hand</u>',
  'a cloud is coming with <u>rain</u>' in (21-ap).
- Locative: 'eat food off <u>the plate</u>'.

In Yidiñ, the applicative derivation may only apply to intransitive verbs. A transitive verb must first be intransitivized (say, by the antipassive derivation) before it can be applicativized (see Dixon 1977a: 309–11).

For some grammars it seems, on the information available, that the applicative derivation has a limited set of meanings and/or is of limited occurrence. For Kisi (Childs 1995: 178–83), it appears that applicative suffix *-(l)ul* is used mainly for G-addition, plus the unusual Locative sense 'in the presence of', in (25-ap). The only meaning illustrated for the applicative prefix *et-* in Jacaltec (Mayan, Guatemala; Craig 1977: 52–3) is Comitative ('dance with <u>you</u>', 'work with <u>him</u>'). Fortescue (1984: 88–9) quotes a single applicative example for West Greenlandic, G-recipient, given at (10-ap).

There is a pervasive areal distribution for those languages with applicatives, concerning whether there is an array of affixes or just one, often with a fair range of meanings. Austronesian languages show both possibilities. Most often, languages in North, Central, and South America have several applicatives whereas those from sub-Saharan Africa and from Australia are content with one. However, there are only tendencies, with a number of exceptions. For instance, a single applicative derivation is common for Mayan languages from Meso-America—including K'iche', illustrated in (13-ap)—and in some South American languages including Yagua (Payne and Payne 1990: 403–6) and those from the small Arawá family, such as Paumarí (Chapman and Derbyshire 1991: 295–7) and Jarawara (Dixon 2004: 255–8), illustrated in (8-ap), (18-ap), and (43-ap).

In some languages, all applicatives are of the canonical variety—where there is a corresponding non-applicative construction, with the applicative argument in peripheral function—whereas other languages only have quasi-applicatives. And there are languages which include a mixture. For instance, in Misantla Totonac, prefix *lu-* for Instrumental, and prefix *puu-* for Locative are canonical applicatives, as illustrated in (1). In contrast, suffix *-ni*, for Goal, is a quasi-applicative. (It is unclear what the status of circumfix *laa-...-na*, Comitative, is.)

  Like other Bantu languages (such as Chichewa, just illustrated), Ndendeule has a single applicative suffix with a wide semantic range. Only for the two Instrumental senses (I-implement and I-reason) is the applicative of the canonical type. When the suffix has a Goal or Locative sense, there is no corresponding non-applicative construction (so that we have quasi-applicatives). Ngonyani (1995, 1997) states that the closely related language Swahili differs from Ndenduele in a small way—in Swahili, the Goal sense is also canonical.

25.5 Syntax

We can now discuss, in the following four sections: the peripheral function of an applicative argument in a non-applicative construction, what function the underlying O argument may go into within an applicative construction, the role of bound pronouns, and whether more than one applicative derivation may apply ('double applicatives').

25.5.1 Peripheral functions for applicative arguments

As stated at the beginning of §25.3, the meaning of a canonical applicative construction relates to the role the applicative argument has when occurring in peripheral function in the original non-applicative construction. If the language has a plentiful set of affixes or adpositions marking peripheral function, then the appropriate label will be used. The applicative argument from a Locative applicative is originally marked by locative case suffix *-da* in Dyirbal, in (3), by locative suffix *-py* in Ayutla Mixe, in (24), and by locative preposition *ana* in Tamambo, in (22). The original marking for the applicative argument from a Comitative applicative is postposition *kantk* 'with' in Yimas, illustrated in (19). The instrumental suffix *-ŋgu* ~ *-ju* in Dyirbal relates to I-implement, I-surface, in (14), and I-material, in (16).

Some languages have an all-purpose adposition which covers a wide range of peripheral functions. In Jarawara, we find postposition *nijaa* the basis for a Goal applicative in (8), and also for a Comitative applicative in (18). Misantla Totonac has a multi-purpose prepositional prefix *laka-*, used for Locative in (1), and also for Instrument, as in 'She peels the apple with (*laka-*) a knife', and for Comitative, and more besides.

All of these applicative arguments (which are placed into AP-O function within the applicative construction) functioned as a peripheral argument within the original non-applicative clause. There is one important variation on this pattern, where the applicative argument was originally modifier within an NP.

In Dyirbal, *-ba* ~ *-bila* is a derivational suffix. When added to a noun it creates an adjective which may modify the head noun in an NP; for example *yara gama-ba* 'man gun-with'. A *-ba*-form agrees in case with the noun it modifies; for example:

(27)   [yara-ŋgu   gama-ba-gu]ₐ   mijiji₀   dirraŋaya-ñu
        man-ERG   gun-WITH-ERG   white.woman:ABS   threaten-PAST
        The man with a gun threatened the white woman

(Verb *dirraŋaya-* means 'threaten with words or gestures'. Indeed it includes within it the noun *dirra* 'word'. The fact of the threatener toting a gun simply adds immediacy to the act.)

   Now consider the intransitive clause (28) and its applicative correspondent (28-ap):

(28)   [bayi   guya-ba]ₛ   ŋurba-ñu
        HE:ABSOLUTIVE   fish-WITH:ABSOLUTIVE   return-PAST
        The man returned with a fish (lit. Man with fish returned)

(28-ap) bangulₐ   guya₀   ŋurbay-ma-n
         HE:ERGATIVE   fish:ABSOLUTIVE   return-APPLICATIVE-PAST
         The man returned with a fish (lit. man returned-with fish)

   Here *guya* 'fish', which is modifier within the S NP of the original sentence, (28), becomes AP-O within the applicative construction, (28-ap), and 'he', the head of the original S NP, makes up the whole of the A NP in (28-ap).

   Note that the same analysis applies to (4) from Dyirbal—the S NP is *bayi barrmba-ba* 'he quartz-with' (note that word order is free in this language)— and to (21) from Yidiñ, where *marun bana-mujay* is the whole S NP 'cloud water-with'.

   In similar fashion, for some languages an applicative argument may be possessive modifier within an NP in the underlying structure. A straightforward example of this is from Chichewa (Baker 1988: 271):

(29)   fisiₐ   a-na-dy-a   [nsomba   z-a   kalulu]₀
        hyena   3sgA-PAST-eat-ASPECT   fish   AGREEMENT-OF   hare
        The hyena ate the hare's fish

(29-ap) fisiₐ   a-na-dy-er-a   kalulu₀   nsomba
         hyena   3sgA-PAST-eat-APPLICATIVE-ASPECT   hare   fish
         The hyena ate the hare's fish (lit. ate-of the hare (its) fish)

The applicative argument, *kalulu* 'hare' is possessor within the O NP in (29) but becomes the whole O NP in (29-ap). The head of the original O NP, *tsomba* 'fish', now makes up a whole NP and is 'second object' (discussed in the next section). Note that object properties are carried by *kalulu*, the AP-O.

25.5.2 What happens to the original O?

When an applicative derivation applies to an intransitive verb, the original S argument takes on A function, and the applicative argument moves from a peripheral function to become AP-O. When applicative applies to a transitive verb, the A argument remains as is, and the applicative argument again moves from a peripheral function to be O. What then happens to the original O argument from the non-applicative construction?

There are, basically, three possibilities (of these, (b) is the most and (a) the least commonly encountered).

(a) **Omitted.**   The original O can no longer be stated as a distinct argument. In Ainu (Bugaeva 2010), for example, the original O is just omitted from the applicative version of an underlying transitive clause.

(b) **Takes peripheral marking.**   This is typically found in languages with a goodly array of marking for non-core NPs. Examples include:

- Original O goes into dative case, -*gu*, in Dyirbal, illustrated for a Locative applicative in (3-ap) and I-surface in (14-ap).
- Original O receives genitive marking, -*e:h*, within the I-implement applicative in K'iche', shown in (13-ap).
- Original O is now marked by preposition *pada* 'at' for the I-implement applicative in Indonesian, at (2-ap).
- In West Greenlandic the applicative argument is the Recipient. We saw in (10-ap) that when this becomes AP-O, the original O (the Gift) takes on allative suffix, -*mut*.

(c) **Becomes 'second object'.**   Looking back at (7), in the Bantu language Chi-mwi:ni, we see that in a plain transitive clause the O NP follows the verb. In the corresponding applicative, (7-ap), the applicative argument (proper name *Nu:ru*) is placed immediately after the verb, being followed by the original O, *xati* 'letter'. Neither NP bears any prepositional marking (as *Nu:ru* did in the non-applicative (7)). On the surface, it looks as if we have two 'object' NPs. However, careful examination shows that only the AP-O, *Nu:ru*, shows prototypical O properties—coming immediately after the verb, being coded by an object bound pronoun on the verb, and being passivizable (Kisseberth and Abasheikh 1977). There *is* only one NP in O function, the AP-O. The original O does not receive any special marking; it is typically called a 'second object' but in fact has peripheral function.

A similar situation is found in other Bantu languages (including Chichewa, Swahili, and Ndendeule) and in some from elsewhere; for example Amharic (Amberber 2000, 2002) and Toba from Argentina (Censabella 2010), illustrated in (9-ap). However, in other Bantu languages, criterial O properties are shared by the applicative argument, AP-O, and the original O. In such languages, applicative constructions based on a transitive verb could sensibly be said to have 'two objects'. For instance, in Kichanga both objects may be coded by a bound pronoun, passivized, and be in reciprocal relation with the A argument. Other languages of this type include Kinyarwanda, Kihaya, and Kimeru. (See Bresnan and Moshi 1990 for discussion and references.)

The Panoan language Shipibo-Konibo is unusual in that the two 'objects' of an extended transitive clause are marked in the same way and have the same syntactic properties. In the sentence 'Who could have given tapir meat to grandmother', both the Gift NP, 'tapir meat', and the Recipient NP, 'grand-mother', are marked with absolutive case, can occur in either order, be com-mon argument within a relative clause construction, function as discourse topic, and so on (Valenzuela 2003: 346–8, 527–32). What more natural than this indeterminacy should extend to the 'two objects' in the applicative derivation from a transitive clause.

In Shipibo-Konibo there are two quasi-applicatives relating to Goal, and also a canonical applicative with Comitative meaning. For example (Valen-zuela 2010: 131):

(30)   tita-n-ra$_A$ wai$_O$ oro-ai   [papa   betan]
       mother-ERG-DIR.EV   farm:ABS   clear-INCOMPL   father   WITH
       Mother clears the farm with father

(30-ap) tita-n-ra$_A$ papa   wai   oro-kiin-ai
         mother-ERG-DIR.EV   father:ABS   farm:ABS   clear-APP-INCOMPL
         Mother helps father clear the farm (lit. clear-with father the farm)

Valenzuela maintains that the AP-O, *papa* 'father' and the original O *wai* 'chacra, or small farm' cannot be distinguished syntactically in (30-ap). Just like Gift and Recipient NPs within an extended transitive clause of giving, each has the same set of criterial properties (see the informative table in Valenzuela 2010: 138).

There are four identificational features for an applicative: (a) the form of the derivational affix to the verb; (b) the applicative meaning; (c) how the applicative argument was marked when in peripheral function in the original non-applicative clause; (d) for an applicative based on a transitive verb, what happens to the original O.

Table 25.1 illustrates these features for the four applicative derivations in Javanese (Suhandano 1994: 50–62). Note that in column (a) lines 1 and 4 employ the same suffix, -*i*, and rows 2 and 3 also employ the same suffix -*ake*. Also, rows 1 and 2 have the same entry in column (d)—'second object'. As in many other languages, the AP-O has all object properties (position, passivization) with the so-called 'second object' being simply a prepositionless peripheral argument.

TABLE 25.1. Applicative derivations in Javanese

(a) APPLICATIVE SUFFIX TO VERB	(b) MEANING	(c) PREPOSITION MARKING APPLICATIVE ARGUMENT WHEN IN ORIGINAL PERIPHERAL FUNCTION	(d) MARKING ON ORIGINAL O IN APPLICATIVE OF TRANSITIVE
1 −*i*	Goal(A)	*marang* 'to'	'second object'
2 -*ake*	Goal(B)	*kanggo* 'for'	'second object'
3 -*ake*	Instrumental	*nganggo* 'with'	*marang* 'to'
4 −*i*	Locative	*ing* 'in, on'	*nganggo* 'with'

Four main prepositions, in column (c), each provides the basis for an applicative. Interestingly, in line 3 the original O takes preposition *marang* 'to', which is the column (c) entry for line 1, and in line 4 the original O is marked by *nganggo* 'with', the column (c) entry for line 3. The four varieties of applicative can now be illustrated. First, line 1, Goal-A, and line 2, Goal-B.

(31)   Bambang$_A$ ngajar   [basa   Inggris]$_O$ [marang   Sri]
         Bambang   teach   language   English   TO   Sri
         Bambang taught the English language to Sri

(31-ap) Bambang$_A$ ngajar-i   Sri$_O$ [basa   Inggris]
         Bambang   teach-GOAL(A).APP   Sri   language   English
         Bambang taught Sri the English language

(32)   Sri$_A$ masak   kue$_O$ [kanggo   bapak]
         Sri   cook   cake   FOR   father
         Sri cooked cakes for father

(32-ap) Sri$_A$ masak-ake   bapak$_O$ kue
         Sri   cook-GOAL(B).APP   father   cake
         Sri cooked father cakes

Suhandano labels line 1 in Table 25.1 as 'indirect object' and line 2 as 'benefactive'. In fact, these applicatives relate to which verbs may occur with peripheral NPs marked by preposition *marang* 'to' and by *kanggo* 'for' respectively; I call them 'Goal(A)' and 'Goal(B)'. It seems that *marang* may only be used with a limited set of verbs, including 'give', 'send', 'entrust', 'teach'; surely these are likely to imply a beneficial effect on the referent of the applicative argument. It appears that, in line 2, a peripheral argument marked by *kanggo* 'for' may occur with a wide selection of verbs; for example 'carry a book for the child', 'buy a new bike for him', 'make a toy for the child'.

We can now illustrate for line 3, Instrumental, which may be used with certain verbs taking an instrumental NP, marked by *nganggo* 'with'. An I-implement applicative can be formed on 'shoot with a gun' or 'hit with that ruler', as in (33-ap), but there is no I-surface applicative based on 'wash with (*nganggo*) soap'.

(33)   Sri$_A$ nuthuk Bambang$_O$ [nganggo garisan iku]
        Sri   hit   Bambang   WITH   ruler   THAT
        Sri hit Bambang with that ruler

(33-ap) Sri$_A$ nuthuk-ake [garisan iku]$_O$ [marang Bambang]
        Sri   hit-INST.APP   ruler   THAT TO   Bambang
        Sri hit Bambang with that ruler (lit. hit that ruler to Bambang)

A spatial milieu can be stated for almost any action or state. Thus the Locative applicative, in line 4, can be used with a wide selection of verbs. For example:

(34)   [Pak Marta]$_A$ nulis [aksara Jawa]$_O$ [ing gepura desa]
        Mr   Marta   write script Java   ON   gate   village
        Mr Marta wrote the Javanese script on the gate of the village

(34-ap) [Pak Marta]$_A$ nulis-i   [gepura desa]$_O$
        Mr   Marta   write-LOCATIVE.APP   gate   village
        [nganggo   aksara Jawa]
        WITH   script Java
        Mr Marta wrote (on) the gate of the village with the Javanese script

25.5.3 The role of bound pronouns

The most typical system of bound pronouns involves coding the S argument in an intransitive and the A and O arguments in a transitive clause. By and large, this applies in a straightforward manner for applicatives. For example, in Nez Perce (Sahaptian, Oregon; Rude 1985: 181, 1986: 142):

(35)   láwtiwaa-yiin hi-túuqi-six   miyóoxat$_S$
        friend-WITH   3.S-smoke-ASPECT   chief
        The chief is smoking with a friend

(35-ap) láwtiwaa-na$_O$ pée-tuqi-twe-ce   miyóoxato-m$_A$
        friend-ACC   3.A:3.O-smoke-APP-ASPECT   chief-ERG
        The chief is smoking-with a friend

An S NP is unmarked, as in (35), while an O NP receives accusative (or 'direct object') suffix *-na* and an A NP takes ergative suffix *-m*, as in (35-ap). In (35) the verb hosts 3rd person S bound pronominal prefix *hi-*. With a transitive clause there is a fused pronominal prefix, combining information on A and O; this is *pée-* for 3rd person A and 3rd person O, as in (35-ap).

Ayutla Mixe operates in a similar manner. In intransitive clause (24), 'A ball entered the corral', there is pronominal prefix *y-* for 3rd person S, and in the applicative (24-ap), 'He entered the car', prefix *t-* indicating 3rd person A combined with 3rd person O. In Amharic, A and O bound pronouns are not fused. In (12-ap), 'The teacher laughed-at the boy', we find 3rd person feminine A suffix *čč*—identical to 3rd person feminine S suffix in (12)—preceding the applicative suffix *-ibb-*, and 3rd person masculine O suffix *-ǝt* following it.

When we look at applicatives of transitives, it is generally the case that the AP-O replaces the original O as regards bound pronominal coding. West Greenlandic has fused A-plus-O forms. In (10), which is literally 'He$_A$ gave Niisi$_O$ with money (plural)', the bound pronominal suffix is *-vaa* for 3sg A ('he') and 3sg O ('Niisi'). However, in the applicative (10-ap)—literally 'He$_A$ gave [money (plural)]$_O$ to Niisi'—the pronominal suffix is *-pai*, for 3sg A (again 'he') and 3pl O ('the money (plural)').

It is good to get an example which includes 1st or 2nd person. The plain transitive (13), 'I hit you with a stick', in K'iche' has 2sg O and 1sg A bound pronominal prefixes. The corresponding applicative, (13-ap), replaces 2sg O prefix *-at-* by the 3sg O form (which has zero realization), coding 'stick'.

There are exceptions to this prototypical scheme. In both Tzutujil (Mayan, Guatemala; Dayley 1985: 354–7) and Metzontla Popoloc (Popolucan, Mexico; Veerman-Leichsenring 2006) there are applicative processes which divest the applicative argument of its peripheral marking and place it in O slot. Nevertheless, bound pronouns still code the original O, not the AP-O. In the Bantu language Ndendeule (Ngonyani 1995), the object bound pronoun codes the AP-O for Goal applicative but the original O for Instrumental and Locative applicatives. This may relate to a preference for using bound pronouns for animate (rather than inanimate) arguments. A Goal applicative argument is likely to have human (or at least animate) reference—for example, 'cook food for the children'—while an Instrumental or Locative applicative argument is likely to have inanimate reference—'cut the boy with a knife' or 'eat food in the office'. And in Bantu languages (such as Kichanga) where the AP-O and the original O share object properties, either may be coded by a bound pronoun.

25.5.4 Several applicatives together

For some languages with an array of applicative processes, more than one can be used with a single verb. For instance in Ainu (Bugaeva 2010), *caranke* means 'argue'. Adding Comitative applicative prefix *ko-*, and then Goal prefix *e-*, we get *e-ko-caranke* 'argue with someone about something'.

As described under III in §25.4, Misantla Totonac has four applicative derivations, two shown by prefixes, one by a suffix and one by a circumfix. Each can be combined with every one of the others. The following example (MacKay 1999: 302) uses both instrumental prefix *lii-* and comitative circumfix *laa-...-na*:

(36-ap²)   kít   ik-laa-lii-laa-yaa-na
        1sg   1sgA:3sgO-COM.APP-INST.APP-cut-IMPERFECTIVE-COM.APP
         hun-mačiitu   hun   Mario
         DETERMINER-machete   DETERMINER   Mario
        I with Mario use the machete to cut something

Misantla Totonac is unusual (unique in the data I have collected) in allowing a single applicative process, Goal suffix *-ni*, to apply twice on a single verb (MacKay 1999: 267):

(37)   wan   'say X, tell X'
           wan-ni   'say/tell X to Y'
           wan-ni-ni   'say/tell X to Y for Z'

An illustration of this double *-ni* is:

(38-ap²)   ut   kin-wan-ni-ni-yaa-na
        3sg   3sgA:1sgO-tell-GOAL.APP-GOAL.APP-IMPERV-3sgA:2sgO
        EITHER   She tells you X for me
        OR   She tells me X for you

This language is unusual in showing some bound pronouns by prefixes, some by suffixes, and some by circumfixes. For combination of 3sg A and 1sg O there is prefix *kin-* while 3sg A and 2sg O uses suffix *-na*. Both bound pronouns are included in (38-ap²) but it is unclear which relates to which applicative, leading to ambiguity (which would be likely to be resolved by pragmatic context).

Olutec (Zavala 2000: 870–6) can combine its various applicatives, shown at array I in §25.4: Comitative *mü:-* plus Goal *-ja:yʔ*, Comitative *mü:-* plus Instrumental *toj-*, Instrumental *toj-* plus Goal *-ja:yʔ*, I-reason *toko-* plus Goal *-ja:yʔ*, and I-reason *tok-* plus G-addition *kuj-*. And this language excels itself in permitting three applicative affixes, Instrumental *toj-*, Comitative *mü:-*, and Goal *-ja:yʔ*, all on a single verb:

(39-ap³)   ta=toj-mü:-mi:nʔ-aʔx-ü-w
         1sgO=INST.APP-COM.APP-come-GOAL.APP-INVERSE-COMPLETIVE
         jeʔ=k   kustat   mo:k
         THAT=ANIMATE   sack   corn
        He brought the corn in a sack for me

'Primary object status is always assigned to the non-subject participant that ranks the highest within the saliency hierarchy (1 > 2 > 3 proximate > 3 obviative)'; here 1sg. 'corn' and 'sack' are then 'second objects'. The inverse marker is used when O is higher than A on the hierarchy, as here.

It should be noted that not every language with more than one applicative derivation permits these to co-occur. Metzontla Popoloc has Comitative and Instrumental verbal suffixes but they 'are mutually exclusive, thus when the clause or sentence contains both an instrumental and a comitative argument, only one of the arguments is encoded in the predicate' with the other being shown by a peripheral NP (Veerman-Leichsenring 2006: 108).

25.6 Functions

Thus far we have dealt with the mechanics of applicatives. But this is a marked construction type, which is employed in specific circumstances. The important feature of any applicative construction lies in its discourse and pragmatic functions.

The Mayan language Tzutujil has a single applicative suffix, with Instrumental meaning. Dayley (1985: 354) states that this derivation is used 'to indicate that the instrument used in a transitive activity is highlighted or in focus'. Specifically, the applicative may be used (1) when the applicative argument is 'in contrastive focus or highly emphatic', (2) when it is questioned, and (3) when it is relativized. As described under I in §25.4, Olutec has five applicative affixes. Zavala (2000: 661) writes that an applicative construction is 'used in syntactic contexts in which the extra-thematic argument [that is, the applicative argument] is treated as a pragmatically salient participant, e.g. clefted constructions, relative clauses, questions and conjoined clauses in which the extra-thematic argument acts as a clausal topic'. He notes also that an applicative construction is triggered by 'the status of the applicative argument in terms of the hierarchy human > animate > inanimate'.

In essence, an applicative construction takes what was an optional peripheral argument and places it in a core function. In some languages, only an argument which is in a core function may be fronted or clefted, questioned, relativized, and so on. In order to take part in such operations a Goal or Instrumental or Comitative or Locative argument must be moved into O function, through an applicative derivation.

Just like passive and antipassive (described in Chapter 23), applicative 'feeds' such syntactic operations, and also feeds topic or pivot requirements. Dyirbal works in terms of an S/O pivot, illustrated at (11) in §23.1. That is, several clauses can only be linked together in one pivot chain if they share an argument and it is in S or O function in each. This was illustrated in discussion of

(4-ap) in §25.1. A further example comes from a story, told by the late Daisy Denham, of how two women went fishing for eels. First of all, they put a woven dilly-bag, *jawun*, into the water hoping that an eel would swim into it; but no luck. This is described by a plain transitive clause:

(40)   jawun$_O$ balagarra-gu$_A$ ŋaba-n   jaban-gu, yimba
          dilly-bag:ABS 3du-ERG   immerse-PAST eel-DATIVE nothing
          The two of them immersed in water the dilly-bag for eels, (but
             there was) nothing.

It is followed by two applicative clauses, each with *jawun* 'dilly-bag' in O function, serving as pivot for this part of the narrative:

(41-ap) jawun$_O$ baŋgun$_A$ waymbarray-mba-n
          dilly-bag:ABS SHE:ERG go.around-APP-PAST
          They (trawled) the dilly-bag around (in the water)
            (lit. went-around-with the dilly-bag)

(42-ap) [jaban-gu   bagul]   gundal-ma-li
          eel-DATIVE HE(eel):DATIVE put.in-APP-PURPOSIVE
          to catch eels in it (lit. to put.in-at (the dilly-bag) to eels)

Dyirbal has single applicative marker, suffix *-ma* ~ *-mba* which covers Instrumental—as in (14-ap) and (16-ap)—Comitative—as in (4-ap), (28-ap), and (41-ap)—and Locative—as in (3-ap) and (42-ap). The plain intransitive clause underlying (41-ap) is:

(41)   [balan   jawun-bila]$_S$ waymbarra-ñu
          SHE:ABS dilly.bag-WITH:ABS go.around-PAST
          They went around with a dilly-bag (lit. they with a dilly-bag went
            around)

The applicative derivation takes *jawun* 'dilly-bag', which is a comitative modifier within the S NP in (41), and puts it into O function in (41-ap) so that it can function as pivot, linked to (40), which also has *jawun* in O function.
   The plain transitive clause underlying (42-ap) is:

(42)   [bayi   jaban]$_O$ baŋgun$_A$ gunda-li   jawun-da
          HE:ABS eel:ABS   SHE-ERG put.in-PURPOSIVE dilly.bag-LOC
          for them to put eels in the dilly-bag

When applicativized, (42) would become *jawun$_O$ baŋgun$_A$ gundal-ma-li [bagul jaban-gu]*. The original O, *bayi jaban* 'eel', is now coded by dative case. We find, in (42-ap), that both *jawun* and *baŋgun* are ellipsed, since they are repeated from the preceding clause, (41-ap). (Note that words can be permuted in almost any order within a Dyirbal sentence.)

In summary, *jawun* 'dilly-bag' is in O function for (40), then in underlying comitative and locative functions (both non-core) for the next two clauses. A Comitative applicative construction is used in (41-ap) and a Locative Application in (42-ap) to place *jawun* in derived O function in each instance, and enable the three clauses to be linked together as a pivot chain.

Languages do vary in terms of the restrictions on their syntactic organization. In Dyirbal two clauses can only be conjoined, to make up a sentence, if they share an argument which is in pivot (S or O) function in each. But any core or peripheral argument may be questioned; there is no need to apply an applicative or antipassive derivation. In a relative clause construction the common argument must be in S or O function within the relative clause; and this is a constraint which is fed by antipassive (putting underlying A into S function) and applicative (putting an underlying non-core argument into O function).

Mithun (2001: 76) describes the three canonical applicatives—Goal, Comitative, and Locative—in the Austronesian language Kapampangan, and then goes on to describe what are here called quasi-applicatives. 'A number of languages contain robust applicative constructions but no evidence of prepositions or postpositions. In fact, they include no oblique beneficiaries, instruments or directions at all.' She illustrates with the Iroquoian language Tuscarora, showing that an instrumental argument, for example, may only be expressed in O function, within an Instrumental applicative construction.

We can also note that a number of languages, which do have bona fide canonical applicatives, exhibit a strong preference for using the applicative rather than the non-applicative alternative. Discussing pairs of constructions in Yimas such as (19) and (19-ap), quoted in §25.3.3, Foley (1991: 304) states that the applicative construction is 'the more common and greatly preferred structure in all cases'.

Often, which construction type is preferred depends on the referents of the arguments involved. In §25.3.4, we quoted a non-applicative, (24), and an applicative, (24-ap), from Ayutla Mixe, both involving the verb 'enter'. The non-applicative is preferred for 'The ball entered the corral' and the applicative for 'He entered (i.e. got into) the car'.

There is a preference, cross-linguistically, for speech act participants to be accorded core functions, and this is an important factor in motivating the use (or the exclusive use) of applicative constructions.

Jarawara has a single applicative prefix, *ka-*, which can be used for G-addition, G-stimulus, G-corporeal, I-implement, Comitative, and Locative. In almost every instance, the applicative argument may be expressed either by a peripheral argument in a non-applicative constructions or as AP-O in an applicative construction. See the examples of G-addition in (8) and (8-ap), and of Comitative in (18) and (18-ap). Now my Jarawara corpus includes the intransitive clause (43) and transitive applicative construction (43-ap), both involving verb *behe* 'overturn' (Dixon 2004: 256):

(43)   kanawaa$_S$ behe   na-waha-ke
         canoe(f)   overturn AUX-NEXT.THING-DECf
         Then the canoe overturned

(43-ap) kanawaa$_A$ mee$_O$ behe   hi-ka-wa   hi-ke
         canoe(f)   3nsg   overturn Oc-APP-NEXT.THING   Oc-DECf
         Then the canoe overturned-with them

I tried extending the intransitive clause, (43), by adding 'them' in a peripheral NP, i.e. *mee ni-jaa*, but was told that it is better to use the applicative version, (43-ap). That is, when the applicative argument is human, and the S/A is inanimate, an applicative construction is preferred, so that the human argument can go into a core function (here, O). (The *hi-* prefix indicates that this is a transitive 'O-construction' in which both A and O are third person and it is the O argument which is pivot within the stretch of discourse in which the clause appears; see §23.1.)

25.7 Further realizations

The great majority of applicative derivations are shown by the morphological process of affixation applying to a verb. There are just a few scattered instances of other kinds of marking.

In §24.2.5 we saw how, in Ngan'gityemerri, exchanging auxiliaries constitutes a causative strategy. There is no provision in Ngan'gityemerri for exchanging auxiliaries being used as an applicative strategy. However we do find an instance of this in Bunuba, another Australian language which has a small set of eleven auxiliary verbs that co-occur with members of a large set of lexical verbs. Consider lexical verb *wula* 'speak' as it is used with monovalent auxiliary *MA* and with divalent auxiliary *RA2* (Rumsey 2000: 77–8):

(40)   wula+MA 'speak',

(44-ap) wula+RA2 'speak to'

As described in §24.2.2, an asymmetrical Serial Verb Construction may represent causation. There are also reports of it having an applicative effect.

In the Papuan language Dumo (Ingram 2006: 214) the extended intransitive verb 'be with' can combine (as minor member) with intransitive verb 'paddle' (the major member) to yield a Comitative applicative SVC 'paddle with':

(45-ap) neh=wor$_A$ [nighe   la-la]$_{SVC}$ nu$_O$
          1sg=EMPHATIC   paddle:1sgA be.with:1sgA-REDUPLICATED 2sg
          I will paddle with you

Other applicative meanings rendered through SVCs include G-recipient with 'give' as minor member, I-implement with 'take', and Locative with 'stay'. SVCs, some with applicative effect, are found in languages from West and south-west Africa, South-east and East Asia, Amazonia and the Pacific (and also in creole languages). See Byrne (1992: 197), and Aikhenvald and Dixon (2006: 26) plus further references therein.

We can now enquire whether an applicative relationship can be recognized involving just lexemes. How about an ambitransitive verb of type S = A? In fact, the transitive version of such a verb is likely to have a quite different profile from the Instrumental applicative derivation of its intransitive version. This can be illustrated schematically for the S = A ambitransitive verb *ori -na-* 'paddle' in Jarawara:

(46)

	PADDLER	CANOE/PASSENGER/RIVER	PADDLE
plain transitive	A	O	peripheral
plain intransitive	S		<u>peripheral</u>
applicative of intransitive	A		<u>O</u>

The O argument for the plain transitive can be the canoe or the passengers in it or the river itself. It cannot be the paddle used which, if stated, must be marked by a peripheral postposition. And it is this peripheral argument which becomes AP-O in the applicative based on the intransitive; the AP-O is quite different from the original O NP of the plain transitive. (Note that in Jarawara applicatives can only be based on intransitive verbs. The actual three sentences will be found in Dixon 2004: 257.)

In English (and no doubt in other languages) we can recognize pairs of intransitive/transitive verbs with rather similar (although not identical) meanings, such that an optional peripheral argument for the intransitive verb corresponds to the obligatory O argument for the transitive. For example:

(47)   John$_S$ thought (about <u>the problem</u>)

(47-ap) John$_A$ considered [the problem]$_O$

Similar pairs (if one considers corresponding meanings of each member) include:

(47) INTRANSITIVE VERB WITH OPTIONAL
     PERIPHERAL ARGUMENT   TRANSITIVE VERB(S)
     look (at)   inspect, scrutinize, examine
     confess (to)   admit
     comment (on)   discuss
     give birth (to)   bear

Just as Dyirbal has causative-type lexical pairs (illustrated at (10) in §24.2.4) so also it has applicative-type pairs, including:

(48)   INTRANSITIVE VERB WITH
           OPTIONAL PERIPHERAL ARGUMENT   TRANSITIVE VERB
     (a)   marri- 'follow' (optional dative NP: banja- 'follow (O: person,
           person, river, track)   river, track)'
     (b)   wurrba- 'speak, talk'   buwa- 'tell (O: addressee or
                                                  news)'
     (c)   mañja- 'eat to satisfy hunger'   janga- 'eat (O: food)'
           (optional instrumental NP: food),
           as in (16)

As mentioned in §24.2.4 (and in §5.1 and §8.1) the 'mother-in-law' speech style, called Jalnguy, has fewer lexemes than the everyday style, Guwal. If the everyday style has a transitive/intransitive verb pair, with similar meanings, then Jalnguy just has a transitive verb, and uses an intransitivized version of this (employing general intransitivizing suffix -(yi)rri- ~ -marri-) to render the intransitive verb in Guwal. In §24.2.4, (12) gave the Jalnguy correspondents of the 'causative pairs' in (10). In similar fashion, (50) gives Jalnguy correspondents of the 'applicative pairs' in (49).

(49)   everyday style   mother-in-law
                             (Guwal)   style (Jalnguy)

     (a) transitive   banja-   gañjama-   'follow'
          intransitive   marri-   gañjama-rri-   'follow'
     (b) transitive   buwa-   wuyuba-   'tell'
          intransitive   wurrba-   wuyuba-rri-   'speak, talk'
     (c) transitive   janga-   yulmi-   'eat'
          intransitive   mañja-   yulmi-marri-   'eat to satisfy
                                                               hunger'

These Jalnguy correspondences show that the verbs in each pair are considered to have roughly the same semantic content, differing in transitivity. But they are by no means exactly synonymous. Each of the intransitive verbs has an applicative form. For example *mañjay-ma-* in (16-ap) still carries with it the sense 'eat to satisfy hunger' (for example, when one has not had anything to eat for a fair while), in contrast to plain transitive *jaŋga-* 'eat (in the normal course of events)'.

25.8 Other functions, other meanings

Some languages include a single affix which can have either applicative or causative effect. The process always increases valency but, operating on an intransitive verb, varies as to whether underlying S becomes A (applicative) or O (causative).

It is not easy to formulate principles for which sense the affix has with which verb. In Yidiñ, suffix *-ŋa-* (which is used only with intransitive verbs) covers a number of applicative functions—listed as array VI in §25.4—and can also have causative meaning. The causative sense is found with a wide range of verbs, but there are specific restrictions (Dixon 1977a: 312–13):

(a) Suffix *-ŋa* cannot have a causative meaning with verbs which form a G-addition, G-stimulus, G-corporeal, or Locative applicative. Thus, with *badi-* 'cry' the derived form *badi-ŋa-* can only have applicative meaning 'cry for'. When I asked how one would express a causative meaning such as 'He made me cry', the response was that one would have to specify what was done to engender the crying, such as 'He teased me and I cried'.

(b) There are a number of 'lexical causative' pairs of verbs which have the same semantic content and differ only in transitivity, on an S = O basis (similar to those quoted in (10) of §24.2.4 for the neighbouring language Dyirbal). They include *jana-* 'stand up' and *jarra-* 'put standing up'; and *bayi-* 'come out' and *daŋga-* 'take out'. When *-ŋa-* is added to the intransitive member of such a pair, the meaning can only be applicative. For example *bayi-ŋa-* may only mean 'come out with', not 'make come out', since there is a transitive verb *daŋga-* 'take out (= make come out)'. However, there is no transitive correspondent for *bila-* 'go in' and as a consequence *bila-ŋa-* is ambiguous between an applicative meaning 'go in with' and a causative one 'put in (= make go in)'.

The Salish language Musqueam has five applicative suffixes (apparently all of the 'quasi-' variety), four for types of Goal and the other for Comitative. The comitative applicative suffix *-stəxʷ* is also used for causative. Suttles (2004: 239) explains that the verb *q'éwəłtən* 'pay' can mean either 'pay penance for sins' or 'pay people'. For the first sense, suffix -*stəxʷ* takes on a causative meaning, and for the second sense it has an applicative meaning:

(50) BASIC VERB   ADDING SUFFIX -*stəxʷ*

| q'éwəłtən | 'pay penance for sins' | q'éwəłtənə-stəxʷ | 'make him pay (punish him)' |
| q'éwəłtən | 'pay people' | q'éwəłtənə-stəxʷ | 'pay for him (pay his way)' |

Quite a number of Australian languages have a single transitivizing affix whose pre-eminent function appears to be causative, with an applicative sense applying for just a few verbs. (Yidiñ is an exception, since for this language the applicative meaning is more common.) In Djabugay (Patz 1991: 284) the only verbs mentioned as taking the applicative sense are 'laugh (at)' and 'be afraid (of)'. The only two in Mparntwe Arrernte (Wilkins 1989: 258) are 'laugh (at someone)' and 'cry (for someone, to mourn someone)'; see §25.3.1. Just a handful of verbs take suffix -*la* in the applicative sense in Arabana-Wangkangurru (Hercus 1994: 148–52); they include 'cry (over)', 'laugh (at)', and 'be pleased (with)'. There is a further handful in Wik-Mungkan (Kilham et al. 1986) including 'laugh (at someone)' and 'cry (with people who are in sorrow)'. It will be seen that, for the Australian cultural area, the G-corporeal verbs 'laugh at' and 'cry for/over/with' are among those most open to be applicativized.

An affix which marks applicative derivation when used with a verb may, in some languages, also be added to a noun or adjective, creating a transitive verbal stem. In (2-ap) above, from Indonesian, suffix -*kan* is added to verb 'hit' and functions as an Instrumental applicative. It can also function as transitive verbalizer with a noun—from *kabar* 'news' we get verb -*kabar-kan* 'to report' and from *libur* 'holiday' there is -*libur-kan* 'to send on holiday' (Sneddon 1996: 76–7). The applicative sense of suffix -*ŋa*- in Yidiñ was illustrated by *gada-ŋa*- 'come with' in (21-ap); it can also be used with an adjective; for example, *gadil* 'small', *gadil-ŋa*- 'make small' (Dixon 1977a: 365).

Applicative affixes may have further special uses in individual languages. One of the most notable is found in Creek, where the two applicative prefixes combine to mark a comparative construction. As described at IV in §25.4, Creek has an invariable Instrumental applicative prefix *(i)s*- and also a Goal applicative prefix which marks person and number of the applicative argument; for example, *an-* ~ *am-* for 1sg. Instrumental and Goal applicative prefixes are applied in this order, with the Goal prefix indicating the person and number of the Standard of Comparison (see §3.23 and Chapter 26). For example (Martin 2011: 379):

(52)   má:h-i:-t   ô:-s
        tall-DURATIVE-THEMATIC be-INDIC
        He/she is tall

(52-cp)   (i)s-am-má:h-i:-t   ô:-s
          INST.APPL-GOAL.APP(1sg)-tall-DURATIVE-THEMATIC   be-INDIC
          He/she is taller than me

One morphological process may have syntactic effect in some circumstances but merely add an element of meaning on other occasions. This was
illustrated for causatives in §24.6.1. In Jarawara, verbal prefix ka- can be used
with an intransitive verb and functions as an applicative, deriving a transitive
stem, as illustrated in (8-ap), (18-ap), and (43-ap). But the same ka- can also
be used with an intransitive or transitive verb, not affecting the transitivity
or the identity of the arguments but instead just adding one of a number of
pieces of semantic information; these include: (a) one of the core participants
is inside something; (b) a container is full of something; (c) an animate S or O
argument has dual reference; (d) the human referent of an S or O argument is
sick. For example:

(53)   okoto$_O$ noki   ti-ka-na!
         1sgPOSS:daughter   wait.for   2sgA-SICK-AUXILIARY:FEMININE
         You wait for my sick daughter!

Omitting the -ka- from (53), the meaning would just be 'You wait for my
daughter!' with no indication that she is sick. Full details and exemplification
will be found in Dixon (2004: 258–65).

25.9 Terminology

The label 'applicative' has been used in study of Bantu languages since the late
nineteenth century. An early mention is Stapleton (1903: 211): 'The Applicative
verb is formed from the verb stem by the addition of a suffix, which imparts
to the Simple idea of the verb the force of one of our prepositions. The sense
of the prepositional idea added must be gathered from the context'. Note that
Stapleton was surveying Bantu languages which have a single applicative suffix
covering a wide range of meanings (see, for example, the account of Chichewa
at V in §25.4).

   The grammatical category, and its label, were extended into general
linguistics—being used to describe non-African languages—only during the
last quarter of the twentieth century. For example, in their *Lingua descriptive series questionnaire*, Comrie and Smith (1977) neither mention the term
'applicative' nor provide any place where such constructions should be discussed.

   Various labels have been used. Mayanists typically refer to 'instrumental
voice' (for example, Dayley 1985: 354–7; Campbell 2000: 278). Dealing with

Ainu, Tamura (2000: 206, translation of 1988 original) described 'prefixes which express case relationships'. Many other labels have been used, including 'object promoting' (Merlan 1983: 47 on Ngalakan), 'promotion to core' (Foley 1991: 303 on Yimas), 'advancement' (all work on Relational Grammar). The grammar of Dyirbal (Dixon 1972) simply spoke of 'instrumental constructions' and 'comitative constructions'.

In his grammar of Musqueam, Suttles (2004: 237) explains that 'the applicative or "redirective" suffixes "redirect" the verb so that what would otherwise have to be in an oblique relationship to it can be its grammatical object'. This grammar was half-a-century in the making; it is likely that, in earlier versions, Suttles just used the label 'redirective'.

The label 'applicative' is now in fairly general employment. But it is used in a variety of different ways. My aim in this chapter has been to try to clarify the topic, so that future work may attain cross-linguistic consistency and clarity.

25.10 Summary

A canonical applicative involves a syntactic derivation whereby an argument (the applicative argument), which is in peripheral function in underlying structure, is placed in O function. An applicative construction is used when the speaker wishes to focus on the applicative argument, or when it needs to be in a core function in order to be available for fronting, questioning, relativizing, or to function as discourse pivot, and so on. Applicative is almost always marked by an affix to the verb; it is never shown periphrastically, and only rather seldom through a serial verb construction, or exchange of auxiliaries.

With an intransitive verb, an applicative derivation derives a transitive form, S becoming A, with the applicative argument moving into O function. When based on a transitive verb, A stays as is, the applicative argument again becomes O, and the original O is most often now marked as a peripheral argument. It can remain unmarked, as 'second object' but—save in rare cases— now exhibits few or no object properties. Or the original O may simply be omitted.

For some languages, the grammar states that there is no corresponding non-applicative construction (and other grammars do not specify whether or not this is to be found). We call these 'quasi-applicatives'—the applicative argument may only be stated in O function within an applicative construction, usurping the underlying O.

It seems that any peripheral argument is available to be an applicative argument, with appropriate choice of verb. But each individual language takes up only some of the possibilities. The meaning of an applicative derivation relates to the original peripheral function of the applicative argument. It is convenient to recognize four broad realms of meaning: Goal, Instrument (each with several subtypes), Comitative, and Locative. 'Benefactive' and 'malefactive' may be secondary facets of varieties of Goal applicative, but are never the primary feature.

Some languages have a single applicative marker, with limited meaning. Others have an array of applicative affixes, each with a fair range of meaning. A further set of languages has a single marker but covering many meanings, comparable to those of languages with an array of markers.

There are examples of several applicative derivations applying to a given verb (generally, but not always, involving different applicative affixes). In a number of languages, one affix can have both causative and applicative meanings; which sense is intended may be clear from the nature of the verb it is used with, or perhaps only from pragmatic and discourse considerations.

25.11 What to investigate

For each applicative derivation, the fieldworker should ascertain the following.

A   What is the formal marking of the derivation? This generally involves a type of affixation but it may be some other morphological process, or a serial verb construction, or changing auxiliaries, or something else.

Does the applicative marking have any further function in the grammar; for example, causative, or a non-valency-changing semantic effect?

B   For a construction to be a canonical applicative, there should be a corresponding non-applicative construction with the applicative argument in peripheral function. It must be checked that this is so. The peripheral function determines the meaning of the applicative.

C   Investigate the factors determining whether an applicative or the corresponding non-applicative is preferred (or required). It may be that the applicative construction is most appropriate when the applicative argument has human, or animate, reference, and the non-applicative when it is inanimate.

D   If the applicative argument can only be coded as object (AP-O) within an applicative construction, and not as peripheral argument in a non-applicative construction, then we have a 'quasi-applicative'. Carefully examine the canonical or 'quasi-' status of each putative applicative. When a language has an array of applicative markings, it may be the case that only some of them are canonical.

E   For each applicative, investigate its full range of meaning, following the scheme in §25.3. For example, if an applicative derivation covers I-implement ('cut the meat with knife') it may be worthwhile looking, in a judicious way, to see whether it may also be used for I-surface ('wipe the surface with a rag') and I-assist ('cook the potatoes with a pan').

Examine how productive each applicative derivation is. For example, whether it applies to all or only some verbs of a certain semantic type (and, if possible, look for conditioning factors which may be involved).

F   For each applicative derivation, check whether it applies to both intransitive and transitive verbs, or just to one of these sets. Also look at extended intransitive and extended transitive subtypes, if the language has these.

G   When an applicative is used with a transitive verb, what happens to the original O from the underlying clause? It may just be omitted. Most often, it is now assigned a peripheral marking. In some languages it takes no new marking and is a 'second object'. Generally, the AP-O now shows criterial object properties (these need to be investigated and listed). Sometimes, object properties are shared between the AP-O and the original O. This should be carefully checked.

A related issue concerns what gets shown by the bound pronouns within an applicative construction.

H   It is unusual to find two applicative derivations with a single verb (or the same derivation twice). The fieldworker should be on the lookout for these turning up in the corpus (I would not recommend trying to elicit them if they have not been observed occurring naturally). If they are found, they should of course be systematically investigated.

J   If it is possible to infer how applicative markers evolved, what they came from, this can be a useful further line of enquiry. For example, an applicative affix may have evolved from an adposition, or from an item such as 'give' or 'take' from within a serial verb construction.

Sources and notes

Apart from Mithun's (2001) short but insightful essay, previous general accounts of applicative constructions have been of uneven or poor quality. Some formal theorists have shown great interest in what happens in those few languages where the original O argument does not take peripheral marking within an applicative construction, and this has tended to skew a number of studies. There has been no systematic study of the meanings of applicatives. A further hindrance has been the well-established but misleading tradition of focussing on 'benefactive' as a main meaning, when it is best regarded as a secondary facet of the more general Goal meaning.

Peterson (2007) includes some useful data, but not always presented correctly. For example, in Yidiñ examples (26–7) on pages 136–7 an 'ACC' form is said to be 'ABS', *wuji-* 'grow up' is glossed as 'bring up', and two tense inflections are unglossed. Peterson (2007: 228) notes an 'apparent tendency for languages with applicative constructions to avoid accusative alignment'; this is not supported by my investigations.

It is hard to imagine more misleading information being included in an article of two (albeit large) pages than Polinsky (2005a). It begins with the following definition: 'In an applicative construction, the number of object arguments selected by the predicate is increased by one with respect to the basic construction'. Not so when, as is most often the case, the original O becomes a peripheral argument. Other unsubstantiable claims include: 'applicatives are commonly found in those languages that have little or no case marking', and 'the intransitive base of applicatives is less common than the transitive base'. Polinsky's sample of 183 languages is said to include only two 'that form applicatives from the intransitive base exclusively'—Fijian (which could not on my criteria be said to have applicatives) and Wambaya (this is correct). My corpus of eighty-two languages with bona fide applicatives includes seventeen 'intransitive-only' and eleven 'transitive-only'. She then 'explains' why applicative is mostly found with transitive verbs (which is untrue) and causative with intransitives.

25.1   Note that 'alternative syntactic frames' such as shown by *give* in English (for example, *Mary gave a parcel to John* and *Mary gave John a parcel*) do not qualify as applicatives since there is no marking on the verb.

A number of grammatical phenomena which have in the literature been described as 'applicatives' do not fall within the scope of the term as employed here, for a variety of reasons. One example concerns the so-called 'applicatives' in the North-west Caucasian language Abaza (O'Herin 2001). This language may have up to two bound pronouns referring to peripheral arguments in addition to the two marking A and O (in a transitive) or S (in an intransitive construction). The so-called 'applicative' prefix does not affect transitivity or the coding of core arguments; it simply adds to the verb a further bound pronoun, relating to a peripheral argument.

Information provided in this chapter on applicatives in Dyirbal is fuller than that in Dixon (1972: 95–9), reflecting a further four decades on work on this language. In order to be maximally reader-friendly, abbreviated glosses are given throughout this chapter for noun markers in Dyirbal. For example, *baŋgul* is glossed as 'HE:ERGATIVE'; more fully it would be *ba-ŋgu-l*, 'THERE-ERGATIVE-MASCULINE'.

25.2   Peterson (2007: 50–1) does not distinguish between canonical and quasi-applicatives. He acknowledges that 'often grammatical descriptions do not identify alternatives for applicative constructions' which would establish canonical status. But he then states that 'if we relied on explicit statements to this effect, we would have far fewer constructions to consider'.

Romero-Méndez (2008: 373–5, 514–18) describes 'benefactive applicative apophony' for Ayulta Mixe (Mixe-Zoque family, Mexico). This is a derivational process involving internal change; for example *ne'ep* 'sow' and its derived form *neejp*. However, it is not clear from the discussion provided that this really qualifies as an applicative.

There is some useful discussion in the literature concerning the diachronic origins of applicative affixes. Two main sources have been identified. The first is from an adposition. Mithun (2001) states that, of the almost fifty forms which serve only as postpositions in the Athabaskan language Navajo (described by Young and Morgan 1987), a dozen appear to have developed into applicative prefixes. Craig and Hale (1988) state that of the nine postpositions in Rama (Chibchan, Nicaragua), five have developed, in reduced form, to be applicative prefixes (although they use the term 'relational preverbs'). This development is illustrated for Nadëb in (23) and (23-ap).

The second source is from a verb. In Yimas, verb *ŋa-* 'give' has given rise to the Goal applicative suffix *-ŋa* (Foley 1991: 308–11). For the Iroquoian language Mohawk, Mithun (1991: 94–5) suggests that Goal applicative suffixes developed from verbs 'lend' and 'give', while in another Iroquoian language, Tuscarora, the two Instrumental applicative suffixes evolved from verbs 'pick up' and 'use'.

Shibatani and Pardeshi (2002: 119) suggest that a 'benefactive' applicative could develop from a 'causer involved' (sometimes called 'sociative') causative (see parameter 9 in §24.4).

Peterson (2007: 123–61) has a chapter on the evolution of applicative constructions. However, it should be consulted with caution. Dixon (1972) states that Dyirbal has a single applicative marker which has Instrumental meaning with transitive and Comitative with intransitive verbs. The language has no causative derivation. On the basis of this data, Peterson (2007: 137), suggests that 'at some point in the past, this [applicative suffix] was very likely a causative marker'. But why stop there? At the present time all affixes in Dyirbal are suffixes. Maybe 'at some point in the past' they were all prefixes.

25.3   For (15-ap), (17-ap), (20-ap), and (25-ap), the sources do not quote corresponding non-applicative constructions in these instances. However, non-applicative/applicative pairs are given for other examples, suggesting that these are canonical (rather than quasi-)applicative constructions.

25.3.2   Other languages which code I-reason in the same way as other Instrumental subtypes include Misantla Totonac (array III in §25.4), Creek (array IV), Popoloc (Veerman-Leichsenring 2006), and the Austronesian language Tukang Besi (Donohue 1999: 225–68). This is mirrored by the fact that in some languages (for example, those of the Slavic subgroup and Tariana from Amazonia) a single nominal case covers both implement instrumental and reason.

25.3.3   It is not uncommon to encounter the same marking on NPs for 'instrument' and 'comitative'; for example, *with* in English. In contrast, for languages with several applicative processes to a verb, there are in most cases different affixes for Instrumental and Comitative.

25.5.1   There are, as would be expected, some rather specialized language-particular peripheral markings found on applicative arguments. Jarawara has a minor postposition *tabijo* 'due to the absence of' (Dixon 2004: 256, 502–4). From intransitive clause 'He$_S$ be.angry [paddle *tabijo*]' can be derived transitive applicative construction 'He$_A$ paddle$_O$ APPLICATIVE-be.angry', both meaning 'He was angry over the absence of the paddle (someone had taken it)'.

Like a number of other Australian languages, Yidiñ (Dixon 1977a: 262–3, 350, 309) has an 'aversive' term in its case system, meaning 'for fear of'; for instance 'You'd better shift camp [high.waves]-AVERSIVE'. The verb 'fear, be frightened of' takes a peripheral NP in aversive case—'Woman$_S$ fears man-AVERSIVE'. An applicative can be formed on this, with the applicative argument, which had been marked by aversive case, now becoming AP-O— 'Woman$_A$ man$_O$ fears-APPLICATIVE'.

There are quite a number of other languages in which a possessor can function as applicative argument. They include Yimas (Foley 1991: 306–8), Motuna (Onishi 2000: 133–6), and Creek (Martin 2011: 188–92).

There are occasional examples of an applicative argument optionally retaining its peripheral marking within what appears to be an applicative construction. For example, in Ayutla Mixe we have the plain transitive 'I sew shirt [with needle]', and the canonical applicative 'I APPLICATIVE-sew shirt needle' where 'needle' has lost its preposition and is now a core argument. But we can also have applicative prefix to the verb and preposition with the instrumental NP: 'I-APPLICATIVE-sew shirt [with needle]'. As Romero-Méndez (2008: 574–5) states 'it is not entirely clear' what the syntactic status of 'needle' is in the last sentence.

25.5.2 Bresnan and Moshi (1990) use labels 'asymmetrical object' for when only the AP-O shows criterial O properties, and 'symmetrical object' for when the AP-O and the original O share these properties. In the late 1970s and 1980s, proponents of various formal theories were much exercised about how to deal with the status of objects in applicative constructions (based on transitive verbs) in Bantu languages. Bresnan and Moshi (1990: 157–71) survey the suggestions of Gary and Keenan, of Perlmutter and Postal, of Marantz, of Baker, of Kiparsky, and then of themselves.

As described in §3.2 and §13.1, some languages have extended intransitive and/or extended transitive verbs with a further core function, E. This can play a role in applicative derivations. Consider the Papuan language Motuna. The applicative object 'this boy' is marked with purposive suffix in the plain intransitive clause (11) and becomes AP-O in the applicative derivation (11-ap). An extended intransitive has S and E arguments. E can be applicative argument, and in an applicative derivation S becomes A and E becomes O. A plain transitive has core NPs in A and O function and may add an applicative argument in peripheral function. In the applicative derivation, the A argument stays as is, the peripheral argument becomes AP-O and the original O goes into E function. (See Onishi 2000: 131–7, which also describes further possibilities.)

25.6 Donohue (2001) presents a detailed and insightful textual study of the reasons for choosing to use an applicative construction in the Austronesian language Tukang Besi.

25.7 Bond (2009: 6) demonstrates two ways of forming an applicative such as 'They brought him an orange' in the Benue-Congo language Eleme. One involves the benefactive suffix -sɛ added to the verb 'buy'; the other is an asymmetrical serial verb construction with 'buy' as major verb and 'give' as minor verb.

25.8 There is some information in Austin (1997) on applicative and causative derivations in Australian languages, both those marked by a single affix and those with distinct affixes. However, the information this study contains was not up-to-date. To mention just three examples, a 1990 draft grammar of Arabana-Wangkangurru was quoted rather than the published version, Hercus (1994). A paper by Blake is referred to in its 1981 manuscript version, although it was published in 1982. And a paper by Austin, 'Word order in a free word order language; the case of Jiwarli', is cited as '1994. To appear in *Language*'; in fact it was published in a Festschrift in 2001. In addition, Austin fails to take account of causative and/or applicative derivations in prefixing languages. For example, there are discussions of applicative derivations in Rembarnga (McKay 1975: 149–52, 266–72), Ngalakan (Merlan 1983: 47–50, 95–6), Ngandi (Heath 1978: 81–3), and Mara (Heath 1981: 202).

Valenzuela (2010: 108) notes that in Shipibo-Konibo a number of 'same subject' markers have the same form as applicative suffixes. They may be an historical connection, but one presumes that these must be regarded as distinct but homonymous forms in analysis of the modern language.

25.9   The term 'applied form of a verb' was used in the first edition of Steere's Swahili grammar (1870: 155), and then Torrend (1891: 276) wrote of 'applicative verbs'. Note that the earliest instance given in the *OED* is Stapleton (1903) but this was simply continuing an established tradition. (I am most grateful to Thilo Schadeberg and Anne Storch for these references.)

The term 'applicative' appears to have been used in a seventeenth-century grammar of a Uto-Aztecan language (see Peterson 2007: 2). But this is simply coincidental. The term was surely (re-)invented ab initio by nineteenth-century Bantuists and it is from them that modern-day usage has developed.

In a book called *Incorporation* (1988), Baker reinterpreted a wide variety of diverse grammatical phenomena (including, for instance, passive) as types of incorporation. Within this line of vision, applicatives were described as involving 'preposition incorporation'. But what of a language in which the applicative argument was marked by a peripheral case in the non-applicative construction. Should this be called 'case incorporation'?

26

Comparative constructions

Comparison, in general terms, involves examining two or more items in order to note similarities and differences between them. Many languages include grammatical means for coding comparison; however, not all do so. §28.2.1 considers the rationale for this.

The prototypical comparative scheme in a grammar involves comparing two participants in terms of the degree of some gradable property relating to them, as in the English sentence *John is more handsome than Felix*. The property is typically expressed by an adjective, in a language with a large open class of adjectives; or else by a stative verb (with an adjective-like meaning).

The prototypical comparative scheme is characterized in §26.1. In §26.2 we see how it may be realized through various types of mono-clausal construction. The discussion is extended, in §26.3, to bi-clausal constructions, and to languages which do not have a dedicated comparative construction as such but instead employ what we can call a comparative strategy (and there is mention of languages which have available a combination of means). §§26.4–6 provide brief discussion of 'less' and 'the same as', of superlatives, and of inherently comparative lexemes.

In §26.7 we look at other schemes of comparison—that involving one participant and two properties (as in *This box is longer than it is wide*, in English), or a comparison of two sets of participant-plus-property (as in *This box is longer than that car is wide*). And there is discussion of 'correlative comparatives', as exemplified by *The more tasks you undertake, the less you'll achieve*. §26.8 explores the possible diachronic origins of markers of comparison and looks at how comparative construction types and their formal markers are particularly liable to be borrowed, and to diffuse. The summary in §26.9 is followed by 'What to investigate', in §26.10.

26.1 The prototypical comparative scheme

There are three basic elements in a prototypical comparative scheme: the two participants being compared, and the property in terms of which they are compared. Consider the English sentence:

(1) John   is more   handsome   than   Felix
      COMPAREE   INDEX PARAMETER MARK STANDARD

The participants are:

COMPAREE—that which is being compared, here *John*
STANDARD of comparison—what the Comparee is being compared
   against, here *Felix*

The property is:

PARAMETER of comparison—here *handsome*

A prototypical comparative scheme will generally (but not invariably) also include a fourth component:

INDEX of comparison—here *more* (with a different choice of English
   adjective, it could have been *-er*, for example, *clever-er*)

Within any clause, there must be marking of the function of each core and peripheral argument. It seems that the Comparee is almost always some kind of subject—copula subject (CS), as in (1), or verbless clause subject (VCS), or intransitive subject (S), or transitive subject (A)—or else the possessor within a subject NP, and is marked as such. The Standard has a wider range of functions. It may be an object (O)—and is then marked as such—or it may be a peripheral argument, as in (1). We then get the fifth element:

MARK of the grammatical function of the Standard—*than* in (1)

Note that in (1), the Parameter, *handsome*, is in copula complement (CC) function, and the clause necessarily includes a copula verb, *is* (the copula verb makes up the whole predicate of the copula clause).

Not every comparative construction is like that in English, and we now investigate the wider possibilities.

26.2 Mono-clausal comparative constructions

In the discussion of adjective classes (Chapter 12), we observed the two main ways in which an adjective may be used to state a property of something— by functioning as copula (or verbless clause) complement, or by functioning as head of an intransitive predicate. Since an adjective is the most common Parameter of comparison, it is natural that two of the major varieties of comparative construction should follow these profiles. What we call type A1 has the Parameter as head of a copula (or verbless clause) complement, and the Index as modifier to it. In type A2 the Parameter is head of an intransitive predicate, and the Index again a modifier to it.

For languages with a serial verb construction (SVC), this may be used for a type B comparative construction, with a verb such as 'surpass' or 'exceed' as minor member within an asymmetrical SVC. We also recognize three less common kinds of mono-clausal comparative construction: type C 'X exceeds Y in property', type D 'X's property exceeds Y's property', and type E 'X is property in opposition to Y'.

Table 26.1 summarizes these types of mono-clausal construction, which are discussed, in turn, in §§26.2.1–7. For each construction type, there is information on:

(a) The possibilities for the Parameter slot. This is typically an adjective but in some languages it may also be an adverb and/or a verb and/or a noun and/or a time word. And there are languages in which the Parameter may only be a noun or a verb (referring to a gradable property), not an adjective.
(b) Other meanings/functions which the Index may have in the language.
(c) Other meanings/functions which the Mark of the standard may have in the language.

26.2.1 Type A1

This involves a copula or verbless clause construction, with the Parameter as copula complement (CC) or as verbless clause complement (VCC). It is generally found in languages in which adjectives (the typical Parameter) cannot function as head of an intransitive predicate but instead may function, alone, as CC or VCC. It is the most common comparative construction in English, and is exemplified in (1).

In English, and in similar languages, a statement that something has a certain property involves an adjective in CC function, as in:

John$_{CS}$ is$_{COPULA:PREDICATE}$ handsome$_{CC}$

The prototypical comparative construction of type A1 adds *more*, the Index of comparison, as modifier to the adjective within the CC, and attaches a peripheral NP referring to the Standard of comparison, marked by *than*. That is:

(1′)   John$_{CS}$ is$_{COP.PRED}$ [more   handsome]$_{CC}$ [than   Felix]$_{PERI}$
          COMPAREE   INDEX   PARAMETER   MARK   STANDARD

Jacaltec, from the Mayan family, is like English save that there is no copula in attributive clauses. Comparative is expressed through a verbless clause construction (Craig 1977: 39):

TABLE 26.1. Mono-clausal grammatical constructions expressing the prototypical comparative scheme

type	COMPAREE participant	STANDARD of comparison participant	PARAMETER of comparison	INDEX of comparison	MARKER of standard
A1	CS/VCS	oblique NP	head of CC/VCC	modifier in CC/VCC	marker of oblique NP
A1-si	CS/VCS	< not stated >	head of CC/VCC	modifier in CC/VCC	—
A2	S	oblique NP	head of intransitive predicate	modifier in intransitive predicate	marker of oblique NP
A2-si	S	< not stated >	head of intransitive predicate	modifier in intransitive predicate	—
B	A	O	open-class verb in an asymmetrical serial verb construction	closed-class verb in an asymmetrical serial verb construction	marker of O
C	A	O	post-predicate constituent	main verb	marker of O
D	possessor in A NP	possessor in O NP	head of A NP (and O NP)	main verb	(marker of O)
E	A	O	head of predicate	derivational suffix to predicate head	marker of O

(2)   [Ka'   icham]$_{VCC}$ hin$_{VCS}$ [s-sataj   naj
       MORE old   I   him-THAN   CLASSIFIER:MAN

       Pel]$_{PERIPHERAL}$
       Peter
    I am older than Peter

Here the Index *ka'* 'more, very' modifies *icham* 'old' within the VCC. The Mark
of the standard is *-sataj*.

The Comparee and Standard are expressed by NPs (and/or bound pronouns) whose head is a noun or pronoun or demonstrative. The head can
be an appropriate abstract noun (as in English *Efficiency is more valuable than
probity in this profession*).

We can now discuss the possibilities for Parameter, Index, and Mark of
standard.

(a) Parameter of comparison. In many languages with a type A1 construction, the Parameter can only be an adjective; for example, Papantla Totonac
(Levy 2004), Finnish, Hungarian, and Turkish. In Brazilian Portuguese, the
Parameter may be an adjective or one of a limited set of nouns (each indicating
something which may be gradable); for instance, one may say *O Fernando é
mais amigo (meu) do que o João* 'Fernando is more of [a] friend (to me) than
João'; Italian is similar. In English a CC cannot be just a noun, and neither can
the Parameter in a comparative construction; one cannot say **Fred is more
friend than John*. (One can use an NP as the Parameter, as in *Fred is more a
friend than John*, although this is usually preferred with an *of*, giving *Fred is
more of a friend than John*.)

(b) Index of comparison. This is sometimes the only function of the form
involved. But in many languages the Index has additional roles in the grammar. For example, in Jacaltec *ka'* is glossed as 'very, more'. Some languages of
type A1 have zero (ø) in the Index slot.

(c) Mark of standard of comparison. This is sometimes the only function
of the form involved. In the majority of languages, the Mark has additional
functions in the grammar. In Jacaltec the preposition *sataj* is, literally, 'in front
of'. The Panoan language Shipibo-Konibo (Valenzuela 2003: 406) is similar in
that its Mark is postposition *-bebon* 'in front of'. In a fair number of languages
the Mark also functions as ablative or locative or genitive marker (this last in
Classical Greek, see §16.1).

A sample of the possibilities for Index and Mark is set out in Table 26.2.
'Special' indicates a form used only in this function. Three of the languages
from Table 26.2 are illustrated in (3–5). Note that in Dhaasanac, the Standard
('me') is in object form.

TABLE 26.2. Examples of Index and Mark in languages of type A1

	Index of comparison	Mark of standard
LANGUAGES WITH COPULA CONSTRUCTIONS		
Somali (Cushitic branch of Afroasiatic)	ø	ablative
Basque (isolate)	special	special
Kurdish (Iranian branch of Indo-European)	special	ablative
LANGUAGES WITH VERBLESS CLAUSES		
Dhaasanac (Cushitic)	ø	'upon'
Bengali (Indic branch of Indo-European)	special	genitive
Jacaltec (Mayan)	'very'	'in front of'

(3) Somali (Tosco 1999b; and see Saeed 1993, 191)

Nínka-nu   [nínká-as   wuu   ká]   wéyn yahay
man-THIS:SUBJ   man-THAT DEC:3m FROM big   be:PRES:3m
This man is taller than that man

(4) Dhaasanac (Tosco 2001: 293)

Máa=l=a   [ye   ɗu]   ɗér
man=THIS=DETERMINER   me   upon   tall
This man is taller than me

(5) Bengali (Onishi 1997)

Ram Tusar-er   [cee   bɔRɔ]
Ram Tusar-GENITIVE COMPARATIVE big
Ram is bigger than Tusar

Ndyuka, an English-based Creole from Surinam, has the unusual feature of Index and Mark being identical, each being shown by the form *moo* (presumably based on English *more*) which is included twice in the construction. Huttar and Huttar (1994: 286) state that *moo* 'has both verb-like and preposition-like characteristics'. An example is:

(6) [A   dagu ya] [moo bigi] [moo den   taa   wan]
      THE:SG dog HERE MORE big   THAN THE:PL other one
      This dog is bigger than the other ones

The Index will generally modify the Parameter within the CC or VCC. However, individual languages show variations. For example, in Kamaiurá

(Tupí-Guaraní branch of Tupí family; Seki 2000: 307), the Index *a'ia'ip* 'more, much' is added to the subject (Comparee) NP constituent if there is one—as in (7), where 2sg free pronoun *ene* is subject NP. Otherwise it is placed after the Parameter, as in (8), a sentence in which the subject is shown just by a bound pronoun attached to the verb.

(7) Ene=a'ia'ip   ne=jey'a   je=wi
     2sg=MORE   2sg=be.tall 1sg=ABLATIVE
     You are taller than me

(8) Ne=jey'a   a'ia'ip je=wi
     2sg=be.tall MORE   1sg=ABLATIVE
     You are taller than me

In some languages, the Standard (plus its Mark) may be omitted in an appropriate discourse context. This applies to Egyptian Colloquial Arabic (Gary and Gamal-Eldin 1982: 47). In English one comes across things like *a crunchier cereal* without any mention of the Standard of comparison. However, in these languages the Standard can be, and usually is, included. There is a subtype of A1 where the Standard is *never* explicitly stated in a comparative construction; this is discussed in the next subsection.

26.2.2 Type A1-si

This is like type A1 save that the Standard is implicit; that is, it is *never* stated within the comparative construction, but is understood from having been mentioned just before in the discourse.

Type A1-si is found in Dyirbal, from north-east Australia, where the Index of comparison is suffix *-bara* added to the Parameter, which is generally an adjective. In one legend the only fire is in the possession of the rainbow serpent, on a high mountain ledge. The scrub turkey tries to snatch it away, and then the pheasant, then the robin; in each instance, the snake sees the bird come and knocks it back. The eagle-hawk (leader of the birds) then asks the chicken-hawk to have a try, saying:

(9) ŋinda$_S$ waynyji;   warrman-bara
     2sg   go.up:IMPERATIVE   fast-COMPARATIVE
     You go up! (to try to snatch the fire away); (you) are faster (than any of
        the birds who have tried before)

The first two words of this utterance constitute an intransitive clause in imperative mood. They are followed by a verbless clause, *ŋinda warrman-bara*, from which the VCS NP, *ŋinda*, is omitted under coreferentiality with the S NP of the first clause. We thus have Comparee *ŋinda* 'you', Parameter *warrman* 'fast', and Index -*bara*. The Standard is not stated in this clause; it is understood to be the birds who have already tried to get the fire, as mentioned earlier in the text.

Other examples involve a comparison between two things. In one conversation, Jimmy Murray mentions that he has carried home some wild honey in a kerosene tin. George Watson asks why he hadn't used a traditional bark bag. Jimmy replies:

(10) Maya! jigal-bara   balan, bigay-bila
      no   good-COMPARATIVE THAT   handle-WITH
      No, that one (kerosene tin) is better, (it is) with a handle (that is, it has
         a handle)

The comparative construction comprises *jigal-bara balan*. *Balan* 'that', referring to the kerosene tin, is the Comparee, *jigal* 'good' is the Parameter, and -*bara* is the Index. The Standard is implicit in this clause; it is the bark bag, referred to in the previous utterance, by George Watson. (The full form of this example, plus further examples and discussion, are in Dixon 1972: 226–8, 252, 263–4.)

It is possible, in elicitation, to add an explicit Standard of comparison; for example, 'I'm big-*bara*, you are small', or 'He's big, I'm big-*bara*'. But in non-elicited data the Standard is never included in a comparative statement, being always understood as the topic of an immediately preceding clause in the discourse.

The Parameter in a Dyirbal comparative construction is typically an adjective, as in these examples. There is no example in the data collected of -*bara* added to a noun. It can, however, be suffixed to a time word (for example, *gilu* 'later today', *gilu-bara* 'even later today') or to a grammatical form referring to distance (for example, -*balbulu* 'long way downriver', -*balbulu-bara* 'further downriver').

26.2.3 Type A2

In languages where an adjective has grammatical properties similar to those of a verb, it functions not as copula complement (or as verbless clause complement) but rather as head of a predicate, going into the same slot—and showing the same morphological and syntactic possibilities—as an intransitive or transitive verb.

As illustrated in §12.3, Fijian (Oceanic branch of Austronesian; Dixon 1988: 89–90) is a language of this kind; a statement that something has a certain property is coded as in:

(11) [E   toto'a]INTRANSITIVE.PREDICATE   [o   Jone]S
      3sgS handsome   ARTICLE John
      John is handsome

Sentence (11) is an intransitive clause, exactly parallel to [*e la'o*]_{INTR.PRED} [*o Jone*]_S 'John is going', in which the intransitive verb *la'o* 'go' functions as predicate head. A variety of modifiers may precede and follow a predicate head, irrespective of whether it is a verb or an adjective (or an NP or a pronoun, which are further possibilities).

Languages with this profile show a comparative construction of type A2, which is parallel to type A1 save that the Parameter is head of an intransitive predicate, rather than being head of a complement argument within a copula construction. The Index is a modifier within the predicate. The Standard is expressed by a peripheral NP, with an appropriate Mark, as in type A1. For example, in Fijian:

	PARAMETER	INDEX		COMPAREE
(12)	[E	toto'a	ca'e]_{INTR.PRED} [o	Jone]_{SI}
	3sgS	handsome	MORE ART	John

	MARK		STANDARD
	[mai	vei	Felise]_{PERIPHERAL}
	FROM	ARTICLE	Felix

John is more handsome than Felix

Here the Index of comparison is a post-head modifier within the predicate, *ca'e*, which outside of a comparative construction has the meaning 'up'. The Mark of the standard is preposition *mai*, which outside of a comparative construction has the meaning 'from'. (A similar example is given at (6) in §12.3.)

We can now consider the possibilities for Parameter, Index, and Mark in a type A2 construction. There are similarities to—and also differences from—these components in type A1.

(a) Parameter of comparison. In languages with a type A1 comparative construction, adjectives typically have grammatical properties rather different from verbs but similar to nouns. It is not uncommon, in such languages, for the Parameter in a comparative construction to be either an adjective or a noun. In contrast, for languages with a type A2 system, adjectives have similar grammatical properties to verbs. In some of these languages, the Parameter can be either an adjective or a verb, as in Ẹdọ (Kwa family, Nigeria; Ọmọruyi 1986). However, in other languages where both verb and adjective can function as predicate head, only an adjective may be Parameter of comparison, with this being a criterial property for distinguishing between the word classes verb and adjective. This applies in Korean (Sohn 2004), Northeast Ambae (Oceanic branch of Austronesian; Hyslop 2004), and Toba-Batak (also Oceanic; Nababan 1981: 71–2).

(b) The Index of comparison in an A2 type construction is generally a special form, but can be zero. In a highly synthetic language, the Index may be shown through an affix to the Parameter, as in Central Alaskan Yupik (Eskimo; Miyaoka 2004: 3):

(13) angya-n$_S$ ange-nru-uq   angya-mni
      boat-2sg:ABS be.big-MORE-3sg:DEC boat-1sg:LOC
      Your (sg) boat is bigger than my boat

The Index is here -*nru*, suffixed to the Parameter *ange*- 'be big'. 3sg declarative suffix at the end of the predicate refers to the S argument, the Comparee 'your boat'. The Standard, 'my boat' bears locative case as its Mark.

(c) The Mark of the standard in an A2 type construction can, as in an A1 type construction, be either a special form, or a form that may be used in non-comparative constructions with a different meaning and/or function. Of a sample of thirty languages with comparative constructions of types A1 and A2, where the Mark was not a special form, slightly more than half of the Marks were an ablative form, 'from'. (Illustrations of the Mark being ablative, dative, locative, 'on' and 'upon', are in Heine and Kuteva 2002: 30–1, 103, 201 and 305–7.)

A sample of the possibilities for Index and Mark are set out in Table 26.3. Indonesian was illustrated by the example in §3.23. Comparative constructions in three further languages are illustrated in (14–16).

(14) Ainu (Tamura 2000: 97)

      En-akkari   eani e-siwente
      1sg:ACCUSATIVE-THAN   2sg   2sg:NOMINATIVE-slow
      You're slower than me

TABLE 26.3. Examples of Index and Mark in languages of type A2

	Index of comparison	Mark of standard
Ainu (isolate, Japan)	∅	special
North-east Ambae (Austronesian)	∅	ablative preposition
Indonesian (Austronesian)	special	ablative preposition
Egyptian Colloquial Arabic (Semitic branch of Afroasiatic)	comparative form of adjective	ablative prefix
Central Alaskan Yupik (Eskimo)	special	locative case
Deiga (Kadugli-Krongo; Sudan)	∅	dative case

(15)   Egyptian Colloquial Arabic (Gary and Gamal-Eldin 1982: 46)

Huwwa₅   ʔatwal   min-haₚₑᵣᵢₚₕₑᵣₐₗ
he   tall:COMPARATIVE   FROM-she
He's taller than her

(16)   Deiga (Reh 1994: 242)

àɓlɔ̀ŋɔ́   [gùɓáayá gìná]₅   [à-dɛ́]ₚₑᵣᵢₚₕₑᵣₐₗ
be.big   glass   THIS   DATIVE-THAT
This glass is bigger than that

We noted above that, in a type A1 construction, the Standard (plus its Mark) may be omitted in an appropriate discourse context. This can also apply for type A2 constructions, for instance that in West Greenlandic Eskimo (Fortescue 1984: 169).

Just as there is a variant of type A1 with the Standard not stated but implicit, so there is a similar subtype of type A2, described in the next subsection.

26.2.4 Type A2-si

In Jarawara (Arawá family, Brazil; Dixon 2004: 172–3), a verb referring to a property (the Parameter) can take the suffix -*nama* (the Index). The Standard is *never* stated in the comparative construction, but its identity is implicit from mention in a recent clause of the discourse. For example, one day speakers were explaining to me the relative distances of three Jarawara villages from the town of Lábrea:

(17)   (a)   [São.Francisco kaa   jama]₅   [jabo-ka-re]ᵢₙₜᵣₐₙₛᵢₜᵢᵥₑ.ₚᵣₑᵤᵢ꜀ₐₜₑ
              village.name   POSS thing(f)   be.far-DECLARATIVE-NEGATIVE:f
              São Francisco (lit. São Francisco's place) is not far

       (b)   [Agua.Branca kaa   jama]₅   [ja-jabo-ke]ᵢₙₜᵣ.ₚᵣₑᵤ
              village.name   POSS thing(f)   REDUPLICATED-be.far-DEC:f
              Agua Branca is a little far

       (c)   [Casa.Nova   kaa   jama]₅   [ja-jabo   nama-ke]ᵢₙₜᵣ.ₚᵣₑᵤ
              village.name   POSS thing(f)   REDUP-be.far   COMP-DEC:f
              Casa Nova is further

The negative suffix in (a) indicates that São Francisco is not far. Reduplication of the verb *jabo-* 'be far' in (b) states that Agua Branca is 'a little bit far'. In (c) the comparative suffix -*nama* is used to state that Casa Nova (Comparee) is further away from Lábrea than the other two villages (implicit Standard). (Note that the verb must be reduplicated with -*nama* and this suffix is added to an auxiliary constituent with the auxiliary verb itself being dropped.)

In (18) there are just two items being compared:

(18) (a) [Makina   one]ₒ   siba   o-na-habone   o-ke;
           machine(f) another:f look.for 1sgA-AUX-INTENT:f 1sg-DEC:f
           I'm going to look for another machine;

      (b) na-nafi   nama   na-aro
           REDUP-be.big/much COMPARATIVE AUX-DEPENDENT:f
           (one) which is bigger

Here the comparative construction is (b) where the S argument (the Compa-ree) is 'another machine', carried over from (a), the Parameter is 'be big/much' and the implicit Standard is the machine which the speaker presently owns.

As described in §12.4. Jarawara has a small class of about fourteen adjectives (including 'big', 'little', 'new', 'old', and 'prototypical, real'). These occur as copula complement and as modifier to a noun within an NP; they may not be used in a comparative construction. Other concepts which are expressed by adjectives in a language like English are coded as verbs in Jarawara. It is some of these which may function as Parameter in a copula construction, together with Index -*nama*.

It appears that only certain property verbs may be used with -*nama*. Those attested include the value term 'be good', dimension term 'be high/tall', phys-ical property terms such as 'be cold', 'be dry', 'be sharp' and 'be sweaty', and also 'be far' and 'be big/much'. However, -*nama* is not accepted with Human Propensity terms such as 'be angry' and 'be happy'.

26.2.5 Type B

A number of languages from many parts of the world (especially Africa, East and South-east Asia, and Oceania) have a Serial Verb Construction (SVC), whereby two or more verbs can function together as a single predicate— without any overt marker of coordination, subordination, or other syntactic linkage—being taken to refer to a single event. (See §3.4 and §24.2.2.) The most common type of SVC is asymmetrical, with a minor component chosen from a restricted set of verbs, and a major component which can be virtually any verb.

Many—but by no means all—languages with SVCs may express the proto-typical comparative scheme in this way. The Parameter of comparison is an adjective or an intransitive verb, which is the major member of the SVC, and the Index of comparison is a verb with meaning such as 'exceed', 'surpass', 'pass', or 'defeat', being the minor member. (There are many examples in Heine and Kuteva 2002: 123–6, 229–30.) Generally the whole SVC is transitive, with the Standard of comparison being in O and the Comparee being in A function, both marked accordingly. An example from Khmer (Austroasiatic family; Jacob 1968: 140) is:

(19) | COMPAREE | | PARAMETER | INDEX | STANDARD | |
|---|---|---|---|---|---|
| [Nì:əŋ | nìh]_A | [lʔɔ: | cìəŋ]_{PREDICATE} | [nì:əŋ | nùh]_O |
| girl | THIS | pretty | exceed | girl | THAT |

This girl is prettier than that one

Here the Comparee and Standard are marked as being in A and O functions, respectively, by their positions before and after the predicate. In Lango (Nilotic family; Noonan 1992: 229) the Comparee, as A argument, is marked by a pronominal prefix on both verbs in the SVC, and the Standard, as O, by a suffix to the final verb:

(20)   À-ryɛ́k   à-kɔ́'t-í
       1sgA-clever:HABITUAL   1sgA-surpass:HABITUAL-2sgO
       I'm cleverer than you

The Index in a type B language is always a member of a small set of verbs. In Ewe (Kwa family, Ghana; Ameka 2006: 136) it can be *wú* 'exceed, surpass', *tó* 'pass', or *gbɔ* 'come back', as in:

(21)   [É-tsi   gbɔ]   [nɔví-á   ŋú]
       3sg-grow   come.back   sibling-DEF   skin
       He has grown more than his sibling

See also the discussion of Kana in §26.4.

The possibilities for the Parameter in a type B construction vary from language to language. In Lao (Tai family; Enfield 2004: 324, 334, 2007a: 24, 256–7), for instance, it can only be an adjective, so that occurrence in a comparative SVC constitutes a criterion for distinguishing between adjectives (which Enfield considers to be a subclass of verbs) and (other) verbs. However, in Wolof (Atlantic family, Senegal and the Gambia; Mc Laughlin 2004: 258), both adjectives, such as *nay* 'miserly' in (22a), and verbs, such as *ligéey* 'work' in (22b), may be used in a comparative SVC with the Index verb *gëna* 'surpass'.

(22) (a) Ibu   moo   gëna   nay   Aamadu
          Ibou   3sg   surpass   miserly   Amadou
          Ibou is more miserly than Amadou

      (b) Maa   la   gëna   ligéey
          1sg   2plO   surpass   work
          I work more than you (plural) do

26.2.6 Types C and D

In types A1 and A2, the Index of comparison is a modifier to the Parameter (which is head either of a copula/verbless clause complement or of an intransitive predicate). In type B, the Index is a verb, of equal status within the predicate to the Parameter, which is also a verb. In type C, the Index is the main verb in a transitive clause, with Comparee and Standard being its A and O arguments (and marked accordingly). The Parameter is expressed by a post-predicate constituent.

A prime example of a type C comparative construction occurs in Hausa (Chadic branch of Afroasiatic family; Newman 2000: 93--6), for example:

(23) COMPAREE   INDEX   STANDARD   PARAMETER
    [Bàlaa   yaa]$_A$ fi   Muusaa$_O$ karfii$_{PERIPHERAL}$
    Bala   HE   exceed   Musa   strength
    Bala is stronger than Musa (lit. Bala exceeds Musa in strength)

The Parameter in a comparative construction in Hausa can be an abstract noun, a verbal noun, or a common noun having a generic meaning. Interestingly, although Hausa has a small class of a dozen or so adjectives, these cannot occur as such in the Parameter slot. There are, however, abstract nouns derived from adjectives. For example, the derived noun *sàabùntaa* 'newness' can be Parameter in a comparative construction, but not the adjective *saaboo* 'new'.

There are a number of verbs which may function as Index. Besides *fi* 'exceed', we can have *daràa* 'exceed slightly' (giving 'be a little more than'), *gazàa* 'fall short of' (giving 'be less than'), and *kai* 'reach', which is a mark of equality, as in:

(24) [tàwadàa   taa]$_A$ kai   àlloo$_O$ bakii$_{PERIPHERAL}$
    ink   IT   reach   blackboard   blackness
    Ink is as black as the blackboard (lit. Ink reaches the blackboard in
    blackness)

There appear also to be type C comparative constructions in Lahu (Tibeto-Burman; Matisoff 1973: 130–1) and in Nkore-Kiga (Bantu; Taylor 1985: 68–70), see (53a) in §26.5. In each language the Parameter is a nominalization.

English shows a comparative construction of type C, as in:

(25) Mary   exceeds   John   [in   intelligence]
    COMPAREE   INDEX   STANDARD   PARAMETER

In (25) *in* is indicator of the Parameter. Again, the Parameter must be in nominal form; in (25) it is a nominalization of adjective *intelligent*. An alternative way of saying (25) is by a type A1 comparative construction, *Mary is more intelligent than John.*

Type D also has the Index as transitive main verb. It differs from type C in that the Parameter is head of both A and O NPs, with Comparee and Standard as possessors within these NPs. It can be illustrated for English:

(26)   [The box's   width]$_A$ [exceeds]$_{TRANSITIVE.PREDICATE}$
          COMPAREE   PARAMETER   INDEX

       [the car's   (width)]$_O$
          STANDARD   PARAMETER

The head of the O NP is here likely to be omitted, under anaphora with the head of the A NP, giving *The box's width exceeds the car's.* Note that the Parameter must be in nominal form (here, *width*, a nominalization of adjective *wide*). An example from Goemai (like Hausa, a Chadic language from West Africa; Hellwig 2004) is:

(27)   PARAMETER   COMPAREE   INDEX   STANDARD
       [k'oom   muk]$_A$ ma   m-mak$_O$
        strength   3sg:POSS   surpass   NOMINALIZER-2sgm:POSS
       His strength surpasses yours

26.2.7 Type E

A rather different comparative construction is found in Ponapean (Austronesian family; Rehg 1981: 249–52) where the Parameter is head of the predicate with the Index being a suffix to it, and appearing to derive a transitive stem.

    First, note that Ponapean has prepositions *ni* 'to, at' and *nan* 'in, on' which govern a peripheral NP. However, 'from' is shown by suffix -*sang* to an intransitive verb of motion or to a transitive verb of 'removing' (such as 'pull out', 'untie'). For example:

(28)   I   papa-sang   wahr-o
       I   swim-FROM   canoe-THAT
       I swam away from that canoe

Ponapean is a language similar to Fijian (see §26.2.3) in which an adjective may, like a verb, function as head of the predicate. When -*sang* is suffixed to an adjective as predicate head, a comparative construction of type E is formed:

(29)   COMPAREE   PARAMETER-INDEX   STANDARD
       Pwihk-e   laud-sang   pwihk-o
       pig-THIS   big-IN.OPPOSITION.TO   pig-THAT
       This pig is bigger than that pig

Rehg's grammar does not specify what the function is of the NP which follows a verb with *-sang*. It is in the position of an O NP, after the predicate. If pronominal, it becomes a bound object pronoun attached to the verb, in the way that an O argument does (Rehg 1981: 229). It seems reasonable to assume that *-sang* increases the valency of the verb it is added to, so that the Comparee is A and the Standard is O.

Ponapean is the only example yet found of a language with type E comparative construction.

26.3 Further grammatical means

The prototypical comparative scheme may be realized through a bi-clausal construction, exemplified in §26.3.1. Languages which have no comparative construction per se are likely to have some way of making a comparison, by what we can call a 'comparative strategy', discussed in §26.3.2. There are quite a few languages which include more than one means for expressing comparison and these are the topic of §26.3.3.

26.3.1 Bi-clausal comparative constructions (type F)

In a number of languages, the prototypical comparative scheme is expressed in a bi-clausal construction, in contrast to types A–E, which are all mono-clausal. Three rather different bi-clausal construction types are illustrated here, from Pilagá (Guaykuruan family, Argentina), from Hua (Gorokan family; Papua New Guinea), and from Dhimal (Tibeto-Burman, Nepal). For ease of reference, bi-clausal comparative constructions will be referred to as Type F.

(a) In Pilagá (Vidal 2001: 350–2), the verb *-ena'am* 'be like' is the Index. Used alone it indicates 'the same as', and with a negator the meaning is 'less than'. The first clause of the construction states that the Parameter applies to the Standard, the second clause then stating that the Comparee is like or not like what is stated of the Standard in the first clause. Thus:

(30)   STANDARD   PARAMETER;   INDEX   COMPAREE
     Ernesto   logeda-ik;   ø-ena'am   Leo
     name   tall-MASC   setA.3-be.like name
     Leo is as tall as Ernesto (lit. Ernesto is tall; Leo is like (him))

(31)   Cacho   logeda-ik;   sa-ø-ena'am   Marcelo
     name   tall-MASC NEG-setA.3-be.like name
     Marcelo is not as tall as Cacho; that is Marcelo is less tall than Cacho,
        or Cacho is taller than Marcelo (lit. Cacho is tall; Marcelo is not
        like (him))

(b) Hua (Haiman 1980: 283) uses a medial verb construction, which recurs in Papuan languages. The first, medial, clause codes Standard, Index, and Comparee, while the final clause ascribes the Parameter to the Comparee.

(32) STANDARD-INDEX-COMPAREE   PARAMETER-COMPAREE
      D-kaso-na;   za'zaf-i-e
      1sgO-exceed-3sg   be.tall-3sg-INDICATIVE
      He is taller than me (lit. He exceeds me; he is tall)

(c) Dhimal (King 2009: 96) has a bi-clausal construction 'looking at (i.e. compared with) Standard, Comparee is Parameter' as in:

(33) STANDARD   COMPAREE PARAMETER
      Bhente   khan-teŋ,   Umpai   poto-ka   hi-hi
      Bhente   look-SEQ   Umpai   short-NOMZR   AUX-PAST
      Umpai is shorter than Bhente (lit. looking at Bhente, Umpai is short)

The verb *khan-* 'look' bears sequential suffix *-teŋ*, appropriate to a non-final verb. Suffix *-hi*, on the auxiliary verb *hi-*, indicates past tense with a non-stative verb but in (33) has present non-imperfective meaning.

A further example of a bi-clausal comparative construction, in Amele, is illustrated in (37–8).

26.3.2 Comparative strategies (type S)

Some languages do not have a comparative construction per se. But there is almost always some way of indicating a comparison; this can be called a 'comparative strategy'. The most straightforward way is simply to juxtapose clauses which impute opposite properties to two participants. Alamblak (Sepik Hill family; Papua New Guinea; Les Bruce personal communication) juxtaposes two copula clauses:

(34) Yiria-r   bro-e-r;   Pian-r   habien-e-r
      Yiria-3sg.M   big-COP-3sg.M   Pian-3sg.M   small-COP-3sg.M
      Yiria is bigger than Pian (lit. Yiria is big; Pian is small)

A similar construction in Kobon (Kalam-Kobon family; Papua New Guinea; Davies 1981: 92) involves the juxtaposing of two verbless clauses, 'that big; that small'.

Examples given for Hixkaryana (Carib family, Brazil; Derbyshire 1979: 67) involve the juxtaposition of two copula clauses, one with the Parameter and the other with the negation of the Parameter:

(35) Kawohra   naha Waraka; kaw naha Kaywerye
      tall:NEGATION he:is Waraka tall he:is Kaywerye
      Waraka is not as tall as Kaywerye (or Kaywerye is taller than Waraka)
          (lit. Waraka is not tall; Kaywerye is tall)

An additional strategy in Hixkaryana adds discourse particles 'more' and 'very much' to the Parameter in non-initial clauses. For example 'monkey is good, tapir is more good; peccary is very much good' (that is, 'peccary is better than tapir which is better than monkey').

Amele (Gum family, Papua New Guinea; Roberts 1987: 135) can use a juxtapositional strategy, similar to (34), 'this house is big; that house is small'. A variant on this (similar to the second strategy described for Hixkaryana) is to repeat the Parameter in two clauses, adding the postposition *ca* (glossed by Roberts as 'add') to its second occurrence:

(36) Jo   i   ben (qa) jo   eu   ben ca
      house THIS   big BUT   house   THAT   big ADD
      That house is bigger than this house (lit. this house is big but that
        house is bigger)

Note the optional inclusion of conjunction *qa* 'but' between the two clauses in (36).

26.3.3 Languages employing more than one grammatical means

In a fair number of languages there are several alternative ways for expressing the prototypical grammatical scheme. Just two languages will be mentioned here.

As described above, Amele has an antonym-type strategy, similar to that illustrated for Alamblak in (34), plus the strategy shown in (36). It also uses a bi-clausal comparative construction, as in (Roberts 1987: 134):

(37) Uqa cecela; ija wol-te-na
      3sg tall   1sg surpass-1sg-3sg:PRESENT
      He is taller than me (lit. he is tall; he surpasses me)

(38) Uqa cecela; ija qa   wol-du-gi-na
      3sg tall   1sg BUT surpass-3sg-1sg-PRESENT
      He is tall but I am taller than him (lit. he is tall; I surpass him)

Note that the conjunction *qa* 'but' must be included if the two clauses have different subjects, as in (38), but not if the subjects are the same, as in (37).

In some languages, only a restricted set of adjectives (or whatever) may function as Parameter in a mono-clausal comparative construction. An appositional strategy may be employed for comparison of other items.

Tamil (Dravidian family; Asher 1985: 88) has a type A1 comparative construction, using a copula clause (with zero Index), as in:

(39) [Eŋka viiṭṭe   viṭa] [avaru viiṭu] pericaa
      our   house:ACC THAN   his   house big
      irrukutu
      be:PRES:3sg.NEUTER
      His house is bigger than our house

The Index is ø in (39) and the Mark of the standard is *viṭa* (which is the verb 'leave') with this requiring accusative case on the preceding Standard. An alternative comparative construction involves a verbless clause, with the Index again ø, and with the Standard marked simply by dative case, as in:

(40) Itukku   atu   nallatu
      THIS:DATIVE THAT good:NOMINALIZER
      That is better than this

Grammars of Tamil do not specify any meaning difference between the two constructions.

As mentioned above, English has a range of comparative constructions (of types A1, C, and D) as indeed do a considerable number of languages.

26.4 'More', 'less', and 'the same as'

In some languages only one form, 'more', can function as Index in a comparative construction. For example, Tzoltzil (Mayan family; Robinson 1999) uses as Index the form *mas* 'more', borrowed from Spanish; but it has not borrowed Spanish *menos* 'less'. However, a number of languages do have a number of forms which can function as Index. It was mentioned in §26.2.6 that Hausa has 'exceed', 'exceed slightly', 'fall short of', and 'reach', roughly corresponding to 'more (than)', 'a bit more (than)', 'less (than)', and 'as . . . as' in English.

In Warao (isolate in Venezuela; Romero-Figueroa 1986: 103), a 'same as' comparison is achieved in exactly the same way as a 'more than' comparison, within a type A1 construction. For example:

(41) Basayanaru tobe   taera   kurarika ta
      ant.eater   jaguar strong MORE   IS
      The jaguar is stronger than the anteater

(42) Hua [ma daka]   irida monuka ta
      John my brother tall   SAME   IS
      My brother and John are the same height

In Kana (Cross River family, Nigeria; Ikoro 1996b), a type B comparative construction involving an SVC can have as Index either *èè* 'surpass', as in (43), or *dòòdòò* 'equal (to)', as in (44).

(43) Léka_A [ku̱i èè]_{PREDICATE} [yē dám]_O
      Leka   fat surpass   her husband
      Leka is fatter than her husband

(44) Léka_A [ku̱i dòòdòò]_{PREDICATE} [yē dám]_O
      Leka   fat equal   her husband
      Leka is as fat as her husband

Teribe (Chibchan family, Costa Rica and Panama; Quesada 2000: 139) has an A1 type comparative construction, with a verbless clause. It appears that the Index is ø, but that 'more than' and 'less than' are expressed by the choice of postposition as Mark of the standard—*kinmo* 'above', as in (45), or *dorko* 'under', as in (46).

(45) [Bor   u]   kégué bopoya kinmo
      1sg.POSS house old   2sg.POSS ABOVE
      My house is older than yours

(46) Kwe   kégué bop dorko
      DEMONSTRATIVE old   2sg UNDER
      That one is less old than you

And 'be the same as' is shown by the same construction type, this time with the Mark of the standard being the adverb *dik* 'like', as in (47):

(47) Maria, e   plú Juan dik
      Maria DEMONSTRATIVE good Juan LIKE
      Maria, she is as good as Juan

As described in §26.3.1, Pilagá uses Index *-ena'am* 'be like' and deals with 'less than' by adding a negator. It expresses 'X is less tall than Y' (or 'Y is taller than X') through 'Y is tall; X is not like him'.

There are languages like English which exhibit a matrix for Index and Marker. For example:

(48) | COMPAREE | INDEX | PARAMETER | INDEX | MARK | STANDARD |
|---|---|---|---|---|---|
| (a) [The spear] is | | long | -er | than | [the sword] |
| (b) [The spear] is less | | long | | than | [the sword] |
| (c) [The spear] is as | | long | | as | [the sword] |

Sentences (a) and (b) can be negated simply by inserting *not* after *is*. However, there are two negative versions of (c), with either *as* or *so* in the Index slot: *The spear is not as long as the sword*, or *The spear is not so long as the sword* (there appears to be no appreciable difference in meaning).

One could, alternatively, use *the same as*, saying *The spear's length is the same as the sword's (length)* or *The spear is the same as the sword in length*, parallel to *The spear's length exceeds the sword's (length)* or *The spear exceeds the sword in length.* (There appears to be no verb whose meaning is opposite to that of *exceed*, so that one can only say *The spear's length is less than the sword's (length)* or *The spear is less than the sword in length.*) Note that constructions of this kind in English all require a nominalization as Parameter (*length*, rather than *long*).

In most languages there is some difference between how one expresses 'more than' and 'the same as'. For example, in Papantla Totonac (Levy 2004: 157), only an adjective can be Parameter in a 'more than' comparative construction, as in (49), and only a nominal may be Parameter in a 'the same as' construction. In (50) the adjective 'small' must be nominalized before it can be used in the equality construction.

(49)   Xla   ma:s   lanka'   katu:ni   akit
       3sg   MORE   big   THAN   1sg
       He (or she) is bigger than me

(50)   Xla   ix-li:-akcu-ná?   la: min-qa'wasa
       3sg   3POSS-INST-small-NOMINALIZER   LIKE   2POSS-son
       He (or she) is as big as your son (lit. He/she, his/her size is like your
           son's)

The majority of languages, across the world, have a grammatical construction for 'the same as' which is quite different from that for 'more than'.

26.5 Comparative and superlative

In English, comparative and superlative forms of adjectives belong to the same morphological paradigm:

handsome	clever
more handsome	clever-er
most handsome	clever-est

However, comparative and superlative have quite different syntactic behaviours. A comparative adjective typically makes up the whole of a copula complement argument, and relates together two participants of similar status, as in *John is more handsome than Felix* (which can be rephrased as *Felix is less handsome than John*).

In contrast, a superlative adjective typically modifies a head noun within an NP which includes the definite article, *the*. It effectively identifies a unique individual, as in:

(51)   John is the most handsome boy (in the class/in Chicago/in the world)

The Mark plus Standard—shown in parentheses in (51)—is optional.

English distinguishes comparative and superlative by (a) the form of the Index; and (b) the inclusion of the definite article before a superlative and a noun after it, but generally neither of these with a comparative. Other European languages use the same Index for both comparative and superlative, with the presence or absence of the definite article being a major distinguishing feature. For example, in French:

(52) (a) Jean est plus   beau   que   Paul
          Jean is INDEX handsome THAN   Paul
          Jean is more handsome than Paul

      (b) Jean est le   plus   beau   (de tous les   garçons/
          Jean is THE INDEX handsome OF   all   THE   boys/
          du   monde)
          OF:THE world
          Jean is the most handsome (of all the boys/ in the world)

Note that, unlike in English, no head noun need be included after *le plus beau*.

Other Romance languages—such as Spanish, Portuguese, and Catalan— behave in the same way. In Basque (genetically unaffiliated but from the same linguistic area), the Index for comparative is suffix *-ago* and that for superlative is *-en*, with superlative requiring the definite article, *-a*.

A fairly small group of languages is like English in having distinct Indexes for comparative and superlative. They include Indonesian, with *lebih* 'more'— illustrated in §3.23—and *paling* (or *ter-*) 'most' (Sneddon 1996: 178–80), and Turkish with *daha* 'more' and *en* 'most'.

Many languages express the superlative by using a comparative construction with the Standard being specified as 'all'. Sentence (53a) shows a comparative and (53b) a superlative in Nkore-Kiga (Taylor 1985: 69), a language with a type C construction:

(53) (a) N-o-n-kira   oburaingwa
          PRESENT.CONTINUOUS-you-me-exceed   height
          You are taller than me (lit. you exceed me in height)

      (b) N-oo-kira   bo-ona   oburaingwa
          PRESENT.CONTINUOUS-you-exceed   them-all height
          You are the tallest (lit. you exceed them all in height)

Similar use of 'all' in a comparative, to convey a superlative meaning, is found in Kannada (Sridhar 1990: 126–8), Kashmiri (Wali and Koul 1997: 134–7), Tamil (Asher 1985: 90), Dumi (van Driem 1993: 78), and Russian. In Hausa, the comparative construction of type C (§2.3.6) is also used for superlative, with the Standard stated as 'everyone' or 'all of them' (Newman 2000: 94).

For languages with a comparative construction of type A1 or A2 but with the Standard of comparison not stated, translation into English may involve a comparative or superlative according to the discourse context. If just two items are involved, then only a comparative can be used—'that one is better (than the other one)' for (10) in Dyirbal, and '(a machine) which is bigger (than the one I have at present)' for (18b) in Jarawara. However, if more than two items are involved, then either a comparative or a superlative can be used in the translation. Sentence (9) in Dyirbal can mean either 'you are faster (than any of the birds who have tried before)' or 'you are the fastest (of the birds)'. And for (17c) in Jarawara either 'Casa Nova is further (than the other two villages)' or 'Casa Nova is the furthest (of the three villages)' is equally appropriate.

26.6 Inherently comparative lexemes

In some languages there are a few lexemes which, effectively, involve a fusion of Parameter and Index; that is, they are inherently comparative.

As described in §26.2.5, Wolof has a type B comparative construction, involving an SVC; for example, verb 'surpass' plus adjective 'miserly' in (22a). There are a few lexemes which are inherently comparative, such as *sut* 'taller / more competent than' (note adjective *njool* 'tall'), and *dàq* 'prettier / better at than' (note adjectives *rafet* 'pretty' and *baax* 'good').

These inherently comparative lexemes do not require the verb *gëna* 'surpass'—see (22a/b)—when used in a comparative construction. For example (Mc Laughlin 2004: 258):

(54) Aamadu   moo   sut   Ibu
      Amadou   3sg   tall:MORE   Ibou
      Amadou is taller than Ibou

In English, *prefer* is an inherently comparative verb. While verb *like* corresponds to adjective *good* (for example *I like jazz* relates to *(I think) jazz is good*), verb *prefer* corresponds to comparative adjective *better* (*I prefer jazz to rock* relates to *(I think) jazz is better than rock*).

There is grammatical support for this; compare:

COMPARATIVE ADJECTIVE	PLAIN VERB	INHERENTLY COMPARATIVE VERB
better	like	prefer
much better	*much like	much prefer
very much better	very much like	very much prefer

The verb *prefer* can be modified by *much*, like a comparative adjective, unlike the corresponding plain verb *like*.

26.7 Other schemes of comparison

The prototypical scheme of comparison involves two participants being examined in terms of a property, as in *John is more handsome than Felix*. Grammatical possibilities for what can be the Parameter vary. In Hausa, it can only be a noun, not an adjective, and in Jarawara only a verb, not an adjective (see §26.2.6 and §26.2.4). However, in most languages the Parameter may be an adjective. In some it can only be an adjective, in some either an adjective or a noun, and in others either an adjective or a verb. This was exemplified in (22a/b) from Wolof with the Parameter being either an adjective, such as 'miserly' or an intransitive verb, such as 'work'.

The Comparee and Standard may each be clauses with shared verb and object (which can be omitted) as in:

(55)   John speaks French better than Felix (speaks French)

The Comparee here is *John speaks French*, with the Standard being *Felix speaks French* and the Parameter *good*. An alternative is for Comparee and Standard to share subject and verb (which may be omitted), as in:

(56)   I speak Koasati better than (I speak) English

Here the Comparee is *I speak Koasati* and Standard is *I speak English*. Kimball (1991: 491) gives this as a comparative construction in the Muskogean language Koasati (note that, unlike (56), this is bi-clausal, and that 'SS' stands for 'same subject switch-reference marker', -*k*):

(57)   Kowassá:ti   na:łí:ka-li-k   ká:no-k   im-má:y   waciná
       Koasati   speak-1sg.SUBJ-SS   be.good-SS 3.DAT-be.more English
       I speak Koasati better than English

Adverbs are typically derived from adjectives, or an adjective may also be used in adverbial function. Naturally, an adverb can function as the Parameter for comparison, as in (58) from Japanese, where the Index is *ø* and the Mark of the standard is *yori* (Onishi 1995):

(58)   [Taroo wa]   [Hanako yori]   hayaku   hasiru
       Taroo TOPIC   Hanako THAN   fast:ADVERB   run
       Taroo runs faster than Hanako

All the examples given thus far have been variants on the prototypical scheme of comparison—of two participants in terms of one property. A rather different scheme is the comparison of:

two properties in relation to one participant

as in:

(59)   John is more loyal than intelligent

The compared properties in (59) are expressed by adjectives. They could alternatively be shown by verbs, as in (60) from Babungo (Bantu family, Cameroon; Schaub 1985: 114):

(60)   ŋwɔ́ gìgísə̄   shɔ́ɔ   fáŋ   ŋwé   fà'
       HE   talk:PROG surpass:PERFV HOW   HE   work:IMPERFV
       He is talking more than working

   Or, the Parameter of comparison can be a verb in a complement clause, as in the SVC in Tetun Dili (Austronesian family, East Timor; Hajek 2006: 250):

(61)   Sira   hatene   dansa   liu   duké   kanta
       3pl   know   dance   pass THAN   sing
       They know how to dance better than they know how to sing

Here verb 'sing' is the Standard, verb 'dance' the Comparee, 'they know how to' the Parameter and verb 'pass' the Index of comparison.
   Going one step further, rather than comparing two participants—as in the prototypical comparative construction—or two properties—as in (60–1)—in some languages one can compare whole clauses. In English one can say:

(62)   You write more quickly than I read

In fact, English allows rather complex comparatives, so long as these are plausible within the discourse context, and the two clauses are both semantically and grammatically compatible. If a conversation has dwelt on how fond Mary is of mangoes and also on the extent to which John can't stand bananas, someone could suggest:

(63)   Mary likes mangoes more than John dislikes bananas

In another conversation, there could have been mention of Mary's unhappiness with excessive noise and the fact that John gets upset when the people around him are insincere. This could lead into people saying:

(64)   Noise annoys Mary more than insincerity angers John

Each of (62), (63), and (64) involves two clauses of similar semantic profile (where the verbs are from the same semantic type, and the subjects have similar reference, such as both being human or both abstract nouns). Note that it is not acceptable to combine clauses with different semantic profiles.

That is, the following are unsuitable sentences: *John is more loyal than Mary likes mangoes* and *Mary likes mangoes more than insincerity angers John*. (For an account of comparative constructions in English, see Dixon 2005b.)

Like other construction types, comparatives typically allow ellipsis of a repeated element. This can lead to ambiguity. Consider the English sentences, given in full with possible omissions in parentheses:

(65) I_A love you$_O$ more than (I_A love) Ana$_O$

(66) I_A love you$_O$ more than Ana$_A$ (loves you$_O$)

When the parenthesized bits are omitted, these both reduce to *I love you more than Ana*, which is ambiguous (between *Ana* being *Ana$_A$* or being *Ana$_O$*).

English marks subject and object NPs by their position, before and after the verb respectively. But when the verb is omitted, as in the reduced versions of (65) and (66), this criterion is lost, giving rise to ambiguity. However, in a language with case marking to show syntactic function, such ambiguity is avoided. The equivalent of (65–6) in Rumanian is (Mallinson 1986: 172):

(67)   Te   lubesc   mai   mult   decât   pe   Ana
        2sg   love:1sg   MORE   MUCH   than   ACCUSATIVE   Ana
        I love you more than (I love) Ana$_O$

(68)   Te   lubesc   mai   mult   decât   Ana
        2sg   love:1sg   MORE   MUCH   than   Ana
        I love you more than Ana$_A$ (loves you)

The fact that Ana is the one who is loved in (67) but the one who does the loving in (68) is shown by the inclusion of accusative preposition *pe* in the first sentence and its absence from the second.

26.7.1 Correlative comparative

English has what is called a 'correlative comparative', in which two comparative clauses, which may both be introduced by *the*, are juxtaposed. For example:

(69)   The riper the cheese, the stronger its/the smell

(70)   The more violence there is, the smaller the chance of peace

Comrie and Smith (1977: 24) include correlative comparison in their 'Lingua Descriptive Series questionnaire', but in fact very few languages have a construction of this type which is similar to simple comparatives. Many of those that do belong to the Indo-European family and/or are spoken in Europe. (Note that Guajiro/Wayuunaiki, an Arawak language spoken in Venezuela and Colombia, does have a correlative comparative construction, but this may well be a calque from Spanish; see Alvarez 2005.)

There is generally a grammatical form which introduces such a construction. This is *com* 'as' in Catalan, *mitä* 'what:PARTITIVE' in Finnish, and *hærci* 'whatever' in Persian:

(71) Catalan (Hualde 1992: 212)

Com més   menja més   gras   es   torna
AS   MORE   eat:3sg MORE   fat:m:sg   3:REFLEXIVE turn:3sg
The more he eats the fatter he gets

(72) Finnish (Sulkala and Karjalainen 1992: 171)

Mitä   kuume-mpi,   sen   parempi
what:PARTITIVE hot-COMPARATIVE it:GEN good:COMPARATIVE
The hotter, the better

(73) Persian (Mahootian 1997: 110)

Hærci   bištær kar-mi-kon-e   kæm-tær
WHATEVER MORE   work-DURATIVE-do-3sg little-COMPARATIVE
      ænjam-me-d-e
      accomplish-DURATIVE-give-3sg
The more she works, the less she accomplishes

Correlative comparatives are also found in Sino-Tibetan languages, for example in the Jieyang dialect of Chaozhou (Sinitic; Xu 2004):

(74) mueʔ$^{5-2}$kiã$^{35-21}$ zu$^{53-35}$ ku^{213} zu$^{53-35}$ bo$^{55-11}$
      thing   EVEN.MORE expensive EVEN.MORE NOT.HAVE
          naŋ$^{55-11}$ poi$^{53-35}$
          people   buy
The more expensive things are, the fewer people will buy them

Similar constructions are reported for the Tibeto-Burman language Lisu (Yu 2004).

26.8 How they may come about

We can now enquire concerning the origin of grammatical elements within a comparative construction, in §26.8.1, and how these constructions may have spread between languages which are in contact, in §26.8.2.

26.8.1 Directions of origin

The non-lexical components of a comparative construction are often related to other elements in the grammar. It was mentioned earlier that the Mark of the standard in an A1 or A2 type comparative construction can be identical with ablative, locative (including 'on' and 'upon'), dative, genitive, or something like 'in front of' or 'above', while the Index of comparison may also be used for 'up' or 'very'. And that the Index of comparison in a type B language can be a verb which, used alone, means 'exceed' or 'surpass' or 'pass'. It is generally assumed (for example, by Heine and Kuteva 2002) that such forms began with a non-comparative meaning, and were then extended to be also used as Index or Mark of standard in a comparative construction. However, it is not impossible that in some cases the extension was in the opposite direction.

Heine and Kuteva (2002: 177) illustrate the development of the interrogative word *wie* 'how' in German, as in (75), to become a Mark of the standard of comparison in Colloquial German (in place of the Standard German *als* 'than'), illustrated in (76).

(75) Wie groß ist er?
      how big   IS   HE
      How big is he?

(76) Er   ist größ-er   wie   [sein Sohn]
      HE   IS   big-MORE   THAN   HIS   son
      He is taller (lit. bigger) than his son

Many languages have grammatical marking for 'degree' on adjectives and/or nouns. For example, in Slave (Athapaskan family; Rice 1989: 238–40):

(77) dih   'chicken' AUGMENTATIVE dih-cho   'rooster'
      łekǫ 'sweet'   DIMINUTIVE   łekǫ-a   'a little sweet'

It is possible that an augmentative or diminutive affix could develop into an Index of comparison. Or that an affix or modifier with a meaning such as 'very', 'really, truly', 'a bit (like English -*ish*)', or 'another' could do likewise. No examples of such a path of development are currently known (aside from *sataj* in (2) from Jacaltec, glossed as 'more' or 'very') but further work may reveal some.

Discussing Indo-European languages, Kuryłowicz 1964: 227) states 'the forms of the comparative go back to two different sources: a pronominal (-*tero*) and a nominal (-*ios*)…A form like **su̯ād(-î)-ios-* had originally an absolute meaning "(very) sweet" and acquired its relative value as "comparative" owing to its being used with the ablative, e.g. **su̯ād(-ī)-ios medhu̯os* "sweet in comparison with mead" (> "sweeter than mead"). On the other hand, -*tero*- implied an opposition between the existence of the given quality ("sweetness") in one object and its absence in the other, thus **su̯ādu-tero*- "the sweet one" as against "the non-sweet one". In the historical languages the two suffixes -*(-ī)ios* and -*tero* became semantically equivalent'.

26.8.2 Diffusion and spread

Some construction types appear to be more likely than others to be borrowed between languages; it appears that comparative construction types are particularly open to this. Thus they may diffuse across all or most of the languages in a linguistic area. For example, Haig (2001: 205–6) undertook a study of four languages in east Anatolia—Turkish (Turkic family), Laz (Kartvelian family), and Kurmanji Kurdish and Zazaki (both from the Iranian branch of Indo-European). He found that a 'feature common to all four languages is the Turkish type of comparative construction'.

The Fijian comparative construction, illustrated in (12) of §26.2.3, is probably a calque from the comparative construction in English, although using Fijian forms (and based on an A2 type of construction since in Fijian an adjective may function as predicate head but not as copula complement). Semelai, an Aslian language spoken in Malaysia, has borrowed a periphrastic comparative construction from the lingua franca of its region, Malay (Kruspe 2004b: 300).

In Dobu, an Austronesian language spoken in Papua New Guinea (Lithgow 1989: 342–4), a comparative construction has been calqued on English, but using native forms. The grammatical element 'enega 'from this, so, then' has been adopted as Mark of the standard (and the index is ø). Thus:

(78) tauna   sinabwa-na   'enega   'abo'agu
      HE   big-3sg   THAN   ME
      He is bigger than me

Lithgow reports what appears to be a similar calque in the related language Bunama, where forms 'abwa and 'oinega 'then, so' are used as Mark of the standard.

It is noteworthy that many languages which have been in contact with Spanish have borrowed its Index of comparison *mas* 'more'—but not, as a rule, *menos* 'less'—together with its comparative construction; see (49) from Papantla Totonac. Other languages with this include Tagalog (in the Philippines), and Tzotzil, Pipil, and San Lucas Quiaviní Zapotec from Meso-America (see Rubino 1998, Robinson 1999, Campbell 1987, and Galant 2004). In (61) from Tetun Dili, spoken in East Timor, we find *duké* 'than', a borrowing from Portuguese *do que* 'than'.

26.9 Summary

For social reasons—see §28.2.1—some communities include a comparative construction in their grammar. The prototypical scheme involves comparing two entities in terms of the degree of some gradable property, which is typically stated through an adjective—'Mathematics (COMPAREE) is more (INDEX) difficult (PARAMETER) than (MARK) knitting (STANDARD)'.

It is thus natural that mono-clausal comparative constructions should reflect the grammatical orientation of adjectives. In a language where an adjective functions as copula (or verbless clause) complement, the Index of comparison (something like English -er or more) will modify the head of this complement NP. Where an adjective functions as head of an intransitive predicate, the Index modifies this predicate head.

There are many variations in individual languages. The Parameter for comparison may be just an adjective, or either adjective or verb, or either adjective or noun, or just verb, or just noun. Comparison may be shown through an asymmetrical serial verb construction, and then the Parameter must be a verb or an adjective that can function as a predicate head. Less frequent varieties of comparative constructions work in terms of nominalizations ('He exceeds me in strength').

There may be a bi-clausal comparative construction ('He exceeds me, he is tall'), or just a comparative strategy involving apposition of complementary descriptions ('Jack is fat, Jill is thin'). A language may have more than one means of expressing comparison; these might have overlapping scope, or they may apply to different sets of Parameters.

Grammatical means for comparison always include 'more than', sometimes also 'less than'. A statement of equivalence 'the same as' may be achieved in a similar way, but most often involves a quite different grammatical technique. A minority of languages have a superlative, sometimes shown in a similar fashion to comparative.

Less frequently, a comparative construction may also be used to compare two properties in terms of one participant—'Uncle Sam is more arrogant than honest'—or may compare two propositions—'Jack cuts the lawn more eagerly than Jill pulls up the weeds'.

It is often possible to trace the origin of the Index of comparison, and/or the Mark of the standard (suggesting the relatively recent evolution of a comparative construction). Typical sources include prepositions, adverbs, intensifiers, and verbs. Finally, forms making up a comparative construction are frequently borrowed, or a construction type may be calqued.

26.10 What to investigate

I   Can a dedicated comparative construction be recognized for your language of study? If so, is it one of the following types:

- A1, Parameter as copula (or verbless clause) complement—§§26.2.1–2
- A2, Parameter as head of intransitive predicate—§§26.2.3–4

- B, Parameter as major member in a serial verb construction, Index as minor member—§26.2.5
- C, Parameter (in nominal form) as post-predicate constituent—§26.2.6
- D, Parameter (again in nominal form) as head of A and O NPs (possessed by Comparee and Standard respectively)—§26.2.6
- E, Parameter as head of predicate, Index as derivational suffix to it—§26.2.7
- F, Bi-clausal construction, as illustrated in §26.3.1

II   For each comparative construction, please specify:

- Which type of lexeme may function as Parameter of comparison. The list may include some or all of: adjectives, nouns, verbs, adverbs, time words. The Parameter may be restricted to just certain types of adjectives (for example, just those referring to value and dimension), nouns (for example, just abstract nouns), verbs (for example, just statives), adverbs (for example, just manner adverbs), etc. It may be restricted to just those forms referring to something considered to be gradable in this language/culture.
- What form(s) may function as the Index of comparison? Are there Indexes for both 'more' and 'less'? And also for 'the same as' (see §26.4)?
    Do these Index forms also occur in other areas of the grammar with different meanings/functions?
- Where the Standard of comparison is shown by a peripheral component, what is the Mark of the standard (corresponding to *than* in English)? Does it occur in other areas of the grammar with different meanings/functions?
- If the Comparee is shown in subject function (S, A, CS, or VCS), does it have all the properties of a subject in other construction types?
- If the Standard is shown in object (O) function, does it have all the properties of an object in other construction types?

III   Does the language have a comparative strategy (e.g. 'X is big, Y is small/not big', see §26.3.2)? If so, please describe it carefully.

IV   If there are several means for expressing comparison, please investigate which values of Parameter each relates to, and factors conditioning its use.

V   Does the language have a superlative construction, as an extension from a comparative construction (see §26.5). If so, describe this, and discuss whether any of the grammatical elements in it have other meanings/functions in other parts of the grammar.

VI   Are there any inherently comparative lexemes (see §26.6)? Which word class(es) do they belong to? What criteria can be invoked to show that they are inherently comparative?

VII   Does the language have any other means for expressing comparison, beyond those outlined in this chapter? Please describe them carefully and show their role within the grammar.

Are there any special types of construction which relate to comparatives? (To mention just one possibility, correlative comparatives, briefly mentioned in §26.7.1.)

VIII   Can you say anything about the diachronic origin of comparative constructions (and of the grammatical elements in them)?

IX   Do you know whether your language has borrowed a comparative construction type and/or forms for Index of comparison, Mark of standard, etc., from a neighbour? Or whether a neighbour has borrowed from this language? Is having a certain type of comparative construction a diagnostic feature for a linguistic area to which the language belongs?

Finally   If there is any analytic problem associated with deciding whether something is or is not a comparative construction, please clearly state the problem, and the pro's and con's of alternative solutions to it.

Sources and notes

This chapter is a revision and expansion of Dixon (2008). I have consulted many previous works on this topic, including Ultan (1972). Heine (1997: 109–30) has been particularly useful. Stassen (1985, 2005) includes a great many examples, but they are not always quoted correctly.

26.1   The contrasting possibilities and roles of comparative suffix -er and syntactic modifier *more* in English are discussed in §4.8; see Table 4.2. Mondorf (2009) provides an insightful account of the different uses of -er and *more* in British and American Englishes.

26.5   If an English superlative involves an article it must be the definite variety. If a comparative occurs in an NP with an article it will normally be indefinite, as in *John is a more handsome boy than Felix*. However, it is possible to have a comparative with a definite article, as in *John is the more handsome of the two*. And a superlative can be used without the definite article or a following head noun, as in *John is (the) handsomest (man) (of all)*. (One can also say *He is a most unusual person*, but *most* is then being used in a different sense, as a degree modifier.)

26.7.1   There are also, in English, idioms based on the correlative comparative construction, including *The longer* (or any other comparative) *the better*. The idiomatic status of this can be seen from the unacceptability of a sentence like *The longer/shorter/hotter/colder the worse*.

27

Questions

As mentioned under (b) in §3.2, there is a correspondence between types of speech act and grammatical means of expressing them:

SPEECH ACT	GRAMMATICAL CATEGORY
statement	declarative (or indicative)
command	imperative
question	interrogative

There are a few examples of non-canonical correspondences between the two columns. For instance, *Could you please close the window?* (said with a friendly intonation) shows interrogative form but has the pragmatic function of a polite command. And *Will you be quiet!*, said in a harsh and annoyed tone, also has interrogative form but is very much a command (which is why I have written it with an exclamation mark rather than a question mark). If I ask something and you reply *Who knows?*, spreading your hands in a gesture of despair, this has interrogative form but the pragmatic status of a statement (meaning 'Nobody knows'). If it does not expect an answer, it is not a true question.

Grammatical values 'declarative', 'imperative', and 'interrogative' are said to constitute the system of 'mood'. 'Declarative' is the default member of the mood system and is typically left unmarked. 'Imperative' is generally shown by verbal affix(es). There are many varieties of interrogative expression, which we shall survey.

Regarded in one way, questions could be said to relate to a special set of construction types. But viewed from another direction, they can be analysed as involving a grammatical **overlay** on declarative clause types. The latter approach will be followed here.

27.1 Confirmation or information—polar and content questions

A person poses a question because they want to know something. This can happen in one of two ways. The person can have an idea of what may or may not pertain, and seeks **confirmation** (or disavowal) of it, as in *Did John resign?* Or they may focus on a particular argument, enquiring whether (as has been rumoured) John was the person involved. The argument *John* may then be stressed (underline is used to indicate that an item is stressed), saying *Did John resign?* Or this could be phrased *Was it John who resigned?*

Alternatively, a person may have limited knowledge of some activity or state, and seek **information** to complete the picture. They may want to know the identity of an argument; for example, *Someone resigned, who was it?* or else just *Who resigned?* Or they may require to know the nature of the predicate, as in *John did something, what was it?* or, more succinctly, *What did John do?*

A question seeking confirmation is sometimes called a 'yes/no question', but this is not appropriate as a general label since, as discussed in §21.8, some languages lack words 'yes' and 'no'. **Polar question** is the preferred label. However, it should not be taken to imply that there are only two possible answers to a question seeking confirmation, these being polar opposites. In fact, there is a range of perfectly legitimate and commonly occurring answers, including 'not really', 'so they say', 'I believe so', and 'it's not clear'.

A question seeking information is generally called a **content question**. Some languages employ an **interrogative word** (alternatively called a 'content question word') to fill an argument slot or the predicate slot—in English: *who, what, where,* and so on. Other languages have, instead, what we can call **indefinite/interrogative words**. They specify that the referent of a particular argument slot is, in the present state of knowledge, unknown, and may simultaneously enquire as to its identity. Like many other Australian languages, Dyirbal has an array of indefinite/interrogative words, including *waña* 'someone, who'. The content question *Waña baniñu?* can be rendered as 'Someone came, who was it?'. This states that the speaker knows someone came but is not sure who, and simultaneously enquires as to their identity.

Before moving on to a cross-linguistic examination of varieties of questions, it will be useful to provide further illustration from English. We can take as basis the statement (which embodies declarative mood):

A [The farmer's wife]$_A$ timidly fed [the two black goats]$_O$ [in the shed]
      1a   1b   2   3   4a 4b   4c   5
  yesterday [because they were hungry]
    6   7

Lexemes are numbered; for those within a clausal constituent, a, b, ... are added. Each lexeme in 1–6 (and the subordinate clause in 7) can be questioned. Note that *the* and *in* are grammatical formatives, and cannot be questioned.

Looking first at polar questions, we can have a **general polar question**, with an interrogative overlay upon the whole of sentence A. This involves moving the first word of the auxiliary to the beginning of the clause. From *The farmer's wife had fed the two black goats*, we get *Had the farmer's wife fed the two black goats?* If there is no auxiliary, as in A, then *do* is inserted, and this carries tense:

A-p   Did the farmer's wife timidly feed the two black goats ...?

A further possibility is that a polar question may **focus** on a specific lexical constituent. To focus on constituent 1, *the farmer's wife*, just this phrase may be stressed:

A-p-1   Did <u>the farmer's wife</u> timidly feed the two black goats ...?

An alternative, not relying on stress, is to say:

A-p-1'   Was it the farmer's wife who fed the two black goats ...?

Here, a question is formed on the copula construction *It was the farmer's wife who fed the two black goats ...*, with sentence A coded as relative clause to the copula clause complement, *the farmer's wife*.

Similarly, to focus on constituent 4, *the two black goats*, the alternatives are:

A-p-4   Did the farmer's wife timidly feed <u>the two black goats</u> ...?
A-p-4'   Was it the two black goats that the farmer's wife timidly fed ...?

Constituents 5, 6, 7, and 2 may also be focussed on through being stressed within A-p, or through a topicalization construction similar to A-p-1' and A-p-4':

A-p-5'   Was it in the shed where/that the farmer's wife timidly fed the two black goats ...?
A-p-6'   Was it yesterday when/that the farmer's wife timidly fed the two black goats ...?
A-p-7'   Was it because they were hungry that the farmer's wife timidly fed the two black goats ...?
A-p-2'   Was it in a timid manner that the farmer's wife fed the two black goats ...?

One could say *Was it timidly ...*, but *Was it in a timid manner ...* is more felicitous.

Either lexeme of constituent 1, *the farmer's wife*, may be placed in focus by being stressed within A-p, or may be topicalized:

A-p-1a' Was it the farmer whose wife timidly fed the two black goats...?

A-p-1b' Was it the wife of the farmer who timidly fed the two black goats...?

Modifiers *two* and *black* within constituent 4 can also be placed in focus by being stressed within A-p, or through topicalization:

A-p-4b' Were they black, the two goats that the farmer's wife timidly fed...?

A-p-4a' Were there two of them (OR: Were they two in number), the black goats that the farmer's wife timidly fed...?

To focus on *goat*, other than by stressing it within A-p, requires a more circuitous (and unwieldy) statement. Something along the lines of:

A-p-4c' Were they goats, the two black animals that the farmer's wife timidly fed...?

Constituent 3, the verb *feed*, may of course be stressed within A-p. The topicalization alternative would be something like:

A-p-3' Was feed them what the farmer's wife did to the two black goats...?

Hungry can be focussed on, by stressing just this word (rather than the whole clause *because they were hungry*) in A-p. However, topicalization of *hungry* from within the subordinate clause to the front of the main clause is scarcely possible.

Other languages have different techniques for creating a polar question. In Dyirbal, it can just involve rising intonation at the end of a sentence. Or the clitic *=ma* can be added to the first word (not the first constituent) of a clause, as in:

(1) ŋinda$_S$=ma   yalay   garrja$_S$ bungi-n?
     2sg=QUESTION HERE.LOCATIVE alright   lie.down-NON.FUTURE
     Are <u>you</u> alright lying down here?

Dyirbal has free ordering of words within a sentence, as exemplified in (1) where the two words making up the NP in S function, pronoun *ŋinda* 'you' and adjective *garrja* 'alright', are separated by locational marker *yalay* 'here'.

   It is this freedom of ordering which allows Dyirbal a simple method for forming focus polar questions—the word in focus is simply placed first in the sentence, and polar question clitic *=ma* attached to it. One story tells of how a transgressor against tribal mores was to be executed with a blow from an axe (and then eaten). The perpetrator enquired of his helpers whether the axe had been placed ready at hand:

(2) barri=ma   bala?
     axe=QUESTION   THERE:ABSOLUTIVE:NEUTER
     Is the <u>axe</u> there?

As described in §1.9 and §12.5.2, a noun in Dyirbal is generally accompanied by a marker showing its noun class. *Barri* 'axe' is neuter and takes noun marker *bala*. Now a noun marker generally precedes the noun. In (2) *barri* comes first so that it can be sentence-initial and take clitic =*ma*, showing that this word is the focus of the polar question.

The transitive verb *manja-l* may describe a bird (A) calling out and by doing so drawing attention to something (O) which is moving through the forest. In one story, a traditional hero is attempting to travel around unnoticed. When a bird calls out, the hero asks:

(3) ŋayguna$_O$=ma   manja-manja-n?
     1sg:ACCUSATIVE=QUESTION   REDUP-draw.attention.to-NON.FUT
     Is attention being drawn to <u>me</u>? (i.e. Am I the one that attention is
        being drawn to?)

The speaker is putting himself in focus for the polar question, and achieves this by placing pronoun *ŋayguna* 'me' first in the sentence, and attaching polar question clitic =*ma* to it.

English has a goodly array of **interrogative words** for content questions. Except in 'echo' questions, an interrogative word must be moved into sentence-initial position. Dealing one by one with the phrases and lexemes from sentence A:

  A-c-1   Who timidly fed the two black goats ...?
  A-c-2   How did the farmer's wife feed the two black goats ...?
  A-c-4   What did the farmer's wife timidly feed ...?
  A-c-5   Where did the farmer's wife timidly fed the two black goats ...?
  A-c-6   When did the farmer's wife timidly feed the two black goats ...?
  A-c-7   Why did the farmer's wife timidly feed the two black goats ...?
  A-c-1a Whose wife timidly fed the two black goats ...?
  A-c-4a How many black goats did the farmer's wife timidly feed ...?
  A-c-4b Which two goats did the farmer's wife timidly feed ...?

Note that *do* (or the first word of the auxiliary, if there is one), plus tense, must be placed immediately after the interrogative word when it is fronted (no fronting is needed when the interrogative word is in subject function, as in A-c-1 and A-c-1a).

Each of these interrogative words relates to a different word class (or subclass). *Who* (together with its possessive form *whose*) is an interrogative pronoun, *what* is an interrogative noun, *which* an interrogative adjective, *how many* is an interrogative member of the subclass of lexical numbers, *where* is a locative expression, *when* a temporal expression, and *how* and *why* are interrogative words relating to different subclasses of adverbs. In addition to the basic word class association, there is an overlay. All of these words share certain properties—being used with a rising final intonation tune, being fronted—which shows that they also belong to the class of interrogative words, which is overlaid across the basic set of word classes (a sort-of pan-basic-word-classes word class).

There is in English no straightforward way of constructing a content question on the head of an NP, leaving aside its modifiers. For 4c, *goats*, one would have to resort to something like: *What sort of animals did the farmer's wife timidly feed two black ones of…?* (but this presupposes that we know she did feed some kind of animal). 1b, *wife*, is even more difficult. One cannot say *what of the farmer. And what relative of the farmer* bears the presupposition that it was a relative (rather then, say, a servant) who did the feeding. It would be interesting to know if other languages fare better in this respect.

Finally, how about an interrogative word relating to constituent 3, the verb? Many languages are like English in lacking an interrogative word which relates to the class of verbs. Instead, one uses *do what* in a transitive clause (dummy verb *do* plus interrogative noun *what* in O function to it) and *do what to* in a ditransitive clause (with the underlying O argument being here marked by preposition *to*):

A-c-3   What did the farmer's wife timidly do to the two black goats…?

However, there is a fair scattering of languages which do include one or more interrogative verbs. Dyirbal has intransitive *wiyama-y* and transitive *wiyama-l* (they belong to different conjugation classes). Used as the sole verb in a predicate, these mean 'do what (to)' as in the transitive clause:

(4)   wiyama-n   ŋinda$_A$ [giyi   yabuju]$_O$?
      DO.WHAT-NON.FUTURE   2sg   THIS.MASCULINE   younger.brother
      What did you do to this younger brother (of yours)?

Used in a serial verb construction with verb X, *wiyama-y/-l* means 'do X how'. A transitive example here is:

(5)   baŋga-n   bayi$_O$ wiyama-n?
      paint-NON.FUTURE   THERE:ABS:MASC   DO.HOW-NON.FUTURE
      How was he painted?

Further discussion of interrogative verbs is under (V) in §27.6.4.

It will be helpful first to outline the ways of asking questions in two sample languages, in §27.2. There is then, in §27.3, discussion of languages which have an interrogative term within an inflectional mood system. §27.4 surveys languages which do (and those which do not) mark polar and content questions in similar ways. We then look in some detail at polar questions and content questions, in §§27.5–6. Interrelation with other grammatical categories is the topic of §27.7. Throughout the chapter we stress the pragmatic aspects of asking questions; this is further discussed in §27.8. There is a summary in §25.9 and suggestions concerning 'what to investigate' in §25.10.

27.2 Two sample languages

Before investigating the parameters which underlie cross-linguistic variation in the structure of questions, it will be useful to summarize the techniques employed in two well-described languages.

(a) **Huallaga Quechua** (Weber 1989: 325–33, 39–40). This language is like many others in employing quite different marking for polar and content questions.

Polar questions are shown by suffix -*chu*. For a general polar question, -*chu* is added to the verb. For a focus polar question, it is added to the constituent in focus, as in:

(6) Hwan-ta-chu   rika-sha?
     John-ACCUSATIVE-POLAR.Q see-PRESENT.PERFECT:3.A:3.O
     Did he see John? (i.e. Was it John—and not someone else—that
        he saw?)

Note that the focussed constituent may occur sentence-initially, as in (6), but does not have to; it can be retained at its normal position in ordering.

Another option is to add topic suffix -*qa* to the constituent in focus and place -*chu* on the verb:

(7) Hwan-ta-qa   rika-sha-chu?
     John-ACCUSATIVE-TOPIC see-PRESENT.PERFECT:3.A:3.O-POLAR.Q
     Did he see John?

A polar question can also be formed by adding tag *aw* 'yes' to a declarative sentence:

(8) Pillku-ta   aywa-yka-nki,   aw?
     Pillku-DIRECT   go-IMPERFECTIVE-2sg.S   YES
     You are going to Pillku, right?

An 'alternative question' has -*chu* on each of the contrasted constituents, linked by *o* 'or' (a loan from Spanish):

(9) qam-chu   o   noqa-chu   aywa-shun?
     2sg-POLAR.Q   OR   1sg-POLAR.Q   go-FUTURE:1inc.S
     Should you or I go?

Turning now to **content questions**, these require both an interrogative word and a suffixal question marker. The interrogative words are:

(10) ima   'what'   pi   'who'
      imay   'when'   may   'where'
      imanir   'why (motive)'   mayqan   'which'
      ayka   'how much/many'

The similarities of form between some of these words are fascinating. We find *ima* as the whole word for 'what' and as the first part of 'when' and 'why (motive)'; *may* is 'where' and also the last part of 'when'; 'which' appears to have -*qan* added to *may* 'where'. Yet none of the forms can be analysed morphologically. That is, there are no other instances of -*y*, -*nir*, *i*-, or -*qan*.

In most—but not all—other languages, a similar situation prevails. That is, there are striking similarities between the forms of interrogative words yet these cannot be analysed into meaningful morphemic elements. (This may have been possible at some time in the past, but diachronic changes have fused forms and obscured history.)

An interrogative word generally occurs sentence-initially and it must take one of two suffixes:

- -*taq* is used when the speaker assumes that the addressee knows the answer to the question
- -*raq* implies no such assumption

Consider:

(11) imay   o:ra-na-taq?
      WHEN   time-NOW-CONTENT.Q
      What time is it?

One might address this to a person who is wearing a watch. However, -*raq* would be substituted for -*taq* if the question were addressed to someone without a watch who could only guess at the time (perhaps, from the position of the sun).

'What for' is expressed with *ima-paq*, which has purposive suffix *-paq* added to *ima* 'what'. And there are two interrogative verbs, formed by compounding *ima* 'what' with *na-* 'do' and *ni-* 'say', giving *ima-na-* 'do what' and *ima-ni-* 'say what'. These do not move to the beginning of the sentence, but—like the words in (10)—they must be suffixed with *-taq* or *-raq*.

In a fair number of languages one form can have both interrogative and indefinite sense (for example, 'what' and 'something'). In others, indefinites are derived from interrogatives—see §27.6.1. In Huallaga Quechua, the forms in (10) can bear suffix *-pis* (in place of interrogative *-taq* or *-raq*) and then have a general indefinite meaning. For example:

(12)   pi-ta-pis   willa-y!
       WHO-ACCUSATIVE-INDEFINITE   tell-IMPERATIVE:2sg
       Tell anyone/whoever!

Weber offers impressions regarding the intonation on questions. Polar questions, but not content questions, generally have rising pitch towards the end of the sentence. With an 'alternative question' there is generally a rise at the end of the first alternative, the second having a decline in pitch and intensity. For a tag question, the sentence itself generally does not have rising intonation, but the tag *aw* 'yes' bears rapidly rising pitch.

(b) **Koasati** (Muskogean; Louisiana; Kimball 1991: 301–2, 423–8, 431, 230–2). This language differs from Huallaga Quechua in that polar and content questions share the same marking. This is a morphological process (which we can call the 'interrogative process') applying to the main verb of the clause. It involves

- infixing a glottal stop between penultimate and final syllables
- according high pitch (shown by ´) to each of these syllables.

When this process is applied to a declarative sentence, it creates a **polar question**. Thus, from

(13)   is-hica-to (2sgA-see-PAST), 'You saw it'

is formed

(14)   is-hi:cá-ʔ-tó?, 'Did you see it?'

(Note that in this instance of the process, the second vowel of the verb becomes lengthened.)

As in many other languages, there is an association between interrogative and specific indefinite words:

(15) ná:si   'what'   ná:si   'something'
      naksó   'who'   naksó, á:ti   'someone'
      naksofá   'which'   —
      naksofón, naksó:n   'where'   naksofá   'somewhere'
                                            naksofón, naksó:n   'to somewhere'
      naksofó:kon   'when'   —

It can be seen that 'what' and 'something', 'who' and 'someone', 'where' and
'to somewhere' have identical forms. They take on an interrogative meaning—
and form a **content question**—in a sentence whose the verb has undergone the
interrogative process, as in (16), and otherwise have an indefinite sense, as in
(17). *Naksofá* 'which' and *naksofá* 'somewhere' are distinguished in a similar
way. (There appears to be no indefinite sense associated with *naksofó:kon*
'when'.)

(16) ná:s-ok$_S$ na:hó-ʔ-sá   ó:la-fa?
      WHAT-SUBJECT.FOCUS   exist:PAST<Q.INFIX>   town-IN
      What is there in town?

(17) ná:s-on$_O$
      SOMETHING-OBJECT.FOCUS   see-SUBJUNCTIVE
      When it sees something (it catches and eats it)

Forms in the lower five rows of (15) all begin with *nakso*, which is the word
for 'what' (leaving aside its high tone). However—similar to the situation in
Huallaga Quechua—they cannot be segmented since the final portions do not
occur elsewhere.

Koasati also has a number of questions marked by tags, each of which
appears to have undergone the interrogative process. These include the plain
tag question marker *-óʔlí*, tag *óʔló* for when a statement is hesitantly questioned by the speaker (as in 'You're eating, aren't you?'), the rather rare desider-
ative tag marker *-Vʔwí* ('Do you want to eat it?'), and the rhetorical question
tag *-háʔwá*, used when the speaker is wondering out loud and does not expect
a reply ('Where indeed has he gone off to?').

There are also interrogative words which are verbs, including *námpó* 'be
how many' (related to *námpon* 'to be so many'), and *(nak)sáʔmí* 'be how'.

27.3 Interrogative mood inflection

Languages with a synthetic profile typically include an inflectional system of
case on nouns, and an inflectional system on verbs which may combine information about tense, aspect, modality, etc. In contrast, an inflectional system

marking mood—with declarative, interrogative, and imperative values—is rather rare.

Eskimo languages provide a clear illustration of an inflectional system of mood. In West Greenlandic (Sadock 1984; Fortescue 1984: 4–24, 23–4, 287–91) we get:

(18)   STATEMENT   neri-vutit

                              eat-DECLARATIVE:2sg

                              You ate

(19)   POLAR QUESTION   neri-vit?

                              eat-INTERROGATIVE:2sg

                              Did you eat?

(20)   CONTENT QUESTION   su-mik   neri-vit?

                              WHAT-INST   eat-INTERROGATIVE:2sg

                              What did you eat?

(21)   COMMAND   neri-git!

                              eat-IMPERATIVE:2sg

                              (You) eat!

It will be seen that each sentence includes a suffix which combines information about mood and person/number of S, or of A and O. There are in fact seven terms in this inflectional system—the three independent moods just illustrated, plus subordinate clause markers conditional ('if'), causal ('because'), and contemporative ('while'), and a participial ending.

In fact, the interrogative suffix differs from declarative only when the S or A argument is 2nd person or when S, or both A and O, are 3rd person. Note that interrogative mood endings are required in both polar and content questions (which involve an interrogative word such as *su-* 'what' or *ki-* 'who').

In a statement, the last three vowel moras 'are respectively high, non-high, and high in pitch'. In a polar question 'this pattern is shifted one mora to the left, so that it is the penultimate mora that bears high pitch, while the last mora is low'. Content questions are like polar questions in that both take interrogative mood inflection, but differ in that content questions typically have the same intonation pattern as statements.

Mangghuer (Mongolic, north-west China; Slater 2003: 115–17, 195–8, 86–7) has an inflectional system on verbs which combines information on mood with aspect/tense (perfective, imperfective, future) and what Slater calls 'subjective' or 'objective' orientation. As mentioned in §14.5.1, the 'subjective' choice is used when the A, S, or CS argument is 1st person and in control in a statement and when it is 2nd person and in control in a polar question.

In all other circumstances, 'objective' is used. (Note that this is similar to 'conjunct'/'disjunct' marking, described in §15.1.10.) Inflectional endings on the verb *ri-* 'come' are:

(22)

		PERFECTIVE	IMPERFECTIVE	FUTURE
STATEMENT OR CONTENT QUESTION	Subjective	ri-ba	ri-la bi	ri-ni
	Objective	ri-jiang	ri-lang	ri-kunang
POLAR QUESTION	Subjective	ri-bu	ri-la biu	ri-nu
	Objective	ri-jinu	ri-leinu	ri-kuninu
'WHY' QUESTION		ri-ji		
COMMAND	Person of subject	2nd: ø; 1st: -a; 3rd: -ge		

The statement in (23) is in perfective aspect. Since the S argument is 1st person and this is in declarative mood, the 'subjective' option must be selected. But when (23) is made into a polar question, in (24), the combination of 1st person S and polar interrogative mood requires the 'objective' suffix to be employed:

(23) biₛ ri-ba
      1sg come:SUBJECTIVE:PERFECTIVE:DECLARATIVE
      I came

(24) biₛ ri-jinu?
      1sg come:OBJECTIVE:PERFECTIVE:POLAR.INTERROGATIVE
      Did I come?

In a content question, the interrogative word—*kan* 'who', *yang* 'what', or *ang* 'where', etc.—appears in the normal syntactic position of the constituent being questioned. And, interestingly, a content question takes inflectional forms not from the polar question rows, but from the same rows as a statement.

Tonkawa (isolate, Texas; Hoijer 1933: 83–94) also treats polar and content questions differently. A mood suffix comes between verb root and the bound pronominal suffix coding core constituents. Thus, in present tense we get *yagb-o:-ga* (hit-DECLARATIVE-2sg.A:3.O) 'You hit him/her'. For imperative, declarative mood suffix *-o:-* is replaced by *-u-*. For polar interrogative, declarative *-o:-* is replaced by *-ʔ-*; thus *yagba-ʔ-ga* (hit-POLAR.INTERROGATIVE-

2sg.A:3.O) 'Did you hit him/her?'. And for a content interrogative, the mood slot is simply left empty.

In Tariana (Arawak; Brazil; Aikhenvald 2003: 311–20, 502–6), there is a rich inflectional system combining the three moods with modalities such as frustrative and apprehensive. Interrogative mood is fused with systems specifying tense (present, past, remote past) and evidentiality (visual, non-visual, inferred). Reminiscent of Tonkawa, an interrogative/tense/evidentiality suffix must be included on the polar question but may be omitted from a content question (if clear from the context). There is optional rising intonation on the last word of a polar question, or on the interrogative word of a content question.

Jarawara, from southern Amazonia (Dixon 2004: 233–4, 402–16), has—as outlined in §19.1—an extensive system of mood suffixes. It includes declarative, four imperatives (positive and negative of immediate and distant), and three interrogatives (each in both feminine and masculine form, agreeing with the gender of the pivot argument; see §23.1). Quoting feminine forms, a general polar interrogative bears suffix -*ini* on the verb, a future polar interrogative uses -*ibana*, and a content interrogative has -*ri*. Compare, with transitive verb -*kaba*- 'eat' (as mentioned in §5.7, all pronouns take feminine agreement):

(25) aba$_O$ ti-kab-ini?
      fish   2sg-eat-POLAR.INTERROGATIVE:FEM
      Did you eat fish?

(26) aba$_O$ ti-kab-ibana?
      fish   2sg-eat-FUTURE:POLAR.INTERROGATIVE:FEM
      Will you eat fish?

(27) himata$_O$ ti-kaba-ri?
      WHAT   2sg-eat-CONTENT.INTERROGATIVE:FEM
      What did you eat?

Further instances of content interrogative suffix -*ri* are in (91) and (94) in §27.6.4. Note that the content interrogative mood suffix is very occasionally omitted.

In a declarative sentence (and in a content question) the final syllable of the main clause is said on rising intonation. A polar question has rising intonation on the penultimate syllable, followed by a fall.

It will be seen that, if there is an inflection for interrogative mood, this is likely to be obligatory for polar questions. Indeed, it may be the only way of marking a polar question. The inflection may be not quite obligatory in the case of content questions, which are in any case shown to be such by the inclusion of an interrogative word.

27.4 Similar marking for polar and content questions

As stated in §27.1, a person asks a question because they want to know something. Polar questions and content questions are two ways of seeking to satisfy this want. In some languages, the two kinds of questions are marked in similar fashion which recognizes them as facets of the overarching category 'question'. In other languages, there is no formal feature common to polar and content questions, the only link between them being pragmatic.

Many grammars state that polar questions have a distinctive intonation (most often, final rising) but say nothing about the intonation of content questions. Others do also deal with the intonation of content questions. There is an exemplary account for Tamambo (Austronesian, Vanuatu; Jauncey 2011: 44): 'With both polar and information-seeking [i.e. content] questions, the pitch rises sharply to a peak on the ante-penultimate syllable, and then falls sharply on the penultimate (usually stressed) syllable.'

Another language in which both types of questions have the same intonation profile is Hixkaryana (Carib, Brazil; Derbyshire 1985: 56–9).

Further examples of similar marking include:

(a) In Sanuma (Yanomami, Brazil and Venezuela; Borgman 1990: 66), there is no significant difference between the intonation pattern of questions and of statements. But 'the distinctive feature common to all questions is the lack of glottal stop at the end of the sentence. The non-interrogative sentences almost always have a sentence-final glottal stop, and when they do not, the context clearly would prohibit the interpretation of the utterance as a question.'

(b) For Takelma (Oregon; Sapir 1922: 277; Culy 1999), interrogative enclitic =ti is used in both polar and content questions. If there is a constituent in focus in a polar question, then =ti is appended to it; in a general polar question it is added to the verb. And in a content question =ti is added to the interrogative word, which appears generally to be in sentence-initial position. The interrogative words also have specific indefinite meaning, with =ti serving to distinguish between the two senses; see §27.6.1.

(c) In Eastern Pomo (Pomoan family, California; McLendon 1996: 528) the clitic =la (relating to realis) or =ti(ši) (relating to irrealis) follows the focussed first constituent of a polar question, and the fronted interrogative word in a content question. For a general polar question (with no constituent in focus), *la* is in sentence-initial position.

(d) As described in §27.2, both varieties of question in Koasati have the 'interrogative process' of glottal stop insertion applying to the verb.

(e) We saw in §27.3 that West Greenlandic uses interrogative mood for both types of question.

(f) In Tariana (§27.3) both kinds of question may take interrogative mood and also rising intonation.

Languages which appear to have no similarity of marking for polar and content questions include three we have just discussed—Huallaga Quechua, Tonkawa, and Jarawara. As a further example, Wolfart (1996: 394–6) shows how, in the Algonquian language Cree, polar and content questions 'differ dramatically' in their properties. For instance, the verb in polar questions is most commonly in the independent form while that in content questions is normally in what is called the 'conjunct' form.

27.5 Polar questions

A true question—as opposed to a rhetorical question, or a command in inter-rogative form—expects an answer. An appropriate response may be vocal, or it may consist simply of a culturally-appropriate gesture. This could be a nod or a shake of the head, or the spreading of arms and palms to imply ignorance.

A question can itself can be without words. In 'The Silence', a short story by Luigi Pirandello, the principal of an Academy calls Cesarino Brei from class with sad news concerning his mother:

'Dear Brei,' he said to him, unexpectedly putting a hand on the boy's shoulder, 'You know that your Mother ...'

'Is she worse?' interrupted Cesarino immediately, raising his eyes to look at him, almost in terror; his school cap dropped from his hand.

'Yes, my boy, it would appear so. You must go home at once.'

Cesarino remained looking at him, in his suppliant eyes a question his lips dared not utter.

'I'm not very sure,' said the principal, understanding the unuttered question.

The question that the boy was not able to say, but was understood by the principal, was whether his mother was already dead. (In fact she was.)

Types of marking for polar questions are surveyed in §27.5.1. There is then discussion of polar questions with focus, types of polar questions (for instance, according to the kind of answer they expect), and alternative questions, in §§27.5.2–4.

27.5.1 Marking

Languages vary greatly in how they mark a polar question. It may be by intonation or pitch, by a distinctive constituent order, by a tag, by a polar question particle, by some special morphological or phonological feature, by mood, or—very often—by a combination of several of these measures. Each of them has been exemplified in the discussion above. It will now be useful to list and discuss them.

(a) **Mood**—where there is an inflectional system of mood, including terms for declarative, interrogative and imperative. This was exemplified in §27.3 for West Greenlandic, Mangghuer, Tonkawa, Tariana, and Jarawara.

(b) **Special phonological or morphological feature.** In §27.4, we noted that in Sanuma non-interrogative sentences generally have a sentence-final glottal stop, but this is omitted from an interrogative. Almost contrariwise, Koasati (§27.2) has a glottal stop infixed into the verb just for interrogatives.

Maale (Omotic, Ethiopia; Amha 2001: 155–7, 147–51) is of particular interest for the way it marks polar questions. First note that a statement is shown by a declarative suffix to the verb: positive -*ne* or negative -*se*. In a statement, perfective aspect is shown by verbal suffix -*é* and imperfective by -*á* (for present) or -*andá* (for future). For example:

(28) ʔ-atsi$_s$ mukk-é-ne
      person-MASC.NOM   come-PERFECTIVE-POSITIVE.DECLARATIVE
      The man came

For a polar question in perfective aspect, the regular aspect suffix -*é* is replaced by -*íya* (and declarative suffix is omitted). Thus:

(29) ʔ-atsi$_s$ mukk-íya?
      person-MASC.NOM   come-PERFECTIVE:POLAR.INTERROGATIVE
      Did the man come?

In contrast, a polar question in imperfective aspect is marked by rising intonation. It retains the normal imperfective suffix. (It does, of course omit the declarative suffix.) Thus:

(30) ʔ-atsi$_s$ mukk-á?   [with rising intonation]
      person-MASC.NOM   come-PRESENT.IMPERFECTIVE
      Is the man coming?

(c) **Polar question particle.** In Slave (Athapaskan; Rice 1989: 1123–38), a general polar question bears a special particle in initial position. The form of the particle varies with dialect. It is *hį* in the Mountain dialect:

(31) hį   golǫ   fehk'é?
      GENERAL.POLAR.QUESTION.PARTICLE   moose   3A:shot
      Did he shoot a moose?

In Japanese, particle *ka* (used for both polar and content questions) is placed
at the end of the sentence (Shibatani 1990: 257–8):

(32) Taroo wa   kita   ka?
      Taroo TOPIC   came   QUESTION.PARTICLE
      Did Taroo come?

When the initial question particle is used in Slave, there is no expectation
as to whether the answer will be positive or negative. Another variety of polar
question involves just rising intonation at the end of the sentence; this expects
a positive answer. In Japanese, sentence-final particle *ka* carries a sharp rise in
intonation. The *ka* may be omitted in informal conversation, and there is then
rising intonation at the end of the sentence.

   In Kana (Benue-Congo, Nigeria; Ikoro 1996a: 319–22) 'there are no pitch
variations or specific interrogative intonation contours'. Polar questions are
marked by *gê*, which is attached to the end of the verb:

(33) wĕé$_A$ yāē-gê   [ló   kpá   ā-mā]$_O$?
      he:PAST buy-POLAR.Q   SPECIFIER.SG book   LOC-ADVERB
      Did he buy this book?

   These are representative examples. A question particle—which can be a
separate word, or a clitic—typically appears after the verb, or at the beginning
or end of the sentence, or after the first constituent or the first word (as in
Dyirbal, illustrated by (1–3) in §27.1).

   (d) **Tag.**   This is added after a statement, which has normal declarative
intonation, and makes it into a question. The tag forms a separate intonation
unit, with its own language-specific tune.

   In most languages, a tag has fixed form. It can be a regular item from the
language, such as *aw* 'yes' in Huallaga Quechua, illustrated in (8) of §27.2.
Indonesian uses *bukan* 'no, not' as a question tag 'either when the speaker,
uncertain as to the truth of the statement, seeks confirmation or, when knowing the statement to be correct, seeks agreement from the addressee.' For
example (Sneddon 1996: 312):

(34) Dia sudah   makan, bukan?
      2sg   already eat   no
      He/she has already eaten, hasn't he/she?

Note that *bukan* can be used after a positive or a negative clause, as in 'You don't have a travel document, *bukan* (do you)'.

In Spanish, '*¿no?* at the end of a statement implies that the asker already knows the answer.' Thus (Butt and Benjamin 2004: 342):

(35) Usted habla inglés, ¿no?
      you   speak English no
      You speak English, don't you?

Tag *illey-aa* in Tamil is made up of clause negator *ille* plus *=aa* which is the polar question enclitic (added to a focused constituent or to the verb in a general polar question). The tag can be added to a positive or a negative clause, and expects the supposition of that clause to be confirmed. Thus (Asher 1985: 5):

(36) Raaman vant-aaru,   illeyaa?
      Raman   come-PAST:3SG.HONORIFIC   TAG
      Raman came, didn't he? [Expects answer: Raman came]

(37) Raaman varale,   illeyaa?
      Raman   come:NEGATIVE   TAG
      Raman didn't come, did he? [Expects answer: Raman didn't come]

As mentioned in §27.2, Koasati has a number of tags, including one for when a statement is hesitantly questioned, one for 'do you want', and one for a question not expecting a response (a kind of rhetorical question).

English has as complicated an array of tags as any language. A tag will normally repeat the subject—as a pronoun—preceded by a copula, or the first word of the auxiliary, or *do* if there is no auxiliary. The prototypical tag will have opposite polarity to the main clause, and expects confirmation of the supposition of the main clause. For example:

TAG QUESTION	EXPECTED ANSWER
(38) John has been sleeping, hasn't he?	Yes, he has been sleeping
(39) Xavier isn't a Republican, is he?	No, Xavier isn't a Republican

An alternative is to have a positive tag with a positive main clause. This adds an attitudinal element, which can be surprise, as in (40), or sarcasm, as in (41).

(40)   Your husband won the prize, did he?

(41)   You expect me to believe that, do you?

(e) **Distinctive constituent order.**   This is quite sparsely attested. There are several instances from languages in Europe, including English—illustrated in §27.1—French, and Finnish (Sulkala and Karjalainen 1992: 8–9).

In Mupun (Chadic branch of Afroasiatic, Nigeria; Frajzyngier 1993: 365–6) a declarative copula construction has the same ordering as in English: copula subject – copula verb – copula complement. To make it into a question, one simply moves the copula verb into initial position, and adds a polar question suffix (see §27.5.3), here -*o*, to the last word of the sentence. Compare:

(42) ha$_{CS}$ a   wat$_{CC}$
      2:MASCULINE   COPULA   thief
      You are a thief

(43) a ha$_{CS}$ wat-o$_{CC}$?
      Are you a thief?

(f) **Intonation or pitch.**   In some languages questions do not differ from statements in intonation—we have mentioned Sanuma (where questions are shown by the lack of a final glottal stop) and Kana (which employs a particle, attached to the verb).

Many languages do have some variety of rising intonation for questions, combining this with another mechanism. Those described above include English, which also has distinctive constituent order; Quechua, which also uses interrogative suffix -*chu*; West Greenlandic, Tariana, and Jarawara, which also have interrogative mood; and Japanese, which also has a sentence-final particle.

And there are languages for which intonation is the main (often the only) marking of a polar question. For example, Rumanian (Mallinson 1986: 4–5), Swahili (Ashton 1947: 151, 23a), the Australian language Yidiñ (Dixon 1977a: 382), Carib languages such as Hixkaryana, and Fijian.

For some languages, a polar question is shown just by a rise in pitch. But this can vary in placement and degree. When engaged on fieldwork in Fiji in 1985, the village chief came into my reed hut early each morning, sat down cross-legged, and chattered away. What he said was fairly inconsequential and I would be half-listening. Then he stopped, and I looked up. The chief's face clearly showed that he was waiting for a response. I quickly replayed in my short-term memory the last thing he had said. It was indeed a question, with rising intonation on the penultimate syllable, followed by a fall. This was slightly different from question intonation in English, so that I had not picked it up. But then I did attune and on future mornings replied without delay.

Intonational marking for polar questions does vary a considerable amount. The constant is that there is *always a rise*, somewhere towards the end of the sentence. Some examples are:

- Swahili (Ashton 1947: 23a): 'stressed mid (or slightly rising) penultimate syllable, followed by a long stressed final syllable, which generally has high falling tone'.

- Hixkaryana (Derbyshire 1985: 56–7): 'rising pitch through the sentence, reaching high on the penultimate syllable, which is stressed, and then falling sharply on the final syllable'.
- West Greenlandic (see §27.3) 'the penultimate mora bears high pitch, while the last mora is low'.
- Tamambo (repeating from §27.4) 'the pitch rises sharply to a peak on the ante-penultimate syllable, and then falls sharply on the penultimate (usually stressed) syllable'.
- Jarawara (§27.3) is unusual in that in a statement, and in a content question, the final syllable of the main clause is said on a rising intonation. A polar question has rising intonation on the penultimate syllable, followed by a fall (Dixon 2004: 410, 530).

In a similar fashion to some spoken languages indicating polar questions entirely by intonation, there are a number of sign languages which show polar questions solely by non-manual means. 'The marking typically involves a combination of several of the following features:

- eyebrows raised
- eyes wide open
- eye contact with the addressee
- head forward position
- forward body posture.'

In a reported question, there is generally lack of eye contact with the addressee. (Zeshan 2004b: 19–20, and see Zeshan 2006a.)

There is no doubt that some of these gestures also play a role in the asking of polar questions in spoken languages. For example, when the Fijian chief uttered a question, his body posture—and the way he looked at me expecting an answer—were integral parts of the speech act.

27.5.2 Polar question with focus

The focus technique is likely to be found in a language where a polar question is shown by a particle, or an interrogative affix. Several illustrations have already been given of this.

In Dyirbal, interrogative enclitic =ma is added to the first word of a polar question; an item in focus is placed sentence-initially and takes this clitic—see (1–3) in §27.1. It was mentioned in §27.4 that in Eastern Pomo a focused constituent must be in initial position and is followed by interrogative clitic =la ~ =ti(ši). For a general polar question, la is placed in sentence-initial position.

We saw in §27.2 that in Huallaga Quechua, suffix *-chu* is added to the verb in a general polar question and in a focus question to the constituent in focus; this does not have to be fronted. In Turkish (Tura and Dede 1982), interrogative particle *mi* comes at the end of a general polar question but follows a constituent which is in focus, which again does not have to be fronted. The same applies for interrogative suffix *-aa* in the Dravidian language Telugu (Krishnamurti and Gwynn 1985: 283–4). Tonkawa (see §27.4) places interrogative clitic *=ti* after the verb in a general polar question or after a constituent in focus; this will generally (but not invariably) be put in sentence-initial position.

Af Tunni, a southern Somali dialect (Tosco 1997: 123–9), is similar to languages just mentioned, except that the interrogative suffix is *-ée* for a general polar question, and is then attached to the verb, as in (44), but has form *-áa* when it is added to a word in focus, as in (45).

(44) áda$_A$ šaléy$_O$ Máryam agart-ée?
      2sg   yesterday Maryam see:2sg-POLAR.QUESTION
      Did you see Maryam yesterday?

(45) áda$_A$ [gèel   bádan-áa]$_O$ qóbtə?
      2sg   camels many-FOCUS.POLAR.QUESTION get:2sg
      Do you have MANY camels?

A fair proportion of grammars do not mention the idea of focus within a polar question. Many—but perhaps not all—of these languages may be like English in being able only to accord stress to a focussed constituent, or to topicalize it (as in 'Is many the quantity of camels that you have?')

27.5.3 Types of polar question

Many times, when someone asks a question they have an expectation of what the answer might be. *Do you think it will rain today?* Or else a hope of what they would like it to be. *We have a picnic planned—do you really think it's going to rain?*

Some languages have a number of types of polar question. These can relate to the kind of answer that is expected, or to the attitude of the questioner or of the questioned.

Tags may carry the expectation of confirmation, as illustrated for Tamil by (36–7) and for English by (38–9). In the Papuan language Amele (Roberts 1987: 17–21), final *fo* on a polar question indicates an expectation that the addressee will agree with the supposition and final *fa* carries an expectation of disagreement (this applies whether the question is phrased as positive or as negative).

(46) [dana eu]$_O$ f-ag-a   fo?
      man   THAT see-2sgA-TODAY.PAST POLAR.QUESTION
      Did you see that man? [Expects answer: '(Yes,) I saw that man']

(47) ija_S qila [cabi   na] nu-ig-en   fa?
      1sg   now   garden TO   go-1sgA-FUTURE POLAR.QUESTION
      Should I go to the garden now? [Expects answer: 'You shouldn't go']

A neutral polar question (with no expectation concerning the answer) has an
'alternative question' structure, with the supposition followed by '*fo* NOT *fo*':

(48) qila   Madang nu-eg-en   fo   qee fo?
      today Masang go-2sgA-FUTURE POLAR.Q NOT POLAR.Q
      Are you going to Madang today or not?

Kobon, another language from the Papuan region (Davies 1981: 5–8) has
a similar system to Amele. Clause-final particle *aka* indicates the expectation
of an answer in agreement with the supposition (whether that was positive or
negative). And particle *ar* ('correct') is used when the speaker has a 'firm belief
in the truth of the proposition contained in the utterance'.

We noted under (c) in §27.5.1 that Slave uses a question-initial particle when
there is no expectation as to whether the answer will be positive or negative,
and just rising intonation (like a sort of echo question) when a positive answer
is expected.

Polar questions in Mupun (Frajzyngier 1993: 359–66) are marked by one of
three suffixes which go onto the last word of the sentence:

(a) Suffix -*e* 'does not carry any presupposition concerning the actual truth
    of the proposition. Nor does it carry any specific attitude of the speaker
    towards the proposition'.
(b) Suffix -*a* indicates 'that the speaker actually believes in the truth of the
    proposition and is looking for confirmation of [their] beliefs'.
(c) Suffix -*o* ~ -*wo* is used 'to seek a confirmation of an unexpected propo-
    sition, surprise, disbelief'. This is illustrated in (43) and:

(49) wur_A   lap   mpuo_O-wo?
      3.MASCULINE marry another-POLAR.QUESTION
      Did he marry another? [Speaker is astonished.]

Another Chadic language, Margi (Hoffmann 1963: 98–9), uses sentence-
final particle *yá* for a neutral polar question, and *rá* for one which expresses
scepticism, as in: 'Can you really write?' (I doubt it). In §27.2, we mentioned
one tag in Koasati which is used when a statement is hesitantly questioned, and
another relating to the addressee's desire ('Do you want to look at it?'). And
sentences (40–1) exemplified how in English a positive tag with a positive main
clause may indicate surprise or sarcasm (among other emotional attitudes).

In §27.3 we exemplified two polar interrogative mood markers in Jarawara, one neutral and the other relating to the future—see (25–6). Other languages deal with the time of a polar question through their regular tense system, or through temporal adverbs.

27.5.4 Alternative questions

In some languages, alternative questions loom large in the grammatical panoply, and come in various types. In others they do not exist at all.

In §27.2, an 'alternative question' was quoted from Huallaga Quechua:

(9) qam-chu   o   noqa-chu   aywa-shun?
     2sg-POLAR.Q OR 1sg-POLAR.Q   go-FUTURE:1inc.S
     Should you or I go?

This could be regarded as a shortening of the disjunction of two simple questions, 'Should you go?' or 'Should I go?', with the pronoun in focus (and marked by -*chu*) in each. The constituent clauses are polar questions, which would be answered by 'yes' or 'no'. The alternative question, (9), is not a polar question and should be answered 'you' or 'me' (with appropriate shift in pronominal reference).

Example (9) has alternative S arguments. Or we can have alternative predicates, as in Longgu (Austronesian, Solomon Islands; Hill 1992: 308):

(50) o$_S$ muha   bwala (o$_S$) ta'akutu?
      2sg be.happy OR   2sg be.sad
      Are you happy or sad?

Note that *bwala* 'or' is homonymous with the independent polarity form *bwala* 'no' (quite different from clausal negator *se* 'not'). For a question in Longgu, 'the intonation rises and then falls on the last syllable'.

In Dhimal (Tibeto-Burman, Nepal; King 2009: 283) a normal structure of polar questions involves 'X not-X'. For example:

(51) ta:-hi   ma-ta:-hi?
      be.tasty-PAST   NEGATIVE-be.tasty-PAST
      Is it tasty? (lit. Is it tasty or not tasty?)

Although this has alternative form, it functions as a polar question. Similar structures are used across Sinitic languages (generally referred to as 'Chinese dialects'). For instance, in Mandarin (Li and Thompson 1981: 532):

(52) ni$_S$ qù bu   qù?
      2sg go NOT go
      Will you go?

In Cantonese (Matthews and Yip 1994: 311), the 'most neutral form' of a polar question involves 'verb-NOT-verb' functioning as a single unit:

(53) léih$_A$ sīk-m̀h-sīk   [ngóh sailóu]$_O$ a?
      2sg   know-NOT-know   my   brother   PARTICLE
      Do you know my brother?

A common variety of alternative question is just to add 'or not' at the end. This was illustrated for Amele in (48). It is also a feature of Indonesian (Sneddon 1996: 313):

(54) ini   jalan ke Rawamangun atau bukan?
      THIS   road   TO Rawamangun OR   NOT
      Is this the road to Rawamangun, or not?

Bukan 'not' is used to negate verbless clauses with a noun as complement, such as the first four words of (54). It is also the independent polarity form 'no'. (*Tidak* 'not' negates other kinds of clause.)

It is normal custom when speaking Fijian to append *se sega* 'or not' to a polar question. On returning from fieldwork I unthinkingly brought this over into my English—*Would you like to come to the theatre, or not?*—only to be rebuked for doing so. What was regarded as good style in Fijian came to be seen (in translation) as rather rude in English.

In Dagbani (Gur family, Ghana; Olawsky 1999: 67) a polar question has alternative form:

(55) a$_S$ ni   kana bee a$_S$ ku   kana?
      2sg FUTURE come OR   2sg NEGATIVE.FUTURE come
      Will you come or not? (lit. Will you come or will you not come?)

Note that *ku* is the regular clausal negator for future tense, with *bi* being employed in past and present.

This can be shortened, so that just the inclusion of *bee* 'or' signals that it is a polar question:

(55') a$_S$ ni   kana bee?
       2sg FUTURE come OR
       Will you come?

Spaulding and Spaulding (1994: 139) quote an even more striking series of polar question constructions in Nankina, a language from the Papuan region. First, we can have a regular alternative question:

(56) kwip-ka   Gwarawon ku-sie   bo ma   ku-sie?
      tomorrow-ASP Gwarawon go-INDEF:2sg OR NOT go-INDEF:2sg
      Tomorrow, will you go to Gwarawon or will you not go?

The second clause may be reduced to a simple negation:

(56′) kwip-ka   Gwarawon ku-sie   bo   woni?
       tomorrow-ASP Gwarawon go-INDEF:2sgS   OR   NO
       Tomorrow, will you go to Gwarawon or not?

Note that *ma* in (56) is the regular clause negator. In (56′) it is replaced by *woni* which functions both as the independent polarity from 'no' and also as a negative modifier within an NP (for example, 'no (*woni*) betel-nut').

A polar question can be further reduced:

(56″) kwip-ka   Gwarawon ku-sie   bo?
       tomorrow-ASP Gwarawon go-INDEF:2sgS   OR
       Tomorrow, will you go to Gwarawon?

The only mark of this being a polar question is the final element, *bo* 'or', similar to Dagbani *bee* in (55′).

27.6 Content questions

A content question includes an interrogative word (or an indefinite/interrogative word)—this is its defining feature. Other facets tend to be viewed as secondary, and are sometimes scarcely noted. For example, one often finds an account of the intonation tune of a polar question, but no mention of what happens with a content question.

We saw in §27.3 that content questions take the same mood marking as polar questions in Tariana and in West Greenlandic (but content questions typically have the same intonation tune as statements in West Greenlandic). Jarawara has special mood suffixes for content questions (different from those on polar questions). The interrogative mood in Mangghuer and in Tonkawa only applies for polar, not for content, questions.

Similar marking for both types of questions was surveyed in §27.4—final glottal stop omission in Sanuma, use of interrogative clitics in Takelma and Eastern Pomo, and the 'interrogative process' of glottal stop infixation in Koasati.

In some languages all types of questions have a similar intonation tune— for example, Tamambo, described in §27.4. In others there are differences— Huallaga Quechua shows rising pitch only in polar questions (and, as described in §27.2, quite different suffixes are used in the two varieties of question).

We will now turn our attention to interrogative words. §27.6.1 considers the relation between interrogatives and indefinites. There is examination of the syntax of content questions in §27.6.2, and then §27.6.3 looks at the forms of interrogative words and how they may fall into paradigms with other types of word, such as demonstratives and locationals. The various kinds of interrogative word (relating to different word classes) is the topic of §27.6.4. Finally, in §27.6.5, we briefly consider the use of an interrogative word to introduce a relative clause.

27.6.1 Indefinites and interrogatives

It is not at all uncommon to find that, in a given language, some or all interrogative words also have an indefinite sense, or that indefinites can be formed from interrogatives by adding an affix.

The first point to note is that the label 'indefinite' is used for two rather different things. Consider:

(57)   Someone in the inner office has the key to the safe

Someone (an alternative is *somebody*) relates to a specific person, but the speaker does not know their identity. This can conveniently be termed a **specific indefinite**.

Compare this with:

(58)   Anyone could solve that puzzle

This means that each person in the world has the ability to solve that puzzle. It could be restricted a bit; for example: *Anyone with a bit of brain ...*, or *Anyone who has studied algebra ...* The label **general indefinite** can be used for *anyone* (or *anybody*); it refers to a general population, of unknown size. (*Everyone* and *everybody* are a slightly different kind of general indefinite.)

In English, interrogatives have different form from specific and general indefinites. We can now look at languages where there is a relationship between (some or all) interrogative words and one or both varieties of indefinites. In a survey of thirty languages in which indefinites either have the same form as interrogatives or are derived from them, specific indefinites are covered in fifteen, general indefinites in ten, and both in five languages.

For Tunica, an isolate from Louisiana, Haas (1941: 83) states that 'the interrogative-indefinite stem *ka*'- has the meaning "what, any, some".' That is, it has interrogative, specific indefinite, and general indefinite, senses. Four interrogative/indefinite words are build on this stem:

(59)   kaˈku   'who, someone, anyone'
       kaˈnahku   'what, something, anything'
       kaˈʔaš   'when, sometime, anytime'
       kaˈta   'where, somewhere, anywhere'

A similar situation is encountered in another isolate, Burushaski, spoken high in the Karakoram mountains of Kashmir. Thus, *bɛsʌn*, for example, can mean 'what' or 'something' or 'anything'. A polar question is marked by suffix *-a* to the verb and this may serve to distinguish interrogative and indefinite senses. Thus (Lorimer 1935: 152):

(60)   bɛsʌn ɛčʌm, What shall I do?

(61)   bɛsʌn ɛčʌm-a, Shall I do anything?

Polar question suffix *-a* is not used on a sentence which involves an interrogative word. Thus, the inclusion of *-a* in (61) indicates that *bɛsʌn* must have an indefinite sense. The absence of *-a* from (60) allows *bɛsʌn* to here have an interrogative sense.

However when a verb ends in *a*, suffix *-a* merges with it and is not discernable. There is then multiple ambiguity. Lorimer states that *bɛsʌn ɛča* may mean 'Thou art doing something' or 'Art thou doing anything?' or 'What art thou doing?'.

Both kinds of indefinites are derived from interrogatives in a further isolate, Ainu (from northern Japan and adjacent parts of Russia). Refsing (1986: 101–10) explains how, in the Shizunai dialect, *-ka* can be added to any interrogative word to form a specific indefinite. For example:

(62)   nen   'who'   nen-ka   'somebody'
       nep   'what'   nep-ka   'something'
       onun   'from where'   onun-ka   'from somewhere'

In addition to these, Refsing has in her corpus two examples of reduplicated forms which appear to have a general indefinite sense—*onun-onun* means 'from various places' and *nen-nen* is 'whoever'. Compare the specific indefinite *nen-ka* 'somebody' in (63) and general indefinite *nen-nen* 'anyone, whoever' in (64).

(63)   [nenka   orwa]   an   e   kik wa…?
       SOMEBODY BY   PASSIVE 2sg hit AND
       Were you hit by somebody, and…?

(64)   nen-nen   payeka yakka,   iokunnuka wa   iunkerayte…
       WHOEVER pass.by CON.CONJ feel.pity   AND give.alms
       No matter whoever passes by, they feel pity and give alms…

Yakka is a 'concessive conditionalizer' (Refsing 1986: 254–5).

In Shoshone (Uto-Aztecan, California and Nevada; Miller 1996: 699, 710–11) there are eight interrogative-indefinite words, including *hakani* 'some way, how' and *hakatin* (subject form) 'someone, who'. If one of these words is placed at the beginning of the sentence, it has interrogative meaning, as in (65), and if it is in the usual position in the sentence, the sense is specific indefinite, as in (66):

(65) hakke_O   in_A puikka?
      WHO:OBJECT   2sg   see
      Who did you see?

(66) ni_A kian   hakke_O   puikka
      1sg   PERHAPS   SOMEONE:OBJECT   see
      I saw someone

In Maricopa (Yuman family, Arizona; Gordon 1986: 61–5), interrogatives and indefinites also have the same form, and this can lead to ambiguity:

(67) mki-sh   have-ii?
      WHO/SOMEONE-SUBJECT   enter-QUESTION.SUFFIX
      Who came in? OR Did someone come in?

Both polar and content questions are marked by rising intonation and by -*ii* suffixed to the verb (if it is consonant-final).

The same sort of ambiguity is found in Tamambo where three of the seven interrogative words also have an indefinite sense. These are *sei* 'who, someone', *sava* 'what, someone', and *avisa* 'how many, some many'. (Those which are exclusively interrogative are 'when', 'where', 'why', and 'how'.) An example of this ambiguity is (Jauncey 1997: 52):

(68) o-sahasaha [mai   sei]?
      2sg-work   WITH   WHO/SOMEONE
      Do you work with someone? OR Who do you work with?

The array at (15) in §27.2 shows that in Koasati just some of the interrogatives also have specific indefinite meaning. They are accorded an interrogative sense when the verb has undergone the interrogative process (of glottal stop infixation) and a specific indefinite sense otherwise. Similar comments apply for Takelma—*nek^h* means 'who' when interrogative clitic =*ti* is attached but 'someone' otherwise, and similarly for the other interrogative/indefinites. (See (b) in §27.4 and Culy 1999.)

Looking now at general indefinites, we find that in Amharic the addition of -*ïmm* to an interrogative word creates a general indefinite—*man* 'who', *man-imm* 'anybody'. Hausa (Newman 2000: 622–3) uses prefix *koo-* to the same effect—*wàà* 'who', *koo-waa* 'everyone, whoever', *yàushè* 'when', *koo-yàushè* 'always, whenever', and so on. In §27.2 we saw that in Huallaga Quechua a content question requires an interrogative word and also suffix -*taq* or -*raq*. If, instead of one of these, -*pis* is used, we get a general indefinite, as illustrated in (12).

In analysing a new language, even a good linguist is likely to be influenced by the structure of their native language and of other languages they have worked on. One notes that a certain word has interrogative meaning and that's that. No need to look further, one might think. But there is such a need.

Consider the example of W. E. Smythe (1948/9: 40), a country doctor in New South Wales who worked with the last generation of speakers of Gumbaynggirr and published a fine grammar. He wrote: 'a peculiar feature of what are usually described as "interrogative" pronouns is that they are interrogative only so long as the right tone of voice is used, otherwise they become impersonal or indefinite' (that is, specific indefinite). Thus *wa:ru* 'who, someone', *mi:nja* 'what, something'. During my first spell of fieldwork, on Dyirbal, I soon recorded the interrogatives; it took quite a while to realize that they also had an indefinite meaning (and that, indeed, this might well be the prior sense).

Differing opinions have been provided concerning what the prior sense is for interrogative/indefinites. Within a general survey volume, Haspelmath (1997b: 176) says 'one thing we know for sure: the interrogative function is always primary, and the indefinite function secondary'. In contrast, Enfield (2007a: 86)—in his study of Lao—considers that 'indefinite reference is semantically simpler than interrogative reference, and is always incorporated within the more complex semantics of interrogatives'. But note that both simple and general indefinites are, in a fair number of languages, formed by addition to interrogatives, whereas there are no examples of derivation in the opposite direction.

In many indigenous Australian communities, social convention requires that one should be as specific as possible, vagueness (in the course of everyday conversation) being looked upon with distaste. At the end §3.7, it was suggested that a form like *wañju* 'who, someone' in Yidiñ carries specific indefinite and interrogative meanings simultaneously. The sentence *Wañju walba yaŋgi:ñ* means 'Someone must have cut that rock, who did it?' In this society, whenever the identity of some person or thing is not known, one should attempt to ascertain it.

As to whether an interrogative or a specific indefinite or a general indefinite sense is primary (if either is), for a multi-sensed word, this may be culturally determined. Detailed studies in the field are needed before it would be proper to embark on inductive typological generalization.

27.6.2 The syntax of content questions

In many languages, a polar question can be viewed as a statement plus an interrogative overlay—special intonation tune, or interrogative process or particle or tag (or a combination of these) And a content question can also be viewed as statement with a different sort of overlay—an interrogative word replaces a regular constituent in a particular functional slot.

In well over half of the several score languages I have examined, an interrogative word remains in the place in order appropriate to its function in the clause. Languages of this type include (mentioning some of those already discussed in this chapter): Koasati, Tamambo, Tamil, Mupun, Japanese, Swahili, Kobon, Chinese, Ainu, and Amharic. Some languages are like English in moving an interrogative word to the beginning of the sentence (often, as a kind of topicalization). This applies to, among others, Hixkaryana, Rumanian, and Hausa. An alternative is for there to be a choice—in languages such as Huallaga Quechua and Slave, an interrogative word can either be in its expected position, or be moved to the beginning of the sentence.

In Kana (Ikoro 1996a: 322, 1996b: 76), an interrogative word will normally be sentence-final, but can be sentence-initial for emphasis. Tolai, an Austronesian language from Papua New Guinea (Franklin, Kerr, and Beaumont 1974: 126) is particularly interesting in that 'who', 'whose', 'what', 'which', 'where', 'when', and 'why' are placed at the beginning of the sentence, 'where to' and a different 'why' at the end, and 'how many' before the word it qualifies. In Amele (Roberts 1987: 21–4), an interrogative word is placed immediately before the verb (except in an echo question).

Just a few languages have a special construction for content questions. In Iraqw (Cushitic, Tanzania; Mous 1993: 283), a content question is phrased as a copula construction, with the interrogative word as copula complement. For example:

(69) [mú-k   aa   qáatl]cs
      people:CONSTRUCT-MASC   3.SUBJECT:PERFECT   die:3sg.MASC:PAST
      a   magá:cc?
      COPULA   HOW.MANY
      How many people have died? (lit. The people (who) have died are how
      many?)

In Salish languages, interrogative words appear as predicate heads within a relative clause construction. An example from Musqueam (Suttles 2004: 394) is:

(70) wét   kʷə   kʷə   ʔi   ƛʼéːnəq?
      WHO   THEN   ARTICLE   AUXILIARY   be.potlaching
      Who is potlaching? (lit. Who then is the one who is potlaching?)

In most languages, it is possible to question either a constituent of a main clause, or one of a subordinate clause. This is particularly straightforward in a language which maintains an interrogative word in its expected place in order, such as Lezgian (North-east Caucasian; Haspelmath 1993: 421–7):

(71)   [Ahmed   wuč   žǧa-j-t'a]CONDITIONAL.CLAUSE
       Ahmed   WHAT:ABSOLUTIVE   find-AORIST.PARTICIPLE-CONDITIONAL
       [ada-z   šad   že-da]MAIN.CLAUSE?
       HE:DATIVE   happy   be-FUTURE
       Literally: If Ahmed finds what, he will be happy?

It can be a trifle tortuous to question something from within a subordinate clause in a language like English, which requires interrogative words to occur in sentence-initial position. For (71), one would have to say something like: 'What is it that if Ahmed finds it, he will be happy?'

Just a few languages have restrictions on how many interrogative words may be included in a clause. For instance, in Hup (Makú or Nadahup family, Brazil; Epps 2008: 778–9), an interrogative word must occur in clause-initial position and only one can be used per clause. However, many languages allow several, as in Manambu (Ndu family, Papua New Guinea; Aikhenvald 2008a: 231):

(72)   akrəl   sə-kə-m   vyak?
       WHERE.TO   WHO-OBLIQUE-ACCUSATIVE   hit:PURPOSIVE
       Where are you going to hit whom?

Fortescue (1984: 17–18) provides similar examples from West Greenlandic. Sentences with several interrogative words are possible (if not always too felicitous) in many European languages. In English, one can say things like *Who took what where?* or *Who gave what to whom?*. However, the possibilities are not unlimited—Kuno and Robinson (1972) and Bolinger (1978) discuss the principles which determine possible combinations of interrogative words in English.

What would be polar or content questions, if used as main clauses, may be embedded as 'interrogative complement clauses' (see §18.4). For example, *I'll decide later whether to go to town tomorrow* and *Mary knows who killed the pig*. These are sometimes called 'indirect questions' but the label is misleading. They are not any kind of question, but rather statements *about* questions.

An unusual construction occurs in Aleut (Eskimo-Aleut family, Alaska; Bergsland 1997: 82–3). This is a polar question about a content question:

(73)   kiins   haqal   ii?
       WHO   came   POLAR.QUESTION
       'Who came?' (is that your question?)

Kiin haqal would be a content question 'Who came?'. The addition of polar question sentence-final particle *ii*, said with a rising tone, queries what the content question was.

27.6.3 The forms of interrogative words

We can recognize eight canonical interrogative words:

(74) who   what   why   where
      which how many/how much how   when

Not every language has separate forms for each of these. As we shall see in §27.6.4, one term may cover both 'who' and 'what', or both 'what' and 'which', or both 'which' and 'where', and so on. And there may be, for instance, several different subtypes of 'why'. In addition, as mentioned in §27.1, a few languages also have interrogative verbs 'do what (to)' and/or 'do how (to)'.

In a few languages we find that some interrogative roots belong in the same paradigm as demonstratives. Such a paradigm for Tamil was presented at (67) in §15.2.2. Some of the demonstratives in Japanese were included in Table 15.3 of §15.2.2, with a note about their interrogative confrères. A fuller paradigm (based on Martin 1988: 1066) is in Table 27.1.

It will be seen that the 'distal' plus 'place' demonstrative is irregular, being a-soko when *a-ko would have been predicted. And 'adverb (of manner)' plus 'distal' would be expected to be á-o; this has become áa.

Languages with similar systems include Lezgian (Haspelmath 1993: 188), Punjabi (Bhatia 1993: 233), and Hup (Epps 2008: 161). In each instance, only *some* interrogative words occur in a paradigm with demonstratives. (For instance, 'who' does not, in Tamil, Japanese, Lezgian, Punjabi, and Hup.)

A partial paradigm is also available for English. Table 27.2 includes, in column A, five interrogative words. For rows I–IV, column B has as reference point something relatively distant from the speaker and column C something relatively near to them (see §15.2.3). Rows I–III are straightforward, referring to position 'at' and motion 'to' and 'from' (forms in Rows II and III are a trifle archaic, but still in general use). Row IV corresponds to I–III but with demonstrative *that* in column B (*this*, in column C, is irregular). In Row V,

TABLE 27.1. Paradigm of demonstratives and indefinite/interrogatives in Japanese

| | DEMONSTRATIVES | | | SPECIFIC INDEFINITE/ |
	PROXIMAL	MEDIAL	DISTAL	INTERROGATIVES
individual	ko-re	so-re	a-re	dó-re 'which one'
adnominal	ko-no	so-no	a-no	dó-no 'which'
similarity	ko-nná	so-nná	a-nná	dó-nná 'what kind of'
place	ko-ko	so-ko	[a-soko]	dó-ko 'where'
direction	ko-tira	so-tira	a-tira	dó-tira 'which way'
adverb (of manner)	kó-o	só-o	áa	dó-o 'how'

TABLE 27.2. Paradigm in English involving interrogative words

	A	B	C
I	wh-ere	th-ere	h-ere
II	wh-ither	th-ither	h-ither
III	wh-ence	th-ence	h-ence
IV	wh-at	th-at	[this]
V	wh-en	th-en	

then refers to a particular point in time (just as *that* refers to a particular person or thing) and *when* enquires about a point in time.

The Cushitic language Hdi (Frajzyngier 2002: 357–78, and personal communication) is unusual in that its interrogative words are pretty different from each other:

(75) wá 'who'   nə́ 'what'   ní-yà 'why' gá 'where'
      nú 'which' kí dàrì 'how many/how much' kí 'how'   yà-wú 'when'

It appears that 'how many/how much' is based on *kí* 'how', and 'why' consists of *nə́* 'what' followed by the copula *yà*, realized as *ní-yà*.

More commonly, we find an array of interrogative words on similar lines to those of Huallaga Quechua, set out in (10) of §27.2. A number of sequences recur—three commence with *ima* and two with *may*—but morphological analysis is not feasible.

Interrogative words in Japanese comprise those from the paradigm in Table 27.1 (all commencing with *dó-*, which we recognized as a morpheme) plus:

(76) dáre 'who'
      náni 'what', náze 'why', nán- (plus classifier) 'how many' (Sino-
        Japanese form)
      ítu 'when', íku- (plus classifier) 'how many' (native form)

We find initial *na-* in three forms and *i-* in two but these cannot be segmented out as morphemes since the remainder of the form does not occur elsewhere.

In Table 27.2, we showed that morphological analysis is appropriate for *wh-ere*, *wh-ither*, *wh-ence*, *wh-at*, and *wh-en*. But no such analysis is feasible for *who*, *what*, and *why*, since *-o*, *-at*, and *-y* do not occur (with similar meaning) in any other words. What is notable about English is that all interrogative words commence with *wh-*, except for *how* (and this does come from an earlier **hwô*, just as *who* comes from **hwoz*, *what* from **hwat*, *where* from **hwǽr*, and so on). A fair number of languages have recurrent segments in their interrogative words, but without morphological analysis being feasible. (In many cases it may relate back to a paradigm in a past stage of the language, whose regularities have been obscured by phonological and other changes.)

And there are languages with a small number of forms, on which all interrogative words are based. Consider the Papuan language Abun (Berry and Berry 1999: 109):

(77)   *u*, 'which' (as modifier to the head noun in an NP)
        je ('person') *u*, 'who'
        mo (locative preposition) *u*, 'where'
        sa ('like') *u*, 'how'
        wa ('for') *sa* ('like') *u*, 'why'
        kap ('time') *u*, 'when'
    suma, 'what'
        wa ('for') *suma*, 'why'
    ot, 'how many' (following noun plus appropriate classifier)
        kap ('time') *ot*, 'when'

Ewe (Kwa family, Ghana; Ameka 1991: 53–4, and personal communication) has the most spartan—perhaps one should say: the most streamlined—way of creating content questions. One simply places *ka* at the end of an NP and it becomes interrogative. Thus 'person *ka*' is 'who', 'thing *ka*' is 'what', 'place *ka*' is 'where', and so on. Note that any noun can take *ka*, so that 'garment *ka*' ('which garment') is of equal status with 'person *ka*' ('which person', 'who'). And there is *néne* 'how many' which may also be placed after any noun. (Ewe has a quite different marker for polar questions; it is particle *à*, at the end of a clause.)

27.6.4 Types of interrogative word

In many languages, each interrogative word is associated with a different word class. In addition to this, the interrogative words are linked together as another kind of class, which is overlaid across the basic set of word classes (a sort-of pan-basic-word-classes word class). That is, the interrogative words share one or more properties. This may be simply that they convert a statement into a content question. But there is usually more—some specific grammatical property or properties that they share.

This can be illustrated for Fijian. The interrogative words comprise:

(a)   *cei* 'who', is related to the class of pronouns.
(b)   *cava* 'what, which' is related to the class of nouns.

Each NP begins with what Fijianists call an 'article'. This is *a* ~ *na* if the head of the NP is a common noun or *cava* 'what', and *o* if the head is a pronoun or proper noun or *cei* 'who'.

Cava functions in a number of other interrogative expressions. They include *baleta a cava* 'concerning what, why', *vu'u ni cava* 'for the cause of what, why', and adverb *va'a-cava* 'do how'.

- (c) *vei* 'where' is a locational word. It only occurs with prepositions *i* 'to, at, in, on' and *mai* 'from', and with the prefix *'ai-* 'native of'.
- (d) *vica* 'how many / how much, some' is the only interrogative word in Fijian to also have an indefinite sense. It clearly relates to the class of lexical numbers. For example, it forms a cardinal by the prefixation of *i'a-*. Compare *tolu* 'three', *i'a-tolu* 'third', with *vica* 'how many/how much, some' and *i'a-vica* 'how-many-th, some-number-th'.
- (e) *'uca(-ta'ini)* 'do what (to)' has the morphological and syntactic profile of a verb; see (92) below.

There are two grammatical properties which link these interrogative words. The first is that modifier *soti* 'a lot, all' may only be used with a negator (which in Fijian are verbs—see §21.2.4 and §21.2.7) or with an interrogative word. Thus *o cei soti* 'who are all of them', *a cava soti* 'what are all of them', and with *vei* 'where':

(78) [i   vei   soti a   vanua] o   na   la'o 'ina?
     AT   WHERE   ALL ART place   2sgS FUTURE   GO   PREP:3sg
     Where are all the places you are going to?

The default marker of a complement clause is *ni* 'that'. But if a complement clause is formed from a polar or a content question, then *ni* must be replaced by *se*. This is the second property common to interrogative words: if one of them occurs in a complement clause, the clause must be marked by *se*.

If a language has interrogative mood (§27.3), this serves as a grammatical link between interrogative words. In Jarawara, for instance, the content interrogative mood—suffix *-ri* in example (27)—is used if and only if the clause includes an interrogative word. Other morphological and syntactic processes that apply to content questions serve a similar function—glottal stop infixation in Koasati, interrogative particles in Takelma and Eastern Pomo, and so on (see the beginning of §27.6).

In the remainder of this section we will briefly survey the eight canonical interrogative words, and interrogative verbs. But note there can be others in individual languages. For example:

- 'what is X's name' in Rukai (Austronesian, Taiwan; Zeitoun 2007: 365–6);
- 'say what, say something' in Choctaw (Muskogean, Mississippi; Broadwell 2006: 105);

- 'how big' in Comanche (Uto-Aztecan, Oklahoma; Charney 1993: 111) and 'what size' in Hungarian (Kenesei, Vago, and Fenyvesi 1998: 280).

(I) 'who', 'what', and 'which'

Languages may have one, two, three (or more) words corresponding to English *what*, *which*, and *who*. We can set the scene by briefly considering the three words in English.

Both *what* and *which* may modify a noun. *Which* implies choice from a **limited** set. Suppose that I have several animals in the house and notice that a piece of fish has been eaten, presumably by one of these animals. I may ask:

(79)   Which animal ate the fish?

But if I am camped in the jungle and hear a horrifying noise in the middle of the night, I might ask:

(80)   What animal made that noise?

Use of *what* implies **unlimited** choice—I have no idea what kind of animal it was.

There is a similar contrast when *which* and *what* modify a noun with human reference. Suppose that a teacher goes into his classroom and finds a rude word written on the board. They may ask:

(81)   Which boy wrote that word on the board?

The use of *which* implies choice from a limited set—all the boys in the room.

Now suppose that someone tells you they heard of a youth having dismembered his sister. You exclaim:

(82)   What boy could do such a thing?

Again, employing *what* implies unlimited choice.

Let us now consider *who*. This cannot be a modifier; it may only function as head of an NP. *Who* could replace *which X* or *what X* if *X* is a noun with human reference. Sentences (81) and (82) could be rephrased: *Who wrote that word on the board?* and *Who could do such a thing?*

What can also function as NP head; instead of (80) one could say just *What made that noise?* The limitlessness of *what* is now extended; rather than the choice being from the potentially unlimited set of all animals, we would now be asking for a choice from all possible entities.

Note that *which* cannot be head of an NP; instead of (79) it is not permissible to say **Which ate the fish?* (It is possible to omit the head of an NP with *which* under anaphoric ellipsis, as in *I have a cat and a dog, which (animal) do you like best?* In this sentence *which* is still a modifier, to the omitted but understood head.)

A fair number of languages have interrogative words that roughly corre-spond to *who*, *what*, and *which* in English. For example, Huallaga Quechua and Koasati—see (10) and (15) in §27.2—Japanese—see Table 27.1 and (76) in §27.6.3—Abun—in (77)—and many European languages. However, the meanings and function of the three interrogative words do vary a good deal between languages and require careful study on a language-specific basis.

In contrast, there are languages with a single interrogative carrying all three meanings. Consider the following sentences involving *yangki* 'who, what, which' in Yawuru, from north-west Australia (Hosokawa 1991: 337):

(83) [yangki   maya] dyunggarra   i-nga-rn?
      WHO/WHAT/WHICH house 2du:GENITIVE 3sg-be-IMPERFECTIVE
      Which house is yours (dual)?

(84) yangki   mi-nga-ny-ngany   dyuyu-ni?
      WHO/WHAT/WHICH 2sg-be-IMPERFECTIVE-COM 2sg-ERGATIVE
      What are you (sg) holding?

(85) yangki-ni   nyamba i-na-ka-nda-dyiya?
      WHO/WHAT/WHICH-ERG THIS   3sg-TR-carry-PERFECTIVE-2sg:DAT
      Who brought this to you (sg)?

In (83), *yangki* occurs in an NP with *maya* 'house' and thus means 'which'. The interpretations 'what' in (84) and 'who' in (85) are inferred from the meaning of the sentences—it is people, not things, who bring something, and a person is more likely to hold something than someone. But the sense of *yangki* can be indeterminate, and ambiguity is then likely to be resolved by pragmatic factors.

In Gurr-goni, another Australian language (Green 1995: 151–2), -*nji* covers 'who', 'what', and 'which'. This is a bound form, which takes a noun class prefix indicating which type of entity is being questioned, for example *mi-nji* 'which kind of food'. If the semantic domain of the referent of -*nji* is not known, the default prefix from noun class 1 is employed.

As mentioned above, Fijian has *cei* 'who' and *cava* which covers both 'what' and 'which'. A fair number of languages are reported to have a single interrogative covering both 'who' and 'what'. And a number where the form for 'who' appears to be based on that for 'what'. For example, Indonesian (Sneddon 1996: 314–17, 141–2) has *apa* 'what' and *siapa* 'who', where the *si*- may be the diminutive prefix which is also used as a personifier (for example, a character in folk tales is called *si Kancil* 'person mouse-deer'). There are just a few examples of 'what' appearing to be based on 'who'; in Panyjima (Australian, Dench 1991: 164–5) we find *ngana* 'who, someone' and *ngananha* 'what, something'.

In many languages, 'who' is related to the small grammatical system of pro-nouns and 'what' to the open lexical class of nouns. In Dyirbal, for instance, *waña* 'who, someone' has separate forms for S, A, and O functions (like 1sg and 2sg pronouns in the southern dialect) whereas *miña* 'what, something' inflects on an absolutive-ergative basis, like nouns and adjectives. We described in §5.1 how the Dyirbal avoidance style—called Jalnguy—has the same grammar as the everyday style but employs a different form for almost every lexeme. In keeping with this, *waña* 'who, someone' is like pronouns in having the same form across both styles, whereas 'what, something' differs, being *miña* in the everyday style and *mindirr* in Jalnguy.

Languages do differ in the word-class associations of interrogative words. In Jarawara, for instance, personal pronouns are basically bound forms. As a consequence, the interrogatives *hibaka* (feminine), *hibeke* (masculine) 'who', and *himata* 'what', which are free forms, both behave like nouns.

(II)   'how many' and 'how much'

Some languages have distinct interrogative forms for 'how many', referring to countables, and 'how much', for non-countables (and sometimes more besides). For example:

- Thai *kìi* 'how many', *thâwrày* 'how much' (Iwasaki and Ingkaphi-rom 2005: 291).
- Tagalog: *ilan* 'how many', *gaano* 'how much (quantity)', *magkano* 'how much (price)' (Schachter and Otanes 1972: 506).
- Tamil: *ettane* 'how many', *evvaḷavu* 'how much'.

The truncated paradigm of demonstratives and interrogatives for Tamil at (67) in §15.2.2 includes *e-ttane*. It can be extended by a further row: *i-vvaḷavu* 'this much', *a-vvaḷavu* 'that much', and *e-vvaḷavu* 'how much' (Asher 1985: 150).

There are many languages in which a single form is used for both 'how many' and 'how much'. These include (from languages already discussed in this chapter): Huallaga Quechua (see (10) in §27.2), Hixkaryana (Derbyshire 1985: 58), and Indonesian (Sneddon 1996: 315); and see the list of languages with this feature in §20.9.1.

In a few languages, 'how many, how much' is a verb; for instance, *námpó* 'be how many' in Koasati (§27.2). In §20.9.1, we explained how the general interrogative verb *ee(-na-)* 'what about' in Jarawara can be taken to mean 'be how many' in appropriate circumstances; there are examples from other languages in §20.9.1.

Cross-linguistically, there are many kinds of similarities of form between different interrogative words. For instance, in the Australian language Djapu, *nhaamuñ?* 'how many' appears to involve an increment to *nhaa* 'what, something' (Morphy 1983: 55–6), and in Yukulta, also from Australia, *t^{y}inamulu* 'how many' appears to involve an increment to *t^{y}ina* 'where at' (Keen 1983: 243).

'How many/much' generally relates to the class (or subclass) of lexical number words, and behaves like it in many ways. For instance, if a number word requires a classifier, then so will 'how many/much'. In Tukang Besi (Austronesian, Indonesia; Donohue 1999: 105–10), a number must be suffixed by one of a set of twelve classifiers, and so must *pia-* 'how many'. For example, *pia-mia* 'how many people', *pia-'ulu* 'how many animals'. And see (f) in §27.7.

And if there is some morphological process for deriving an ordinal from a cardinal number, it is likely that this will also apply to 'how many/much'. The ordinal prefix *i'a-* in Fijian was mentioned at the beginning of this section; added to *vica* 'how many, some number', it forms *i'a-vica* 'the how-many-th, the some-number-th'. In Hungarian, an ordinal number is formed from a cardinal by suffixing *-(V)dik*; thus *hat* 'six', *hat-odik* 'sixth'. This suffix is also used with *hány* 'how many', giving *hány-adik* 'how-many-th'. In Latin, parallel to the derivation of ordinal numbers from cardinals (such as *sex* 'six', *sextus* 'sixth') we find *quot* 'how many' and *quot-us*, explained in a bilingual dictionary as 'having what position in a numerical series'. And similarly in many other languages.

English is rather unusual in not having a straightforward interrogative word referring to quantity. In place of this, it employs a construction which can combine *how* with virtually any adjective, including *many* and *much* (and *few* and *little*). Alongside *how many* and *how much*, one can also enquire *how big*, *how hot*, *how old*, *how clever*, *how likely*, and so on. It is surely related to the fact that English does not have a single word meaning 'how many', that it lacks the sort of ordinal just illustrated for Fijian, Hungarian, and Latin.

(III) 'why' and 'how'

Mandarin Chinese is unusual in that one interrogative, *zěnme*, can mean either 'how' or 'why'. The following sentence is ambiguous:

(86) nǐ$_A$ zěnme   xiě   xiǎshuō$_O$?
      2sg HOW/WHY write novel
      EITHER How do you write novels? OR Why do you write novels?

Li and Thompson (1981: 522–4) explain that 'how' is a manner adverbal ('pertaining to the manner in which the action of the verb is carried out'), which can only occur before the verb, whereas 'why' is a sentential adverbal ('requesting the respondent to provide a semantic frame for the entire sentence'), which can occur either before the verb or sentence-initially. Thus, if *zěnme* is moved to the beginning of the sentence, only the 'why' interpretation is possible.

Most languages have quite different ways of expressing 'why' and 'how'. There may be distinct interrogative words, as in Japanese (see (76) and Table 27.1), and Hdi, shown in (75). Quite often, 'why' is based on 'what'. We find *de ce* 'for what', with preposition *de* 'for', in Rumanian (Mallinson 1986:

267), and similarly in Abun, see (77). Dative suffix *-fí* can be added to *máalí* 'what' in Oromo (Cushitic branch of Afroasiatic, Ethiopia and Kenya; Owens 1985: 116, 205), dative *-gu* to *miña* 'what' in Dyirbal (and similarly in many other Australian languages), again creating 'what for' = 'why'.

In Supyire (Gur family, Mali; Carlson 1994: 537), 'why' is shown through *ñàhá* 'what' and a postposition—either *ná* 'on' or *kúrúgó* 'along, by means of, because', as in:

(87) ñàhá   kúrúgó   pi   màha   ñìŋke   yaa   yɛ?
      WHAT   BECAUSE.OF 3pl   HABITUAL earth:DEF repair QUESTION
      Why do they restore the earth? (lit. Because of what ... ?)

Similarly, in Fijian *baleta a cava* 'concerning what' is used for 'why' (Dixon 1988: 172).

Jarawara has three ways of expressing 'why', all based on *himata* 'what'. One can use *himata ebe -na-* 'for what purpose' (e.g. 'is the boy crying?'), or *himata ihi* 'due to what' (e.g. 'are you calling out?'), or by combining *himata* 'what' with postposition *tabijo* 'due to the absence/lack of' (e.g. 'are you angry with me?'); see Dixon (2004: 405).

Many languages have a monomorphemic form for 'how', but in others it is based on another interrogative. We saw, in (77), that for Abun 'why' is, literally 'for like which' or 'for what'. In quite a few languages, 'how' is rendered by an interrogative verb—see (V) below.

Just as some languages have a number of different varieties of 'why', so some include several articulations of 'how'. In Rukai (Zeitoun 2007: 375–6) we find three 'how' interrogatives (synchronically distinct, but etymologically related):

- *amokoa*, referring to a degree or quality, e.g. 'how fast/good/cold is it?'
- *apokoa*, referring to a means in realis, e.g. 'How did you go to Wanshan?'
- *pikoa*, referring to a means in irrealis, e.g. 'How will you go to Wanshan?'

(IV) 'where' and 'when'

There may be several interrogatives 'where', and they may be in a paradigm with local adverbial demonstratives. There is *where/whither/whence* in English, shown in Table 27.2, and a similar array in Dyirbal (Dixon 1972: 87–8):

(88)

	WHERE	HERE	THERE
AT	wuñjay	yalay	balay
TO (TOWARDS A PLACE)	wuñjarru	yalu	balu
TO (IN A DIRECTION)	wuñjarri	yali	bali
FROM	wuñjaŋum	yaŋum	baŋum

In the Papuan language Amele (Roberts 1987: 21), *ai* is used for 'which' and also for 'where', 'when the location is proximal, i.e. within view', with *ana* being used for 'where' when 'the location is not proximal, i.e. not necessarily within view'.

'Where' and 'when' may have different forms, as in Japanese—see Table 27.1 and (76)—and in Tunica—see (59). In the Australian language Guugu Yimidhirr (Haviland 1979: 71) *wanhdhaa* is 'where' and its reduplicated form *wanhdhaa-wanhdhaa* is 'when'. Sometimes both 'where' and 'when' appear to relate in form to other interrogatives. We saw in (15) that, for Koasati, *naksofó:kon* 'when' appears to be based on *naksofón ~ naksó:n* 'where', which in turn appears to be based on *naksó* 'who' (although these forms are not morphologically segmentable).

In Abun, several interrogatives are based on *u* 'which'—see (77). 'Where' is rendered by locative preposition *mo* plus *u*, and 'when' by *kap* 'time' plus *u*. Manambu (Aikhenvald 2008a: 225–7) uses *akə* for 'where'; if it is followed by *səkər* 'time', this indicates 'when' (literally, 'where time').

'Where' is sometimes based on noun 'place' and—rather more often—'when' on 'time' or a similar noun. For example, 'when' is interrogative 'what' plus noun 'time' in Amele (Roberts 1987: 21), in Turkish (Göksel and Kerslake 2005: 302–3) and in Tzotzil (Robinson 1999: 79).

In Yidiñ, there are two temporal interrogatives, both based on *wañjirri* 'how many'. Adding *-may* produces *wañjirrimay* 'when' and *-m* gives *wañjiirrim* 'how long' (this is the only place in the grammar where suffixes *-may* and *-m* occur). Thus (Dixon 1977a: 201):

(89) ñundu_S wanjirrimay gada-ŋ?
      2sg   WHEN   come-NON.PAST
      When will you come?

(90) ñundu_S wanjiirrim wuna-ŋ?
      2sg   HOW.LONG   sleep-NON.PAST
      How long are you going to sleep for?

One does encounter languages with two different words for 'when'—one referring to the past and one to the future. For example the Austronesian language Tukang Besi (Donohue 1999: 105) and the Muskogean language Choctaw (Broadwell 2006: 112).

There are languages which have no general word 'when'. It is, however, always possible to enquire about time. In Jarawara, a question relating to today ('When will you eat?) is phrased in terms of the position of the sun; literally, 'At where will the sun be sitting in the sky, will you eat?' Questions about time outside today may involve 'how many' plus 'days' (literally 'sleeps') or 'months' ('moons') or 'years' ('wet seasons'). One day, a Jarawara man asked when I would be returning to the village. What he said was (Dixon 2004: 409):

(91) [[tika amo-ni]ₛ   ee   ni]   jaa
        2sgS sleep-AUX.COMP WHAT.ABOUT AUX.NOMZR IN
        ti-ka-ma-ri-be   [Kasanofa   jaa]?
        2sgS-in.motion-BACK-CONTENT.Q.f-FUT.f   Casa.Nova TO
      In how many days will you return to Casa Nova? (Lit. In how many of
        your sleeps will you return to Casa Nova?)

In this sentence, 'how many' is expressed by the general interrogative verb *ee (-na-)* 'what about' (discussed in §20.9.1). Since the sentence includes a content interrogative word (verb *ee -na-*), albeit in a subordinate clause, the main verb is marked by content interrogative mood suffix *-ri* (feminine form because *ti-* 'you', like all pronouns, takes feminine agreement), as in (27) above.

(V) Interrogative verbs

Just about every language allows one to ask about a person or a thing, a place or a time, but rather few have an interrogative verb—to query an action or state. (I don't know why this is so.)

Fijian is like English in that it is a straightforward matter to question an argument—for example, *Who*ₛ *laughed?*, *Who*ₐ *hit you*ₒ? and *Who*ₒ *did Harry*ₐ *hit?* It differs in that it also has an interrogative verb, intransitive form *'uca* 'do what' and transitive form *'uca-ta'ini* 'do what to', as in (Dixon 1988: 174):

(92) [e   'uca-ta'ini   i'o]ₚREDICATE [o   Ari]ₐ?
        3sgA DO.WHAT-TRANSITIVE 2sgO   ARTICLE Harry
      What did Harry do to you? (lit. Harry did what to you?)

In Fijian, 'how' is shown not by a verb but by *va'a-cava*, in which adverb-creating prefix *va'a-* is added to *cava* 'what'; literally 'what-ly'.

As discussed in §27.1, Dyirbal has interrogative verbs which can make up the whole of a predicate—intransitive *wiyama-y* 'do what' and transitive *wiyama-l* 'do what to?', shown in (4). These can also be used together with a lexical verb, in a serial verb construction, and then mean 'do how (to)', illustrated in (5).

There are languages in which an interrogative verb is formed from an interrogative nominal by regular process of derivation. In the Australian language Kayardild (Evans 1995: 282–3, 371), the addition of inchoative *-wa-tha* to a nominal creates a verb; for example, *ngarrku* 'strong', *ngarrku-wa-tha* 'become strong, recover from illness'. When the inchoative process applies to *ngaaka* 'who, what', we get intransitive verb *ngaaka-wa-tha* 'do what'. In Yidiñ, also from Australia (Dixon 1977a: 364–8), both inchoative verbalizer *-daga-n* and causative verbalizer -ŋa-l can be added to wañin 'what, something', giving intransitive wañin-daga-n 'do what' and transitive wañin-ŋa-l 'do what to'.

There may be interrogative verbs with other meanings. In Tinrin (Austronesian, New Caledonia; Osumi 1995: 233), trò 'what is the matter with' functions 'as a verb, indicating that something is wrong with the subject and that the speaker is concerned about the matter'. (Note that 'the subject cannot be first person'.) For instance:

(93) nrâ trò   nrâ   rroto?
      3sg WHAT'S.THE.MATTER.WITH SUBJECT.MARKER car
      What's the matter with the car?

As mentioned in §27.6.2, in Salish languages all interrogative words appear as predicate heads within a relative clause construction; one could say that they are all verbs. Other languages have several verbs and several non-verbs among their interrogatives. For Jamul Tiipay (Diegueño branch of Yuman; California), Miller (2001: 174–9) lists three 'interrogative/indefinite pronouns':

- me'a   'where, somewhere'
- me'ap   'who, someone'
- maayiich   'what, something, anything'

and also five interrogative verbs (four of which also have an indefinite sense):

- ch-i   'to say what, to say something'
- ch-'i   'to be how many'
- ma'wi   'to do how, to do what, to do somehow, to do something'
- mu'yu(u)   'to be how, to be somehow'
- mu'yu(u)-i 'to be/do why, to be/do for some reason'

Or there can be just one interrogative verb with a wide range of meaning. In §20.9.1 we mentioned intransitive ee (-na-) in Jarawara which can, according to context, be taken to mean 'where' or 'how many'—see (91) above—or 'how are (you)' or 'is there any X'. The general meaning of 'X ee?' is 'what about X?'. One day I was helping two Jarawara men scoop out an itaúba tree to make a dug-out canoe. A third man came into the clearing and asked (Dixon 2004: 407):

(94) ee-ri   kanawaa$_S$?
      WHAT.ABOUT-CONTENT.Q:f canoe(f)
      How's the canoe coming on? (lit. What about the canoe?)

But most languages are like English, with no interrogative verbs at all. One has to use a transitive construction such as 'do WHAT$_O$' to convey what would be rendered by an intransitive interrogative verb in a language like Fijian or Dyirbal or Kayardild or Jamul Tiipay, and a ditransitive construction 'do WHAT_O to X' to translate a transitive interrogative verb.

27.6.5 Interrogative words as markers of relative clauses

What are often called *wh*-words in English comprise: *who* (with forms *whom* and *whose*), *what*, *which*, *why*, *how*, *where*, and *when*. They have a number of functions:

(a) As interrogative words.
(b) Introducing a *wh*-complement clause; for example, I_A *know* [*what John would like for his birthday*]$_{CoCl:O}$ and *We*$_A$ *didn't hear* [*why Mary resigned*]$_{CoCl:O}$.
(c) As marker of a relative clause, such as I_A *don't like* [*the man* [*who Mary married*]$_{RC}$]$_O$.
(d) As fusion of part of an NP and a relative clause marker. For example, I_A *noted down* [*the things* [*which she said*]$_{RC}$]$_O$ can be reduced to *I noted down what she said*. Suffix *-(so)ever* can be added to a *wh*-word in function (d), producing a more general meaning. Thus, *I noted down what(so)ever she said* relates to I_A *noted down* [*everything* [*which she said*]$_{RC}$]$_O$.

All of the *wh*-words may be used in (a) and (b) but *what* and *how* do not occur in function (c). These exceptions do have an explanation. In the discussion of 'who', 'what', and 'which' under (I) in §27.6.4, we contrasted the meanings of *what* and *which* as modifiers. It was noted that use of *what* implies unlimited choice (*what animal* could be any animal at all) while *which* indicates choice from a limited set (*which animal*, say of the pets in the house). A relative clause has specific reference and only admits the 'limited' form *which* (not 'unlimited' *what*). One would say I_A *like the car* [*which you bought*]$_{RC}$]$_O$, and not—in standard English—**I like the car what you bought*. And the exclusion of *how* from being the marker of a relative clause is due to the fact that it functions as an adverb, and adverbs do not occur as common arguments in relative clause constructions.

Most *wh*-words can occur in function (d). By virtue of being modifiers within an NP, *which* and *whose* lack this function. Also, *why* can be used as fused relative—*She*$_A$ *noted down* [*the reason* [*that he resigned*]$_{RC}$]$_O$ and *She noted down why he resigned*—but *whyever* is not so used.

The employment of interrogative words as relative clause markers is a feature of Indo-European languages, although it is not found in all of them (for example, not in Welsh). This trait is also found (sometimes only in limited form) in languages which are in contact with Indo-European tongues, in many cases presumably by calquing from them. For instance, Basque, Hebrew, Kabardian (North-west Caucasian family; Colarusso 1992: 69–71), Estonian, and Finnish (although here only *mikä* 'what' marks a relative clause: Sulkala and Karjalainen 1992: 285–7). In Georgian (Vogt 1971: 49), adding *-c(a)* to an interrogative word creates a relative clause marker, and in Hungarian (Kenesei, Vago, and Fenyvesi 1998: 281–2), adding prefix *a-* fulfils the same role. (And see §17.3.1.)

And the influence may be indirect. A number of East Tucanoan and Arawak languages in the Vaupes River basin of Brazil use interrogative words as markers of relative clauses. It is likely that they adopted this from Nhêengatú (or Língua Geral, a creolized version of Tupínambá), the erstwhile lingua franca of the area, which in turn would have calqued it from Portuguese, the language of the colonial invaders. (See Aikhenvald 2002: 165–6.)

27.7 Interrelations with other grammatical categories

Previous chapters have mentioned links between questions and other categories, which we can refer back to as appropriate.

(a) **Negation** is linked in a number of ways with questions. In §21.1 we saw that Karo has one negator for both imperatives and content questions, different from that for polar questions which is in turn different from that for declaratives. It was also noted—in §§21.1–2—that in Kham negator prefix *ma-* has developed a second function as marker of a polar question and that, in some varieties of Quechua, *-chu* is used as a negator and also to form polar questions.

In Rukai, the normal polar question construction involves negator *-ka* followed by a genitive pronoun (Zeitoun 2007: 355–6):

(95)   o-kane-nga-ka-'o?
       DYNAMIC-eat-ALREADY-NEGATOR-2sg:GENITIVE
       Have you already eaten?

Note that a 'dynamic' verb (such as 'eat' or 'jump' or 'give') takes prefix *o-* while a stative verb (such as 'ache', 'forget', 'be thirsty') takes prefix *ma-*.

In quite a number of languages, it is most polite to phrase a polar question in the negative—saying 'May I not enter?' rather than 'May I enter?'. This applies in, for instance, Ute (Givón 1984: 224–5), Japanese, Danish, and Russian (but not in Dutch or German). (See Chisholm 1984: 270–1.)

(b) **Person** is closely linked with interrogativity in conjunct/disjunct systems, described in §15.1.10. Conjunct marking is used with 1st person subject in statements and with 2nd person subject in questions. 'Subjective' and 'objective' marking in Mangghuer (described in §27.3) operates on a similar principle.

Discussing the West Greenlandic mood system, in §27.3, we noted that interrogative and declarative suffixes differ only when the S or A argument is 2nd person or when S, or both A and O, are 3rd person. In Jamul Tiipay (Miller 2001: 196–7), the clause-final interrogative clitic =chu ~ =chu'u ~ = chuum is used in polar and content questions, but only with 1st or 3rd person subject; for 2nd person subject, an auxiliary construction must be used instead.

Manipuri (Tibeto-Burman; Bhat and Ningomba 1997: 324) forms polar questions from declaratives by attaching -rə to the predicate. 'The question marker can also occur after imperative and prohibitive sentences, but in such a usage, they can only have a 1st person actor; that is, the questions are used by the speaker for obtaining permission for carrying out (or not carrying out) the relevant action, rather than for eliciting information'. For example:

(96) əy_A maŋon-də   ləphoy_O pi-yu-rə?
     1sg 3sg-LOCATIVE banana   give-IMPERATIVE-QUESTION
     Shall I give him/her a banana?

(c) **Number** distinctions are shown for some interrogative words in some languages. For example, there are separate singular and plural forms for 'who' and 'which' (but not for 'what') in Amele and Amharic; just for 'which' (not for 'who' and 'what') in Hausa; and singular, dual, and plural forms just for 'who' (with no number distinction for 'what, something') in Comanche. In Swahili, only 'which' and 'how many'—which are modifiers—take noun class prefixes, which include a specification for singular/plural. 'Which' in Supyire has forms marking simple/emphatic and five noun classes, with a singular/plural distinction in the three noun classes whose members are countable. Yagua (Peru; Payne 1990: 310–11) marks animate/inanimate on 'which' and, if animate, singular/dual/plural. In Tagalog all interrogative words have a plural form—created by reduplication—except for 'why' and 'where'.

When there is a number system applying to interrogatives, it may differ from the number system on pronouns—see the examples discussed in §20.4 and §20.6.2.

(d) **Tense and aspect** can interrelate with questions in several ways. They may determine the type of interrogative marking. In Ika (Chibchan,

Colombia; Frank 1990: 79) both polar and content questions are marked by a verb-phrase-final suffix or particle, with *-e* being employed for a question referring to recent past time, and *-o* or *no* for one referring to the present, future, or distant past. Under (b) in §27.5.1, we saw how in Maale question marking depends on aspect choice, illustrated in (29–30).

Secondly, there may be a reduced number of tense and/or aspect and/or modality choices in questions. In Hua (Papuan region; Haiman 1980: 165) the distinction between future indicative and subjunctive is neutralized in both polar and content questions. In Mojave (Yuman, California; Munro 1976: 72, 78, 88) present and past tense suffixes may not be included in content questions or 'neutral' polar questions (they do occur in a type of confirmatory polar question which expects an affirmative answer; this just involves particle *va:* added to a declarative sentence).

In §19.3, there was mention of the fascinating system in Kham, whereby *-ke* marks perfect and *-ya* future in a declarative clause, with these being reversed in an interrogative clause.

(e) **Evidentiality** may, as mentioned in §19.13, involve a system with fewer choices in questions than in statements. For instance, Tucano has a four-term system, {visual, non-visual sensory, inferred, reported}, in statements but there is no 'reported' term in the three-term system employed in questions. There is ample exemplification for this and other languages in Aikhenvald (2004: 72, 82, 85, 97–8, 103, 242–9, 255, and see further references therein).

When a statement with evidentiality specified is questioned, languages vary as to whether the information source is questioned from the point of view of the speaker or of the addressee (see Aikhenvald 2004: 242–9).

Declarative clauses in Jarawara may choose from three past tenses, {immediate past, recent past, far past}, with each being specified for eyewitness or non-eyewitness evidentiality. This six-term system is neutralized in certain subordinate clauses and in content questions, with just the immediate past non-eyewitness suffix being used (Dixon 2004: 196, 403).

(f) **Gender, noun classes and classifiers** may relate to questions in a number of ways. We saw in §27.3 that in Jarawara each inflection for mood—which include declarative, four imperatives, content interrogative, and two varieties of polar interrogative—agrees in gender with the pivot argument in the clause. Thus, 'Did John go?' takes the masculine and 'Did Mary go?' takes the feminine form of the neutral polar interrogative mood suffix.

Since 'who' has human reference, it is more likely than 'what' to have distinct masculine and feminine forms. Jarawara provides an instance of this—we have feminine *hibaka* and masculine *hibeke* for 'who', but gender-unspecified *himata* for 'what'.

In languages where a noun class system is marked on a number of word classes by affixation, some interrogatives may be included in the web. In §27.6.4, we saw that in Gurr-goni the wide-meaning interrogative -*nji* 'who, what, which' takes a noun class prefix indicating the kind of entity that is being asked about. And in the section just above on 'number', we noted that noun class is marked on 'which' and 'how many' in Swahili, and on 'which' in Supyire.

An interrogative 'how many' generally relates to the class of lexical number words. In languages where these must be accompanied by a 'numeral classifier', this also applies for 'how many', as mentioned above for Japanese—in (76)—and for Abun—in (77)—and for Tukang Besi—under (II) in §27.6.4.

In §5.7, there was discussion of how, in neutral circumstances, an interrogative which is not itself marked for gender will take on agreement for the unmarked member of the system of gender in that language. This was exemplified for masculine in Portuguese and feminine in Jarawara.

Yidiñ has two interrogatives 'what, something', at different levels of generality. *Wañi* is used to enquire about something about which nothing is known. *Wañirra* is employed when one knows what classifier something comes under and is enquiring about its species; it typically occurs with a classifier—for example, *wañirra miña* 'what kind of edible animal' or *wañirra mayi* 'what type of vegetable food' (Dixon 1977a: 184–5, 1982: 190–1).

(g) **Case inflection** on interrogatives is usually parallel to that on the word classes they correspond to. But interrogatives may show less, or else more, case distinctions. In Georgian, nouns have a six-term inflectional system—nominative, ergative, dative, genitive, instrumental, and adverbial. 'What' accords with this pattern. In contrast, 'who' has only two forms, one covering both nominative and ergative, and the other both dative and genitive (with nothing for instrumental or adverbial). Note that the 1sg pronoun has a single form for nominative, ergative, and dative, and a different one for genitive (Vogt 1971: 17–45).

In Dyirbal, 'what' inflects on an absolutive (S/O) – ergative (A) pattern, just like nouns and adjectives. In contest, 'who' has separate forms for the three core functions: S, A, and O. Singular pronouns also have three distinct forms in the southernmost dialect, Girramay, but non-singular pronouns in Girramay, and all pronouns in other dialects, show a nominative (S/A) – accusative (O) paradigm. Thus 'who' here has more case distinctions than pronouns, whereas it has fewer in Georgian.

(h) **Imperative** may be in a mood system with interrogative (the two terms being complementary). However, Whitney (1924: 215) shows how, in Sanskrit, 'the imperative is now and then used in an interrogative sentence'.

Tags are prototypically used in questions but English also has a kind of same-polarity tag which can be added to a command and keeps it as a command; it uses auxiliary *will*, as in *Go away, will you!* (see Aikhenvald 2010: 67–8, 284–5). Also, an interrogative construction can be used as a type of command; for example *Why don't you shut up!*

A rare example of structural similarity comes from the Tibeto-Burman language Mao Naga (Giridhar 1994: 451). The unmarked constituent orders in declarative clauses are AVO, SV but in imperatives and interrogatives orders OVA, VS are 'pretty common'. See also the techniques for negation in Karo,— mentioned under 'negation' above (and in §21.1)—linking imperatives with content questions; and the marking of an imperative with question suffix in Manipuri, illustrated in (96).

27.8 Pragmatic aspects

Questions—like commands—involve much more than segmental elements of speech. Nuances of intensity, rhythm, and timbre provide colour to a question, making it gentle or peremptory, perhaps expecting confirmation or denial. And in addition to actual sounds, one should pay attention to facial expression, direction of eye gaze, bodily gesture (such as splaying of the hands), and suchlike. Many factors need to be studied for a full understanding of the practical intent and effect of a question.

Communities with a strong politeness parameter in their culture, and thus in the grammar of their language, naturally extend this to questions. For example, in Japanese (Hinds 1984: 157) 'questions are either polite or nonpolite. In polite questions the morpheme *-masu* or *desu* is attached to a verbal, and the question particle *ka* follows. In nonpolite questions, the plain form of the verbal occurs, followed by the particle *ka*.' Under (a) in §27.7, we mentioned languages in which it is most polite to cast a polar question in the negative.

At the beginning of this chapter, we drew attention to some non-canonical correspondences between type of speech act and grammatical category. For example, a sentence in interrogative form may not expect an answer; it is often called a 'rhetorical question' (although it is not, strictly speaking, a question at all). For example, *Who am I to complain?* and *Why does it always rain just after we put the washing out to dry?* Quite a number of languages have a special rhetorical question marker; for example, the tag *-háʔwá* in Koasati was mentioned at the end of §27.2.

Greetings frequently have interrogative form, but are rhetorical in nature, expecting a phatic response rather than any informative answer. The greeting in English *How are you?* should be accorded a conventional response along the lines of *Pretty good, how are you?* (One would not, in normal circumstances, launch into an account of one's minor ailments.)

In other languages, greetings may be questions which do require an answer. In many Oceanic societies, when two people meet outside a village one will ask the other 'Where are you going?' (or, if it is clear that they are just about to enter a village, 'Where have you come from?'). The fieldworker is soon made to realize that the answer given must be truthful. Or else the fieldworker learns to get in quickly and be the person to ask the greeting question, in which case they need not disclose information about their own travelling intentions.

Questions should always be employed judiciously. To bombard someone with questions may be disconcerting, and sometimes appear to be threatening or even accusatory. Most people prefer to give out information at their own pace, rather than on demand. For example, in some Australian Aboriginal societies the conventional way to elicit information from another person is to first provide that information about oneself. Rather than enquire 'Where are you from?', one would say 'I'm from Biliyana', and the other person would naturally reply 'I'm from Labalaba'.

A full account of the pragmatics of questions would be a considerable undertaking. And there is also the matter of how different societies conventionally provide an answer to a question. For instance, in §3.11 we mentioned that in the Australian language Yidiñ, a reply to a question must be a full clause, with predicate and appropriate core arguments. In contrast, its southerly neighbour Dyirbal will prefer a single word response (often just 'yes' or 'no').

One fascinating matter is the choices available in various grammatical categories for questions and their corresponding responses. For example, in the Tucanoan language Tuyuca, a question—like a statement—may choose any of the five evidentiality values. However, when a response is employed as a 'conversation sustainer', only three choices are available. Thus (Aikhenvald 2004: 86–7):

(97)　EVIDENTIALITY　　　CORRESPONDING SPECIFICATION
　　　 SPECIFICATION IN　　IN 'CONVERSATION SUSTAINER'
　　　 QUESTION　　　　　　RESPONSES

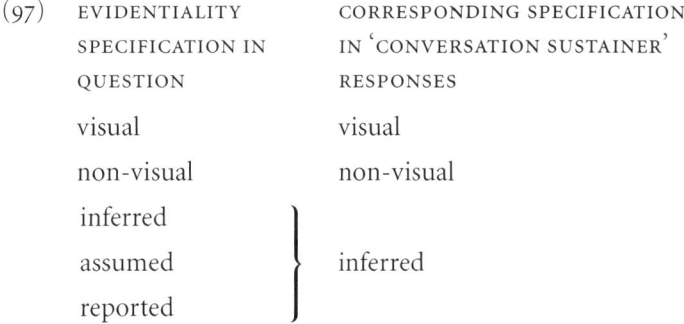

EVIDENTIALITY SPECIFICATION IN QUESTION	CORRESPONDING SPECIFICATION IN 'CONVERSATION SUSTAINER' RESPONSES
visual	visual
non-visual	non-visual
inferred	
assumed	inferred
reported	

27.9 Summary

Curiosity is a characteristic of all humankind. One way of gaining information is through asking questions. It appears that every language has two types of question. There are polar (or 'yes/no') questions which present a statement and seek confirmation (or denial) of it. And there are content questions which seek information about an argument of a clause (or about the predicate).

A polar question may be general in scope ('Did John steal a Honda?'), or it may be focussed, enquiring about the reference of a particular constituent ('Was it a Honda that John stole?'). Some languages make much use of alternative questions, 'Is it this or is it that?'

Just a few languages have an inflectional system of mood, which includes one or more interrogative terms. Otherwise, polar questions may be marked with a special phonological or morphological feature, a particle, a tag, a distinctive constituent order, or just a special intonation tune. This last always involves rising pitch somewhere towards the end of the sentence (it may be followed by a final fall).

A content question includes an interrogative word, such as 'who', 'what', 'which', 'how many/much', 'why', 'how', 'where', or 'when'. Quite often, such words also have a specific or general indefinite sense—for example, 'who, someone' or 'who, anyone'. In a very limited set of languages, the marker of a relative clause may have the same form as an interrogative word. A content question may also—but need not—be indicated in some other way, essentially covering the same possibilities as polar questions. There may be the same or different marking for the two varieties of question.

There can be intricate interrelations between questions and various grammatical categories, including negation; person; number; tense and aspect; evidentiality; gender, noun class and classifiers; case; and imperatives.

Vocal timbre and bodily comportment play a large role in the pragmatic effect of questions. Some desired piece of information is often best obtained by gentle or indirect means, rather than through officious interrogation.

27.10 What to investigate

I. Perhaps the easiest place to begin is with the identification of **interrogative words**. As discussed in §27.6.3, we can recognize eight canonical forms:

who   what   why   where
which   how many/how much   how   when

Not every language has exactly this set. For example, 'why' may be rendered by 'for what'. In English 'how many' involves *how* plus the number adjective *many*, parallel to *how big* and *how clever*. Not infrequently, one form combines 'what' and 'which'; and in a few languages 'who' and 'what' are two senses of a single interrogative word.

Some languages also have interrogative verb(s) 'do what (to)' and 'do how (to)'.

Matters to study include:

(a) Do some or all interrogative words also have an **indefinite sense**? If so, is it **specific indefinite** (for example, 'someone') or **general indefinite** ('anyone', 'everyone'), or both? Can reasons be given for the interrogative sense being primary, or the indefinite sense being primary, or the two senses being of equal significance?

(b) What **word class** does each interrogative word relate to, in terms of its system of inflection or other grammatical properties? For instance 'how many' is typically linked to the set of lexical numbers, and may form an ordinal in the same way as them ('the how-many-th', parallel to 'the fifth', and so on). 'What' is generally associated with the class of nouns. 'Who' patterns like a pronoun in some languages but like a noun in others.

(c) In addition to their association with regular word classes, all interrogative words will **share certain features**, establishing them as a pan-basic-word-classes word class. Attention should be paid to identifying these features.

(d) What are the **syntactic possibilities** for interrogative words? In many languages an interrogative word occupies the position in surface structure appropriate to its function. In a smaller number of languages, it must be moved to the front of the sentence (as a kind of topicalization). In a few cases there is a special (often, copula-type) construction (for example, 'The people who voted are who?').

(e) Only rather seldom does each interrogative word have a totally distinct **form**. There are typically one or more recurrent elements (such as *wh-* in English), although these may not be susceptible to morphological analysis. A number of languages have some interrogative words in a **paradigm** with demonstratives ('this one' and 'that one' patterning like 'which one', and so on). These possibilities should be investigated.

(f) Investigate what **other functions** (if any) interrogative words have in the grammar. For example, in a few languages some interrogative words (or their homonyms) may introduce relative clauses. In §27.6.5—building on what was said under (I) in §27.6.4—we explained why in standard English *which* can mark a relative clause whereas *what* cannot do so.

II.   A **polar question** lacks anything like an interrogative word and must thus have some distinctive marking. Investigate the possibilities, which may include one or more of:

- a special phonological or morphological feature
- a polar question particle
- a tag
- distinctive constituent order
- special intonation or pitch pattern

Note that it is not sufficient just to describe the intonation tunes of questions. These must be always contrasted with the intonational possibilities for statements and commands.

One of the devices for marking polar questions may also apply for content questions, or the two varieties of question may employ a similar means with different form. This matter should be carefully examined. If an interrogative word also has an indefinite sense, then employment of a question-marking stratagem should assist in disambiguation.

Just a few languages have an inflectional system for mood marking— declarative, imperative, interrogative (and there may be further terms in the system). Study whether interrogative mood inflection applies just for polar questions, or for both polar and content varieties, or whether there are two interrogative mood inflections, one for each type of question.

III.   Study the **subtypes of polar question**. First, there should be some way of focussing on one constituent, and this must be looked into. It may involve a special marker, or just stress (an example from English is *Did McTavish eat the haggis yesterday?*).

Some languages have a range of polar question markers, relating to such things as whether confirmation or denial is expected, whether there is an element of surprise or disbelief, and so on. Alternative questions are a favourite construction type in some languages—either of the type 'Are you going or staying?' or 'Are you going or not going?' If these can be identified, their structure and conditions for use require careful examination.

IV.   If anything can be stated about the **historical origin** of interrogative elements, this is of course useful information. Very little has been said on it in the present chapter. We did note, in §27.5.4, that 'or' from an alternative question may develop into a straightforward polar question marker.

It is also relevant to study the areal distribution of types of interrogative patternings, to investigate what is likely to diffuse as a consequence of language contact.

V.   As a natural aspect of writing a comprehensive and integrated grammar, the **interrelations** between questions and all manner of other grammatical categories should be studied. In §27.7 we briefly surveyed: negation; person;

number; tense and aspect; evidentiality; gender, noun class and classifiers; case; and imperatives. There may be more besides.

VI.   The manner in which people in a particular speech community provide **answers** to questions is something else to be investigated.

The **pragmatic effect** of a question, or of an answer, depends on the way it is delivered—construction type chosen, timbre of voice, and also associated facial and bodily gestures. This is a matter to which few grammars have paid any attention. It will provide a fertile domain for study.

VII.   A number of other topics are suitable for study. These include: sentences in interrogative form which do not expect an answer (so-called 'rhetorical questions'), interrogative sentences used as a type of command, and 'echo questions'.

Sources and notes

There have been few general, cross-linguistic discussions of questions. Chisholm (1984) is a most useful compilation, including studies of 'seven diverse languages'. Ultan (1978) is based on a limited sample of languages and lacks depth. Huddleston (2002) provides an instructive account of questions in English.

27.1   A variety of other labels have been employed for polar and content questions. For example, they have been referred to as 'closed' and 'open' questions respectively. In English, all interrogative words (except for *how*) begin with *wh-* and, as a consequence, content questions are often referred to as '*wh*-questions'. Unfortunately, there has arisen the deplorable habit of using '*wh*-questions' to label content questions in languages other than English (whose interrogative words do not begin with *wh-*).

Sometimes, the term 'interrogative pronouns' is misleadingly used for all interrogative words, irrespective of which major word class they relate to; see §15.1.

Most grammatical elements (forms belonging to small, closed classes) cannot be questioned. But those terms which can be head of an NP—pronouns and demonstratives—may be questioned in the same way as nouns.

Further examples of interrogative verbs *wiyama-y/-l* in Dyirbal will be found in Dixon (1972: 55–6).

27.2   In §21.2, we drew attention to the association between negative and polar question marking in another variety of Quechua, Imbabura Quechua. Examples (72–3) in §21.3.2 illustrate negation in Huallaga Quechua.

The grammar of Koasati (Kimball 1991) makes no mention of the intonation for questions. It could be inferred that there is no special intonation tune. Certainly, with the glottal-insertion morphological process for marking both polar and content questions, nothing else is needed.

27.3   In Lyons (1977. ii: 748, my italicization) we read: 'in none of the languages with which traditional grammar has been concerned, *and possibly in no attested language*, is there a distinct mood that stands in the same relation to questions as the imperative does to [com]mands'. Lyons was just not familiar with the literature; the Tonkawa grammar had been published more than forty years before, and informed descriptions of Eskimo had been available for a couple of hundred years.

Fortescue (1984: 4–24) provides detailed information on the intonation of questions in West Greenlandic. Note that mood inflections apply only to verbal (not verbless clauses) and are linked to polarity marking. Sadock (1984) gives details of all this and also of questioning from subordinate clauses, etc.

For Mangghuer, Slater (2003: 353) states: 'due to a lack of natural information data, the important suprasegmental feature of intonation will not be treated in this book.'

Mithun (1999: 171–2) provides examples of interrogative mood inflections in two further North American languages, Maidu and Cheyenne.

27.5.1   Maale (Amha 2001: 126–8, 155–8) has three varieties of imperative ('regular', 'polite', and 'impolite'), each marked by a verbal suffix (which replaces the declarative suffix). This language could be said to have a mood system, albeit with rather unusual realization of interrogative.

Quirk et al. (1985: 810–14) and Huddleston (2002: 891–7) have informative accounts of tags in English. 'Using an extensive corpus of conversational data', Geluykens (1988) shows 'that the role of Rising intonation ... in polar questions [in English] is overrated'. See (h) in §27.7 for mention of tags used with imperatives in English.

There have been reports of languages where the marking for polar questions does not involve any rise in intonation. In a note to their account of questions in Mandarin Chinese, Li and Thompson (1984: 60) state: 'the opposite of marking questions with a rising intonation is found in Chitimacha, an American Indian language of Louisiana, where declarative sentences have a rising intonation and questions have a falling intonation.' (No reference is given for this information on Chitimacha). Siemund (2001: 1013) repeats this misinformation: 'in Chitimacha, apparently, interrogative intonation has a falling contour whereas declarative intonation has a rising contour'. (Again no reference is given and note the inclusive of 'apparently', perhaps indicating a modicum of doubt.) In fact, Swadeshs's (1934: 353–4) account of the Musko-gean language Chitimacha states that a question or a command bears high pitch on the penultimate or ante-penultimate syllable (this being phonolog-ically conditioned), with the pitch then falling. Just like Hixkaryana, West Greenlandic, Tamambo, and Jarawara, there *is* a rise on pitch, and it comes just before the end of the sentence.

Looking just at page 121 of the short grammar of Lote (Austronesian, Papua New Guinea; Pearson 2008) one reads that polar questions 'are signalled by a falling intonation on the last syllable of the sentence.' However, page 14 states: 'questions end on a high + low falling tone contour. Statements and commands end on a low tone.' Once more there is high pitch involved in the marking of a polar question. It is, of course, not impossible that a language will be found with a distinctive intonation tune for polar questions (differing from that for statements) which does not involve any sort of high pitch, but none is known to me at present.

27.5.3 Enfield (2007a: 44–52) describes and exemplifies a variety of polar question particles in Lao. One is unmarked, another asks 'do I rightly take this to be the case', a third is 'surely I'm correct in thinking this to be the case', a fourth is 'this is the case, don't you agree' (and there are three or more further possibilities).

27.6.1 Bhat (2000b) provides a thoughtful discussion of what he called 'the indefinite-interrogative puzzle'.

Lehmann (1993: 102–9, 233) lists eighteen interrogative words in Tamil. Adding -*oo* to these forms a specific indefinite—thus *yaar* 'who' and *yaar-oo* 'someone'. And adding -*aavatu* creates what Lehmann calls a 'non-specific indefinite referential'—*yaar-aavatu* 'someone or other' (as in 'Someone or other will build a house here'). This appears to be something between a specific and a general indefinite.

Many other languages have interrogative words which also carry an indef-inite sense. Indeed, Szemerényi (1996: 208–10) states that in proto-Indo-European the interrogative pronoun 'also served as indefinite'. He adds that in some languages 'it is used additionally as relative, either without … or with formal differentiation'.

27.6.3 Diessel (2003) provides further examples of languages with interroga-tives and demonstratives in the same paradigm.

Ashéninka Perené (Arawak, Peru; Mihas 2010: 175–81) has *niNka* 'who' and a general interrogative word *tsika* in terms of which all other interrogative con-cepts are expressed. Cysouw (2007) shows how the related Pichis Ashéninka lacks *niNka* so that here *tsika* is the sole base for all interrogative words (see his informative table 1). We now await a full account of Pichis Ashéninka, so that the interrogative system can be viewed in proper grammatical perspective.

Iraqw (Mous 1993: 120–1) has interrogative words, *milá* 'what' and *magá* 'how many'. Apart from these, it is like Ewe is adding interrogative marker *-má* or *-lá* to a noun, e.g. *aamá* 'where' from *aamo* 'place', *heemá* 'who' from *hee* 'man (male human)'.

27.6.4   Fuller details of interrogatives in Boumaa Fijian are in Dixon 1988: 169–74, 114–16, 96–7, 270–1). There is also *naica* 'when'. I did not encounter this with *soti* nor in a complement clause; however, further research may well uncover these properties.

Hagége (2008) includes information on interrogative verbs. However, all the materials he quotes require to be checked against primary sources (for instance the 'Dyirbal' forms in his table 3 are not recognizable as coming from that language).

27.6.5   *What* is in fact used with function (c) in some low-prestige dialects of English, for example, *I like the car what you bought*. There is extensive discussion of relative clauses in English in Huddleston, Pullum and Peterson (2002).

In India, one can observe the expansion of using interrogative words as relative clause markers. Bhat (1989a: 356) remarks: 'most of the grammarians of Dravidian languages consider the corelative relative clauses, containing wh-words functioning as relative pronouns, to have developed rather recently as a result of Indo-Aryan influence. They also consider these constructions to be marginal and unnatural in these Dravidian languages'. There is a similar construction in Ho, a Munda language spoken in India: 'this device of attaching the yes-no question particle to wh- words to form relative pronouns can also be used in Ho, but according to Deeney (1975), such constructions are used only by "people who become accustomed to thinking in Hindi and Hindi thought patterns" ' (Bhat 1989a: 484).

27.7   Currently, I know of no language which has a negator for polar and content questions that is of different form from negators for other clause types. However, I would not be at all surprised were such a language to be uncovered.

Mithun (1999: 173–80) has a fine account of the relations between realis/irrealis and questions in North American languages. The note to §19.4 states that in Caddo content questions are marked as realis but polar questions as irrealis.

The notes to §19.3 mention Munro's (1987: 127) claim that Chickasaw appears to have more tense/aspect distinctions in polar interrogatives than in declaratives.

Vogt's (1971) 'nominative' case in Georgian corresponds to 'absolutive' in more modern usage.

Nasilov, Isxakova, Safarov, and Nevskaja (2001: 217) mention that, in some Turkic languages, 'a rhetorical question can also be expressed with imperative verb forms of the 1st or 3rd person sg/pl, and an interrogative pronoun'.

27.8   Enfield, Stivers, and Levinson (2010) provides insightful studies of question-response sequences in conversation across ten languages.

28

Language and the world— explanations now and needed

For all human beings, using language is an integral part of living. Language plays a fundamental role in satisfying physical needs, ensuring social integration, and maintaining a mental balance. Language is an essential tool as we interact with the world around.

The important point in all this is that language only has existence with respect to the physical and mental order of things. Language is not any sort of independent system, to be tapped into as required. Aspect of language have significance only as they relate to aspects of the world.

A description of a language must indicate the role it plays for its community of users. Investigation of why some parameter within a language is the way it is should seek for an explanation partly within the overall structure of the language and partly in the way that language correlates with things outside it. Prediction of how a language may be likely to change in the future will pay attention to internal forces and also to outside, societal, pressures. Evaluation of the relative worth of several languages must take account not only of their communicative content, but also of how well these relate to the needs and predispositions of their communities of speakers.

All human beings share a commonality of activities. Everyone eats and drinks; walks, runs and jumps; sits and stands; laughs and cries; hits and cuts and burns someone or something; tells a piece of news and tells lies; feels happy or jealous or ashamed.

There are also significant points of difference between societies. Only some have the idea of a supreme being, a god, and the habit of praying to it. Only some embrace a classificatory kinship system where everyone in a community is related—by a kind of algorithm—to everyone else in the community, with each type of relationship carrying a specific set of social obligations. Many societies embrace the custom of competition between people (and between teams of people) with concomitant ideas of winning and losing; such a practice is entirely alien to many other societies. One community may consider it quite improper to sit on a pillow, an object on which one's head has lain. And so on. All of these differences are reflected in language.

Each language is just a partial means of expression, being able to directly convey only a portion of possible meaning contrasts (that is, only a portion of the sum of meaning contrasts added up over all known languages). A semantic distinction is likely to be coded in a language if it is salient for the people using that language. As Sapir (1912: 230) puts it: 'everything naturally depends on the point of view, as determined by interest'.

Just as what speakers code in their language relates to the way in which they view the world, so the way in which a linguist describes a language is dependent upon their interests and inclinations. There is, of course, the difference between the aims and methods of 'formalists' and those of scholars who treat linguistics as a science, with a cumulative theory built up by inductive generalization (see §1.2). We are here only concerned with the latter.

Across Africa, Asia, North America, Meso-America, South America, and New Guinea, there are some thousands of 'tone languages', which employ pitch variation to carry lexical and grammatical meanings. Such languages are spoken by peoples inhabiting widely different environments and with every kind of culture. There is no correlation between 'having a system of tones' and any extra-linguistic parameter, such as lifestyle.

Some languages in northern Europe show 'pitch accent' but most scholars would agree that, properly speaking, there are no tone languages in Europe. Most linguists come from a European-style background. As a consequence, there is a tendency to view tone systems as rather exotic, something outside the normal run of things, perhaps as a sort of optional extra to the grammatical and lexical apparatus of a language.

Such a Eurocentric attitude is misguided. Tones are a wonderful vehicle for conveying meaning. As the distinguished linguist Yuen Ren Chao (1976: 88) put it: 'since every word has some pitch pattern anyway, we might as well make use of it without any extra cost in time. A Chinese word is a sort of ice-cream cone; since you have paid for the cone as well as for the ice-cream, you might as well eat it'.

Attitudes to adjective classes also tend to show a decidedly Eurocentric bias. As described in Chapter 12, an adjective class can have grammatical properties in common with nouns—as in the familiar languages of Europe—or with verbs (or, less often, with both or with neither). When documenting a previously undescribed language, linguists are happy to use the label 'adjective' for a word class grammatically similar to nouns, but are often reluctant to employ this label for a word class grammatically similar to verbs (and thus markedly different from adjective classes in European languages). Instead of 'adjectives', labels such as 'statives' and 'descriptive verbs' have been employed (see §12.2).

A few languages have two adjective classes, one grammatically similar to nouns and the other to verbs. This is found in the Tibeto-Burman language Manange. In their detailed and instructive account of this language, Genetti and Hildebrandt (2004) call the former class just 'adjectives' and the latter one 'verb-like adjectives'. It is as if being noun-like does not have to be stated, since it is taken to be the default profile.

These treatments of tone and of adjective classes are current. Further in the past, attitudes to reduplication were quaintly Eurocentric. What could be more straightforward and useful than a grammatical process which involves repeating all or part of a form before or after (or in the middle of) it, and can convey any of a range of meanings? (See (2) in §3.13.) A productive process of reduplication is not found in the well-known languages of Europe. When Europeans began to explore the linguistic riches of Africa, Asia, and the Pacific they found that almost every language there makes copious use of this process. It was condemned as simplistic and childish, only what one would expect from a society at an early stage of civilization, speaking a language that was in many cases branded as 'primitive'.

But suppose that reduplication had been a characteristic of the languages of Europe and almost unknown elsewhere. It would surely then have been regarded as the acme of morphological sophistication, and the lack of reduplication in the languages of peoples whose skins were not altogether white would have been taken as an index of their primitiveness. (Tails I win, heads you lose.)

The reader needs to be made aware of such biases (of which only a sample have been mentioned). We can now move on to cross-linguistic investigations, which are made (hopefully) on a balanced basis.

28.1 What we can say

Explanations begin at home. One part of a grammar naturally relates to the whole. We can begin by recapitulating some earlier observations.

In §3.19, there was a survey of dependencies between grammatical systems, whereby the range of choices available in one system may depend on the choice that is made from a further system. A number of dependencies were noted, and shown to have a principled basis. Systems of person, number, and noun class (call these set III) are all associated with the noun phrase; there can be dependencies in any direction between them. Tense, aspect, and evidentiality (set II) relate equally to predicate and to clause; there can be dependencies in any direction between them. The contrast between positive and negative (polarity, set I) relates to the clause.

A clause includes a predicate which takes a number of arguments, realized by NPs. This chain of requirement provides a natural explanation for inter-set dependencies—systems in set III may depend upon those in set II or set I, and those in set II may depend upon polarity in set I.

The topic of transitivity profile (Chapter 13) is linked with that of syntactic derivations which change valency (Chapters 22–5). In a language whose verbs have strict transitivity, there are likely to be a number of ways of deriving a transitive stem from an intransitive root and/or vice versa. Such derivations are less needed, and are less likely to be encountered, in a language where many verbs are ambitransitive (of type S = O or S = A), occurring in both intransitive and transitive clause types.

In similar vein, a language for which many verbs have secondary function as head of an NP is likely to have a less rich set of nominalizing derivations than one in which a verb may only function as predicate head. And, contrariwise, if a fair number of nouns have secondary function as head of an intransitive predicate, there are likely to be fewer verbalizing derivations than in a language where nouns are restricted to being NP heads.

Why do some language have passive derivations, some antipassives, a few both and others neither (Chapter 23)? Both types of derivation have a range of functions, which include 'feeding' a pivot requirement. Passive may feed an S/A pivot and thus is often—although by no means exclusively—found in languages of this ilk. Similarly for antipassive and S/O; languages which work in terms of an S/O pivot are extremely likely to include an antipassive derivation which will feed the pivot.

All observations of the last few paragraphs deal in tendencies. Unlike the hard sciences, the science of linguistics includes few absolutely definitive tenets. Rather, each language can be characterized as the intertwining of a series of pervasive proclivities.

However, there are a few universal features. One of these is the distinction between grammar and lexicon, two complementary but interlocking components of every language; see §1.11.

The main components of a grammar are closed systems (of limited size). Each term in a system has meaning with respect to the others. It can be specified as not being any of the others. For example, in a three-term number system something which is 'not singular' and 'not plural' must be 'dual'. Looking at the system of demonstratives in English, something which is 'not this', 'not those' and 'not these' must be 'that'. Grammatical values can be expressed by affixes and other morphological processes or by separate words (like demonstratives in English and other languages). Or a grammatical item may only be *written* as a word (in terms of the orthographic conventions of its language; see §10.2). For example, in the great majority of its occurrences, *the* in English is not a separate phonological word at all, but an unstressed proclitic, ðə= (as in ðə=*mæn* 'the man').

In contrast, a lexicon involves listing the members of open word classes, such as noun, verb, and adjective, each of which has a potentially unlimited set of members. A dictionary is an alphabetical list of all lexemes in the language. Ideally, grammar and dictionary should be compiled in concert with cross-referencing between them. It is inappropriate to include grammatical items in a dictionary, since their paradigmatic associations and functional roles in the language will be fully specified in the grammar. Unfortunately, grammars and dictionaries of well-spoken languages tend to be compiled by different groups, working quite apart from each other. An example to be followed is Capell's (1941) bilingual dictionary and Churchward's (1941) grammar of Fijian. Typically, an English dictionary will include the grammatical form *the*, treating it as if it were a lexeme (something that is absolutely unsatisfactory). But for the 'common article' *na* in Fijian, Capell's (1941: 152) sensibly refers the reader to §§I.3.1–4 of Churchward's grammar.

There are many manifestations of the distinction between grammar and lexicon. As pointed out in §27.1, it is generally possible to directly question each lexeme in a sentence, but not most grammatical forms and values. Individual languages can manifest the grammar/lexicon distinction in fascinating ways. The avoidance (or 'mother-in-law') style of Dyirbal, mentioned in §5.1, had to be used in the presence of any of a set of tabooed relatives. The avoidance style has the same phonology, grammar (including affixes and separate grammatical words such as pronouns, demonstratives, and particles like *gulu* 'not' and *yanda* 'tried but failed') and proper names as the everyday language style. But all lexemes—verbs, adjectives, and common nouns (except for the four grandparent terms)—have different forms in the two speech styles. (This is illustrated by (1) in §5.1.)

We have been mainly focussing, in these volumes, on the underlying organization of a language, rather than on its surface manifestation. But it is interesting to enquire concerning motivation for different orders of constituents.

The predicate is the heart of a clause, determining how many core arguments there should be, and their nature. For instance, intransitive verb *laugh* calls for a single core argument, whose referent should be a person or certain kinds of animal or bird. Transitive verb *drink* entails an O argument referring to a liquid, and an animate A argument. Logically, it would surely be ideal to state the predicate first in a clause, and follow it with the core arguments.

But a remarkably small number of languages are predicate-initial. Why is this so? The answer lies in the fact that discourse is organized around a topic, and there is a cross-linguistic preference (although not unanimity) that the topic should be stated before anything else. Let us first of all know what is being talked about, and then find out what is being said about it. The subject (in S or A function) tends to be the favoured sentence-commencer (although in languages with an S/O pivot, it may be an argument in one of these functions).

What about types of affix? Much has been written (none of it fully convincing) about why suffixing is more common cross-linguistically than prefixing. One should really focus on the kinds of grammatical information realized through affixes. Case affixes which mark the core argument status of a noun (phrase) are predominantly suffixes. First one wants to know what the NP refers to, and then what its function is with respect to the predicate. In a fair number of languages, case suffixes for core arguments occur together with prepositions for marking peripheral arguments. 'Mary-NOMINATIVE planted roses-ACCUSATIVE' is the core of the sentence. Then where did she do it? 'In (PREPOSITION)' - ah, in something, in what? 'The front garden'. But this explanation is rather ad hoc. The topic requires detailed study, not looking at prefixing/suffixing in general, but investigating what happens for each type of grammatical item.

28.2 Why things are the way they are

As outlined in §1.6. the make-up of a language stems from a combination of factors. First there is genetic history; each language inherits certain features—but may have lost others—from the ancestral proto-language. Secondly, social contact between speakers of adjacent languages leads to structural patterns, and techniques of semantic organization, diffusing from one to the other. The third factor is that each language is likely to mirror, to some extent, the habitat of the speech community and the way in which its speakers live and view the world.

These factors interrelate. What is kept and lost in terms of genetic inheritance may be motivated by contact issues and by the need to reflect habitual activities and attitudes. If adjacent language communities share certain rituals, they may evolve similar linguistic protocols in connection with them.

There are a couple of environmental factors which are often reflected in a grammar. As illustrated in §1.6, a language spoken in hilly country may specify not only relative distance ('here' versus 'there') but also relative height ('lower', 'on same level', or 'higher' than speaker). And there is sometimes grammatical specification with respect to water: out to sea versus towards the inland; away from or towards a major river; upstream or downstream. It would be instructive to investigate whether there are other ways in which the type of country inhabited by a community is reflected in their grammar.

Small societies are often divided into subsistence types, such as 'hunters and gatherers' and 'agriculturalists'. If such categorization has any validity, it does not (as far as I have been able to ascertain) carry any structural linguistic implications. Even lexical distinctions are slight. Hunters and gatherers harvest, prepare, and cook foodstuffs. It is true that agriculturalists need words for 'plant' and 'weed'. But the verb 'plant' may also be used for 'set a stick upright in the ground (as when building a house frame)', a verb also needed by hunters and gatherers.

The following sections outline the ways in which lifestyle may be reflected in language—habitual activities (§28.2.1), social organization and kinship (§28.2.2), religion (§28.2.3), ways of viewing the world (§28.2.4), and modes of speaking (§28.2.5). Then, in §28.2.6, we consider the different make-ups of languages spoken by large and by small populations.

28.2.1 Habitual activities

The lexicon of a language reflects what its speakers engage in. As mentioned in §1.6, cattle herders have an elaborate vocabulary for types of livestock and the many kinds of skin coloration and patterning by which they may be identified. A society in which weaving plays a major role will have nouns and verbs describing every aspect of this activity.

Hunting equipment varies between cultures. Spears are the major implement in Australia; six specialized verbs of spearing in Dyirbal were set out in §6.5. The Jarawara in Amazonia lack spears, instead using blow-guns and bows and arrows (these are unknown in Australia), with an appropriate set of verbs.

Both Dyirbal and Jarawara live in rainforest and gather the rich variety of fruit and vegetables which grow there. Speakers of Dyirbal simply pick and dig. But trees in the Jarawara's forest are considerably taller than in Australia, and additional techniques have been devised. For instance, one sense of the verb *jaa -na-* is '(climb a tree and) stand on a branch, shaking it with one's foot so that fruit attached to the branch fall to earth'. In a story about a woman gathering fruit, we hear:

(1) to-ko-misa,   akori$_o$ jaa   na,   wa-re
     AWAY-in.motion-UP:f fruit   shake   AUX:f stand-RAISED.SURFACE
     She climbed up (a tree), and shook akori fruit off, she was standing on
        a branch (lit. She went up, she shook the fruit off, she was standing
        on a raised surface (that is, a tree branch))

Across the world, many societies—both large and small—are imbued with the notion of 'competition'. This can relate to races or other sports, or just to prowess in daily activities. One person tries to be better than another, to win. Naturally, there is then an appropriate stock of lexemes: 'race', 'compete', 'win', 'lose', 'victor', 'victory', and so on. In contrast, there any many small egalitarian communities—including both Dyirbal and Jarawara—for which ideas of competition, or winning, or triumphing, are totally alien. They simply lack such lexemes.

This may also have consequences within the grammar. Chapter 26 describes a wide variety of comparative constructions, along the lines of 'John is cleverer/taller than Felix'. Languages whose speakers indulge in competition are likely to use a grammar which includes a specific comparative construction, be it mono-clausal (§26.2) or bi-clausal (§26.3.1). By and large, languages whose speakers eschew explicit competition are likely to lack a comparative construction and instead employ a strategy such as 'John is clever, Felix is stupid' or 'Felix is clever; John is very clever' (§26.3.2).

I am not suggesting that there is a one-to-one connection between notions of competitiveness and having a comparative construction. Like most linguistic generalizations, we have here a tendency.

Extra-linguistic considerations can be stated more widely. From examination of many languages and peoples, the following tentative inductive generalization may be put forward. The more complex a society is, in terms of (a) material culture; (b) a stratified economic and political system, with money, an articulated social hierarchy, and the like, the more likely it is to have one or more dedicated comparative constructions. Competitiveness tends to be linked in with (a) and, more especially, (b).

28.2.2 Social organization and kinship

The manner in which something is stated depends on the profiles of speaker and addressee, the relationship between them, and also the nature of what is being discussed.

Suppose that John has just received a welcome message from a grant-giving body. First he calls his mum, talking to her in the way he always does:

(2) I've been given a pile of dough to find out why lingos die

Then, at a faculty meeting later that day he informs his colleagues by saying:

(3) I have just been awarded a substantial grant to study language death

In fact the summary at the beginning of the application for this grant reads:

(4)   The project will pursue a transgenetic methodology encompassing both investigation of the circumstances pertaining to linguistic obsolescence and factors militating against post-demise resuscitation

Each of these is rather posher than the previous one. High-flown speech in English is characterized by using many words of Romance origin (from various stages of French, or directly from Latin). A straightforward statement uses mostly native words, of Germanic origin.

All the words in (2) are Germanic except for the colloquial *lingo* (which came originally from Latin). In (3) there is a single Germanic lexeme, *death*, the remainder being all of Romance origin. In the actual application, (4), John attempted (successfully) to impress by sticking entirely to non-native lexemes.

Every language has varying styles for speaking to different types of people. (One universal feature is that there is always a simplified mode for addressing a small child.) But why, one may ask, should it be prestigious in English to use a profusion of long, non-Germanic words? The answer goes back almost a thousand years. When William the Conqueror vanquished speakers of Old English (in 1066), he brought with him a new culture. For a couple of centuries, the people in power spoke Anglo-Norman, a variety of French. When everyone began to speak English, about 1400 CE, the increasing Romance element continued to merit esteem. And so it continues today.

The differences between (2), (3), and (4) are motivated by the nature of the addressee. Many languages go further; the relative social status of speakers—and the nature of the interaction between them—is shown in the grammar. There may be a single indicator, as in a number of modern European languages which have a distinction of formality in the 2nd person pronoun. In French, for instance, *tu* is used to address relatives, children, servants, and friends, with *vous* being used otherwise. (A difficulty concerns deciding when a friendship is ripe enough to switch from formal *vous* to more intimate *tu*.)

How do such distinctions arise, and why may they be lost? We can attempt an answer in the case of English. For Old English there was, originally, simply a distinction of number for 2nd person pronouns—*thou* (nominative), *thee* (accusative), *thy* (possessive) in the singular, and *ye* (nominative), *you* (accusative), *your* (possessive) in the plural. In the thirteenth century, when high-echelon speakers began to use English as well as (and then instead of) Anglo-Norman, a formality contrast for 2nd person was taken over from French: 'the singular forms (*thou*, *thee*, *thy*) were used among familiars and in addressing children or persons of inferior rank, while the plural forms (*ye*, *you*, *your*) began to be used as a mark of respect in addressing a superior' (Baugh 1959: 292–3). Over the next couple of centuries, as Sweet (1892: 102) describes it, the use of *you* 'was so much extended that it became the usual polite form of address' with *thou* 'being used mainly to express familiarity and contempt, which latter use brought about its complete disuse in the spoken language'. By the sixteenth century *thou* survived only in archaic-sounding high-flown poetry and prose, and in sundry religious contexts.

A number of large-scale societies in South, South-east, and East Asia have an articulated system of social hierarchies, and grammatical markers to express these. Illustration was provided in §1.6 for Bengali, which has distinct 'intimate', 'ordinary', and 'honorific' forms for the 2nd person pronoun (in both singular and plural), and also 'ordinary' and 'honorific' forms for 3sg and 3pl. And in §15.1.5, 'Social niceties', we mentioned languages such as Japanese, Thai, and Khmer. In addition to honorific pronouns, there may be special forms used between specific speech act participants (such as a layman speaking to a monk, a monk speaking to a layman).

Sohn (1994: 9–10, 33; 1999: 413) enumerates no less than seven 'speech levels' in Korean. But, as Korean society changes, so is the number of 'politeness' distinctions being reduced. For instance the 'superpolite' level 'is no longer used in spoken Korean', surviving only 'in religious prayer, poems and in extremely formal and deferential letters'. The blunt level, 'sometimes used by a boss to his subordinates' is also on the wane 'probably due to its blunt connotation'. Sohn states that 'many contemporary Koreans, including the author of this book, have not used the level at all in their life'. Note that employment of speech levels may also be grammatically conditioned. For example, polar echo questions in Korean are restricted to just two levels (intimate and polite).

Many small-scale societies have a classificatory kinship system. There are perhaps twenty kin categories such that, by applying a series of equivalence rules, each member of the society is placed in one category with respect to ego. In pre-contact days, the Dyirbal-speaking tribe would have had about five hundred members. Each person would have had about two dozen relatives in each category. The *gumbu* class included mother's mother, her sisters and brothers, and (reciprocally) a woman's daughter's children, and so on. For a male ego, the *waymin* class included mother's elder brother's daughters, father's elder sister's daughters, and other more distant relatives calculated through the equivalence rules. (For full details see Dixon 1989.)

Each type of relationship carries a specific social role. For instance, a woman can look to a *gaya*, mother's younger brother, for friendship and guidance. And permitted marriage partners are determined by the kinship system—a man should marry the daughter of a woman in the *waymin* category (that is a cross-cousin through elder sibling link in the parent's generation). There is strict avoidance behaviour between a man and any *waymin* (any potential mother-in-law) and—reciprocally—between a woman and any potential son-in-law (also, although a little less strongly, between potential father-in-laws and daughter-in-laws). I was told that the avoidance was to prevent sexual contact between these two relatives. It was realized in several ways. A boy would never look at a *waymin*, and vice versa. He would never speak directly to her, but only through an intermediary (such as his wife).

Most important of all, a special speech style had to be used when in the presence of (or within earshot) of an avoidance relative. The Dyirbal 'mother-in-law' language style (this is a name bestowed by bilingual speakers) has to be employed in these circumstances. As briefly mentioned in §5.1, in §8.1, and also in §28.1 just above, the avoidance style, Jalnguy, has exactly the same phonetics, phonology, and grammar as the everyday style, Guwal, but every single lexeme is different (except for *gumbu* and three other grandparent terms).

A many-to-one relationship holds between Guwal and Jalnguy vocabularies. For example, there may be distinct names for half-a-dozen varieties of kangaroo in Guwal, but a single generic term in Jalnguy. The special style is purposely vague, in keeping with the nature of the avoidance relationship.

Avoidance behaviour of this kind is pervasive among speakers of the 250 or so distinct languages of Australia. Many communities are like Dyirbal in having a special avoidance speech style but in most instances there are just a couple of score special lexemes, the remainder being the same as in the everyday style. Only in Dyirbal and a few neighbouring languages of north-east Queensland, has the avoidance vocabulary extended to almost every lexeme. Why is this? Why have just a few languages elaborated their avoidance styles? The answer is that this was an aesthetic and intellectual endeavour. Just as some communities revel in grand opera, or crossword puzzles, or proverbs, or tracing genealogies way back, so speakers of these Australian languages take delight in creating a second semantic system.

Large societies may have an authority structure which is reflected in the language. Small societies with a classificatory kinship system may, in their language use, reflect which kind of relative is being addressed or referred to. And some communities of medium size can have both. The situation in Fijian was illustrated in §15.1.5. Here the pronoun system has four numbers (in all three persons): singular, dual, paucal, and plural. Generally, a single person is addressed with the 2sg pronoun. In terms of the classificatory kinship system, there are two kinds of avoidance relation. The 2dual pronoun is used for a single person belonging to one set (mother-in-law, father-in-law, son-in-law, and daughter-in-law) and the 2paucal pronoun for a single person belonging to the other set (an actual or classificatory brother-in-law or sister-in-law of the opposite sex). Fijian society also has a clear hierarchy. Great respect must be accorded to a village chief, who wields considerable power. In keeping with this, a chief is addressed with the 2pl pronoun.

28.2.3 Religion

Every society has some kind of religion—a belief in gods or spirits which have a supernatural character. There is typically a special speech style (sometimes, a different language) associated with religious practices. Why should this be? As with most things, there is a combination of reasons.

Spoken language is continually changing and evolving. Written versions change too, but at a somewhat slower rate. In contrast, the language of religious routines may be immutable. If some holy writings were cast in (or first translated into) a particular style of language, then it is that which is designated as appropriate for dealings in the religion. For example, the Ethiopian Church uses Ge'ez (the ancestor of some modern Southern Peripheral Semitic languages). This is the language into which the Bible was translated, between the fifth and seventh centuries. It ceased to be used as a spoken language of everyday life about a thousand years ago, and is unintelligible to Amharic-speaking churchgoers in Ethiopia nowadays. In similar fashion, the Koran was written in Classical Arabic, which is therefore the language for the Moslem religion, although it is not mutually intelligible with any of the varieties of Arabic in daily use today.

Another factor is the feeling that religion, being a somewhat separate business, should be solemnified by using at least a special style of language (if not a separate language). The language of the King James Bible was archaic when this translation appeared in 1611, and has become more so over the centuries (with its *ye* and *you*, *thou*, *thee*, and *thy*). For that reason, many Christians prefer it over more colloquial modern translations.

A further illustration comes from Fiji. There are many distinct dialects and early missionaries (in the mid-nineteenth century) started translations into individual varieties. Daunted by this task, they then pooled their efforts and aimed for a single translation which was intended to be in Bauan, a dialect which had something of the status of a lingua franca. Only in several respects it wasn't proper Bauan at all. The missionaries had come from Tonga via the Lau islands and some elements of the Lau dialect were (probably unwittingly) mixed in. The missionaries also simplified the language and introduced new features, either in a conscious attempt to regularize paradigms, or because they had not achieved a full understanding of the language. The resulting 'church language' has been whimsically referred to by linguist Paul Geraghty (1984: 41) as 'Old High Fijian' (and described by him as 'a truly crude and impoverished variety'). The point is that Fijians today like having this special style for use in church. 'God wants to be spoken to in this way', I was told.

Systems of religion in Australia typically involve initiation ceremonies for young men—when they undergo circumcision or have cicatrices cut, and are instructed in secret spiritual matters. Some communities have a special speech style, taught to youths at the ceremony and then used between initiated men. The initiation style of one tribe involves replacing each lexeme and pronoun by a designated 'opposite'. For example, the assertion 'I am sitting on the ground' is rendered by 'You are standing in the sky'. Another group uses a special phonology, involving clicks (the only instance of these outside southern Africa). (See Hale 1971, 1973: 442–6; Hale and Nash 1997, and Dixon 2002: 91–2.)

Religion involves special acts and attitudes. There will be lexemes to describe supplicating oneself before an imagined supernatural being, praying, and perhaps performing a sacrifice. Each local religion has its own proclivities. For example, every speaker of Dyirbal is identified with an animal or plant as their totem. Before an important occasion (such as a fighting corroboree), a man or woman would stretch and by mental power take on the identity of their totem, saying something like (using the specialized verb *wurrali-* 'identify with one's totem'):

(5) ŋajaₛ miyaburₛ   wurrali-ñu
    1sg   red.silky.oak identify-NON.FUTURE
    I am now a red silky oak tree (*Carnavionia araliifolia*) (and will have the
       might of an oak tree in the forthcoming fight)

Many societies, across the world, have a class of shamans, who combine the roles of priest and healer. They are able to control spirits who may cause a person's death, unless chased away by the spirits of a stronger shaman. Shamans are sometimes credited with the ability for telekinesis (that is, being able to move objects solely by mental power), and for extrasensory perception. Language has to be used in a special way to describe the doings of these powerful beings. To mention just one example, an ordinary speaker of Tariana will describe a dream using the non-eyewitness evidential since it belongs to an unreal imaginary world. 'In contrast, Tariana shamans have prophetic dreams, which are part of their supernatural experience. Accounts of such dreams are cast in visual evidential' (Aikhenvald 2004: 346–7).

This illustrates choice from a grammatical system being motivated by religious belief. Such belief may also constrain the applicability of a construction type. In §1.6, we saw how Old Order Mennonites do not permit the verb 'want' to be used with a potential-type complement clause (as in 'I want to come'). Their brand of religion subordinates self to the will of God and, as a consequence, no individual should want something for themselves.

28.2.4 Ways of viewing the world

The category of 'evidentiality', whereby a speaker must indicate—through an obligatory grammatical system—the evidence on which each statement is made, accords with a certain kind of world view. Evidentiality seems exotic and fascinating for speakers of languages which lack it. What if it were necessary to specify information source for every sentence in English? This would surely make things easier for police engaged in a criminal investigation. And it would without doubt discombobulate our politicians—no more vague answers, but instead a need to be fully explicit. However, we don't have a grammatical system of evidentiality in English, in part because it wouldn't really tally with the way we view the world and with our principles of behaviour.

Other societies operate in a different way. Across Amazonia, there is held to be an explicit cause for everything that happens. As mentioned in §1.6, if someone dies, it is never believed to be through 'natural causes'. There must be a perpetrator (often, employing sorcery) who should be sought out and dispatched. So as not to be blamed for something they had no responsibility for, a speaker should always be absolutely explicit about what they have done. This is achieved through an obligatory system of evidentiality marking. (See Aikhenvald 2004: 332–63.)

A similar situation appertains up in the Andes. Weber (1986: 138) lists the following maxims for speakers of Quechua:

1. (Only) one's own experience is reliable.
2. Avoid unnecessary risk, as by assuming responsibility for information of which one is not absolutely sure.
3. Don't be gullible. (Witness the many Quechua folktales in which the victim is foiled because of his gullibility.)
4. Assume responsibility only if is safe to do so. (The successful assumption of responsibility builds stature in the community.)

The necessity of having always to make a choice from the grammatical system of evidentiality values assists in satisfying these requirements.

There are languages in most parts of the world which have a subclass of nouns for which a possessor has to be specified (see Chapter 16). This naturally includes body parts. Unless it is detached, one can only talk of 'my leg', 'your leg', 'her leg', and so on. Parts of an object may also be included in the 'inalienably possessed' subclass. And so may kin terms, since a mother must always be someone's mother. Or it could just be blood relations and not those through marriage, for whom the link may be severed through divorce or desertion.

This much is fairly straightforward. But there may be other nouns classed as inalienably possessed, these reflecting the way in which the world is viewed by that culture. One recurrent member is 'name'; many people consider name to be an indissoluble attribute, a token of their individuality. Other examples were mentioned in §16.5.1, including 'home', 'friend', and 'clothing'.

In the Caucasian mountains, blood feuds were common and 'vengeance for the killing of a kinsman was an obligation that was marked as inalienably possessed in West Circassian dialects' (Colarusso 1992: 5).

A network of beliefs and legends may motivate the way in which objects in the real world are mapped into grammar. The system of four noun classes in Dyirbal was briefly expounded in §1.9. 'Sun' and 'moon' are in the feminine and masculine classes, respectively, since they are considered as wife and husband. Willy wagtail birds feature as legendary men, and are thus classed as masculine. Other birds are held to be the spirits of dead human females, and so are feminine. And so on. In order to understand the rationale for noun class membership in Dyirbal one has, essentially, to learn to view the world as its speakers do.

In addition to their everyday style, called Guwal, speakers of Dyirbal have a so-called 'mother-in-law' style, Jalnguy, which had to be used in the presence of a relative with whom contact should be minimized. In keeping with its 'avoidance' role, Jalnguy is purposely vague, dealing just in generic terms (see §8.1 and §28.2.2 just above). In contrast, when speaking Guwal one must always be as specific as possible. To report that a snake has been seen, the species name should be used (this is particularly important since some of the most dangerous snakes in the world are found in this territory). The generic term *bayi wadam* 'snake' would only be employed if, say, just a snake's tail were espied so that the snake could not be identified.

We said in §1.6 that Dyirbal lacks a verb 'know', simply because this would be too vague. It is necessary to specify *how* one knows a thing; for instance, I saw it happen, or someone told me. In similar fashion, there is in this language no causative construction, in part because of the requirement for specificity.

One cannot just say, in Dyirbal, 'John made me laugh' but must specify what was done to achieve this result; for instance, 'John told me a funny story and I laughed' or 'John tickled me and I laughed' or 'John tripped over and I laughed at his clumsiness'. The valency-changing derivation marked by verbal suffix -*ma*- generally has applicative effect, with intransitive S becoming transitive A argument (as illustrated by examples (3-ap), (4-ap), (14-ap), (16-ap), (41-ap), and (42-ap) in Chapter 25). There is just the occasional example where S becomes O. For instance, we get intransitive verb *wuji* 'grow up (as of a child)' and applicative *wuji-ma*- 'bring up, rear (as a parent does of a child)'. This process of nurturing could scarcely be regarded as an instance of causation.

Another reason for the absence of a causative construction in Dyirbal is that one person simply does not *make* another do something in this society. There are no words with meanings such as 'control' or 'command' or 'order', or 'obey'. There is the transitive verb of speaking *giga-*, variously glossed as 'let do', 'ask to do', and 'tell to do', but it always implies that the referent of the O argument is acting voluntarily.

In some societies—including Japan and Korea—one should not presume to intrude into the mind of another. As Sohn (1994: 99) describes it for Korean: 'sensory adjectives denote only an unobservable internal state of mind and, therefore, are in principle used only with first person subject in declaratives and with second person subject with interrogatives'. That is, one can state 'I am sad' or ask 'Are you sad?' but should not venture to assert 'You are sad' (however strong the physical manifestations of such a state may be). Neither is it permissible to say 'You envy Nani' (only 'I envy Nani' or 'Do you envy Nani?').

Some of the characteristics just described illustrate varying ways languages have for reflecting a certain type of contrast or attitude. As just mentioned, Korean treats speaking about the states of mind of oneself and of someone else as quite different matters. The same contrast is expressed through the evidentiality system in a language such as Tariana. 'I am sad' has to be coded with the 'non-visual' evidential (which cover hearing, smelling, and feeling), never 'visual'. But if one observes from their expression that someone is sad, one can say to them 'You are sad' and should then employ 'visual' (never 'non-visual'), or you can say to someone else 'He/she is sad' and would then use the 'inferred (from visual evidence)' choice.

The pragmatic role of a grammatical category of evidentiality is to prevent vagueness or ambiguity. Speakers of Dyirbal have a similar predilection (for their everyday language style) but this is achieved in a different way, by avoiding lexemes with vague and underspecified meanings (such as 'know' and 'make (do)') and requiring full details to be provided.

28.2.5 Modes of speaking

When a linguist gets chatting with an ordinary person and mentions that they have just returned from a period of intensive fieldwork on some out-of-the-way language, the question often asked is: 'How do they say "yes" and "no"?' The appropriate response is sometimes: 'They don't'. This may engender doubt as to the worth of the linguist, or of the language. 'Surely every language must be able to say simple straightforward "yes" and "no"!' But some *do* lack this. How can it be?

It is simply that in such languages an answer to a question or a response to a statement must have the structure of a sentence, with (at the least) predicate and core arguments. This was discussed and illustrated in §21.8. In Jarawara, for instance, the only negator is verbal suffix *-ra*. When I asked 'Has Okomobi returned?', the negative answer could only be 'Okomobi has not returned', given as (120) in §21.8.

Dyirbal and Yidiñ are two adjacent (but not closely genetically related) Australian languages. In both of them, nouns inflect on an absolutive-ergative principle and pronouns on a nominative-accusative one. As described in §23.1, the syntactic pivot for Dyirbal works on an S/O basis, irrespective of whether the argument linking two clauses is noun or pronoun. However, Yidiñ operates with an S/O pivot for coordination of nouns but an S/A one for pronouns. Why should this be? The answer lies in the nature of discourse organization.

Narratives in Dyirbal are rather similar to those in English, being generally told in 3rd person. But for a tale in Yidiñ the narrator typically assumes the identity of the main character, and the story is told in 1st person. If the original main character drops out and a new one comes in then, after a couple of clauses of transition, the narrator assumes the identity of this new person. As a consequence, 1st (and 2nd) person pronouns are much more common in my recordings of Yidiñ than in those for Dyirbal. And this is undoubtedly a major factor why clauses in Yidiñ which are linked through a pronominal argument operate with an S/A pivot (reflecting the nominative/accusative morphology of pronouns). (A full account is in Dixon (1977b.)

In §15.3.4 we considered the dialogue in English: *John hadn't been at the six o'clock meeting, We wondered why. Then Kofi said **he** had left at five o'clock.* The *he* in the last sentence is ambiguous; it could be taken to refer back to Kofi or to John. Then we mentioned that ambiguity of this sort is avoided by the use of 'logophoric pronouns' in a broad belt of about thirty languages across central Africa. A logophoric pronoun is used in a complement cause when it relates to the subject of the main clause (that is, when *he* refers to Kofi), and a neutral pronoun in other circumstances (when *he* refers to John). Why should it be that just these languages have such a useful grammatical device? An insightful explanation was provided by Ameka (2004). Repeating from §15.3.4: there is, in the logophoric belt, a tradition of indirect (or 'triadic') communication. If A wants to communicate with B, they are likely to use an intermediary— A tells C who in turn tells B, rather than A speaking directly to B. It is—in large part—to avoid the possibility of ambiguous reference of an anaphoric pronoun in such complex speech situations that logophoric pronouns are needed.

This exemplifies the way in which a language spoken by a group which is socially homogeneous may differ from a 'world language'—such as English or Spanish—which is spoken in many regions by varied types of social groups. We now turn to comparison of languages with larger and smaller numbers of speakers.

28.2.6 Large and small language communities

We have seen how a language may reflect (to a small extent) the geographical terrain in which it is spoken and (to a much larger extent) the habitual activities, social organization, and kinship system of its speakers, plus their way of viewing the world, and modes of speaking.

When a language is spoken in a small area, by a limited population, these possibilities are immense. The further one moves away from them, so a number of the possibilities are likely to diminish. A small community—of just a few hundred or a few thousand people—may live in a single sort of landscape. If this is mountainous, their language may include a grammatical category indicating 'up' and 'down'. A large community consisting of tens of millions of people will necessarily be spread over a wide range of territory, which precludes an obligatory grammatical system (which applies across all dialects of the language) relating to any particular type of terrain.

Classificatory kinship systems are most likely to be found among peoples who live in small villages. By applying the 'kinship algorithms' a relationship is established between one person (call them 'ego') and every other person in their village. Once a kinship link is established with someone in a neighbouring village, every other person in that village is also in a specified relationship with ego.

Classificatory kinship is associated with special pronominal systems, such as the harmonic/disharmonic contrast for Lardil, described in §1.6. In another Australian language, Adnjamathanha, there can be up to ten different forms for a given person and number combination, depending on moiety, generation level, and kinship relation. For example, the 2du pronoun 'you two' is *nhuwadnbila* if said by a woman talking to her own children or her sister's children, *valdu* if said by a woman speaking to the children of her brothers, either *nhuwatalanbi* or *watalanbi* for talking to a married couple of the generation above or below the speaker, and so on. (Full details are in Schebeck, Hercus, and White 1973.) Such a socially-appropriate pronominal system could only be found in the language of a small community with a classificatory kinship system.

'Avoidance language styles' were discussed in §28.2.2 and 'initiation styles' in §28.2.3. Both of these are associated with small languages communities. There is often no strict social hierarchy in such groups. If a language is used by a fair number of people, its speakers are likely to be arranged in social ranks and there may then be levels of politeness, as described for Korean in §28.2.2. Or, on a much more simplistic level, the use of *sir* when addressing a male superior in England. Overall, things tend to balance out. Large and small communities each have their own speech style, reflecting individual types of social organization.

As mentioned in 'Sources and notes' to §15.2.4, there does seem to be some sort of inverse correlation between size of a demonstrative system and size of a language community. A distinction between alienable and inalienable possessive is predominantly found in languages spoken by a smallish number of people. (As mentioned in §28.2.4, there can be cultural extensions of inalienability, to such things as name, home, clothing, and even personal wrongdoer.) Tense systems incorporating multiple division of past and future time (see §1.7 and §19.3) are almost all found in local languages.

An inclusive/exclusive distinction for non-singular first person pronouns is found most often—but not solely—in languages with a small or medium number of speakers. This contrast can be reconstructed for the proto-language of the extensive Austronesian family, which was presumably spoken by a fairly small population. And it is retained in most modern descendents, including such multi-million-speaker tongues as Malay, Indonesian, and Tagalog.

At the end of §20.11, attention was drawn to what might appear to be an inverse correlation between the size of a number system within grammar and the complexity of a class of lexical number words. We suggested that the connection here is of a social rather than a linguistic nature. In small language communities, value may be placed on whether someone is coming alone or with one other person or with a few or with many, shown by singular, dual, paucal, and plural pronouns. Such societies often have few (or no) lexical numbers, lacking any social need for counting or arithmetical operations. Larger language communities indulge in buying and selling, establishing prices, assigning marks, paying taxes, and the like. For all these purposes, an intricate set of lexical number words is needed.

McWhorter (2007) has shown that a number of languages with many speakers is each considerably simpler in its phonology and morphology than genetically related languages spoken by smaller communities. He compares Mandarin with other Sinitic languages (so-called 'Chinese dialects'), Malay with 'Indonesian-type' relatives, Persian with other Iranian languages, and English with other Germanic tongues.

We have provided some examples of grammatical systems which tend to be maximally rich in local languages (and McWhorter uses other parameters). However, this does not apply to every category. For instance, the number of techniques for negation varies widely across languages spoken by both large and small communities, with a preponderance towards there being more for larger groups. The richest set of techniques for negation that I know of is in English.

It is not the case, as sometimes seems to be implied, that the major languages of the world today—Mandarin, English, Hindi, and so on—are relatively simply in structure. Each is a complex linguistic entity, not at all easy to learn. What may have been lost at the phonological and/or morphological levels may be, at least in part, compensated for by intricacies of syntactic organization and by richness of lexical resources.

Finally, we can ask what happens when people change languages. Suppose, for instance, that—in the fullness of time—members of a number of ethnic groups across central Africa should switch to speaking just a local dialect of English or French. They would lose the distinctive device of logophoric pronouns. As described in §28.2.5, this appears to be related to a system of triadic (or indirect) communication. That mode of speaking would undoubtedly become problematic without logophoric pronouns to assist in efficient comprehension. Language shift might well lead to change in this culturally-characteristic method of communication. (Many similar examples could be described.) Change towards a global profile may be a mixed blessing.

28.3 The challenge ahead

We have explored a few possible explanations for linguistic phenomena in terms of the relation between language and the world. From Chapters 10 through 27 there are hundreds more interesting descriptive facts begging for explanation (and many more for topics beyond those covered here). Simply as a sample, a linguist's dozen of these are listed here.

(a) Why do some languages have one or more morphological processes of **reduplication**, while others lack this? (See 2 in §3.13, and §6.4.) When there is reduplication, why does it sometimes involve the whole form, sometimes just a part of it? Why is the reduplicand sometimes placed before, sometimes after, and sometimes in the middle of the basic form? What motivates the varying semantic effects of reduplication (with nouns, with verbs, with adjectives)?

(b) Why is it that some languages spoken in hilly country code 'up' and 'down' in their grammar (§1.6), while others—although spoken in similar terrain—don't do this? (Perhaps the latter sort only moved into the hills rather recently, and in the course of time an 'up/down' category may be developed. Or there could be many other reasons.)

(c) A **three-term demonstrative system** is sometimes {near speaker, mid-distant from speaker, far from speaker} and other times {near speaker, near addressee, not near speaker or addressee} (see (a) in §15.2.4). What motivates choice between these two types?

(d) Every language has nominal and local adverbial demonstratives ('this', 'here', 'there'). Every language has interrogative words 'who', 'what', 'where', and so on. Why do so few languages have **verbal demonstratives** ('do like this (to)') and/or **interrogative verbs** ('do what/how (to)')? (See (c) in §15.2.1 and in (V) in §27.6.4.)

(e) Why do some languages include in their grammar a system directly indicating **definite/indefinite** reference while others have to convey such information in a somewhat circuitous manner? (§3.18.)

(f) Why do some languages have a large open class of **adjectives** while others are restricted to just a small closed class? (Chapter 12.)

(g) Why do some languages (for example, Armenian) lack **genders** while others which are genetically related to them, and have a similar structural profile, do include this category in their grammar? (§3.16.)

(h) Why do some languages have a **tense system**, while others indicate temporal reference in other ways? (§19.3.)

(i) Why, in some languages with a tense system, are there **several past tenses**, while others have a single past tense (or perhaps one term combining past and present reference)?

(j) What motivates the different treatments of **reference to future time**— through a tense value in some languages and just through modalities in others? (§19.2.1.)

(k) Why have some languages developed a specialized verb '**have**' for predicative possession, while others make secondary use of various means (copula construction, verb 'exist', etc.)? (§16.9.)

(l) In a number of languages a **double negative** may simply emphasize the negative meaning; for example, *I didn't see nothing* in colloquial English and similar instances in Newar. In others, such as Tuyuca, a double negative may create 'a semantically strong positive statement' (§21.5). What is the reason for the difference?

(m) Some languages lack any special **reflexive construction** (simply saying things like 'I$_A$ cut me$_O$'). A large group employ a reflexive pronoun in a transitive clause (as in English, *I$_A$ cut myself$_O$*). And many languages have a reflexive verbal process which derives an intransitive stem (literally 'I$_S$ cut-REFLEXIVE'). What motivates this? There are similar possibilities for **reciprocals**, and the same question can be asked. (Chapter 22.)

(n) Some languages have a single **causative derivation**, while others have several with contrasting meanings (whether or not causee does it willingly, whether the causer acts directly or indirectly, and so on). Why? (Chapter 24.)

(o) Languages from several parts of the world—predominantly Africa, but also the Americas, Asia, New Guinea, and Australia—have a well-defined class of **ideophones**. These typically have special phonological features, they frequently involve inherent reduplication and are often onomatopoeic. Ideophones may relate to 'manner, colour, sound, smell, action, state or intensity' (§8.3). Why do ideophones occur in certain languages but not in others? Do they reflect a common mind-set, or cultural trait, for speakers of languages in which they occur?

These are just a small fraction of the things for which explanations could be sought. It is unlikely that, even in the furthest reaches of time, everything could be provided with a reason. Some may be due to chance, or collective whim. But if explanations are not looked for, none will be found.

The future agenda, for a linguist working in the scientific mould, is both challenging and invigorating.

Sources and notes

28.1   One can directly question a lexeme. Relating to *Burglars ransacked our house*, one can ask *Who ransacked our house?* or *What did burglars do to our house?* or *What did burglars ransack?* (here the complete NP *our house* has to be questioned, rather than just its head noun *house*). Pronouns (and demonstratives) do constitute grammatical systems, but they can be questioned—*Whose house did burglars ransack?*

It is not possible to directly question most grammatical items, such as plural suffix -*s* in *burglars*. However, one can question the information a grammatical item conveys—*Was it one or more burglars who ransacked our house?*

Among the many discussions on suffixing versus prefixing are Cutler, Hawkins, and Gilligan (1983), Bybee, Pagliuca, and Perkins (1990), and Mithun (2003).

28.2.2   Earlier chapters included several further references to the grammatical implications of kinship systems. In §1.2 there was mention of different possessive constructions for consanguineal and affinal kin in Lango, and for kin in authority and those not in authority over one in Gapapaiwa.

Further information on the Jalnguy avoidance style of Dyirbal is in Dixon 1971 (revised version 1982). See Dixon (2002: 91–6) for a brief survey of special speech styles in Australia, and reference to other surveys and to primary sources.

Enfield (2007b) is a wonderfully insightful account of pronominal use in Lao, in terms of a variety of social parameters.

28.2.4   See also an account of the limited nature of 'causation' in Semelai, under 4 in §24.4.

28.2.6   There are occasional instances of a bit of grammar from a local language infiltrating into a lingua franca. For example, several regional varieties of Spanish in South America have introduced grammatical particle *dizque* (from original *diz que* 'say that') as a reported marker, bringing into their Spanish one element from the complex evidential systems in languages of the area. See, among others, Travis (2006), Aikhenvald (2012: Chapter 9), and further references therein.

Appendix 1 Source materials

It may be useful to list here some of the handbooks and grammar series which, by and large, provide sound source materials as a basis for inductive typological study. Note that the listing is far from exhaustive.

Handbook of American Indian languages, edited by Franz Boas.

Classic grammar sketches (some quite lengthy), basically framed on a common pattern: grammatical processes, ideas expressed by grammatical processes/categories, and so on. Each grammar (except for Zuni, in Volume 3), includes one or more glossed texts.

Part 1. 1911 (Smithsonian Institution, Bulletin 40). Introduction (a brilliant essay) by Franz Boas; Athapascan (Hupa), by Pliny Earle Goddard; Tlingit and Haida, both by John R. Swanton; Tsimshian, Kwakiutl, and Chinook, all by Franz Boas; Maidu, by Roland B. Dixon; Alqonquian (Fox), by William Jones (revised by Truman Michelson); Siouan (Dakota), by Franz Boas and John R. Swanton; Eskimo, by William Thalbitzer.

Part 2. 1922 (Smithsonian Institution, Bulletin 40). The Takelma language of southwestern Oregon, by Edward Sapir; Coos and Siuslawan (Lower Umpqa), both by Leo J. Frachtenberg; Chukchee, by Waldemar Bogoras.

Volume III. 1933. Columbia University Press, New York. Tonkawa, an Indian language of Texas, by Harry Hoijer; Quileute, by Manuel J. Andrade; Yuchi, by Günter Wagner; Zuni, by Ruth L. Bunzel; Coeur d'Alene, by Gladys A. Reichard.

Volume IV. 1941. J. J. Augustin, New York. Only one part was issued: Tunica, by Mary R. Haas.
Note that there have been various reissues of some of these volumes.

Handbook of Australian languages, edited by R. M. W. Dixon and Barry J. Blake. Volumes 1–3 from Australian National University Press, Canberra, and John Benjamins, Amsterdam; volumes 4–5 (title now commencing with *The*) from Oxford University Press, Melbourne.

Each grammar follows the traditional order: phonology, morphology, syntax. Also included is a vocabulary, by semantic fields and also alphabetically and, where available, a glossed text.

Volume 1. 1979. Guugu Yimidhirr, by John Haviland; Pitta-Pitta, by Barry J. Blake; Gumbaynggir, by Diana Eades; Yaygir, by Terry Crowley.

Volume 2. 1981. Wargamay, by R. M. W. Dixon; The Mpakwithi dialect of Anguthimri, by Terry Crowley; Watjarri, by Wilfrid H. Douglas; Margany and Gunya, by J. G. Breen; Tasmanian, by Terry Crowley and R. M. W. Dixon.

Volume 3. 1983. Djapu, a Yolngu dialect, by Frances Morphy; Yukulta, by Sandra Keen; Uradhi, by Terry Crowley; Nyawaygi, by R. M. W. Dixon.

Volume 4. 1991. Woiwurrung, the Melbourne language, by Barry J. Blake; Panyjima, by Alan Dench; Djabugay, by Elisabeth Patz; Mbabaram, by R. M. W. Dixon.

Volume 5. 2000. Bunuba, by Alan Rumsey; Ndjébbana, by Graham McKay; Kugu Nganhcara, by Ian Smith and Steve Johnson.

Handbook of Amazonian languages, edited by Desmond C. Derbyshire and Geoffrey K. Pullum, Mouton de Gruyter, Berlin.

A valuable set of volumes, featuring a number of grammars which are, for the most part, of good to very good quality. However, this *Handbook* would have been even more useful if its contributors had not been constrained to follow an idiosyncratic order of presentation, commencing with syntax, and within that constituent order (called 'word order'). That this is far from ideal is apparent from the fact that, in five of the grammars, the whole of '23, Morphology' consists of a single sentence along the lines 'This has been treated in earlier sections' (but at different places in each grammar). There are some chapters on general topics; only the grammatical sketches are listed here. Note that a glossed text is provided for Sanuma, Yagua, Macushi, Wai Wai, and Warekena.

Volume 1. 1986. Apalai, by Edward and Sally Koehn; Canela-Krahô, by Jack and Jo Popjes; Pirahã, by Daniel L. Everett; Urubu-Kaapor, by James Kakumasu.

Volume 2. 1990. Sanuma, by Donald M. Borgman; Yagua, by Doris L. Payne and Thomas E. Payne.

Volume 3. 1991. Macushi, by Miriam Abbott; Paumarí, by Shirley Chapman and Desmond C. Derbyshire.

Volume 4. 1998. Wai Wai, by Robert E. Hawkins; Warekena, by Alexandra Y. Aikhenvald.

Lingua/Croom Helm descriptive studies

Bernard Comrie and Norval Smith published a 'Lingua descriptive studies questionnaire' as pp. 1–72 of *Lingua*, volume 42, 1977, setting out the method of organization to be followed by each grammar in the series. This was slightly idiosyncratic, commencing with syntax, and within that direct and indirect speech, and then questions. North-Holland (in Amsterdam), publishers of *Lingua*, put out only volumes 1–6. They then sold the project to Croom Helm (in London) who published volumes 7–16 under the series title *Croom Helm Descriptive Grammars*. Croom Helm was then taken over by Routledge who published volumes 17–36, with the series title shortened just to *Descriptive Grammars* for 19–36. Series editors were Comrie and Smith for volumes 1–16 and after that just Comrie. Note that one advertised volume, *Haruai* by Bernard Comrie, was never published.

The questionnaire employed had its strong and weak points. For instance, no less than 192 possibilities were canvassed for relations between antecedent and reflexive in a reflexive construction (and similarly for reciprocal) but there was no mention of, or place for, applicative constructions.

Note that most grammars in the series are good and reliable. There are just a few which do not quite measure up, and which I would be reluctant to quote from.

I have supplied volume numbers after 1–6.

1. 1979. *Hixkaryana*, by Desmond C. Derbyshire
2. 1979. *Abkhaz*, by B. G. Hewitt
3. 1981. *Kobon*, by John Davies
4. 1982. *Mangarayi*, by Francesca Merlan
5. 1982. *Imbabura Quechua*, by Peter Cole
6. 1982. *Cairene Egyptian Colloquial Arabic*, by Judith Olmsted Gary and Saad Gamal-Eldin
7. 1984. *West Greenlandic*, by Michael Fortescue
8. 1985. *Tamil*, by R. E. Asher
9. 1985. *Nkore-Kiga*, by Charles Taylor
10. 1985. *Babungo*, by Willi Schaub
11. 1986. *Japanese*, by John Hinds
12. 1986. *Rumanian*, by Graham Mallinson
13. 1987. *Modern Greek*, by Brian Joseph and Irene Philippaki-Warburton
14. 1987. *Amele*, by John R. Roberts
15. 1988. *Basque*, by Mario Saltarelli
16. 1990. *Gulf Arabic*, by Clive Holes
17. 1990. *Kannada*, by S. N. Sridhar
18. 1992. *Finnish*, by Helena Sulkala and Merja Karjalainen

19. 1992. *Catalan*, by José Ignacio Hualde
20. 1993. *Punjabi, a cognitive-descriptive grammar*, by Tej K. Bhatia
21. 1993. *Maori*, by Winifred Bauer
22. 1994. *Korean*, by Ho-min Sohn
23. 1994. *Ndyuka*, by George L. Huttar and Mary L. Huttar
24. 1996. *Rapanui*, by Veronica Du Feu
25. 1996. *Nigerian Pidgin*, by Nicholas G. Faraclas
26. 1997. *Wari', the Pacaas Novos language of western Brazil*, by Daniel L. Everett and Barbara Kern
27. 1997. *Evenki*, by Igor Nedjalkov
28. 1997. *Maltese*, by Albert Borg and Marie Azzopardi-Alexander
29. 1997. *Kashmiri, a cognitive-descriptive grammar*, by Kashi Wali and Omkar N. Koul
30. 1997. *Koromfe*, by John R. Rennison
31. 1997. *Persian*, by Shahrzad Mahootian
32. 1997. *Marathi*, by Rajeshwari V. Pandharipande
33. 1997. *Malayalam*, by R. E. Asher and T. C. Kumari
34. 1997. *Turkish*, by Jaklin Kornfilt
35. 1998. *Hungarian*, by István Kenesei, Robert M. Vago, and Anna Fenyvesi
36. 2000. *Tuvaluan, a Polynesian language of the central Pacific*, by Niko Besnier

Mouton grammar library

German publisher de Gruyter has provided an immense service to permanent scholarship through this series of grammars. It commenced in 1985 and is continuing today, with more than fifty volumes issued so far. Full details are on the website <http://www.degruyter.de>. Series editors have always included Georg Bossong, together with (at various times), Wallace Chafe, Bernard Comrie, and Matthew Dryer.

   Most of the grammars in the series are of good to very good quality, with just a few falling short (see, for example, critical comments by Storch 2005: 35, and Adelaar 2006 on grammars in the series).

Cambridge Grammatical Descriptions

In the 1990s, I persuaded Cambridge University Press to publish a series of top-class grammars (edited by myself and Keren Rice). Of the fair number of submissions, only the very best were considered appropriate for the series. After just three volumes, all very well received, CUP decided to scrap the series, apparently on the grounds that sales were meagre. (But so are the sales of similar series from other publishers, such as the Mouton Grammar Library.)

   Each grammar includes a selection of texts and a vocabulary.

- 2002. *A grammar of Kham*, by David E. Watters.
- 2003. *A grammar of Tariana, from northwest Amazonia*, by Alexandra Y. Aikhenvald.
- 2004. *A grammar of Semelai*, by Nicole Kruspe.

All these volumes have now been reissued in paperback, at a cheaper price.

Amongst other publishers who have put out a number of first-class grammars are University of California Press, University of Nebraska Press, Brill in Leiden, and Rüdiger Köppe in Cologne. Over a fifty-year period, from 1961 to 2011, Pacific Linguistics in Canberra published many grammars, a significant proportion of them being of high quality; from 2012, Pacific Linguistics is to be absorbed into de Gruyter.

The world atlas of language structures (WALS)

The aim of *WALS* is to 'display the structural properties of the world's languages' through 142 world maps (and many local maps) with an accompanying text for each map.

A project of this magnitude is wonderfully ambitious. To properly achieve it would involve decades of work by a team of high-quality linguists (closely supervised by the editors) with entries being double-checked in primary sources and also cross-checked with experts in languages of a particular area. Unfortunately, such a procedure has not been followed. To an outsider, *WALS* might appear to 'set a new standard in linguistic typology'. However, to a linguist who examines with care the principles followed, the parameters employed, and the data entries, such a judgment is not justified.

A number of reviewers praise the book overall, but have found disturbing errors concerning language areas that they know well. For instance, Schulze (2007) undertook 'a very superficial test of *WALS* concerning the region of the Caucasus. In sum, 22 maps contain problematic or even false classifications'. Bright (2007) notes errors in eight maps relating to languages of California or central Mexico and suggests that users of *WALS* should 'double-check the data'. However, this would not be an easy matter—bibliographic references are not given for the individual entries on maps, so that one does not know what sources the compiler used.

There are also countless errors in reading and quoting data sources. For instance, Map 30 shows Paumarí as having four genders. In fact this language has two distinct and independent systems, one with two genders and another consisting of two classifiers (see Chapman and Derbyshire 1991: 254–9).

In summary, difficulties with *WALS* include:

- Including in its database languages for which the materials available are poor and unreliable, while omitting some excellent sources.
- Variable coverage—some maps include a little over 100 languages, other more than 500. Plainly, some contributors put in more work than others.
- Criteria used are often idiosyncratic. For instance, two clauses linked by 'because' (as in 'Pedro did it because Carmen came to the class') are said to constitute a 'causative construction' (p. 446). And see also Sources and Notes to §25.0 for comment on the 'Applicatives' section.
- There are many omissions—for a certain category, one region is left white whereas this category *is* found in languages from that region. (In some cases a language from the area with this feature was included in the list of languages prescribed for contributors, but has plainly not been examined.)
- Some of the contributors are not familiar with the relevant general literature on the topic they are writing about.

(See also Sources and Notes to §15.1, §20.6.4, and §24.0.)

Unfortunately—but as might be expected—some linguists and many people on the periphery of the discipline have accepted *WALS* as an accurate and reliable resource. To mention just one of a multiplying number of instances, psychologists Lupyan and Dale (2010), in an examination of whether 'language structure is partly determined by social structure', base their work on the information in *WALS*.

Overall, *WALS* is an unfortunate document. It gives a false picture, an illusion; it would be better for the field if it had not been produced. If *WALS* is accepted uncritically, it will hinder or even set back sound typological scholarship.

Appendix 2 How many languages?

How many languages are there in the world today, either spoken on a daily basis or well remembered? Before answering this question, we must explain that the term 'language' is used in two quite different ways—there is the 'linguistic' sense and the 'political' sense.

In the scientific usage of linguists, two modes of speaking are regarded as dialects of a single language if they are mutually intelligible; we can call this 'S-language'. Sometimes we get a chain of dialects each of which is mutually intelligible with several neighbours in each direction, but dialects at the extreme ends of the chain are not immediately intelligible to each other's speakers (although it would take only a few weeks' immersion for this to be achieved). It is possible—and most economical—to write just one overall grammar for an S-language, with notes on dialect variation.

The political use of the term 'language' is that any ethnic group may decide to call their way of speaking a language, and perhaps get it recognized as such by the national government; we can call this 'P-language'.

In 1961, the Summer Institute of Linguistics (also called Wycliffe Bible Translators) first produced *Ethnologue*, a listing of world languages. This was intended for SIL/WBT needs, with the main purpose of indicating where there is considered to be need for translation of the Christian Bible. A revised edition has been issued about every four years, with the sixteenth edition appearing in 2009. The volume is uneven in scope and reliability, and also in consistency with respect to what is an (S-)language and what is a dialect.

It is a fact that, across the world, languages are passing into extinction at a depressing rate. The number of languages being spoken or remembered is steadily falling. Yet the number of languages listed in successive editions or *Ethnologue* is steadily rising—5,445 in the tenth edition (Grimes 1984), 6,703 in the thirteenth edition (Grimes 1996), up again to 6,805 in the fourteenth edition (Grimes 2000), a further rise to 6,912 in the fifteenth edition (Gordon 2005), and then a tiny drop to 6,909 in the sixteenth edition (Lewis 2009). Why this rise in *Ethnologue* numbers when languages are continuing to die?

There is a combination of reasons. One is that S-languages have in many instances been replaced by P-languages in the catalogue. For example, three languages were listed for the Netherlands in 1984, six in 1996, and no less than sixteen in 2005. (The number is down to fifteen in 2009, with two P-languages omitted, two more added, while 'East Veluws' and 'North Veluws' were accorded separate entries in 2005 but are combined into just 'Veluws' in 2009.) Most of these are mutually intelligible dialects of the Dutch (S-)language, but speakers have decided that their dialects should be called (P-)languages (and lobbied the Dutch government for such recognition). There are many other examples of a similar nature. As a result, *Ethnologue* has a mixture of S-languages and P-languages. (But note that if every tribal dialect were accorded 'language' status—as many groups of speakers would no doubt like if they were informed of the situation—then the number of entries in *Ethnologue* would rise to be several tens of thousands.)

As stated, the purpose of *Ethnologue* is to assist in planning Bible translation, and decisions about what is a language and what is a dialect may shift as policies change. This can be illustrated by an instance from my own fieldwork area. In 1984, *Ethnologue* listed a single language: 'Jamamadí (Yamamadí)— 400 including 150 Jaruára, 100 in Banawá.' At that time there was a just one SIL team working in this language, concentrating on the Jamamadí dialect. In the late 1980s the SIL introduced two further teams, to translate the Bible into Banawá and Jarawara respectively. The 1996 edition lists the three dialects as distinct languages, saying for Banawá 'not as close to Jamamadí linguistically as previously thought' and for 'Jaruára (Jarawara)' 'formerly considered a dialect of Jamamadí.' There is in fact no doubt that these are dialects of one language. I have seen Jarawara people and Banawá people living in the same house and, on another occasion, Jarawara people and Jamamadí people living in the same house; in each instance they were able to communicate freely. Indeed, from my knowledge of Jarawara I am able to understand both Jamamadí and Banawá. SIL/WBT decided to have one translation team for each dialect, and at that time promoted the dialects to be (P-)languages in the *Ethnologue* listing.

Even the 1984 figure of 5,445 'languages' is far too high. For example, more that 200 languages are listed for Australia (many labelled 'nearly extinct' or even 'extinct', although *Ethnologue* maintains that it includes only 'living languages'), but 60 would be an optimistic estimate for the number which are actually still spoken (or else well remembered).

There is no authoritative list, or overall number, for extant S-languages (in the linguists' sense of the term), across the world today. The *Ethnologue* listing is useful but far from definitive. If one counts S-languages, and not dialects/P-languages, my estimate is that the figure is not more than 4,000, and probably a good deal less than this. And it is falling at a slow but steady rate.

Glossary

Definitions are provided for a number of technical terms which recur in these volumes. For some entries there is reference to the chapter or section in which they are discussed. Note that Chapters 1–9 are in Volume 1, Chapters 10–18 are in Volume 2, while Chapters 19–28 comprise Volume 3. Complementary terms are cross-referenced by 'Compl.'

A: subject of a transitive verb, a syntactic core argument.

ABLATIVE: marker indicating movement away from the referent of the noun phrase to which it is attached.

ABSOLUTIVE: case inflection marking intransitive subject (S) and transitive object (O). Compl. ergative. §3.9, §13.2, §13.5.4.

ACCENT, see stress.

ACCUSATIVE: case inflection marking transitive object (O). Compl. nominative. §3.9, §13.2, §13.5.4.

ACTIVE/STATIVE: label covering split-S and fluid-S systems.

ADJECTIVE: class of words which typically refer to properties and have two main roles: (a) make a statement that something has a certain property through functioning in intransitive predicate slot or in copula complement slot; and (b) help to specify the referent of the head noun in an NP by functioning as modifier to it. §3.6, §4.5, §6.1, §8.3.2, Chapter 12.

ADPOSITION: a marker of a (predominantly peripheral) grammatical relation which is realized as a separate phonological word or as a clitic, not as an affix. §5.4.

AFFINAL: kinship relation which involves a link by marriage. Compl. consanguineal. §1.3, §16.1.

AFFIX: a bound form added to a root or stem. §5.4.

AFFIXATION: morphological process which involves adding an affix to a root or stem. §3.13.

AGGLUTINATIVE: a type of language whose words are readily segmentable into a sequence of morphemes, each of which typically conveys one piece of information. §5.5.

AGREEMENT: when two words (for example, noun and modifying adjective within an NP) are marked for the same grammatical category. §5.6.

AIRSTREAM MECHANISM: a system for initiating a flow of air which will facilitate speech; see pulmonic, glottalic. §7.2.

ALIENABLE POSSESSION: when the possessed does not have an inherent connection with the possessor. §1.3, §16.5.

ALLATIVE: marker indicating movement towards the referent of the noun phrase to which it is attached.

ALLOMORPH: one of several alternative forms of a morpheme. §5.2.

ALLOPHONE: one possible pronunciation of a phoneme. §7.1.

AMBITRANSITIVE: verb which can function in both a transitive and an intransitive clause; of type S = A or S = O. §3.3, §13.3.

ANALYTIC: language whose words generally each have a small number of grammatical components. Compl. synthetic. §5.5.

ANAPHORA: a pronoun or demonstrative referring to something which was explicitly stated earlier in the discourse, such as *he* in *John came in and he sat down*. §15.3.

ANTIPASSIVE: valency-reducing derivation which puts underlying A argument into derived S function, and places underlying O argument in a peripheral function. §3.20, Chapter 23.

APPLICATIVE: valency-increasing derivation which can operate on an intransitive clause, putting the original S argument into A function and moving an erstwhile peripheral argument into O function. And/or it may operate on a transitive clause, again putting an original peripheral argument into O function, and dealing in various ways with the original O argument. See Chapter 25.

ARCHIPHONEME: unit resulting from the neutralization of a phonological contrast in a certain environment. §7.2.

ARGUMENT, CORE: an obligatory argument for a specific verb, which must be either stated or understood from the context. §3.2, §3.9, §5.6, §13.2.

ARGUMENT, PERIPHERAL: non-core argument, which is optional; typically includes instrument, accompaniment, recipient, beneficiary, time, place, manner. §3.9, §5.6.

ARTICLE: a type of determiner, whose prototypical role is to mark an NP as definite or indefinite. The label is used in special ways for particular languages; for instance the tradition in Fijian linguistics is to use 'article' for the first word of an NP, which is *a* or *na* if the NP head is a common noun and *o* if the head is a proper name or pronoun. §3.4, §3.18.

ARTICULATORS: an active articulator (for example, tongue tip) is brought into contact with—or into approximation with—a passive articulator (for example, the teeth). §7.2.

ASPECT: term used for composition (perfective/imperfective), sometimes also for boundedness, completion, etc. §3.15, §19.10.

ASSIMILATION: a process by which one sound changes to become more similar to a neighbouring sound, for example *-nb-* becoming *-mb-*.

ATELIC: an event is unbounded and has no definite end point. Compl. telic. §3.15, §19.8.

AUGMENTED: pronoun paradigm in which one or more further participants are added to each term in a minimal paradigm. Compl. minimal. §3.7, §15.1.2.

AUXILIARY: a grammatical form (sometimes called an auxiliary verb) which occurs together with a lexical verb. It typically inflects for some non-spatial setting categories, instead of the verb inflecting for these categories.

AVERSIVE: case which is added to a noun or pronoun referring to something for fear of which the action described by the verb of the clause takes place or should take place. For example, 'Come away from the fire for fear of the flying sparks'.

BENEFICIARY: peripheral argument referring to someone who will benefit from an action, as in *John wrote the letter [for Mary]*BENEFICIARY.

BOUND FORM: form which cannot occur alone but must be attached to some other form, e.g. *un-* in English. Compl. free form. §5.2.

BOUNDEDNESS (or telicity): grammatical category indicating whether or not an activity has a definite end point; see telic, atelic. §3.15, §19.8.

CASE: a system of nominal inflections, marking the syntactic function of a noun phrase in its clause. §1.5, §1.10, §13.2.

CATAPHORA: a pronoun or demonstrative referring to something which is explicitly stated later in the discourse, such as *he* in *After he stopped smoking, John lived to a ripe old age*. §15.3.

CAUSAL: peripheral argument whose referent is responsible for a state or activity, as in *John is sick [from eating rotten meat]*CAUSAL.

CAUSATIVE: valency-increasing derivation which prototypically operates on an intransitive clause, putting underlying S argument into O function and introducing a 'causer' as A argument. §3.20, Chapter 24.

CIRCUMFIX: a type of affix made up of one part which precedes the root or stem (like a prefix) and one part which follows (like a suffix). §5.2.

CLASSIFIERS: a set of (free or bound) forms which serve to categorize most of the nouns of a language, typically in terms of shape, composition, arrangement, or function/use. §3.16.

CLAUSE: the description of some activity, state or property. Consists of an obligatory predicate which requires certain core arguments and may also have peripheral arguments. §3.2.

CLITIC: a surface element part-way between a word and an affix in its properties. It is typically a separate grammatical word which is attached to a contiguous phonological word. §5.4, §10.5.

COGNATES: two forms which are historically related; that is, go back to a single original form.

COMITATIVE: an affix (generally derivational, sometimes inflectional) added to a form with reference X, giving the meaning 'with (accompanied by) an X' or 'having an X'. Comp. privative.

COMITATIVE APPLICATIVE: an applicative construction in which an original comitative argument is placed in O function. Chapter 25.

COMMON ARGUMENT: an argument shared, in their underlying structures, by main clause and relative clause within a relative clause construction. Chapter 17.

COMPARATIVE CONSTRUCTION: typically involves comparing two participants (the comparee and the standard) in terms of some property (the parameter) this being marked by an index. §3.23, Chapter 26.

COMPLEMENT CLAUSE: clause which fills a (normally core) argument slot in a higher clause. §1.9, §3.10, Chapter 18.

COMPLEMENT-TAKING VERB: a verb which may have a complement clause filling one of its (generally, core) argument slots. Chapter 18.

COMPLEMENTARY DISTRIBUTION: the occurrence of each of two or more items (sounds or forms) in mutually exclusive environments.

COMPLEMENTIZER: grammatical form which marks a complement clause. Chapter 18.

COMPLETION: grammatical category covering perfect and imperfect. §3.15, §19.7.

COMPOSITION: grammatical category covering perfective and imperfective. §3.15, §19.10.

COMPOUNDING: morphological process which joins two roots to form one stem. §3.13.

CONCORD: when two words (for example, noun and modifying adjective within an NP) are marked for the same grammatical category. §5.6.

CONJUGATION: a class of verbs all of which take the same inflectional allomorphs.

CONJUNCT: grammatical element showing that the subject is 1st person in a statement and 2nd person in a question. Compl. disjunct. §15.1.10.

CONSANGUINEAL: kinship relation which does not involve marriage but is entirely through descent (a 'blood relation'). Compl. affinal. §1.3, §16.1.

CONSTITUENT: anything which fills a slot in a syntactic structure. §5.6.

CONSTITUENT ORDER: the order in which phrasal constituents occur within a clause (often mistermed 'word order'). §2.4, §5.6.

CONSTRUCTION: type of clause (or, sometimes, phrase) with specified properties. §5.6.

CONTENT QUESTION: question which enquires concerning a core or peripheral argument (including time, place, and manner), or predicate (referring to an action or state or property), through employing an interrogative word. §3.7, Chapter 27.

CONTINUOUS, see durative.

COPULA CLAUSE: indicating a relational meaning between CS (copula subject) and CC (copula complement) functions. §3.2, Chapter 14.

COPULA COMPLEMENT (CC): the argument in a copula clause which is shown to be in a specified relation to the copula subject (typically, may be realized as a plain NP, an NP marked with a preposition, a possessive clause, an adjective, or a complement clause). Chapter 14.

COPULA SUBJECT (CS): that argument in a copula clause which is topic for the discourse in which it occurs (generally realized by an NP or a complement clause). Chapter 14.

CORE ARGUMENT: an obligatory argument for a specific verb, which must be either stated or understood from the context. §3.2, §3.9, §5.6, §13.2.

COVERB: word (generally non-inflecting) which may be combined with an inflecting verb to form a complex verbal lexeme. §1.11.

DATIVE: a case which typically marks the beneficiary of 'give', the addressee of 'tell', and the person to whom something is shown for 'show'.

DECLARATIVE: choice from a mood system used in a statement. §3.2.

DEICTIC REFERENCE: pointing to some participant, activity, or place within the context of speaking. §15.2.

DEMONSTRATIVE: grammatical element whose primary function is to point to an object in the situation of discourse; may also have anaphoric and/or cataphoric function. §3.7, §§15.2–3.

DERIVATION: optional morphological process which applies to a root or stem and derives a stem; may or may not change word class. §§3.13–14, §5.3.

DETERMINER: grammatical modifier within an NP, typically including demonstratives and articles.

DIACHRONIC DESCRIPTION: description of how a language system changes through time. Compl. synchronic description.

DIPHTHONG: vowel phoneme which has two or more phonetic components. §4.9.

DIRECT SPEECH: verbatim (or almost verbatim) quotation of what was said.

DISJUNCT: grammatical element showing that the subject is not 1st person in a statement and not 2nd person in a question. Compl. conjunct. §15.1.10.

DISSIMILATION: change by which one sound becomes more dissimilar to some neighbouring sound.

DUAL: term in a grammatical number system referring to two entities. §20.2.

DURATIVE (also called continuous or progressive): an event seen as unfolding over a period of time. Compl. punctual. §3.15, §19.9.

E: a syntactic function which constitutes an extension to the core in an extended intransitive or an extended transitive clause. §3.2, §13.1.

ENCLITIC: clitic which is attached to the end of a word. §5.4, §10.5.

ERGATIVE: case inflection marking transitive subject (A). Compl. absolutive. §3.9, §13.2, §13.5.4.

EVIDENTIALITY: grammatical system providing information about the evidence on which a report is based. §1.5, §3.15, §19.13.

EXCLUSIVE: non-singular first person pronoun, referring to speaker and one or more other people who do not include the addressee. Compl. inclusive. §15.1.2.

EXTENDED INTRANSITIVE: clause type with two core arguments, in S (intransitive subject) and E (extension to core) functions. Verb which occurs in the predicate of such a clause. §3.2, §13.1.

EXTENDED TRANSITIVE (or ditransitive): clause type with three core arguments, in A (transitive subject), O (transitive object), and E (extension to core) functions. Verb which occurs in the predicate of such a clause. §3.2, §13.1.

EXTENT: grammatical category covering punctual and durative. §3.15, §19.9.

FLUID-S: system where some verbs may have their S argument marked like A (Sa) or like O (So) with a (generally, predictable) difference in meaning. §3.9, §13.2, §13.5.4.

FOCAL CLAUSE: that clause in a linking construction which carries the mood of the sentence. §3.11.

FOCUS: an argument accorded prominence within a clause. §3.21.

FORMAL MARKEDNESS: if a term in a grammatical system has zero realization (or a zero allomorph) it is said to be formally unmarked. Other terms in the system are formally marked. §5.7.

FREE FORM: a form which constitutes a grammatical word without any morphological processes having to be applied. §5.2.

FUNCTIONAL LOAD of a contrast: the extent to which that contrast is utilized within that language.

FUNCTIONAL MARKEDNESS: a term in a grammatical system which is employed in neutral or unspecified circumstances (or when a contrast is neutralized) is said to be functionally unmarked. Other terms in the system are functionally marked. §5.7.

FUSIONAL: a type of language whose words involve a number of grammatical elements fused together (that is, not segmentable in surface structure). §5.5.

GENDER: small closed system of noun classes one of whose semantic distinctions is masculine/feminine. See noun classes. §1.5, §1.10, §3.16.

GENITIVE: marker of an intra-NP possessive relation, which is added to the possessor item. Compl. pertensive. §1.10, §16.2.

GLOTTALIC AIRSTREAM MECHANISM: air movement initiated at the glottis. §7.2.

GOAL APPLICATIVE: an applicative construction in which an original goal argument is placed in O function. Chapter 25.

GRAMMATICAL WORD: a unit on the hierarchy of grammatical units (just below phrase) defined on grammatical criteria. Generally (but not necessarily always) coinciding with phonological word. Chapter 10.

HEAD: obligatory nucleus of a phrase which determines the grammatical profile of the whole phrase (for example, gender of a noun phrase). §3.4, §5.6, §16.8, §17.2.

HETERORGANIC: sequence of sounds which have different place of articulation, for example -nb-.

HOMORGANIC: sequence of sounds which have the same place of articulation, for example -mb-.

IDEOPHONE: word class which generally has special phonology (often involving inherent reduplication and onomatopoeia). Typically relating to manner, colour, sound, smell, action, state, or intensity. §8.3.

IMPERATIVE: choice from a mood system used in a direct command. §1.5, §3.2.

IMPERFECT: something which began in the past and is still continuing. Compl. perfect. §3.15, §19.7.

IMPERFECTIVE ASPECT: focussing on the temporal make-up of an event. Compl. perfective aspect. §3.15, §19.10.

INALIENABLE POSSESSION: when the possessed has an inherent connection with the possessor, and cannot be given away. §1.3, §16.5.

INCLUSIVE: non-singular first person pronoun, referring to speaker and one or more other people who do include the addressee. Compl. exclusive. §15.1.2.

INDIRECT SPEECH: a report of what someone else has said (often cast into the reporter's own words).

INFLECTION: morphological process which obligatorily applies to a root or derived stem of a certain word class, producing a grammatical word. §3.13, §5.3.

INSTRUMENTAL: case inflection marking the referent of the NP to which it is attached as weapon, tool, or material used in the activity described by the verb. §4.3, §13.2.1.

INSTRUMENTAL APPLICATIVE: an applicative construction in which an original instrumental argument is placed in O function. Chapter 25.

INTERJECTION: a conventionalized cry, typically indicating the speaker's emotional response to something that has happened to them, or something which they have observed or become aware of. §10.7.

INTERNAL CHANGE: morphological process which involves changing a vowel (or, less frequently, a consonant) in the middle of a word, for instance, from *take* /teik/ to *took* /tuk/ in English. §3.13.

INTERROGATIVE: choice from a mood system used in a (content or polar) question. §3.2, §3.7, Chapter 27.

INTERROGATIVE WORD: word occurring in a content question which establishes it as a question. Chapter 27.

INTONATION: type of prosody realized by pitch, generally applying over clause or sentence. §7.6.

INTRANSITIVE: clause type with one core argument, in S (intransitive subject) function. Verb which occurs in the predicate of such a clause. §3.2, §5.6, Chapter 13.

IRREALIS: referring to something that didn't happen (but could have happened) or which might happen. Compl. realis. §3.15, §19.4.

ISOLATING: a type of language most of whose words consist of one morpheme. §5.5.

LABILE: older name for ambitransitive.

LANGUAGE: in the technical sense of linguists, a number of forms of speech are said to constitute a single language if they are mutually intelligible.

LENITION: the replacement of a sound by another sound that has weaker manner of articulation (involving less muscular tension).

LEXEME (or LEXICAL ITEM): a root or underlying form. §10.2.

LOCATIVE: marker indicating position of rest at, on, or near the referent of the noun phrase to which it is attached.

LOCATIVE APPLICATIVE: an applicative construction in which an original locative argument is placed in O function. Chapter 25.

LOGOPHORIC PRONOUN: used in a complement clause, this refers back to the subject of the matrix clause. §15.3.4.

MARKEDNESS: see formal markedness, functional markedness. §5.7.

MINIMAL: pronoun paradigm in which 'me and you' is a term on a par with 1st person singular and 2nd person singular (and, in some languages, 3rd person singular). Compl. augmented. §3.7, §15.1.2.

MODAL VERB: a verb which indicates a modality.

MODALITY: one of a number of choices (within irrealis) referring to some aspect of the future. §3.15, §19.4.1.

MOOD: grammatical system indicating the pragmatic function of a sentence, covering indicative (for a statement), interrogative (for a question), and imperative (for a command). §3.2, §27.0.

MORA: unit between phoneme and syllable, variously defined. §7.6.

MORPHEME: the minimum meaningful unit of speech. §5.2.

MORPHOLOGICAL PROCESS: process which applies to a root, forming a stem. §3.13.

MORPHOLOGY: that part of grammar which studies the structure of words. Compl. syntax. §3.13, §5.2.

NEUTRALIZATION: when a certain grammatical or phonological contrast may not apply in a certain environment, it is then said to be neutralized. §5.7, §7.2, §15.1.3.

NOMINAL HIERARCHY: hierarchy of items which can be head of an NP, according as how likely they are to be in A rather than in O function. §3.9, §13.5.4.

NOMINALIZATION: morphological derivation which forms a noun stem from a verb or adjective root or stem. §3.14.

NOMINATIVE: case inflection marking intransitive subject (S) and transitive subject (A). Compl. accusative. §3.9, §13.2, §13.5.4.

NON-CANONICAL MARKING OF CORE ARGUMENTS: when most of the instances of a core argument receive a certain marking, but there are a minority of instances which attract a different marking, this is termed non-canonical. §13.6.

NON-SPATIAL SETTING: covers the range of parameters which describe the setting for an activity or state other than those referring to spatial location. It typically includes evidentiality, reality, degree of certainty, phase of activity, completion, boundedness, temporal extent, composition (some of the last three, and more besides, may be called aspect), and tense. §3.15, Chapter 19.

NOUN: word class whose primary function is as head of an NP; many of its members refer to concrete objects. §3.3, §8.3.1, Chapter 11.

NOUN CLASSES: grouping of all the nouns of a language into a number of small classes which comprise a small closed grammatical system. Noun class membership must be marked somewhere outside the noun itself. And see gender. §1.9, §3.16.

NOUN INCORPORATION: the incorporation of a noun (generally in underlying S or O function) into a verb to create a compound stem.

NOUN PHRASE (NP): a constituent which can fill an argument slot in clause structure. It has a noun or pronoun or demonstrative, etc. as head. §3.4, §5.6, §11.4.

NP, see NOUN PHRASE.

NUMBER: grammatical system referring to quantity of referents, one of whose terms is singular. There will be one or more further terms. §1.4, Chapter 20.

O: object of a transitive verb, a syntactic core argument.

PASSIVE: valency-reducing syntactic derivation which puts underlying O argument into derived S function and places underlying A argument in a peripheral function. §3.20, Chapter 23.

PAUCAL NUMBER: referring to a relatively smaller number, greater than two, in a {singular, dual, paucal, plural} grammatical number system. §20.2.

PERFECT: a past action which is completed but still has present relevance. Compl. imperfect. §3.15, §19.7.

PERFECTIVE ASPECT: an event regarded as a whole, without regard for its temporal constituency. Compl. imperfective aspect. §3.15, §19.10.

PERIPHERAL ARGUMENT: a non-core argument, which is optional. Typically includes instrument, accompaniment, recipient, beneficiary, time, place, manner. §3.9, §5.6.

PERSON: speech act participants; always including 1st person (speaker) and 2nd person (addressee), and sometimes also 3rd person (neither speaker nor addressee). §15.1.1.

PERTENSIVE: marker of an intra-NP possessive relation, which is added to the possessed item. Compl. genitive. §16.2, §19.10.

PHASE OF ACTIVITY: whether beginning, continuing, ending, etc. §3.15, §19.6.

PHONEME: the minimum segmentable unit of phonology. §7.1.

PHONETICS: articulatory and/or acoustic study of the sounds of speech.

PHONOLOGICAL WORD: a unit on the hierarchy of phonological units (just above syllable). defined on phonological criteria. Generally (but not necessarily always) coinciding with grammatical word. Chapter 10.

PHONOLOGY: description of the phonetic contrasts which are used to distinguish between distinct words in a given language. Chapter 7.

PHONOTACTICS: statement of which consonants and vowels may correspond to each structural slot in syllable (and word) structure. §7.4.

PHRASE: a constituent which can fill a slot in clause structure—noun phrase in an argument slot and verb phrase in predicate slot. §3.4.

PIVOT: a topic which a recognizable as such by its grammatical properties. §3.21, §23.1.

PLURAL: can have absolute or relative reference, depending on the type of number system it occurs in; all is explained in §20.2.

POCHAL: a relatively smaller number greater than one, in a {singular, pochal, plural} grammatical system of number. §20.2.

POLAR INTERROGATIVE: question enquiring whether or not a proffered statement is correct. Can be answered by 'yes' or 'no' in languages which have such words (not all do). §3.2, Chapter 27.

POLARITY: grammatical system whose terms are positive and negative. §3.12, Chapter 21.

POLYSYNTHETIC: highly synthetic. §5.5.

POSSESSIVE PHRASE: a type of NP which is included within a larger NP and indicates the possessor with respect to the head of the larger NP, which is the possessed. §3.4, Chapter 16.

POSTPOSITION: an adposition which follows the constituent for which it provides grammatical marking. §5.4.

PRAGMATICS: the practical consequences of the use of a given portion of language.

PREDICATE: the central (and obligatory) structural element of a clause, generally realized by a verb phrase (with verb as head). It determines the number and type of core arguments required in the clause. §2.5, §3.2, §11.5.

PREFIX: an affix which precedes a root or stem.

PREPOSITION: an adposition which precedes the constituent for which it provides grammatical marking. §5.4.

PRIMARY VERBS: refer directly to an activity or state. Compl. secondary verbs. §1.11, §18.5.

PRIVATIVE: an affix (generally derivational, sometimes inflectional) added to a form with referent X, giving the meaning 'without an X'. Comp. comitative.

PROCLITIC: clitic which is attached to the beginning of a word. §5.4, §10.5.

PROGRESSIVE, see durative.

PRONOUN: small closed class of grammatical items which relate to person (and usually also to number). Can be free forms or bound forms. §3.7, §15.1.

PROSODY: a system of phonological contrasts which has scope over a sequence of segments. §7.5.

PROTO-LANGUAGE: putative single ancestor language for a group of modern languages that are held to be genetically related, each having developed by regular changes from the proto-language.

PULMONIC AIRSTREAM MECHANISM: air movement initiated in the lungs. §7.2.

PUNCTUAL: an event which happens more-or-less instantaneously. Compl. durative. §3.15, §19.9.

QUASI-APPLICATIVE: a type of applicative construction for which there is no underlying construction in which the applicative argument appears in peripheral function. §25.2.

REALIS: referring to something that is believed to have happened or to be happening. Compl. irrealis. §3.15, §19.4.

REALITY STATUS: grammatical category covering realis and irrealis. §3.15, §19.4.

RECIPROCAL CONSTRUCTION: clause describing several instances of an activity such that what is A argument in one instance is O argument in another. §3.22, Chapter 22.

REDUPLICATION: morphological process which involves repeating all or part of a root (or stem or full word) before, after, or in the middle of it. §3.13.

REFLEXIVE CONSTRUCTION: clause in which underlying A and O arguments have the same reference. §3.22, Chapter 22.

RELATIVE CLAUSE: clause which modifies the head of an NP. Relative clause and main clause share, in their underlying structures, a common argument. Chapter 17.

ROOT: unanalysable lexical element.

S: subject of an intransitive verb, a syntactic core argument.

S = A AMBITRANSITIVE: the S argument, when the verb is used intransitively, corresponds to the A argument, when it is used transitively. §3.3, §13.3.

S = O AMBITRANSITIVE: the S argument, when the verb is used intransitively, corresponds to the O argument, when it is used transitively. §3.3, §13.3.

Sa: subject of an intransitive verb (S) which is marked in the same way as the subject of a transitive verb (A). §3.9, §13.5.4.

SECONDARY CONCEPTS: provide modification for a primary verb. May be realized as an affix or as a verb (a secondary verb). Compl. primary verb. §1.11, §18.5.

SEMANTIC ROLE: the types of participant involved with verbs of a certain semantic type. §1.9, §3.3, §13.5.1.

SEMANTIC TYPE: a set of words with similar meanings and grammatical properties. §1.9, §1.11, §3.3, §8.3, §12.4, §13.5.1, §18.5.

SEMANTICS: study of the meaning relations conveyed by the grammatical systems and lexical contrasts of a language.

SENTENCE: no simple definition is feasible—see §3.11.

SERIAL VERB CONSTRUCTION: has a predicate consisting of two (or more) verbs, each of which could make up a predicate on its own, and whose combination is conceived of as describing a single action; there must be a single subject applying to the whole. §18.6.1, §21.3, §24.2.2.

SHIFTER: grammatical item whose reference changes depending on who is speaking (pronouns) or what the place or time is. §3.7.

So: subject of an intransitive verb (S) which is marked in the same way as the object of a transitive verb (O). §3.9, §13.5.4.

SPLIT-S: system where the S argument for some verbs is marked like A (Sa) and for other verbs S is marked like O (So); also called active/stative. §3.9, §13.2, §13.5.4.

STATIVE/ACTIVE: label covering split-S and fluid-S systems.

STEM: the nucleus of a word, to which an inflectional process applies, forming a word.

STRESS (or accent): a contrastive prosody generally having scope over a word, characterized by some or all of: loudness, vowel quality, pitch, and length. §7.6.

SUBGROUP: set of languages within a language family which descend from a single ancestor language, this being itself a descendent of the proto-language for the whole language family.

SUBTRACTION: morphological process which involves deleting something from a root. §3.13.

SUFFIX: an affix which follows a root or stem.

SUPPLETION: when a lexeme has two forms which are not cognate (as *go* and *went* in English).

SUPPORTING CLAUSE: that clause in a linking construction which does not carry the mood of the sentence. §3.11.

SYLLABLE: a phonological unit centred on a nucleus (typically a vowel) which may be preceded and/or followed by one or more consonants. §1.4, §6.3, §7.4.

SYNCHRONIC DESCRIPTION: description of a language system at one point in time, without taking account of historical changes. Compl. diachronic description.

SYNTAX: study of the organization and interrelation of the components of a grammar above the level of word.

SYNTHETIC: language whose words generally each have a large number of grammatical components. Compl. analytic. §5.5.

TELIC: an event which is bounded and has a definite end point. Compl. atelic. §3.15, §19.8.

TEMPORAL EXTENT: grammatical category covering punctual and durative. §3.15, §19.9.

TENSE: grammatical category, with shifting reference, which refers to time. §1.5, §1.7, §1.10, §3.15, §19.3.

TOPIC: an argument which occurs in a succession of clauses in a discourse and binds them together. §3.21, §23.1.

TRANSITIVE: clause type with two core arguments, in A (transitive subject) and O (transitive object) functions. Verb which occurs in the predicate of such a clause. §3.2, §5.6, Chapter 13.

TRIAL: term in a grammatical number system referring to three entities. §20.2.

TRIPARITE MARKING: when each of transitive subject (A), intransitive subject (S), and transitive object (O) receives a distinct surface marking. §3.9, §13.2.

UNMARKED: see formal markedness, functional markedness.

VALENCY: the number of core arguments a verb requires.

VALENCY-CHANGING: derivations which may increase valency (causative, applicative) or decrease it (passive, antipassive, some varieties of reflexive and reciprocal, etc.). §3.20, Chapters 22–25.

VERB: word class whose primary function is as head of a predicate. Most of its members refer to actions and states. §3.3, §8.3.3, Chapter 11.

VERB PHRASE: a constituent which can fill the predicate slot within a clause. Typically has a verb as its head. §3.4, §5.6.

VERBALIZATION: morphological derivation which forms a verb stem from a noun or adjective root or stem. §3.14.

VERBLESS CLAUSE: similar to a copula clause but with the predicate slot left blank. It indicates a relational meaning between verbless clause subject and verbless clause complement. Chapter 14.

VERBLESS CLAUSE COMPLEMENT (VCC): the argument in a verbless clause which is shown to be in a specified relation to the verbless clause subject (typically, may be realized as a plain NP, an NP marked with a preposition, a possessive clause, an adjective, or a complement clause). Chapter 14.

VERBLESS CLAUSE SUBJECT (VCS): that argument in a verbless clause which is topic for the discourse in which it occurs (generally realized by an NP or a complement clause). Chapter 14.

WORD: the result of applying optional derivational processes to a root, and then any obligatory inflectional process to the resulting stem. Subtypes: phonological word, grammatical word. Unit at the intersection of morphology and syntax. §3.1, Chapter 10.

WORD ORDER: the order in which words must or may occur in a phrase, in a clause, or in a sentence. (This label is often misleadingly used for (phrasal) constituent order.) §2.4, §5.6.

YES/NO QUESTION: see polar question.

ZERO: when one term in a grammatical system has no explicit marking it is said to have zero realization (ø). For example, in English a noun with singular number reference receives zero marking (for instance *horse-ø*) whereas one with plural reference is marked by orthographic *-s* (*horse-s*). §3.13, §5.3.

ZERO ANAPHORA: when anaphora is shown simply by leaving a gap. Compare anaphoric *he* in *John came in and he sat down* with anaphoric *ø* in *John came in and ø sat down.* §15.3.

ZERO DERIVATION: a word-class-changing derivation with zero marking. Compare noun *hospital* and verbalization *hospital-ize*, marked by *-ize*, with noun *market* and verbalization *market-ø*, with zero marking. §3.5, §3.13, §11.3.

References

Abbott, Miriam. 1991. 'Macushi', pp. 23–160 of Derbyshire and Pullum 1991.

Abitov, M. L., Balkarov, B. X., Desheriev, Yu. D., Rogava, G. V., El'berdov, X. U., Kardanov, B. M., and Kuasheva, T. X. 1957. *Grammatika kabardino-cherkesskogo literaturnogo jazyka. [A grammar of literary Kabardian-Cherkess.]* Moscow: Akademija Nauk SSSR.

Adelaar, Willem. 1977. *Tarma Quechua: grammar, texts, dictionary.* Lisse: The Peter de Ridder Press.

—— 2006. 'Review of *A grammar of Moseten* by Jeanette Sakel', *Anthropological Linguistics* 48: 191–4.

Aikhenvald, Alexandra Y. 1998. 'Warekena', pp. 225–439 of Derbyshire and Pullum 1998.

—— 2000a. 'Transitivity in Tariana', pp. 145–72 of Dixon and Aikhenvald 2000a.

—— 2000b. *Classifiers: a typology of noun categorization devices.* Oxford: Oxford University Press.

—— 2002. *Language contact in Amazonia.* Oxford: Oxford University Press.

—— 2003. *A grammar of Tariana, from northwest Amazonia.* Cambridge: Cambridge University Press.

—— 2004. *Evidentiality.* Oxford: Oxford University Press.

—— 2006. 'Serial verb constructions in typological perspective', pp. 1–68 of Aikhenvald and Dixon 2006.

—— 2007. 'Reciprocals and reflexives in North-Arawak languages of the Upper Rio Negro (Warekena of Xié, Bare, Baniwa of Içana)', pp. 845–55 of Nedjalkov 2007, Vol. 2.

—— 2008a. *The Manambu language of East Sepik, Papua New Guinea.* Oxford: Oxford University Press.

—— 2008b. 'Reciprocals in the making: Multiple grammaticalization in Manambu', pp. 156–67 of *Studies on Grammaticalization*, edited by Elizabeth Verhoeven, Stavros Skopeteas, Yong-Min Shin, Yoko Nishina, and Johannes Helmbrecht. Berlin: Mouton de Gruyter.

—— 2010. *Imperatives and commands.* Oxford: Oxford University Press.

—— 2011. 'Causatives which do not cause: Non-valency-increasing effects of a valency-increasing derivation', pp. 86–142 of Aikhenvald and Dixon 2011a.

—— 2012. *Languages of the Amazon.* Oxford: Oxford University Press.

—— and Dixon, R. M. W. 2006. Editors of *Serial verb constructions, a cross-linguistic typology.* Oxford: Oxford University Press.

—— —— 2011a. *Language at large: Essays on syntax and semantics.* Leiden: Brill.

—— —— 2011b. 'Non-ergative associations between S and O', pp. 143–69 of Aikhenvald and Dixon 2011a.

Aissen, Judith. 1974. 'Verb raising', *Linguistic Inquiry* 5: 325–66.

Alcalay, R. 1974. *The complete Hebrew-English dictionary*. Bridgeport, CT: Prayer Book Press.

Allen, Barbara J., Gardiner, Donna B., and Frantz, Donald G. 1984. 'Noun incorporation in Southern Tiwa', *International Journal of American Linguistics* 50: 292–311.

Alpatov, Vladimir, Bugaeva, Anna Ju., and Nedjalkov, Vladimir P. 2007. 'Reciprocals and sociatives in Ainu', pp. 1751–822 of Nedjalkov 2007, Vol. 4.

—— and Nedjalkov, Vladimir P. 2007. 'Reciprocal, sociative and competitive constructions in Japanese', pp. 1021–94 of Nedjalkov 2007, Vol. 3.

Alvarez, José. 2005. 'Comparative constructions in Guajiro/Wayuunaiki', *Opción* 47: 9–36.

Amberber, Mengistu. 1996. 'Amharic grammar summary'. RCLT internal document, ANU.

—— 2000. 'Valency-changing and valency-encoding devices in Amharic', pp. 312–32 of Dixon and Aikhenvald 2000a.

—— 2002. *Verb classes and transitivity in Amharic*. Munich: Lincom Europa.

Ameka, Felix K. 1991. 'Ewe: its grammatical constructions and illocutionary devices'. PhD thesis, ANU.

—— 2004. 'Grammar and cultural practices: The grammaticalization of triadic communication in West African languages', *Journal of West African Languages* 30: 5–28.

—— 2006. 'Ewe serial verb constructions in their grammatical context', pp. 124–43 of Aikhenvald and Dixon 2006.

Amha, Azeb. 2001. *The Maale language*. Leiden: CNWS, University of Leiden.

Andersen, Torben. 1988. 'Ergativity in Päri, a Nilotic OVS language', *Lingua* 75: 289–324.

Anderson, Gregory D. S. 1993. 'Obligatory double-marking of morphosyntactic categories', *Chicago Linguistic Society Papers* 29 (1): 1–16.

Anderwald, Lisselotte. 2002. *Negation in non-standard British English: Gaps, regularizations and asymmetries*. London: Routledge.

Andrade, Manuel J. 1933. 'Quileute', pp. 149–292 of Boas 1933.

Arokianathan, S. 1987. *Tangkhul Naga grammar*. Mysore: Central Institute for Indian Languages.

Aronson, Howard I. 1991. 'Modern Georgian', pp. 219–312 of *The indigenous languages of the Caucasus*, Vol. 1, *The Kartvelian languages*, edited by Alice C. Harris. Delmark, NY: Caravan Books.

Asher, R. E. 1985. *Tamil*. London: Croom Helm.

Ashton, E. O. 1947. *Swahili grammar (including intonation)*, 2nd edition. London: Longmans.

Austin, Peter. 1981a. *A grammar of Diyari, South Australia*. Cambridge: Cambridge University Press.

—— 1981b. 'Switch-reference in Australia', *Language* 57: 309–34.

—— 1997. 'Causatives and applicatives in Australian Aboriginal languages', pp. 165–225 of *The dative and related phenomena*, edited by Kazuto Matsamura and Tooru Hayasi. Tokyo: Hituzi Syobo.

—— 2001. 'Word order in a free word order language: the case of Jiwarli', pp. 305–23 of *Forty years on: Ken Hale and Australian languages*, edited by Jane Simpson, David Nash, Mary Laughren, and Peter Austin. Canberra: Pacific Linguistics.

Azevedo, Milton M. 2005. *Portuguese: A linguistic introduction*. Cambridge: Cambridge University Press.

Baker, C. L. 1995. 'Contrast discourse prominence and intensification with special reference to locally free reflexives in British English', *Language* 71: 63–101.

Baker, Mark C. 1988. *Incorporation: A theory of grammatical function changing*. Chicago: University of Chicago Press.

Baker-Shenk, Charlotte and Cokley, Dennis. 1996. *American sign language: A teacher's resource text on grammar and culture*. Washington DC: Gallaudet University Press.

Barnes, Janet. 1994. 'Tuyuca', pp. 325–42 of Kahrel and van den Berg 1994.

Bauer, Winifred. 1993. *Maori*. London: Routledge.

Baugh, Albert C. 1959. *A history of the English language*, 2nd edition. London: Routledge and Kegan Paul.

Baxter, Alan N. 1988. *A grammar of Kristang (Malacca Creole Portuguese)*. Canberra: Pacific Linguistics.

Bennett, David C., Bynon, Theodora, and Hewitt, George. 1995. Editors of *Subject, voice and ergativity: Selected essays*. London: School of Oriental and African Studies.

Berg, René van den. 1989. *A grammar of the Muna language*. Dordrecht: Foris.

Bergsland, Knut. 1997. *Aleut grammar, Unangam Tunuganaan Achixaasix̂*. Fairbanks: Alaska Native Language Center.

Bernini, Giuliano and Ramat, Paolo. 1996. *Negative sentences in the languages of Europe: A typological approach*. Berlin: Mouton de Gruyter.

Berry, Keith and Christine. 1999. *A description of Abun, a West Papuan language of Irian Jaya*. Canberra: Pacific Linguistics.

Bhat, D. N. S. 1989a. *An introduction to Indian grammars*, Part 2, *Wh-words*. A report being submitted to the University Grants Commission (India).

—— 1989b. *The prominence of tense, aspect and mood*. Amsterdam: John Benjamins.

—— 2000a. *Introducing grammatical notions*. Pune: Centre for Advanced Study in Sanskrit, University of Pune.

—— 2000b. 'The indefinite-interrogative puzzle', *Linguistic Typology* 4: 365–400.

—— and Ningomba, M. S. 1997. *Manipuri grammar*. Munich: Lincom Europa.

Bhatia, Tej K. 1993. *Punjabi, a cognitive-descriptive grammar*. London: Routledge.

Bittner, Maria. 1987. 'On the semantics of the Greenlandic antipassive and related constructions', *International Journal of American Linguistics* 53: 194–231.

Blake, Barry J, 1982. 'The absolutive: its scope in English and in Kalkatungu', pp. 71–94 of *Studies in transitivity (Syntax and semantics*, Vol. 15), edited by Paul J. Hopper and Sandra A. Thompson. New York: Academic Press.

Bloomfield, Leonard. 1917. *Tagalog texts with grammatical analysis*. Urbana, IL: University of Illinois.

Boas, Franz. 1911a. Editor of *Handbook of American Indian languages*, Part 1 (Smithsonian Institution, Bureau of American Ethnology, Bulletin 40). Washington DC: Government Printing Office.

Boas, Franz. 1911b. 'Introduction', pp. 1–83 of Boas 1911a.

—— 1911c. 'Kwakiutl', pp. 423–557 of Boas 1911a.

—— 1911d. 'Chinook', pp. 559–667 of Boas 1911a.

—— 1922. Editor of *Handbook of American Indian languages*, Part 2 (Smithsonian Institution, Bureau of American Ethnology, Bulletin 40). Washington DC: Government Printing Office.

—— 1933. Editor of *Handbook of American Indian languages*, Vol. III. New York: Columbia University Press.

—— 1947. 'Kwakiutl grammar, with a glossary of the suffixes', *Transactions of the American Philosophical Society*, new series 37: 201–377.

—— and Deloria, Ella. 1941. *Dakota grammar*. Washington DC: Government Printing Office.

Bolinger, Dwight. 1977. *Meaning and form*. London: Longman.

—— 1978. 'Asking more than one thing at a time', pp. 107–50 of *Questions*, edited by Henry Hiz. Dordrecht: Reidel.

Bond, Oliver. 2009. 'The locative-applicative in Eleme', *Transactions of the Philological Society* 107: 1–30.

Borgman, Donald M. 1990. 'Sanuma', pp. 15–248 of Derbyshire and Pullum 1990.

Breen, J. G. 1981. 'Margany and Gunya', pp. 274–393 of Dixon and Blake 1981.

Bresnan, Joan and Moshi, Lioba. 1990. 'Object asymmetries in comparative Bantu syntax', *Linguistic Inquiry* 21: 147–85.

Bright, William. 2007. 'Review of *The world atlas of language structures*, edited by Martin Haspelmath, Matthew S. Dryer, David Gil and Bernard Comrie', *International Journal of American Linguistics* 73: 241–54.

Bril, Isabelle. 2007. 'Reciprocal constructions in Nêlêmwa (New Caledonia)', pp. 1479–509 of Nedjalkov 2007, Vol. 3.

Broadwell, George A. 2006. *A Choctaw reference grammar*. Lincoln: University of Nebraska Press.

Bruce, Les. 1984. *The Alamblak language of Papua New Guinea (East Sepik)*. Canberra: Pacific Linguistics.

Bugaeva, Anna. 2004. *Grammar and folklore texts of the Chitose dialect of Ainu (idiolect of Ito Oda)*. Kyoto: Endangered languages of the Pacific Rim.

—— 2010. 'Ainu applicatives in typological perspective', *Studies in Language* 34: 749–801.

Bull, W. E. 1968. *Time, tense and the verb: A study in theoretical and applied linguistics, with particular attention to Spanish*. Berkeley and Los Angeles: University of California Press.

Bursill-Hall, G. L. 1972. *Grammatica Speculativa of Thomas of Erfurt*. London: Longman.

Butt, John and Benjamin, Carmen. 2004. *A new reference grammar of modern Spanish*, 4th edition. London: Hodder Arnold.

Bybee, Joan and Fleischman, Suzanne. 1995. Editors of *Modality in grammar and discourse*. Amsterdam: John Benjamins.

—— Haiman, John, and Thompson, Sandra A. 1997. Editors of *Essays on language function and language type, dedicated to T. Givón*. Amsterdam: John Benjamins.

Bybee, Joan L., Pagliuca, William, and Perkins, Revere D. 1990. 'On the asymmetries in the affixation of grammatical material', pp. 1–39 of *Studies in typology and diachrony* 1, edited by William Croft, Keith Denning, and Suzanne Kemmer. Amsterdam: John Benjamins.

Byrne, Francis. 1992. 'Tense, scope and spreading in Saramaccan', *Journal of Pidgin and Creole Languages* 7: 195–221.

Campbell, Lyle. 1987. 'Syntactic change in Pipil', *International Journal of American Linguistics* 53: 253–80.

—— 2000. 'Valency-changing derivations in K'iche', pp. 236–81 of Dixon and Aikhenvald 2000a.

Capell, A. 1941. *A new Fijian dictionary*. Suva: Government Printer.

—— 1984. 'The Laragia language', pp. 55–106 of *Papers in Australian Linguistics*, No. 16. Canberra: Pacific Linguistics.

—— and Coate, H. H. J. 1984. *Comparative studies in Northern Kimberley languages*. Canberra: Pacific Linguistics.

—— and Hinch, H. E. 1970. *Maung grammar, texts and vocabulary*. The Hague: Mouton.

Carlson, Robert. 1994. *A grammar of Supyire*. Berlin: Mouton de Gruyter.

Censabella, Marisa. 2010. 'Beneficiaries and recipients in Toba (Guaycurú)', pp. 185–201 of *Benefactives and malefactives: Typological perspectives and case studies*, edited by Fernando Zúñiga and Seppo Kittilä. Amsterdam: John Benjamins.

Chafe, Wallace. 1995. 'The realis-irrealis distinction in Caddo, the northern Iroquoian languages, and English', pp. 349–65 of Bybee and Fleischman 1995.

Chao, Yuen Ren. 1976. 'Chinese as symbolic system', pp. 84–96 of *Aspects of Chinese sociolinguistics, Essays by Yuen Ren Chao*, selected and introduced by Anwar S. Dil. Stanford: Stanford University Press. [Paper first published in 1973.]

Chapman, Shirley and Derbyshire, Desmond C. 1991. 'Paumari', pp. 161–332 of Derbyshire and Pullum 1991.

Chappell, Hilary. 1980. 'Is the get-passive adversative?', *Papers in Linguistics* 13: 411–52.

Charney, Jean O. 1993. *A grammar of Comanche*. Lincoln: University of Nebraska Press.

Childs, G. Tucker. 1995. *A grammar of Kisi, a southern Atlantic language*. Berlin: Mouton de Gruyter.

Chisholm, William S., Jr. 1984. Editor of *Interrogativity: A colloquium on the grammar, typology and pragmatics of questions in seven diverse languages*. Amsterdam: John Benjamins.

Christaller, J. G. 1875. *A grammar of the Asante and Fante language called Tshi (Chwee, Twi) based on the Akuapem dialect with reference to the other (Akan/Fante) dialects*. Basel: The Basel Evangelical Missionary Society.

Chumbow, Robert S. and Tamanji, Pius N. 1994. 'Bafut', pp. 211–36 of Kahrel and van den Berg 1994.

Chung, Sandra and Timberlake, Alan. 1985. 'Tense, aspect, and mood', pp. 202–58 of Shopen 1985, Vol. III.

Churchward, C. Maxwell. 1941. *A new Fijian grammar*. Sydney: Australasian Medical Publishing Company.

Churchward, C. Maxwell. 1953. *Tongan grammar*. London: Oxford University Press.

Clendon, Mark. 2000. 'Topics in Worora grammar'. PhD thesis, University of Adelaide.

Clynes, Adrian. 1992. 'Negation in Balinese'. Handout for presentation at Workshop on Negation, ANU.

Coetzee, J. M. 2000. *Disgrace*. London: Vintage.

Colarusso, John. 1992. *A grammar of the Kabardian language*. Calgary: University of Calgary Press.

Cole, Peter. 1976. 'A causative construction in Modern Hebrew: Theoretical implications', pp. 99–128 of *Studies in Modern Hebrew syntax and semantics: The transformational-generative approach*, edited by Peter Cole. Amsterdam: North-Holland.

—— 1982. *Imbabura Quechua*. Amsterdam: North-Holland.

—— 1983. 'The grammatical role of the causee in universal grammar', *International Journal of American Linguistics* 49: 115–33.

Comrie, Bernard. 1975. 'Causatives and universal grammar', *Transactions of the Philological Society for 1974*, pp. 1–32.

—— 1976a. 'The syntax of causative constructions: cross-language similarities and divergences', pp. 261–312 of Shibatani 1976a.

—— 1976b. *Aspect*. Cambridge: Cambridge University Press.

—— 1981. *Language universals and linguistic typology, syntax and morphology*. Oxford: Blackwell.

—— 1985a. 'Causative verb formation and other verb-deriving morphology', pp. 309–48 of Shopen 1985, Vol. III.

—— 1985b. *Tense*. Cambridge: Cambridge University Press.

—— 1989. *Language universals and linguistic typology, syntax and morphology*. 2nd edition. Oxford: Basil Blackwell.

—— 2000. 'Valency-changing derivations in Tsez', pp. 360–74 of Dixon and Aikhenvald 2000a.

—— 2005. 'Endangered numeral systems', pp. 203–30 of *Bedrohte Vielfalt Aspekte des Sprach(en)tods: Aspects of language death*, edited by Jan Wohlgemut and Tyro Dirksmeyer. Berlin: Weissensee.

—— and Polinsky, Maria. 1993. Editors of *Causatives and transitivity*. Amsterdam: John Benjamins.

—— and Smith, Norval. 1977. 'Lingua descriptive series: questionnaire', *Lingua* 42: 1–72.

Cooreman, Ann. 1994. 'A functional typology of antipassives', pp. 49–88 of Fox and Hopper 1994.

Corbett, Greville G. 1978. 'Universals in the syntax of cardinal numbers', *Lingua* 46: 355–68.

—— 2000. *Number*. Cambridge: Cambridge University Press.

—— and Hayward, Richard J. 1987. 'Gender and number in Bayso', *Lingua* 73: 1–28.

Craig, Colette G. 1977. *The structure of Jacaltec*. Austin: University of Texas Press.

—— and Hale, Kenneth L. 1988. 'Relational preverbs in some languages of the Americas: Typological and historical perspectives', *Language* 64: 312–44.

Crapo, Richley H. and Aitken, Percy. 1986. *Bolivian Quechua reader and grammar-dictionary*. Ann Arbor, MI: Karoma.

Crowley, Terry. 1978. *The middle Clarence dialects of Bandjalang*. Canberra: Australian Institute of Aboriginal Studies.

—— 1982. *The Paamese language of Vanuatu*. Canberra: Pacific Linguistics.

—— 1983. 'Uradhi', pp. 306–428 of Dixon and Blake 1983.

Culy, Christopher. 1999. 'Questions and focus in Takelma', *International Journal of American Linguistics* 65: 251–74.

Curnow, Timothy J. 1993. 'Semantics of Spanish causatives involving *hacer*', *Australian Journal of Linguistics* 13: 165–84.

—— 1997. 'A grammar of Awa Pit (Cuaiquer), an indigenous language of southwestern Colombia'. PhD thesis, ANU.

Cutler, Anne, Hawkins, John A., and Gilligan, Garry. 1983. 'The suffixing preference: A processing explanation', *Linguistics* 23: 723–58.

Cysouw, Michael. 2007. 'Content interrogatives in Pichis Ashéninka: Corpus study and typological comparison', *International Journal of American Linguistics* 73: 133–63.

Dahl, Osten. 1979. 'Typology of sentence negation', *Linguistics* 17: 79–106.

Dahlstrom, Amy. n.d. 'Grammar of Fox'. Ms.

Davies, John. 1981. *Kobon*. Amsterdam: North-Holland.

Davies, William D. 2000. 'Events in Madurese reciprocals', *Oceanic Linguistics* 39: 123–43.

Davis, Henry. 2005. 'On the syntax and semantics of negation in Salish', *International Journal of American Linguistics* 71: 1–55.

Dayley, Jon P. 1978. 'Voice in Tzutujil', *Journal of Mayan Linguistics* 1(1): 20–52. [A later version appeared as pp. 192–226 of Nichols and Woodbury 1985.]

—— 1981. 'Voice and ergativity in Mayan languages', *Journal of Mayan Linguistics* 2(2): 3–82.

—— 1985. *Tzutujil grammar*. Berkeley and Los Angeles: University of California Press.

De Wolf, Charles M. 1988. 'Voice in Austronesian languages of Philippine type: passive, ergative or neither?', pp. 143–93 of Shibatani 1988a.

Deeney, S. J. J. 1975. *Ho grammar and vocabulary*. Chaibasa: Xavier Publications.

Dench, Alan. 1991. 'Panyjima', pp. 124–243 of Dixon and Blake 1991.

—— 1995. *Martuthunira, a language of the Pilbara region of Western Australia*. Canberra: Pacific Linguistics.

Derbyshire, Desmond C. 1979. *Hixkaryana*. Amsterdam: North-Holland.

—— 1985. *Hixkaryana and linguistic typology*. Dallas: Summer Institute of Linguistics and University of Texas at Arlington.

—— and Pullum, Geoffrey K. 1986–1998. Editors of *Handbook of Amazonian languages*, Vol. 1, 1986; Vol. 2, 1990; Vol. 3, 1991; Vol. 4, 1998. Berlin: Mouton de Gruyter.

Diakonoff, I. M. 1988. *Afrasian languages*. Moscow: Nauka.

Dickens, Patrick. n.d. 'Juù'hoan grammar'. Ms.

Diessel, Holger. 2003. 'The relationship between demonstratives and interrogatives', *Studies in Language* 27: 635–55.

Dimmendaal, Gerrit J. 1983. *The Turkana language*. Dordrecht: Foris.

Dineen, Anne. 1992. 'Reciprocals in Mawng'. Handout for presentation at Local Workshop on Reflexives and Reciprocals, ANU.

Dixon, R. M. W. 1971. 'A method of semantic description', pp. 436–71 of Steinberg and Jakobovits 1971. [Revised version as pp. 63–115 of Dixon 1982.]

—— 1972. *The Dyirbal language of North Queensland*. Cambridge: Cambridge University Press.

—— 1977a. *A grammar of Yidiɲ*. Cambridge: Cambridge University Press.

—— 1977b. 'The syntactic development of Australian languages', pp. 365–415 of *Mechanisms of syntactic change*, edited by Charles N. Li. Austin: University of Texas Press.

—— 1980. *The languages of Australia*. Cambridge: Cambridge University Press.

—— 1981. 'Wargamay', pp. 1–144 of Dixon and Blake 1981.

—— 1982. *Where have all the adjectives gone? and other essays in semantics and syntax*. Berlin: Mouton.

—— 1983. 'Nyawaygi', pp. 430–525 of Dixon and Blake 1983.

—— 1988. *A grammar of Boumaa Fijian*. Chicago: University of Chicago Press.

—— 1989. 'The Dyirbal kinship system', *Oceania* 59: 245–68.

—— 1991a. *A new approach to English grammar, on semantic principles*. Oxford: Clarendon Press.

—— 1991b. *Words of our country: Stories, place names and vocabulary in Yidiny, the Aboriginal language of the Cairns-Yarrabah region*. St Lucia: University of Queensland Press.

—— 1994. *Ergativity*. Cambridge: Cambridge University Press.

—— 2000a. 'A typology of causatives: form, syntax and meaning', pp. 30–83 of Dixon and Aikhenvald 2000a.

—— 2000b. 'A-constructions and O-constructions in Jarawara', *International Journal of American Linguistics* 66: 22–56.

—— 2002. *Australian languages: Their nature and development*. Cambridge: Cambridge University Press.

—— 2004. *The Jarawara language of southern Amazonia*. Oxford: Oxford University Press.

—— 2005a. *A semantic approach to English grammar*. Oxford: Oxford University Press. [Revision of Dixon 1991a, with three chapters added.]

—— 2005b. 'Comparative constructions in English', *Studia Anglica Posnaniensia* 41: 6–27. [Reprinted as pp. 472–93 of Aikhenvald and Dixon 2011a.]

—— 2006a. Complement clauses and complementation strategies in typological perspective', pp. 1–48 of Dixon and Aikhenvald 2006.

—— 2006b. 'Complementation strategies in Dyirbal', pp. 263–79 of Dixon and Aikhenvald 2006.

—— 2008. 'Comparative constructions: A cross-linguistic typology', *Studies in Language* 32: 787–817.

Dixon, R. M. W. and Aikhenvald, Alexandra Y. 1997. 'A typology of argument-determined constructions', pp. 71–113 of Bybee, Haiman, and Thompson 1997.

————— 2000a. Editors of *Changing valency: Case studies in transitivity*. Cambridge: Cambridge University Press.

————— 2000b. 'Introduction', pp. 1–29 of Dixon and Aikhenvald 2000a.

————— 2004. Editors of *Adjective classes: A cross-linguistic typology*. Oxford: Oxford University Press.

————— 2006. Editors of *Complementation: A cross-linguistic typology*. Oxford: Oxford University Press.

—— and Blake, Barry J. 1979–83. Editors of *Handbook of Australian languages* Vol. 1, 1979; Vol. 2, 1981; Vol. 3, 1983. Canberra: The Australian National University Press and Amsterdam: John Benjamins.

————— 1991–2000. Editors of *The handbook of Australian languages* Vol. 4, 1991; Vol. 5, 2000. Melbourne: Oxford University Press.

Dobrushina, N. R. 1999. 'Formy irrealnogo naklonenija' ['Forms of irrealis'], pp. 262–8 of *Elementy tsakhurskogo jazyka v tipologicheskom osvetshenii* [*Elements of Tsakhur language in typological perspective*], edited by A. E. Kibrik and Ya. G. Testelec. Moscow: Nasledie.

Donaldson, Tamsin. 1980. *Ngiyambaa, the language of the Wangaaybuwan of New South Wales*. Cambridge: Cambridge University Press.

Donohue, Mark. 1999. *A grammar of Tukang Besi*. Berlin: Mouton de Gruyter.

—— 2001. 'Coding choices in argument structure: Austronesian applicatives in texts', *Studies in Language* 25: 217–54.

Driem, George van. 1993. *A grammar of Dumi*. Berlin: Mouton de Gruyter.

Dubinsky, Stanley, Lloret, Maria-Rosa, and Newman, Paul. 1988. 'Lexical and syntactic causatives in Oromo', *Language* 64: 485–500.

Duff-Tripp, Martha. 1997. *Gramatica del idioma Yanesha' (Amuesha)*. Lima: Instiiuto Lingüístico de Verano.

Dunn, Ernest F. 1968. *An introduction to Bini*. Michigan State University: African Studies Center.

Durie, Mark. 1985. *A grammar of Acehnese, on the basis of a dialect of North Aceh*. Dordrecht: Foris.

—— 1986. 'The grammaticization of number as a verbal category', *Berkeley Linguistics Society Proceedings* 12: 355–70.

Eades, Diana. 1979. 'Gumbaynggir', pp. 244–361 of Dixon and Blake 1979.

Early, Robert. 1994. 'Lewo', pp. 65–92 of Kahrel and van den Berg 1994.

Elliott, Jennifer R. 2000. 'Realis and irrealis: Forms and concepts of the grammaticalisation of reality', *Linguistic Typology* 4: 55–90.

Emenanjo, E. Nolue. 1978. *Elements of modern Igbo grammar, a descriptive approach*. Ibadan: Oxford University Press.

Enfield, N. J. 2004. 'Adjectives in Lao', pp. 323–47 of Dixon and Aikhenvald 2004.

—— 2007a. *A grammar of Lao*. Berlin: Mouton de Gruyter.

—— 2007b. 'Meanings of the unmarked: how "default" person reference does more than just refer', pp. 97–120 of *Person reference in interaction: Linguistic, cultural, and social perspectives*, edited by N. J. Enfield and Tanya Stivers. Cambridge: Cambridge University Press.

Enfield, N. J., Stivers, T., and Levinson S. C. 2010. 'Question-response sequences in conversation across ten languages', *Journal of Pragmatics* 42: 2613–798.

England, Nora C. 1983. *A grammar of Mam, a Mayan language*. Austin: University of Texas Press.

——1988. 'Mam voice', pp. 525–45 of Shibatani 1988a.

Epps, Patience. 2006. 'Growing a number system: The historical development of numerals in an Amazonian language family', *Diachronica* 2003: 259–88.

——2008. *A grammar of Hup*. Berlin: Mouton de Gruyter.

Erades, P. A. 1950. 'Points of Modern English Syntax XII', *English Studies* 31: 153–7.

Erelt, Mati. 2007. Editor of *Estonian language*, 2nd edition. Tallinn: Estonian Academy Publishers.

Éva, Hompó. 1990. 'Grammatical relations in Gamo: A pilot sketch', pp. 356–405 of *Omotic language studies*, edited by Richard J. Hayward. London: School of Oriental and African Studies.

Evans, Nicholas D. 1995. *A grammar of Kayardild, with historical-comparative notes on Tangkic*. Berlin: Mouton de Gruyter.

——2008. 'Reciprocal constructions: towards a structural typology', pp. 33–103 of *Reciprocals and reflexives: Theoretical and typological explorations*, edited by Ekkehard König and Volker Gast. Berlin: Mouton de Gruyter.

——2009. 'Two plus one makes thirteen: Senary numbers in the Morehead/Maro region', *Linguistic Typology* 13: 321–35.

——Gaby, Alice, and Nordlinger, Rachel. 2007. 'Valency mismatches and the coding or reciprocity in Australian languages', *Linguistic Typology* 11: 541–97.

Everett, Caleb. 2006. 'Patterns in Karitiana: Articulation, perception and grammar'. PhD dissertation, Rice University.

Everett, Dan and Kern, Barbara. 1997. *Wari', the Pacas Novos language of western Brazil*. London: Routledge.

Faltz, Leonard M. 1985. *Reflexivization: A study in universal syntax*. New York: Garland.

Farr, Jim. 1991. 'Reflexivization and reciprocity in Korafe'. Handout for presentation at Local Workshop on Reflexives and Reciprocals, ANU.

Feldman, Harry. 1986. *A grammar of Awtuw*. Canberra: Pacific Linguistics.

Feldpausch, Tom and Feldpausch, Becky. 1992. 'Namia grammar essentials', pp. 1–97 of *Namia and Amanab grammar essentials*, edited by John R. Roberts. Ukarumpa, Papua New Guinea: Summer Institute of Linguistics.

Fleck, David. 2003. 'A grammar of Matses'. PhD dissertation, Rice University.

——2006. 'Antipassives in Matses', *Studies in Language* 30: 541–73.

Fleisch, Axel. 2005. 'Agent phrases in Bantu passives', pp. 93–111 of *Studies in African linguistic typology*, edited by F. K. Erhard Voeltz. Amsterdam: John Benjamins.

Fodor, J. A. 1970. 'Three reasons for not deriving "kill" from "cause to die"', *Linguistic Inquiry* 1: 429–38.

Foley, William A. 1991. *The Yimas language of New Guinea*. Stanford: Stanford University Press.

—— and Van Valin, Robert D. 1984. *Functional syntax and universal grammar*. Cambridge: Cambridge University Press.

Ford, Lysbeth J. 1998. 'A description of the Emmi language of the Northern Territory of Australia'. PhD thesis, ANU.

Foris, David P. 2000. *A grammar of Sochiapan Chinantec*. Dallas: SIL International and the University of Texas at Arlington.

Fortescue, Michael. 1984. *West Greenlandic*. London: Croom Helm.

—— 2007. 'Reciprocals in West Greenlandic Eskimo', pp. 813–42 of Nedjalkov 2007, Vol. 2.

Fox, Barbara and Hopper, Paul J. 1994. Editors of *Voice: Form and function*. Amsterdam: John Benjamins.

Frajzyngier, Zygmunt. 1993. *A grammar of Mupun*. Berlin: Dietrich Reimer.

—— 2002. *A grammar of Hdi*. Berlin: Mouton de Gruyter,

—— and Curl, Trace S. 2000. Editors of *Reciprocals: Forms and functions*. Amsterdam: John Benjamins.

Francis, Dick. 1982. *Banker*. London: Michael Joseph.

Frank, Paul. 1990. *Ika syntax*. Dallas: Summer Institute of Linguistics and University of Texas at Arlington.

Franklin, Karl J., Kerr, Harland B., and Beaumont, Clive. 1974. *Tolai language course*. Huntington Beach, CA: Summer Institute of Linguistics.

Frawley, William. 1992. *Linguistic semantics*. Hillsdale, NJ: Lawrence Erlbaum.

Gabas, Nilson, Jr. 1999. 'A grammar of Karo, Tupí (Brazil)'. PhD dissertation, University of California at Santa Barbara.

Gair, James W. 1970. *Colloquial Sinhalese clause structure*. The Hague: Mouton.

Galant, Michael. 2004. 'The nature of the standard of comparison in San Lucas Quiaviní Zapotec', pp. 59–74 of *Report 13, Survey of Californian and other Indian languages, Conference on Otomanguean and Oaxacan languages*, edited by Rosemary B. de Azcona and Mary Paster. Berkeley: University of California at Berkeley.

Gallagher, Steve and Baehr, Peirce. 2005. *Bariai grammar sketch*. Ukarumpa, Papua New Guinea: Summer Institute of Linguistics.

Galloway, Brent D. 1993. *A grammar of Upriver Halkomelem*. Berkeley and Los Angeles: University of California Press.

Galucio, Ana Vilacy. 2001. 'The morphosyntax of Mekens (Tupi)'. PhD dissertation, University of Chicago.

Garey, Howard B. 1957. 'Verbal aspect in French', *Language* 57: 91–110.

Gary, Judith O. and Gamal-Eldin, Saad. 1982. *Cairene Egyptian Colloquial Arabic*. Amsterdam: North-Holland.

—— and Keenan, Edward L. 1977. 'On collapsing grammatical relations in universal grammar', pp. 83–120 of *Syntax and semantics 8: Grammatical relations*, edited by Peter Cole and Jerrold M. Sadock. New York: Academic Press. [Reprinted in Keenan 1987, pp. 121–65.]

Geluykens, Ronald. 1988. 'On the myth of rising intonation in polar questions', *Journal of Pragmatics* 12: 467–85.

Genetti, Carol and Hildebrandt, Kristine. 2004. 'The two adjective classes in Manange', pp. 74–96 of Dixon and Aikhenvald 2004.

Geniušienė, Emma. 1987. *The typology of reflexives*. Berlin: Mouton de Gruyter.

—— 2007. 'Reflexive and reciprocal constructions in Lithuanian (with references to Latvian)', pp. 633–72 of Nedjalkov 2007, Vol. 2.

Geraghty, Paul. 1984. 'Language policy in Fiji and Rotuma', pp. 32–84 of *Duivosavosa, Fiji's languages: Their use and their future*, edited by G. B. Milner, D. G. Arms, and P. Geraghty. Bulletin No. 8. Suva: Fiji Museum.

Gerdts, Donna B. 2000. 'Combinatory restrictions on Halkomelem reflexives and reciprocals', pp. 133–60 of Frajzyngier and Curl 2000.

Gibson, Jeanne D. 1980. 'Clause union in Chamorro and universal grammar'. PhD dissertation, University of California at San Diego.

Giridhar, P. P. 1980. *Angami grammar*. Mysore: Central Institute of Indian Languages.

—— 1994. *Mao Naga grammar*. Mysore: Central Institute of Indian Languages.

Givón, T. 1979. *On understanding grammar*. New York: Academic Press.

—— 1980. *Ute reference grammar*. Ignacio, CO: Ute Press.

—— 1984. 'Ute', pp. 215–43 of Chisholm 1984.

—— 1990. *Syntax: A functional-typological introduction*, Vol. II. Amsterdam: John Benjamins.

—— 1994. Editor of *Voice and inversion*. Amsterdam: John Benjamins.

—— 2001. *Syntax: An introduction*, Vol. II. Amsterdam: John Benjamins.

—— and Yang, Lynne. 1994. 'The rise of the English GET-passive', pp. 119–49 of Fox and Hopper 1994.

Glasgow, Kathleen. 1964. 'Frame of reference for two Burera tenses', p. 118 of *Papers on the languages of the Australian Aborigines*, edited by Richard Pitman and Harland Kerr. Canberra: Australian Institute of Aboriginal Studies.

Goddard, Ives. 1996. Editor of *Handbook of North American Indians*, Vol. 17, *Languages*. Washington DC: Smithsonian Institution.

Göksel, Asli and Kerslake, Celia. 2005. *Turkish: A comprehensive grammar*. London: Routledge.

Golovko, Evgeniy V. 1993. 'On non-causative effects of causativity in Aleut', pp. 385–90 of Comrie and Polinsky 1993.

Gordon, Lynn. 1986. *Maricopa morphology and syntax*. Berkeley and Los Angeles: University of California Press.

Gordon, R. G. 2005. Editor of *Ethnologue: Languages of the world*, 15th edition. Dallas: SIL International.

Graczyk, Randolph. 2007. *A grammar of Crow: Apsáalooke Aliláau*. Lincoln: University of Nebraska Press.

Gray, Louis H. 1934. *Introduction to Semitic comparative linguistics*. New York: Columbia University Press.

Green, Diana. 1993. 'Palikur numerals'. Ms.

Green, Ian. 1991. 'Reflexive constructions in Daly languages'. Handout for presentation at Local Workshop on Reflexives and Reciprocals, ANU.

Green, Rebecca. 1995. 'A grammar of Gurr-goni (North Central Arnhem Land)'. PhD thesis, ANU.

Greenberg, Joseph H. 1978. 'Generalizations about numeral systems', pp. 249–95 of *Universals of human language*, Vol. 3, *Word structure*, edited by Joseph H. Greenberg. Stanford: Stanford University Press.

Grimes, Barbara F. 1984. Editor of *Ethnologue: Languages of the world*, 10th edition. Dallas: Wycliffe Bible Translators.

—— 1996. Editor of *Ethnologue: Languages of the world*, 13th edition. Dallas: Summer Institute of Linguistics.

—— 2000. Editor of *Ethnologue: Languages of the world*, 14th edition. Dallas: SIL International.

Grimes, Charles E. 1991. *The Buru languages of eastern Indonesia*. PhD thesis, ANU.

Grondona, Verónica M. 1998. 'A grammar of Mocovi'. PhD dissertation, University of Pittsburgh.

Groot, Caspar de. 1994. 'Hungarian', pp. 143–62 of Kahrel and van den Berg 1994.

Guentchéva, Zlatka and Rivière, Nicole. 2007. 'Reciprocal constructions in French', pp. 561–607 of Nedjalkov 2007, Vol. 2.

Guillaume, Antoine. 2008. *A grammar of Cavineña*. Berlin: Mouton de Gruyter.

—— and Rose, Françoise, 2010. 'Sociative causative markers in South American languages: A possible areal feature', pp. 383–402 of *Essais de typologie et de linguistique générale: Mélanges offerts à Denis Creissels*, edited by Franck Floricic. Lyons: ENS editions.

Guirardello, Raquel. 1999a. 'Trumai', pp. 351–3 of *The Amazonian Languages,* edited by R.M.W. Dixon and Alexandra Y. Aikhenvald. Cambridge: Cambridge University Press.

—— 1999b. 'A reference grammar of Trumai'. PhD dissertation, Rice University.

Gurubasave Gonda, K. S. 1975. *Ao grammar*. Mysore: Central Institute of Indian Languages.

Haas, Mary R. 1941. *Tunica*. New York: J. J. Augustin.

Hagége, Claude. 2008. 'Towards a typology of interrogative verbs', *Linguistic Typology* 12: 1–44.

Haig, Geoffrey. 1999. 'Turkish grammar summary'. RCLT internal document, ANU.

—— 2001. 'Linguistic diffusion in present-day East Anatolia: From top to bottom', pp. 195–224 of *Areal diffusion and genetic inheritance: Problems in comparative linguistics*, edited by Alexandra Y. Aikhenvald and R. M. W. Dixon. Oxford: Oxford University Press.

Haiman, John. 1980. *Hua: a Papuan language of the eastern highlands of New Guinea*. Amsterdam: John Benjamins.

—— 1983. 'Iconic and Economic Motivation', *Language* 59: 781–819.

—— 1985. *Natural syntax*. Cambridge: Cambridge University Press.

—— and Munro, Pamela. 1983. Editors of *Switch reference and universal grammar*. Amsterdam: John Benjamins.

Hajek, John. 2006, 'Serial verbs in Tetun Dili', pp. 239–53 of Aikhenvald and Dixon 2006.

Hale, Austin and Shrestha, Kedar P. 2006. *Newār (Nepāl Bhāṣā)*. Munich: Lincom Europa.

Hale, Kenneth. 1971. 'A note on a Walbiri tradition of antonymy', pp. 472–82 of Steinberg and Jakobovits 1971.

—— 1973. 'Deep-surface canonical disparities in relation to analysis and change: An Australian example', pp. 401–58 of *Current Trends in Linguistics*, Vol. 11—*Diachronic, areal and typological linguistics*, edited by Thomas A. Sebeok. The Hague: Mouton.

—— 1975. 'Gaps in grammar and culture', pp. 296–311 of *Linguistics and anthropology, in honor of C. F. Voegelin*, edited by M. Dale Kinkade, Kenneth L. Hale, and Osward Werner. Lisse: Peter de Ridder.

—— 1997a. 'The Misumalpan causative construction', pp. 199–216 of Bybee, Haiman, and Thompson 1997.

—— 1997b. 'Some observations on the contributions of local languages to linguistic science', *Lingua* 100: 71–89.

—— and Nash, David. 1997. 'Damin and Lardil phonotactics', pp. 247–59 of *Boundary rider: Essays in honour of Geoffrey O'Grady*, edited by Darrell Tryon and Michael Walsh. Canberra: Pacific Linguistics.

—— and Storto, Luciana. 1997. 'Agreement and spurious antipassives', *ABRALIN (Boletim da Associação Brasiliera de Lingüística)* 20: 61–89.

Hansen, K. C. and Hansen, L. E. 1974. *Pintupi dictionary*. Darwin: Summer Institute of Linguistics, Australian Aborigines Branch.

——— 1992. *Pintupi/Luritja dictionary*. 3rd edition. Alice Springs: Institute for Aboriginal Development.

Harris, Alice C. 1981. *Georgian syntax: A study in relational grammar*. Cambridge: Cambridge University Press.

Harris, Kyle. 1990. 'Nend grammar essentials', pp. 73–156 of *Two grammatical studies*, edited by John. R. Roberts. (Data Papers on Papua New Guinea Languages, Vol. 37.) Ukarumpa: Summer Institute of Linguistics.

Hartzler, Margaret. 1994. 'Sentani', pp. 51–64 of Kahrel and van den Berg 1994.

Haspelmath, Martin. 1993. *A grammar of Lezgian*. Berlin: Mouton de Gruyter.

—— 1997a. *From space to time: Temporal adverbials in the world's languages*. Munich: Lincom Europa.

—— 1997b. *Indefinite pronouns*. Oxford: Clarendon Press.

—— 2007. 'Further remarks on reciprocal constructions', pp. 2087–115 of Nedjalkov 2007, Vol. 4.

—— Dryer, Matthew S., Gill, David, and Comrie, Bernard. 2005. *The world atlas of language structures*. Oxford: Oxford University Press.

Haviland, John. 1979. 'Guugu Yimidhirr', pp. 1–180 of Dixon and Blake 1979.

—— 1981. *Sk'op sotz'leb: El Tzotzil de San Lorenzo Zinacantán*. Mexico City: Universidad Nacional Autónoma de México.

Hayward, Dick. 1984. *The Arbore language: A first investigation*. Hamburg: Helmut Buske.

Heath, Jeffrey. 1976. 'Antipassivization: a functional typology', *Berkeley Linguistics Society Proceedings* 2: 202–11.

——1978. *Ngandi grammar, texts and dictionary*. Canberra: Australian Institute of Aboriginal Studies.

——1981. *Basic materials in Mara: Grammar, texts and dictionary*. Canberra: Pacific Linguistics.

Heine, Bernd. 1997. *Cognitive foundations of grammar*. New York: Oxford University Press.

——2000. 'Polysemy involving reflexive and reciprocal markers in African languages', pp. 1–29 of Frajzyngier and Curl 2000.

——and Kuteva, Tania. 2002. *World Lexicon of Grammaticalization*. Cambridge: Cambridge University Press.

Hellwig, Birgit. 2004. 'Comparative structures in Goemai'. Handout for presentation in Workshop on Comparative Constructions, RCLT.

Hercus, Luise A. 1994. *A grammar of the Arabana-Wangkanguru language, Lake Eyre Basin, South Australia*. Canberra: Pacific Linguistics.

Hetzron, Robert. 1976. 'On the Hungarian causative verb and its syntax', pp. 371–98 of Shibatani 1976a.

Hewitt, B. G. 1979. *Abkhaz*. Amsterdam: North-Holland.

——1982. ' "Anti-passive" and "labile" constructions in North Caucasian', *General Linguistics* 22: 158–71.

——1983. 'The causative: Daghestanian variations on a theme', *Papers in Linguistics* 16: 171–202.

Hidalgo, Raquel. 1994. 'The pragmatics of de-transitive voice in Spanish: from passive to inverse', pp. 160–86 of Givón 1994.

Hill, Deborah. 1992. 'Longgu grammar'. PhD thesis, ANU.

——1997. 'Longgu grammar summary'. RCLT internal document, ANU.

Hinds, John. 1984. 'Japanese', pp. 145–88 of Chisholm 1984.

——1986. *Japanese*. London: Croom Helm.

Hinton, Leanne. 1982. 'How to cause in Mixtec', *Berkeley Linguistics Society Proceedings* 8: 354–63.

Hirtle, W. H. 1988. 'Some and any: Exploring the system', *Linguistics* 26: 443–77.

Hladký, Josef. 1976. 'A brief comment on some previous works on modality', *Brno Studies in English* 12: 85–92.

Hoa, Monique, Nedjalkov, Vladimir P., and Nikitina, Tamara N. 2007. 'Reciprocal constructions in Modern Chinese (with data from wényán)', pp. 1985–2083 of Nedjalkov 2007, Vol.4.

Hoffmann, Carl. 1963. *A grammar of the Margi language*. London: Oxford University Press.

Hoijer, Harry. 1933. 'Tonkawa, an Indian language of Texas', pp. 1–148 of Boas 1933.

Holes, Clive. 1990. *Gulf Arabic*. London: Routledge.

Holisky, Dee Ann. 1981. *Aspect and Georgian medial verbs*. Delmar, NY: Caravan.

Hollenbach, Barbara E. 1984. 'Reflexives and reciprocals in Copala Trique', *International Journal of American Linguistics* 50: 272–91.

Horn, Laurence R. 1989. *A natural history of negation*. Chicago: University of Chicago Press.

Hosokawa, K. 1991. 'The Yawuru language of West Kimberley: A meaning-based description'. PhD thesis, ANU.

Hualde, Jose Ignacio. 1992. *Catalan*. London: Routledge.

Huddleston, Rodney. 2002. 'Clause type and illocutionary force', pp. 851–945 of Huddleston and Pullum 2002.

——and Pullum, Geoffrey K. 2002. Chief authors of *The Cambridge grammar of the English language*. Cambridge: Cambridge University Press.

————and Peterson, Peter. 2002. 'Relative constructions and unbounded dependencies', pp. 1031–96 of Huddleston and Pullum 2002.

Hudson, Grover. 1997. 'Amharic and Argobba', pp. 457–85 of The *Semitic languages*, edited by Robert Hetzron. London: Routledge.

Hudson, Joyce. 1978. *The core of Walmatjari grammar*. Canberra: Australian Institute of Aboriginal Studies.

Hurford, James R. 1975. *The linguistic theory of numerals*. Cambridge: Cambridge University Press.

——1987. *Language and number: The emergence of a cognitive system*. Oxford: Basil Blackwell.

Hutchisson, Don. 1986. 'Sursurunga pronouns and the special uses of quadral number', pp. 1–20 of Wiesemann 1986.

Huttar, George L. and Huttar, Mary L. 1994. *Ndyuka*. London: Routledge.

Hyman, Larry M. and Duranti, Alessandro. 1982. 'On the object relation in Bantu', pp. 217–39 of *Syntax and semantics* 15: *Studies in transitivity*, edited by Paul J. Hopper and Sandra A. Thompson. New York: Academic Press.

Hymes, Virginia D. 1955. 'Athapaskan numeral systems', *International Journal of American Linguistics* 21: 26–45.

Hyslop, Catriona. 2001. *The Lolovoli dialect of the North-east Ambae language, Vanuatu*. Canberra: Pacific Linguistics.

——2004. 'Adjectives in North-east Ambae', pp. 263–82 of Dixon and Aikhenvald 2004.

Ikoro, Suanu. 1996a. *The Kana language*. Leiden: CNWS.

——1996b. 'Kana grammar summary'. RCLT internal document, ANU.

Ingram, Andrew. 2006. 'Serial verb constructions in Dumo', pp. 202–22 of Aikhenvald and Dixon 2006.

Iwasaki, Shoichi and Ingkaphirom, Preeya. 2005. *A reference grammar of Thai*. Cambridge: Cambridge University Press.

Jacob, Judith M. 1968. *Introduction to Cambodian*. London: Oxford University Press.

Jacobsen, William H., Jr. 1964. 'A grammar of the Washo language'. PhD dissertation, University of California at Berkeley.

——1967. 'Switch-reference in Hokan-Coahuiltecan', pp. 238–63 of *Studies in southwestern ethnolinguistics*, edited by Dell H. Hymes and William E. Bittle. The Hague: Mouton.

——1985. 'The analog of the passive transformation in ergative-type languages', pp. 176–91 of Nichols and Woodbury 1985.

Jagger, Philip J. 2001. 'Reflexives in Hausa', pp. 213–28 of *Von Ägypten zum Tscadsee: Eine linguistische Reise durch Africa*, edited by Dymitr Ibriszimov, Rudolf Leger, and Uwe Seibert. Würzburg: Deutsche Morgenländische.

Jauncey, Dorothy. 1997. 'Tamambo, Malo Island, Vanuatu grammar summary', RCLT internal document, ANU.

——2011. *Tamambo, the languages of west Malo, Vanuatu*, Canberra: Pacific Linguistics.

Jespersen, Otto. 1914. *A Modern English grammar on historical principles*, Part II, *Syntax*, Vol. 1. Heidelberg: Winter.

——1917. *Negation in English and other languages*. Copenhagen: Det. Kgl. Danske Videnskabernes Selskab. Historisk-filologiske Meddelelser. [Reprinted as pp. 3–151 of *Selected writings of Otto Jespersen*. London: Allen and Unwin and Tokyo: Senjo, 1962.]

——1924. *The philosophy of grammar*. London: Allen and Unwin.

——1937. *Analytic syntax*. Copenhagen: Levin and Munksgaard, and London: Allen and Unwin.

——1940. *A Modern English grammar on historical principles*. Part V, *Syntax*, Vol. 4. Copenhagen: Munksgaard.

Jeyapaul, V. Y. 1987. *Karbi grammar*. Mysore: Central Institute for Indian Languages.

Johnson, Allen. 2003. *Families of the forest: The Matsigenka Indians of the Peruvian Amazon*. Berkeley and Los Angeles: University of California Press.

Jones, Morris and Thomas, Alan R. 1977. *The Welsh language: Studies in its syntax and semantics*. Cardiff: University of Wales Press.

Joseph, Brian D. and Philippaki-Warburton, Irene. 1987. *Modern Greek*. London: Croom Helm.

Joseph, U. V. 2005. 'Causatives in Rabha', *Linguistics of the Tibeto-Burman Area* 28: 79–106.

Kachru. Yamuna. 1976. 'On the semantics of the causative construction in Hindi-Urdu', pp. 353–69 of Shibatani 1976a.

Kahrel, Peter and van den Berg, René. 1994. Editors of *Typological studies in negation*. Amsterdam: John Benjamins.

Kakumasu, James. 1986. 'Urubu-Kaapor', pp. 326–403 of Derbyshire and Pullum 1986.

Kazenin, Konstantin I. 2007. 'Reciprocals, comitatives, sociatives and reflexives in Kabardian', pp. 739–71 of Nedjalkov 2007, Vol. 2.

Keen, Sandra. 1983. 'Yukulta', pp. 190–304 of Dixon and Blake 1983.

Keenan, Edward L. 1985. 'Passive in the world's languages', pp. 243–81 of Shopen 1985, Vol. I.

——1987. *Universal grammar: 15 essays*. London: Croom Helm.

——and Comrie, Bernard. 1977. 'Noun phrase accessibility and universal grammar', *Linguistic Inquiry* 8: 63–99.

——and Dryer, Matthew S. 2007. 'Passive in the world's languages', pp. 325–61 of *Language typology and syntactic description*, Vol. I, *Grammatical categories and the lexicon*, 2nd edition, edited by Timothy Shopen. Cambridge: Cambridge University Press.

Kemmer, Suzanne. 1993. *The middle voice*. Amsterdam: John Benjamins.

Kenesei, István, Vago, Robert M., and Fenyvesi, Anna. 1998. *Hungarian*. London: Routledge.

Kennedy, Benjamin H. 1962. *The revised Latin primer*, edited and further revised by James Mountford. London: Longmans.

Khanmagomedov, B. G.-K. 1967. 'Tabasaranskij jazyk (Tabasaran language)', pp. 545–61 of *Jazyki narodov SSSR (Languages of the USSR)*, Vol. 4, *Iberijsko-kavkazskie jazyki (Ibero-Caucasian languages)*, chief editor V. V. Vinogradov. Moscow: Nauka.

——2001. 'Tabasaranskij jazyk (Tabasaran language)', pp. 385–98 *of Jazyki mira. Kavkazskije jazyki. (Languages of the world. Caucasian languages)*, edited by V. N. Jartseva, V. M. Solntsev, and N. I. Tolstoj. Moscow: Academia.

Kibrik, A. E. 1990. 'As línguas semanticamente ergativas na perspectiva da tipologia sintática geral', *Cadernos de estudos lingüísticos* (Universidade Estadual de Campinas) 18: 15–36.

Kilham, Christine, Pamulkan, Mabel, Pootchemunka, Jennifer, and Wolmby, Topsy. 1986. *Dictionary and source book of the Wik Mungkan language*. Darwin: Summer Institute of Linguistics.

Kilian-Hatz, Christa. 2006. 'Serial verb constructions in Khwe (Central-Khoisan)', pp. 108–23 of Aikhenvald and Dixon 2006.

Kimball, Geoffrey D. 1991. *Koasati grammar*. Lincoln: University of Nebraska Press.

King, Gareth. 2008. *Modern Welsh: A comprehensive grammar*. 2nd edition. London: Routledge.

King, John T. 2009. *A grammar of Dhimal*. Leiden: Brill.

Kinkade, M. Dale. 1977. 'Singular versus plural roots in Salish', pp. 147–56 of *Papers from the XII International Conference on Salish languages*.

Kisseberth, Charles W. and Abasheikh, Mohammad I. 1977. 'The object relationship in Chi-mwi:ni, a Bantu language', pp. 179–218 of *Syntax and semantics*, Vol. 8, *Grammatical relations*, edited by Peter Cole and Jerrold M. Sadock. New York: Academic Press.

Klaiman, M. H. 1991. *Grammatical voice*. Cambridge: Cambridge University Press.

Klima, Edward S. 1964. 'Negation in English', pp. 246–323 of *The structure of language: Readings in the philosophy of language*, edited by Jerry A. Fodor and Jerrold J. Katz. Englewood Cliffs, NJ: Prentice-Hall.

Klumpp, Deloris. 1990. *Piapoco grammar*. Typescript (Colombia: Summer Institute of Linguistics).

Koehn, Edward and Sally. 1986. 'Apalai', pp. 33–127 of Derbyshire and Pullum 1986.

Kornfilt, Jaklin. 1997. *Turkish*. London: Routledge.

Kozinsky, Isaac, and Polinsky, Maria. 1993. 'Causee and patient in the causative of transitive: Coding conflict or doubling of grammatical relations', pp. 177–240 of Comrie and Polinsky 1993.

Kraft, C. H. and Kirk-Greene, A. H. M. 1973. *Hausa* (Teach Yourself Books). London: Hodder and Stoughton.

Krishnamurti, Bh. and Gwynn, J. P. L. 1985. *A grammar of Modern Telugu*. Delhi: Oxford University Press.

Kruspe, Nicole. 2004a. *A grammar of Semelai*. Cambridge: Cambridge University Press.

—— 2004b. 'Adjectives in Semelai', pp. 283–305 of Dixon and Aikhenvald 2004.

Kuipers, Aert H. 1974. *The Shuswap language: Grammar, texts, dictionary*. The Hague: Mouton.

Kulikov, Leonid I. 1993. 'The "second causative": A typological sketch', pp. 121–54 of Comrie and Polinsky 1993.

—— 1999. 'Remarks on double causatives in Tuvan and other Turkic languages', *Journal de la Société Finno-Ougrienne* 88: 49–58.

—— 2001. '66. Causatives', pp. 886–98 of *Language typology and language universals, an international handbook*, edited by Martin Haspelmath, Ekkehard König, Wulf Oesterreicher, and Wolfgang Raible. Berlin: Walter de Gruyter.

Kuno, Susumu. 1973. *The structure of the Japanese language*. Cambridge, MA: MIT Press.

—— and Robinson, Jane J. 1972. 'Multiple Wh questions', *Linguistic Inquiry* 3: 463–87.

Kuryłowicz, Jerzy. 1964. *The inflectional categories of Indo-European*. Heidelberg: Carl Winter.

Kwak, Inhee Lee. 1994. 'The pragmatics of voice in Korean', pp. 261–82 of Givón 1994.

Laidig, Wyn D. and Laidig, Carol J. 1990. 'Larike pronouns: duals and trials in a Central Moluccan language', *Oceanic Linguistics* 29: 87–109.

Lakoff, Robin. 1969. 'Some reasons why there can't be any some-any rule', *Language* 45: 608–15.

Landin, David J. 1984. 'An outline of the syntactic structure of Karitiâna sentences', pp. 219–54 of *Estudos sobre línguas tupí do Brasil* (Série Lingüística No. 11), edited by Robert A. Dooley. Brasília: Summer Institute of Linguistics.

Laughren, Mary. 1981. 'Number strand——Warlpiri'. Ms.

Lehmann, Thomas. 1993. *A grammar of Modern Tamil*. Pondicherry: Pondicherry Institute of Linguistics and Culture.

Levy, Paulette. 2004. 'Adjectives in Papantla Totonac', pp. 147–76 of Dixon and Aikhenvald 2004.

Lewis, Geoffrey. 2000. *Turkish grammar*, 2nd edition. Oxford: Oxford University Press.

Lewis, M. Paul. 2009. Editor of *Ethnologue: Languages of the world*, 15th edition. Dallas: SIL International.

Li, Charles N. and Thompson, Sandra A. 1976. 'Development of the causative in Mandarin Chinese: Interaction of diachronic processes in syntax', pp. 477–92 of Shibatani 1976a.

—— —— 1981. *Mandarin Chinese: A functional reference grammar*. Berkeley and Los Angeles: University of California Press.

—— —— 1984. 'Mandarin', pp. 47–61 of Chisholm 1984.

Lichtenberk, Frantisek. 1983. *A grammar of Manam*. Honolulu: University of Hawaii Press.

Lichtenberk, Frantisek. 1985. 'Multiple uses of reciprocal constructions', *Australian Journal of Linguistics* 5: 19–41.

—— 2000. 'Reciprocals without reflexives', pp. 31–62 of Frajzyngier and Curl 2000.

Lithgow, David. 1989. 'Influence of English grammar on Dobu and Bunama', pp. 335–47 of *VICAL 1, Oceanic Languages, Papers from the Fifth International Conference on Austronesian Linguistics*, edited by Ray Harlow and Robin Hooper. Auckland: Linguistic Society of New Zealand.

Liu, Meichun. 2000. 'Reciprocal marking with deictic verbs come and go in Mandarin', pp. 123–32 of Frajzyngier and Curl 2000.

Lockwood, W. B. 1969. *Indo-European philology, historical and comparative*. London: Hutchinson.

Loogman, Alfons. 1965. *Swahili grammar and syntax*. Pittsburgh, PA: Duquesne University Press.

Lorimer, D. L. R. 1935. *The Burushaski language*, Vol. 1, *Introduction and grammar*. Oslo: Aschenhoug.

Love, J. R. B. 2000. *The grammatical structure of the Worora language of north-western Australia*. Munich: Lincom Europa. [Publication of 1932 MA thesis from the University of Adelaide.]

Lucas, Christopher. 2007. 'Jespersen's cycle in Arabic and Berber', *Transactions of the Philological Society* 105: 398–431.

Luo, Yongxian. 2008. 'Zhuang', pp. 317–77 of *The Tai-Kadai languages*, edited by Anthony V. N. Diller, Jerold A. Edmondson, and Yongxian Luo. London: Routledge.

Lupyan, Gary and Dale, Rick. 2010. 'Language structure is partly determined by social structure'. PLoS ONE 5(1): e8559.doi:10.1371/journal. pone.0008559.

Lyons, John. 1968. *Introduction to theoretical linguistics*. Cambridge: Cambridge University Press.

—— 1977. *Semantics*, 2 vols. Cambridge: Cambridge University Press.

MacKay, Carolyn J. 1999. *A grammar of Misantla Totonac*. Salt Lake City: University of Utah Press.

McKay, Graham R. 1975. 'Rembarnga: A language of Central Arnhem Land'. PhD thesis, ANU.

Mc Laughlin, Fiona. 2004. 'Is there an adjective class in Wolof?', pp. 242–62 of Dixon and Aikhenvald, 2004.

McLendon, Sally. 1996. 'Sketch of Eastern Pomo, a Pomoan language', pp. 507–50 of Goddard 1996.

McWhorter, John. 2007. *Language interrupted: Signs of non-native acquisition in standard language grammars*. New York: Oxford University Press.

Mahootian, Shahrzad. 1997. *Persian*. London: Routledge.

Mallinson, Graham. 1986. *Rumanian*. London: Croom Helm.

Maran, La Raw and Clifton, John M. 1976. 'The causative mechanism in Jinghpaw', pp. 443–58 of Shibatani, 1976a.

Marantz, Alec. 1984. *On the nature of grammatical relations*. Cambridge, MA: MIT Press.

Marchand, Hans. 1969. *The categories and types of present-day English word-formation*. Munich: C. H. Beck.

Marchese, Lynell. 1986. 'The pronominal system of Godié', pp. 217–55 of Wiesemann 1986.

Martin, Jack B. 1991. 'Lexical and semantic aspects of Creek causatives', *International Journal of American Linguistics* 57: 194–229.

—— 2000. 'Creek voice: beyond valency', pp. 375–403 of Dixon and Aikhenvald 2000a.

—— 2011. *A grammar of Creek (Muskogee)*. Lincoln: University of Nebraska Press.

Martin, Samuel E. 1988. *A reference grammar of Japanese*, 2nd edition. Rutland, VT: Charles E. Tuttle.

Martins, Silvana and Martins, Valteir. 1999. 'Makú', pp. 251–67 of *The Amazonian languages*, edited by R. M. W. Dixon and Alexandra Y. Aikhenvald. Cambridge: Cambridge University Press.

Masica, Colin P. 1976. *Defining a linguistic area: South Asia*. Chicago: University of Chicago Press.

Maslova, Elena. 2000. 'Reciprocals and set construal', pp. 161–78 of Frajzyngier and Curl 2000.

Matisoff, James A. 1973. *The grammar of Lahu*. Berkeley and Los Angeles: University of California Press.

Matthews, P. H. 1997. *The concise Oxford dictionary of linguistics*. Oxford: Oxford University Press.

Matthews, Stephen and Yip, Virginia. 1994. *Cantonese: A comprehensive grammar*. London: Routledge.

Maxmudova, S. M. 1999. 'Kauzativ v rutul'skom jazyke [The causative in Rutul]', pp. 222–35 of *Studies in Caucasian linguistics, selected papers from the eighth Caucasian colloquium*, edited by Helma van den Berg. Leiden: CNWS.

Mazaudon, Martine. 2009. 'Number-building in Tibeto-Burman languages', pp. 117–48 of *Northeast Indian linguistics*, Vol. 2. edited by Stephen Morey and Mark Post. Delhi: Foundation (Cambridge University Press India).

Mchombo, Sam. 2004. *The syntax of Chichewa*. Cambridge: Cambridge University Press.

Merlan, Francesca. 1982. *Mangarayi*. Amsterdam: North-Holland.

—— 1983. *Ngalakan grammar, texts and vocabulary*. Canberra: Pacific Linguistics.

—— 1994. *A grammar of Wardaman, a language of the Northern Territory of Australia*. Berlin: Mouton de Gruyter.

Mettouchi, Amina. 2005. 'Nonverbal and verbal negations in Kabyle (Berber): A typological perspective', pp. 263–76 of *Studies in African linguistic typology*, edited by F. K. Erhard Voeltz. Amsterdam: John Benjamins.

Michael, Ian. 1970. *English grammatical categories, and the tradition to 1800*. Cambridge: Cambridge University Press.

Michael, Lev D. 2008. 'Nanti evidential practice: Language, knowledge, and social action in an Amazonian society'. PhD dissertation, University of Texas at Austin.

Miestamo, Matti. 2005. *Standard negation: The negation of declarative verbal main clauses in a typological perspective*. Berlin: Mouton de Gruyter.

Mihas, Elena. 2010. 'Essentials of Ashéninka Perené grammar'. PhD dissertation, University of Wisconsin-Milwaukee.

Miller, Amy. 2001. *A grammar of Jamul Tiipay*. Berlin: Mouton de Gruyter.

Miller, Wick R. 1996. 'Sketch of Shoshone, a Uto-Aztecan language', pp. 693–720 of Goddard 1996.

Mithun, Marianne. 1984. 'The evolution of noun incorporation', *Language* 60: 847–94.

——1986a. 'On the nature of noun incorporation', *Language* 62: 32–7.

——1986b. 'The convergence of noun classification systems', pp. 379–97 of *Noun classes and noun classification*, edited by Colette Craig. Amsterdam: John Benjamins.

——1995. 'On the relativity of irreality', pp. 367–88 of Bybee and Fleischman 1995.

——1999. *The languages of native North America*. Cambridge: Cambridge University Press.

——2000. 'Valency-changing derivation in Central Alaskan Yup'ik', pp. 84–114 of Dixon and Aikhenvald 2000a.

——2001. 'Understanding and explaining applicatives', *Chicago Linguistic Society Papers* 37(2): 73–97.

——2003. 'Why prefixes?', *Acta Linguistica Hungarica* 50: 155–85.

——and Ali, Elizabeth. 1996. 'The elaboration of aspectual categories: Central Alaskan Yup'ik', *Folia Linguistica* 30: 111–27.

Miyaoka, Osahito. 2004. 'Comparative constructions in Central Alaskan Yupik'. Handout for presentation in Workshop on Comparative Constructions, RCLT.

Mondloch, James L. 1978. 'Disambiguating subjects and objects in Quiche', *Journal of Mayan Linguistics* 1(1): 3–19.

Mondorf, Britta. 2009. 'Synthetic and analytic comparatives', pp. 86–107 of *One language, two grammars? Differences between British and American English*, edited by Günter Rohdenburg and Julia Schlüter. Cambridge: Cambridge University Press.

Monserrat, Ruth. 2000. 'A lingua do povo Mỹky'. PhD dissertation, Universidade Federal de Rio de Janeiro.

——and Dixon, R. M. W. 2003. 'Evidentiality in Mỹky', pp. 237–41 of *Studies in evidentiality*, edited by Alexandra Y. Aikhenvald and R. M. W. Dixon. Amsterdam: John Benjamins.

Moravcsik, Edith. 2003. 'A semantic analysis of associative plurals', *Studies in Language* 27: 469–503.

Morphy, Frances. 1983. 'Djapu, a Yolngu dialect', pp. 1–188 of Dixon and Blake 1983.

Mosel, Ulrike. 1984. *Tolai syntax and its historical development*. Canberra: Pacific Linguistics.

Mous, Maarten. 1993. *A grammar of Iraqw*. Hamburg: Helmut Buske.

Moyse-Faurie, Claire. 2007. 'Reciprocal, sociative, middle and iterative constructions in East Futunan', pp. 1511–43 of Nedjalkov 2007, Vol. 3.

Munro, Pamela. 1976. *Mojave syntax*. New York: Garland.

——1987. 'Some morphological differences between Chickasaw and Choctaw', pp. 119–33 of *Muskogean linguistics*, edited by Pamela Munro and George A. Broadwell. Los Angeles: UCLA.

Nababan, P. W. J. 1981. *A grammar of Toba-Batak*. Canberra: Pacific Linguistics.

Nasilov, Dimitri M., Isxakova, Xoršid F., Safarov, Šaxrijor S., and Nevskaja, Irina A. 2001. 'Imperative sentences in Turkic languages', pp. 181–220 of *Typology of imperative constructions*, edited by Victor S. Xrakovskij. Munich: Lincom Europa.

Nedjalkov, Igor V. 1994. 'Evenki', pp. 1–34 of Kahrel and van den Berg 1994.

—— 1997. *Evenki*. London: Routledge.

—— and Nedjalkov, Vladimir P. 2007a. 'Reciprocals, sociatives, comitatives, and assistives in Yakut', pp. 1095–161 of Nedjalkov 2007, Vol. 3.

—— —— 2007b. 'Reciprocal, sociative and competitive constructions in Karachay-Balkar', pp. 969–1019 of Nedjalkov 2007, Vol. 3.

Nedjalkov, Vladimir P. 2007. Editor of *Reciprocal constructions*. 5 vols. Amsterdam: John Benjamins.

—— and Geniušienė. Emma. 2007. 'Questionnaire on reciprocals', pp. 379–434 of Nedjalkov 2007, Vol. 1.

—— Otaina, G. A., and Xolodovič, A. A. 1995. 'Morphological and lexical causatives in Nivkh', pp. 60–81 of Bennett, Bynon, and Hewitt 1995.

—— and Silnitsky, G. G. 1973. 'The typology of morphological and lexical causatives', pp. 1–32 of *Trends in Soviet theoretical linguistics*, edited by F. Keifer. Dordrecht: Reidel.

Nevalainen, Teritu. 1996. 'Social mobility and the decline of multiple negation in Early Modern English', pp. 264–91 of *English historical linguistics 1996*, edited by M. Krygier and Jacek Fisiak. Berlin: Mouton de Gruyter.

Newman, Paul. 2000. *The Hausa language: An encyclopedic reference grammar*. New Haven: Yale University Press.

Ngonyani, Deo. 1995. 'Towards a typology of applicatives in Bantu'. Paper presented at the 26th Annual Conference on African Linguistics. 24–6 March 1995, Los Angeles.

—— 1997. 'Towards a typology of applicatives in Bantu', pp. 249–58 of *Language history and linguistic description in Africa*, edited by Ian Maddieson and Thomas J. Hinnebusch. Trenton, NJ: Africa World Press. [This is a much shortened version of the 1995 paper.]

Nichols, Johanna. 1985. 'Switch-reference causatives', *Chicago Linguistic Society Papers* 21(2): 193–203.

—— and Woodbury, Anthony C. 1985. Editors of *Grammar inside and outside the clause: Some approaches to theory from the field*. Cambridge: Cambridge University Press.

Nicklas, T. Dale. 1972. 'The elements of Choctaw'. PhD dissertation, University of Michigan.

Nida, Eugene A. 1984. *Towards a science of translating, with special reference to principles and procedures involved in Bible translation*. Leiden: Brill.

Nikolaeva, Irina. 2007. 'Reciprocals and sociatives in Udehe', pp. 933–67 of Nedjalkov 2007, Vol. 3.

Noonan, Michael. 1992. *A grammar of Lango*. Berlin: Mouton de Gruyter.

Nordlinger, Rachel. 1998. *A grammar of Wambaya*. Canberra: Pacific Linguistics.

—— and Sadler, Louisa. 2004. 'Nominal tense in cross-linguistic perspective', *Language* 80: 776–806.

O'Connor, Mary C. 1992. *Topics in Northern Pomo Grammar*. New York: Garland.

Ogunbọwale, P. O. 1970. *The essentials of the Yoruba language*. London: University of London Press.

O'Herin, Brian O. 2001. 'Abaza applicatives', *Language* 77: 477–93.

Olawsky, Knut J. 1999. *Aspects of Dagbani grammar, with special emphasis on phonology and morphology*. Munich: Lincom Europa.

—— 2006. *A grammar of Urarina*. Berlin: Mouton de Gruyter.

Ọmọruyi, Thomas O. 1986. 'Adjectives and adjectivalization processes in Edo', *Studies in African Linguistics* 17: 83–302.

Onishi, Masayuki. 1994. 'A grammar of Motuna (Bougainville, Papua New Guinea)'. PhD thesis, ANU.

—— 1995. 'Japanese grammar summary'. RCLT internal document, ANU.

—— 1997. 'Bengali grammar summary'. RCLT internal document, ANU.

—— 2000. 'Transitivity and valency-changing derivations in Motuna', pp. 115–44 of Dixon and Aikhenvald 2000a.

Osumi, Midori. 1995. *Tinrin grammar*. Honolulu: University of Hawai'i Press.

Oswalt, Robert L. 1977. 'The causative as a reference switching mechanism in Western Pomo', *Berkeley Linguistic Society Proceedings* 3: 46–54.

Otaina, Galina A. and Nedjalkov, Vladimir P. 2007. 'Reciprocal constructions in Nivkh (Gilyak)', pp. 1715–47 of Nedjalkov 2007, Vol. 4.

Overall, Simon, 2007. 'A grammar of Aguaruna'. PhD thesis, La Trobe University.

Owens, Jonathan. 1985. *A grammar of Harar Oromo (northeastern Ethiopia), including a text and glossary*. Hamburg: Helmut Buske.

Pacheco, Frantomé Bezerra. 1997. 'Aspectos da Gramática Ikpeng (Carib)'. MA thesis, Universidade Estadual de Campinas.

Pacon, W. F. 1971. *Ambrym (Lonwolwol) grammar*. Canberra: Pacific Linguistics.

Palmer, F. R. 1984. *Grammar*, 2nd edition. Harmondsworth: Penguin.

—— 1986. *Mood and modality*. Cambridge: Cambridge University Press.

—— 1994. *Grammatical roles and relations*. Cambridge: Cambridge University Press.

Pandharipande, Rajeshwari V. 1997. *Marathi*. London: Routledge.

Patz. Elisabeth. 1991. 'Djabugay', pp. 245–347 of Dixon and Blake 1991.

—— 2002. *A grammar of the Kuku Yalanji language of North Queensland*. Canberra: Pacific Linguistics.

Pawley, Andrew. 1972. 'On the internal relationships of Eastern Oceanic languages', pp. 1–142 of *Studies in Oceanic culture history*, Vol. 3, edited by R. C. Green and M. Kelly. Honolulu: Department of Anthropology, Bernice P. Bishop Museum.

—— 1995. 'Number in Kalam', presentation to Workshop on Number Systems. Research Centre for Linguistic Typology, ANU.

Payne, David. 2002. 'Causatives in Asheninka, the case for a sociative source', pp. 485–505 of Shibatani 2002.

Payne, Doris L. 1990. 'Morphological characteristics of Lowland South American languages', pp. 213–41 of *Amazonian Linguistics: Studies in Lowland South American languages*, edited by Doris L. Payne. Austin: University of Texas Press.

—— and Payne, Thomas E. 1990. 'Yagua', pp. 249–474 of Derbyshire and Pullum 1990.

Payne, John R. 1985. 'Negation', pp. 197–242 of Shopen 1985, Vol. I.

Payne, Thomas E. 1982. 'Subject in Guaymi', pp. 45–76 of *Estudios varios sobre les lenguas Chibchas de Costa Rica*, by Adolfo Constenla Umaña, Enrique Margery Peña, Thomas E. Payne, Raymond E. Schlabach, and Stephen H. Levinsohn. San José, Costa Rica: Universidad de Costa Rica.

—— 1997. *Describing morphosyntax: A guide for field linguists*. Cambridge: Cambridge University Press.

—— and Payne, Doris L. 1999. 'Panare: A Cariban language of Central Venezuela grammar summary'. RCLT internal document, ANU.

Pearson, Greg. 2008. *Lote grammar sketch*. Ukarumpa: SIL-PNG.

Peterson, David A. 2007. *Applicative constructions*. Oxford: Oxford University Press.

Piper, Nick. 1989. 'A sketch grammar of Meryam Mir'. MA thesis, ANU.

Pires, Nadia N. 1992. 'Estudo da gramática da língua Jeoromitxi (Jabutí), aspectos sintáticos das cláusulas matrizes'. MA thesis, Universidade Estadual de Campinas.

Polinsky, Maria. 2005a. 'Applicative constructions', pp. 442–5 of Haspelmath et al. 2005.

—— 2005b. 'Antipassive constructions', pp. 438–41 of Haspelmath et al. 2005.

Popjes, Jack and Popjes, Jo. 1986. 'Canela-Krahô', pp. 128–99 of Derbyshire and Pullum 1986.

Pullum, Geoffrey K. and Huddleston, Rodney D. 2002. 'Negation', pp. 785–849 of Huddleston and Pullum 2002.

Quesada, J. Diego. 2000. *A grammar of Teribe*. Munich: Lincom Europa.

Quirk, Randolph, Greenbaum, Sidney, Leech, Geoffrey, and Svartvik, Jan. 1985. *A comprehensive grammar of the English language*. London: Longman.

Randolph, Vance. 1927. 'The grammar of the Ozark dialect', *American Speech* 3: 1–11.

Reece, Laurie. 1970. *Grammar of the Wailbri language of central Australia*. Oceania Linguistic Monographs No. 13. Sydney: University of Sydney.

Refsing, Kirsten. 1986. *The Ainu language: The morphology and syntax of the Shizunai dialect*. Aarhus: Aarhus University Press.

Reh, Mechthild. 1994. 'A grammatical sketch of Deiga', *Afrika und Übersee* 77: 197–261.

—— 1996. *Anywa language: Description and internal reconstructions*. Cologne: Rüdiger Köppe.

Rehg, Kenneth L. 1981. *Ponapean reference grammar*. Honolulu: University of Hawaii Press.

Reid, Nicholas. 2000. 'Complex verb collocations in Ngan'gityemerri: A non-derivational strategy for encoding valency alternations', pp. 333–59 of Dixon and Aikhenvald 2000a.

Rice, Keren. 1989. *A grammar of Slave*. Berlin: Mouton de Gruyter.

—— 2000. 'Voice and valency in the Athapaskan family', pp. 173–235 of Dixon and Aikhenvald 2000a.

Roberts, John R. 1987. *Amele*. London: Croom Helm.

—— 1997. 'Switch-reference in Papua New Guinea: A preliminary survey', pp. 101–241 of *Papers in Papuan linguistics*, Vol. 3, edited by Andrew Pawley. Canberra: Pacific Linguistics.

Robinson, Stuart P. 1999. 'Tzotzil (dialect of Zinacantan) grammar summary'. RCLT internal document, ANU.

Romero-Figueroa, Andrés. 1986. 'Warao comparatives', *Studies in Language* 10: 97–108.

Romero-Méndez, Rodrigo. 2008. 'A reference grammar of Ayutla Mixe (Tukyo'm Ayuujk)'. PhD dissertation, State University of New York at Buffalo.

Rowlands, E. C. 1969. *Yoruba* (Teach Yourself Books). London: Hodder and Stoughton.

Rubino, Carl. 1998. 'Tagalog grammar summary'. RCLT internal document, ANU.

Rude, Noel. 1982. 'Promotion and topicality of Nez Perce objects', *Berkeley Linguistics Society Proceedings* 8: 363–83.

——1985. 'Studies in Nez Perce grammar and discourse'. PhD dissertation, University of Oregon.

——1986. 'Topicality, transitivity, and the direct object in Nez Perce', *International Journal of American Linguistics* 52: 124–53.

Rumsey, Alan. 1982. *An intra-sentence grammar of Ungarinjin, North-Western Australia.* Canberra: Pacific Linguistics.

——2000. 'Bunuba', pp. 34–152 of Dixon and Blake 2000.

Sadock, Jerrold M. 1984. 'West Greenlandic', pp. 189–214 of Chisholm 1984.

Saeed, John I. 1993. *Somali reference grammar*, 2nd revised edition. Kensington, MD: Dunwoody Press.

Safford, William E. 1909. *The Chamorro language of Guam.* Washington DC: W. H. Lowdermilk.

Saksena, Anuradha. 1982. 'Contact in causation', *Language* 58: 820–31.

Saltarelli, Mario. 1988. *Basque.* London: Routledge.

Sapir, Edward. 1912. 'Language and environment', *American Anthropologist* n.s. 14: 226–42. [Reprinted as pp. 89–103 of *Selected writings of Edward Sapir in language, culture and personality*, edited by David G. Mandelbaum. Berkeley and Los Angeles: University of California Press, 1949.]

——1921. *Language: an introduction to the study of speech.* New York: Harcourt Brace.

——1922. 'The Takelma language of south western Oregon', pp. 1–296 of Boas 1922.

——1930–1. 'The Southern Paiute language', *Proceedings of the American Academy of Science* Vol. 65, Nos. 1–3.

——1994. *The psychology of culture, a course of lectures.* Reconstructed and edited by Judith T. Irvine. Berlin: Mouton de Gruyter.

Sastry, G. Devi Prasada. 1984. *Mishmi grammar.* Mysore: Central Institute of Indian Languages.

Saxe, Geoffrey B. 1981. 'Body parts as numerals: A developmental analysis of numeration among the Oksapmin in Papua New Guinea', *Child Development* 52: 306–16.

Schachter, Paul and Otanes, Fe T. 1972. *Tagalog reference grammar.* Berkeley and Los Angeles: University of California Press.

Schaub, Willi. 1985. *Babungo.* London: Croom Helm.

Schebeck, B., Hercus, L. A., and White, I. M. 1973. 'The Adnjamathanha personal pronoun and the "Wailpi" kinship system' and 'Perception of kinship structure reflected in the Adnjamathanha pronouns', making up *Papers in Australian linguistics*, No. 6. Canberra: Pacific Linguistics.

Schulze, Wolfgang M. 2007. 'Review of *The world atlas of language structures*, edited by Martin Haspelmath, Matthew S. Dryer, David Gil and Bernard Comrie', *Studies in Language* 31: 445–63.

Schwenter, Scott A. 2005. 'The pragmatics of negation in Brazilian Portuguese', *Lingua* 115: 1427–56.

Seidenberg. A. 1960. 'The diffusion of counting practices', *University of California Publications in Mathematics* 3(4): 215–99.

Seifert, Stephan and Weite, Werner. 1987. *A basic bibliography on negation in natural languages*. Tübingen: Gunter Narr.

Seki, Lucy. 2000. *Gramatica da língua Kamaiurá, lingua Tupí-Guaraní de Alto Xingu*. Campinas: Editora da Unicamp.

Senn, Alfred M. 1966. *Handbuch der Litauischen Sprache*, Band 1, *Grammatik*. Heidelberg: Winter.

Seyoum, Mulugeta. 2008. *A grammar of Dime*. Utrecht: LOT.

Sharma, Jagdish C. 1982. *Gojri grammar*. Mysore: Central Institute for Indian Languages.

Sharp, Janet. 2004. *Nyangumarta: A language of the Pilbara region of Western Australia*. Canberra: Pacific Linguistics.

Shibatani, Masayoshi. 1976a. Editor of *Syntax and semantics*, Vol. 6, *The grammar of causative constructions*. New York: Academic Press.

——1976b. 'The grammar of causative constructions: a conspectus', pp. 1–40 of Shibatani 1976a.

——1988a. Editor of *Passive and voice*. Amsterdam: John Benjamins.

——1988b. 'Voice in Philippine languages', pp. 85–142 of Shibatani 1988a.

——1990. *The languages of Japan*. Cambridge: Cambridge University Press.

——2002. Editor of *The grammar of causation and interpersonal manipulation*. Amsterdam: John Benjamins.

——and Pardeshi, Prashant, 2002. 'The causative continuum', pp. 85–128 of Shibatani 2002.

Shopen, Timothy. 1985. Editor of *Language typology and syntactic description*, Vol. I, *Clause structure*; Vol. II, *Complex constructions*; Vol. III, *Grammatical categories and the lexicon*. Cambridge: Cambridge University Press.

——and Konaré, Mamadou. 1970. 'Sonrai causatives and passives: Transformational versus lexical derivations for propositional heads', *African Linguistics* 1: 211–54.

Siemund, Peter. 2001. 'Interrogative constructions', pp. 1010–28 of *Language typology and language universals: An international handbook*, edited by Martin Haspelmath, Ekkehard König, Wulf Oesterreicher, and Wolfgang Raible. Berlin: Walter de Gruyter.

Siewierska, Anna. 1984. *The passive: A comparative linguistic analysis*. London: Croom Helm.

——2005. 'Passive constructions', pp. 434–7 of Haspelmath et al. 2005.

Singh, Rajendra. 1973. 'Multiple negation in Shakespeare', *Journal of English Linguistics* 7: 50–6.

Slater, Keith W. 2003. *A grammar of Mangghuer, A Mongolic language of China's Qinghai-Gansu Sprachbund*. London: RoutledgeCurzon.

Smith, Ian and Johnson, Steve. 2000. 'Kugu Nganhcara', pp. 355–489 of Dixon and Blake 2000.

Smith-Stark, T. Cedric, 1974. 'The plurality split', *Chicago Linguistic Society Papers* 10: 657–71.

Smythe, W. E. 1948/9. *Elementary grammar of the Gumbáiŋgar language (north coast, N. S. W.)*. Oceania Monograph, 8. Sydney: Australian National Research Council. [Reprinted from *Oceania* 1948–9, 19: 130–91, 254–99; 20: 29–65.]

Sneddon, James N. 1996. *Indonesian reference grammar*. Sydney: Allen and Unwin.

Sohn, Ho-Min. 1994. *Korean*. London: Routledge.

—— 1999. *The Korean language*. Cambridge: Cambridge University Press.

—— 2004. 'The adjective class in Korean', pp. 223–41 of Dixon and Aikhenvald 2004.

Sohn, Joong-Sun. 1995. 'The reflexive suffix -v in Hualapai', *Kansas Working Papers in Linguistics* 20: 149–63.

Song, Jae Jung. 1996. *Causatives and causation*. London: Longman.

—— 2005a. 'Periphrastic causative constructions', pp. 446–9 of Haspelmath et al. 2005.

—— 2005b. 'Nonperiphrastic causative constructions', pp. 450–3 of Haspelmath et al. 2005.

Spaulding, Craig and Pat. 1994. *Phonology and grammar of Nankina*. Ukarumpa: SIL-PNG.

Sprott, Robert. 1992. 'Jemez syntax'. PhD dissertation, University of Chicago.

Sridhar, S. N. 1979. 'Dative subjects and the notion of subject', *Lingua* 49: 99–125.

—— 1990. *Kannada*. London: Routledge.

Stapleton, Walter H. 1903. *Comparative handbook of Congo languages*. Yakusu, Stanley Falls. Congo Independent State.

Stassen, Leon. 1985. *Comparison and universal grammar*. Oxford: Basil Blackwell.

—— 2005. 'Comparative constructions', pp. 490–3 of Haspelmath et al. 2005.

Stebbins, Tonya N. Forthcoming. *Mali (Baining) grammar*. Canberra: Pacific Linguistics.

Steere, Edward. 1870. *A handbook of the Swahili language – as spoken at Zanzibar*. London: Bell and Daldy.

Steinberg, Danny D. and Jakobovits, Leon A. 1971. Editors of *Semantics: An interdisciplinary reader in philosophy, linguistics and psychology*. Cambridge: Cambridge University Press.

Stirling, Lesley and Huddleston, Rodney. 2002. 'Deixis and anaphora', pp. 1449–564 of Huddleston and Pullum 2002.

Stokes, Bronwyn, 1982. 'A description of Nyigina, a language of the West Kimberley, Western Australia'. PhD thesis, ANU.

Storch, Anne. 2005. *The noun morphology of Western Nilotic*. Cologne: Rüdiger Köppe.

Storto, Luciana R. 1999. 'Aspects of a Karitiana grammar'. PhD dissertation, MIT.

Subrahmanyam, P. S. 1968. *A descriptive grammar of Gondi*. Annamalainagar: Annamalai University.

Suhandano. 1994. 'Grammatical relations in Javanese: A short description'. MA thesis, ANU.

Sulkala, Helena and Karjalainen, Merja. 1992. *Finnish*. London: Routledge.

Sumbatova, Nina R. 1993. 'Causative constructions in Svan: Further evidence for role domination', pp. 253–70 of Comrie and Polinsky 1993.

Sun, Jackson T.-S. 2007. 'The irrealis category in rGyalrong', *Language and Linguistics* 8: 797–819.

Suttles, Wayne. 2004. *Musqueam reference grammar*. Vancouver: UBC Press.

Sutton, Peter. 1978. 'Wik: Aboriginal society, territory and language at Cape Kerweer, Cape York Peninsula, Australia', PhD thesis, University of Queensland.

Sutton-Spence, Rachel and Woll, Bencie. 1999. *The linguistics of British Sign Language: An introduction*. Cambridge: Cambridge University Press.

Svantesson, Jan-Olof. 1983. *Kammu phonology and morphology*. Traveaux de l'institut de linguistique de Lund, No. 18.

Svartvik, Jan. 1966. *On voice in the English verb*. The Hague: Mouton.

Swadesh, Morris. 1934. 'The phonetics of Chitimacha', *Language* 10: 345–62.

Swanton, John R. 1911. 'Tlingit', pp. 159–204 of Boas 1911a.

Sweet, Henry. 1892. *A short historical English grammar*. London: Oxford University Press.

Szemerényi, Oswald J. L. 1996. *Introduction to Indo-European linguistics*. Oxford: Clarendon Press.

Tampubolon, D. P. 1983. *Verbal affixations in Indonesian: A semantic exploration*. Canberra: Pacific Linguistics.

Tamura, Suzuko. 2000. *The Ainu language*. Tokyo: Sanseido. [English translation of article 'Ainu-go' (The Ainu language) from *Gengogaku-dai-jiten* (*The Sanseido Encyclopaedia of Linguistics*), Vol. 1, Part 1, 1988.]

Tavares, Petronila. 1995. 'Causation in Wayâna (Cariban)'. Handout for paper presented at a meeting of the Society for the Study of the Indigenous Languages of the Americas, held at the University of New Mexico.

Taylor, Charles. 1985. *Nkore-Kiga*. London: Croom Helm.

Thiesen, Wesley and Weber, David. 2000. 'A grammar of Bora'. Ms.

Thomas, David D. 1971. *Chrau grammar*. Honolulu: University of Hawaii Press.

Thomas, Dorothy M. 1969. 'Chrau affixes', *Mon-Khmer Studies* 3: 90–107.

Thompson, Laurence C. 1965. *A Vietnamese grammar*. Seattle: University of Washington Press.

Thompson, Sandra A. 1987. 'The passive in English: a discourse perspective', pp. 497–511 of *In honor of Ilse Lehiste*, edited by R. Channon and L. Shockley. Dordrecht: Foris.

—— Park, Joseph Sung-Yul, and Li, Charles N. 2006. *A reference grammar of Wappo*. Berkeley and Los Angeles: University of California Press.

Thomsen, Marie-Louise. 1984. *The Sumerian language*. Copenhagen: Akademisk Forlag.

Thornes, Timothy J. 2003. 'A Northern Paiute grammar with texts'. PhD dissertation, University of Oregon.

Tonoike, Shigeo. 1978. 'On the causative constructions in Japanese', pp. 3–29 of *Problems in Japanese syntax and semantics*, edited by J. Hinds and I. Howard. Tokyo: Kaitakusha.

Topping, Donald M. 1973. *Chamorro reference grammar*. Honolulu: University of Hawaii Press.

Torrend, Julius. 1891. *Comparative grammar of the South African Bantu languages*... London: Kegan Paul, Trench, Trubner.

Tosco, Mauro. 1997. *Af Tunni: Grammar, texts and glossary of a southern Somali dialect*. Cologne: Rüdiger Köppe.

——1999a. 'Dhaasanac (Cushitic) grammar summary'. RCLT internal document, ANU.

——1999b. 'Somali (Cushitic) grammar summary'. RCLT internal document, ANU.

——2001. *The Dhaasanac language*. Cologne: Rudiger Köppe.

Trask, R. L. 1993. *A dictionary of grammatical terms in linguistics*. London: Routledge.

Travis, Catherine. 2006. 'Dizque, a Columbian evidentiality strategy', *Linguistics* 44: 1269–97.

Trithart, Mary L. 1977. 'Relational grammar and Chichewa subjectivization', PhD dissertation, UCLA.

Tsujimura, Natsuko. 1996. *An introduction to Japanese linguistics*. Oxford: Blackwell.

Tura, Sabahat and Dede, Müşerref. 1982. 'Sentential and constituent questions in Turkish', pp. 228–36 of *Papers from the parasession on declaratives*, edited by Robinson Schneider, Kevin Tuite, and Robert Chametzky. Chicago: Chicago Linguistic Society.

Ultan, Russell. 1972. 'Some features of basic comparative constructions', *Working papers on language* (Stanford) 9: 117–62.

——1978. 'Some general characteristics of interrogative systems', pp. 41–63 of *Universals of human languages*, Vol. 4, *Syntax*. edited by Joseph H. Greenberg. Stanford: Stanford University Press.

Urton, Gary. 1997. *The social life of numbers: A Quechua ontology of numbers and philosophy of arithmetic*. Austin: University of Texas Press.

Valenzuela, Pilar. 2003. 'Transitivity in Shipibo-Konibo grammar'. PhD dissertation, University of Oregon.

——2010. 'Applicative constructions in Shipibo-Konibo (Panoan)', *International Journal of American Linguistics* 76: 101–44.

van den Berg, René. 1989. *A grammar of the Muna language*. Dordrecht: Foris.

van Eijk, Jan. 1997. *The Lillooet language: Phonology, morphology, syntax*. Vancouver: UBC Press.

Veerman-Leichsenring, Annette. 2006. 'Valency-changing devices in Metzontla Popoloc', pp. 93–118 of *What's in a verb? Studies in the verbal morphology of the languages of the Americas*, edited by Grazyna J. Rowicka and Ethne B. Carlin. Utrecht: LOT.

Veselinova, Ljuba. 2003. 'Suppletion in verb paradigms: Bits and pieces of a puzzle'. PhD dissertation, Stockholm University.

——2005. 'Verbal number and suppletion', pp. 326–9 of Haspelmath et al. 2005.

Vidal, Alexandra. 2001. 'Pilagá grammar (Guaykuruan family, Argentina)'. PhD dissertation, University of Oregon.

Vitale, Anthony J. 1981. *Swahili syntax*. Dordrecht: Foris.

Vogt, Hans. 1971. *Grammaire de la langue Géorgienne*. Oslo: Universitetforlaget.

Voort, Hein van der. 2004. *A grammar of Kwaza*. Berlin: Mouton de Gruyter.

Wade, Terence. 1992. *A comprehensive Russian grammar*, edited by Michael J. de K. Holnan. Oxford: Blackwell.

Wagner, Günter. 1934. 'Yuchi', pp. 293–384 of Boas 1933.

Wali, Kashi and Koul, Omkar N. 1997. *Kashmiri, a cognitive-descriptive grammar*. London: Routledge.

Ward, Gregory, Birner, Betty, and Huddleston, Rodney. 2002. 'Information packaging', pp. 1363–447 of Huddleston and Pullum 2002.

Watanabe, Honoré. 2003. *A morphological description of Sliammon, Mainland Comox Salish, with a sketch of syntax*. Osaka: Endangered Languages of the Pacific Rim.

Watkins, Calvert. 1985. *The American heritage dictionary of Indo-European roots*. Boston: Houghton Mifflin.

Watkins, Laurel J. 1984. *A grammar of Kiowa*. Lincoln: University of Nebraska Press.

Watters, David E. 2002. *A grammar of Kham*. Cambridge: Cambridge University Press.

Weber, David J. 1986. 'Information perspective, profile, and patterns in Quechua', pp. 137–55 of *Evidentiality: the linguistic coding of epistemology*, edited by Wallace Chafe and Johanna Nichols. Norwood, NJ: Ablex.

——1989. *A grammar of Huallaga (Huánuco) Quechua*. Berkeley and Los Angeles: University of California Press.

Weir, E. M. Helen. 1986. 'Footprints of yesterday's syntax: Diachronic development of certain verb prefixes in an OSV language (Nadëb)', *Lingua* 68: 291–316.

Wells, H. G. 1909. *Ann Veronica*. London: Fisher Unwin.

Whistler, K. W. 1985. 'Focus, perspective, and inverse marking in Nootka', pp. 227–65 of Nichols and Woodbury 1985.

Whitely, W. H. 1970. 'Notes on the syntax of the passive in Swahili', *African Language Studies* 11: 391–404.

Whitney, William D. 1924. *Sanskrit grammar, including both the classical language and the older dialects of Veda and Brāhmana*, 5th edition. Leipzig: Breitkopf and Härtel.

Wiemer, Björn and Nedjalkov, Vladimir P. 'Reciprocal and reflexive constructions in German', pp. 455–512 of Nedjalkov 2007, Vol. 2.

Wiesemann, Ursula. 1986. Editor of *Pronominal systems*. Tübingen: Gunter Narr.

Wijayawardhana, G. D., Wickramasinghe, Daya, and Byron, Theodora. 1995. 'Passive-related constructions in Colloquial Sinhala', pp. 105–41 of Bennett, Bynon, and Hewitt 1995.

Wilkins, David. 1989. 'Mparntwe Arrernte (Aranda): Studies in the structure and semantics of grammar'. PhD thesis, ANU.

Wise, Mary Ruth. 1986. 'Grammatical characteristics of PreAndine Arawakan languages of Peru', pp. 567–642 of Derbyshire and Pullum 1986.

Wise, Mary Ruth. 2002. 'Applicative affixes in Peruvian Amazonian languages', pp. 329–44 of *Current studies in South American languages*, edited by Mily Crevels, Simon van de Kerke, Sérgio Meira, and Hein van der Voort. Leiden: CNWS.

Wolfart, H. C. 1996. 'Sketch of Cree, an Algonquian language', pp. 390–439 of Goddard 1996.

Xu, Hui Ling. 2004. 'Comparative constructions in the Jieyang dialect'. Handout for presentation in Workshop on Comparative Constructions, RCLT.

—— 2007. *Aspect of Chaozhou grammar: A synchronic description of the Jieyang variety.* Journal of Chinese Linguistics, Monograph series No. 22.

Young, Robert W. and Morgan, William, Sr. 1987. *The Navajo language: A grammar and colloquial dictionary.* Revised edition. Albuquerque: University of New Mexico Press.

Yu, Defen. 2004. 'Comparative constructions in Lisu'. Handout for presentation in Workshop on Comparative Constructions, RCLT.

Zaborski, Andrzej. 1986. *The morphology of nominal plural in the Cushitic languages, Beiträge zur Afrikanistik* Band 28. Vienna.

Zavala, Roberto. 2000. 'Inversion and other topics in the grammar of Olutec (Mixean)'. PhD dissertation, University of Oregon.

Zeitoun, Elizabeth. 2007. *A grammar of Mantauran (Rukai).* Taipei: Institute of Linguistics, Academia Sinica.

Zeshan, Ulrike. 2000. 'American sign language (ASL) grammar summary'. RCLT internal document, ANU.

—— 2004a. 'Hand, head and face: Negative constructions in sign languages', *Linguistic Typology* 8: 1–58.

—— 2004b. 'Interrogative constructions in signed languages: Cross-linguistic perspectives', *Language* 80: 7–39.'

—— 2006a. Editor of *Interrogative and negative constructions in sign languages.* Nijmegen: Ishara Press.

—— 2006b. 'Negative and interrogative constructions in sign languages: A case study in sign language typology', pp. 28–68 of Zeshan 2006a.

Author Index

The indices cover all of Volume 1 (shown by **1:**), Volume 2 (shown by **2:**), and Volume 3 (shown by **3:**). Note that grammars and their authors listed in Appendix 1 to Volume 3 are not indexed.

Language Index

Subject Index

Note that entries in the glossary (which appears in all three volumes) are not included in this index.

Books by R. M. W. Dixon

BOOKS ON LINGUISTICS
Linguistic science and logic
What *is* language? A new approach to linguistic description
The Dyirbal language of North Queensland
A grammar of Yidiɲ
The languages of Australia
Where have all the adjectives gone? and other essays in semantics and syntax
Searching for Aboriginal languages: Memoirs of a field worker
A grammar of Boumaa Fijian
A new approach to English grammar, on semantic principles
Words of our country: Stories, place names and vocabulary in Yidiny,
the Aboriginal language of the Cairns-Yarrabah region
Ergativity
The rise and fall of languages
Australian languages: Their nature and development
The Jarawara language of southern Amazonia
A semantic approach to English grammar
I am a linguist

with Alexandra Y. Aikhenvald
Language at large: Essays on syntax and semantics

with Grace Koch
Dyirbal song poetry: The oral literature of an Australian rainforest people

with Bruce Moore, W. S. Ramson and Mandy Thomas
Australian Aboriginal words in English, their origin and meaning

BOOKS ON MUSIC
with John Godrich
Recording the blues

with John Godrich and Howard Rye
Blues and gospel records, 1890–1943

NOVELS *(under the name Hosanna Brown)*
I spy, you die
Death upon a spear

EDITOR OF BOOKS ON LINGUISTICS
Grammatical categories in Australian languages
Studies in ergativity

with Barry J. Blake
Handbook of Australian languages, Vols 1–5

with Martin Duwell
The honey ant men's love song and other Aboriginal song poems
Little Eva at Moonlight Creek and other Aboriginal song poems

with Alexandra Y. Aikhenvald
The Amazonian languages
Changing valency: Case studies in transitivity
Areal diffusion and genetic inheritance: Problems in comparative linguistics
Word: A cross-linguistic typology
Studies in evidentiality
Adjective classes: A cross-linguistic typology
Serial verb constructions: A cross-linguistic typology
Complementation: A cross-linguistic typology
Grammars in contact: A cross-linguistic typology
The semantics of clause-linking: A cross-linguistic typology
Possession and ownership: A cross-linguistic typology

with Alexandra Y. Aikhenvald and Masayuki Onishi
Non-canonical marking of subjects and objects